D0284886

Devonport & the Northwest p204

Launceston & Around p176

The East Coast p141

| BT | CH | PD | GR | PN | DON |

R 919.46

CANCELLE

BANKSTOWN CITY LIBRARY

Midlands & Lake Country p129

Cradle Country & the West p244

Hobart & Around p44

Tasman Peninsula & Port Arthur p90

The Southeast p102

PAGE 309 | SURVIVAL GUIDE

VITAL PRACTICAL INFORMATION TO HELP YOU HAVE A SMOOTH TRIP

Directory A-Z 310
Transport 320
Index 328
Map Legend 335

THIS EDITION WRITTEN AND RESEARCHED BY

Brett Atkinson

Gabi Mocatta

welcome to
Tasmania

Remembering History

To understand Australian history, you'll first need to understand Tasmanian history. The often tragic story of Van Diemen's Land is told through the haunting stories surrounding the colony's first convict ships. The beautiful Tasman Peninsula scenery around the Port Arthur Historic Site only serves to reinforce the area's grim history, both in the 19th century and in more recent times. In Hobart's bustling waterfront pubs it's still very easy to conjure up memories of the port's raffish and rambunctious past. Elsewhere on the island, the legacy of convict labour has produced Tasmanian architectural treasures, including the elegant bridges at Ross, Richmond and Campbell Town.

Tasting Tasmania

At first it was all about apples, but now Tasmania's contribution to the world of food extends to premium seafood, artisan cheese, bread, honey and Australia's most intensely flavoured cool-climate wines. Many smaller producers are owned and operated by passionate foodies, and Tasmania is ideal for a leisurely driving holiday visiting farm-gate suppliers and providores. After you've sampled Tassie produce at its just-picked freshest, visit one of the excellent restaurants to see how local chefs respect the state's natural bounty with their delicious creations.

Mainland Australia's quirky and rugged southern neighbour celebrates its relative isolation with a laid-back ambience, an emerging gourmet food scene, and some of the planet's most astounding wilderness and scenery.

(left) Views over the Bruny Neck isthmus (p105)
(below) Salamanca Square, Hobart (p49)

Festival Frenzy

From celebrations of food, wine and beer, to internationally renowned arts and music festivals, Tasmania fits a packed schedule of celebrations into its annual calendar. How many more reasons do you need to escape for a long weekend from mainland Australia? Hobart's beautiful harbourfront hosts many events ranging from the flavour-packed The Taste to the heritage glories of the Australian Wooden Boat Festival. Art and culture are showcased over the summer months during MONA FOMA and Ten Days on the Island. In winter the Lumina Festival fills Hobart's streets and squares with yet more food and wine, and the joys of the human voice.

Wild by Nature

From the cobalt waters and pristine coves and headlands of the east coast, to the rugged alpine vistas of the Cradle Mountain-Lake St Clair National Park, Tasmania is a definite overachiever when it comes to natural beauty. The opportunities to explore Tasmania by foot range from easygoing strolls to forested waterfalls to the challenge of the Overland Track. Tassie's rugged coastline and rivers can be accessed by kayak, raft, yacht or cruiser, with plenty of opportunity to encounter the island's idiosyncratic wildlife. Spy on gorging Tasmanian devils after dark, share the Southern Ocean swell with seals and dolphins, or welcome penguins home at dusk.

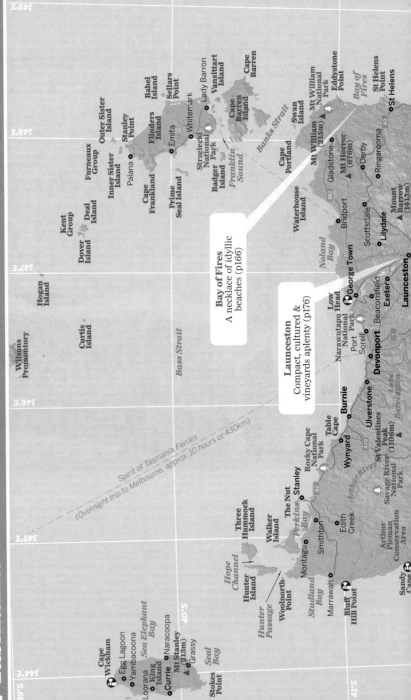

Bay of Fires
A necklace of idyllic beaches (p166)

Launceston
Compact, cultured & vineyards aplenty (p176)

Spirit of Tasmania Ferries
(Overnight trip to Melbourne, approx. 10 hours or 430km)

Cradle Mountain
Superb views from a Tasmanian icon (p264)

Franklin River
Negotiating Tasmania's wild, forested heart (p262)

Mt Field National Park
Waterfalls, wildlife & wonderful walking (p85)

Bathurst Harbour
Kayaking amid gloriously remote isolation (p273)

Bruny Island
Hushed seclusion & artisan foods (p105)

MONA
Unique, challenging & utterly world-class (p53)

Hobart & Salamanca Market
Harbourside with a heritage vibe (p45)

Port Arthur Historic Site
Melancholy memories & stunning scenery (p97)

Tasman Peninsula
Rugged & beautiful coastal scenery (p90)

Maria Island
Wildlife up close & personal (p144)

Freycinet National Park
Walking & kayaking amid dazzling landscapes (p150)

TASMAN SEA

SOUTHERN OCEAN

42°S

43°S

ELEVATION

| 2500m |
| 2000m |
| 1500m |
| 1000m |
| 750m |
| 500m |
| 250m |
| 0 |

0 — 40 km
0 — 20 miles

15 TOP
EXPERIENCES

MONA

1 A ferry ride from Hobart's harbour, Moorilla Estate's Museum of Old & New Art (MONA; p53) is an innovative and truly world-class institution. Designed by architect, Nonda Katsalidis, MONA's three levels of spectacular underground galleries showcase more than 400 often challenging and controversial works of art. Owner, Hobart philanthropist David Walsh, describes it as a 'subversive adult Disneyland'. Visitors may not like everything they see, but it's guaranteed that intense conversation will be on the agenda after viewing one of Australia's unique arts experiences.

ANDREW BAIN/LONELY PLANET IMAGES ©

Hobart & Salamanca Market

2 Historic, harbourside Hobart (p44) is a city that's made for exploration. Kick off with a stroll through the buskers, crafts stalls, and ethnic and local food options of Saturday morning's Salamanca Market (p53), before delving into history-rich Battery Point. More essential Tasmanian heritage is revealed at the Cascade Brewery and the sombre Female Factory, both nestled under Mt Wellington Don't miss the views from the summit, and definitely travel by mountain bike to return thrillingly to Hobart's waterfront.

Constitution Dock, Hobart

Port Arthur Historic Site

3 Tasmania's number one tourist drawcard, the Port Arthur Historic Site (p97), is a compelling mix of stunning coastal scenery and the sombre legacy of the past – engrossing, quiet and disquieting. Take a walking tour to understand the site's grand layout before exploring in-depth the separate ruined buildings and constructions. While Port Arthur's overall scale impresses, it's the personal histories of the former prisoners that leave the strongest impression. Join a guided tour of the Isle of the Dead Cemetery and the Point Puer Boys' Prison to uncover the most poignant memories.

Gourmet Produce

4 Salty-fresh seafood, plump cherries and crisp apples, artisan cheese, premium wine, beer and whisky: for the curious foodie, Tasmania offers plenty of reasons for a mouth-watering visit. Festivals and farmers' markets showcase the best of the Tassie food scene, often with visiting mainland chefs envious of the glorious produce on tap for local restaurant owners. At the excellent cookery schools at the Agrarian Kitchen (p81) and the Red Feather Inn (p198), visitors have the opportunity to get creative with some of Australia's – and the world's – best natural produce.

Bruny Island

5 Just a 15-minute ferry ride from Kettering – on 'the other side' as islanders refer to the Tasmanian mainland – windswept Bruny (p105) is a sparsely populated microcosm of the best of Tasmania. A thriving gourmet food scene produces fine artisan cheeses, shuckingly fresh oysters, delicately smoked seafood, and Australia's most southerly wines. Wildlife watching includes penguins, seals and ocean-going marine birds, and the best accommodation usually comes with an absolute beachfront location to ensure a relax-at-all-costs approach to any visit.

Nebraska Beach, Bruny Island

Bushwalking & the Outdoors

6 From short, alpine moorland strolls in the Hartz Mountains National Park (p117) to the iconic five-day Overland Track in the Cradle Mountain–Lake St Clair National Park (p264), Tasmania is nirvana for bushwalkers. Strike out solo or take a luxury guided walk fuelled by Tasmanian food and wine. Either way, you'll soon start considering other ways to explore the Tasmanian outdoors, including kayaking on remote Bathurst Harbour, sailing on the Gordon River, or embarking on a 10-day rafting trip on the Franklin River (p263). Welcome to Australia's hub for outdoor adventure. South Coast Track

Tasman Peninsula

7 Although tinged with the undeniable sadness of the Port Arthur Historic Site, the Tasman Peninsula (p90) offers much more than colonial history and convict ruins. Check out the 300m sea cliffs – amongst the highest on the planet – that soar above cobalt waters straight from the southern ocean. Cruising sea eagles and albatrosses patrol the skies above, and seals, dolphins and whales are regular marine visitors. Explore the superb Tasman Coastal Trail (p94), or paddle around the monumental coastline in a sea kayak. Black-faced cormorants, Tasman National Park

Rafting on the Franklin River

8 This may be the ultimate wilderness journey in Tasmania. It's deep immersion in nature, where you feel as far from the rest of humanity as it's possible to get. You can spend up to 10 days on the Franklin (p263), navigating as the river dictates: sometimes floating in a world of reflections, then battling surging white-water rapids, or sliding through deep, echoing gorges. Nights are spent in rainforest-fringed camp sites where the river hushes you to sleep. It's a truly amazing adventure, one of the best things you'll ever do.

ANDRE W BAIN/LONELY PLANET IMAGES ©

Cradle Mountain

9 A precipitous comb of rock carved out by millennia of ice and wind, crescent-shaped Cradle Mountain (p264) is Tasmania's most recognisable – and spectacular – mountain peak. It's an all-day walk (and boulder scramble) to the summit and back, for unbelievable panoramas over Tasmania's alpine heart. Or you can stand in awe below and fill your camera with the perfect views across Dove Lake to the mountain. If the peak has disappeared in clouds or snow, warm yourself by the fire in one of the nearby lodges...and come back tomorrow.

KAREN TRIST/LONELY PLANET IMAGES ©

10 Ice-blue water, powder-white beaches, craggy granite headlands, splashed by flaming orange lichen, the Freycinet Peninsula (p150) is a gorgeous natural domain. It's also home to Tasmania's most photographed beach: Wineglass Bay (p154). Climb to the lookout over the bay then descend to the beach to swim in Caribbean-clear seas. To escape the crowds, trek the three-day peninsula circuit. Camp under whispering she-oaks...you may be the only soul around. Or explore Freycinet by cruise boat, kayak or joy flight, and stay in the luxury accommodation on its doorstep. Wineglass Bay from Mt Amos

ANDREW WATSON / LONELY PLANET IMAGES ©

Bay of Fires

11 This string of idyllic beaches washed by azure seas is possibly the most gorgeous slice of coastal Tasmania. Remote, rural, fringed with pasture-or-eucalypt green, the Bay of Fires beaches (p166) are places to hike, fish, camp and contemplate. Visit Binalong Bay (p167) in the south for its fine surf and swimming beach, and dive sites full of crayfish and abalone. Mt William National Park (p169) in the north has abundant wildlife, waterfront camping, and peace. Visit the bay under your own steam or be guided by the experts at the Bay of Fires Walk (p167).

GLENN VAN DER KNIJFF/LONELY PLANET IMAGES ©

Launceston

12 Launceston (p176) is a friendly, arty place that's shed its country-bumpkin air and is now the perfect pocket-sized city in Tasmania's north. It's graced with wonderful architecture, green parks, and the wilds of Cataract Gorge cut right into its heart. These days Launceston is a foodie's delight: there are top-notch restaurants, cafes and patisseries. Providores source the fabulous fresh produce of the Tamar Valley – stock up here for picnics – then get out into the valley yourself to taste the wines that make this place famous. Gardens, Cataract Gorge

GLENN VAN DER KNIJFF/LONELY PLANET IMAGES ©

HOLGER LEUE/LONELY PLANET IMAGES ©

Maria Island National Park

13 Beautiful Maria Island (p144)is like an island zoo – minus the fences. You don't even need to leave the historic settlement of Darlington (p145) to see Forester kangaroos, pademelons and wombats up close, and stroll among Cape Barren geese. On a forest walk you might spot a prickly echidna, and keep your eyes peeled for the spotted pardalote, one of Tasmania's rare birds. (Oh, and did we say historic? There's World Heritage history here and an ex-penitentiary you can stay in, complete with convict ghosts.) Painted Cliffs, Maria Island National Park

Mt Field National Park

14 Tasmania's wild beauty has never been so accessible. Just 80km northwest of Hobart, the Mt Field area (p85) was declared a national park in 1916. The combination of mountain scenery, alpine moorlands, lakes, rainforest, waterfalls and wildlife is a favourite escape for Hobartians. Enjoy the beautifully hushed 20-minute circuit to the 40m-high cascade of Russell Falls (p85), or stroll through the high country, punctuated by steep cliffs, deep valleys and shimmering lakes. You can be back in a cosy Hobart pub come sundown. Russell Falls

RICHARD I'ANSON/LONELY PLANET IMAGES ©

Bathurst Harbour & Port Davey

15 Bathurst Harbour and Port Davey are true natural wonders. There can be few places left in the world quite as wild. Perched on Tasmania's furthest southwest rim, this extensive inland waterway is as remote as it gets, and yet, amazingly, it's accessible too. Fly in by light plane from Hobart to the gravel airstrip at Melaleuca (an adventure in itself; p275), then sea kayak and camp your way around this incredible watery wilderness. Expect memories to last a lifetime.

GABI MOCATTA/LONELY PLANET IMAGES ©

need to know

Currency
» Australian dollars ($)

Language
» English

When to Go

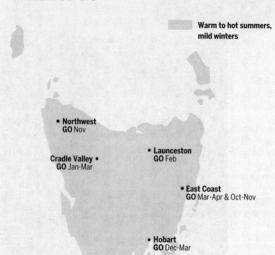

Warm to hot summers, mild winters

• **Northwest**
GO Nov

Cradle Valley •
GO Jan-Mar

• **Launceston**
GO Feb

• **East Coast**
GO Mar-Apr & Oct-Nov

• **Hobart**
GO Dec-Mar

High Season
(Dec & Jan)

» Accommodation prices are at a peak.

» Book ahead for accommodation and transport.

» Expect crowds at high-profile destinations.

Shoulder Season
(Feb–Apr, Oct & Nov)

» Easter is busy with holidaying Australian families.

» Book ahead for campgrounds, motels and ferries at this time.

» Farmers markets from October to April.

Low Season
(May–Sep)

» Accommodation prices are the lowest of the year.

» Outside Hobart and Launceston, some eating and accommodation options may be closed.

» Snowfall can close bushwalking tracks.

Your Daily Budget

Budget
$50–75

» Hostel dorm beds: $25–30

» Supermarkets and farmers markets for self-catering

» No charge for many sights

Midrange
$75–250

» Double room in a motel or B&B: $100–150

» Competition keeps rental-car prices low

» Lunch and dinner in cafes or local pubs

Top end over
$250

» Rent luxury lodges or with friends

» Self-cater with excellent local produce and wine

» Dine at world-class restaurants in Hobart and Launceston

Money

» ATMs widely available. Credit cards widely accepted.

Visas

» All visitors to Australia need a pre-travel visa (New Zealand nationals are exempt but receive a visa on arrival). See www.immi.gov.au.

Mobile Phones

» Local SIM cards will work in British and European phones, but other phones must be set to roaming. Telstra has the best coverage in Tasmania.

Driving/ Transport

» Drive on the left; steering wheel on right-hand side of the car.

Websites

» **Lonely Planet** (www. lonelyplanet.com/ australia/tasmania) Destination info, hotel bookings, forum.

» **Tourism Tasmania** (www. discovertasmania.com) Official site.

» **Tasmanian Travel Centre** (www. hobarttravelcentre. com.au) Info and bookings.

» **Parks & Wildlife** (www.parks.tas.gov.au) Essential info about the outdoors.

» **Rita's Bite** (www. pc-rita.blogspot.com) Reviews the restaurant scene.

Exchange Rates

Canada	C$1	$0.98
Euro zone	€1	$1.30
Japan	¥100	$1.20
New Zealand	NZ$1	$0.76
UK	UK£1	$1.52
US	US$1	$0.98

For current exchange rates see www.xe.com

Important Numbers

Ambulance, fire & police	☏000
Australia country code	☏61
Directory assistance	☏1223
International access code	☏0011
Tourism Tasmania	☏1300 827 743 Information line in Australia

Arriving in Tasmania

» **Hobart Airport**
Buses – Services to central Hobart meet every flight
Taxis – $40 to $50, around 20 minutes to the city

» **Launceston Airport**
Buses – Services to central Launceston meet every flight
Taxis – $35, around 20 minutes to the city

» **Devonport Spirit of Tasmania Ferry Terminal**
Buses – A Redline bus departs 7.40am Monday to Friday and 9.05am Saturday and Sunday to Hobart via Launceston

Ferry or Fly?

For many mainland Australian visitors to Tasmania, a major planning consideration is whether to fly to Hobart and pick up a rental car, or drive down to Victoria and cross Bass Strait on the *Spirit of Tasmania* ferry from Melbourne. Check airfares, ferry costs and car-rental prices when you're planning, as prices fluctuate throughout the year, but the following breakdown will give you some indication.

For a couple travelling for one week in Tasmania, a combination of Melbourne to Hobart return flights and a rental car will cost around $900 to $1000. Driving your own vehicle – excluding fuel costs – and crossing on the ferry in a cabin will total around $800 to $900. If you're happy to spend the overnight crossing in a standard reclining chair, the cost for two people will be around $500.

if you like...

Gourmet Food

Renowned Australian mainland chefs are passionate advocates of Tasmania's fine produce and seafood. Local restaurant owners also showcase Tassie's natural bounty to good effect in eateries regularly voted among the country's best.

Hobart Treat yourself at Marque IV (p69) or Restaurant 373 (p71)

Cygnet This small town harbours the superb Red Velvet Lounge (p112) and the surprising Lotus Eaters Café (p113)

Cooking Courses Get creative with local produce at the Agrarian Kitchen (p81) or learn to cook the slow-food way at the Red Feather Inn (p198)

Freycinet Marine Farm Enjoy briny fresh oysters, mussels, marinated octopus, crayfish and other marine delicacies on the deck at this fresh-from-the-sea outlet (p151)

Stillwater Settle back with a long, lazy lunch or linger over dinner at Launceston's best eatery (p187)

Wild Café Restaurant Head to Penguin to discover the best food on the northwest coast at this local institution (p223)

Bushwalking

For a relatively compact island, Tasmania crams in many different natural landscapes, usually best enjoyed at a steady walking pace and surrounded by venerable old forests or some of the planet's most audacious coastal scenery. The six-day 65km Overland Track offers the state's biggest bragging rights, but other shorter walks still provide spectacular insights into the great Tasmanian outdoors.

Cradle Mountain Allow eight hours to reach the summit of this iconic mountain (p264)

Wineglass Bay The Isthmus Track takes in some of Tasmania's most beautiful coastal scenery (p154)

Bay of Fires Join a four-day guided walk with all the benefits of luxury accommodation and gourmet food (p166)

Mt Wellington Explore plenty of challenging tracks a mere stone's throw from harbourfront Hobart (p52)

Mt Field National Park In spring and summer, Mt Field's high-country tracks showcase lakes, tarns and waterfalls (p85)

Beer, Wine & Whisky

Hobart's Cascade and Launceston's Boag's are now being joined by smaller microbreweries offering surprising craft beers. Quality is also the focus for Tasmanian wine producers and the smoothest of single malt whisky distilleries, an enterprise entirely appropriate for Tasmania's brooding landscapes. See also p293.

Jansz Wine Room For delightful Tassie sparkling wine (p197)

Tasmanian Whisky Create your own single malt taste test at Lark (p50), Nant (p136) and Hellyers Road (p224)

Seven Sheds Willie Simpson's Railton microbrewery is home to organically brewed boutique beers (p220)

New Sydney Hotel Hobart's best Irish pub offers the best of Tasmanian craft beers (p74)

Coal River Valley Sample Meadowbank Estate's fine wines with a gourmet lunch or picnic at the Puddleduck Vineyard (p80)

Bruny Island Premium Wines Partner excellent wines from Australia's southernmost vineyard with Bruny Island oysters and superb local cheeses (p107)

GRANT DIXON/LONELY PLANET IMAGES ©

» Snowcapped Cradle Mountain (p264)

History

Often overlaid with moody and melancholy weather, Tasmania is layered with poignant reminders of an often tragic and challenging past; a heritage that is also an essential component of colonial Australian history.

Port Arthur Historic Site Beautiful coastal scenery (almost) masks the tragic melancholy infused in every building (p97)

Callington Mill Organic flour from this meticulously restored mill in Oatlands is transformed into baked treats by the nearby Companion Bakery (p131)

Hobart's Heritage Secrets Take a guided walking tour to discover the stories abounding in Australia's second-oldest capital city (p58)

Midland (Heritage) Hwy Tasmania's past comes alive in the beautiful heritage towns of Ross, Hamilton, Oatlands and Bothwell (p131)

Launceston Ghost Tour Get spooked with spine-tingling stories of ghoulish spectres and severed heads (p183)

Maria Island Penitentiary Reputed to be haunted by the ghosts of interned convicts, but also a good place to stay the night. Boo! (p146)

Wildlife

The rambunctious Tasmanian devil is the island's most iconic wild creature, but Tasmania also abounds in other wildlife-watching opportunities, especially in the roiling waters along the rugged southern coast. Quolls, platypus, bettongs and echidnas also throw out the Tassie welcome mat.

Maria Island For all things furry and feathered. You can get up really close, and the wombats are supersized (p144)

Mt William National Park For spotting wildlife in the open grasslands behind the beaches. Rare Forester kangaroos are the standout species (p169)

Devil spotting The best on the island is at Marrawah with local Geoff King (p237)

Tasman Island Stunning coastal scenery and the opportunity to see seals, dolphins and the occasional whale (p94)

Bruny Island Superb birdwatching including the penguins and mutton birds of the Bruny Island Neck Game Reserve (p105)

Devil Conservation Support the work being undertaken by Something Wild (p85) and the Tasmanian Devil Conservation Park (p95)

Getting Out on the Water

Freshwater or saltwater? Opportunities to get active or take it easy on the water abound in Tasmania, and visitors are guaranteed the bonus of some of Australia's finest landscapes and seascapes. Another bonus of kayaking or rafting is that you're really earning another Tasmanian gourmet meal at the end of the day.

Bruny Island Check out vertigo-inducing sea cliffs, towering wind- and ocean-eroded rocks, and the wild expanse of the Great Southern Ocean (p107)

Wineglass Bay Cruise into the bay's perfect curve of sand and liquid turquoise (p154)

Kayaking Bathurst Harbour Join Roaring 40s Ocean Kayaking for a remote expedition in Tasmania's southwest (p273)

Gordon River Take a leisurely cruise downriver on the yacht *Stormbreaker* (p255)

Rafting the Franklin River Unwind on a classic, remote, 10-day river journey (p263)

Sailing on the Derwent Sign on to crew a majestic tall ship leaving from old Hobart town (p58)

ANDREW PEACOCK/LONELY PLANET IMAGES ©

» Denison Beach, near Bicheno (p157)

Beaches & Swimming

For more than a few months of the year, the waters surrounding Tasmania may be a tad too cold for swimming, but what doesn't change from winter to summer are the improbably scenic landscapes, and the very real chance that you'll have an entire expanse of sand all to yourself.

Boat Harbour Beach Water so clear and blue you could think you're in the Caribbean, but for the 'brrr' factor (p229)

Ocean Beach Long, wild beach walks, giant waves and stunning sunsets (p251)

Wineglass Bay Well-known, yes, but still undeniably spectacular, and well worth the sweaty walk in (p154)

Douglas-Apsley National Park Dip into the park's sparkling emerald waterholes (p161)

Seven Mile Beach Hobart's best beach features consistent waves, undulating dunes and good campgrounds in close proximity. Righto, that's summer sorted (p87)

Fortescue Bay Wonderfully isolated, and definitely worth paying a national park entrance fee to access (p96)

Activities for Children

From wildlife and the great outdoors, to hands-on learning and heritage whimsy, Tasmania packs in plenty of attractions for the younger traveller. The state's compact footprint means you'll find something to excite young minds within a short drive .

Pandemonium Indoor creative play and science discovery at Devonport's best kid-friendly option if you're waiting to catch the *Spirit of Tasmania* (p205)

Beaconsfield Mine & Heritage Centre Thrilling, hands-on displays and plenty of heritage lessons, too (p193)

Village of Lower Crackpot A wacky and whimsical fantasyland for the little ones at Tasmazia (p217)

Fossicking for 'diamonds' Well, semiprecious topaz anyway, but they still look pretty flash at Killiecrankie Bay on Flinders Island (p174)

Tassie's unique wildlife Making eye contact with the local fauna in the best of Tasmania's wildlife parks (p294)

Mountain biking down Mt Wellington An active, downhill alternative for adventurous kids. The view's damn fine too (p52)

Luxury

Either enjoyed romantically as a couple, or in the company of a few good friends, Tasmania excels at luxury accommodation, often in stunning and remote locations. Equip the kitchen with lots of Tassie wine and produce, and you may not need to venture out at all.

Peninsula Relaxed isolation at this modern and spacious restored homestead (p117)

Red Feather Inn Gorgeous accommodation and slow-food cookery classes at Hadspen's finest (p198)

Saffire Hands-down Tasmania's most spectacular accommodation, located amid the improbable landscapes of the Freycinet Peninsula (p153)

Priory Country Lodge Rural ambience meets urban sophistication at this stately restored manor in Bothwell (p137)

Rocky Hills Retreat A bush-clad luxury opportunity designed for doing not much at all – very, very slowly (p147)

Avalon Coastal Retreat 'Beach house' is such an inadequate description of this glass-and-steel haven with endless ocean views (p148)

month by month

Top Events

1   **The Taste,** December–January

2   **MONA FOMA,** January

3   **Launceston Festivale,** February

4   **Ten Days on the Island,** March

5   **Australian Wooden Boat Festival,** February

January

The summer festival season kicks off with two very different, but equally interesting, events. It's school holiday time in Australia, so expect high demand for family-friendly accommodation such as motels and campgrounds.

Cygnet Folk Festival

The sleepy town of Cygnet comes alive for three days with a celebration of folk, country, blues and roots music, and great food (www. cygnetfolkfestival.com.au). Catering is provided by two of Tasmania's best cafes, the Red Velvet Lounge and Lotus Eaters Café.

MONA FOMA
Tasmania's most eclectic music and arts festival (www.mofo.net.au) brings internationally re-spected guests to the island. Past artists-in-residence have included Nick Cave, John Cale and Philip Glass. The event is curated by proud Hobart resident, Brian Ritchie, formerly bass player with the Violent Femmes.

February

Hobart's maritime heritage is celebrated on and off the water, while Launceston's biggest party of the year is a chance to try wines from the nearby Tamar Valley. Book ahead for accommodation, especially on weekends.

Launceston Festivale

Launceston's City Park hosts three days of eating, drink-ing, arts and entertainment (www.festivale.com.au). It's a laid-back spot to explore the best of Tasmania's food, wine and beer, and there are regular live gigs from stars of decades past such as Diesel and Jenny Morris.

Evandale Village Fair
The National Penny Farthing Championships have been held at the an-nual Evandale Village Fair (www.evandalevillagefair. com) since 1983. Between breakneck races around Evandale's streets, there are heritage markets and the occasional musical interlude from pipe bands.

Australian Wooden Boat Festival

This biennial gathering of beautifully crafted yachts, dinghies and tall ships fills Hobart's waterfront with a heritage ambience (www. australianwoodenboatfes tival.com.au). Upcoming events are in 2011 and 2013. After admiring the boats, adjourn for a whisky at the suitably maritime Lark Distillery.

Royal Hobart Regatta

This three-day extravaganza sees Hobart's Derwent River filled with aquatic craft of all shapes and sizes (www. royalhobartregatta.com). It's a good chance to get up close and personal with Hobart's resident tall ships, the *Lady Nelson* and the *Windeward Bound.*

March

Summer's warm weather is the perfect backdrop for an island-wide celebration of music and arts, while in Tasmania's rural heartland, roadside stalls are crammed with fresh produce. Book

ahead for accommodation during Easter.

 Ten Days on the Island

Ten Days on the Island (www.tendaysontheisland. org) fills Tasmania from late March with an inspired program of theatre, music, visual arts, literature and film. It's held every second year – upcoming events are in 2011 and 2013.

 Celebrating the Huon's Harvest

Huonville's Ranelagh show-grounds host a two-day showcase of the best of Huon Valley produce (www. tasteofthehuon.com). With apples, cherries, wine and salmon on offer, no-one goes home hungry. It's also a good time to explore the Huon Valley's many road-side stalls.

April

Cooler weather may commence later in the month, and if Easter falls in April, ferry crossings, motels and campgrounds should be booked in advance at this time. Lumina's Winter of Festivals commences in April and runs until August.

 A Winter of Festivals

The Lumina Festival (www. lumina.discovertasmania. com) kicked off in 2010, and from April to August more than 100 events now show-case everything from food and wine to Shakespeare and the arts.

May

Cool blue-sky days – with a bit of Tasmanian luck – make this time of year perfect for visiting the island. The light will be stellar for photography, and accommodation owners are sometimes offering off-peak discounts. Hobart's cosy eateries host the annual Savour Tasmania Festival.

 Tasmanian Food Winter-Style

A vital component of the Lumina Festival, Savour Tasmania (www.savour tasmania.com) showcases Tasmanian produce and fine foodie creations from local and international chefs. The tasty event is held in Hobart for four days in late May, and then moves up to Burnie and Launceston in early June.

July

Batten down the hatches for cooler weather and enjoy the indoor pleasures of a cappella music, choirs and chocolate. Outside of Hobart and Launceston, expect some accommodation to be closed, especially in coastal areas.

 Latrobe Chocolate Winterfest

Chocolate in all its forms is a tasty way to warm the heart in the middle of a Tasmanian winter. The town of Latrobe hosts some chocolate-inspired festivities (www.chocolatewinterfest.

com.au), including the essential 'Chocolate High Tea'.

 Festival of Voices

This top winter festival (www.festivalofvoices.com) brings beautiful music to the streets and concert venues of Hobart. Gospel music, choirs and a cappella groups showcase just how amazing and versatile the human voice is.

August

Snow brings skiing and snowboarding to Tasmania, but hiking and bushwalking opportunities on certain tracks may be limited and only for very experienced walkers.

 Hitting the Snow at Ben Lomond

The snow-sports season in Ben Lomond National Park usually lasts from July to September; snow coverage is changeable so be sure to check the latest on snow and weather conditions (www. skibenlomond.com.au).

October

Spring is signalled with (usually) more settled weather, and two of Tasmania's smaller festivals. In Hobart and Launceston, the cities' Royal Shows put pressure on accommodation during 'Show Week'. Book ahead if possible.

Table Cape Tulip Festival

Celebrate that spring is well and truly here with food, music and dancing at the Table Cape Tulip Farm's annual Tulip Festival (www.bloomintulips.com. au). Bring your camera as it's a stunning spectacle. Floral fans should also visit www.bloomingtasmania. com for details of other garden events around Tassie throughout the rest of the year.

The Country Comes to Town

Tasmania's rural heritage combines with all the fun of the fair at the Royal Hobart Show and the Royal Launceston Show. (Re) discover your inner child with a bulging show bag full of stuff you probably don't need, and the 'Mum, I feel sick' memories of candy floss and hot dogs.

Birdwatching on Bruny

The gloriously isolated seascapes and landscapes of Bruny Island host the annual three-day Bruny Island Bird Festival. The inaugural event was organised in 2010 by the Bruny Island Environmental Network (www. bien.org.au) and included an expedition to the seabird colony on Pedra Branca.

November

Accommodation is still well-priced before the peak tourist season from mid-December to January. Tasmania's weather can be fickle, but you're just as likely to get crisp blue-sky days.

Getting Crafty in Deloraine

Running for four days before the first Monday in November, Deloraine's Tasmanian Craft Fair (www. tascraftfair.com.au) draws up to 30,000 arty types from around Australia. Pottery, textiles, glassware and sculpture are all celebrated.

Brewing Up a Storm

The best of Tasmania's beer is showcased at Hobart's annual Tasmanian Beerfest (www.tasmanianbeerfest. com.au). Apart from Tassie brews, you can try almost 200 beers from all around the world. Beer and food matching masterclasses are also available. Educate me now.

December

Accommodation is at a premium, especially after Christmas and around New Year's Eve, when the best of Hobart's festivals take place. Book accommodation well in advance, especially for inner-city hotels.

Hobart Summer Festival

No other Australian city experiences as great a contrast between winter and summer – a good reason for Hobartians to kick back for two weeks around New Year's Eve. Activities include partying with contestants in the Sydney to Hobart Yacht Race, live theatre performances, kids' events, and buskers.

The Taste

Part of the annual Hobart Summer Festival, but nevertheless worthy of its own mention, The Taste (www.tastefestival.com.au) is a week-long celebration of Tasmania's food and wine scene. For seven days around New Year's Eve, Hobart's waterfront is filled with scores of stalls of the island's finest produce.

Sydney to Hobart Yacht Race

Australia's biggest and most exciting yacht race departs Sydney on Boxing Day, and the winners usually sail up the Derwent around December 29. Four days at sea is a pretty good reason for a party, especially when New Year's Eve is just around the corner.

Music at Marion Bay

Tasmania's ultimate multi-day musical celebration, the annual Falls Music & Arts Festival (www.fallsfestival. com.au) is a must-attend for indie-music lovers. Recent visitors to the Marion Bay site northeast of Hobart have included Interpol and The National, and Australasian stars such as Paul Kelly, Dan Sultan and Ladyhawke.

Summer's Harvest in Sorell

Pick your own summer bounty at the Sorell Fruit Farm (www.sorellfruitfarm. com). December and January are the best months, but some fruit is best harvested at other times of the year; the website has a handy harvest calendar.

Walking in Tasmania

Spotting Wildlife

Maria Island For Cape Barren geese, wallabies, pademelons, wombats and echidnas
Mt William National Park To spot the rare Forester Kangaroo

Family Friendly

The easy 20-minute (pram and wheelchair friendly) boardwalk track to **Cape Tourville Lighthouse** lookout
Enchanted Nature Walk, Cradle Mountain
Creepy Crawly Nature Trail, Southwest National Park

Spectacular Scenery

Climbing **Mt Strzelecki**
Summitting Frenchmans Cap – peer over the cliffs if you dare
Ascending **Cradle Mountain** for views of Tasmania's alpine heart
Negotiating the improbably scenic **Tasman Coastal Trail**

Challenging Yourself

The quartzite spire of **Federation Peak**, known as Australia's toughest bushwalk
The 10-day traverse of the whole of the **Western Arthurs** in Tasmania's remote southwest
Flying in to the bush airstrip at Melaleuca to walk out along the rugged **South Coast Track**

Forget a fascinating convict history and a great food and wine scene. For many visitors, Tasmania's unique appeal is bushwalking through the state's idiosyncratic and challenging wilderness areas, often quite different from the Australian mainland to the north. Arguably, no other destination on the planet – Hello, New Zealand? – packs as much diversity for outdoor buffs into such a small area. So break out the thermals, tent and Primus stove and get walking. If you're after a tad more luxury with your scenic highlights, Tasmania can also provide guided walks where you'll get to experience great local food and wine after rewarding days on the trail. And while Tasmania is renowned for its superb, multi-day bushwalking challenges, many shorter and more accessible tracks also dot the island. Look forward to scenic wilderness thrills and a good night's sleep.

Planning

When to Go

Choosing when to visit Tasmania for bushwalking is a decision involving track popularity, visitor numbers and climate conditions. Bear in mind that Tasmania's notoriously fickle weather can deliver many surprises, so definitely come prepared. See the 'Before You Go' section on www.parks.tas.gov.au for more on the best timing for bushwalking.

Summer

Although summer – from December to February – offers long days and a higher likelihood of warmer, settled weather (but no guarantees, OK) it is also the peak season and popular tracks can be crowded on weekends. Try and depart midweek to avoid crowding. An exception is the Overland Track, which has instigated a booking system and one-way walking to alleviate congestion. In alpine regions, snow is still possible during summer, so look forward to experiencing Tasmania's archetypal changeable weather in these areas.

Autumn

Mild weather and the gorgeous golden tones of autumn – from March to May – are a great time to experience the Tasmanian wilderness. Anzac Day (April 25) and Easter (timing varies year to year) sees higher walker numbers on popular tracks, so plan accordingly.

Winter

Winter – from June to August – is a mixed bag with the likelihood of crisp, blue-sky mornings balanced with the very real possibility of snow, especially in the highlands. Days are short with reduced daylight, and deep snow can make some tracks inaccessible. Winter in Tasmania is definitely only for the intrepid and the very experienced.

Spring

Rain and wind can be the defining characteristics of spring – from September to November – in Tasmania. Tracks can be muddier and more slippery, and the addition of melting snow into the climatic equation means that river levels can be at their highest.

Pre-Walk Planning Information

Books & Brochures

Lonely Planet's *Walking in Australia* has info on some of Tasmania's best (longer) walks. Available free from visitor centres is Australian Geographic's *Great Walks of Tasmania* – covering Tasmania's five most iconic multi-day walks – and the Parks & Wildlife Service's *60 Great Short Walks* brochure listing the state's best quick ambles, with durations from 10 minutes to all day.

Other compilations of walks throughout the state include *A Visitor's Guide to Tasmania's National Parks* by Greg Buckman, *120 Walks in Tasmania* by Tyrone Thomas, which covers a wide variety of short and multi-day walks, or *Day Walks Tasmania* by John Chapman and Monica Chapman. There are also detailed guides to specific walks or areas, including *South West Tasmania* by John Chapman and *Cradle Mountain–Lake St Clair & Walls of Jerusalem National Parks* by John Chapman and John Siseman. Jan Hardy and Bert Elson's short-walk books are also worth hunting down (covering Hobart, Mt Wellington, Launceston, the Northeast and the Northwest).

Online

Check the **Parks & Wildlife Service's** (www.parks.tas.gov.au) website for essential pre-departure information including safety

PLAN YOUR TRIP WALKING IN TASMANIA

TASMANIA'S GREAT WALKS

Tasmania's most iconic multi-day walks have been handily grouped together for marketing purposes. All together they cover around 300km, encompassing rainforest, subalpine areas, and beautiful coastal scenery. See www.greatwalkstasmania.com for information, including details of companies offering guided experiences of the following 'Great Walks'.

» Maria Island Walk
» Bay of Fires Walk
» Freycinet Experience Walk
» South Coast Track
» Tarkine Rainforest Track
» Walls of Jerusalem Experience
» Cradle Mountain

Tasmania's other iconic wilderness experience is the Overland Track. See www.overlandtrack.com.au for information and booking details. Another track for the Tasmanian outdoor completist is the 480km Tasmanian Trail trek from Devonport to Dover. It's also popular with mountain bikers and horseriders. See p32.

TASMANIA'S TOP 10 WALKS

Walking is absolutely the best way to see Tasmania's wilderness in its full glory (and it's not a bad way to walk off all that great local food and wine, either). Pack comfy walking shoes, thick socks and hit the tracks. Following are our favourite walks, ranging in length from 20 minutes to six days:

» **Overland Track** A stunning week-long endeavour through the Cradle Mountain-Lake St Clair National Park

» **Wineglass Bay** Climb up over the saddle and lookout to Freycinet Peninsula's famous beach, a very scenic return walk of around three hours

» **Cataract Gorge Walk** Explore Launceston's gorgeous gorge that actually cuts through the heart of the town

» **Tasman Coastal Trail** Awesome three- to five-day trail along the Tasman Peninsula clifftops. Keep an eye out for migrating whales.

» **Truganini Track** A hilly, two-hour return climb through sclerophyll bushland between the southern suburbs of Taroona and Mt Nelson

» **Russell Falls Walk** A short jaunt from the car park at Mt Field National Park

» **Dove Lake Circuit** A three-hour lake lap at Cradle Mountain–Lake St Clair National Park

» **South Coast Track** An 85km epic along the south coast in the Southwest National Park

» **The Nut** Sweat it out on the steep slopes of the Nut in Stanley

» **Tahune AirWalk** Take a knee-trembling treetop walk about 1½ hours south of Hobart

hints and equipment checklists. This superb resource also includes information on what weather to expect, updates on bushfires and track closures, and a whole raft of podcasts, downloadable track notes, and fact sheets. Other online information sources include:

» **www.overlandtrack.com.au** For information on Tasmania's most iconic wilderness experience

» **www.bushwalk.com** Visit the 'Forum' section for Tasmania for up-to-date trip reports and feedback from experienced local bushwalkers.

» **www.bushwalktasmania.com** Lots of information on tracks and transport

National Parks Fees & Track Bookings

Visitors' fees apply to all national parks. See p295 for details. Because of its popularity, there is a limit on the number of walkers and a booking system on the Overland Track from November to April. Across that period, the compulsory direction to walk the Overland Track is from north to south. Bookings can be made on www.parks.tas.gov.au and www.overlandtrack.com.au. See p266 for further information.

Prior booking of other tracks and walks in Tasmania is not possible.

On the Trail

Maps & Track Notes

Tasmap produces excellent maps available from visitor centres and Parks & Wildlife Service offices. In Hobart you'll also find them at Service Tasmania (p76) and the Tasmanian Map Centre (p76), as well as statewide outdoors stores. To order online, see www.dpiw.tas.gov.au.

Track notes for the Overland Track, the Tasmanian Coastal Trail, the Freycinet Peninsula Circuit, the Frenchmans Cap Circuit and the South Coast Track are available on the Parks & Wildlife Service (www.parks.tas. gov.au) website.

Gear & Equipment

Shops specialising in bushwalking gear and outdoors equipment proliferate around the state. In Hobart, most shops congregate on Elizabeth St between Bathurst St and Melville St. Most shops can also hire gear as well. To arrange hire of any bushwalking gear before you reach Tasmania contact Tasmanian Wilderness Experiences (1300 882 293; www.twe.travel).

The Challenges of Tasmania's Weather

In Tasmania (particularly in the west and southwest), a fine day can quickly become cold and stormy at any time of year – always carry warm clothing, waterproof gear and a compass. In addition, you should always carry a tent, rather than relying on finding a bed in a hut, particularly on popular walks such as the Overland Track.

On all extended walks, you must carry extra food in case you have to sit out a few days of particularly inclement weather. This is a very important point, as the Parks & Wildlife Service routinely hears of walkers running out of food in such instances and having to rely on the goodwill of better-prepared people they meet along the way to supplement their supplies. In the worst of circumstances, such lack of preparation puts risk at risk: if the bad weather continues for long enough, everyone suffers.

Tasmanian walks are famous for their mud, so be prepared: waterproof your boots, wear gaiters and watch where you're putting your feet. Even on the Overland Track, long sections of which are covered by boardwalk, you can sometimes find yourself up to your hips in mud if you're not careful.

Guided Walks

Many companies offer guided walks ranging from one-day excursions to multi-day epics involving accommodation in everything from tents to upmarket lodges, plus trips that blend foot power with time on a bike, bus or canoe. Also see the 'Activities' section of www.discovertasmania.com.au for more information.

» **Tasmanian Expeditions** (☎1300 666 856; www.tas-ex.com) Rafting, biking and climbing also available

» **Bay of Fires Walks** (☎6392 2211; www. bayoffires.com.au) A four-day, luxury walk along this photogenic, rock-strewn stretch of coast in the northeast

» **Tasmanian Wilderness Experiences** (☎1300 882 293; www.twe.travel) Lots of one- and multi-day walks across the island. Bushwalking gear is also for sale and for hire.

» **Tarkine Trails** (☎6223 5320; www. tarkinetrails.com.au) Multi-day experiences in the Tarkine Wilderness

» **Cradle Mountain Huts** (☎6392 2211; www.cradlehuts.com.au) Six-day walk along the Overland Track, staying in private huts

» **Freycinet Experience** (☎1800 506 003; www.freycinet.com.au) A fully catered, lodge-based, four-day stroll down the famous peninsula

» **Maria Island Walk** (☎6227 8800; www. mariaislandwalk.com.au) Another four-day option, this time on Maria Island

Responsible Bushwalking

To help preserve the ecology and beauty of Tasmania, consider the following when bushwalking.

Code of Ethics

The **Parks & Wildlife Service** (☎6233 6191; www.parks.tas.gov.au) publishes a booklet

---

KEEPING SAFE #1 – BUSHFIRES & BLIZZARDS

Bushfires are a regular occurrence in Australia and Tasmania is no exception. In hot, dry and windy weather, be extremely careful with any naked flame and don't throw cigarette butts out of car windows. On a total fire ban day it's illegal to use even a camping stove in the open.

When a total fire ban is in place (common from November onwards), bushwalkers should delay their trip until the weather improves. Get updates from the **Tasmania Fire Service** (www.fire.tas.gov.au). If you're out in the bush and you see smoke, even a long way away, take it seriously – bushfires move very quickly and change direction with the wind. Go to the nearest open space, downhill if possible. A forested ridge, on the other hand, is the most dangerous place to be.

At the other end of the elemental scale, blizzards can occur in Tasmania's mountains at any time of year. Bushwalkers should certainly be prepared for such freezing eventualities, particularly in remote areas. Take warm clothing such as thermals and jackets, plus windproof and waterproof garments. Carry a high-quality tent suitable for snow camping and enough food for two extra days, in case you get held up by bad weather.

called *Tasmania's Wilderness World Heritage Area: Essential Bushwalking Guide & Trip Planner,* which has sections on the basics of planning, minimal impact bushwalking, first aid and what gear you need to bring to cope with Tasmania's changeable weather. The booklet is available online on the Parks & Wildlife Service's website. You can also pick up PWS literature at Service Tasmania (p76), or national park visitor centres or ranger stations.

Safety First

» Bushwalkers should stick to established trails. Avoid cutting corners and taking short cuts, and stay on hard ground where possible.

» Before tackling a long or remote walk, tell someone about your plans and arrange to contact them when you return. Make sure you sign a Parks & Wildlife Service (PWS) register at the start and finish of your walk.

» Keep bushwalking parties small.

Camping & Walking on Private Property

» When camping, always use designated campgrounds. When bush camping, try to find a natural clearing to set up your tent.

» Always seek permission to camp from landowners.

Rubbish Disposal

» Carry all your rubbish out with you; don't burn or bury it.

» Don't overlook easily forgotten items, such as silver paper, orange peel, cigarette butts and plastic wrappers.

» Make an effort to carry out rubbish left by others.

» Never bury your rubbish. Digging disturbs soil and ground cover and encourages erosion. Buried rubbish will likely be dug up by animals who may be injured or poisoned by it.

» Minimise waste by taking minimal packaging and no more food than you will need.

» Sanitary napkins, tampons, condoms and toilet paper should be carried out despite the inconvenience. They burn and decompose poorly.

Human Waste Disposal

» Use toilets provided; otherwise bury human waste.

» Dig a small hole 15cm (6in) deep and at least 100m (320ft) from any watercourse. Cover the waste with soil and a rock.

» In snow, dig down to the soil.

» Ensure that these guidelines are applied to a portable toilet tent if one is being used by a large bushwalking party. Encourage all party members to use the site.

Washing

» Don't use detergents or toothpaste in or near watercourses, even if they are biodegradable.

» For personal washing, use biodegradable soap and a water container (or even a lightweight, portable basin) at least 50m (160ft) away from

---

SHORT BUT SWEET

Here's concise proof that walking in Tasmania is not just suited to gung-ho outdoor types with industrial-strength thermals and a week's worth of powdered milk and instant noodles. If you like what you see here, hunt out the *Tasmania's Great Short Walks* brochure. It's freely available at visitor centres, and lists 60 of the state's best short walks, with durations from 10 minutes to all day. Search for 'Great Walks' on www.parks.tas.gov.au to get the same information before you leave home.

» Isthmus circuit to **Wineglass Bay**

» Boardwalk track to **Cape Tourville Lighthouse** lookout

» The forest wander to **Liffey Falls**

» **Russell Falls** walk

» **Coal Mines Historic Site** on the Tasman Peninsula

» **Hartz Peak** in the Hartz Mountains National Park

» **Cape Hauy** near Fortescue Bay

» **Waterfall Bluff** near Eaglehawk Neck

» **Organ Pipes** walk on Hobart's Mt Wellington

» **Labillardiere Peninsula** on Bruny Island

KEEPING SAFE #2 – HYPOTHERMIA & CREEPY CRAWLIES

Hypothermia is a significant risk, especially during the winter months in southern parts of Australia – and especially in Tasmania. Strong winds produce a high chill factor that can result in hypothermia even in moderately cool temperatures. Early signs include the inability to perform fine movements (such as doing up buttons), shivering and a bad case of the 'umbles' (fumbles, mumbles, grumbles and stumbles). The key elements of treatment include moving out of the cold, changing out of any wet clothing into dry clothes with windproof and waterproof layers, adding insulation and providing fuel (water and carbohydrate) to allow shivering, which builds the internal temperature. In severe hypothermia, shivering actually stops: this is a medical emergency requiring rapid evacuation in addition to the above measures.

For information on other environmental hazards including leeches, spiders and snakes see p312.

the watercourse. Disperse the waste water widely to allow the soil to filter it fully.

» Wash cooking utensils 50m (160ft) from watercourses using a scourer, sand or snow instead of detergent.

Erosion

» Hillsides and mountain slopes, especially at high altitudes, are prone to erosion.

» If a well-used track passes through a mud patch, walk through the mud so as not to increase the size of the patch.

» Avoid removing the plant life that keeps topsoils in place.

» Stick to existing tracks and avoid short cuts.

Fires & Low-Impact Cooking

» Don't depend on open fires for cooking. The cutting of wood for fires in popular trekking areas can cause rapid deforestation.

» Cook on a light-weight kerosene, alcohol or Shellite (white gas) stove and avoid those powered by disposable butane gas canisters.

» Boil all water for 10 minutes before drinking it, or use water-purifying tablets.

» If you are trekking with a group, supply stoves for the whole team. In alpine areas, ensure that all members are outfitted with enough clothing so that fires are not a necessity for warmth.

» Fires may be acceptable below the tree line in areas that get very few visitors. If you light a fire, use an existing fireplace. Don't surround fires with rocks. Use only dead, fallen wood. Leave wood for the next person.

» Ensure that you fully extinguish a fire after use. Spread the embers and flood them with water.

» National parks are 'fuel stove only' areas.

» Don't light fires in any bush environment, and use only fuel stoves for cooking.

» On days of total fire ban, don't light any fire whatsoever, including fuel stoves.

Wildlife Conservation

» Do not engage in or encourage hunting. It is illegal in all Tasmanian national parks.

» Don't attempt to exterminate animals in huts. In wild places, they are likely to be protected species.

» Discourage the presence of wildlife by not leaving food scraps behind you. Place gear out of reach and tie packs to rafters or trees.

» Do not feed the wildlife as this can lead to animals becoming dependent on hand-outs, to unbalanced populations and to diseases.

» Don't harm native birds or animals; these are protected by law.

» Don't feed native animals.

» Don't take pets into national parks.

Outdoor Adventures

Family Fun

Take-it-easy **summer camping** at Richardson's Beach
Rugging up for winter **ski and snowboard** thrills at Ben Lomond National Park
Sailing on Hobart's Derwent River, on the elegant tall ship the *Windeward Bound*

Daredevil Thrills

Abseiling down the 140m-high wall of the Gordon Dam
Cable hang-gliding near Launceston
Descending Mt Wellington by **mountain bike** through four seasons in one hour

Taking it Easy

Cruising the Gordon River on the yacht *Stormbreaker*
Casting a trout fly across the Lake Country's serene waters
Paddling a slow-moving **canoe** on the southwest's Pieman River

Rivers, Lakes & Ocean

Rafting the Franklin River, a classic, remote 10-day river journey
Sea-kayaking amid the glorious southwest isolation of Bathurst Harbour and Port Davey
Diving through sea caves and giant underwater kelp forests around the Tasman Peninsula

If Tasmania were a person, it would be very much the 'outdoors type'. The bushwalks are among Australia's best (and most taxing), while white-water rafting on the Franklin River is charged with much environmental grandeur and excitement. Abseiling and rock-climbing on the Tasman and Freycinet Peninsulas is a thrill a minute, and cycling is a great way to see the countryside.

Less demanding is boating on the Arthur and Pieman Rivers in the northwest, sea-kayaking in the southeast, and walks through the Hastings Caves in the south. Yachties can spend lazy days exploring the bays and inlets of the D'Entrecasteaux Channel, and trout fishers will find plenty of fish in the remote Lake Country.

For information on staying safe in the outdoors see p25 and p27. Checking out the Health section in the Directory (p314) would also be a sensible precautionary measure.

On the Water

Canoeing

For sedate paddles, try the Arthur and Pieman Rivers in the northwest, and the Ansons River in the northeast. You can rent canoes at Arthur River. The Huon, Weld, Leven and North Esk Rivers also attract their fair share of canoes and rafts.

Rafting

Tasmania is famed for white-knuckle white-water rafting on the Franklin River. Other rivers offering rapid thrills include the Derwent (upstream from Hobart), the Picton (southwest of Hobart) and the Mersey in the north. See Aardvark Adventures (☏6273 7722; www.aardvarkadventures.com.au) for details of rafting trips down south. Search for 'rafting' on www.parks.tas.gov.au for lots of good advice.

Sea-Kayaking

Sea-kayaking centres include Kettering, southeast of Hobart, from where you can explore the D'Entrecasteaux Channel, Bruny Island and the south coast; and Coles Bay, the launching place for Freycinet Peninsula explorations. Multiday expeditions exploring the Tasman Peninsula and the isolated Bathurst Harbour through Roaring 40s Tasmania (www.roaring40skayaking.com.au).

You can also have a paddle around the Hobart docks, and even end with an alfresco, on the water feast of fish and chips. See p55.

Search for 'kayaking' on www.parks.tas. gov.au for tips on how to tackle sea-kayaking in a sustainable way.

Sailing

The D'Entrecasteaux Channel and Huon River south of Hobart are wide, deep and tantalising places to set sail, with more inlets and harbours than you could swing a boom at (although conditions can be difficult south of Gordon). Fleets of white sails often dot Hobart's Derwent River in summer – many Hobartians own yachts and consider the city's nautical opportunities among its greatest assets. See p58 for details of heritage-style tall ships plying the Derwent.

Yacht Hire & Moorings

For casual berths in Hobart (overnight or weekly), contact the Royal Yacht Club of Tasmania (☏03-6223 4599; www.ryct.org.au) in Sandy Bay. North of the bridge, you can anchor in Cornelian Bay or New Town Bay. There's a great marina at Kettering, in the channel south of Hobart, but it's usually crowded so finding a mooring isn't easy.

If you're an experienced sailor, hire a yacht from Yachting Holidays (☏0417 550 879; www.yachtingholidays.com.au), based in Hobart. Charter of a six-berth vessel is around $700 per day, with reduced rates for long rentals or in the off-peak (April to November) period.

For cruising and trailer boat owners, a useful publication is *Cruising Southern Tasmania* ($27.50), available online from Tasmap (www.tasmap.com.au).

Ocean Fishing

Rod fishing in saltwater is allowed year-round without a permit, but size restrictions and bag limits apply. If you're diving for abalone, rock lobsters or scallops, or fishing with a net, recreational sea fishing licences are required. These are available from post offices, Service Tasmania or online from the Department of Primary Industries & Water (www.dpiw.tas.gov.au). There are on-the-spot fines for breaches of fishing regulations.

See Tasmanian Wilderness Fishing (www.tasmaniawildernessfishing.com.au) for exciting seven-day live-aboard fishing trips from Hobart to Port Davey.

Read the bimonthly *Tasmanian Fishing & Boating News*, available online at www.tasfish.com, and scan the online back issues for coverage of ocean fishing in Tasmania.

Scuba Diving & Snorkelling

Where to Dive

National Geographic reckons Tasmania offers the 'most accessible underwater wilderness in the world'. You may well find yourself in agreement. Visibility ranges from 12m in summer to 40m in winter, with temperate waters offering unique biodiversity. There are excellent scuba-diving opportunities around Rocky Cape on the north coast, on the east coast, and around the shipwrecks of King and Flinders Islands. At Tinderbox near Hobart and off Maria Island there are marked underwater snorkelling trails. There's also an artificial dive site created by the scuttling of the *Troy D* off the west coast of Maria Island; see www.troyd.com.au for info.

Information

Discover Tasmania (www.discovertasmania.com) has info on diving in Tasmania including the PDF download *Tasmania's Dive Trail*, also available at visitor information centres. The website also lists diving businesses and equipment hire around the state.

See this book's coverage of Eaglehawk Neck, Bicheno, Binalong Bay and Wynyard.

Learning to Dive

Eaglehawk Dive Centre (☑6250 3566; www.eaglehawkdive.com.au; 178 Pirates Bay Dr) is on the Tasman Peninsula.

Surfing
Where to Surf

Tasmania has dozens of great surf beaches, but the water is damn cold – BYO steamer wetsuit. Close to Hobart, the most reliable spots are Clifton Beach and Goats Beach (unsigned) en route to South Arm. Eaglehawk Neck on the Tasman Peninsula is also worth checking out. The southern beaches on Bruny Island – particularly Cloudy Bay – offer consistent swells.

The east coast from Bicheno north to St Helens has solid beach breaks when conditions are working. Binalong Bay on the Bay of Fires is good. The east coast from Ironhouse Point south to Spring and Shelly Beaches near Orford has consistent surf, and King Island also gets its share. At Marrawah on the west coast the waves are often towering, and Australia's heaviest wave, Shipstern Bluff off the south coast, isn't recommended for anyone other than serious pros.

Island Surf School (☑6265 9776, 0400 830 237; www.islandsurfschool.com.au) offers lessons at Park Beach near Sorell.

TOP TASSIE BEACHES

Pack your swimsuit, brace yourself for a cold-water collision, and jump right in! Also see p18 for other slices of primo Tassie sand.

» **Binalong Bay** Binalong time since you had a dip? Head for this long crescent of sand just north of St Helens.

» **Boat Harbour Beach** The drive down the steep access road offers postcard-perfect views of this divine little bay.

» **Marrawah** Hardcore ocean surf for harder-core surfers.

» **Fortescue Bay** A little slice of heaven, complete with low-key camping ground.

» **Trousers Point** A kooky name indeed, but this magnificent beach makes the waters of Bass Strait look unfeasibly alluring.

Information

See the following for surf reports and live webcams:

» Magic Seaweed (www.magicseaweed.com)
» Surf Tasmania (www.surftasmania.com)
» Tassie Surf (www.tassiesurf.com)

Swimming

The north and east coasts have plenty of sheltered, white-sand beaches offering excellent swimming, although the water is (to understate it) rather cold. There are also sheltered beaches near Hobart, including Bellerive and Sandy Bay, but these tend to receive some urban pollution – things will be less soupy further south at Kingston and Blackmans Bay, or east at Seven Mile Beach. On the west coast, the surf can be ferocious and the beaches aren't patrolled – play it safe.

On the Land

See p25 for information on reducing your environmental impact while outdoors.

Caving

Tasmania's limestone karst caves are among the most impressive in Australia. The caves at Mole Creek, Gunns Plains and Hastings are open to the public daily. Both Mole Creek and Hastings offer the chance to get troglodytic on cave tours – see regional chapters for details.

Trout Fishing

Brown trout were introduced into Tasmania's Plenty River in 1866, and into Lake Sorell in 1867. Innumerable lakes and rivers have subsequently been stocked, including artificial lakes built by Hydro Tasmania for hydroelectricity production. Trout have thrived, and today anglers make the most of the state's inland fisheries.

Where to Fish

The sparsely populated Lake Country on Tasmania's Central Plateau is a region of glacial lakes and streams, and is home to the state's best-known spots for brown and rainbow trout: Arthurs Lake, Great Lake, Little Pine Lagoon (fly-fishing only), Western Lakes (including Lake St Clair), Lake Sorell and the Lake Pedder impoundment. On some parts of Great Lake you're only allowed to use artificial lures, and you're not allowed to fish any of the streams flowing into Great Lake. For more information on fishing in Tasmania's lakes, see p138.

The Tamar River is another great fishing area, with a series of 10 fishing pontoons (accessible by fishers with disabilities) between Launceston and George Town. The George Town area is particularly good for both freshwater and saltwater fishing.

Information & Gear

To bone up on Tassie trout before you unpack your rod, get a copy of *Tasmanian Trout Waters* by Greg French. Also worth a look is the bimonthly *Tasmanian Fishing & Boating News* ($4), available online at www.tasfish.com. The website features plenty of articles from back issues.

In Hobart, the spot for spot-on lures and fishing info is Spot On Fishing Tackle (p75).

Learning to Fish

Tasmanian trout (brown and rainbow) can be difficult to catch as they're fickle about what they eat; the right lures are needed for the right river, lake, season or weather. If you find you just can't hook them yourself, there are dozens of operators offering guides, lessons and fishing trips; **Trout Guides & Lodges Tasmania** (www.troutguidestasmania.com.au) is a great starting point.

Licences & Costs

A licence is required to fish Tasmania's inland waters; there are bag, season and size limits on most fish. Licence costs vary from $20 for 48 hours to $66.50 for the full season, and are available from sports stores, Service Tasmania outlets, post offices, visitor centres and some country shops and petrol stations. In general, inland waters open for fishing on the Saturday closest to 1 August and close on the Sunday nearest 30 April; the best fishing is between October and April. Different dates apply to some places and these (plus other essential bits of information) are all detailed in the *Fishing Code* brochure you'll be given when you buy your licence. Also see the **Inland Fisheries Service** (www.ifs.tas.gov.au) website for a ton of information about fishing on Tasmanian lakes and rivers.

Rock Climbing & Abseiling

Although clear skies are desirable for rock climbing and Tasmania's weather is often wet, the sport nonetheless thrives around the state, as does abseiling. There are some excellent cliffs for climbing, particularly along the east coast, where the weather is usually best. The Organ Pipes on Mt Wellington above Hobart, the Hazards at Coles Bay, the cliffs on Mt Killiecrankie on Flinders Island, and Launceston's Cataract Gorge offer brilliant climbing on solid rock. Climbing fiends often see images of the magnificent rock formations on the Tasman Peninsula and head straight for that region, but the coastal cliffs there are impossible to climb if the ocean swell is too big.

Courses

It's possible to climb or abseil with an experienced instructor. Some recommended outfits:

» **Aardvark Adventures** (6273 7722; www.aardvarkadventures.com.au)

» **Freycinet Adventures** (6257 0500; www.freycinetadventures.com.au)

» **Tasmanian Expeditions** (1300 666 856, 6339 3999; www.tas-ex.com)

Skiing

There are two petite ski resorts in Tasmania: Ben Lomond, 55km southeast of Launceston, and Mt Mawson in Mt Field National Park, 80km northwest of Hobart. Both offer cheaper, though much less developed, ski facilities than at mainland resorts in Victoria and New South Wales (rope tows are still used on some runs!). The ski season usually runs from July to September, but despite the state's southerly latitude, snowfalls tend to be patchy and unreliable.

See www.ski.com.au for snow conditions. For gear hire, including snow chains for your car, contact Skigia & Surf in Hobart (p75).

Cycling & Mountain Biking

Cycling is a terrific way to tour Tasmania and engage with the island landscapes, especially on the dry east coast. To cycle between Hobart and Launceston via either coast, allow between 10 and 14 days. For a 'lap of the map' by bike, allow between 18 and 28 days.

Information

» **Bicycle Tasmania** (www.biketas.org.au) A solid source of information. Click on 'Routes to

Ride by Region' for details of two- and three-week circuits.

» Discover Tasmania (www.discover tasmania.com) Download the *Self Guided Touring in Tasmania* PDF or ask for it at the Hobart visitor information centre.

Information centres and Discover Tasmania can also supply the excellent *Your Guide to Cycling Touring* detailing west-coast and east-coast routes and including terrain profiles.

See p322 for further cycle-touring tips.

Bike Rental

Short- and long-term bike rental is available in Hobart (p55) and in Launceston (p190).

Tours

» Green Island Tours (✆6376 3080; www.cycling-tasmania.com)

» Island Cycle Tours (✆6234 9558; www.islandcycletours.com)

» Mountainbike Tasmania (✆0447 712 638; www.mountainbiketasmania.com.au)

» Tasmanian Expeditions (✆1300 666 856; www.tas-ex.com)

Mountain Biking

There are no dedicated mountain-biking trails within parks in Tasmania, but there are plenty of fire trails and off-the-beaten-track tracks around to explore – ask at bike shops. On the competition front, check out

---

THE TASMANIAN TRAIL

The Tasmanian Trail is a 480km route from Devonport to Dover, geared towards walkers, horse riders and mountain bikers. Most of the trail is on forestry roads, fire trails or country roads; it passes towns, pastoral land and forests, and there are camping spots about every 30km. All the information you need to follow the trail is in the *Tasmanian Trail Guide Book*, available in bookshops, outdoor-equipment stores and online from www.tasmaniantrail.com. au. Also see www.parks.tas.gov.au for more information.

January's four-day, 200km Wildside Mountain Bike Race (www.wildsidemtb.com), which wheels through the west-coast wilderness from Cradle Mountain to Strahan. There's also the multisport Freycinet Lodge Challenge (www.tasultra.org), held in Freycinet National Park every October.

An essential part of any visit to Hobart should be a knobbly two-wheeled descent of Mt Wellington. See p54. Mountainbike Tasmania (see Tours opposite) run excellent tours around northern Tasmania.

For information on low-impact mountain biking, search for 'Mountain Biking' on www.parks.tas.gov.au, and see Discover Tasmania (www.discovertasmania.com).

itineraries

Whether you've got six days or 60, these itineraries provide a starting point for the trip of a lifetime. Want more inspiration? Head online to www.lonelyplanet. com/thorntree to chat with other travellers.

One Week to 10 Days
East Coaster

> Spend a few days enjoying the cosmopolitan ambience in Hobart, combining great pubs and cafes, brilliant restaurants, and a heritage vibe. Explore the city's vibrant arts scene, including the eclectic and dramatic Museum of Old & New Art (MONA). Head south to the dramatic coastal crags of the **Tasman Peninsula** and to experience the grim convict stories of **Port Arthur**. Wind your way back north, stopping to say g'day to the Tasmanian devils in **Taranna** and to pick fresh fruit at **Sorell**. Near Copping, take the shortcut to the east coast via Wielangta Forest Drive. Take a boat out to **Maria Island** for camping, bushwalking and wildlife spotting on some rare west-facing east-coast beaches. Get your camera ready for **Freycinet National Park** and **Wineglass Bay**, and indulge in sea kayaking and oyster appreciation at **Coles Bay**. Continue north to the chilled-out fishing town of **Bicheno** for penguin spotting, before checking out the rocky lagoons and headlands of the **Bay of Fires**.

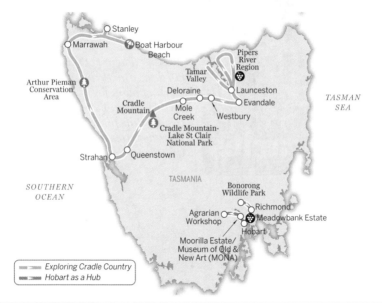

Exploring Cradle Country
Hobart as a Hub

Three to Four Days
Hobart as a Hub

Take advantage of Tasmania's relatively small driving distances by using **Hobart** as a hub for a variety of day trips out and about around the Tasmanian state capital, maybe as a long weekend escape from the Aussie mainland. Commence with a day-long outing to the relaxed heritage streets of **Richmond**. Don't miss the graceful Richmond Bridge before checking out the **Bonorong Wildlife Centre** followed by a leisurely lunch at **Meadowbank Estate** in the Coal River Valley. Next, catch a ferry from the Hobart waterfront up the Derwent River to the **Moorilla Estate**. Make it a day filled with all things gourmet and cultural, including wine and beer tasting, lunch at the Source restaurant, and diving into the pleasantly bewildering **Museum of Old & New Art (MONA)**. Continue the gourmet and foodie theme with a booking at the **Agrarian Kitchen** cookery school near New Norfolk. Its most popular class is 'The Agrarian Experience', a day-long celebration of the seasons commencing with choosing the freshest of fruit and veggies in its very own orchard and garden.

10 Days to Two Weeks
Exploring Cradle Country

Kick off in **Launceston** with a stroll through Lonnie's Cataract Gorge, before exploring the excellent Queen Victoria Museum & Art Gallery (QVMAG). Discover the eclectic attractions of the **Tamar Valley**, including seahorses, gold mines, lighthouses and wineries. Don't miss having lunch at one the vineyard restaurants around the **Pipers River region**. Loop through the historic towns of **Evandale** and **Westbury** before drifting west to **Deloraine** and the caves at **Mole Creek.** A roundabout route (via Moina) takes you to iconic **Cradle Mountain–Lake St Clair National Park,** arguably Australia's top national park. Spend a few days here bushwalking, including the popular two-hour return track to Crater Lake. From Cradle Mountain, drive southwest to the lunar landscapes of **Queenstown** and ride the West Coast Wilderness Railway to **Strahan**. From Strahan, track north through the vast **Arthur Pieman Conservation Area**, spy devils in the wild around **Marrawah**, and clamber up the Nut in **Stanley**. An ocean dip at idyllic **Boat Harbour Beach** is the perfect journey's end.

Up the Guts
Southern Ramblings

One Week to 10 Days
Up the Guts

Kick off in **Hobart** with a walk around Battery Point and the waterfront. Try to visit on a weekend to experience Saturday's sensational Salamanca Market. From Hobart travel northwest through New Norfolk en route to excellent bushwalking in the **Mt Field National Park**. Visit the Something Wild wildlife park at **Westerway**, before diverting via Ellendale through the Derwent Valley to sleepy **Hamilton** and easygoing **Bothwell**, maybe for a round of golf on Australia's oldest course. Continue east to join the Midland (Heritage) Highway and linger for a few nights in sandstone-built towns complete with country pubs, tearooms and colonial accommodation. **Oatlands** has the restored Callington Mill and more Georgian sandstone buildings than any other town in Australia; **Ross** is a gorgeous colonial town with a great bakery, a historic bridge, a friendly pub and plenty of places to stay; and **Campbell Town** makes a handy pit stop en route to laid-back **Launceston**. Reward yourself with a tour and a taste at the hallowed Boag's brewery and dinner at the excellent Stillwater.

One Week to 10 Days
Southern Ramblings

From **Hobart**, trundle south to **Kettering** to catch the ferry across to windswept and easygoing **Bruny Island**. Allow at least three nights to appreciate Bruny's laid-back charm, including artisan cheeses, Australia's southernmost vineyard, and exciting excursions to the Southern Ocean for seals and spectacular scenery. Don't miss the fairy penguins on **'The Neck'**. Return to the Tasmanian 'mainland', and divert west to funky **Cygnet** for two of the island's best little cafes, Red Velvet Lounge and Lotus Eaters. Continue north along the scenic Huon River to **Huonville**. Lots of summer fruit – apples, cherries and more – and lunch at the Home Hill Winery Restaurant are tasty distractions. Travel south down the river's opposite bank to **Geeveston**. Spend some time in the treetops at **Tahune Forest AirWalk**, before bushwalking in the **Hartz Mountains National Park.** Continue south to Dover, an excellent southern base for day trips: go underground at **Hastings Caves & Thermal Springs**, or negotiate the winding, unsealed road out to the end-of-the-road ambience of **Recherche Bay** and **Cockle Creek**.

Travel with Children

Best Regions for Kids

Hobart & Around

Treat the kids to harbourside fish and chips before feeding your family's minds at the Tasmanian Museum & Art Gallery. Balance things out with mountain biking down Mt Wellington.

Tasman Peninsula & Port Arthur

Get spooked on the Historic Ghost Tour at Port Arthur or enjoy 'pick your own' fruit at the Sorell Fruit Farm. Meet the furred and feathered Tassie locals at Taranna's Tasmanian Devil Conservation Park.

The Southeast

Explore Bruny Island's spectacular coastline by boat. Near sleepy Geeveston is the exciting Tahune Forest AirWalk.

The East Coast

Kayak the sheltered waters of Coles Bay, and welcome Bicheno's penguins home at dusk. Hit the region's beaches for laid-back family fun.

Launceston & Around

Meet City Park's energetic Japanese macaques, and ponder on the odd little creatures at Seahorse World. Ride the Cataract Gorge chairlift before burning off energy at Kids Paradise.

Tasmania for Kids

Tasmania's a naturally active kind of place that will provide challenges, fun and exercise for children of all ages. Take a cruise past stunning coastal scenery to spy on seals and dolphins, or get paddling in a kayak around Hobart's inner harbour. Take to the hills for adventures through the forest canopy, or rush on a mountain bike down the imposing hulk of Mt Wellington. On the gentler side is the bike path following Hobart's Derwent River, or feeding time at Tassie's excellent wildlife parks, with animals that can be difficult to see in other parts of Australia. And when the kids have hiked, biked and kayaked all day, treat them to superfresh local fruit from a roadside stall, or an alfresco feast of fish and chips around Hobart's docks. Just mind the occasional nosy seagull, OK?

Not all of Tasmania's historic buildings and museums will hold the interest of kids, but there are still plenty of historical, natural or science-based exhibits to get them thinking.

See p58 and p185 for the best kid-friendly ways to experience Hobart and Launceston; other highlights of experiencing Tasmania through children's eyes are listed on p18.

Accommodation

Many motels and better-equipped caravan parks can supply cots and baby baths and offer playgrounds, sandpits, minigolf, games rooms, swimming pools or lots of grass to run around on, at the very least. Top-end and some midrange hotels are well versed

A fantastic program of free, family-friendly 'Discovery Ranger' activities, including guided walks, spotlight tours, slide shows, quiz nights and games, is held at the most popular national parks during the peak season (usually from the week before Christmas until the start of school in early February).

National parks that stage these activities include Cradle Mountain-Lake St Clair, Freycinet, Maria Island, Tasman, Mt Field, Narawntapu and South Bruny. There are also nature-based events scheduled in Hobart and Launceston. Ask at visitor centres, or search for 'Discovery Ranger' on the Parks & Wildlife Service website (www.parks.tas.gov.au).

in the needs of guests with children; some may also have in-house children's videos and child-minding services. B&Bs, on the other hand, often market themselves as blissfully child-free – it's a good idea to ask if this is the policy. Where relevant, mention of this policy has been included in accommodation reviews in this book.

Eating Out with Children

Dining with children in Tasmania is relatively easy. If you avoid the flashiest places, children are generally welcomed, particularly at Asian, Greek or Italian restaurants. It's usually fine to take kids to cafes, and you'll see families dining early in bistros and pub dining rooms.

Many places that do welcome children don't have separate kids' menus. It's better to find something on the regular menu and ask to have the kitchen adapt it slightly to your children's needs. Places catering to kids usually offer everything straight from the deep fryer. It's usually fine to bring toddler food in with you.

It can be difficult to dine with kids in some better restaurants and booking in for the earliest sitting is one way to tackle this. While some cafes lack a specialised children's menu, many will provide small serves from the main menu if you ask. Some also supply high chairs.

Good news for travelling families, weather permitting, is that there are plenty of picnic spots, and sometimes free or coin-operated barbecues in parks. During summer, Tassie's also a great spot to pick up juicy-fresh fruit. See p290.

Breastfeeding & Nappy Changing

Most Tasmanians have a relaxed attitude about breastfeeding or nappy changing in public, and it's common to change the baby's nappy in the open boot of the car. Hobart and most major towns have centrally located public rooms where parents can go to nurse or feed their baby or change his or her nappy; check with the local visitor centre or city council for details. The area around Salamanca Sq in Hobart can be difficult, as few restaurants and cafes offer nappy-changing facilities. Items such as infant formula and disposable nappies are widely available in urban centres.

Babysitting

In Hobart, contact the **Mobile Nanny Service** (☑6273 3773, 0437 504 064) or check out the statewide listings on www.babysittersrus.com.au or www.bubhub.com.au.

Admission Fees & Discounts

Child concessions (and family rates) often apply for such things as accommodation, tours, admission fees, and air and bus transport, with discounts as high as 50% of the adult rate. Nearly all tourist attractions offer significant discounts for children, with the very young often admitted free. However, the definition of 'child' can vary: from under 12 to under 18 years. Accommodation concessions generally apply to children under 12 years sharing the same room as adults. On the major airlines, infants travel free provided they don't occupy a seat – child fares usually apply between the ages of two and 11 years. Major car-hire companies will supply and fit booster seats for you for a minimal rate, sometimes for free.

Children's Highlights
Beaches & Swimming

» Seven Mile Beach

» Boat Harbour Beach

» Douglas-Apsley National Park

» Fortescue Bay

» Binalong Bay

We're Hungry, Mum

» Fish and chips at Hobart's Constitution Dock
» Sorell Fruit Farm
» Cadbury Chocolate Factory in Claremont
» Honey Farm in Chudleigh
» Devonport's House of Anvers Chocolate Factory

Getting Active

» Walking in Mt Field National Park
» Tahune Forest AirWalk
» Mountain biking down Mt Wellington
» Snow play at Ben Lomond
» Hollybank Treetops Adventure near Lilydale

A History Lesson

» Port Arthur's Historic Ghost Tour
» Ida Bay Railway
» Richmond's Old Hobart Town Historic Model Village
» Oatland's Callington Mill
» Low Head Pilot Station

Meeting the Locals

» Something Wild Wildlife Park near Mt Field
» Taranna's Tasmanian Devil Conservation Park
» Bonorong Wildlife Centre
» Bicheno Penguin Tours
» Seahorse World and Platypus House in Beauty Point

Mucking Around in Boats

» Bruny Island and Tasman Peninsula cruises
» Tall-ship sailing on the Derwent River
» Kayaking around Coles Bay
» Jet-boat rides in New Norfolk

Planning

Lonely Planet's *Travel with Children* contains plenty of useful information for travel with young ones. Also see www.holidays withkids.com.au.

When to Go

When it comes to family holidays, Tasmania is definitely a summer destination. While some parents may value the cultural and intellectual boost given to their children with a cavalcade of museums and historic sites, it won't be too long before little Lachlan and Lilly are bored silly. Having said that, the Australian school holidays and long holiday weekends are peak tourist times in Tasmania, and booking ahead for transport and accommodation is highly recommended. This is especially true for interstate flights, rental cars, the *Spirit of Tasmania* ferry, and budget accommodation like campgrounds and motels. To find out when Australian school holidays are scheduled, search for 'School Term Dates' on www.australia.gov.au.

If the weather does turn to custard, see the rain-day activities recommended on p58 and p185.

What to Pack

Tasmania's weather can be highly changeable, even in summer, so a wide diversity of clothing and footwear is recommended. Definitely pack beach-friendly gear like aqua socks and UV-protection all-in-one suits, but also throw in a few easily layered items like thermal or polypropylene pullovers. If you're planning a beach holiday, a compact and easily assembled beach tent is handy given Tasmania's sometimes capricious winds. Don't forget hats and sunnies – essential for Tasmania's vibrant southern light.

Regions at a Glance

Hobart & Around

Arts Scene ✓✓✓
Gourmet Travel ✓✓✓
History ✓✓✓

Festival Frenzy

For a compact city at the southern edge of the planet, Hobart hosts an amazing range of world-class festivals and arts events. January's eclectic MONA FOMA festival always includes a truly iconic 'artist in residence', and the Ten Days on the Island festival in March spreads the arty good vibes through the rest of Tasmania. Between the city's regular festival frenzies, Hobart's galleries support an energetic and innovative community of local artists.

Eating Well

Visit to enjoy one of Hobart's excellent food and wine festivals, such as The Taste or Savour Tasmania, or experience the innovation and skill of local chefs any time of the year. Dine in superb restaurants, eat casually at Saturday's Salamanca Market or have fish and chips from the Constitution Dock seafood punts. Make sure you find time to sample Tasmania's emerging crop of craft beers at the New Sydney Hotel. Actually, make that eating *and* drinking well.

Historic Port

Hobart is Australia's second-oldest capital city, and the lanes and buildings of Salamanca Place and the winding streets of Battery Point are awash with the stories and memories of a challenging past. Huddled under Mt Wellington, southwest of the historic harbour, the Cascade Brewery and former site of the Female Factory present very different aspects of Tasmania's colonial times.

p44

Tasman Peninsula & Port Arthur

Activities ✓✓
History ✓✓✓
Wildlife ✓✓✓

Coastal Exploring

Experience the rugged coastal landscapes of the Tasman Peninsula either in a sea kayak or on a surfboard, or take it more leisurely by walking around the vertiginous Tasman Coastal Trail or camping at remote Fortescue Bay.

Port Arthur & Beyond

Port Arthur's compelling combination of tragic past and stunning coastal setting is only the starting point for history buffs. Explore the underrated Coal Mines Historic Site at Saltwater River and the fascinating history of the Dogline at Eaglehawk Neck.

Wildlife Wonders

Get up close and personal with Tassie's wildlife icon at the Tasmanian Devil Conservation Park, and seek out the best of marine mammals including seals, dolphins and whales on a rock and rolling cruise around Tasman Island.

p90

The Southeast

Birdwatching ✓✓
Gourmet Travel ✓✓✓
Natural Landscapes ✓✓

Birds of Every Feather
Penguins and muttonbirds are the immediate stars on Bruny Island, but an in-depth birdwatching excursion with Inala Nature Tours also reveals a variety of pelagic species. Visit in October for the annual Bruny Island Bird Festival.

Stop the Car!
Throw your schedule out the window – stop off at the Southeast's vineyards, roadside fruit stalls, and two of Tasmania's best regional eateries in the arty town of Cygnet. Across on Bruny Island, smoked seafood, fresh oysters and artisan cheeses are further temptations.

Underground & Above Ground
Explore the subterranean caverns of the Hastings Caves and Thermal Springs area, and venture through the glacial peaks and glacial tarns of the Hartz Mountains National Peak. Equally exciting are the airborne thrills of the Tahune Eagle Glide.

p102

Midlands & Lake Country

History ✓✓✓
Fishing ✓✓✓
Whisky ✓✓✓

History's Highway
The Heritage Hwy traverses through some of Tasmania's finest colonial architecture. The Callington Mill stands out even amid Oatlands' procession of fine heritage buildings, and the Ross Bridge is a delicate entry point to the sleepy little town for which it's named.

Trout-fishing Nirvana
The isolated lakes of Tasmania's central plateau almost feel otherworldly, and the trout fishing is out of this world, too. Reminisce at cosy lakeside pubs about the one that didn't get away, or take on the rivers around Tarraleah.

Singleminded About Single Malt
The renovated heritage mill at Bothwell's Nant Distillery is worth a trip in itself. Then you taste Nant's amazing single malt. After a round on Australia's oldest golf course, venture to Tarraleah and experience the Lodge's collection of over 200 single malt whiskies.

p129

The East Coast

Beaches ✓✓✓
Gourmet Travel ✓✓✓
Wildlife ✓✓✓

Beaut Beaches
Wineglass Bay and the Bay of Fires may get the limelight, but equally deserving are Binalong Bay, Spring Beach and Honeymoon Bay. Cool off after a robust walk in, or hire a sea kayak in Coles Bay to explore the Freycinet Peninsula.

Securing Nature's Bounty
The East Coast is a great hunting ground for switched-on foodies with seasonal berries, artisan cheeses, oysters, fresh fish and seafood all on offer. Craft beer and excellent wines also make it to the menu for summer's best beach picnics.

On Land & in the Sea
Head to Maria Island for a mini-selection from Dr Dolittle's contact list with wallabies, pademelons, wombats, echidna and rare-as-hen's-teeth Cape Barren geese. Boat trips from Coles Bay often serve up sightings of penguins, seals, dolphins and (sometimes) whales.

p141

Launceston & Around

Arts Scene ✓✓
History ✓✓
Wine ✓✓✓

Arty Events
Festivale is Launceston's annual summer arts festival, and the city also showcases events during the Tasmania-wide Ten Days on the Island. The best of local design is celebrated year round at Launceston's Design Centre of Tasmania.

Historic Launceston
Tasmania's second city has a compelling architectural heritage, including the historic Pilot Station and lighthouse at Low Head, and the diverse public edifices dotting the centre. Join a guided walking tour for the lowdown on Launceston's city and architecture.

Tamar Valley Wines
The vineyards of the Tamar Valley are renowned for producing premium dry wines of international quality. At pretty riverside Rosevears, the Ninth Island Vineyard cascades down a gentle hillside and the attached Strathlynn restaurant is an essential lunch stop.

p176

Devonport & the Northwest

Gourmet Travel ✓✓✓
Bushwalking ✓✓✓
Arts Scene ✓✓

Beer, Chocolate & Whisky
At least three major food groups are covered on yet another of Tasmania's excellent food trails. In between sampling chocolate, single malt whisky, and craft beers from Seven Sheds in Railton, leave room for locally produced smoked salmon, cheese and fresh berries.

Camping & Caving
Head to the Walls of Jerusalem National Park for superb bushwalking – camping here is particularly dramatic in a snow-covered winter – and say g'day to the glow worms in the Mole Creek Karst National Park.

Nurturing a Creative Heritage
Small, historic towns such as Deloraine and Sheffield showcase creative arts and expansive murals amid lovingly restored Georgian and Victorian architecture, and Burnie's Creative Paper continues to push the boundaries of papermaking with its output on show at the Makers' Workshop.

p204

Cradle Country & the West

Bushwalking ✓✓✓
Kayaking ✓✓✓
History ✓✓

Tasmania's Alpine Heart
The island's wild southwest provides endless opportunities for bushwalking; choose from established or less-commonly walked trails. The ascent of Cradle Mountain is a robust eight hours return, and the Overland Track is a well-marked and spectacular six-day adventure.

Remote Waters
Venture by kayak onto isolated Bathurst Harbour or cruise under sail on the remote Gordon and Pieman Rivers. For rafting thrills, the 10-day journey on the Franklin River is one of the planet's finest excursions involving inflatable boats.

Riding the Rails
Venture through the rainforest between Queenstown and Strahan on the West Coast Wilderness Railway. Compare and contrast the town's different heritage makeovers – Queenstown's rugged and authentic mining ambience, and Strahan's cutesy, but undeniably lovely, harbourside location.

p244

Look out for these icons:

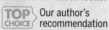 Our author's recommendation

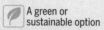 A green or sustainable option

 No payment required

HOBART & AROUND 44
Hobart 45
AROUND HOBART 77
Richmond & Around 77
New Norfolk & Around ... 81
New Norfolk to Mt Field ..84
Mt Field National Park....85
Seven Mile Beach........ 87
Channel Highway 88

TASMAN PENINSULA & PORT ARTHUR ... 90
Sorell 92
Dunalley................ 93
Eaglehawk Neck......... 93
Taranna 95
Fortescue Bay & Tasman National Park....96
Port Arthur 96
Remarkable Cave....... 100
Koonya & Nubeena 100

THE SOUTHEAST ...102
Margate 104
Kettering 104
Bruny Island 105
Woodbridge............ 110
Cygnet 111
Huonville & Around 113
Geeveston 115
Arve Road & Tahune Forest Reserve 116
Hartz Mountains National Park 117
Dover 117

Southport 118
Hastings Caves & Thermal Springs........ 119
Lune River 119
Cockle Creek...........120

MIDLANDS & LAKE COUNTRY 129
Midland (Heritage) Hwy . 131
Oatlands 131
Ross 132
Campbell Town.........134
Lake Country 136
Bothwell................136
The Lakes 137
Derwent Valley 138
Hamilton 138
Tarraleah 139

THE EAST COAST...141
Orford................. 143
Triabunna.............. 143
Maria Island National Park 144
Swansea............... 146
Coles Bay & Freycinet National Park 150
Bicheno 157
Douglas-Apsley National Park 161
St Marys 162
Scamander & Beaumaris...........163
St Helens.............. 163
Bay of Fires..........166
Binalong Bay...........167
Weldborough..........168

On the Road

Mt William National Park 169
Derby 169
Scottsdale & Around 171
Bridport 172
Flinders Island 173

LAUNCESTON & AROUND 176
Launceston 178
Tamar Valley 191
Legana & Rosevears 192
Exeter 193
Batman Bridge 193
Beaconsfield & Around . . 193
Beauty Point 194
Narawntapu National Park 195
George Town 195
Low Head 196
Pipers River Region 197
Lilydale 197
Hadspen & Carrick 198
Westbury 199
Liffey Valley 200
Longford 200
Evandale 201
Ben Lomond National Park 203

DEVONPORT & THE NORTHWEST 204
Devonport 205
Latrobe 212
Deloraine 213
Chudleigh 215

Mole Creek 215
Walls of Jerusalem National Park 216
Gowrie Park 217
Lake Barrington & Around 217
Sheffield 218
Ulverstone 220
Penguin 221
Burnie 223
Wynyard & Around 227
Boat Harbour Beach 229
Rocky Cape National Park 229
Stanley 230
Smithton & Around 234
Marrawah 236
Arthur River 237
The Tarkine Wilderness . .238
Western Explorer (C249) & Arthur Pieman Conservation Area 239
Corinna & the Pieman River 240
Waratah 241
King Island 241

CRADLE COUNTRY & THE WEST 244
Tullah 245
Rosebery 248
Zeehan 249
Strahan 250
Queenstown 259
Franklin-Gordon Wild Rivers National Park 262

CRADLE MOUNTAIN– LAKE ST CLAIR NATIONAL PARK 264
The Overland Track 265
THE SOUTHWEST 270
Maydena 271
Lake Pedder Impoundment 271
Strathgordon 273
Southwest National Park 274
Melaleuca 275

Hobart & Around

Includes »

Hobart 45
Richmond & Around . . 77
New Norfolk &
Around 81
New Norfolk to
Mt Field 84
Mt Field National
Park 85
Seven Mile Beach 87
Channel Highway 88

Best Places to Eat

» Pigeon Hole (p71)

» Marque IV (p69)

» Meadowbank Estate (p80)

» Restaurant 373 (p71)

» Chado The Way of Tea
(p68)

» Taste Café (p68)

Best Places to Stay

» The Islington (p66)

» Tree Tops Cascades (p65)

» Astor Private Hotel (p63)

» Grande Vue Private Hotel
(p65)

Why Go?

Australia's second-oldest city and southernmost capital, Hobart dapples the foothills of Mt Wellington, angling down to the slate-grey Derwent River. The town's rich colonial heritage and natural charms are complemented by great festivals and top-notch food and drink.

It's a gorgeous place, but until quite recently Hobart was far from cosmopolitan or self-assured. It's taken a while for Hobartians to feel comfortable in their own skins, and some locals did become protective of their town, shouting 'Hypocrites!' at big city escapees who invested in Hobart's Georgian and Federation houses.

The mainland attitude to Hobart has now shifted from derision to delight, with investors recognising that Tassie's abundant water, stress-free pace and cool climate are precious commodities. The city's waterfront, architecture, market, mountain and river have always been here, but these days Hobart is boutique, not backward. And not far out of town are some great beaches, mountains and historic villages.

When to Go?

Hobart's weather is at its best from November to March, the same time the city hosts a wide variety of festivals showcasing everything from beer, food and wine, through to art, music and culture. The city's maritime roots are also celebrated with the Royal Hobart Regatta, the Australian Wooden Boat Festival, and the culmination of the Sydney to Hobart yacht race. A visit from May to October will be in chillier, more challenging weather, still, a damn fine reason to cosy up in Hobart's excellent pubs, cafes and restaurants.

Hobart

POP 212,000

No doubt about it, Hobart's future is looking rosy. Tourism is booming and the old town is treading confidently onto the world stage. Plan on staying a while – you'll need at least a few days to savour the full range of beers flowing from the city's pubs.

Rising high above the city is Mt Wellington, a wild and rugged monolith perfect for mountain and bushwalking. Stretched out below the mountain, the Derwent River is a vital link to Hobart's maritime past. Every February the Royal Hobart Regatta fills the historical expanse of water with boats of all kinds, and sailing on graceful tall ships is possible year-round.

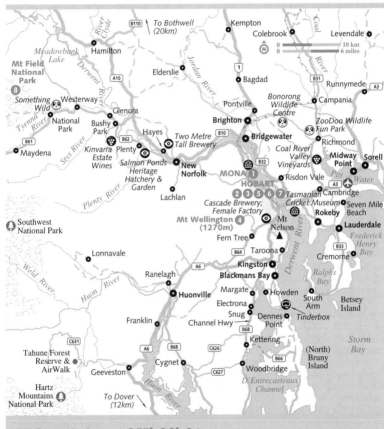

Hobart & Around Highlights

1 Being simultaneously educated and entertained at Moorilla Estate's astounding **Museum of Old & New Art (MONA)** (p53)

2 Losing yourself in the crowds at Hobart's Saturday **Salamanca Market** (p53)

3 Boning up on architectural history on a walking tour through historic **Battery Point** (p51)

4 Careering on two wheels from the summit of **Mt Wellington** (p52)

5 Sampling Tasmanian microbrews at the **New Sydney Hotel** (p74)

6 Devouring freshly fried seafood and chips from

Constitution Dock's **floating fish restaurants** (p69)

7 Discovering what's new along the ever-evolving **North Hobart restaurant strip** (p71)

8 Bracing yourself for the cold-water spray of Russell Falls in **Mt Field National Park** (p85)

Tasmania's growing reputation as a centre of food and wine excellence is on display every Saturday at the famous Salamanca Market, and the cafes, bars and restaurants of Salamanca and the nearby waterfront showcase the best of Tassie produce.

There's more great eating in historical Battery Point, cashed-up Sandy Bay and along dynamic Elizabeth St in bohemian North Hobart. Salamanca is also a vital hub for cultural and arts festivals in summer and winter.

History

Hobart's original inhabitants were the semi-nomadic Mouheneenner band of the Southeast tribe, who called the area Nibberloonne. In 1803 Van Diemen Land's first European settlers pitched their tents at Risdon Cove on the Derwent's eastern shore, which became the site of the first massacre of the Mouheneenner (Risdon Cove was returned to the Aboriginal community by the state government in 1995). The colony relocated a year later to the site of present-day Hobart, where water running off Mt Wellington was plentiful.

When Britain's gaols overflowed with sinners in the 1820s, Hobart's isolation loomed as a major selling point. Tens of thousands of convicts were chained into rotting hulks and shipped down to Hobart Town to serve their sentences in vile conditions. In the 1840s, Hobart's sailors, soldiers, whalers and rapscallions boozed and brawled shamelessly in countless harbourside pubs.

With the abolition of convict transportation to Tasmania in 1853, Hobart started to toe a slightly more moral line, and the town came to rely on the apple and wool industries for its fiscal fortitude.

In the 20th century Hobart stuttered through the Great Depression and World Wars, relying more heavily on industry (paper, zinc and chocolate production, most notably) and the deep-water Derwent River harbour to sustain it.

Hobart has always been a key Australian port. Unlike inland cities, ports look outwards to the world, and bring the world to them via trade and travellers. Harbourside pubs sustain this traffic with the same free-floating spirit, and the day Hobart's waterfront is no longer the place to go for a beer is the day Hobart loses its sea-born soul.

Indeed, the city has only ever partially sobered up, but today's convicts are more likely to be white-collared than bad company at the bar. Skeletons rattle in Hobart's closet – Indigenous Tasmanians and thousands of convicts suffered here – but the old town's shimmering beauty and relaxed vibe scare away the ghosts of the past.

◉ Sights

Most of Hobart's big-ticket sights are in or near the city centre and waterfront area, within easy walking distance of each other. On the city outskirts are historic houses, wineries, the famous Cascade Brewery, and of course, the omnipresent bulk of Mt Wellington.

CITY CENTRE

TOP CHOICE Penitentiary Chapel Historic Site
HISTORIC SITE
(Map p48; ☑6231 0911; www.penitentiarychapel. com; cnr Brisbane & Campbell Sts; tours adult/ concession & child/family $10/8/20; ⊙tours 10am, 11.30am, 1pm, 2.30pm Sun-Fri & 1pm, 2.30pm Sat) Ruminating over the court rooms, cells and gallows writer TG Ford mused, 'As the Devil was going through Hobart Gaol, he saw a solitary cell; and the Devil was pleased for it gave him a hint, for improving the prisons in hell.' Take the excellent National Trust-run tour, or the one-hour **Penitentiary Chapel Ghost Tour** (☑0417-361 392; www.hobartghosts. com; adult/child/concession $10/6/8; ⊙8.30pm) held most nights (bookings essential).

Parliament House HISTORIC BUILDING
(Map p50; www.parliament.tas.gov.au; Salamanca Pl; 45min tours free; ⊙tours 10am & 2pm Mon-Fri) Presiding over an oak-studded park adjacent to Salamanca Pl is Tasmania's sandstone Parliament House, completed in 1840 and originally used as a customs house. No-one knows what it was used for, but there's a tunnel under Murray St from the building to the Customs House Hotel opposite. No tours when parliament sits.

Theatre Royal HISTORIC BUILDING
(Map p48; www.theatreroyal.com.au; 29 Campbell St; 1hr tours adult/concession & child $10/8; ⊙tours 11am Mon, Wed & Fri) Take a backstage tour of Hobart's most prestigious theatre. Built in 1837, it's actually Australia's oldest continuously operating theatre.

Maritime Museum of Tasmania MUSEUM
(Map p56; www.maritimetas.org; 16 Argyle St; adult/child $7/3; ⊙9am-5pm) Celebrating Hobart's unbreakable bond with the sea, the excellent Maritime Museum of Tasmania has a fascinating, salt-encrusted collection of photos, paintings, models and relics (try

to resist ringing the huge brass bell from the *Rhexenor*). Upstairs is the council-run **Carnegie Gallery** (admission free; ⊘9am-5pm), exhibiting contemporary Tasmanian art, craft, design and photography.

Hobart's Real Tennis Club HISTORIC BUILDING
(Royal Tennis Club; Map p56; ☑6231 1781; www.hobarttennis.com.au; 45 Davey St; ⊘9am-6pm Mon-Fri) Dating from 1875, this is one of only five such courts in the southern hemisphere (the others are in Melbourne, Ballarat, Sydney and Romsey in country Victoria). Real (or 'Royal') tennis is an archaic form of the highly strung game, played in a jaunty four-walled indoor court. Visitors can watch, take a lesson ($45) or hire the court ($15 per hour).

Allport Library & Museum of Fine Arts MUSEUM
(Map p56; ☑6233 7484; www.statelibrary.tas.gov.au; 91 Murray St; admission free; ⊘9.30am-5pm Mon-Fri, to 2.30pm last Sat of the month) At the State Library is this collection of rare books on the Australia-Pacific region, plus colonial paintings, antiques, and a special collection of artworks it dusts off for display several times a year.

Well-Preserved Old Buildings HISTORIC BUILDINGS
Hobart's cache of amazingly well-preserved old buildings makes it exceptional among Australian cities. There are more than 90 buildings classified by the National Trust here – 60 of these are on Macquarie and Davey Sts. The intersection of Macquarie and Murray Sts features a gorgeous sandstone edifice on each corner. For detailed information contact the **National Trust** (Map p48; ☑6223 5200; www.nationaltrust.org.au; cnr Brisbane & Campbell Sts; ⊘9am-1pm Mon-Fri), or pick up the *Hobart's Historic Places* brochure from the visitor centre. Other notable edifices in the central city include the 1864 **Town Hall** (Map p56; 50 Macquarie St), which takes its architectural prompts from the Palazzo Farnese in Rome, and the austere **St David's Cathedral** (Map p56; cnr Murray & Macquarie Sts).

WATERFRONT & SALAMANCA PLACE

TOP CHOICE **Salamanca Place** HISTORIC AREA
This picturesque row of four-storey sandstone warehouses on Sullivans Cove (Map p50) is a classic example of Australian

---

HOBART IN...

Two Days

Get your head into history mode with a stroll around **Battery Point** – coffee and cake at **Jackman & McRoss** will sustain your afternoon explorations of nearby **Salamanca Place.** It's worth stumping up for a guided walking tour to get the stories behind the history. Bone up on Hobart's maritime heritage at the **Maritime Museum of Tasmania** before a promenade along the Sullivans Cove waterfront and fish and chips for dinner from **Flippers Fish Punt.** Mind those pesky seagulls. Wash it down with a few Cascades at **Knopwood's Retreat**, the quintessential Hobart pub, or a few single malts at the **Lark Distillery**.

On day two recuperate over a big breakfast at **Machine Laundry Cafe** then blow out the cobwebs with a mountain bike ride down **Mt Wellington** – on a clear day the views are jaw-dropping. Come down to earth with dinner, drinks and some live music at **Republic Bar & Café**, North Hobart's happening hub.

Four Days

If you've got a bit more time on your hands, take a **river cruise** – perhaps on a tall ship like the **Windeward Bound**, followed by the combination of the **Museum of Old & New Art** (MONA), and a wine-splashed lunch at **Moorilla Estate**. If beer is more your vice, take a tour of the legendary **Cascade Brewery** in South Hobart. Snooze the afternoon away on the sunny lawns of the **Botanical Gardens** before a classy dinner at **Marque IV**.

Still feeling energetic? Have a crack **sea-kayaking** around the Hobart docks – you can even get to eat more seafood while safely parked in your kayak. More sedate is a photo-worthy day trip to nearby **Richmond** or the waterfalls and peaks of **Mt Field National Park**. Wine buffs should strongly consider the short hop to the **Coal River Valley** wine region.

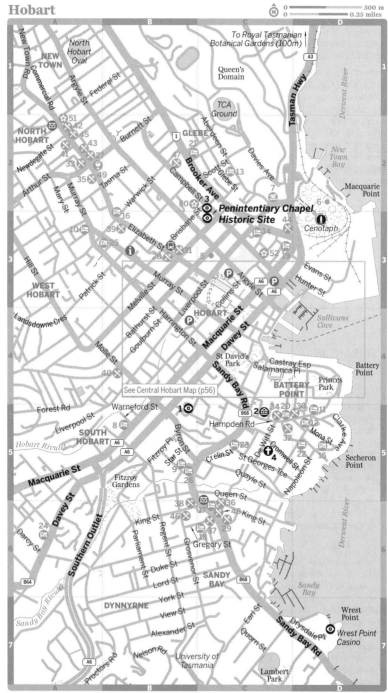

Hobart

500 m
0.25 miles

To Royal Tasmanian
Botanical Gardens (100m)

North
Hobart
Oval

NEW
TOWN

Queen's
Domain

Derwent River

TCA
Ground

New
Town
Bay

NORTH
HOBART

GLEBE

Macquarie
Point

**Penintentiary Chapel
Historic Site**

Cenotaph

WEST
HOBART

HOBART

Sullivans
Cove

Landsdowne Cres

St David's
Park

Castray Esp
Salamanca Pl

Battery
Point

See Central Hobart Map (p56)

BATTERY
POINT

Princes
Park

Forest Rd

Warneford St

Hampden Rd

SOUTH
HOBART

Hobart Rivulet

Secheron
Point

Macquarie St

Fitzroy
Gardens

St Georges Tce

Quayle St

Queen St

King St

Gregory St

SANDY
BAY

DYNNYRNE

Sandy Bay Rivulet

Sandy
Bay

Wrest
Point

Wrest Point
Casino

University of
Tasmania

Lambert
Park

⊙ **Top Sights**
Penintentiary Chapel Historic
Site...C3

⊙ **Sights**
1 Anglesea Barracks B5
Military Museum of Tasmania.......(see 1)
2 Narryna Heritage Museum C5
3 National Trust...C2
4 St George's Anglican Church C5
Theatre Royal.............................(see 52)

Activities, Courses & Tours
5 Climbing Edge..C3
6 Derwent Bike Hire.................................D2
7 Hobart Aquatic Centre.........................C2

🛏 **Sleeping**
8 2 on Warneford......................................B5
9 Apartments on Star...............................B5
10 Apple Isle Cottages...............................A3
11 Battery Point Boutique
Accommodation....................................D5
12 Coopers Cottage D5
13 Corinda's Cottages................................C2
14 Fountainside C3
15 Grande Vue Private Hotel D5
16 Lodge on Elizabeth................................B3
17 Mayfair Plaza Motel...............................C6
18 Merre Be's..C6
19 Old Woolstore C3
20 Prince of Wales Hotel............................C5
21 Quest Trinity House B2
22 Shipwright's Arms Hotel.......................D5
23 St Ives Motel..C5

24 The Islington..A6
25 Waratah Hotel B3
26 Woolmers Inn B5

🍴 **Eating**
27 Annapurna..A2
28 Chado The Way of Tea...........................B3
29 Coles Supermarket................................C6
30 Da Angelo...D5
31 Farmer's Market....................................B3
32 Francisco's on Hampden.......................C5
33 Fresco Market A2
34 Jackman & McRoss C5
35 Mai Ake A2
36 Me Wah C6
37 Metz C6
38 Mykonos B6
39 Pasha's...B3
40 Pigeon Hole..B4
41 Rain Check Lounge A2
42 Restaurant 373.......................................A2
43 Sweet Envy A2
44 Taste Café..C3
45 Vanidol's...A2
46 Woolworths Supermarket.....................B6
47 Woolworths Supermarket.....................B2
48 Written On Tea.......................................C6

🍷 **Drinking**
49 Republic Bar & Café...............................A2

🎭 **Entertainment**
50 Brisbane Hotel.......................................B2
51 State Cinema..A2
52 Theatre Royal C3

colonial architecture. Dating back to the whaling days of the 1830s, Salamanca Pl was the hub of Hobart Town's trade and commerce, but by the mid-20th century many of the buildings had fallen into ruin. The 1970s saw the dawning of Tasmania's sense of 'heritage', from which flowed a push to revive the warehouses to house restaurants, cafes, bars and shops – an evolution that continues today. The development of the quarry behind the warehouses into **Salamanca Square** has bolstered the atmosphere. The eastern end of Salamanca Pl has been the subject of major developments in recent years, including the conversion of four old wheat silos into luxury apartment towers. Concealed in one of the silos is the excellent Blue Eye seafood restaurant (p69).

Operating behind the scenes here is a vibrant and creative arts community. The nonprofit **Salamanca Arts Centre** (Map p50; ☑6234 8414; www.salarts.org.au; 77 Salamanca Pl; ⊙shops & galleries 9am-6pm) occupies seven Salamanca warehouses, home to 75-plus arts organisations and individuals, including shops, galleries, studios, performing arts venues (including the Peacock Theatre) and versatile public spaces. Check the website for the latest happenings.

To reach Salamanca Pl from Battery Point, descend the well-weathered **Kelly's Steps**, wedged between warehouses halfway along the main block of buildings.

TOP CHOICE **Waterfront**   HISTORIC AREA
Hobartians flock to the city's waterfront like seagulls to chips. Centred around

HOBART & AROUND

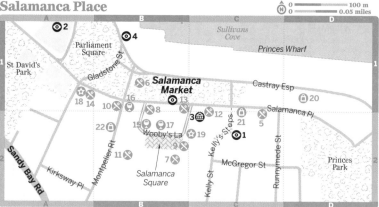

Victoria Dock (Map p56; a working fishing harbour) and **Constitution Dock** (Map p56; chock-full of floating takeaway-seafood punts), it's a brilliant place to explore. The obligatory Hobart experience is to sit in the sun, munch some fresh fish and chips and watch the harbour hubbub. If you'd prefer something with a knife and fork, there are some superb restaurants around here too – head for nearby Elizabeth St Pier.

Celebrations surrounding the finish of the annual **Sydney to Hobart Yacht Race** also revolve around Constitution Dock at New Year. The fabulous food festival, 'The Taste', is also in full swing around this time. There are so many people around the waterfront, Hobart feels like it could be Monaco! The waterfront on New Year's Eve is both an exhilarating and nauseating place (depending on how late you stay out).

Hunter St has a row of fine Georgian warehouses, most of which comprised the old Henry Jones IXL jam factory. It's occupied these days by the Art School division of the University of Tasmania and Hobart's glam-est hotel, the uber-swish **Henry Jones Art Hotel** and its affiliated restaurants and galleries. These developments have remained true to the area's heritage and retain the original facades, but not all of the hotel's neighbours can make the same claim. It's no secret that the design of the large, modern hotel and apartment complex at the corner of Davey and Hunter Sts has few admirers; many Hobartians consider it totally inappropriate for the historic area (and you'd be forgiven for feeling the same

way about the naff hotel and concert hall opposite too).

Most of the Hobart waterfront area is built on reclaimed land. When the town was first settled, Davey St marked the shoreline and the Hunter St area was an island used to store food and imported goods. Subsequent projects filled in the shallow waters and created the land upon which the Hunter St and Salamanca Pl warehouses were constructed. On Hunter St itself, there are markers indicating the position of the original causeway, which was built in 1820 to link Hunter Island with the long-since-demolished suburb of Wapping.

Lark Distillery   DISTILLERY
(Map p56; ✆6231 9088; www.larkdistillery.com. au; 14 Davey St; admission free, tours per person $15; ☉10am-6pm Sun-Wed, 10am-late Thu-Sat) The Lark Distillery, located near the visitor centre, produces fruit liqueurs (free tastings) and single malt whisky ($2.50 per tasting). Distillery tours happen at 11.30am and 2.30pm, Monday to Saturday. You can also get a bite to eat here, and it morphs into a lounge bar with live music on Friday and Saturday nights. Expect blues, country and Americana beats with your Moo Brew Pilsner or smooth single malt. Lark Distillery also runs whisky tours (1/2/4 days $195/375/2100) diving gloriously into Tasmania's emerging whisky scene. See the website for details.

Tasmanian Museum & Art Gallery   MUSEUM
(Map p56; www.tmag.tas.gov.au; 40 Macquarie St; admission free; ☉10am-5pm) Incorporating Hobart's oldest building, the Commissariat

◎ Top Sights
Salamanca Market................................B1

◎ Sights
1 Kelly's Steps.......................................C2
2 Parliament House..............................A1
3 Salamanca Arts Centre.......................C2
4 Wild Thing...B1

⊗ Eating
5 Ball & Chain Grill..............................C2
6 Blue Eye..B1
7 Machine Laundry Café.......................B2
8 Maldini..B1
9 Mezethes...B2
10 Retro Café...B1
11 Salamanca Bakehouse.......................B2
Salamanca Fresh Fruit
Market....................................(see 16)
12 Tricycle Café Bar...............................C2

13 Vietnamese Kitchen..............................B1
14 Zum Salamanca.....................................A1

◎ Drinking
15 Bar Celona...B2
16 Knopwood's Retreat.............................B1
Quarry...(see 14)
17 The Squire's Bounty..............................B2

◎ Entertainment
18 Irish Murphy's.......................................A1
Peacock Theatre............................(see 3)
19 Salamanca Arts Centre
Courtyard...C2
Syrup..(see 16)

◎ Shopping
20 Despard Gallery.....................................D1
21 Handmark Gallery..................................C2
22 Wursthaus...B2

Store (1808), the museum features Aboriginal displays and colonial relics; the gallery curates a collection of Tasmanian colonial art. There are free guided tours at 2.30pm from Wednesday to Sunday (hordes of school kids might be a little less interested in proceedings than you are). There's a cool cafe here too.

BATTERY POINT, SANDY BAY & SOUTH HOBART

TOP CHOICE **Battery Point** HISTORIC AREA

An empty rum bottle's throw from the once-notorious Sullivans Cove waterfront, the old maritime village of **Battery Point** (Map p56; www.batterypoint.net) is a nest of tiny lanes and 19th-century cottages, packed together like shanghaied landlubbers in a ship's belly. Its name derives from the 1818 gun battery that stood on the promontory, protecting Hobart Town from nautical threats both real and imagined. Built in 1818, the guardhouse is now Battery Point's oldest building. The guns were never used in battle and the only damage they inflicted was on nearby windowpanes when fired during practice.

During colonial times Battery Point was a salty maritime enclave, home to master mariners, shipwrights, sailors, whalers, coopers and merchants. Architectural styles here reflect the original occupants' varying jobs (and salaries), ranging from one- and two-room fishermen's cottages (like those around Arthur Circus), to lace-festooned mansions. Most houses are still occupied by Hobartians; many are now guesthouses where you can stay (usually for a pretty penny) and absorb the village atmosphere.

While away an afternoon exploring on your own, or follow our walking tour (p59). Stumble up **Kelly's Steps** (Map p50) from Salamanca Pl and dogleg into **South St** where the red lights once burned night and day and many a lonesome sailor sheltered from the storm. Spin around the picturesque **Arthur Circus** then explore **Hampden Rd** (Map p48) where slick cafes and restaurants cater to a more dignified clientele than the ale houses of the past. Check out **St George's Anglican Church** (Map p48) on Cromwell St or shamble down **Napoleon St** (Map p48) to the waterfront where yachts strain against their moorings in the tide. For a fortifying stout, duck into the **Shipwright's Arms Hotel** (Map p48).

The **Anglesea Barracks** (Map p48) were built adjacent to Battery Point in 1811. Still used by the army, this is the oldest military establishment in Australia. Inside is the volunteer-staffed **Military Museum of Tasmania** (Map p48; www.militarymuseum tasmania.org.au; cnr Davey & Byron Sts; adult/family $5/10; ◎9am-2pm Tue & 9am-1pm Thu). Free 45-minute guided tours of the buildings and grounds depart the front gates at 11am every Tuesday.

SYDNEY TO HOBART YACHT RACE

Arguably the world's greatest and most treacherous open-ocean yacht race, the **Sydney to Hobart Yacht Race** (www.rolexsydneyhobart.com) winds up at Hobart's Constitution Dock every New Year's Eve. As the storm-battered maxis limp across the finish line, champagne corks pop and weary sailors turn the town upside down. On New Year's Day, find a sunny spot by the harbour, munch some lunch from The Taste food festival and count the spinnakers on the river. New Year's resolutions? What New Year's resolutions?

Narryna Heritage Museum MUSEUM
(Map p48; ☑6234 2791; www.narryna.com.au; 103 Hampden Rd; adult/child $6/3; ☉10.30am-5pm Tue-Fri, 2-5pm Sat & Sun, closed Jul) This stately Georgian sandstone-fronted mansion (pronounced 'Narinna'), built in 1836, is set in established grounds and contains a treasure-trove of domestic colonial artefacts.

TOP CHOICE Cascade Brewery HISTORIC BUILDING
(☑6224 1117; www.cascadebrewery.com. au; 140 Cascade Rd, South Hobart; 2hr brewery tours adult/child $20/10, 1hr garden tours adult/child $15/12; ☉brewery tours 11am, 1pm & 2.30pm, garden tours 12.30pm & 2.30pm Mon-Fri) Around a bend in South Hobart, standing in startling, Gothic isolation is Australia's oldest brewery. Cacscade was established in 1832 next to the clean-running Hobart Rivulet, and is still pumping out superb beer and soft drinks today. Tours involve plenty of stair climbing, with tastings at the end (including Cascade Premium, the global sales smash). Wear flat, enclosed shoes and long trousers (no shorts or skirts). You can take a tour on weekends, but none of the machinery will be operating (brewers have weekends too). A full-of-history one-hour wander around Cascade's lovely gardens is also on offer. Online bookings or by phone are essential. To get here, take bus 43, 44, 46 or 49 from Elizabeth St at Franklin Sq and jump ship at stop 18.

See p293 for more on the local beer scene.

Female Factory HISTORIC SITE
(☑6233 6656; www.femalefactory.com.au; 16 Degraves St, South Hobart; Historic Heritage tour adult/child $15/5, Tea with the Matron tour per person $12, Matron's Cottage adult/child $5/1; ☉9am-5pm Mon-Fri) Finally being recognised as an important historic site (one in four convicts transported to Van Diemen's Land was a woman!), this was where Hobart's female convicts were incarcerated. Major archaeological work is ongoing. Tour bookings are essential; phone to confirm the latest tour schedule.

It's not far from the Cascade Brewery – combining the two makes for a fascinating afternoon . To get here by public transport, take bus 43, 44, 46 or 49 and jump off at stop 16.

Mt Wellington PARK
(www.wellingtonpark.org.au) Cloaked in winter snow, Mt Wellington peaks at 1270m, towering over Hobart like a benevolent overlord. The citizens find reassurance in its constant, solid presence, while outdoorsy types find the space to hike and bike on its leafy flanks. And the view from the top is unbelievable! Don't be deterred if the sky is overcast – often the peak rises above cloud level and looks out over a magic carpet of cotton-topped clouds.

Hacked out of the mountainside during the Great Depression, the 22km road to the top winds up from the city through thick temperate forest, opening out to lunar rockscapes at the summit. If you don't have wheels, local buses 48 and 49 stop at Fern Tree halfway up the hill, from where it's a five- to six-hour return walk to the top via Fern Glade Track, Radfords Track, Pinnacle Track, then the steep Zig Zag Track. The Organ Pipes walk from the Chalet (en route to the summit) is a flat track below these amazing cliffs. Pick up the *Mt Wellington Walks* map ($4.10 from the visitor centre) as a guide or download PDF maps at www.wellingtonpark.com.au. Alternatively, Mt Wellington Walks (p60) runs organised hikes on the mountain from easy to adventurous.

Some bus-tour companies include Mt Wellington in their itineraries (see p58). Another option is the Mt Wellington Shuttle Bus Service (☑0408-341 804; per person return $25), departing the visitor centre at 10.15am and 1.30pm daily. City pick-ups by arrangement; call to book.

Feeling more intrepid? Bomb down the slopes on a mountain bike with **Mt Wellington Descent** (☑6274 1880; www.mtwellingtondescent.com.au; adult/child $75/65). Kick off with a van ride to the summit, followed by more than 21km of downhill cruising (mostly on sealed roads, but with off-road options). Tours depart at 9.30am and 1pm daily, with an additional 4pm departure in January and February.

Mt Nelson
PARK

If Mt Wellington is cloud shrouded, the **Old Signal Station** atop Mt Nelson, which is much lower, provides immaculate views over the city and Derwent estuary. When Port Arthur was operating as a penal site, a series of semaphore stations were positioned atop hills to transmit messages across the colony. The one on Mt Nelson – established in 1811 – was the major link between Hobart and the rest of the colony.

There's a pretty good restaurant beside the signal station, and there are barbecues and picnic tables here too. To get here, drive up Davey St then take the Southern Outlet towards Kingston and turn left at the top of the hill. Local buses 57, 58 and 156-8 also come here. Alternatively, you can walk to the top via the 90-minute return **Truganini Track** which starts at Cartwright Reserve beside the Channel Hwy in Taroona.

NORTH & WEST HOBART

TOP CHOICE **Moorilla Estate**
MUSEUM
(☑6277 9900; www.moorilla.com.au; 655 Main Rd, Berriedale; tastings free; ☺10am-5pm) Twelve kilometres north of Hobart's centre, Moorilla occupies a saucepan-shaped peninsula jutting into the Derwent River. Founded in the 1950s, Moorilla plays a prominent role in Hobart society. Stop by for wine and 'Moo Brew' beer tastings, have lunch or dinner at the outstanding restaurant, the **Source** (mains $30-42; ☺lunch daily & dinner Tue-Sat), or catch a summer concert on the lawns. Maybe splash out for a night in the uber-swish accommodation (p67).

Moorilla's newest attraction is **MONA** (☑6277 9900; www.mona.net.au; ☺11am-7pm), the $75 million Museum of Old and New Art, which Moorilla owner David Walsh describes as 'a subversive adult Disneyland'. The extraordinary installation is arrayed across three underground levels concealed inside a sheer rock face. Ancient antiquities are showcased next to more recent works by Sir Sidney Nolan and British *enfant terrible*, Damien Hirst. Even if you're not an art fan, don't miss this eccentric, but world-class, museum.

To get here catch the Moorilla ferry from Hobart's Brooke St Pier (each way $15, 45 minutes).

Moorilla is also the driving force behind Hobart's annual MONA FOMA arts and music festival (p61).

Queen's Domain
PARK

(Map p48) When Hobart was settled, the leafy hill on the city's northern side was the Governor's private playground, which prevented housing being built. Today the hillock is called the Queen's Domain and is public parkland, strewn with cricket grounds, an athletics stadium, native grasslands and hilltop lookouts. Pedestrian overpasses on the western side provide easy access to North Hobart.

On the hill's eastern side is the small but beguiling **Royal Tasmanian Botanical Gardens** (Map p48; ☑6236 3076; www.rtbg.tas.gov.au; Queens Domain; admission free, 1hr tours per person $5; ☺8am-6.30pm Oct-Mar, to 5.30pm Apr & Sep, to 5pm May-Aug). Established in 1818, it features more than 6000 exotic and native plant species over 14 hectares. Tours

---

DON'T MISS

SALAMANCA MARKET

Every Saturday morning since 1972, the open-air **Salamanca Market** (Map p50; ☑6238 2843; www.hobartcity.com.au; ☺8.30am-3pm Sat) has lured hippies and craft merchants from the foothills to fill the tree-lined expanses of Salamanca Pl with their stalls. Fresh organic produce, secondhand clothes and books, tacky tourist souvenirs, ceramics and woodwork, CDs, cheap sunglasses, antiques, exuberant buskers, quality food and drink – it's all here, but people-watching is the real name of the game. Rain or shine – don't miss it! See www.salamanca.com.au to download a handy guide and map of the market, and get planning to maximise your time in this labyrinth of bargains, ethnic food, and arts and crafts.

FOUR SEASONS IN ONE DAY *BRETT ATKINSON*

Melbourne's changeable weather was allegedly the inspiration for the Crowded House song *Four Seasons in One Day*, but I reckon if Neil Finn had moved south to Hobart, the iconic tune would have been *Four Seasons in One Hour*.

My climatic confusion evolves while careening on a mountain bike down Hobart's Mt Wellington. I'd spied a light dusting of snow on the summit when I arrived in town, but didn't expect a full-on snowstorm to emerge just as I depart down the winding summit road. The first stage of the descent is relatively steep, and after just 15 minutes the wintery mists part, and Hobart emerges in spring sunshine. A few downhill moments later the sweet, summer smell of golden wattle infuses the air, and mist wafts from the warm tarmac.

I quickly consider jettisoning a few layers, but by the time the off-road section through a forest begins, I'm ensconced in a full-on autumn squall and my knobbly tyres are finding their own way through rocky grooves filled with water. Cue lighter spring rain around the time of a snack stop in the gardens of the Cascade Brewery, and the Crowded House hit is complete.

Actually, make that *Four Seasons in 45 Minutes...*

run at 11am Monday, Tuesday and Thursday. Explore the flora in detail at the **Botanical Discovery Centre** (admission free; ⊙9am-5pm), which also houses a gift shop, kiosk and restaurant.

Next door to the Botanical Gardens is palatial **Government House**, the state governor's digs. It's not open to the public and not visible from the road, but you can get a good view of the turrets and towers from high on Queen's Domain.

Bus 17 runs daily to the Botanical Gardens.

Cadbury Chocolate Factory　　LANDMARK
(☑1800 627 367; www.cadbury.com.au; Cadbury Rd, Claremont; adult/child/family $7.50/4/17.50; ⊙9am-4pm Mon-Fri) A must-see for sweettooths and Willy Wonka wannabes is the Cadbury Chocolate Factory, 15km north of the city centre. You can enjoy samples, invest in low-priced choc products and watch a chocolate-making video.

Some companies offer day trips and river cruises incorporating the Cadbury tour, or book directly with Cadbury by phone or online and make your own way here on bus 37, 38 or 39 to Claremont from stop E on Elizabeth St. Closed public holidays.

Runnymede　　HISTORIC BUILDING
(☑6278 1269; www.nationaltrusttas.org.au; 61 Bay Rd, New Town; adult/concession $10/8; ⊙10am-4.30pm Tue-Fri & noon-4.30pm Sun) This gracious 1840 sandstone-and-slate residence is 5km north of the city centre. It was built for Robert Pitcairn, the first lawyer to qualify in Tasmania, and named by a later owner, Captain Charles Bayley, after his favourite ship.

It's now managed by the National Trust, and through 2010 considerable archaeological investigation was undertaken to uncover the building's history. Guided tours (adult/child $25/12.50) run at 10.30am and 1.30pm Tuesday to Thursday, October to March; and Special 'Twilight' guided tours (adult/child $35/17.50) run at 6pm from January to March; bookings essential. To get here, take bus 15 or 20.

Tasmanian Transport Museum　　MUSEUM
(☑6272 7721; www.railtasmania.com/ttms; Anfield St, Glenorchy; adult/child $6/3; ⊙1-5pm Sat & Sun) Train rides are available on the first and third Sundays of each month at this mecca for trainspotters. When the trains run, admission increases to $8/4 per adult/child. At other times, mourn the loss of Tasmania's passenger train network, which called it a day in the mid-1970s. Take bus X1 from stop F on Elizabeth St: the museum is a short walk from Glenorchy bus station.

Moonah Arts Centre　　ART GALLERY
FREE (☑6214 7633; www.mac.gcc.tas.gov.au; 65 Hopkins St, Moonah; ⊙12.30-5pm Mon-Fri, 10am-2pm Sat) This community arts centre stages everything from indigenous arts exhibitions and concerts to workshops and special events. Buses departing stop E on Elizabeth St go to groovy Moonah.

Lady Franklin Gallery　　ART GALLERY
FREE (☑6228 0076; www.artstas.com; Ancanthe Park, 268 Lenah Valley Rd; ⊙1.30-5pm Sat & Sun) In a colonnaded 1842 sandstone

building called Ancanthe (Greek for 'Vale of Flowers'), the Lady Franklin Gallery displays work by Tasmanian artists. To travel here take bus 6, 7, 8, 9 or 10 to the Lenah Valley terminus from stop G on Elizabeth St.

EAST HOBART

Tasmanian Cricket Museum MUSEUM
(☑6211 4000; www.tascricket.com.au; cnr Church & Derwent Sts, Bellerive; adult/child $2/1; ☺1-3pm match days, plus 10am-3pm Tue-Thu, 10am-noon Fri) Cricket fans should steer a well-directed cover drive towards Bellerive Oval on Hobart's eastern shore. Oval and museum tours run at 10am on Tuesday (except on match days) and cost $10/3 for adults/children. Don't miss the special corner of the museum dedicated to the achievements of Tassie's-own Ricky Ponting. There's still no commemoration of David Boon's record of 52 cans of beer on a Sydney to London flight in 1989 though. Buses 285 and 287 service Bellerive Oval.

🏃 Activities

See also p22 and p28 for information on bushwalking, canoeing and rafting, caving, fishing, sailing, skiing, scuba diving and snorkelling around Hobart.

Cycling

A useful navigational tool is the *Hobart Bike Map* ($4 from the visitor centre and most bike shops), detailing cycle paths and road routes. Pick up a pair of wheels from either of the following.

Bike Hire Tasmania (Appleby Cycles; Map p56; ☑6234 4166, 0400 256 588; www.bikehiretasmania.com.au; 109 Elizabeth St; ☺8.30am-6pm Mon-Fri, 9am-4pm Sat) Quality mountain/road bikes from around $45 per day.

Derwent Bike Hire (Map p48; ☑6260 4426, 0428 899 169, www.derwentbikehire.com; Regatta Grounds Cycleway; ☺10am-4pm Sat & Sun Sep-Nov, Apr & May, daily Dec-Mar) Mountain and touring bikes from $25/140 per day/week.

Indoor Climbing

A converted warehouse, **Climbing Edge** (Map p48; ☑6234 3575; www.theclimbingedge.com.au; 54 Bathurst St; adult/child $14/10; ☺noon-9pm Mon-Fri & 10am-5pm Sat) offers world-class climbing walls. Don your nifty rubber shoes, chalk up your paws and up you go. Shoe and harness hire is $10.

Sea-Kayaking

Kayaking around the docks in Hobart, particularly at twilight, is a lovely way to get a

---

LOCAL KNOWLEDGE

DAVID BUTTON – BUSHWALKING ARCHITECT

David Button is a Hobart architect and all-round Tassie enthusiast, with a penchant for national parks, bushwalking and the good life.

Top Places to See Colonial Architecture

Tasmania has some of Australia's best early-colonial architecture. The standouts are Port Arthur, Evandale, and Ross. In Hobart there's Battery Point, and the Penitentiary Chapel Historic Site. It's a bit grim, but it is an intact remnant of early Hobart Town.

Enjoying Tasmania's National Parks

The beaches on the east coast are great, especially around Freycinet Peninsula National Park. Maria Island National Park is great for camping, and there are a couple of mountains to climb, lovely beaches and some tranquil, isolated spots.

Great Short Walks

In Hobart, walk from the city around Sullivans Cove, through the docks, around Battery Point and down to Sandy Bay Beach. Get a bus to Fern Tree and explore Mt Wellington. Bring warm clothing, water and food, and allow a day to make a good job of it.

In Tasmania's southeast, walk from Cockle Creek to South Cape Bay. It's a pretty easy two-hour walk – some of it along boardwalks – to one of the wildest ocean beaches in the world. The Southern Ocean swell crashes in with huge surf on the edge of a primeval forest.

As related to Charles Rawlings-Way

Central Hobart

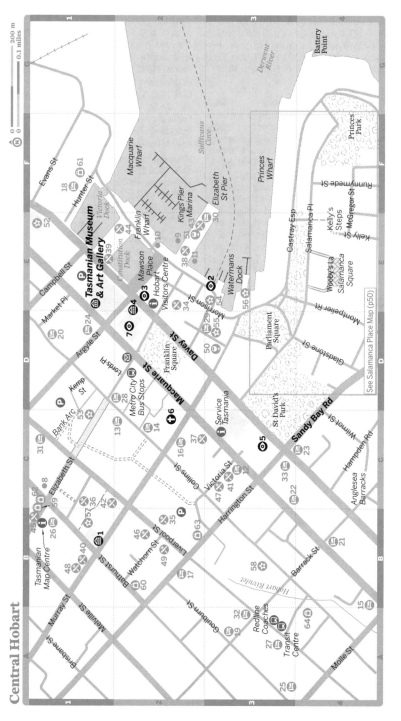

N
0   200 m
0   0.1 miles

See Salamanca Place Map (p50)

◉ **Top Sights**

Tasmanian Museum & Art
Gallery E1

◉ **Sights**

1 Allport Library & Museum of
Fine Arts B1
2 Boat Cruise Booking Offices.................E3
Carnegie Gallery ....(see 4)
3 Lark Distillery.....................................E2
4 Maritime Museum of Tasmania E2
5 Hobart's Real Tennis Club C3
6 St David's Cathedral............................C2
7 Town Hall...D2

Activities, Courses & Tours

8 Bike Hire Tasmania (Appleby
Cycles)...C1
Captain Fell's Historic Ferries........(see 2)
9 Lady Nelson E2
Navigators ....(see 2)
Peppermint Bay Cruise..................(see 2)
10 Tasman & Bruny Island Cruises............E2
11 Windeward Bound E2

🛏 **Sleeping**

12 Astor Private Hotel...............................C3
13 Central Café Bar C2
14 Central City Backpackers......................C2
15 Edinburgh Gallery.................................B4
16 Grand Mercure Hadleys Hotel..............C2
17 Harrington's 102...................................B2
18 Henry Jones Art Hotel...........................F1
19 Hobart Hostel.......................................A3
20 Hotel Collins...D1
21 Jackson Townhouse...............................B4
22 Macquarie Manor C3
23 Mantra One C4
24 Montgomery's Private Hotel &
YHA..D1
25 Narrara Backpackers A3
26 New Sydney Hotel B1
27 Pickled Frog A3
28 Quest Savoy D2
29 Quest Waterfront...................................D3
30 Somerset on the Pier E3

31 Tassie Backpackers...............................C1
32 Transit Centre Backpackers A3
33 Welcome Stranger Hotel.......................C3

🍴 **Eating**

34 Catch...E2
35 City Supermarket..................................B2
36 Criterion St Cafè...................................C1
37 Dev'lish...C2
38 Fish Frenzy E2
39 Flippers Fish Punt E1
40 Garagistes...B1
Henry's Harbourside...................(see 18)
41 Jackman & McRoss C3
Jam Packed ....(see 18)
42 Kafe Kara C1
43 Marque IV E2
44 Mures E2
45 Nourish...B1
46 R. Takagi Sushi.....................................B2
47 Sirens C3
48 The Cupping Room B1
49 Vanny's B2

🍷 **Drinking**

IXL Long Bar ....(see 18)
50 Lower House..D3
51 T-42°...E2

🎭 **Entertainment**

52 Federation Concert Hall E1
53 Halo C1
54 Isobar E3
55 Mobius D3
New Sydney Hotel........................(see 26)
56 Observatory...E3
57 Playhouse Theatre B1
58 Village Cinemas....................................B3

🛍 **Shopping**

59 Antiques Market....................................C1
60 Antiques to Retro..................................B2
61 Art Mob...F1
62 Skigia & Surf C1
63 Spot On Fishing Tackle.........................B2
64 Tasmanian Wine Centre........................A4

feel for the city. **Blackaby's Sea-Kayaks & Tours** (📞0418 124 072; www.blackabyseakayaks .com) have morning, afternoon or sunset paddles around the Hobart waterfront with fish and chips or wood-fired pizza to finish; $65 per person. Ask about paddling adventures further afield at Port Arthur, Fortescue Bay, the Coal Mines Historic Site on Tasman Peninsula, and the Gordon River. Also available is a 'Peddle & Paddle' combo including a descent by mountain bike of Mt Wellington (per person $135).

Swimming & Surfing

Hobart's city beaches look inviting, especially at Bellerive and Sandy Bay, but the water here tends to get a bit soupy. For a safe, clean swim, you'll be better off heading further south to Kingston and Blackmans Bay. The most reliable local surfing spots are Clifton Beach and Goats Beach en route to South Arm.

The **Hobart Aquatic Centre** (Map p48; ☑6222 6999; www.hobartcity.com.au; 1 Davies Ave; adult/child $6.90/4.50; ☺6am-10pm Mon-Fri, 8am-6pm Sat & Sun) offers recreational moisture when it's raining outside. Inside are leisure pools and pools for lap swimming etc. There's also a spa, sauna, steam room, aqua-aerobics and aerobics for land-lubbers.

Tall Ship Sailing

Explore the Derwent under sail on these gracious, heritage vessels. You'll find them both docked near the Elizabeth St Pier.

Lady Nelson (Map p56; ☑6234 3348; www.ladynelson.org.au; per person from $35) Trips on a replica of the surprisingly compact brig, the *Lady Nelson*, one of the first colonial ships to sail to Tasmania. Longer overnight trips are also on offer.

Windeward Bound (Map p56; ☑6231 6941; www.windewardbound.com; three-hour sail incl lunch adult/child $65/30) An elegant replica tall ship with lots of opportunities to get involved with the sailing. Also runs occasional eight-day voyages around Port Davey and Recherche Bay (per person $2750).

Hobart for Children

Parents won't break the bank keeping the troops entertained in Hobart. The free Friday-night music in the courtyard at the Salamanca Arts Centre is a family-friendly affair, while the street performers, buskers and visual smorgasbord of Saturday's Salamanca Market captivate kids of all ages. There's always something interesting going on around the waterfront – fishing boats chugging in and out of Victoria Dock, yachts tacking and jibing in Sullivans Cove – and you can feed the whole family on a budget at the floating fish punts on Constitution Dock.

Rainy-day attractions to satisfy your child (or inner child) include the Tasmanian Museum & Art Gallery, the Maritime Museum of Tasmania, the Cadbury Chocolate Factory,

and the Discovery Centre at the Royal Tasmanian Botanical Gardens.

Hobart is a naturally active kinda town: take a boat cruise up or down the river; assail the heights of Mt Wellington or Mt Nelson; rent a bike and explore the cycling paths; pack the teens into the Kombi and go surfing at Clifton Beach. The minute you head out of town the child-friendly options increase, with an abundance of animal parks, beaches, caves, nature walks and mazes to explore.

If you're needing a romantic dinner date just for two, contact the **Mobile Nanny Service** (☑6273 3773, 0437 504 064) to look after the sprogs for a few hours.

Tours

Most cruises and bus and walking tours run daily during summer (December to February), but schedules and prices vary with the season and demand; call in advance to confirm. Several boat-cruise companies operate from the Brooke St Pier and Watermans Dock area cruising around the harbour and up and down the river.

Captain Fell's Historic Ferries CRUISES (Map p56; ☑6223 5893; www.captainfellshistoricferries.com.au) Good-value lunch (from $30 per adult) and dinner ($53) cruises on cute old ferries. Also runs coach or double-decker bus sightseeing trips around town and to Mt Wellington, the Cadbury Chocolate Factory and Richmond.

Gray Line SIGHTSEEING (☑6234 3336, 1300 858 687; www.grayline.com.au) City coach tours (from $42/21 per adult/child), plus longer tours to destinations including Mt Wellington ($47/23.50), Mt Field National Park ($111/55), Bruny Island ($165/110) and the Huon Valley ($146/73). Free hotel pick-ups.

Ghost Tours of Hobart & Battery Point HISTORICAL (☑0439 335 696; www.ghosttoursofhobart.com.au) Walking tours oozing ectoplasmic tall tales departing The Bakehouse in Salamanca Sq at dusk. Bookings essential; $25 per person.

Herbaceous Tours FOOD (☑041 697 0699; www.herbaceoustours.com.au; per person from $130) Specialist food and wine tours across Tasmania including Hobart, the Coal River Valley wine region, Bruny Island and the Huon Valley. Look

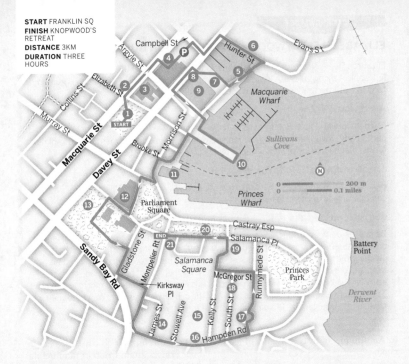

Campbell St

Argyle St

Elizabeth St

Collins St

Murray St

Macquarie St

Davey St

Brooke St

Morrison St

Hunter St

Evans St

Macquarie Wharf

Sullivans Cove

Princes Wharf

Castray Esp

Salamanca Pl

Salamanca Square

McGregor St

Kirksway Pl

James St

Stowell Ave

Kelly St

South St

Hampden Rd

Runnymede St

Princes Park

Battery Point

Derwent River

Parliament Square

Montpellier Rt

Gladstone St

Sandy Bay Rd

0   200 m
0   0.1 miles

Walking Tour
Hobart

Launch your expedition at ❶ **Franklin Square** under the statue of Governor Sir John Franklin. Track northeast down Macquarie St past the 1906 sandstone clock tower of the ❷ **General Post Office**, the 1864 ❸ **Town Hall** and into the ❹ **Tasmanian Museum & Art Gallery**. Exit through the cafe into the courtyard and across the car park. Navigate across Campbell and Davey Sts to the fishing boats at ❺ **Victoria Dock**.

Check out the renovated ❻ **Henry Jones Art Hotel**. Formerly the IXL jam factory headed by the entrepreneurial Henry Jones, it was once Tasmania's largest private employer. Cross the swing bridge and fishtail towards ❼ **Mures** or ❽ **Flippers Fish Punt** for lunch by ❾ **Constitution Dock**. On New Year's Eve this is party central for yachties completing the famous Sydney to Hobart Yacht Race.

Next stop is the slickly reworked ❿ **Elizabeth St Pier** jutting into Sullivans Cove – classy accommodation upstairs, restaurants and bars downstairs. If the tide is out, take the low-road steps around ⓫ **Watermans Dock**. Cross Morrison St then wander through Parliament Sq in front of ⓬ **Parliament House**.

Resist the photogenic façades of Salamanca Pl for now, turning right instead to detour through ⓭ **St David's Park**, with its picturesque pergola and walls of colonial gravestones; formerly Hobart Town's original cemetery. Cut through Salamanca Mews, jag right onto Gladstone St, left onto Kirksway Pl then right onto Montpellier Retreat, arcing uphill towards the colonial delights of ⓮ **Narryna Heritage Museum**, built in 1836.

Hampden Rd leads you into the heart of ⓯ **Battery Point**, Hobart's oldest residential area. Reconstitute with coffee and cake at ⓰ **Jackman & McRoss**, then turn left into Runnymede St to check out ⓱ **Arthur Circus**, an improbably quaint roundabout lined with eave-free Georgian cottages. Continue down Runnymede St and turn left into McGregor St, casting an eye up well-preserved ⓲ **South St**. Turn right onto Kelly St and bumble down ⓳ **Kelly's Steps**, an 1839 sandstone link between Battery Point and the redeveloped warehouses of ⓴ **Salamanca Place**. Nearby is Hobart's best pub, ㉑ **Knopwood's Retreat**, and a well-earned cold beer.

LOCAL KNOWLEDGE

ELIZABETH FLEETWOOD – WALKING TOUR GUIDE

Elizabeth Fleetwood from Hobart Historic Tours (p60) is one of the city's most know ledgeable walking guides. A leisurely stroll around Hobart's heritage environs is guaranteed to feature a few lesser-known facts and quirky stories about the city.

A Famous Visitor

Charles Darwin visited Hobart in 1836. It is said that it was his studies of our geology, particularly while walking along the foreshore at Bellerive, and our many curious animal forms, that helped lay the foundations for his theories on evolution.

The Truth About Hobart's Weather

Here's a fact about Hobart that takes many visitors by surprise. Of all of Australia's state capitals, only Adelaide gets less rain.

Just one more beer, OK?

Before the Derwent Bridge was completed, a fellow called Burt was a well-known regular on the trans-Derwent ferry. He liked to have a few beers at the waterfront pubs before catching the ferry home from work. One day he got a bit too enthusiastically into his beer, and only had half the money for his fare. He appealed to the ferryman, saying he knew him well and that he would provide the missing amount the next morning. Half way across the river, the ferry came to a halt, and the captain announced: 'We've stopped here so Burt can get off. He's only paid for half the journey.'

forward to lots of tasty sampling of foodie goodies.

Hobart Historic Tours   HISTORICAL
(☑6278 3338, 0429 843 150; www.hobarthistoric tours.com.au; per tour $30) Highly informative walking tours of Hobart (9.30am Tue, Thu, Sat & Sun) and historic Battery Point (11.30am Sat). Also available is an Old Hobart Pub Tour (5pm Tue, Thu & Sat) taking in waterfront watering holes. Restricted winter dates. Bookings essential.

Louisa's Walk   HISTORICAL
(☑6229 8959, 0437 276 417; www.livehistory hobart.com.au; 1½hr tour adult/child/family $30/15/75) Engaging tours of Hobart's female convict heritage at the Female Factory; interpreted through 'strolling theatre'. Tours depart Cascade Brewery at 2pm. Great feedback from readers.

Mt Wellington Walks   WALKING
(☑0439 551 197; www.mtwellingtonwalks.com.au; half-day walk adult/child $75/60) Runs organised hikes on Hobart's high hill, from easy to adventurous.

Navigators   CRUISES
(Map p56; ☑6223 1914; www.navigators.net .au) Slick ships sailing north to Moorilla Estate and the Museum of Old & New Art (adult/child return $30/20), and south to Port Arthur ($159/128, including site entry and return coach trip). Also harbour cruises around Hobart (adult/child $32/26).

Par Avion   FLIGHTSEEING
(☑6248 5390; www.paravion.com.au) Scenic flights into the southwest from Cambridge Aerodrome near Hobart Airport. A four-hour Southwest World Heritage Tour including a boat ride on Bathurst Harbour costs $240/210 per adult/child; an eight-hour Day In The Wilderness tour costs $350/310, including lunch and a visit to Port Davey.

Penitentiary Chapel Ghost Tour   HISTORICAL
Historic hauntings at Hobart's old gaol (p60).

Peppermint Bay Cruise   CRUISES
(Map p56; ☑1800 751 229; www.peppermint-bay.com.au) A five-hour float down the D'Entrecasteaux Channel to the sassy Peppermint Bay development at Woodbridge. Prices start at $118/68 per adult/child, including lunch on board; cruise only, from $98/58.

Red Decker   SIGHTSEEING
(☑6236 9116; www.reddecker.com.au) Commentated sightseeing on an old London double-decker bus. Buy a 20-stop, hop-on-hop-off pass (adult/child/concession

$25/15/23), or do the tour as a 90-minute loop. Pay a bit more and add a Cascade Brewery tour ($44/25/42) or river cruise ($48/37/46) to the deal.

Rotor-Lift Helicopters   FLIGHTSEEING
(✆6248 4117; www.rotorlift.com.au) Twenty-minute helicopter flights over Hobart and Mt Wellington for $195, or one-hour sightseeing over Hobart and the Tasman Peninsula for $595. Departing Hobart Airport.

Sullivans Cove Walks   HISTORICAL
(✆6245 1208; www.sullivanscovewalks.com.au; adult/family $20/45; ⏱Mon-Sat) Hobart's maritime history comes alive on these interesting walking tours.

Tasair   FLIGHTSEEING
(✆6248 5088; www.tasair.com.au) Thirty-minute flights over Hobart for $115 per person, plus longer flights to the Tasman Peninsula ($155), Bruny Island ($385) and the Southwest ($298). Departing Hobart Airport.

Tasman Island Cruises   CRUISES
(Map p56; ✆6250 2200; www.tasmancruises.com.au; full-day tour adult/child $195/150) Take a bus to Port Arthur for a three-hour ecocruise around Tasman Island, then explore the Port Arthur Historic Site and bus it back to town. Includes morning tea, lunch and Port Arthur admission. Departs Hobart at 7.45am; bookings required. Other options incorporate a visit to the Tasmanian Devil Conservation Park. Day trips to Bruny Island are also possible from Hobart (see p107). Tasman Island Cruises has its own harbourside booking office.

Tours Tasmania   SIGHTSEEING
(✆1800 777 103; www.tourstas.com.au; tours $120-140) Small-group, backpacker-oriented full-day trips from Hobart: Cradle Mountain, Wineglass Bay or Mt Field National Park. Also longer two- to five-day itineraries.

Wild Thing   JET BOAT
(Map p50; ✆1300 137 919; www.wildthing adventures.com.au) A speedy red boat churning up the froth around the Derwent ($39 per person).

🎭 Festivals & Events

Hobart hosts a cavalcade of festivals and events throughout the year.

Hobart Summer Festival   ART & MUSIC
(www.hobartsummerfestival.com.au) Hobart's premier festival, focussed around the waterfront: two weeks of theatre, kids' activities, concerts, buskers, New Year's Eve shenanigans and The Taste festival.

Sydney to Hobart Yacht Race   SAILING
(www.rolexsydneyhobart.com) Yachts competing in this annual race start arriving in Hobart around 29 December – just in time for New Year's Eve! (Yachties sure can party...)

The Taste   FOOD & WINE
(www.tastefestival.com.au) On either side of New Year's Eve, this week-long harbourside event is a celebration of Tassie's gastronomic prowess. The seafood, wines and cheeses are predictably fabulous, or branch out into mushrooms, truffles and raspberries! Stalls are a who's who of the Hobart restaurant scene.

MONA FOMA   CULTURAL
(www.mofo.net.au) January's wonderfully eclectic array of music, arts and culture with a high-profile 'Eminent Artist in Residence' every year. Previous 'EARs' have included John Cale and Nick Cave.

Australian Wooden Boat Festival   HERITAGE
(www.australianwoodenboatfestival.com.au) Biennial event in mid-February (odd-numbered years) to coincide with the Royal Hobart Regatta. The festival showcases Tasmania's boat-building heritage and maritime traditions.

Royal Hobart Regatta   SAILING
(www.royalhobartregatta.com) Three days of aquatic yacht-watching and mayhem

---

WHALES IN THE DERWENT

In the 1830s Hobartians joked about walking across the Derwent River on the backs of whales and complained about being kept awake at night by the noise of the ocean giants cavorting offshore. In typical Tasmanian style, the ensuing whaling boom was catastrophic, driving local populations of southern right and humpback whales to near extinction. Though still endangered, the occasional forgiving whale returns to the Derwent during June-July northbound and October-November southbound migration. If you spy one, call the **Parks & Wildlife Service Whale Hotline** (✆0427 942 537).

HOBART'S ANTARCTIC LINKS

Tasmania was the last chunk of Gondwanaland to break free from Antarctica, which is now about 2500km south of Hobart across the Southern Ocean. Hobart is arguably the world's leading Antarctic gateway city, and has become a centre for Antarctic and Southern Ocean science: the Australian Antarctic Division has its headquarters at suburban Kingston; the Commonwealth Scientific and Industrial Research Organisation (CSIRO) Division of Marine Research is in Battery Point; and the Institute of Antarctic & Southern Ocean Studies and the Antarctic Climate & Ecosystems Cooperative Research Centre reside on the University of Tasmania campus. Down on the waterfront, the Antarctic Division's garish orange research vessel *Aurora Australis* and the CSIRO's boats *Southern Surveyor* and *MV Franklin* often dock at Hobart's wharves, alongside international research ships.

Pick up a copy of the free *Polar Pathways* brochure from the Hobart visitor centre, which details the key Antarctic sites around town on walking and driving tours. For a sense of Antarctic life, check out the climate-controlled Subantarctic Plant House at Hobart's Royal Tasmanian Botanical Gardens which re-creates the flora (and soundtrack!) of Tasmania's Macquarie Island, en route to Antarctica.

on the Derwent River. Held annually in mid-February so it coincides with the Australian Wooden Boat Festival every second year.

Ten Days on the Island   CULTURAL
(www.tendaysontheisland.com) Tasmania's premier cultural festival – a biennial event (odd-numbered years, usually late March to early April), celebrating arts. Music and culture at state-wide venues. Concerts, exhibitions, dance, film, theatre and workshops.

Lumina   CULTURAL
(www.lumina.discovertasmania.com) Tasmania's newest festival – inaugurated in 2010 – and including lots of winter events such as May's **Savour Tasmania Food festival** (www.savourtasmania.com) and July's **Festival of Voices** (www.festivalofvoices.com).

Royal Hobart Show   ENTERTAINMENT
(www.hobartshowground.com.au) Enduring rural-meets-urban festival in October showcasing Tassie's primary industries. Bulging showbags, hold-onto-your-lunch rides and the fecund aromas of nature.

Tasmanian Beerfest   BEER
(www.tasmanianbeerfest.com.au) More than 200 brews from around Australia and the world, and lots of opportunities for waterfront snacking and imbibing.

Falls Festival   MUSIC
(www.fallsfestival.com.au) The Tasmanian version of the Victorian rock festival is a winner! Three days from December 29 to January 1 of live Oz and international

tunes (Paul Kelly, Dan Sultan, Interpol, the National) at Marion Bay, an hour south of Hobart.

🛏 Sleeping

The pumping-est areas to stay in Hobart are the Sullivans Cove waterfront and Salamanca Pl (and to a lesser extent Battery Point), though prices here are usually sky-high and vacancy rates low. The CBD has less atmosphere, but most of the backpacker hostels, pubs with accommodation, and midrange hotels are here. Note that rooms above pubs can be pretty noisy, especially on weekends with live music.

To the north of the city centre are suburban North Hobart and New Town, where apartments and B&Bs are within walking distance of the North Hobart restaurants. Accommodation in waterside Sandy Bay is surprisingly well priced, but it's a fair hike from town (check that you won't be in for a long walk). Most of Hobart's motels are out of town along Brooker Ave heading into the city from the north (those listed here are closer in).

Top-end Hobart accommodation can be quite reasonable. If your budget stretches to around $200 you can afford something quite special: designer hotels, historic guesthouses and modern waterside apartments.

Like the rest of Tasmania, midrange accommodation here isn't exactly a bargain. If you're visiting in January, book as far in advance as humanly possible. Hobart accommodation also gets busy when the city's various festivals and events like the Royal

Hobart Show and the Australian Wooden Boat Festival take place. Try and book ahead for these periods.

Outside peak season, holidays and festivals, many plush hotels offer weekend accommodation and dinner deals and walk-in rates, while luxury B&Bs also slash prices.

CITY CENTRE

TOP CHOICE Astor Private Hotel
HOTEL $$

(Map p56; ✆6234 6611; www.astorprivate hotel.com.au; 157 Macquarie St; s from $77, d $93-140; ☞) A rambling, downtown, 1920s charmer, the Astor retains much of its character: stained-glass windows, old furniture, ceiling roses and the irrepressible Tildy at the helm. Older-style rooms have shared facilities; newer en suite rooms top the price range. Strict 'No Bogans' policy! Breakfast included.

2 on Warneford
APARTMENTS $$$

(Map p48; ✆0408-991 063; www.2onwarneford. com.au; 2 Warneford St; apt $230-350; ☞) In a quiet inner suburban street a 15-minute walk from Salamanca, 2 on Warneford fills a lovely brick villa with two modern self-contained apartments. Lots of natural light showcases stunning decor and quality furnishings; kitchens and bathrooms both look transplanted direct from the Home Show.

Hotel Collins
HOTEL $$$

(Map p56; ✆6226 1111; www.hotelcollins.com.au; 58 Collins St; d $220-240, apt 335; ☞) One of Hobart's newest hotels effortlessly shows up other places around town as a little old and tired. A youthful energy at reception flows through to spacious rooms and apartments, many with sterling views of Mt Wellington's imposing bulk. Downstairs is the relaxed fifty8 cafe and bar.

Jackson Townhouse
APARTMENTS $$

(Map p56; ✆040 009 2710; www.jacksontown house.com.au; cnr Macquarie & Barrack Sts; d $180-200; ☞) Still close enough to reach Salamanca on foot, the Jackson Townhouse enjoys a fringe CBD location opposite a great heritage pub. The two self-contained apartments both turn the heritage charm up to eleven, but they're definitely not chintzy. Choose from the sun-filled two-bedroom townhouse or the cosy and compact one-bedroom 'Garret'. Extra person costs $45.

Macquarie Manor
BOUTIQUE HOTEL $$$

(Map p56; ✆6224 4999; www.macmanor.com .au; 172 Macquarie St; r $210-315; ☞) Plush,

high-ceilinged heritage rooms and cooked breakfast buffets are the order of the day at this central, well-groomed, Regency-style guesthouse. Enough chesterfields and mahogany writing desks to fill three gentlemen's clubs.

Fountainside
HOTEL $$

(Map p48; ✆6213 2999; www.fountainside. com.au; 40 Brooker Ave; d $189; ☞) Venture past the old school 1980s reception and exterior to discover newly renovated rooms that are surprisingly modern and spacious. The building hugs a busy roundabout, but well-insulated windows easily combat most traffic noise. Flash new rooftop rooms have some of the best views in town.

Edinburgh Gallery
B&B $$

(Map p56; ✆6224 9229; www.artaccom.com.au; 211 Macquarie St; r $90-230;@☞) This funky, art-filled boutique hotel puts an eclectic stamp on an old Federation home, just to the west of the CBD. Some rooms share immaculate bathrooms, all have quirky, artsy decor (try for a verandah suite).

Mantra One
APARTMENTS $$

(Map p56; ✆6221 6000; www.mantraonesandy bayroad.com.au; 1 Sandy Bay Rd; d from $149; ☞) These spacious and stylish loft apartments in a restored heritage building are a short stroll from both Salamanca and Battery Point. Lots of restaurants on tap up and down the road mean you probably won't need the sleek kitchenettes. Ask for a room on the building's southern side to negate occasional road noise from busy Davey St.

Grand Mercure Hadleys Hotel
HOTEL $$

(Map p56; ✆6223 4355; www.grandmercurehadleys hotel.com.au; 34 Murray St; d from $190;@☞) This sumptuous place has clocked up more than 150 years of hospitality in the heart of the CBD – ideal for meeting-plagued business-people. It's acquired plenty of modern embellishments since its colonial beginnings, including a restaurant and lobby bar. Some rooms are a tad compact, but at the time of writing, a flash new annexe was being added. Check online for hearty discounts.

Old Woolstore
HOTEL $$$

(Map p48; ✆6235 5355, 1800 814 676; www.old woolstore.com.au; 1 Macquarie St; d from $229, apt d from $289;@☞) Oodles of parking and super friendly staff are the first things you'll notice at this large, lavish hotel-apartment complex. You won't notice much wool lying around – it hasn't been a wool store for 100 years. Spend up on a roomy apartment (up to three bedrooms), with kitchen, laundry, stereo and video. Look online for killer discounts. Extra person in apartment is $40.

Quest Savoy
HOTEL $$

(Map p56; ☎6220 2300; www.questapartments.com.au; 38 Elizabeth St; r $165-250;@🖬🛜✹) The Savoy offers super-duper modern studios – all with kitchenette and living/dining area – smack-bang in the middle of downtown Hobart. If you're travel-weary, there's a therapeutic spa on site. **Quest Waterfront** (3 Brooke St) and **Quest Trinity House** (149 Brooker Ave, Glebe) offer similar rates. See online for good last-minute deals.

Central Café Bar
HOTEL $$

(Map p56; ☎6234 4419; www.centralcafebar.com; 73 Collins St; d & tw $120; 🛜) Downstairs is a classic Aussie pub with gaming machines and big screen sport, but upstairs are surprisingly modern double rooms with flat screen TVs and designer furniture. You'll struggle to find anywhere more central, so the name's a definite winner.

New Sydney Hotel
PUB $

(Map p56; ☎6234 4516; www.newsydneyhotel.com.au; 87 Bathurst St; dm $27) Casual, ebullient downtown pub with small, basic dorms upstairs. Good pub grub, and live music most nights (see p74), so don't expect a monastic retreat. The New Sydney's also a great place to try lots of different Tasmanian craft beers, so that's shelter and sustenance sorted then.

Hobart Hostel
HOSTEL $

(Map p56; ☎1300 252 192; www.hobarthostel.com; cnr Goulburn & Barrack Sts; dm $23-30, d/tw/tr from $80/80/99;@🛜) In a former pub (the ever-rockin' Doghouse), Hobart Hostel offers clean, recently redecorated dorms, with better value twins and doubles upstairs. Downstairs are huge red sofas and, just maybe, Hobart's biggest big-screen TV.

Harrington's 102
HOTEL $$

(Map p56; ☎6234 9277; www.harringtons102.com.au; 102 Harrington St; d incl breakfast $125-195) After the shock of the naff postmodern office facade subsides, you'll find the rooms here well equipped but a tad small. Still, the price is good given that continental breakfast is included and you're within walking distance of good central Hobart restaurants. Extra person costs $35.

Narrara Backpackers
HOSTEL $

(Map p56; ☎6234 8801; www.narraraback packers.com; 88 Goulburn St; dm $23-27, s/d/tw/f $60/69/69/119;@🛜) In a three-level townhouse on the city fringe, the laidback Narrara has brightly coloured rooms with newish beds and recently redecorated bathrooms. Travellers slump on couches in front of the TV, working through the pain of last night's efforts.

Welcome Stranger Hotel
HOTEL $

(Map p56; ☎6223 6655; www.welcomestranger hotel.com.au; cnr Harrington & Davey Sts; s/d incl breakfast from $105/125) Only a discerning eye will appreciate the aesthetic qualities of this modern redbrick pub, but upstairs there are decent pub rooms with en suite, and a few shared bathroom options for budget travellers. It's on a noisy intersection, but windows are double-glazed. Downstairs is a pretty decent pool hall.

Pickled Frog
HOSTEL $

(Map p56; ☎6234 7977; www.thepickledfrog.com; 281 Liverpool St; dm $24-28, s/d $62/67;@🛜) Not for the moderate or meek, this huge, ramshackle hostel fills an old pub on the CBD fringe with party vibes. Cheap beer, big-screen TVs, pool table, slightly homesick backpackers checking out Facebook – you get the picture.

Tassie Backpackers
HOSTEL $

(Map p56; ☎6234 4981; www.tassiebackpackers.com; Brunswick Hotel, 67 Liverpool St; dm $23-25, d/tw $65-85; 🛜) The venerable old Brunswick Hotel has been reinvented as Hobart's newest hostel. There's plenty of shared spaces including a kitchen and laundry, and the energetic young management team also operates an excellent bar downstairs. Some of the original sandstone walls date back to 1816.

Montgomery's Private Hotel & YHA
HOSTEL $

(Map p56; ☎6231 2660; www.montgomerys.com.au; 9 Argyle St; dm $28-30, s & d with/without bathroom $130/112;@) Attached to Montgomery's pub, this YHA offers clean, bright, secure accommodation right in the middle of town. Spread over three levels are dorms of all sizes, and nifty en suite singles and doubles; family-sized rooms also available. Look forward to karaoke downstairs on Friday and Saturday nights. It's your call if that's a good thing or a bad thing.

Central City Backpackers
HOSTEL $

(Map p56; ☑1800 811 507; www.centralcityhobart.com; 138 Collins St; dm $23-27, s/d $55/69;@☎) Smack-bang in the middle of the city, this mazelike hostel has loads of communal space, a great kitchen, OK rooms, friendly staff and extras such as baggage storage and tour desk. Linen costs extra in dorms.

Transit Centre Backpackers
HOSTEL $

(Map p56; ☑6231 2400; www.transitbackpackers.com; 251 Liverpool St; dm $23-26, tw/d $56/64;@) Recently relocated, this friendly spot has rooms leading off a huge communal area, strewn with shared couches, bookshelves and a kitchen and laundry. The vibe is inclusive and relaxed, and the helpful owners host regular barbecues to encourage lots of international socialising.

Waratah Hotel
PUB $

(Map p48; ☑6234 3685; www.thewaratah.com; 272 Murray St; s/d $80/100) Known as 'W Block' to truant students from the nearby college, the red-brick Waratah pub is short on charisma. It's nowhere near as pretty as its namesake native flower, but offers good-value beds a short walk from town. Pub meals are available downstairs, and there's a pool table or two. It's a shortish stroll to the North Hobart restaurant strip if you're after something flasher for dinner. Extra person $40.

WATERFRONT & SALAMANCA PLACE

Henry Jones Art Hotel
BOUTIQUE HOTEL $$$

(Map p56; ☑6210 7700; www.thehenryjones.com; 25 Hunter St; d $320-420, ste $400-850;@☎) Since opening in 2004, superswish HJs has become a beacon of sophistication. Absolute waterfront in a restored jam factory, it oozes class but is far from intimidating (this is Hobart after all, not Sydney). Modern art enlivens the walls, while facilities and downstairs distractions (bar, restaurant, cafe) are world class. The hotel also makes smart use of recycled materials.

Somerset on the Pier
HOTEL $$$

(Map p56; ☑6220 6600, 1800 766 377; www.somerset.com; Elizabeth St Pier; apt from $275;@☎) In a definitively Hobart location on the upper level of the Elizabeth Pier, this stylish complex offers luxurious apartments with beaut harbour views and breezy, contemporary design. You'll pay more for a balcony, but with these views you won't need to do any other sightseeing! Check online for best rates.

Tree Tops Cascades
TOP CHOICE
RENTAL HOUSE $$

(☑6223 2839; www.treetopscascades.com.au; 165 Strickland Ave, South Hobart; d $150-160; ☎) Book ahead for this superb three-bedroom house in an idyllic bush setting, 6km from town near Cascade Brewery. Built on 6 acres, there's a zoo-full of wildlife about: possums, bandicoots and tame kookaburras (which you can feed on the barbecue deck). The three bedrooms means lots of room for families and groups; extra person $25. Buses 46, 47 and 49 run here from bus stop M on Elizabeth St next to Franklin Sq.

Apartments on Star
APARTMENTS $$$

(Map p48; ☑6225 4799; www.apartmentsonstar.com.au; 22 Star St, Sandy Bay; apt $200-250; ☎) This block of 1970s flats in Sandy Bay is now four thoroughly 21st-century apartments with Sandy Bay's buzzing restaurant scene just down the hill. That's if you can pull yourself away from rustling up something special in the designer kitchens and enjoying a Tassie wine with maritime views.

Grande Vue Private Hotel
B&B $$$

(Map p48; ☑6223 8216; www.grande-vue-hotel.com; 8 Mona St, Battery Point; r incl breakfast $220-280; ☎) The 'vues' from this lovingly restored brick mansion take in the sweep of Sandy Bay and the Wrest Point casino. Sleek new bathrooms and superfriendly service lift Grande Vue above other similar, nearby accommodation. Breakfast ($12.50) includes still-warm freshly baked goodies from Jackman & McRoss.

Coopers Cottage
RENTAL HOUSE $$

(Map p48; ☑6224 0355; www.cooperscottage.com.au; 44a Hampden Rd, Battery Point; r $165) Nestled in behind an old-time Hampden Rd shopfront is this self-contained option, perfect for two or three, with extras such as DVD player, CD player and washing machine. The Gods of Decor do not ordain the carpet. Reception is next door at the Village Café.

Shipwright's Arms Hotel
HOTEL $$

(Map p48; ☑6223 5551; www.shipwrightsarms.com.au; 29 Trumpeter St, Battery Point; d with bathroom $150, s/d without bathroom $75/80) Concealed in the backstreets of Battery Point, 'Shippies' is one of the best old pubs in town. Soak yourself in maritime heritage at the bar, then retire to your clean, aboveboard berth upstairs or in the newer, more modern wing. Great pub meals in the beer garden too.

Hugo's B&B
B&B $$

(☑6225 1902; www.hugosbb.com.au; 22 Edith Ave, Sandy Bay; s/d incl breakfast from $100/120) Down south in Sandy Bay is Hugo's, a modern, unobtrusive B&B with a one-bedroom and a two-bedroom unit, both with sensational Derwent River views. Extra adult/child is $35/25. To get here take Regent St (which becomes Churchill Ave) off Davey St, then turn right onto Edith Ave after 2.5km.

Motel 429
MOTEL $$

(☑6225 2511; www.motel429.com.au; 429 Sandy Bay Rd, Sandy Bay; d $130-170;[@☎]) This motel's recent facelift has given most rooms a sleek designer sheen. The staff are friendly, everything's clean and shipshape, and the restaurants of Sandy Bay are just a short drive away. The Deluxe rooms are supercomfortable, and the Wrest Point Casino is nearby if you're feeling lucky.

Battery Point Boutique Accommodation
APARTMENTS $$

(Map p48; ☑6224 2244; www.batterypoint accommodation.com.au; 27-29 Hampden Rd, Battery Point; d $175; ☎) Yet more colonial midrangery, this time in a block of four salmon-coloured serviced apartments (sleeping three, with full kitchens; extra person $35) in Battery Point's heart (somewhere near the left ventricle). Off-street parking is a bonus.

Merre Be's
B&B $$

(Map p48; ☑6224 2900; www.merrebes.com. au; 17 Gregory St, Sandy Bay; d incl breakfast from $140) On a quiet street close to the Sandy Bay shopping strip, this 1901 colonial house has been transformed into an upmarket B&B with large rooms (some with spa), and almost-as-large bathrooms. Colonial interiors are on the tasteful side of excessive; breakfast is a full buffet affair. Lots of good restaurants are 200m away.

St Ives Motel
MOTEL $$

(Map p48; ☑6221 5555; www.stivesmotel.com.au; 67 St Georges Tce, Battery Point; d $135-175; ☎) Within walking distance of Battery Point and the city is this excellent option – a curvalicious '80s building with dozens of rooms, all with kitchens. A recent flash makeover has introduced the property to the 21st century. Good last-minute deals online.

Woolmers Inn
MOTEL $$

(Map p48; ☑6223 7355, 1800 030 780; www.wool mersinn.com; 123-127 Sandy Bay Rd, Sandy Bay; d from $140) A solid choice not too far from the action, despite lashings of brown-brick colonial coach-house style. Spacious studio and two-bedroom units, all with kitchenette, cable TV and DVD player. Some disabled-access units too.

Mayfair Plaza Motel
MOTEL $$

(Map p48; ☑6220 9900; www.mayfairplaza.com.au; 236 Sandy Bay Rd, Sandy Bay; d from $149) The redevelopment of the Mayfair in the '90s sent Sandy Bay into an architectural tailspin, but if that doesn't bother you, these cavernous modern rooms are well located and offer pretty good value. There are lots of eating options in the area and plenty of parking.

Prince of Wales Hotel
HOTEL $$

(Map p48; ☑6223 6355; www.princeofwaleshotel. net.au; 55 Hampden Rd, Battery Point; r incl breakfast $130-210; ☎) A severe '60s glitch in Battery Point's urban planning (would Charles and Camilla approve?), the POW is nonetheless exquisitely located and offers cheery, spotlessly clean pub-style rooms, all with en suite. Off-street parking and Moo Brew on tap are two more ticks.

NORTH & WEST HOBART

The Islington
BOUTIQUE HOTEL $$$

(Map p48; ☑6220 2123; www.islingtonhotel.com; 321 Davey St; d $350-550;☎) One of Hobart's best, The Islington effortlessly combines a heritage building with interesting antique furniture, contemporary art and a glorious garden. Service is attentive but understated, and breakfast is served in an expansive conservatory. Choose from the guest library, study/music room or drawing room to wind down with a wine after exploring Hobart. Exquisite private dinners are also available. The Islington is a sister property of The Priory in the Midlands town of Bothwell, and package deals combining both are available.

Corinda's Cottages
B&B $$$

(Map p48; ☑6234 1590; www.corindascottages .com.au; 17 Glebe St, Glebe; d incl breakfast $195-250) Gorgeous Corinda, a renovated Victorian mansion with meticulously maintained parterre gardens, sits high on the Glebe hillside a short (steep!) walk from town. Three self-contained cottages (garden, coach house or servants' quarters) provide contemporary comforts with none of the twee, olde-worlde guff so many

Tasmanian accommodations wallow in. Breakfast is DIY gourmet (eggs, muffins, fresh coffee etc).

Moorilla Estate Suites & Chalets
BOUTIQUE HOTEL $$$

(☑6277 9900; www.moorilla.com.au; 655 Main Rd, Berriedale; d $490-950; @🛜🐕) For a slice of luxury, rent a secluded uberchic chalet at Moorilla Estate 12km north of the city. These modern self-contained pavilions (one- and two-bedroom) are superbly equipped, featuring private balconies, wine cellars, river views and oh-so-discreet service. An indoor swimming pool is an essential aid to relaxation, and the stunning Museum of Old & Modern Art (MONA) is truly in your backyard.

Apple Isle Cottages
RENTAL HOUSE $$$

(Map p48; ☑0407 932 394; www.appleisle.com. au; 9 Devonshire Sq & 310 Murray St, North Hobart; d $200-220) These restored heritage cottages just a stroll from the North Hobart restaurant strip are ideal for families or two couples travelling together. Cute-as-a-button Murray Cottage sleeps up to six, and nearby Devonshire Cottage is a rambling two-storey home with barbecue-friendly gardens and excellent views of both old and new Hobart town. Extra person $55 to 65.

Lodge on Elizabeth
B&B $$

(Map p48; ☑6231 3830; www.thelodge.com.au; 249 Elizabeth St, North Hobart; r incl breakfast from $150-170, self-contained cottage $195;@) Built in 1829, this old-timer has been a school house, a boarding house and a halfway house, but now opens its doors as a value-for-money guesthouse. Rooms are dotted with antiques (not for the modernists); all have en suites. The self-contained cottage overlooks the courtyard out the back (two-night minimum stay).

Elms of Hobart
B&B $$$

(☑6231 3277; www.theelmsofhobart.com; 452 Elizabeth St, North Hobart; d incl breakfast $170-250;@🛜) Built in 1917 for the Palfreymans, a haughty Hobart merchant family, this self-assured mansion features beaut gardens (perfect for sunny afternoon gin and tonics), six luxurious rooms and cooked breakfasts. Pro: close to the North Hobart restaurant action. Con: no kids under seven.

Bay View Villas
MOTEL $$

(☑6234 7611, 1800 061 505; www.bayviewvillas. com; 34 Poets Rd, West Hobart; d $100-219;@🛜🐕) Two kilometres up the steep West Hobart

slopes from the city, this family-focussed option offers a games room, playground, indoor pool and spa. Twelve brand new and stylish one-bedroom units have exceptional views of the harbour and the city, and are well suited to couples seeking privacy. Extra person $20.

Graham Court Apartments
MOTEL $$

(☑6278 1333, 1800 811 915; www.grahamcourt. com.au; 15 Pirie St, New Town; d $145-170) One of Hobart's best-value self-contained options, this block of 23 well-maintained apartments sits amid established gardens in the subdued northern suburbs. Units range from one to three bedrooms (extra person $25), and decor ranges from 1970s to the 1990s. A playground, cots, high chairs and on-call babysitters make it another good option for families. Wheelchair-accessible units are also available.

Waterfront Lodge
MOTEL $$

(☑6228 4748; www.waterfrontnewtownbay.com; 153 Risdon Rd, New Town; d $80-120;🐕) Overlooking the semi-industrial New Town Bay and the Cornelian Bay Cemetery 5km north of the centre, this funky renovated motel has spotless, modern units, all with kitchenette. There's also a guest kitchen. Great value if you don't mind the outlook or the drive. Extra person $20.

Adelphi Court YHA
HOSTEL $

(☑6228 4829; www.yha.com.au; 17 Stoke St, New Town; dm $26-29, d & tw with/without bathroom from $88/74) Rooms here occupy a spruced-up 1950s-style apartment block built around a courtyard behind a Federation manor. It's out of the way – 2.5km from the city – but reasonably close to the North Hobart strip. Limited reception hours, so call ahead. Take bus 15 or 16 from stop H in Elizabeth St to stop 8, or any bus leaving stop E to stop 13, which is close to Stoke St.

OUTSIDE THE CITY

Hobart Cabins & Cottages
CABINS $$

(☑6272 7115; www.hobartcabinscottages.com.au; 19 Goodwood Rd, Glenorchy; cabins & cottages $95-125, 3-bedroom house per d $200; 🛜) About 8km north of the centre, with a range of cottages and cabins, and a three-bedroom house sleeping up to 10 people.

Barilla Holiday Park
CAMPGROUND $

(☑1800 465 453; www.barilla.com.au; 75 Richmond Rd, Cambridge; sites $26-30; cabins $85-160;@🛜🐕) A decent option for those with wheels, Barilla is midway between Hobart

(12km) and Richmond (14km). It's close to the airport, the Coal River Valley wineries, and a couple of good wildlife parks around Richmond. The river-plains grounds are dotted with well-kept cabins, plus minigolf and an on-site restaurant serving wood-fired pizzas should keep the kids happy.

✗ Eating

Downtown Hobart proffers some classy brunch and lunch venues, but when the sun sinks behind the mountain, the city streets are sometimes overrun with 'bogans' (Hobart's version of standard, low-IQ, pugilistic hoons), stuck on an endless petrol-wasting loop of the city block.

The waterfront streets, docks and piers are the collective epicentre of the city's culinary scene, and quality seafood is everywhere you look. Salamanca Pl is an almost unbroken string of excellent cafes and restaurants, and is especially busy during Saturday morning market festivities. Battery Point's Hampden Rd restaurants are always worth a look, while Elizabeth St in North Hobart has evolved into a diverse collection of cosmopolitan cafes. A few rascally locals have even started calling it 'NoHo'. Sandy Bay is another emerging dining destination. So far it doesn't have a cool-sounding nickname. Any ideas?

For Hobart's best pub food, head to the New Sydney Hotel, the Shipwright's Arms, or the Republic Bar & Café.

CITY CENTRE

TOP CHOICE **Garagistes** MODERN AUSTRALIAN **$$$**
(Map p56; ☑6231 0558; www.garagistes. com.au; 103 Murray St; Sunday lunch $65, dinner small plates $17-32; ⊙lunch Sun & dinner Wed-Sat) The very fine Garagistes delivers truly innovative small plates in a simple, yet dramatic, dining room that was formerly a rental car garage. Owner Luke Burgess pushes the culinary envelope with dishes including salted cabbage, ricotta and barley salad and raw jack mackerel with pickles, young elderberries and rhubarb. Dive into the stellar wine and beer list as you discover just how surprising his food is. Sunday lunch is four highly recommended courses. Bookings essential.

TOP CHOICE **Taste Café** CAFE **$**
(Map p48; Baha'i Centre, 1 Tasman Hwy; mains $10-12; ⊙9am-4pm Mon-Fri & 9am-3pm Sat) Concealed within Hobart's Baha'i Centre is this terrific daytime cafe that's a

favourite of journos from the nearby ABC. The prices are low and the ever-changing menu is always fresh and interesting. Look forward to dishes like Bratwurst Scotch eggs or roasted pumpkin and ricotta gnocchi. Try a zingy glass of nonalcoholic Rhu Brew – made from rhubarb and proudly Tassie's own.

Chado The Way of Tea ASIAN FUSION **$$**
(Map p48; ☑6231 6411; 134 Elizabeth St; mains $15-25; ⊙lunch Tue-Sat) Part Zen teahouse and part pan-Asian restaurant, Chado presents mainly Japanese and Sri Lankan flavours with a healthy organic bent. The cool guy playing the Japanese flute is bound to be local muso Brian Ritchie, also the curator of the eclectic MONA FOMA music and arts festival.

Sirens VEGETARIAN **$$**
(Map p56; ☑6234 2634; 6 Victoria St; mains $21-24; ⊙dinner Mon-Sat; ☑) Sirens serves up creative vegetarian and vegan food in a warm, welcoming space, offset by excellent service and impeccable ethics. But it's not all earnest Birkenstock-wearers stirring lentils, and there's some sophisticated cooking going on in the kitchen. Try the three-cheese beetroot ravioli in champagne, dill and pink peppercorn cream. Bookings recommended.

Dev'Lish CAFE **$**
(Map p56; 137 Macquarie St; meals $7-10; ⊙breakfast & dinner Mon-Fri) Have a coffee at this cosy espresso nook and tuck into great-value cafe fare including hearty macaroni cheese, Asian-tinged salads and gluten-free wraps. Every purchase supports the Save the Tasmanian Devil program (www.tassiedevil. com.au). We like that.

R. Takagi Sushi JAPANESE **$**
(Map p56; 155 Liverpool St; sushi $7-10; ⊙lunch Mon-Sat) Hobart's best sushi spot makes the most of Tasmania's great seafood. Udon noodles and miso also feature at this sleek, compact eatery that's a favourite of central Hobart desk jockeys.

The Cupping Room CAFE **$**
(Map p56; 105 Murray St; mains $10-18; ⊙breakfast & lunch Tue-Sat) It's coffee wonderland time at this hip cafe and coffee roastery. Take your pick from an international selection of beans – Mexican Chiapas, Tanzanian Peaberry – and partner it with funky cupcakes and macarons, or robust brunch and lunch

AGRARIAN KITCHEN: COOKING SCHOOL

Rodney Dunn and Séverine Demanet run the Agrarian Kitchen (p81), Tasmania's highly regarded farm-based cooking school. Classes are run by Rodney, a former food editor of *Australian Gourmet Traveller* magazine, and a one-time apprentice to iconic Australian chef, Tetsuya Wakuda. To follow are the Agrarian Kitchen's recommendations for Hobart-bound foodies.

Hobart's Don't Miss

Visitors should definitely check out the following places. **Garagistes** in central Hobart is run by Luke Burgess who also teaches our charcuterie class. He's another chef who has worked with Tetsuya Wakuda. Up in North Hobart there's **Sweet Envy**, a tiny patisserie with superb pastries and desserts. Its chef, Alistair Wise, used to work at Gordon Ramsay's restaurant at 'The London' in New York.

Coffee, Tea & More

Other places we love in Hobart are **Tricycle Café Bar**, **Chado The Way of Tea** and **Pigeon Hole**.

Craft Beer in the Country

The **Two Metre Tall Brewery** in the Derwent Valley near New Norfolk only uses hops and barley grown on its property to make its ales. Apparently it's the only microbrewery in the world to do this. Its onsite 'Farm Bar' is open every Friday night between spring and summer.

options. The wagyu beef burger is truly a wonderful thing.

Criterion Street Café   CAFE **$**
(Map p56; 10 Criterion St; mains $10-14; ⊙breakfast & lunch Mon-Sat) It's a short menu on a short street, but Criterion Street Café effortlessly keeps both breakfast and lunch fans happy, and caffeine fiends buzzing through the day. Try the Spanish omelette or the supercreamy cinnamon porridge.

Nourish   CAFE **$**
(Map p56; 129 Elizabeth St; meals $9-14; ⊙breakfast & lunch Mon-Sat, dinner to 8pm Thu & Fri; ⍟) Don't eat wheat? Dairy's scary? Nourish is a God-sent cafe for the allergic and intolerant, serving curries, salads, stir-fries, risottos and burgers – all gluten-free, and mostly dairy-free too. Vegetarians and vegans are also catered for.

Kafe Kara   CAFE **$**
(Map p56; 119 Liverpool St; mains $10-19; ⊙lunch & dinner Mon-Sat) A pioneering Hobart cafe with a loyal following, offering early breakfasts and all-day eating in its stylish *looooong* room. There'd be a riot if they ever took the chicken salad off the menu. If they do, order a *panini*, pasta or risotto.

Vanny's   ASIAN **$**
(Map p56; 181 Liverpool St; meals $8-14; ⊙lunch & dinner Mon-Fri) Supermodest cafe-takeaway plating up cheap Cambodian-style curries and satays, including vegetarian options. Lots of fluoro lights and hearty chilli channels your last trip to Southeast Asia.

WATERFRONT & SALAMANCA PLACE

Blue Eye   SEAFOOD **$$**
(Map p50; ✆6223 5297; 1 Castray Esplanade; mains $20-32; ⊙lunch & dinner) Ignore the slightly clinical decor and dive into some of Hobart's best seafood. Standouts include chargrilled salmon, chilli salt squid, and a terrific seafood-packed risotto with roasted fennel. Moo Brew and Two Metre Tall Cleansing Ale on tap, and a Tassie-skewed wine list complete the tasty picture. The restaurant is housed in an old grain silo.

Marque IV   MODERN AUSTRALIAN **$$$**
(Map p56; ✆6224 4428; Elizabeth St Pier; lunch mains $18-33, dinner $35-37; ⊙lunch & dinner Tue-Sat) High-class dining hits waterfront Hobart at Marque IV, a discrete food emporium halfway along Elizabeth St Pier. You could start with an 'amuse' but, at these prices it doesn't pay to dally. Begin with freshly shucked Bruny Island oysters with limoncello and chilli, followed by slow-roasted

pork belly with feta and almond tortellini. Desserts? Sensational. Wine list? Superb. Romantic dinner? Sorted.

Retro Café · CAFE $
(Map p50; 31 Salamanca Pl; mains $10-18; ⊙breakfast & lunch) So popular it hurts, funky Retro is ground zero for Saturday brunch among the market stalls. Masterful breakfasts, bagels, salads and burgers interweave with laughing staff, chilled-out jazz and the whirr and bang of the coffee machine. A classic Hobart cafe.

Tricycle Café Bar · CAFE $
(p50; 71 Salamanca Pl; mains $10-18; ⊙breakfast & lunch Mon-Sat) This cosy red-painted nook near the Salamanca Arts Centre serves up a range of cafe classics (BLTs, toasties, free-range scrambled eggs, salads and Fair Trade coffee). Sip wine by the glass from the mirror-backed bar.

Jam Packed · CAFE $$
(Map p56; 27 Hunter St; mains $10-25; ⊙breakfast & lunch) Inside the redeveloped IXL jam factory atrium next to the Henry Jones Art Hotel, this cafe is jam-packed at breakfast time. If you're sporting a hangover of some description, the 'Big JP Breakfast' is the perfect reintroduction to civilisation, while the Med-style lamb burger with haloumi makes a filling lunch.

Machine Laundry Café · CAFE $
(Map p50; 12 Salamanca Sq; mains $10-18; ⊙breakfast & lunch) Hypnotise yourself watching the tumble dryers spin at this bright, retro-style cafe, where you can wash your dirty clothes while discreetly adding fresh juice, soup or coffee stains to your clean ones. Five dollars per load, and don't miss trying the chilli-infused roti wrap for breakfast.

Fish Frenzy · SEAFOOD $$
(Map p56; Elizabeth St Pier; meals $15-28; ⊙lunch & dinner) A casual, waterside fish nook, perennially overflowing with fish fiends and brimming with fish and chips, fishy salads (spicy calamari, smoked salmon and brie) and fish burgers. The eponymous 'Fish Frenzy' ($16) delivers a little bit of everything. Food-wise, Fish Frenzy can be a little inconsistent, but the buzzy harbourside ambience is great. No bookings.

Flippers Fish Punt · SEAFOOD $
(Map p56; ☑6234 3101; Constitution Dock; meals $8-15; ⊙lunch & dinner) With its voluptuous fish-shaped profile and alluring sea-blue paint job, floating Flippers is a Hobart institution. Not to mention the awesome fish and chips! Fillets of flathead and curls of calamari – straight from the deep blue sea and into the deep fryer. And remember, be firm with the occasionally annoying seagulls who'll want to steal your chips.

Mures · SEAFOOD $$
(Map p56; ☑6231 2121; www.mures.com.au; Victoria Dock; ⊙lunch & dinner) Mures and Hobart seafood are synonymous. On the ground level you will find a fishmonger (selling the Mures fleet's daily catch), a sushi bar, ice-cream parlour and the hectic, family-focussed bistro Lower Deck (mains $8-16), serving meals for the masses (fish and chips, salmon burgers, crumbed scallops). The Upper Deck (mains $30-45) is a sassier bookable affair, where patrons can take in silvery dockside views and à la carte seafood dishes.

Mezethes · GREEK $$
(Map p50; ☑6224 4601; Salamanca Sq; mains $17-30; ⊙breakfast, lunch & dinner) Tried and true Greek dishes and Adonis-like staff come together perfectly at Mezethes. All the classics (moussaka, souvlaki, lamb, fish, *saganaki,* baklava) plus, in true Hellenic style, a dazzling array of starters. The entrée platter ($28 for two) is hard to beat.

Maldini · ITALIAN $$
(Map p50; ☑6223 4460; 47 Salamanca Pl; mains $24-34; ⊙breakfast, lunch & dinner) A midrange Italian joint trying to climb the culinary rungs, with essential pasta and risotto dishes, Maldini also has mains such as Sicilian fish stew, osso bucco and baked calamari. Tiramisu and grappa polishes the palate and closes out the night.

Henry's Harbourside · MODERN AUSTRALIAN $$$
(Map p56; ☑6210 7700; 25 Hunter St; lunch $19-32, dinner $30-38; ⊙breakfast, lunch & dinner) Inside the flash Henry Jones Art Hotel is this better-than-most lobby eatery. Breakfast is pricey (up to $23); lunch is better value (pan-seared salmon, seafood pie); and dinner sees prices escalate again, but the food is high-quality stuff. Aim for an atrium table.

Catch · SEAFOOD $$
(Map p56; ☑6234 3490; www.catchrestaurant.com.au; 11 Morrison St; mains $26-42; ⊙lunch Tue-Fri & dinner Tue-Sat) Inside the flamboyantly renovated City Mill (cast-iron columns, white-painted timber, black-and-white stripy chairs) is this sharp but relaxed eatery serving up seafood straight from the deep blue sea.

Zum Salamanca
CAFE $$

(Map p50; Salamanca Pl; meals $10-22; ⊘breakfast, lunch & dinner Wed-Sat) A long, lantern-lit space segueing to a courtyard where energised young staff serve get-up-and-go breakfasts (muffins, ricotta hotcakes, egg-and-bacon *panini),* moving on to risotto and pasta later in the day.

Ball & Chain Grill
STEAKHOUSE $$

(Map p50; ☑6223 2655; 87 Salamanca Pl; mains $25-40; ⊘lunch Sun-Fri, dinner nightly) This carnivorous cave has been here so long, it's almost convict-era. Predictable, yes, but when you're onto a good thing, stick with it. Steaks, grilled game, gourmet sausages, chicken and seafood with perfectly paired wines.

Vietnamese Kitchen
VIETNAMESE $

(Map p50; 61 Salamanca Pl; mains $9-15; ⊘lunch & dinner; ✍) With slick waterfront eateries closing in on all sides, it's refreshing to discover this cheap, kitsch kitchen, with its glowing drinks fridge and plastic-coated photos of steaming soups and stir-fries. Eat in or take-away.

Salamanca Bakehouse
BAKERY $

(Map p50; ☑6224 6300; 5 Salamanca Sq; items $3-8; ⊘24hr) Open 24/7, with pies, pastries and rolls to soak up the beer and build a better tomorrow for nocturnal drinkers. The curried scallop pies are great any time of the day (or night).

NORTH & WEST HOBART

TOP CHOICE / Pigeon Hole
CAFE $

(Map p48; 93 Goulburn St; mains $8-13; ⊘breakfast & lunch Tue-Sat) This funky and friendly cafe is the kind of place every inner-city neighbourhood should have. A serious attitude to coffee is mixed with cafe food that's definitely a cut above. The freshly-baked *panini* are the best you'll have, and the foodie owners always concoct innovative spins on traditional cafe fare. Try the baked eggs *en cocotte* with serrano ham for a lazy brunch.

Sweet Envy
CAFE $

(Map p48; 341 Elizabeth St, North Hobart; snacks & cakes $4-8; ⊘breakfast & lunch Mon-Sat) A delicate diversion along North Hobart's restaurant strip, Sweet Envy conjures up gossamer-light macarons, madaleines and cupcakes. Gourmet pies and sausage rolls – try the lamb and harissa– and fantastic ice-creams and sorbets are made right on the

premises. Ever-changing ice-cream flavours include the surprising Beer and Peach.

Restaurant 373
MODERN AUSTRALIAN $$$

(Map p48; ☑6231 9031; 373 Elizabeth St, North Hobart; mains $32-37; ⊘dinner Tue-Sat) Artsy, high-end eatery on the Elizabeth St strip in a lovely old shopfront with wide floorboards and splashes of dark red paint and white linen. The young owners give local produce an innovative twist – try the Longford eye fillet or the duck breast with foie gras dumplings. Excellent service, a brilliant wine list and desserts, plus a seasonal multi-course tasting menu ($100) if you're looking to really push the boat out.

Rain Check Lounge
CAFE $$

(Map p48; ☑6234 5975; 392 Elizabeth St, North Hobart; mains $12-28; ⊘breakfast, lunch & dinner) A slice of urban cool, Rain Check's Moroccan-styled room and sidewalk tables see punters sipping coffee, reconstituting over big breakfasts and conversing over tasty treats like venison and mushroom pie. Mix and match with a selection of tapas ($7.50 to $10).

Lebrina
MODERN AUSTRALIAN $$$

(☑6228 7775; 155 New Town Rd, New Town; mains $35-48; ⊘dinner Tue-Sat) Foodies effuse about Lebrina. Concealed in Hobart's northern reaches, it looks small and unremarkable from the outside, but inside it's sheer dining pleasure, from the decor to the service to the wine list – and of course the creative modern food. Bookings essential.

Annapurna
INDIAN $$

(Map p48; ☑6236 9500; 305 Elizabeth St, North Hobart; mains $15-19; ⊘lunch Mon-Fri & dinner Mon-Sun) It seems like half of Hobart lists Annapurna as their favourite eatery (bookings advised). Northern and southern Indian options are served with absolute proficiency. The *masala dosa* (south Indian crepe filled with curried potato) is a crowd favourite. BYO and takeaway available. Also at 93 Salamanca Pl if you're staying near the harbour.

Mai Ake
THAI $$

(Map p48; ☑6231 5557; www.maiakethai.com; 322 Elizabeth St, North Hobart; mains $20-28; ⊘dinner nightly) An elegant, but buzzy, destination for some of Hobart's best Thai flavours. Abundant use of fresh, fragrant herbs give curries and salads authentic zing and punch, and a steady stream of takeaway customers introduces diners to Mai Ake's loyal regulars.

Vanidol's
ASIAN **$$**

(Map p48; ☑6234 9307; 353 Elizabeth St, North Hobart; mains $15-28; ☺dinner Tue-Sun; ☒) A pioneering North Hobart restaurant, Vanidol's diverse menu travels effortlessly around Asia with dishes including spicy Thai beef salad, Nepalese lamb curry, and Balinese chicken. Expect a well-thumbed passport full of vegetarian dishes too.

Pasha's
TURKISH **$$**

(Map p48; ☑6234 6300; 216-218 Elizabeth St; mains $16-28; ☺lunch & dinner Tue-Sat) More interesting than your average Turkish eatery, Pasha's menu incorporates the expected Ottoman goodies – *pide, dolma, kofte*– with a few more surprising dishes from southeastern Anatolia. Turkish dips to takeaway are a good place to start if you're planning a picnic.

BATTERY POINT, SANDY BAY & SOUTH HOBART

TOP CHOICE Jackman & McRoss
BAKERY **$**

(Map p48; 57-59 Hampden Rd, Battery Point; meals $8-13; ☺breakfast & lunch) Be sure to swing by this conversational, neighbourhood bakery-cafe, even if it's just to gawk at the display cabinet full of delectable pies, tarts, baguettes and pastries. Early-morning cake and coffee may evolve into quiche or soup for lunch. Staff stay cheery despite being run off their feet. There's another **branch** (Map p56; 4 Victoria St; meals $8-13; ☺breakfast & lunch) in central Hobart.

Me Wah
CHINESE **$$$**

(Map p48; ☑6223 3688; www.mewah.com.au; Suite 16 Magnet Ct, Sandy Bay Rd, Sandy Bay; mains $25-38; ☺lunch Tue-Sun & dinner nightly) Clever or what? From the outside, Me Wah's location looks just like a suburban shopping mall. Inside the restaurant is an elegant confection of Chinoiserie, almost bordering on over the top. The food is equally stellar including terrific ways with seafood and world-famous-in-Hobart yum cha sessions from 11am on weekends.

Written on Tea
CHINESE **$**

(Map p48; 236 Sandy Bay Rd, Sandy Bay; mains $10-16; ☺lunch & dinner) Excellent steamed dumplings, squid studded with ginger and spring onion, and roast duck feature at this humble suburban eatery delivering the authentic flavours of the owners' Chinese hometown of Nanjing. Ask for a table downstairs for (slightly) flasher ambience.

Macquarie St Food Store
CAFE **$**

(356 Macquarie St, South Hobart; meals $10-17; ☺breakfast & lunch) OK, so it's a little way out of the city centre, but an excursion to the Food Store will reward the intrepid traveller. It's an old shopfront cafe full of booths, bookish students, brunching friends and kids mooching under the tables. A mod-rock soundtrack competes with the coffee machine running at fever pitch. Truly yummy *quesadillas*. Stop in before or after a visit to the Cascade Brewery.

Metz
GASTROPUB **$$**

(Map p48; ☑6224 4444; 217 Sandy Bay Rd, Sandy Bay; mains $18-30; ☺breakfast, lunch & diner) If you haven't been in Hobart for a few years, you'll be forgiven for looking twice at superslick Metz, once a grungy student bar with rotten floorboards. Today it's an all-day cafe with a huge outdoor deck, transforming nightly into a bar (DJs Wednesday night and Sunday afternoon). Less surprising is the menu: salads, pastas, wood-fired pizza, plus upmarket dinner mains.

Francisco's on Hampden
TAPAS **$$**

(Map p48; ☑6224 7124; 60 Hampden Rd, Battery Point; tapas $10-12, mains $27-30; ☺lunch Fri, dinner Tue-Sun) Upbeat, noisy tapas bar of the fertile Spanish persuasion, adorned with posters of toreadors and dusky dancing maidens. Try some snacky tapas washed down with Rioja, or a larger meal (paella, seafood or meat platters) if you want a plate all to yourself.

Beach House Café, Bar & Restaurant
CAFE **$$**

(Sandy Bay Rd, Lower Sandy Bay; mains $17-35; ☺breakfast, lunch & dinner) A rockin' pub in the '70s, the Beach House is now a classy cafe. Wander along the beach before retiring for creative seafood and pasta, Tasmanian wines and good vegetarian options.

Da Angelo
ITALIAN **$$**

(Map p48; ☑6223 7011; 47 Hampden Rd, Battery Point; mains $20-32; ☺dinner) An enduring (and endearing) Italian *ristorante,* Da Angelo presents an impressively long menu of homemade pastas, veal and chicken dishes, calzone and pizza with 20 different toppings. Colosseum and Carlton Football Club team photos add authenticity. Takeaway and BYO.

Mykonos
FAST FOOD **$**

(Map p48; 165 Sandy Bay Rd, Sandy Bay; snacks $8-12; ☺lunch & dinner) Late night/early morning destination for souvlaki, potato cakes and another assorted fried goodies that taste best around 3am. A stone cold Hobart icon, that's even got its own fervent fast food following on Facebook.

OUTSIDE THE CITY

Prosser's on the Beach   SEAFOOD **$$**
(✆6225 2276; www.prossersonthebeach.com; Beach Rd, Lower Sandy Bay; mains $28-35; ☺lunch Fri & Sun, dinner Mon-Sat) A glass-fronted pavilion by the water on Sandy Bay Point, classy Prosser's is BIG on seafood: try a fresh crayfish and avocado cocktail with warm citrus dressing, or the Catalan fish stew with mussels, scallops and chorizo. It's a taxi ride from town, but worth the trip. Bookings recommended, and from Monday to Friday they'll even pay your taxi fare to get there.

**Cornelian Bay
Boathouse**   MODERN AUSTRALIAN **$$**
(✆6228 9289; www.theboathouse.com.au; Queen's Walk, Cornelian Bay; lunch $14-30, dinner $26-31; ☺lunch daily, dinner Mon-Sat) Hip, stylish restaurant-bar in a converted beach pavilion on shallow Cornelian Bay, 3km north of town. On the menu is contemporary cuisine starring quality local produce and delivered with great service. Try the Boathouse chowder followed by some seared Tasmanian lamb or Asian-style duck breast salad.

**Mt Nelson Signal Station Café
Restaurant**   CAFE **$$**
(✆6223 3407; 700 Nelson Rd, Mt Nelson; lunch $12-22, dinner $20-32; ☺breakfast & lunch daily, dinner Fri & Sat) Try for a window table at this elegant restaurant with awesome D'Entrecasteaux views, inside Mt Nelson's historic signalman's house. On offer are morning and afternoon teas, lunch, and dinner later in the week (dinner bookings essential in winter). Try the Thai chicken curry or the rustic signalman's beef and burgundy pie.

SELF CATERING

The most central self-catering option is **City Supermarket** (Map p56; 148 Liverpool St). Hobart's best **farmers' market** (Map p48; www.tasfarmgate.com.au; cnr Melville & Elizabeth Sts; ☺9am-1pm Sun) takes place Sunday morning.

Gourmet self-caterers should head to **Wursthaus** (p75) for deli produce or the **Salamanca Fresh Fruit Market** (Map p50; 41 Salamanca Pl) for fruit and groceries.

Fresco Market (Map p48; 346 Elizabeth St, North Hobart) and **Woolworths Supermarket** (Map p48; 189 Campbell St, North Hobart) are handy for North Hobart. **Coles Supermarket** (Map p48; 246 Sandy Bay Rd, Sandy Bay) or nearby **Woolworths Supermarket** (Map p48; 57 King St, Sandy Bay) are mainstream supermarkets handy if you're staying around Sandy Bay. In South Hobart, the **Salad Bowl** (✆6223 7728; 362 Macquarie St, South Hobart) stocks picnic fodder, wine, cakes, fresh groceries and deli delights.

🍷 Drinking

Hobart's younger drinkers are 10,000 leagues removed from the rum-addled whalers of the past, but the general intentions remain true – drink a bit, relax a lot and maybe get lucky and take someone home. Salamanca Pl and the waterfront host a slew of pubs and bars with outdoor imbibing on summer evenings and open fires in winter. North Hobart (aka 'NoHo') is another solid (or rather, liquid) option.

Knopwood's Retreat   PUB
(Map p50; 39 Salamanca Pl) Adhere to the 'when in Rome...' dictum and head for Knoppies, Hobart's best pub, which has been serving ales to seagoing types since the convict era. For most of the week it's a cosy watering hole with an open fire. On Friday nights the city workers swarm and the crowd spills across the street. It's also a good spot to look for craft beers from the rather wonderful Van Dieman Brewing.

T-42°   BAR
(Map p56; Elizabeth St Pier; ☺9am-late) Waterfront T-42° makes a big splash with its food, but also draws late-week barflies with its minimalist interior, spinnaker-shaped bar and ambient tunes. If you stay out late enough, it does breakfast too.

Bar Celona   BAR
(Map p50; Salamanca Sq) Lots of different beers on tap, a slick wine list, and well-priced bistro-style food make this one of Salamanca's most versatile drinking spots. The outdoor tables are perfect for people-watching Salamanca Square-style.

IXL Long Bar   BAR
(Map p56; 25 Hunter St; ☺5pm-late) Prop yourself at the glowing bar at the Henry Jones Art Hotel and check out Hobart's fashionistas over cocktails. If there are no spare stools at the not-so-long bar, flop onto the leather

FRIDAY NIGHT FANDANGO

Some of Hobart's best live music airs every Friday year-round from 5.30pm to 7.30pm at the Salamanca Arts Centre courtyard, just off Wooby's Lane. It's a free community event that started in about 2000, with the adopted name 'Rektango', borrowed from a band that sometimes plays here. Acts vary from month to month – expect anything from African beats to rockabilly, folk or gypsy-Latino. Drinks essential (sangria in summer, mulled wine in winter); dancing optional.

couches in the lobby. Moo Brew on tap is another tasty diversion.

The Squire's Bounty   PUB
(Map p50; Salamanca Sq) Yes, it is another James Squire concept pub, but the range of frosty beers is as wide as Bass Strait, and the bar snacks even taste good after a single beer. The big-screen tellys are perfect if you're in town and you want to watch your favourite footy team.

Lower House   BAR
(Map p56; 9-11 Murray St; ☺noon-late Mon-Sat) Across the road from Parliament House is this hip basement bar, keeping escapee MPs lubricated with top-shelf whiskies, cocktails and a massive wine list. Mature crowd and occasional DJs.

Quarry   BAR
(Map p50; 27 Salamanca Pl) Yet another slick Salamanca renovation, this place lures swarms of sassy Hobart young 'uns, encircled by predatory, ageing musos and bombastic businessmen itching their wedding rings.

See also the Shipwright's Arms Hotel (p65), New Sydney Hotel, Republic Bar & Café and Lark Distillery (p50).

☆ Entertainment

Republic Bar & Café   LIVE MUSIC
(Map p48; www.republicbar.com; 299 Elizabeth St, North Hobart) The Republic is a raucous art deco pub hosting live music every night (often free entry). It's the number-one live-music pub in town, with an always-interesting line-up including international visitors. With loads of different beers and excellent food, it's the kind of place you'd love to call your local.

New Sydney Hotel   LIVE MUSIC
(Map p56; www.newsydneyhotel.com.au; 87 Bathurst St) Low-key folk, jazz, blues and comedy playing Tuesday to Sunday nights (usually free). See the website for gig listings. Great pub food and a terrific selection of beer, including an always tasty and ever-changing array of Tassie microbrews.

Brisbane Hotel   LIVE MUSIC
(Map p48; 3 Brisbane St) The bad old Brisbane has dragged itself up from the pit of old-man, sticky-carpet alcoholism to reinvent itself as a progressive live-music venue. This is where anyone doing anything original, off-beat or uncommercial gets stage time: punk, metal, hip-hop and singer-songwriters.

Isobar   NIGHTCLUB
(Map p56; www.isobar.com.au; 11a Franklin Wharf; admission free Wed, $5/8 Fri/Sat; ☺10pm-5am Wed, Fri & Sat) Downstairs here is a slick bar (open 5pm Friday, 7pm Saturday), while Isobar itself – the club upstairs – plays commercial dance and blows hot and cold with the locals. Check the website for listings.

Observatory   NIGHTCLUB
(Map p56; L1, Murray St Pier; ☺3pm-late Wed-Sun) Sip a 'Big O' cocktail as you swan between loungy nooks. DJs kick in on Friday and Saturday, and don't dress down as the bouncers are quite choosy.

Irish Murphy's   LIVE MUSIC
(Map p50; 21 Salamanca Pl) Pretty much what you'd expect from any out-of-the-box Irish pub: crowded, lively, affable and dripping with Guinness. Free live music of varying repute from Wednesday to Sunday night, with original acts on Thursday.

Syrup   NIGHTCLUB
(Map p50; www.syrupclub.com; 39 Salamanca Pl; ☺9pm-late Thu-Sat) Over two floors above Knopwood's Retreat, this is an ace place for late-night drinks and DJs playing to the techno-house crowd.

Mobius   NIGHTCLUB
(Map p56; 7 Despard St; ☺9pm-late Thu-Sat) A pumping, clubby dungeon meets cool lounge bar behind the main waterfront area. Occasional name DJs.

Halo   NIGHTCLUB
(Map p56; 37a Elizabeth St; ☺10pm-late Wed-Sun) Hobart's best-credentialed club is Halo, which sees touring and local DJs spinning acid, hard trance, electro and hip-hop. Access is off Purdy's Mart.

Federation Concert Hall CONCERT HALL
(Map p56; ☑1800 001 190; www.tso.com.au; 1 Davey St; ☺box office 9am-5pm Mon-Fri) Welded to the Hotel Grand Chancellor, this concert hall resembles a huge aluminium can leaking insulation from gaps in the panelling. Inside, the Tasmanian Symphony Orchestra does what it does best.

Theatre Royal THEATRE
(Map p48; ☑6233 2299, 1800 650 277; www.theatreroyal.com.au; 29 Campbell St; shows $20-60; ☺box office 10am-5pm) This venerable old stager is Australia's oldest continuously operating theatre, actors first cracking the boards back in 1837. Expect a range of music, ballet, theatre, opera and university revues. See p46 for backstage tour information.

State Cinema CINEMA
(Map p48; ☑6234 6318; www.statecinema.com.au; 375 Elizabeth St, North Hobart) Saved from the wrecking ball in the '90s, the State shows independent and arthouse flicks from local and international film-makers. There's a great cafe and bar on site, and the foodie temptations of the North Hobart restaurant strip just outside.

Village Cinemas CINEMA
(Map p56; ☑1300 555 400; www.villagecinemas.com.au; 181 Collins St) An inner-city multiplex screening mainstream releases. Cheap-arse Tuesday tickets $10.

Playhouse Theatre THEATRE
(Map p56; ☑6234 1536; www.playhouse.org.au; 106 Bathurst St; tickets from $25; ☺box office 7-8.30pm performance nights) Home of the Hobart Repertory Theatre Society (musicals, Shakespeare, kids' plays).

Peacock Theatre THEATRE
(Map p50; ☑6234 8414; www.salarts.org.au; 77 Salamanca Pl; ☺box office 9am-6pm) This intimate theatre is inside the Salamanca Arts Centre, along with a handful of other small performance spaces.

🛍 Shopping

Head to Salamanca Pl for shops and galleries stocking Huon pine knick-knacks, hand-knitted beanies, local cheeses, sauces, jams, fudge and other assorted edibles. The hyperactive Salamanca Market is held here every Saturday.

On Elizabeth St between Melville St and Bathurst St is a swathe of stores catering to the active types if you're heading into the great Tassie outdoors.

There are good antique stores in the city centre and around the junction of Hampden Rd and Sandy Bay Rd in Battery Point. Pick up the free *Antique Shops of Hobart* and *Antiquarian & Secondhand Booksellers & Printsellers in Hobart* brochures from the visitor centre. Also grab a copy of the *Gallery Guide* brochure from the visitor centre to guide you around Hobart's arty hot spots.

Antiques Market ANTIQUES
(Map p56; ☑6234 4425; www.theantiquesmarket.com.au; 125 Elizabeth St; ☺10am-5.30pm Mon-Fri, to 4pm Sat, noon-3pm Sun)

Antiques to Retro ANTIQUES
(Map p56; ☑6236 9422; www.antique-art.com.au; 128 Bathurst St; ☺10am-5pm Mon-Fri, to 1pm Sat)

Art Mob ART
(Map p56; ☑6236 9200; www.artmob.com.au; 29 Hunter St; ☺10am-late) Aboriginal fine arts.

Despard Gallery ART
(Map p50; ☑6223 8266; www.despard-gallery.com.au; 15 Castray Esplanade, Battery Point; ☺11am-6pm Mon-Fri, noon-5pm Sat) Top-notch contemporary Tasmanian arts.

Handmark Gallery ART
(Map p50; ☑6223 7895; www.handmarkgallery.com; 77 Salamanca Pl; ☺10am-6pm) Exquisite local ceramics, glass, wood, jewellery and textiles, plus paintings and sculpture.

Spot On Fishing Tackle FISHING
(Map p56; ☑6234 4880; www.spotonfishing.com.au; 89-91 Harrington St; ☺9am-5.30pm Mon-Fri, to 3.45pm Sat) Fishing supplies and licences.

Tasmanian Wine Centre WINE
(Map p56; ☑6234 9995; www.tasmanian-wine.com.au; 201 Collins St; ☺8am-6pm Mon-Fri, 9.30am-5pm Sat) Stocks a hefty range of Tassie wines; also organises shipping, winery tours and educational tastings for groups.

Wursthaus DELICATESSAN
(Map p50; www.wursthaus.com.au; 1 Montpelier Retreat, Battery Point; ☺8am-6pm Mon-Fri, to 5pm Sat, 9.30am-4pm Sun) Fine-food showcase off Salamanca Pl selling speciality smallgoods, cheeses, breads, wines and pre-prepared meals.

Skigia & Surf SKIING
(Map p56; ☑6234 6688; 123 Elizabeth St; ☺9.30am-6pm Mon-Fri, to 4pm Sat) Hire ski and snowsports equipment and chains for your car if you're heading to Mt Mawson or Ben Lomond.

ℹ Information

Emergency

Police, Fire & Ambulance (☑000)

Hobart Police Station (☑6230 2111; www.police.tas.gov.au; 43 Liverpool St; ☺24hr)

Internet Access

Expect to pay around $6 per hour at internet cafes.

Drifters Internet Café (Shop 9/33 Salamanca Pl; ☺9am-6.30pm) Printing, scanning and faxing available.

Outzone (1st fl, 3/66 Murray St; ☺10am-7pm)

State Library (91 Murray St; ☺9.30am-6pm Mon-Thu, to 9pm Fri, to 12.30pm Sat) Thirty minutes free for Australian citizens; $6 for international visitors.

Internet Resources

Hobart City (www.hobartcity.com.au) City council website.

Rita's Bite (www.pc-rita.blogspot.com) Excellent food blog covering the Hobart eating out scene.

The Dwarf (www.thedwarf.com.au) Online gig guide.

Welcome to Hobart (www.welcometohobart.com.au) Official visitors guide.

Maps

The visitor centre supplies basic city maps. For more comprehensive coverage try the *Hobart & Surrounds Street Directory* ($18) or the UBD *Tasmania Country Road Atlas* ($31), available at larger newsagents and bookshops. Travellers with disabilities should check out the useful *Hobart CBD Mobility Map* from the visitor centre.

Hobart visitor centre (☑6230 8233; www.hobarttravelcentre.com.au; cnr Davey & Elizabeth Sts; ☺8.30am-5.30pm Mon-Fri, 9am-5pm Sat, Sun & public holidays;@)

Royal Automobile Club of Tasmania (www.ract.com.au; cnr Murray & Patrick Sts; ☺8.45am-5pm Mon-Fri)

Service Tasmania (www.service.tas.gov.au; 134 Macquarie St; ☺8.15am-5pm Mon-Fri)

Tasmanian Map Centre (www.map-centre.com.au; 100 Elizabeth St; ☺9.30am-5.30pm Mon-Fri, 10am-4pm Sat) Good for bushwalking maps.

Media

The visitor centre stocks free Tassie tourist publications highlighting Hobart's attractions. Hobart's long-running newspaper the *Mercury* (aka 'the Mockery') is handy for discovering what's on where. The Thursday edition lists entertainment options.

Medical Services

Australian Dental Association Emergency Service (☑6248 1546) Advice for dental emergencies.

Chemist on Collins (93 Collins St)

City Doctors & Travel Clinic (☑6231 3003; www.citydoctors.com.au; 93 Collins St)

Macquarie Pharmacy (180 Macquarie St; ☺8am-10pm)

Royal Hobart Hospital (☑6222 8423; www.dhhs.tas.gov.au; 48 Liverpool St; ☺24hr) Argyle St emergency entry.

Salamanca Medical Centre (☑6223 8181; 5a Gladstone St; ☺8.30am-6pm Mon-Fri, 10am-3pm Sat, noon-3pm Sun)

Money

The major banks all have branches and ATMs around Elizabeth St Mall.

Post

General Post Office (cnr Elizabeth & Macquarie Sts)

North Hobart (412 Elizabeth St)

Sandy Bay (cnr Sandy Bay Rd & King St)

Tourist Information

Hobart visitor centre (☑6230 8233; www.hobarttravelcentre.com.au; cnr Davey & Elizabeth Sts; ☺8.30am-5.30pm Mon-Fri, 9am-5pm Sat, Sun & public holidays) Brochures, maps, information and statewide tour and accommodation bookings. Collect a copy of the useful *Hobart and Surrounds* booklet.

Useful Organisations

Parks & Wildlife Service (☑1300 135 513; www.parks.tas.gov.au; 134 Macquarie St; ☺9am-5pm Mon-Fri) Information and fact sheets for bushwalking and all national parks; inside the Service Tasmania office.

Wilderness Society Office (☑6224 1550; www.wilderness.org.au; 130 Davey St; ☺9.30am-5pm Mon-Fri) Head office on the outskirts of the city.

ℹ Getting There & Away

Air

For information on domestic flights to/from Hobart, see p320.

Bus

There are two main intrastate bus companies operating to/from Hobart:

Redline Coaches (230 Liverpool St; www.redlinecoaches.com.au) Operates from the Transit Centre.

Tassielink (www.tassielink.com.au; 64 Brisbane St) Operates from the Hobart Bus Terminal.

Additionally, **Hobart Coaches** (☑132 201) has regular services to/from Richmond, New Norfolk and Kingston, south along the D'Entrecasteaux Channel and to Cygnet. See those towns for specific timetable and fare info, check online or visit Metro Tasmania's Metro Shop inside the General Post Office on the corner of Elizabeth and Macquarie Sts.

❶ Getting Around

To/From the Airport

Hobart Airport (www.hobartairpt.com.au) is at Cambridge, 16km east of town. The **Airporter Shuttle Bus** (☑1300 385 511; www.redline coaches.com.au; one-way/return $15/25) scoots between the Transit Centre and the airport (via various city pick-up points), connecting with all flights. Bookings essential. A cheaper option is the **Ten Buck Bus** (www.tenbuckbus. com.au; one way/return $10/20). Book online for an airport pick-up.

A taxi between the airport and the city centre will cost around $38 between 6am and 8pm weekdays, and around $46 at other times.

Bicycle

See p55 for details of bike-rental places in Hobart.

Bus

Metro Tasmania (www.metrotas.com.au) operates the local bus network, which is reliable but infrequent outside of business hours. The **Metro Shop** (⊘8.30am-5.30pm Mon-Fri), inside the General Post Office on the corner of Elizabeth and Macquarie Sts, handles ticketing and enquiries. Most buses depart this section of Elizabeth St, or from nearby Franklin Sq.

One-way fares vary with distances ('sections') travelled (from $2.50 to $5.60). For $4.60 you can buy an unlimited-travel Day Rover ticket, valid after 9am Monday to Friday, and all day Saturday, Sunday and public holidays. Buy one-way tickets from the driver (exact change required) or ticket agents (newsagents and most post offices); day passes are only available from ticket agents.

Car

Timed, metered parking predominates in the CBD and tourist areas like Salamanca and the waterfront. For longer-term parking, large CBD garages (clearly signposted) offer inexpensive rates.

The big-boy rental firms have airport desks and city offices.

AutoRent-Hertz (☑1800 030 222; www.au torent.com.au; cnr Bathurst & Harrington Sts)

Avis (☑6234 4222; www.avis.com.au; 125 Bathurst St)

Budget (☑6234 5222, 1300 362 848; www. budget.com.au; 96 Harrington St)

Europcar (☑6231 1077, 1300 131 390; www. europcar.com.au; 112 Harrington St)

Cheaper local firms offering daily rental rates from as low as $30 include the following.

Bargain Car Rentals (☑6234 6959, 1300 729 230; www.bargaincarrentals.com.au; 173 Harrington St)

Rent For Less (☑6231 6844; www.rentforless. com.au; 92 Harrington St)

Selective Car Rentals (☑6234 3311, 1800 300 102; www.selectivecarrentals.com.au; 47 Bathurst St)

Taxi

City Cabs (☑13 10 08)

Maxi-Taxi Services (☑6274 3140; www. hobartmaxitaxi.com.au) Wheelchair-accessible vehicles.

AROUND HOBART

You won't have to travel too far from Hobart to swap cityscapes for natural panoramas, sandy beaches and historic sites. Reminders of Tasmania's convict history await at Richmond, and the waterfalls, wildlife and fantastic short walks at Mt Field National Park make an easy day trip. New Norfolk is a curious place to visit, while Seven Mile Beach and the Channel Hwy towns are great for an estuarine escape.

See p58 for info on companies offering day trips out of Hobart.

Richmond & Around

POP 750

Straddling the Coal River 27km northeast of Hobart, historic Richmond was once a strategic military post and convict station on the road to Port Arthur. Riddled with 19th-century buildings, it's arguably Tasmania's premier historic town, but like the Rocks in Sydney and Hahndorf in Adelaide, it's in danger of becoming a parody of itself with no actual 'life', just a passing tourist trade picking over the bones of the colonial past.

That said, Richmond is undeniably picturesque, and kids love chasing the ducks around the riverbanks. It's also quite close to the airport – a happy overnight option if you're on an early flight. There are no banks in town, but both main street supermarkets have ATMs. Hobart is only 20 minutes away,

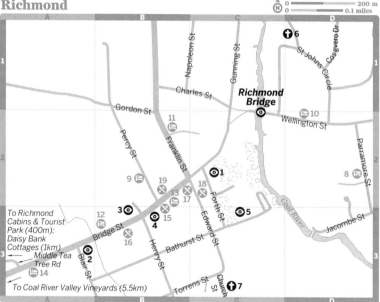

so it can be worthwhile considering Richmond as a base for accommodation.

See www.richmondvillage.com.au for more information.

◉ Sights & Activities

Richmond Bridge   LANDMARK
(Wellington St) This chunky but not inelegant bridge still funnels traffic across the Coal River, and is the town's proud centrepiece. Built by convicts in 1823 (making it the oldest road bridge in Australia), it's purportedly haunted by the 'Flagellator of Richmond', George Grover, who died here in 1832.

Richmond Gaol   HISTORIC BUILDING
(37 Bathurst St; adult/child/family $7/4/18; ⊙9am-5pm) The northern wing of the remarkably well-preserved gaol was built in 1825, five years before the penitentiary at Port Arthur. Like Port Arthur, fascinating historic insights abound, but the mood is pretty sombre.

**Old Hobart Town Historic
Model Village**   HISTORIC PARK
(www.oldhobarttown.com; 21a Bridge St; adult/family $14/30; ⊙9am-5pm) A painstaking re-creation of Hobart Town in the 1820s built from the city's original plans. The kids will love it.

Oak Lodge   HISTORIC BUILDING
(www.nationaltrust.org.au; 18 Bridge St; admission by gold-coin donation; ⊙11am-3.30pm) One of Richmond's oldest homes (c 1831), Oak Lodge is now owned by the National Trust and operated by the Coal River Historic Society. Inside is a museum illuminating colonial life.

Other interesting historic places in Richmond include the following.

St John's Church   CHURCH
(Wellington St) 1836; the first Roman Catholic church in Australia.

St Luke's Church of England   CHURCH
(Edward St) 1834.

Courthouse   HISTORIC BUILDING
(Forth St) 1825.

Old Post Office   HISTORIC BUILDING
(Bridge St) 1826.

Richmond Arms Hotel   HISTORIC BUILDING
(Bridge St) 1888.

ZooDoo Wildlife Fun Park   WILDLIFE PARK
(Map p77; www.zoodoo.com.au; 620 Middle Tea Tree Rd; adult/child $19/10; ⊙9am-5pm) Six kilometres west of Richmond on the road to Brighton (Middle Tea Tree Rd), ZooDoo has 'safari bus' rides, playgrounds, picnic areas

◉ **Top Sights**
   Richmond Bridge.................................C2

◉ **Sights**
   1 Courthouse...C2
   2 Oak Lodge..A3
   3 Old Hobart Town Historic Model
      Village..B3
   4 Old Post Office.....................................B3
      Richmond Arms Hotel................(see 13)
   5 Richmond Gaol.....................................C3
   6 St John's Church..................................D1
   7 St Luke's Church of England..............C3

◉ **Sleeping**
   8 Geraldine Cottage..............................D2

   9 Hollyhock Cottage...............................B2
  10 Laurel Cottage.....................................D2
  11 Mrs Currie's House B2
  12 Red Brier Cottage &
      Villa...B3
  13 Richmond Arms Hotel B2
  14 Richmond Cottages.............................A3

◉ **Eating**
  15 Anton's...B3
  16 Ashmore on Bridge
      Street...B3
  17 Ma Foosies...B2
      Richmond Arms Hotel ....(see 13)
  18 Richmond Bakery..................................C2
  19 Richmond Wine Centre.......................B2

and half of Dr Dolittle's appointment book including tigers, llamas, Tasmanian devils and wallabies. Hungry lions chow down at 11am, 1pm and 3pm.

Bonorong Wildlife Centre WILDLIFE PARK (Map p77; www.bonorong.com.au; 593 Briggs Rd, Brighton; adult/child $18/9; ◎9am-5pm) This place is about 17km west of Richmond (or alternatively, signposted off Hwy 1 at Brighton). From Richmond, take Middle Tea Tree Rd, and turn left into Tea Tree Rd after 11km. 'Bonorong' derives from an Aboriginal word meaning 'native companion' – look forward to Tasmanian devils, koalas, wombats, echidnas and quolls. The emphasis here is on conservation, education and the rehabilitation of injured animals.

🛏 Sleeping

TOP CHOICE **Daisy Bank Cottages** RENTAL HOUSE **$$** (6260 2390; www.daisybankcottages.com; Daisy Bank; d $150-160) This place is a rural delight: two spotless, self-contained units (one with spa) in a converted 1840s sandstone barn. There are loft bedrooms, views of the Richmond rooftops and plenty of farm-oriented distractions for the kids. The surrounding farmland has a few interpretative walks, and it's also a top spot to spy birds of prey. Off Middle Tea Tree Rd.

Mrs Currie's House B&B **$$** (6260 2766; www.mrscurrieshouse.com.au; 4 Franklin St; d incl breakfast $150) The oldest part of this accommodation was once the Prince of Wales Inn, a rammed-earth structure

dating from the 1820s. On offer are four tastefully furnished rooms, plus cooked breakfasts, open fires and snooker-table-flat lawns. And yes, Mrs Currie did live here for 80 years last century. Extra person $35.

Hollyhock Cottage RENTAL HOUSE **$$** (6260 1079; www.hollyhockcottage.com.au; 3 Percy St; d $160) Hollyhock is a cutesy National Trust-listed brick-and-timber cottage off the main street, renovated using original materials, with a few modern indulgences like a double spa. Breakfast provisions supplied. Mind your head on the convict-height doors.

Laurel Cottage RENTAL HOUSE **$$** (6260 2397; www.laurelcottages.com.au; 9 Wellington St; s/d $120/130) Ramshackle, two-bedroom convict-brick cottage beside the bridge, with a wood fire. Self-catering kitchen; breakfast provisions supplied. Kids welcome. Extra adult/child $30/20.

Geraldine Cottage RENTAL HOUSE **$$** (6260 2397; www.laurelcottages.com.au; 12 Parramore St; s/d $140/150) Run by the same folks as Laurel Cottage (and with similar rates), Geraldine – a former schoolhouse – is a bit bigger, a bit more refined and a bit newer (yeah, like 1839 is new). More flowers in the garden than a busy bee could ever service. Extra adult/child $30/20.

Red Brier Cottage & Villa RENTAL HOUSE **$$** (6260 2349; www.redbriercottage.com.au; 15 Bridge St; d cottage/villa $163/230) There are two modern accommodation styles on offer here: an intimate, fully equipped cedar cottage lashed with heritage decor, and a plush modern villa with king-size beds, two en suites, spa, flat-screen TVs, sound system and fantastic private garden with barbecue. Both sleep four and an extra person is $20/40 in the cottage/villa.

Richmond Cottages   RENTAL HOUSE $$

(6260 2561; www.richmondcottages.com; 12 Bridge St; d from $135) Just can't get enough colonial accommodation? On offer here are two self-contained abodes. Ivy Cottage is a family-friendly, three-bedroom home (complete with claw-foot bath), and behind it The Stables is a rustic one-bedroom cottage with spa. Extra adult/child $25/15.

Richmond Arms Hotel   PUB $$

(6260 2109; www.richmondarmshotel.com.au; 42 Bridge St; d from $110) The grand old Richmond pub has four good-quality motel-style units in the adjacent former stables. Onsite there's the dual attraction of the cosy dining room and sunny garden bar.

Richmond Cabins & Tourist
Park   CAMPGROUND $

(6260 2192; www.richmondcabins.com; 48 Middle Tea Tree Rd; unpowered/powered sites $24/30, cabins $75-130;) This place, 1km south of town, provides affordable accommodation in neat, no-frills cabins. Kids will be happy with the indoor pool and games room.

Eating

Ashmore on Bridge Street   CAFE $$

(6260 2238; 34 Bridge St; mains $14-20; breakfast & lunch daily, dinner Tue) Cheery corner food room with the sun streaming in through small-paned windows. Order up a big breakfast (scrambled eggs, cinnamon French toast with berry compote), and zingy lunches (beef lasagne, garlic prawns, Caesar salad). The best coffee in town too. Bookings essential for Tuesday night dinners.

Richmond Arms Hotel   PUB $$

(42 Bridge St; mains $15-25; lunch & dinner) This laid-back sandstone pub, popular with day-tripping, moustachioed bikers, has a reliable pub-grub menu (including meals for kids). The streetside tables are where you want to be. Coal River Valley wines are available.

Anton's   PIZZA $

(42a Bridge St; mains $11-19; lunch Wed-Sun, dinner Fri-Sun) Next to the pub, this small shop churns out first-class pizzas (try the Indian curry and lamb), plus pasta, antipasto, salads, desserts and *gelati*. Grab some picnic fixings and head for the river, or there are a couple of tables inside and out.

Richmond Wine Centre   RESTAURANT $$

(27 Bridge St; mains $13-28; breakfast & lunch daily, dinner Thu-Mon) Don't be duped by the name because this place dedicates itself to fine food as well as wine. Slink up to an outdoor table then peruse the menu. Tassie produce reigns supreme.

Ma Foosies   CAFE $

(46 Bridge St; dishes $8-21; breakfast & lunch) Cosy tearoom serving breakfast till 11.30am (pancakes, stuffed croissants, bacon and eggs) and an array of light meals, including

---

WINE TOURING IN THE COAL RIVER VALLEY

Richmond is also the centre of Tasmania's fastest-growing wine region, the Coal River Valley. Some operations are sophisticated affairs with gourmet restaurants, while others are small family-owned vineyards, with their cellar doors open by appointment. See winesouth.com.au for more information. Here's a few spots to get you started.

Meadowbank Estate (6248 4484; www.meadowbankwines.com.au; 699 Richmond Rd, Cambridge; mains $32-34; 10am-5pm) Overlooking the Mt Pleasant Observatory 9km southwest of Richmond, Meadowbank's acclaimed restaurant serves lunch daily; bookings are recommended, especially on weekends. Don't miss *Flawed History,* an in-floor jigsaw by local artist Tom Samek. Award-winning Pinot Gris, Sauvignon Blanc and Pinot Noir. There's also an art gallery and kids play area.

Craigow Vineyard (www.craigow.com.au; 528 Richmond Rd, Cambridge; 11am-5pm Jan-Mar) Opposite Meadowbank, offering tastings in a colonial cottage. Great whites including Riesling, Chardonnay and Sauvignon Blanc.

Puddleduck Vineyard (www.puddleduckvineyard.com.au; 992 Richmond Rd, Richmond; 10am-5pm) Small family-run vineyard producing just 1000 cases per year. Riesling, Merlot, Chardonnay and 'Bubbleduck' sparkling white. Cheese platters ($15) are for sale, or fire up its barbecues with your own steak, salad and sausages.

COOKING UP A STORM

Tasmania is rapidly becoming renowned globally as a destination for passionate, foodie travellers. The state's fruit and vegetables, seafood and meat, and wine and beer are held in high regard by star mainland chefs like Tetsuya Wakuda, and local chefs are also forging an international reputation. It's the kind of superior produce that any self-respecting home cook would love to get into. Here's your chance...

Agrarian Kitchen (www.theagrariankitchen.com) Located in a 19th-century schoolhouse in the Derwent Valley village of Lachlan, about 45-minutes' drive from Hobart, the Agrarian Kitchen is Tasmania's first – and only – hands-on, farm-based cookery school. The surrounding 5-acres provide sustainably- and organically grown vegetables, fruit, berries and herbs. Other ingredients are sourced from local farmers, fishermen and artisanal producers.

One of the most popular classes is 'The Agrarian Experience' (per person $295), a day-long celebration of the seasons commencing with choosing the freshest of fruit and vegies in the farm's garden, and then cooking up a storm before settling in for lunch with Tasmanian wines and beers from the nearby Two Metre Tall Brewery. Other classes specialise in charcuterie and gourmet sausage making, pastries and pasta, bread making and desserts.

The Agrarian Kitchen was voted Australia's No 1 Gourmet Experience by *Australian Traveller* magazine, and is a great way to improve your cooking skills surrounded by great Tassie produce and the rolling hills of the Derwen9t Valley.

If you're travelling in the north of Tasmania, Hadspen's **Red Feather Inn** also offers cookery classes, this time inspired by the Slow-Food movement.

See p69 for Hobart restaurant recommendations from the owners of the Agrarian Kitchen, Rodney Dunn and Séverine Demanet.

---

ploughman's lunch, grilled *panini,* quiche and lasagne. Gluten-free menu available.

Richmond Bakery BAKERY **$**
(off Edward St; items $4-8; ⊙breakfast & lunch) Pies, pastries, sandwiches, croissants, muffins and cakes – take away or munch in the courtyard. If the main street is empty, chances are everyone is in here.

❶ Getting There & Away

BUS **Tassielink** (☑1300 653 633; www.tassielink.com.au) run from the Hobart Bus Terminal, Monday to Friday at 8am, 8.30am, 10.30am, 12.30pm and 2.30pm (one way $7.20, 45 minutes). On Saturday and Sunday, buses leave Hobart at 8.55am and 2.10pm.

Richmond Tourist Bus (☑0408 341 804; per person return $25) runs a twice-daily service from Hobart at 9.15am and 12.20pm, with three hours to explore Richmond before returning. Call for bookings and pick-up locations.

CAR Richmond is a 20-minute drive from Hobart.

New Norfolk & Around
POP 9000

Cropping up unexpectedly amid the lush, rolling countryside (and heavy industry) of the Derwent Valley is New Norfolk, disarmingly referred to by locals as 'Norfick'. Here, 38km north of Hobart, the Derwent River narrows to just a few hundred metres across, and black swans rubberneck across the water. An Irish ex-con was so impressed, he knocked up the first house here in 1808. By the 1860s the valley had become a hop-growing hub, which explains all the old oast houses dotted around the valley (used for drying the plant). Hops, which give beer its bitterness, are sensitive to wind, so banks of trees were planted as wind barriers. Today, distinctive rows of tall poplars mark the boundaries of former hop fields.

Through the 20th century, New Norfolk was sculpted (and stigmatised) by two forces – the insane asylum Willow Court and the Boyer newspaper print mill, just downstream. Hobart viewed New Norfolk as mainland Australians viewed Hobart: somehow lesser, reduced, utterly working class and morally debased. These days the asylum is no more, and New Norfolk is an easygoing mix of colonial remnants and a smalltown, rural sensibility.

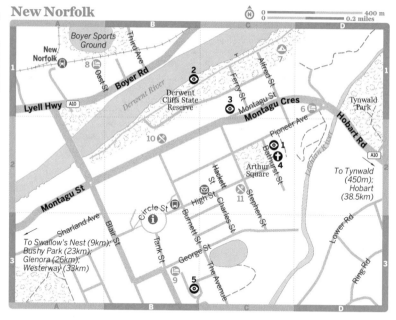

◉ Sights & Activities

St Matthew's Church   CHURCH
(www.newnorfolk.org/~st_matthews; 6 Bathurst
St; ☺service 9.30am Sun) Built in 1824, St Matthew's is Tasmania's oldest Anglican church.
It's been extensively altered since it first
rose from the ground, and its best features
today are the impressive stained-glass windows. In the adjacent St Matthew's Close
is a sporadically staffed **Craft Shop** that
raises money for the church's restoration.
On one wall is a massive clock face from
the tower (long since demolished) of Willow Court asylum, around which the town
evolved in the 1850s.

Willow Court Historic Site   HISTORIC BUILDING
(www.newnorfolk.org/~willow_court; George St;
☺daylight hr) The infamous Willow Court
Historic Site dates from the 1820s, and
housed invalid convicts before it became
part of the state's mental-health program.
In 1968 it housed 1000 patients, but by
the 1980s asylums began to be phased out
in favour of community-based treatment
and housing. In 2000 the asylum was finally closed. The stately old buildings are
slowly being revitalised, and now include
a hostel and a budget motel, a garden restaurant, and a rambling and abundant
antiques shop. See www.royalderwent.com

for the latest on Willow Court's ongoing
restoration.

Old Colony Inn   HISTORIC BUILDING
(☎6261 2731; www.newnorfolk.org/~old_colony_inn; 21 Montagu St; adult/child $2/50c;
☺10am-5pm) Built in 1815 as a hop shed, this
higgledy-piggledy, black-and-white-striped
museum is full of colonial furnishings
and artefacts. It's on a one-way street, so
prepare to make a tight U-turn at the top
end of the road division on Montagu St if
you're approaching from Hobart. There's
also recently renovated accommodation
here.

Pulpit Rock Lookout   LANDMARK
For camera-conducive views over New Norfolk and a sweeping Derwent River bend,
take the road along the northern side of
the river eastward for 1km, then up a steep,
unsealed side road to this popular lookout
spot.

Devil Jet   WATER SPORTS
(☎6261 3460; www.deviljet.com.au; Esplanade;
trips per adult/child $60/35; ☺9am-4pm)
30-minute jet-boat rides on the river propels
you 10km upstream and back. Be prepared
for 80km/h over shallows, traversing rapids
and 360-degree spins. Trips depart on the
hour, and bookings are recommended.

◎ Sights

1	Craft Shop	C2
2	Devil Jet	B1
3	Old Colony Inn	C1
4	St Matthew's Church	C2
5	Willow Court Historic Site	B3

◎ ◎ Sleeping

6	Junction	D1

7 New Norfolk Esplanade Caravan
    Park C1
    Old Colony Inn .... (see 3)
8 Rosie's Inn A1
9 Willow Court Motel B3

◎ Eating

10	Bush Inn	B2
11	New Norfolk Hotel	C2

🛏 Sleeping

Heimat Chalets   RENTAL HOUSE **$$**
[TOP CHOICE] (☑6261 2843; www.heimatchalets.com; 430 Black Hills Rd, Black Hills; powered sites $35, chalets d $145) About 9km out of town (signposted off Lyell Hwy west of the bridge) is Heimat, offering family-friendly accommodation in an amenable rural setting with friendly alpacas. There are two powered, ensuite sites, and two self-contained chalets, plus a playground, all-weather barbecue hut and chalet breakfast provisions. Pop in around October to December for handsdown Tasmania's cutest lambs. Extra person in chalet $35.

Swallow's Nest   B&B **$$**
(☑6286 1144; www.swallowsnestguesthouse. com.au; 1358 Glenora Rd, Plenty; d incl breakfast $120-135) With a quiet riverside location 15 minutes from New Norfolk en route to Mt Field National Park, Swallow's Nest features a cosy B&B room and a one-bedroom apartment in a restored oast house over 100 years old. There's plenty of birdlife, a few resident platypuses, and the opportunity to paint to your heart's content in the adjacent studio (cost of art materials is extra). Follow the road to Glenora along the Derwent River for 9km from New Norfolk.

Tynwald   B&B **$$**
(☑6261 2667; www.tynwaldtasmania.com.au; 1 Tynwald St; d incl breakfast $165-220; @☒) Tynwald is a turreted, three-storey 1830s mansion overlooking the river, with six antique-furnished guest rooms, a heated swimming pool, extensive gardens, tennis court and cooked breakfasts. There's also a self-contained stone cottage on the grounds, and the restaurant here is the best in 'Norfick'. It's open to outside guests, but you'll need to book ahead.

Junction   MOTEL **$$**
(☑6261 4029; www.junctionmotel.com.au; 50 Pioneer Ave; d $99-125; �) This recently refurbished motel complex has spotless rooms – including a few Asian-themed luxury options – and energetic ex-Sydney and New Zealand owners forging a new life in Tasmania. Recommended as a counterpoint to the overly chintzy styling of some other New Norfolk accommodation. There's an onsite restaurant (only available to motel guests).

Base Camp Tasmania   CABINS **$**
(☑1300 882 293; www.twe.travel; 959 Glenfern Rd, Glenfern; tent per person $15, dm $36, cabin $60) Just 14km from New Norfolk, and about an hour from Hobart, but Base Camp Tasmania feels like a thousand miles from anywhere. The final windy mountain road reveals rustic but comfortable dorms and cabins. One self-contained cabin suits families, and other cabins and dorms share the spotless kitchen and dining facilities. Look forward to loads of wildlife roaming the surrounding forest, as the site is a protected reserve. It's used as a base for bushwalking groups from Tasmanian Wilderness Experiences, but casual guests are also welcome. Phone ahead to make sure they've got room.

Rosie's Inn   B&B **$$**
(☑6261 1171; www.rosiesinn.com.au; 5 Oast St; d $120-180) Quiet, motel-like B&B with welcoming hosts and an improbably floral garden. A cooked breakfast is $10. The building used to be a workers' hostel, and a certain institutional ambience does linger.

Old Colony Inn   B&B **$$**
(☑6261 2731; www.newnorfolk.org/~old_colony_inn; 21 Montagu St; d incl breakfast $110-120) Set in picture-perfect gardens, the Old Colony Inn has recently redecorated rooms offering just the right mix of heritage – the building dates back to 1815 – and modern comfort with new bathrooms and flat-screen TVs. There's

also a lovely onsite tearoom and more than a few rooms of antiques.

Willow Court Motel
MOTEL $

(☑6261 4281; www.willowcourt.com.au; 15 George St; dm $30, d $60-80; @) Part of the ongoing Willow Court redevelopment is this newish motel and hostel, offering affordable accommodation in bright, simple rooms. It's a rambling, immaculately maintained place, with TVs in most rooms, internet access, and asylum-strength metal bunks. There's also the on-site Olive Tree restaurant with pasta, burgers and salads (mains $12 to $25).

New Norfolk Esplanade Caravan Park
CAMPGROUND $

(☑6261 1268; www.newnorfolk.org/~caravan_park; Esplanade; sites $20-25, on-site vans $45, cabins $60-90) Shady, poplar-studded grounds on the Derwent's south bank. There are only four cabins, which have toilets – everyone else uses the spotless amenities blocks.

✗ Eating & Drinking

Bush Inn
PUB $$

(49 Montagu St; mains $15-25; ⊙lunch & dinner) This old pub has a classic menu of seafood and meat-heavy pub favourites, including surf 'n' turf (steak topped with prawns), rump steak, roast of the day and chicken kiev. There's a kids' menu too, plus an outdoor deck with dreamy river views. It's also renowned as Aussie's oldest pub, established in 1815.

Tynwald
RESTAURANT $$

(☑6261 2667; Tynwald St; mains $27-33; ⊙dinner) In addition to accommodation, Tynwald has an outstanding, seasonally shifting menu. Look forward to French influences, and an emphasis on game meats (rabbit, hare, venison) and Tasmanian seafood. Desserts raise the bar even higher. Bookings essential.

Two Metre Tall
BREWERY

(Map p77; www.2mt.com.au; 2862 Lyell Hwy, Hayes; ⊙from 4pm Fri, Sep-Apr) On of Tassie's best microbreweries throws open its gates every Friday afternoon from September to April. Two Metre Tall 'Farm Bar' sessions feature hand pumped real ale and cider, and there's barbecues available to make a night of it (BYO gourmet sausages, marinated chicken breasts and salad fixings). Brewer Ashley Huntington strives to make beer with an authentic stamp of the surrounding area, and hops and barley are sourced from Two Metre Tall's own farm in the Derwent Valley. And if you're wondering where the name came from, let's just say Ashley may have been a dab hand at basketball in his younger days.

New Norfolk Hotel
PUB $$

(cnr Stephen & High Sts; mains $15-25; ⊙lunch & dinner) Amid the jingle jangle of the poker machines there's standard pub fare here with fish and chips, steaks and chicken schnitzels, plus the odd oddity like flounder fillets. Big serves and a kids menu. It's the local's favourite, but the views and ambience are better at the Bush Inn.

❶ Information

Derwent Valley visitor centre (☑6261 3700; www.riversrun.net.au; Circle St; ⊙10.30am-4pm) is behind the courthouse, and handles accommodation bookings and local lowdown. The free brochure *Historic Walks of New Norfolk* will guide you around the old-time sights.

Online see www.newnorfolk.org and www.derwentvalley.net.au.

❶ Getting There & Away

Hobart Coaches (☑13 22 01) is the main operator between Hobart and New Norfolk (buses 130 and 134), and provides five services a day in both directions on weekdays, and three on Saturday ($8 one way, 50 minutes). In New Norfolk, the buses leave from Burnett St. In Hobart they depart from stop F on Elizabeth St.

New Norfolk to Mt Field

Further west en route to Mt Field National Park, the road travels through the three historic rural towns of Bushy Park, Glenora and Westerway. Here you can see old barns, a water wheel and rambling hop fields. The shingled buildings are typical of the local farms built in the 19th century. Hop-growing has vanished from much of Tasmania, but it's still pursued commercially around Bushy Park, the largest hops-producing town in the southern hemisphere. In late summer and autumn you can see hops vines winding up thin leader strings.

◉ Sights

Salmon Ponds Heritage Hatchery & Garden
GARDEN

(☑6261 5663; www.salmonponds.com.au; Salmon Ponds Rd, Plenty; adult/child/family $8/6/22; ⊙9am-5pm) In 1864, rainbow and brown trout were bred for the first time in the southern hemisphere at this hatchery 9km west of New Norfolk at Plenty. You can feed the fish in the display ponds, visit the hatchery and check out the angling museum. The restaurant here, **Pancakes by the Ponds** (meals $8-19), specialises in sweet and savoury crepes, plus island wines and decent coffee.

Kinvarra Estate Wines VINEYARD
(☑6286 1333; www.kinvarra.com.au; 1211 Glenora Rd, Plenty; ⊙by appointment) About 5km further west after the Salmon Ponds, Kinvarra offers wine tastings and sales in a lovely 1827 homestead. Riesling, Pinot Noir and sparkling whites are the tipples of choice. It tends to open and close on a whim, so call for an appointment.

Something Wild WILDLIFE PARK
(☑6288 1013; www.somethingwild.com.au; 2080 Gordon River Rd; adult/child $14/7; ⊙10am-5pm) On the Tyenna River 4km before Mt Field, this wildlife sanctuary rehabilitates orphaned and injured wildlife, and provides a home for animals unable to be released. Visit the animal nursery, see native wildlife (devils, wombats, quolls), and maybe spot a platypus sniffing around the grounds. Something Wild is visited by several companies offering day trips from Hobart; see p58).

🛏 Sleeping & Eating

Platypus Playground RENTAL HOUSE $$
(☑0413 833 700; www.riverside-cottage.com; 1658 Gordon River Rd, Westerway; d $150) You can't miss this cute, red riverside cottage at Westerway, offering ecofriendly accommodation. Winning features include an outdoor deck over the river and the chance to spot a platypus or hook a trout. The owners make it a priority to minimise guests' environmental impact, and ecofriendly toiletries and detergents are supplied to protect the adjacent river.

Duffy's Country
Accommodation RENTAL HOUSE $$
(☑6288 1373; www.duffyscountry.com; 49 Clark's Rd, Westerway; d $125-135; @) Overlooking a field of raspberry canes are two immaculate self-contained cabins, one a studio-style cabin for couples, the other a two-bedroom relocated rangers' hut from Mt Field National Park. Breakfast provisions are provided including toast, eggs and homemade raspberry jam. Extra adult/child $25/15.

Hamlet Downs B&B $$
(☑6288 1212; www.hamletdowns.com; 50 Gully Rd, Fentonbury; d $155) Amid rural quiet and spectacular flowerbeds around 3km northwest of Westerway at Fentonbury, Hamlet Downs is a gracious 1860s homestead transformed into three self-contained apartments. Take a walk down to Fentonbury Creek to look for a platypus. Dinner, bed and breakfast packages featuring terrific Greek food are $230 for two people (extra adult/child from $40/25). Mt Field is just 10km away, and Hamlet Downs is a great option if you're heading northeast to Hamilton and Bothwell, or northwest to Tasmania's Lake Country.

Possum Shed CAFE $
(1654 Gordon River Rd, Westerway; meals $10-20; ⊙breakfast & lunch, closed Tue Apr-Sep) At Westerway en route to Mt Field is this brilliant riverside haunt, with outdoor seating, a resident platypus (sightings not guaranteed) and locally sourced lunches and snacks (salads, pancakes, wraps, BLTs). The coffee is good too.

Mt Field National Park

POP 170 (NATIONAL PARK TOWNSHIP)
Mt Field, 80km northwest of Hobart (and 7km beyond Westerway), was declared a national park in 1916 and is famed for its mountain scenery, alpine moorlands, lakes, rainforest, waterfalls and abundant wildlife. To many locals it's simply known as National Park, a moniker given to the small town at its entrance. It's an accessible place to visit for a day, or to bunk down overnight with the kids.

Walks

Pick up a copy of the *Welcome to Mt Field National Park* brochure, which details walks in the park, from the visitor centre.

Short Walks

The park's most touted attraction is the cascading, 40m-high **Russell Falls**, which is in the valley close to the park entrance. It's an easy 20-minute circuit walk from the car park along a wheelchair-suitable path. From Russell Falls, you can continue past **Horseshoe Falls** and **Tall Trees Circuit** to **Lady Barron Falls**, a two-hour return walk past mountain ash (*Eucalyptus regnans*, the world's tallest flowering plants).

The 15-minute **Lyrebird Nature Walk** starts 7km up Lake Dobson Rd. It's a pocket-sized introduction to park flora and fauna – great for kids – with numbers along the track corresponding to information in a brochure from the visitor centre.

For kids (and adults!) who don't mind a longer walk, there's the **Pandani Grove Nature Walk**, which traces the edge of Lake Dobson through magical stands of endemic pandani palms that grow up to 12m high before toppling over. This walk takes 40 minutes. Park at Lake Dobson car park, 16km from the park entrance.

High-Country Walks

There are some awesome walks at the top of the range, where glaciation has sculpted steep cliffs and bruised deep valleys into what was once a continuous plateau. Shimmering lakes perforate the valley floors, and smaller tarns adorn the ridge-tops.

If you're setting out on a walk to the high country, take waterproof gear and warm clothing – the weather is changeable year-round, so check weather and track conditions with the visitor centre before you set out. Walks here include those to **Lake Nicholls**, **Seagers Lookout** and **Lake Seal Lookout** (all two hours return), the **Mt Field East Circuit** (four to five hours return) and **Lake Belcher** (five to six hours return).

Tarn Shelf Track

The **Tarn Shelf Track** is a brilliant walk year-round in clear weather. In summer the temperature is mild, and in autumn deciduous beech leaves along the way turn golden. In winter you may need skis or snowshoes, and in spring the sound of melting snow trickling beneath the boardwalk enhances the silence.

There's a 4WD gravel road from Lake Dobson to the ski fields and Tarn Shelf, but this is only open to authorised vehicles. Most people walk from the Lake Dobson car

park along the Urquhart Track to its junction with the gravel road. Both the track and the road are steep. Continue along the road to the ski fields, at the top of which is the start of the Tarn Shelf Track.

The track is fairly level with a boardwalk protecting delicate vegetation and keeping walkers out of the mud. Either continue as far as you like along the track and then return via the same route, or take one of two routes branching off at Lake Newdegate then circle back to the ski fields. If you travel east past Twisted Tarn, Twilight Tarn and Lake Webster, the walk takes five or six hours return from the car park, while the wonderful Rodway Range circuit to the west takes six or seven hours return.

Skiing

Skiing was first attempted here on **Mt Mawson** in 1922. A low-key resort with clubby huts and rope tows has evolved, and when nature sees fit to offload some snow (infrequently in recent years) it makes a lowkey change from the commercial ski fields on mainland Australia. The ski field is open 10am to 4pm weekends and school holidays, weather permitting. The cost for a day's snowploughing is $30/15 per adult/child. Up-to-date snow reports are available online at www.ski.com.au/reports/mawson, or via a recorded message service (☑6288 1166).

There are no ski-equipment hire outlets here; hire ski and snowboard gear in Hobart at **Skigia & Surf** (p75).

🛏 Sleeping & Eating

There's also accommodation at Maydena, 12km west of Mt Field National Park village, and around Westerway, 7km east.

Land of the Giants Campground

CAMPGROUND $

(☑6288 1526; unpowered/powered sites $20/28) A privately run, self-registration campground with adequate facilities (toilets, showers, laundry and free barbecues), it's just inside the park gates. Bookings not required. Site prices are additional to national park entry fees.

Lake Dobson Cabins

CABINS $

(☑6288 1149; www.parks.tas.gov.au; Lake Dobson Rd; cabins up to 6 people $45) Get back to your pure mountaintop essence at these three simple, six-bed cabins about 14km inside the park. All are equipped with mattresses, cold water, wood stove and firewood (there's no

WINTER ROAD WARNING

If you're staying in the Lake Dobson huts, skiing Mt Mawson or trampling the Pandani Grove Nature Walk or other high-country walks, you'll have to drive the 16km, unsealed Lake Dobson Rd. In winter, despite climate change's best efforts, you'll need chains and anti-freeze for your car. Hire them in Hobart at **Skigia & Surf** (p75).

CROWN PRINCESS MARY OF DENMARK (AKA MARY DONALDSON OF TAROONA)

A few Tasmanians have found themselves in the spotlight recently, but no-one has garnered more international attention than Mary Donaldson, the girl from Taroona now living a modern-day fairy tale in Europe. Mary was born in Hobart in 1972 to Scots who had emigrated to Australia a decade earlier. The youngest of four children, she attended Taroona High School before graduating from the University of Tasmania (commerce and law) in 1993. Mary moved to Melbourne and worked in advertising, then travelled through Europe and the US before returning to Australia to live in Sydney.

Mary met Denmark's Crown Prince Frederik at the Slip Inn pub in Sydney during the 2000 Olympic Games; the prince was in Oz with the Danish sailing team. The pair sailed into a relationship that sent the gossip mags into a frenzy of speculation until Mary and Fred announced their engagement in 2003. They married in a lavish ceremony in Copenhagen in 2004 with a sea of well-wishers lining the streets, waving Danish and Australian flags. Interest in Tasmania as a holiday destination for the Danes has skyrocketed, and Tassie produce has found a new export market in Denmark.

'Our Mary' is never far from the covers of Danish and Australian gossip mags, as journos dissect every aspect of her life. Is she too thin? Does she own too many shoes? How's her Danish coming along? Of course, the real show-stoppers have been Frederick and Mary's four children: HRH Prince Christian, born October 2005, HRH Princess Isabella, born April 2007, and the most recent Danish double whammy of Prince Vincent and Princess Josephine, twins born on January 8, 2011. Give or take a few months that made it four kiddies under age five for Frederik and Mary. No doubt she's getting a bit of help at home though.

power), and have a communal toilet block. Visitors will need to bring gas lamps and cookers, plus utensils. Book at the visitor centre.

Waterfalls Cafe   CAFE **$**
(66 Lake Dobson Rd; meals $10-12; ⊘lunch) Simple eatery next to the visitor centre, serving up reasonable cafe fare (burgers, nachos, soup and schnitzels).

National Park Hotel   PUB **$$**
(Gordon River Rd; mains $15-30; ⊘dinner) This relaxed rural pub, 300m past the park turn-off, cooks up mixed grills, chicken dishes and steaks. The barmaid shakes her head and says, 'They love their meat round here...'

❶ Information

The **Mt Field National Park visitor centre** (☑6288 1149; www.parks.tas.gov.au; 66 Lake Dobson Rd; ⊘8.30am-5pm Nov-Apr, 9am-4pm May-Oct) houses a cafe and displays on the park's origins, and has reams of information on walks and ranger-led activities held from late December until early February. There are excellent day-use facilities in the park, including barbecues, shelters and a children's playground.

See p295 for national park entry fees.

❶ Getting There & Away

The drive to Mt Field through the Derwent River Valley and Bushy Park is an absolute stunner with river rapids, hop fields, rows of poplars and hawthorn hedgerows. Public transport connections to the park are limited to **Tassielink** (☑1300 300 520; www.tassielink.com.au) services, running on Tuesday, Thursday and Saturday ($30, 3½ hours) from December to March. Some Hobart-based tour operators offer Mt Field day trips, usually taking in the Something Wild wildlife sanctuary as well as the national park.

Seven Mile Beach

POP 450

Out near the airport, 15km east of Hobart, is this brilliant, safe swimming beach (Map p44) backed by shacks, a corner store and pine-punctured dunes. When the swell is working, the point break here is magic.

Follow Surf Rd out past the airport runway and around to the left for 2km and you'll come to **Barilla Bay Oyster Farm** (☑6248 5458; www.barillabay.com.au; 1388 Tasman Hwy, Cambridge; tours adult/child $10/5, mains $28-35; ⊘lunch daily, dinner daily Oct-Apr & Thu-Sun May-Sep). Hit the slick restaurant, or grab a dozen shucked oysters ($10) washed down with some Oyster Stout. Tours run most days, so call for bookings and to confirm times.

To get to Seven Mile Beach, drive towards the airport and follow the signs. Local buses 191, 192, 291 and 293 also run here.

Channel Highway

The convoluted Channel Hwy is the continuation of Sandy Bay Rd, mimicking the D'Entrecasteaux Channel coastline as it flows south. It was once the main southbound road out of Hobart, but was relegated to a pleasant tourist drive once the Southern Outlet (Hwy A6) from Hobart to Kingston opened in 1985. Drive slowly and check out the views, hilltop houses and gardens en route south.

TAROONA
POP 2000

Ten kilometres from Hobart is snoozy Taroona, its name derived from an Aboriginal word meaning 'seashell'.

On the suburb's southern fringe stands the **Shot Tower** (Channel Hwy; adult/child $7/3; ⊙9am-5pm), a 48m-high, circular sandstone turret - each block precisely curved and tapered - built in 1870 to make lead shot for firearms. Molten lead was dribbled from the top, forming perfect spheres on its way down to a cooling vat of water at the bottom. The river views from atop the 318 steps (we're pretty sure we counted them correctly...) are wondrous. The tower is surrounded by leafy grounds and has a snug **tearoom** (light meals $5-10; ⊙11am-3pm) downstairs. If it's sunny, devour a Devonshire tea on the stone rampart outside.

On the northern fringe of Taroona is Truganini Reserve and the bottom end of the Truganini Track which leads up a wooded valley to Mt Nelson Signal Station.

A great detour from Hobart for lunch or dinner is the **Taroona Lounge Bar** (⊘6227 8886; www.taroonaloungebar.com.au; 178 Channel Hwy; mains $15-32; ⊙11am-late), a funky reworking of a 1970s pub with terrific wood-fired pizza and superior versions of Aussie classics like tempura-battered fish and chips and Black Angus Scotch Fillet. You'll find the Taroona Lounge Bar at the northern end of town around 8km from central Hobart. It's very popular at the weekend, so it might pay to book.

To get to Taroona from Hobart, take **Metro Tasmania** (⊘13 22 01; www.metrotas.com.au) bus 56, 61-3, 67, 68, 94, 162, 167 or 168 from Franklin Sq stop O. A one-way adult fare is $3.30.

KINGSTON
POP 13,000

Sprawling Kingston, 12km south of Hobart, is a booming outer suburb of the city. It started to evolve from a sleepy beach enclave when the Southern Outlet roadway established a rocket-shot route into town. The beach here is a super spot to laze away a sunny afternoon. A couple of good eating options make it a worthwhile day trip from Hobart.

◉ Sights

Kingston Beach   BEACH

This popular swimming and sailing spot has steep wooded cliffs at each end of a long arc of sand. There's a picnic area at the northern end, accessed by a pedestrian bridge over the pollution-prone, nonswimmable (and therefore aptly named) Browns River. Behind the sailing clubhouse at the southern end of the beach is a track leading to a beaut little swimming spot called **Boronia Beach**, which has a deep rock pool. Note that sections of this track are heavily eroded.

DETOUR: TINDERBOX

Make time to drive through Blackmans Bay and a further 10km to Tinderbox. The views along the way are eye-popping, and at Tinderbox itself is a small beach bordering **Tinderbox Nature Marine Reserve** (www.parks.tas.gov.au). Here you can snorkel along an underwater trail running alongside a sandstone reef, marked with submerged information plates explaining the rich local ecosystem. Bruny Island is just across the water, and locals often launch their boats here and skim across to Dennes Point for a barbecue.

From Tinderbox, continue around the peninsula to Howden and back to Kingston via the Channel Hwy.

Blackmans Bay
BEACH

About 3km from Kingston Beach, Blackmans has another decent beach and a blowhole (down Blowhole Rd). The water at both these beaches is usually quite cold, and there's rarely any surf.

Australian Antarctic Division
MUSEUM

(www.antarctica.gov.au; 203 Channel Hwy; admission free; ☺8.30am-5pm Mon-Fri) Beside the Channel Hwy south of Kingston is the headquarters of the government department administering Australia's 42% wedge of the frozen continent. Australia has a long history of exploration and scientific study of Antarctica, and it's one of the original 12 nations that ratified the Antarctic Treaty in 1961. Visitors can check out the displays here, which feature Antarctic equipment, clothing and scientific vehicles, plus ecological info and some brilliant photographs. The centre's cafeteria is open to the public.

✖️ Eating

Citrus Moon Café
CAFE $

(23 Beach Rd; mains $10-17; ☺breakfast & lunch; 🖉) Bright, retro cafe with a predominantly vegetarian menu. Devour brekky until noon, then choose from burgers, bagels or salads for lunch, or swing by for coffee and homemade cake (vegan, flourless or regular options available). If you *must,* there are a few tasty beef, chicken and fish dishes as well.

The Beach
CAFE $$

(Ocean Esplanade, Blackmans Bay; mains $20-30; ☺lunch & dinner) On a sunny day there's no better spot than the outdoor terrace of this angular, metal-finned cafe-bar, south of Kingston opposite Blackmans Bay beach. Wood-fired pizzas, risotto, lamb shanks and pasta, all done with flair. Good coffee and cake too.

❶ Getting There & Away

BUS To get to Kingston from Hobart take **Metro Tasmania** (🖉13 22 01; www.metrotas.com.au) bus 61, 62, 63, 67, 68, 94, 162, 167 or 168 via Taroona, or bus 174, 184 or 185 via the Southern Outlet. Buses depart from Hobart's Franklin Sq stop O; a one-way adult fare is $3.30.

Hobart Coaches (🖉13 22 01) runs regular services (buses 89, 90, 92-4, 96 and 98) from Hobart to Kingston. Bus 89 continues to Blackmans Bay. The fare to both destinations is $3.10 one way.

CAR As you branch off from the Southern Outlet and approach Kingston, continue straight ahead at the first set of lights instead of turning right onto the Channel Hwy; this road takes you down to the beach. If you're trundling down the Channel Hwy from Taroona, turn left at these lights.

Tasman Peninsula & Port Arthur

Includes »
Sorell 92
Dunalley 93
Eaglehawk Neck 93
Taranna 95
Fortescue Bay 96
Port Arthur 96
Remarkable Cave 100
Koonya & Nubeena . . 100

Best Places to Eat

» Sorell Providore (p93)

» Dunalley Waterfront Café (p93)

» Taylor's Restaurant (p99)

» Lucky Ducks (p101)

Best Places to Stay

» Drovers Daughter (p92)

» Casilda House (p93)

» Taranna Cottages & Campervan Park (p95)

» Norfolk Bay Convict Station (p95)

» Harpers on the Beach (p101)

» Larus Waterfront Cottage (p101)

Why Go?

Just an hour from Hobart are the staggering coastal landscapes, sandy surf beaches and historic sites of the Tasman Peninsula. Bushwalking, surfing, sea-kayaking, scuba-diving and rock-climbing opportunities abound – all good reasons to extend your visit beyond a hurried day trip from Hobart.

Don't miss visiting the peninsula's legendary 300m-high sea cliffs, which will dose you up on natural awe. Most of the cliffs are protected by Tasman National Park, a coastal enclave embracing chunky offshore islands and underwater kelp forests. The cliffs are a safe haven for seabirds, while the fertile waters below throng with seals, dolphins and whales.

Waiting portentously at the end of Arthur Hwy is Port Arthur, the infamous and allegedly escape-proof penal colony in the mid-19th century. Today kids kick footballs and dads poke sausages on BBQs there, but it's impossible to forget this is a tragic place, both historically and more recently.

When to Go

The Tasman Peninsula's weather is at its best from November to March, but from December to February you'll need to be prepared for crowds at the Port Arthur Historic Site, especially on weekends. Lovers of fresh fruit should visit from December to January, when the Sorell Fruit Farm is awash with juicy varieties. Negotiating the Tasman Peninsula's many walking tracks is definitely a summer activity, best undertaken from December to April.

⚲ Tours

If you don't have wheels, you can take a coach or ferry tour to the Tasman Peninsula from Hobart. Many operators run trips to Port Arthur.

Tasman Island Adventure Cruises   SIGHTSEEING, CRUISE
(☑6253 5325; www.tasmanadventurecruises.com.au; full-day tour adult/child from $169/110)

Trips departing Hobart and incorporating a three-hour adventure cruise, the Tasman Peninsula's most spectacular coastal scenery, and the option of exploring Port Arthur. The cruise can also be joined from Eaglehawk Neck (adult/child $100/55).

Gray Line   SIGHTSEEING, CRUISE
(☑1300 858 687; www.grayline.com.au; full-day tour adult/child from $100/50) Coach tours

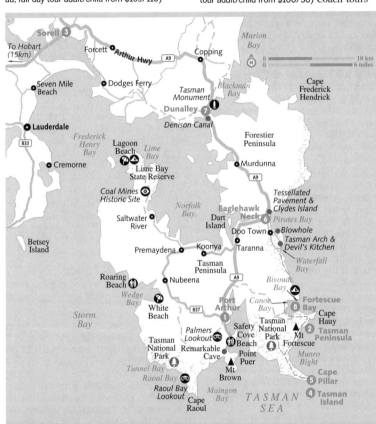

Tasman Peninsula & Port Arthur Highlights

❶ Paying your respects to the past, both distant and recent, at the **Port Arthur Historic Site** (p97)

❷ **Sea-kayaking** (p94) around the Tasman Peninsula's broken coastline

❸ Getting your hands dirty picking fresh raspberries, apricots and silvanberries at the **Sorell Fruit Farm** (p92)

❹ Spotting seals, dolphins and maybe even a whale on a cruise around **Tasman Island** (p94) from Port Arthur

❺ Battling vertigo atop the southern hemisphere's highest sea cliffs at Cape Pillar on the **Tasman Coastal Trail** (p94)

❻ Diving the clear, cool waters of the Tasman Peninsula from **Eaglehawk Neck** (p94)

❼ Chowing down on local seafood at the **Dunalley Waterfront Café** (p93)

❽ Pitching your tent at remote **Fortescue Bay** (p96) and falling asleep to the lull of the waves

ex-Hobart, including a harbour cruise around the Isle of the Dead, Port Arthur admission and guided tour, and pit stops at Tasman Arch and the Devil's Kitchen.

Navigators SIGHTSEEING, CRUISE
(☑6223 1914; www.navigators.net.au; Brooke St Pier, Hobart; full-day tour adult/child from $159/128; ⊘Wed, Fri & Sat Oct-May) Cruises from Hobart to Port Arthur, returning on a coach. Includes entrance to the historic site, guided tour and morning tea. Also offers cruises around Tasman Island from Port Arthur.

Roaring 40s Ocean Kayaking KAYAKING
(☑6267 5000; www.roaring40stours.com.au; 1-/3-day tour $255/1250) Based in Kettering, Roaring 40s also conducts epic sea-kayaking tours around the Tasman Peninsula, paddling past the monumental coastline. Prices include equipment, meals, accommodation and transfers from Hobart.

Tasman Island Cruises SIGHTSEEING, CRUISE
(☑6250 2200; www.tasmancruises.com.au; full-day tour adult/child from $165/110) Take a bus to Port Arthur for a three-hour ecocruise around Tasman Island, then explore the Port Arthur Historic Site and bus it back to town. Includes morning tea, lunch and Port Arthur admission. You can also take just the cruise from Port Arthur (adult/child $100/55).

Tours Tasmania SIGHTSEEING
(☑1800 777 103; www.tourstas.com.au; full-day tours $100-110; ⊘Tue, Wed, Fri & Sat) Small-group day trips to Port Arthur and the Tasmanian Devil Conservation Park, or Port Arthur combined with Remarkable Cave and Tasman Arch. Longer two- to five-day trips to Mt Field, Wineglass Bay and Cradle Mountain. Backpacker focused.

Sorell

POP 1730

Sorell is one of Tasmania's oldest towns, settled in 1808 primarily to supply locally processed wheat and flour to the rest of the colony, but its historic aura has tarnished over time. These days it's a T-junction service town with more petrol stations and fast-food joints than anything else, but it's still the gateway to the Tasman Peninsula.

A handful of 19th-century buildings have survived near the centre of town and

are worth a look. The 1841 **Scots Uniting Church** (Arthur St) is behind the high school. Also near the school are the **Sorell Barracks** (31 Walker St), now colonial accommodation, and the 1829 **Blue Bell Inn** (cnr Somerville & Walker Sts). On the main drag is the 1884 **St George's Anglican Church** (Gordon St), its adjacent **graveyard** propped with the headstones of early settlers.

The perfect pit stop is the **Sorell Fruit Farm** (☑6265 3100; www.sorellfruitfarm.com; 174 Pawleena Rd; pay per kilo picked, minimum purchase berries/cherries $6/11; ⊘8.30am-5pm late Oct-May), where you can pick your own fruit from its intensively planted 12.5 acres. There are 15 different kinds of edibles on offer, including strawberries, raspberries, cherries, apricots, peaches and apples, and more exotic varieties like loganberries, tayberries and silvanberries. December and January are the best months for variety, but different fruits are in season at different times – check the website for a nifty chart. Afterwards, enjoy a snack or a mellow coffee in the **tearooms** (light meals $8-11), or choose from a wide range of fruity jams, chutneys, sauces, wines and liqueurs for sale. To get here, head east through Sorell towards Port Arthur. After exiting the town you'll see Pawleena signposted on your left.

🛏 Sleeping & Eating

Given its proximity to the airport, Sorell makes a handy overnight stop if you have an early flight.

Drovers Daughter B&B $$
(☑6253 5452; www.droversdaughter.com.au; 2124 Arthur Hwy; d $140-150, extra person $20; @) This rambling modern homestead set on 5 acres has two swish rooms with adjoining verandahs ideal for taking in the relaxed rural views. Keep your eyes peeled for local personalities 'Cuddles' the echidna and 'Fat Boy' the kookaburra. Picnic and cheese platters are available, with evening meals on request.

Cherry Park Estate B&B $$
(☑6265 2271; www.cherryparkestate.com.au; 114 Pawleena Rd; d $140-150; @🛜) Close to Sorell Fruit Farm, Cherry Park has three recently renovated rooms with antique furniture and spacious bathrooms. There's 7 hectares of surrounding open space, including gardens, an orchard and a compact vineyard. Breakfast includes homemade jams and free-range eggs.

Sorell Providore
CAFE **$$**

(21 Gordon St; breakfast & lunch mains $8-15, dinner mains $26-30; ☺breakfast & lunch daily, dinner Fri & Sat; ☎) Another of Tasmania's emerging hybrids, combining cafe and delicatessen. Look forward to terrific eggy breakfasts, interesting counter food, and a small dinner menu on Friday and Saturday nights. With a great range of Tassie beer and wine, and artisan bread and cheese for sale, it's a perfect spot for compiling a relaxed Tasman Peninsula picnic. There's also free wi-fi with any purchase.

❶ Information

Sorell visitor centre (☑6265 6438; www.tasmanregion.com.au; 16 Main Rd; ☺9am-4pm May, 10am-4pm Jun-Sep, 9am-5pm Oct Apr) For maps and peninsula info. Pick up the *Tasman – The Essence of Tasmania* and the *Convict Trail* booklets, which cover the peninsula's key historic sites.

❶ Getting There & Away

BUS The **Tassielink** (www.tassielink.com.au) service down the Tasman Peninsula from Hobart stops at Sorell ($7.20, 40 minutes). **Redline Coaches** (www.redlinecoaches.com.au) also operates some weekday services between Hobart and Sorell.

Dunalley

POP 290

The thickly timbered Forestier Peninsula – the precursor peninsula you'll cross en route to the Tasman Peninsula – is connected to mainland Tasmanian soil by the isthmus town Dunalley. Gouged out in 1905, the **Denison Canal**, complete with a raiseable bridge, bisects the isthmus, providing a short cut for small boats. There's not much to see here, but there are a few good places to stay and eat.

🛏 Sleeping & Eating

Casilda House
B&B **$$**

(☑6253 5265; www.casildahouse.com.au; 18 Imlay St; d $140; ☎) Originally built in 1880, this waterfront heritage cottage is just a short stroll to the Dunalley Waterfront Café. Home-baked bread tops off tasty cooked breakfasts, and free use of kayaks and fishing gear makes it easy to enjoy Dunalley's laid-back charm. Fire up the barbecue or use the shared kitchen if you're in self-catering mode.

Potters Croft
B&B **$$**

(☑6253 5469; www.potterscroft.com.au; Arthur Hwy; s/d from $100/146, extra person $25) At Dunalley's northern end is this convict-brick, family-run estate, tripling as a craft gallery, local wine outlet and provider of snug accommodation. There are four en-suite rooms that share a large kitchen and lounge area, and a self-contained cottage that sleeps four.

TOP CHOICE Dunalley Waterfront Café
CAFE **$$**

(☑6253 5122; 4 Imlay St; meals $17-30; ☺lunch & dinner Wed-Mon) With its broad outdoor deck and views across the water, this elegant cafe is Dunalley's cultural and culinary hot spot. The menu ranges from Mediterranean seafood stew to salt-and-pepper prawns, and the homemade cakes, brilliant coffee and Tassie wines are all good reasons to linger awhile. Energetic new owners have added a funky gallery showcasing local artists.

Dunalley Fish Market
SEAFOOD **$**

(1 Fulham Rd; light meals $10-15; ☺lunch & dinner) Quite possibly the best fish and chips for a considerable distance. Grab some takeaway, sit beside the canal and commune with the occasional local seagull. Oysters and lobsters also make an appearance in season. To find the fish market, rather than turning left across the bridge to Port Arthur, continue straight on for a further 300m.

❶ Getting There & Away

BUS The **Tassielink** (☑1300 300 520; www.tassielink.com.au) Tasman Peninsula service will take you to Dunalley from Hobart ($13, one hour). **Redline Coaches** (☑1300 360 000; www.redlinecoaches.com.au) also operates some weekday services between Hobart and Dunalley.

Eaglehawk Neck

POP 100

Eaglehawk Neck is the second isthmus you'll cross heading south to Port Arthur, this one connecting the Forestier Peninsula to the Tasman Peninsula. Its historical importance harks back to the days of convicts at Port Arthur, when the 100m-wide Neck had a row of ornery dogs chained across it to prevent escape – the infamous Dogline. Timber platforms were also built in narrow Eaglehawk Bay to the west, and stocked with yet more ferocious dogs to prevent convicts from wading around the

Dogline. To discourage swimming, rumours were circulated that the waters were shark infested – the occasional white pointer does indeed shimmy through these waters, but 'infested' is an overstatement. Remarkably, despite these efforts, several convicts made successful bids for freedom. The key convict sites are now protected as the Eaglehawk Neck Historic Site (www.parks.tas.gov.au – see 'Fact Sheets' on the website).

◉ Sights

Lookout LANDMARK
As you approach Eaglehawk Neck from the north, turn east onto Pirates Bay Dr for an astonishing view of Pirates Bay, the Neck and the rugged coastline beyond.

FREE **Officers Quarters** HISTORIC BUILDING
(⊙9am-4.30pm) Down on the isthmus you'll find the only remaining structure from the convict days in 1832. The oldest wooden military building in Australia, it also operates as a historical museum.

Tessellated Pavement LANDMARK
At the northern end of Pirates Bay is a rocky terrace that has eroded into what looks like tiled paving. At low tide you can walk along the foreshore to Clydes Island, where there are wicked coastline panoramas and several graves. You can see as far south as Cape Hauy.

Blowhole, Tasman Arch & the Devil's Kitchen LANDMARKS
Follow the signposted side roads to the Blowhole, Tasman Arch and Devil's Kitchen for some close-up views of spectacular coastal cliffs. Watch out for sporadic bursts at the Blowhole, and keep behind the fences at the other sites – the cliff edges are prone to decay. The Eaglehawk Neck jetty is opposite the Blowhole car park.

On the road to the Blowhole look out for the signposted turn-off to the 4km gravel road leading to Waterfall Bay, which has yet more camera-conducive views. Equally spectacular are the Devil's Kitchen, a rugged 60m deep cleft in the coastal cliffs, and the cavern-like Tasman Arch.

🏃 Activities

Waterfall Bluff BUSHWALKING
From the car park at Waterfall Bay, take the 1½-hour return hike to Waterfall Bluff. Much of the walk is through a forest of tall, slender trees that somewhat obscure the view, but the track stays close to the water

and there are plenty of places to stop and gawp at the magnificent scenery from the clifftops (unfenced, except at the car park). Make sure you continue to the spectacular bluff itself before returning to the part of the walk that takes you down past the falls.

Tasman Coastal Trail BUSHWALKING
(www.parks.tas.gov.au/recreation/tracknotes/tasman.html) Waterfall Bay is also the gateway to this trail, which climbs over Tatnells Hill then follows the coast to Fortescue Bay, out to Cape Hauy and on to Cape Pillar. Walkers should allow three to five days for the one-way trip.

If you'd rather tackle a one-day walk, traipse along the coast from Waterfall Bay to Bivouac Bay (six hours) or on to Fortescue Bay (eight hours), with camping available at both bays. If you're looking for a hike that lets you return to your car, only walk as far as Tatnells Hill (around four hours there and back), from which there's an amazing view all the way from Eaglehawk Neck to the craggy rock formations of Cape Hauy.

Island Surf School SURFING
(☑6265 9776, 0400 830 237; www.islandsurfschool.com.au; 2hr group lessons $40) Lessons are held at Park Beach near Sorel. All gear including wetsuits is provided and bookings are essential. Check the website for lesson times.

Eaglehawk Dive Centre DIVING
(☑6250 3566; www.eaglehawkdive.com.au; 178 Pirates Bay Dr) This excellent company conducts underwater explorations (sea caves, giant kelp forests, a sea-lion colony and shipwrecks) and a range of PADI courses. A one-day introduction to scuba diving costs $199 (no experience necessary). Equipment rental is $85 per day; two boat dives with equipment costs $190. They provide free Hobart pick-ups, and dorm accommodation for divers for $25 per night. A private double room is $80.

👉 Tours

Tasman Island Adventure Cruises WILDLIFE
(☑6253 5325; www.tasmanadventurecruises.com.au; 3hr cruises adult/child $100/55; ⊙10am year round & 2pm Jan-Mar) The Tasman Peninsula's longest-established cruise company takes in the peninsula's dramatic east coast from Eaglehawk Neck to Cape Hauy, with bountiful sea life along the way – bring your camera. Tours depart from the Doolishus food caravan at the Eaglehawk Neck jetty. Book-

DOO TOWN

No one is really sure how it all started, but the raggedy collection of fishing shacks at Doo Town (3km south of Eaglehawk Neck on the way to the Blowhole) all contain the word 'Doo' in their names. There's the sexy 'Doo Me', the approving 'We Doo', the Beatles-esque 'Love Me Doo', and (our favourite) the melancholic 'Doo Write'. The overly pedantic 'Xanadu' doesn't seem to get the joke. We doo hope the new breed of architecturally adventurous beach houses here maintain the tradition.

At the Blowhole car park, the **'Doolishus' food caravan** (snacks $5-10) dishes up fresh berry smoothies, great gourmet pies – try the scallop or rabbit flavours – and superlative fish and chips.

Definitely worth a dootour.

ings essential. The trip can also be joined in Hobart (from $169/110 per adult/child).

Personalised Sea Charters   FISHING
(☑6250 3370; www.personalisedseacharters.com; 322 Blowhole Rd, Eaglehawk Neck; per person half/full day from $110/180) Takes small groups game, deep-sea, reef or bay fishing. All gear supplied.

❶ Getting There & Away

BUS Tassielink (☑1300 300 520; www.tassielink.com.au) can bus you from Hobart to Eaglehawk Neck in 1½ hours; the one-way fare is $20.

Taranna

POP 160

Taranna is a small town strung out along the shores of Norfolk Bay about 10km north of Port Arthur, its name coming from an Aboriginal word meaning 'hunting ground'. Historically important, it was once the terminus for Australia's first railway, which ran from Long Bay, near Port Arthur, to here. This public transport was powered by convicts, who pushed the carriages uphill, then jumped on for the ride down. In those days Taranna was called Old Norfolk. Not far offshore, **Dart Island** was used as a semaphore station to relay messages from Port Arthur to Hobart. Today, the waters near the island are used for oyster farming.

Taranna's main attraction is the **Tasmanian Devil Conservation Park** (www.tasmaniandevilpark.com; adult/child/family $24/13/59; Arthur Hwy; ☺9am-6pm Oct-Mar, to 5pm Apr-Sep), which functions as a quarantined breeding centre for devils to help protect against Devil Facial Tumour Disease (for more information see p300). It's also a breeding centre for endangered birds of

prey. There are plenty of other native species here too, with feedings throughout the day: devils at 10am, 11am, 12.15pm, 1.30pm, 3pm and 5pm, and kangaroos at 10.30am and 2.30pm. There's also a 'Kings of the Wild' birds of prey show at 11.15am and 3.30pm. Other wildlife includes eastern quolls and pademelons.

FREE **Federation Chocolate Factory** (2 South St; ☺9am-5pm Mon-Sat) sits alluringly close to Taranna. Check out chocolate being handmade and chew on some traditional favourites (such as honeycomb or caramel nougat) or try some intriguingly flavoured delights (the surprisingly good apple flavour, or perhaps liquorice or brandied apricot). Inside the factory is a museum of blacksmithing and sawmilling equipment.

🛏 Sleeping & Eating

TOP CHOICE **Taranna Cottages & Campervan Park**   CABINS **$**
(☑6250 3436; www.tarannacottages.com.au; 996 Arthur Hwy; d $95, extra adult/child $20/10, unpowered sites $20) Perhaps the best-value accommodation on the peninsula, this enterprise at the southern end of Taranna features three neat-as-a-pin self-contained apple-pickers cottages. They exude basic, rustic charm in a quiet bush setting and have open fires. Breakfast provisions (free-range eggs, homemade jams) are a few dollars extra. There's parking for self-contained campervans, and at the time of writing the friendly owners were planning the addition of a pioneer museum.

Norfolk Bay Convict Station   B&B **$$**
(☑6250 3487; www.convictstation.com; 5862 Arthur Hwy; d incl breakfast $160-180) Built in 1838 and once the railway's port terminus (as well as the first pub on the Tasman

Peninsula, the Tasman Hotel), this gorgeous old place is now a top-quality waterfront B&B. Eclectic rooms come with homemade buffet breakfasts and complimentary port. Fishing gear and a dinghy are for hire, and the owners have a wealth of knowledge on the area's fascinating history.

Abs by the Bay   MOTEL **$$**
(☑6250 3719; www.absbythebay.com; 5730 Arthur Hwy; d $80-120, extra person $20) Abalone? Abdominals? We suspect it's the former, although the water-view deck here affords the opportunity to relax the latter after a busy day's sightseeing. Flexible configurations can accommodate two couples or two singles in suburbanite units.

Mason's Cottages   MOTEL **$$**
(☑6250 3323; 5741 Arthur Hwy; d $100-110) On the highway at the northern edge of town, this place has a huddle of suburban-looking, two-bedroom brick units available for your self-contained discretion. A recent renovation spruce-up makes them good value.

❶ Getting There & Away

BUS The **Tassielink** (☑1300 300 520; www. tassielink.com.au) Tasman Peninsula service calls in at Taranna ($20, 1¾ hours) en route from Hobart to Port Arthur.

Fortescue Bay & Tasman National Park

Sequestered 12km down a gravel road from the highway (the turn-off is halfway between Taranna and Port Arthur) is becalmed Fortescue Bay, with a sweeping sandy arc backed by thickly forested slopes. The sheltered bay was one of the semaphore-station sites used during the convict period to relay messages to and from Eaglehawk Neck. Early last century a timber mill was in operation, and the boilers and jetty ruins are still visible near Mill Creek, as are the remains of some of the tramways used to collect the timber. The mill closed in 1952.

Fortescue Bay is one of the main access points for **Tasman National Park** (www. parks.tas.gov.au), encompassing the territory around Cape Raoul, Cape Hauy, Cape Pillar, Tasman Island and up the rugged coast north to Eaglehawk Neck. Offshore, dolphins, seals, penguins and whales are regular passers-by. The usual national park entry fees (p295) apply.

◉ Sights & Activities

Apart from swimming and lazing around on the beach, most people come here to launch their fishing boats or do some **bushwalking**. Several walking tracks kick off at Fortescue Bay. To the north, a solid track traces the shoreline to **Canoe Bay** (two hours return) and **Bivouac Bay** (four hours return), continuing all the way to the Devil's Kitchen car park at **Eaglehawk Neck** (10 hours one way). To the east, a track meanders out to **Cape Hauy** (four to five hours return) – a well-used path leading out to sea cliffs with sensational views of the famous sea stacks **The Candlestick** and **Totem Pole**. To get into some rainforest, follow the same track towards Cape Hauy, then take the steep side track to **Mt Fortescue** (six to seven hours return). Another track extends all the way to **Cape Pillar** near Tasman Island, where the sea cliffs are 300m high – purportedly the highest in the southern hemisphere. You'll need two to three days return to knock off the Cape Pillar track. For detailed track notes, see Lonely Planet's *Walking in Australia*.

🛌 Sleeping

Fortescue Bay Campground   CAMPGROUND **$**
(www.parks.tas.gov.au; Tasman National Park; sites $26) Dream the night away to the sound of gentle surf. There are no powered sites and showers are cold, but fireplaces and gas BBQs compensate. National park fees apply in addition to camping fees; book ahead during summer. There are no shops here so BYO food and drink.

Port Arthur

POP 200

Port Arthur is the name of the small settlement that has grown up around the Port Arthur Historic Site. In 1830 Governor Arthur chose the Tasman Peninsula to confine prisoners who had committed further crimes in the colony. A 'natural penitentiary' – the peninsula is connected to the mainland by a strip of land less than 100m wide, Eaglehawk Neck – where ferocious guard dogs and tales of shark-infested waters deterred escape.

Between 1830 and 1877, 12,500 convicts did hard, brutal prison time at Port Arthur. For most it was hell on earth, but those who behaved often enjoyed better conditions than they'd endured in England and Ire-

Admission to the Port Arthur Historic Site is via a fairly complex hierarchy of passes: either a Bronze, Silver, Gold or After Dark Pass. It's possible to prebook passes and tours on www.portarthur.org.au, or phone 1800 659 101; this is recommended during peak periods like school holidays.

Bronze Pass (adult/child/concession/family $30/15/25/75) Includes admission to the site, a guided tour and a harbour cruise. Suits visitors here for half a day or so.

Silver Pass (adult/child/concession $68/49/63) Includes all of the above plus a tour of the Isle of the Dead or Point Puer, an audio tour and lunch at either the Museum Café or the Port Café. Suits visitors here for a full day.

Gold Pass (adult/child/concession $100/77/95) Includes all the Silver Pass offers, but you get to do both the Point Puer and the Isle of the Dead tour, and have morning and afternoon tea. If you're staying overnight in the area, this is the pass for you (it's valid for two days).

After Dark Pass (adult $61) Gets you onto the Historic Ghost Tour and snares you a two-course meal at Felons Bistro.

land. Port Arthur became the hub of a network of penal stations on the peninsula, its fine buildings sustaining thriving convict-labour industries, including timber milling, shipbuilding, coal mining, shoemaking and brick and nail production.

Australia's first railway literally 'ran' the 7km between Norfolk Bay at Taranna and Long Bay near Port Arthur: convicts pushed the carriages along the tracks. A semaphore telegraph system allowed speedy communication between Port Arthur, other peninsula outstations and Hobart. Convict farms provided fresh vegetables, a boys' prison was built at Point Puer to reform and educate juvenile convicts, and a church was erected.

Despite its redemption as a major tourist site, Port Arthur is a sombre place. Don't come here expecting to remain unaffected by what you see. There's a sadness that's undeniable, and a gothic pall of woe that can cloud your senses on the sunniest of days. Compounding this, in April 1996 a young gunman fired bullets indiscriminately at the community, murdering 35 people and injuring 37 more. After burning down a guesthouse, he was finally captured and remains imprisoned north of Hobart.

rant and a gift shop (which stocks some interesting convict-focused publications). Downstairs is an interpretative gallery where you can follow the convicts' journey from England to Tasmania. Buggy transport around the site can be arranged for people with restricted mobility – ask at the information counter. The ferry plying the harbour is also wheelchair accessible.

Beyond the main building are dozens of restored structures, most of which you visit on the guided tour. The **Port Arthur Museum**, containing numerous displays and a cafe, was originally an asylum, housing patients from throughout the colony. The **Separate Prison** was built as a place of punishment for difficult prisoners, following a decision to 'reform' prisoners by isolation and sensory deprivation rather than by flogging. The **Church** was built in 1836 but was destroyed by fire in 1884, while the **Penitentiary**, converted from a granary in 1857, was also damaged by fire in 1897. The Broad Arrow Café, scene of many of the 1996 shootings, was gutted following the massacre. Today, the shell of the building has been preserved and a **Memorial Garden** established around it.

⊙ Sights

TOP CHOICE **Port Arthur Historic Site**

HISTORIC SITE

(☑6251 2310, 1800 659 101; www.portarthur.org.au; Arthur Hwy; ⊙tours & buildings 9am-5pm, grounds 8.30am-dusk) This is one of Tasmania's busiest tourist attractions. Inside the main entry building is a visitor centre, a cafe, a restau-

☞ Tours

Tours of the Port Arthur Historic Site are included in the price of admission. Bookings for all other tours are highly recommended and can be made either online at www.portarthur.org.au or at the **visitor centre** (☑1800 659 101).

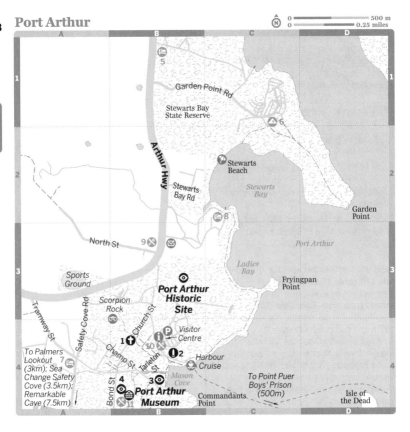

Port Arthur Historic Site   HISTORIC SITE

This 40-minute guided tour leaves regularly from the Port Arthur visitor centre. It's an excellent introduction to the site, visiting all the old buildings. Also included in the price of your ticket is a 25-minute harbour cruise (with commentary) past Point Puer and the Isle of the Dead. When you buy your ticket you'll be told the times of the next tour and cruise.

Isle of the Dead Cemetery Tour   CEMETERY

(adult/child/family $12/8/34) A detailed guided tour through Port Arthur's old burial ground on an island in the harbour.

Point Puer Boys' Prison Tour   PRISON

(adult/child/family $12/8/34) This tour visits the first reformatory in the British Empire built for juvenile male convicts (aged nine to 18).

Historic Ghost Tour   GHOST

(adult/child/family $22/12/60) This 90-minute, lantern-lit, very popular tour leaves from the visitor centre nightly at dusk (rain or shine) and visits a number of historic buildings, with guides relating spine-chilling occurrences. Bookings essential.

🛏 Sleeping

Given the iconic status of Port Arthur to Tasmania's tourism, it's surprising to find limited quality accommodation or dining offerings down here. Bland, dated motel units and cheesy B&Bs prevail, with a few notable exceptions. If you're driving, consider staying in Taranna or around Koonya and Nubeena.

Sea Change Safety Cove   B&B $$

(✉6250 2719; www.safetycove.com; 425 Safety Cove Rd; d $160-200) Whichever way you look from this guesthouse there are fantastic views – misty cliffs, sea-wracked beach or

Port Arthur

◎ **Top Sights**

Port Arthur Historic Site B3
Port Arthur Museum B4

◎ **Sights**

1 Church...B4
2 Memorial Garden B4
3 Penitentiary B4
4 Separate Prison B4

😴 **Sleeping**

5 Fox & Hounds Inn............................. B1
6 Port Arthur Caravan & Cabin
    Park...C1
7 Port Arthur Villas A4
8 Stewarts Bay Lodge C2

✴ **Eating**

9 Eucalypt B3
10 Felons Bistro..................................B4
    Fox & Hounds Inn........................(see 5)
11 Museum Café B4
    Port Café ....(see 10)
    Taylor's Restaurant ....(see 8)

scrubby bushland. It's 4km south of Port Arthur, just off the sandy sweep of Safety Cove Beach. There's a beaut communal deck, a couple of B&B rooms inside the house, plus a large self-contained unit that sleeps five. Two viewing platforms, complete with barbecues and telescopes, are where you'll be enjoying end-of-day drinks.

Stewarts Bay Lodge　　　HOTEL $$$

(✆6250 2888; www.stewartsbaylodge.com.au; 6955 Arthur Hwy; d $235-420; @🐕) Arrayed around a gorgeous hidden cove – just made for swimming and kayaking – Stewarts Bay Lodge combines older, more rustic units with brand new deluxe accommodation, some with private spa baths. Modern kitchens are great for making the most of good local produce, but you'll probably spend more time in the sleek Taylor's Restaurant overlooking the bay.

Port Arthur Villas　　　MOTEL $$

(✆6250 2239, 1800 815 775; www.portarthurvillas. com.au; 52 Safety Cove Rd; d $160-190) This place has reasonable self-contained units sleeping up to four, horseshoeing around the garden and outdoor barbecue area. Externally it's all faux-Victorian lace and brickwork, but inside things are a little more stylish. Walking distance to the historic site.

Fox & Hounds Inn　　　MOTEL $$

(✆6250 2217; www.foxandhounds.com.au; 6789 Arthur Hwy; d $120-200) *Ewww*, mock Tudor! Still, the rooms off to the side of the main building are the cheapest motel doubles south of Eaglehawk Neck (especially in winter), and it's a matter of seconds from the Port Arthur gates. You can get a bang-up pub meal here amid the faux splendour of old Blighty, and the new two-bedroom apartments are a wise choice for travelling families.

Port Arthur Caravan & Cabin Park　　　CAMPGROUND $

(✆6250 2340; www.portarthurcaravan-cabinpark. com.au; Garden Point Rd; dm $20, sites $24-35; cabins $110-120) Spacious with plenty of greenery, this park with plenty of facilities (including camp kitchen, wood BBQs and shop) is 2km before Port Arthur, not far from a sheltered beach. The best (and only) budget option.

✖ Eating

Taylor's Restaurant　　　RESTAURANT $$

(✆6250 2771; Stewarts Bay Lodge, 6955 Arthur Hwy; mains $26-31; ◷breakfast, lunch & dinner; 🐕) Housed in a modern glass-and-wood pavilion with water views, Taylor's showcases local produce with Eaglehawk Neck oysters, Pirates Bay octopus, and quail served with pesto mash and Mediterranean vegetables. Definitely worth a detour if you're overnighting anywhere on the peninsula. Bookings recommended in summer.

Eucalypt　　　CAFE $$

(6962 Arthur Hwy; mains $10-20; ◷breakfast & lunch year round, dinner Dec-Mar) A versatile spot near the turn-off to Port Arthur, Eucalypt does robust breakfasts, the area's best coffee and hearty lunches, including scallop pot pie. The owners were planning weekend 'Curry Nights' at the time of writing, and a small on-site shop showcases locally made handicrafts and gourmet produce.

Felons Bistro　　　RESTAURANT $$

(✆1800 659 101; visitor centre; mains $27; ◷dinner) In a wing of the visitor centre, Felons is a worthy choice before you head off on the ghost tour. Up-market, creative dinners with a seafood bias (including tuna and salmon) reinforce Felons' catchy slogan: 'Dine with Conviction'. Hungry carnivores should try the Tasmanian mixed grill with local wallaby, lamb cutlet and venison sausages. Reservations advised.

Fox & Hounds Inn　　　PUB $$

(6789 Arthur Hwy; mains $17-34; ◷lunch Dec-Mar, dinner nightly) This restaurant at the Fox &

Hounds does reputable meals in its dated, ye-olde-themed dining room, mostly from the pub-menu roll call of timeless classics (reef 'n' beef, mixed grill, lamb cutlets, curried scallops). It also has a children's menu, and oceans of cold Cascade on tap.

There are a couple of daytime food options at the historic site: the Museum Café in the Old Asylum and the hectic Port Café inside the visitor centre.

❶ Getting There & Away

BUS Regional public-transport connections are surprisingly poor. Tassielink (☎1300 300 520; www.tassielink.com.au) runs a weekday evening bus from Hobart to Port Arthur ($25, 2¼ hours) during school terms, reducing to Monday, Wednesday and Friday mornings during school holidays. Buses stop at the main towns en route.

CAR Take care driving down the peninsula to Port Arthur if you're behind the wheel, as plenty of gnarly accidents have occurred on the Arthur Hwy. It's a wiggly, narrow road in places, with exits hidden behind hills and around corners.

Remarkable Cave

About 5km south of Port Arthur is Remarkable Cave, a long tunnel eroded from the base of a collapsed gully, under a cliff and out to sea. A boardwalk and stairs provide access to a metal viewing platform above the gully, a few minutes' amble from the car park. Believe it or not, hardcore surfers brave the turbulent swell surging in through the cave, paddling out through the opening to surf the offshore reefs beyond.

You can also follow the coast east from the car park to Maingon Blowhole (one hour return) or further on to Mt Brown (four hours return), from which there are awesome views. On the way back it's worth deviating to Palmers Lookout for majestic views of the entire Port Arthur and Safety Cove area.

Koonya & Nubeena

There's not a whole lot of shakin' going on in diminutive Koonya (population 100), apart from accommodation at the nearby Cascades and the Seaview Riding Ranch (☎6250 3110; 60 Firetower Rd; 1/2hr rides from $30/55), signposted off the main road from Taranna. On offer is horse riding for all ages and skill levels, with scenic rides led by long-time locals.

About 12km further along the road is Nubeena (population 300), the largest town on the peninsula, fanned out along the shore of Wedge Bay. It's much more low-key than Port Arthur – it's really just an easygoing holiday destination for locals – but if all the other accommodation on the peninsula is booked out (trust us, it happens), you might be able to find a bed here. There are also a couple of good options for eating, often recommended by accommodation owners across the peninsula.

The main things to do here are swimming and chilling out on White Beach, or fishing from the jetty or foreshore. Down a side road 3km south of town is some energetic walking to Tunnel Bay (five hours return), Raoul

---

WORTH A TRIP

SALTWATER RIVER & LIME BAY

At Premaydena, take the signposted turn-off (the C431) 13km northwest to Saltwater River and the restored ruins at the Coal Mines Historic Site (www.parks.tas.gov.au; admission free; ☉dawn-dusk), a powerful reminder of the colonial past. Excavated in 1833, the coal mines were used to punish the worst of the convicts, who worked there in abominable conditions. The poorly managed mining operation wasn't economically viable, and in 1848 it was sold to private enterprise. Within 10 years it was abandoned. Some buildings were demolished, while fire and weather put paid to the rest.

A low-key contrast to Port Arthur, the old mines site is interesting to wander around, following a trail of interpretive panels. Don't go burrowing into any old mine shafts – they haven't been stabilised and are potentially dangerous. You can snoop around the well-preserved solitary confinement cells, which are torturously small and dark.

Not far away is Lime Bay State Reserve, a beautiful area aflutter with rare birds and butterflies, and with some lazy coastal walks. From Lime Bay, the 2½-hour return journey to Lagoon Beach is an untaxing amble. There's free bush camping to the north along a sandy track. Camping is very basic, with pit toilets. BYO drinking water and fuel stoves.

Bay Lookout (two hours return) and the exquisitely named Cape Raoul (five hours return). To the north is Roaring Beach, which gets wicked surf but isn't safe for swimming.

🛏 Sleeping & Eating

TOP CHOICE **Harpers on the Beach**   B&B $$
(✏6250 2933; www.harpersonthebeach.com.au; 91 White Beach Rd, Nubeena; d $160-240, cottage $160-220; ☎) Get ready to get sand between your toes – 'on the beach' means exactly that at this friendly, classy bed and breakfast. The emphasis is as much on good food and wine, with a wood-fired oven for homemade bread and pizza, an organic vegie garden, and restaurant-quality three-course dinners ($45). Elegant rooms are decked out in muted tones and have ocean-facing decks. The adjoining cottage with wooden floors and maritime touches is a lovely reminder of sleepy beach holidays in days gone by.

Larus Waterfront Cottage   RENTAL HOUSE $$
(✏0457 758 711; www.larus.com.au; 576 White Beach Rd, Nubeena; d $145) Contemporary design, audacious views and all mod-cons (big-screen TV, iPod dock and a flash barbecue) add up to a great Tasman Peninsula bolthole. It's in a quiet location, but only 30 minutes' drive from Port Arthur. Bring along lots of edible goodies because you'll be spending a lot of time admiring the sunset from the wraparound deck.

Cascades   B&B $$
(✏6250 3873; www.cascadescolonial.com.au; 533 Main Rd, Koonya; d $180-230) This old property was originally an outstation for Port Arthur, with around 400 convicts working here at one time. Some of the buildings have been restored in period style to become snug, self-contained cottages (including one luxury option with spa). Full breakfast provisions and entry to a private museum included.

Parson's Bay Retreat   MOTEL $$
(✏6250 2000; www.parsonsbayretreat.com.au; 1583 Nubeena Rd, Nubeena; d $98-138, f $158; @☎☒) A good option for families, this place offers an indoor pool and spa, tennis courts, barbecues and a games room. Comfortable motel units or self-catering apartments with modern kitchens add up to excellent value. The on-site restaurant, Hub (mains $5-20; ⊙breakfast, lunch & dinner), keeps up the good-value focus with regular themed nights including all-you-can-eat pizza, and surprisingly good Thai and Indian curries. Port Arthur is just 15 minutes by car.

White Beach Tourist Park   CAMPGROUND $
(✏6250 2142; www.whitebeachtouristpark.com.au; 128 White Beach Rd, Nubeena; sites $22-26, cabins $95-100) Beachfront park in quiet, ghost gum–dotted surrounds south of Nubeena. Facilities include laundry, shop, petrol bowser, playground and barbecue areas with impossibly well-manicured lawns. Ask about local walks and cheaper off-season rates.

TOP CHOICE **Lucky Ducks**   CAFE $
(Main Rd, Nubeena; meals $15-25; ⊙breakfast, lunch & dinner) With huge picture windows, this modern waterfront spot is perfect for coffee and cake, a beer, or a glass of wine. Other options include excellent gourmet pies and a chicken, chorizo and bacon terrine. The huge farmer's lunch with marinated mushrooms is also recommended for nonrural types.

ℹ Getting There & Away

BUS **Tassielink** (✏1300 300 520; www.tassielink.com.au) will take you from Hobart to Koonya in 1¾ hours; the one-way fare is $23. The bus continues to Nubeena ($23, two hours).

The Southeast

Includes »

Kettering 104
Bruny Island 105
Woodbridge 110
Cygnet 111
Huonville & Around . . 113
Geeveston 115
Hartz Mountains
National Park 117
Dover 117
Southport 118
Hastings Caves &
Thermal Springs 119
Lune River 119
Cockle Creek 120

Best Places to Eat

» Bruny Island Smokehouse (p109)
» Red Velvet Lounge (p112)
» Lotus Eaters Café (p113)
» Franklin Woodfired Pizza (p114)
» Post Office 6985 (p118)

Best Places to Stay

» Beachfront on Bruny (p108)
» Woodbridge Hill Hideaway (p111)
» Old Bank B&B (p112)
» Huon Bush Retreats (p114)
» Jetty House (p118)

Why Go?

The quiet harbours and verdant valleys of Tasmania's southeast have much to offer, particularly if you enjoy snacking leisurely from roadside produce stores. Once the apple-producing heart of the Apple Isle, the southeast is now abundant with cherries, apricots, Atlantic salmon, wines, mushrooms and cheese.

The fruit-filled hillsides of the Huon Valley give way to the sparkling inlets of the D'Entrecasteaux Channel, and Bruny Island awaits enticingly offshore. Hartz Mountains National Park is not far inland, and further south the South Coast Track kicks off at magnificent Recherche Bay.

French explorers Bruni d'Entrecasteaux and Nicolas Baudin charted much of the region's coastline in the 1790s and early 1800s, Entrecasteaux arriving a good decade before the Brits hoisted the Union Jack at Risdon Cove near Hobart in 1803.

The wide Huon River remains the region's lifeblood. Courtesy of the southern latitudes and abundant waterways, the southeast is also known for its rainbows.

When to Go?

Summer – from December to March – is definitely the time to visit the southeast. The Huon Valley will be jam-packed with fresh produce, including juicy cherries and crisp apples, and the cool southern waters around Bruny Island will be more inviting in the summer sunshine. January is the time to be in funky Cygnet for the annual folk music festival, and birdwatching fans should wing it to Bruny Island in October for the island's annual Bird Festival.

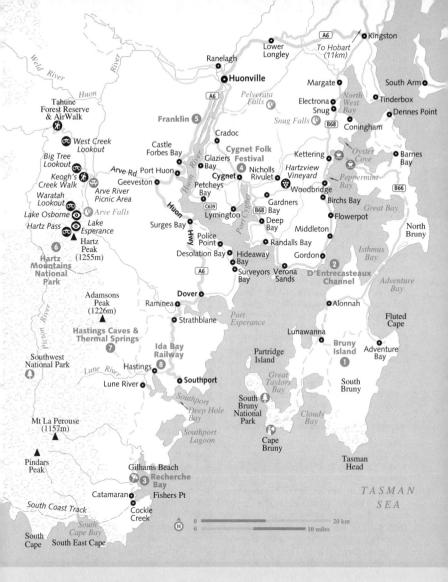

Southeast Highlights

1 Forgetting the office, courtesy of a couple of days on **Bruny Island** (p105)

2 Paddling a sea-kayak over **D'Entrecasteaux Channel** (p104)

3 Conjuring up images of French explorers' tall ships anchored in remote **Recherche Bay** (p119)

4 Tuning in to the twang, shimmy and stomp of the **Cygnet Folk Festival** (p112), a funky January jamboree

5 Inspecting a Huon pine hull under construction at Franklin's **Wooden Boat Centre** (p114)

6 Smiling at your reflection in an alpine moorland tarn at **Hartz Mountains National Park** (p117)

7 Spelunking into the subterranean gloom at **Hastings Caves & Thermal Springs** (p119)

8 Riding the **Ida Bay Railway** (p119), Australia's southernmost railway, to the end of the line

☞ Tours

Gray Line SIGHTSEEING
(☎1300 858 687; www.grayline.com.au; tours
adult/child $146/73) Huon Valley day tours vis-
iting Huonville, Franklin, Geeveston and the
Tahune Forest AirWalk.

Peppermint Bay Cruises CRUISE
(☎1300 137 919; www.peppermintbay.com.au;
Brooke St Pier, Hobart) A five-hour cruise down
the D'Entrecasteaux Channel to Woodbridge
(see p111).

❶ Getting There & Around

BUS **Hobart Coaches** (☎13 22 01) runs several
buses each weekday from Hobart south through
Margate, Snug and Kettering to Woodbridge. A
bus also runs once each weekday from Hobart
to Snug and inland across to Cygnet. There are
no weekend services. **Tassielink** (☎1300 300
520; www.tassielink.com.au) runs buses along
the Huon Hwy from Hobart through Huonville,
Franklin and Geeveston to Dover.

CAR The views from the Channel Hwy between
Hobart and Woodbridge are lovely. The road
from Woodbridge to Gardners Bay en route to
Cygnet is also spectacular. You can also follow
the coast from Woodbridge through Verona
Sands to Cygnet, occasionally passing very
close to the channel.

Further south, some sections of the side
route from Surges Bay through Police Point are
surfaced with coarse gravel. Check your tyres
before you leave.

Margate

POP 745
About 23km south of Hobart is small-town
Margate.

FREE **Margate Train** (1567 Channel Hwy;
◷9am-4.30pm) is a chance for
trainspotters to scrutinise the last passenger
train used in Tasmania. It stands idly on a
redundant section of track by the highway
on the northern side of town, and houses
craft shops, antique dealers and the **Pancake Train Café** (mains $10-22; ◷breakfast
& lunch), serving pancakes and light meals.
There's a good **providore** here for picnics.

Behind the train is **Inverawe Native Gardens** (www.inverawe.com.au; 1565 Channel Hwy;
adult/child $12/4; ◷9am-sunset Sep-May), a pri-
vate, 9.5-hectare property with landscaped
native gardens, trails, water views and 80
species of blow-through birds, including the
12 species endemic to Tassie. Last entrance
is at 6pm.

Closer to town is the fabulous **Brookfield
Vineyard** (☎6267 2880; www.brookfieldvineyard.
com; 1640 Channel Hwy; mains $16-20; ◷9am-
6pm, to midnight Fri & Sat), Margate's multifac-
eted hub of all things good: wine, gourmet
fare, live music and artsy design. Breakfast
is served until 3pm, and crepes, salads and
pasta feature on the wider menu. Regular
highlights include a Wednesday craft market, and live music with a rootsy, Americana
bent on Friday and Saturday nights.

Hobart Coaches (☎13 22 01) offers several bus runs from Hobart through Kingston
to Margate ($6.50, 20 to 30 minutes) Mon-
day to Friday, plus two services on Saturday.

Kettering

POP 300
Blessed with photogenic looks, the lethargic
port of Kettering shelters fishing boats and
yachts in Oyster Cove Marina, next to the
Bruny Island ferry terminal. Most folks just
blow through here en route to Bruny, but it's
an essential stop for sea-kayakers.

The **Bruny D'Entrecasteaux visitor
centre** (☎693 2096; www.tasmaniaholiday.com;
81 Ferry Rd; ◷9am-5pm), by the ferry terminal,
has information on accommodation and
services on Bruny Island, including walking
maps and a self-guided driving tour.

At the marina is **Roaring 40s Ocean
Kayaking** (☎6267 5000; www.roaring40skayak
ing.com.au; Oyster Cove Marina, Ferry Rd; ◷closed
Aug-Sep), Tassie's leading sea-kayaking tour
operator. It offers gear rental to kayakers,
and organises a smorgasbord of kayaking
trips to suit all levels of experience. A half-
day paddle around Oyster Cove costs $95; a
full day on the D'Entrecasteaux Channel is
$160, including lunch and return transport
from Hobart. A full day around the Tasman
Peninsula costs $255. Extended three- and
seven-day trips around the Tasman Peninsula and the southwest are also available.

ᵴ Sleeping & Eating

Herons Rise Vineyard RENTAL HOUSE $$
(☎6267 4339; www.heronsrise.com.au; 1000
Saddle Rd; d $125, incl breakfast $140, extra per-
son $30) Just north of town, Herons Rise
has three upmarket self-contained cot-
tages set among Pinot Noir vines. All three
have log fires, and we especially like the
view-friendly spacious apartment above the
wine cellar. It's ideal for a family or two cou-
ples. Dinners are available by arrangement

(per person $37.50). Muller Thurgau and Pinot Noir wines are available for purchase, and the whole operation is overseen by the four-legged and shaggy Toby.

Rosie's
CAFE $

(cnr Channel Hwy & Saddle Rd; mains $15-20; ⊙10am-5pm, closed Wed) Lots of gluten-free baked items – slices, muffins, quiche – feature at the friendly and sunny Rosie's. During summer there's an extended emphasis on robust Aussie mains, including garlic prawns and lamb shanks.

ⓘ Getting There & Away

Weekday-only buses from Hobart run by **Hobart Coaches** (☑13 22 01) stop at Kettering ($11, 50 minutes, four daily).

Bruny Island

POP 600

Bruny Island is almost two islands, joined by a narrow, 5km sandy isthmus called the Neck. Renowned for its wildlife (fairy penguins, echidnas, mutton birds), it's a windswept, sparsely populated retreat, blown by ocean rains in the south, and dry and beachy in the north.

Bruny's coastal scenery is magical. There are countless swimming and surf beaches, plus good sea and freshwater fishing. South Bruny is home to the steep, forested South Bruny National Park, which has some beaut walking tracks, especially around Labillardiere Peninsula and Fluted Cape.

The island was spied by Abel Tasman's beady eyes in 1642, and between 1770 and 1790 was visited by Furneaux, Cook, Bligh and Cox. It was named after Rear Admiral Bruni d'Entrecasteaux, who explored the area in 1792. Strangely, confusion reigned about the spelling – in 1918 it was changed from Bruni to Bruny.

Tasmanian Aborigines of the Nuenonne band called the island Lunawanna-Alonnah, a name given contemporary recognition (albeit broken in two) as the names of two island towns. Among their numbers was Truganini, daughter of Mangana, chief of the Nuenonne band. Truganini left Bruny in the 1830s to accompany George Robinson on his infamous statewide journey to win the trust of all the Tasmanian Aborigines. Many of Bruny's landmarks, including Mt Mangana, are named after the isle's original inhabitants. For more on Truganini, see p284.

The island has endured several commercial ventures. Sandstone was mined here and used for the Post Office and Houses of Parliament in Melbourne, and coal was also exhumed here. Both industries gradually declined due to lofty transportation costs. Only farming and forestry have had long-term viability.

Tourism is becoming increasingly important to the island's economy but remains fairly low-key. There are (as yet) no homogenised resorts, just plenty of interesting cottages and houses, most self-contained. Too many visitors try unsuccessfully to cram their Bruny experience into one day. If you can handle the peace and quiet, definitely plan to stay a few days. It's the kind of place that takes hold slowly, and then tends not to let go. Note that mobile-phone coverage on Bruny Island is limited to Telstra, and even that's patchy. Your best bet will be to park yourself on Adventure Bay beach and point your mobile device at the sky.

◎ Sights & Activities

South Bruny National Park NATIONAL PARK

At **Fluted Cape**, east of the Adventure Bay township, an easy trail winds past **Grass Point** (1½ hours return), a brilliant breakfast spot on a sunny morning. From here walk along the shore to **Penguin Island**, accessible at low tide, or complete a more difficult circuit climbing the cape itself (2½ hours return).

The park's southwestern portion comprises the **Labillardiere Peninsula** featuring jagged coastal scenery and a lighthouse. Walks here range from leisurely beach meanderings to a seven-hour circuit of the entire peninsula (starting and finishing at Jetty Beach camping ground).

For up-to-date information on the national park walks, plus other walks around the island, consult the Bruny D'Entrecasteaux visitor centre, or check out www.bruny island.net.au/Walks/brunywalks.html or www.parks.tas.gov.au. For national park entry fees, see p295.

Bruny Island Neck Game Reserve NATURE RESERVE

(www.brunyisland.net.au/Neck/neck.html) The isthmus between North and South Bruny is home to mutton birds and little (fairy) penguins that nest in the dunes. The best time and place to see the penguins is at dusk in the warmer months at **Highest Hummock Lookout**.

THE SOUTHEAST

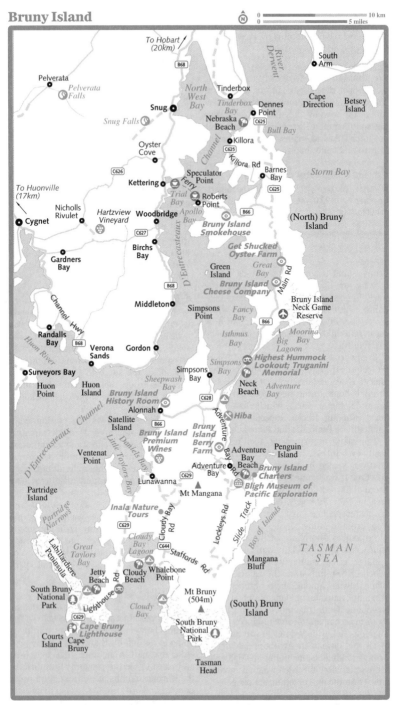

Some of the interesting folk drawn to Bruny by the island's rugged beauty are also at the forefront of the destination's growing reputation for top-quality food and wine. At the time of writing, we also heard rumours of a microbrewery starting up, so keep your taste buds on standby when you get off the ferry. Here's the best of Bruny's foodie experiences to get you started.

If you're hankering for a quivering sliver of goat's or cow's milk cheese, head to the **Bruny Island Cheese Company** (www.brunyislandcheese.com.au; 1087 Main Rd, Great Bay; ☺11am-4pm). Kiwi cheesemaker Nick Haddow is inspired by working and travelling in France, Spain, Italy and the UK. Artisan bread and local wines are also for sale.

Another brilliant Bruny business is the **Get Shucked Oyster Farm** (www.getshucked. com.au; 1650 Main Rd, Great Bay; ☺10am-5pm Oct-May, to 4pm Mon-Fri Jun-Sep), cultivating the 'fuel for love' in these chilly southern waters. Visit its humble caravan and wolf down a half dozen ($8) with lemon juice and Tabasco and a bottle of nonalcoholic chilli beer. Shuckingly good.

If you're still working up a thirst, **Bruny Island Premium Wines** (☎6293 1008; www. brunyislandwine.com; 4391 Main Rd, Lunawanna; ☺11am-4pm) offers cellar door sales at Australia's most southerly vineyard. Opening hours can change – call ahead to guarantee your tasting. Pinot Noir and Chardonnay rule the roost.

Go berry crazy with strawberries, blackberries, boysenberries and more at the **Bruny Island Berry Farm** (www.brunyislandberryfarm.com.au; 562 Adventure Bay Rd, Adventure Bay; ☺10am-5pm late Oct-late Apr). 'Pick your own' or enjoy the farm's juicy seasonal produce with ice cream, scones or pancakes.

Carry on up the hill to **Hiba** (53 Adventure Bay Rd; ☺10am-4pm), a smart little providore with a fine selection of silky-smooth Bruny Island Fudge.

At the **Bruny Island Smokehouse** (☎6260 6344; brunyislandsmokehouse1@bigpond. com; 360 Lennon Rd; ☺lunch & dinner daily Nov-Easter, to 5pm Thu-Sat rest of yr), salmon, trout, wallaby, duck and mussels are all carefully smoked. Homemade salad dressings and interesting preserves are also available for purchase. It's also a terrific restaurant and bar with superior marine views. Don't blame us if you miss the last ferry back to Kettering. Phone ahead as hours may vary.

Park at the Bruny Island Neck Game Reserve sign and climb the 273 steps to the **Truganini Memorial** for broad views of both ends of the island. Another timber walkway crosses the Neck to the beach on the other side. Keep to the boardwalk in this area.

Bligh Museum of Pacific Exploration   MUSEUM
(www.brunyisland.net.au/Adventure_Bay/blighmuseum.html; 876 Main Rd, Adventure Bay; adult/child/family $4/2/10; ☺10am-4pm) This curiosity-arousing museum details the local exploits of explorers Bligh, Cook, Furneaux and, of course, Bruni D'Entrecasteaux. The engaging collection includes maps, charts and manuscripts, many of them originals or 1st editions.

Cape Bruny Lighthouse   LANDMARK
(☎6298 3114; www.brunyisland.net.au/Cape_Bruny/Lightstation/lighthouse.html; tours adult/child $5/2) Worth visiting is the 1836 stone lighthouse on South Bruny – Australia's second-oldest. Take a tour (one day's advance booking required) or wander the surrounding **reserve** (☺10am-4pm).

FREE **Bruny Island History Room**   MUSEUM
(www.brunyisland.net.au/Alonnah/history-room.html; Main Rd, Alonnah; ☺10am-3pm) At the council offices in Alonnah is this wee, volunteer-run museum, displaying newspaper clippings, photos and records of the island community's past, plus info on walks and attractions around Bruny.

☞ Tours

Bruny Island Charters   WILDLIFE
(☎6293 1465; www.brunycharters.com.au; adult/child/family $100/55/300) This highly recommended three-hour tour of the island's awesome southeast coastline takes in rookeries, seal colonies, bays, caves and towering sea cliffs. Trips depart Adventure Bay jetty at 11am daily. You can also take the tour as a full-day trip from Kettering or Hobart

($165 per adult and $110 per child, including lunch and transfers).

Inala Nature Tours WILDLIFE
(2 6293 1217; www.inalabruny.com.au; 320 Cloudy Bay Rd; tours per person from $140) These highly regarded personalised walking and 4WD tours of the island (from half day to three days) focus on flora and fauna. The tour leader is a botanist, zoologist and conservationist; her 250-hectare property is home to almost 140 bird species. There are also two farm cottages to rent (doubles $220).

In 2010, Inala was instrumental in establishing the annual **Bruny Island Bird Festival**, a three-day celebration of all things avian in late October. The 2010 programme included half- and full-day birdwatching tours. See the website of the Bruny Island Environmental Network (www.bien.org.au) for information.

Ol' Kid FISHING
(2 6293 1128; www.capcookolkid.com.au) Other options include fishing charters, with all equipment provided, run by and operating from Captain James Cook Memorial Caravan Park in Adventure Bay. Three-hour charters including all equipment are $100 per person (minimum two people). Full-day charters are also available.

🛏 Sleeping

Self-contained cottages abound on Bruny, most suitable for midsize groups and offering economical weekly rates. Adventure Bay has the lion's share of accommodation, but there are places at Alonnah (the other main settlement on South Bruny), and at Barnes Bay and Dennes Point (pronounced 'Denz') on North Bruny.

Bookings are essential, as owners/managers and their keys aren't always easily located; the Bruny D'Entrecasteaux visitor centre is a good starting point. Online, see the booking and information portals www.brunyisland.com and www.brunyisland.net.au. Most accommodation options do *not* offer wi-fi access.

If you have a vehicle and a tent, the cheapest island accommodations are the free bush campgrounds. Camping on Bruny is restricted to sites within South Bruny National Park (national park passes required); at Jetty Beach, a beautiful sheltered cove 3km north of the lighthouse; and at Cloudy Bay. There's also a camp site outside the national park at Neck Beach, at the southern

end of the Neck. All sites have pit toilets and fireplaces; BYO firewood and water.

Beachfront on Bruny RENTAL HOUSE **$$**
(2 6293 1271; www.brunyisland.com; 1848 Bruny Island Main Rd, Great Bay; d $195, extra person $25) Nestled in the dunes on a private bay, this cosy whitewashed abode features lots of recycled timber, a terrific upstairs bedroom with expansive views, and a courtyard garden packed with native birds. The simple but stylish decor couldn't be more perfect for an island escape.

All Angels Church House RENTAL HOUSE **$$**
(2 6293 1271; www.brunyisland.com; 4561 Bruny Island Main Rd, Lunawanna; d $195, extra person $25) Your prayers have been answered with this restored church, now rental accommodation with three bedrooms and a high-ceilinged open-plan lounge. Fire up the barbecue in the sheltered garden, eat alfresco on the picnic table or dine inside on the huge shared table.

Eversley RENTAL HOUSE **$$**
(2 6293 1088; www.brunyislandvillas.com; 4391 Bruny Island Main Rd, Lunawanna; d $170) Recently refurbished, this modern two-bedroom house is operated by the adjacent Bruny Island Premium Wines. Classy decor and high-end appliances, including a huge flat-screen TV, all prove the operators are as fussy about their accommodation as they are about their Pinot Noir and Chardonnay.

Aquarius Retreat RENTAL HOUSE **$$$**
(2 6293 1271; www.brunyisland.com; Lighthouse Rd; d $245, extra person $25) The luxurious Aquarius Retreat features modern, open-plan living in a sleek glass-and-wooden pavilion. Two bedrooms make it perfect for families or two couples, and solar power makes it totally self-sufficient. Private walking tracks lead to an equally private hide for viewing the abundant bird life.

Morella Island Retreats RENTAL HOUSE **$$**
(2 6293 1131; www.morella-island.com; 46 Adventure Bay Rd, Adventure Bay; d $180-280) For a special occasion, book one of these unique, sequestered cottages 6km north of Adventure Bay (they also have beachfront cottages down by the Neck). Cottages range from sexy retreats for couples (complete with garden bath and hammock for two) to family-size holiday homes. All are self-contained, and design and decor could be described as 'classic castaway'. Prices drop by $30 for stays longer than one night.

Tree House
RENTAL HOUSE **$$**

(✆0405 192 892; www.thetreehouse.com.au; Alonnah; d $190, extra person $30) This is a good-lookin', open-plan timber place overlooking the agriculturally named Sheep Wash Bay. It has two bedrooms, all the mod cons and super-dooper views. The price drops to $180 for stays of two nights or more.

St Clairs
RENTAL HOUSE **$$**

(✆6293 1300; www.stclairs.com; Lighthouse Rd, Lunawanna; d $210) On the road to the lighthouse (just past the Explorers' Cottages) is this plush (but not pretentious) getaway cottage built for two, surrounded by bushland. Rent it and you'll get a spa and cooked-breakfast provisions; dinner by arrangement.

Bruny Beach House
RENTAL HOUSE **$$**

(✆0419 315 626; www.brunybeachhouse.com; 91 Nebraska Rd, Dennes Point; d $145, extra person $20) Above the sandy sliver of Nebraska Beach in the north is this large, good-value beach house sleeping four. It's got all the requisite facilities, a wood heater and a super deck on which to sip and scan. BYO supplies; two-night minimum stay.

Mickeys Bay Eco Retreat
RENTAL HOUSE **$$**

(✆1300 889 557; www.mickeysbay.com; 736 Lighthouse Rd, Lunawanna; d $150, extra person $25) About 12km south of Lunawanna en route to the lighthouse is this self-contained, open-plan studio apartment sleeping up to six. It has a hip, modern design, with polished floorboards, handmade furniture, a BBQ and a private beach. Perfect for families.

Wainui
RENTAL HOUSE **$$**

(✆6293 2096, 1300 889 557; www.wainuibandb.com; 87 Main Rd, Dennes Point; r $195, extra person $40) Spacious, open-plan living and outdoor deck views are the main selling points of this modern home at Dennes Point in the island's north. Fire up the barbecue and make the most of the vista. The name means 'big water' in New Zealand's Maori language, and we can only agree. There's a minimum two-night stay.

Lumeah
RENTAL HOUSE **$$**

(✆6293 1265; www.lumeah-island.com.au; Adventure Bay Rd, Adventure Bay; d $140, extra person $25) Lumeah, an Adventure Bay sawmiller's cottage knocked up 115 years ago, offers accommodation perfect for two couples or two families: two double rooms, two bathrooms and a bunk room sleeping six (maximum 10 guests). It's fully self-contained, 50m from

the beach, and has a barbecue area and spa. Nice one.

Explorers' Cottages
MOTEL **$$**

(✆6293 1271; www.brunyisland.com; 20 Lighthouse Rd, Lunawanna; d $175, extra person $25) Just south of Lunawanna on the way to the lighthouse, these bright, beachy, self-contained cottages sleep four, with lounge areas, log fires, board games and outdoor decks. You'll need to like the posse of incredibly friendly ducks who roam the expansive grounds. We found a combination of Arnott's Salada crackers and two-day old bread went down pretty well with them.

Captain James Cook Memorial Caravan Park
CAMPGROUND **$**

(✆6293 1128; www.capcookolkid.com.au; 786 Main Rd, Adventure Bay; unpowered/powered sites $20/23, on-site vans $44-55, cabins $140; ☜) Right by the beach, this grandly named park could do with a few trees but has decent facilities, including some swish new one-bedroom cabins with private decks. Fishing charters are available.

✖ Eating

Pick up provisions and takeaways at the island's general stores. Don't miss the gourmet pies at the Lunawanna store.

Bruny Island Smokehouse
TOP CHOICE CAFE **$$**

(360 Lennon Rd, North Bruny; pizzas $18-24; ☺lunch & dinner daily Nov-Easter, to 5pm Thu-Sat rest of yr) Managed with pizazz, 'BISH' is a winner – gourmet pizzas, smoked fish and meats, cakes, decent coffee and astounding views from the deck. It's hands down the best place on Bruny for a few cold ones, other than your own deck, of course. The shared platters ($65 to $68) are great value for groups.

Hothouse Café
CAFE **$$**

(✆6293 1131; 46 Adventure Bay Rd, South Bruny; meals $10-23; ☺breakfast & lunch from 10am, dinner by arrangement) This cafe at Morella Island Retreat occupies a converted hothouse (sit inside on a sunny day and you'll start to sprout). Isthmus views and flappy bird life distract you from the menu of interesting snacks and mains, including gourmet burgers and seafood chowder. Bookings essential for dinner. Also a top spot for a beer or wine.

Jetty Café at the Point
CAFE **$$**

(✆6260 6245; Dennes Pt, North Bruny; mains $18-24; ☺breakfast & lunch daily, dinner summer weekends) Part cafe-restaurant, part providore and part art gallery specialising in local artists, the stylish Jetty Café is a great addition to Bruny's dining scene. Pop in for a coffee, or book for lunch or dinner – seasonal menus showcase local produce. Phone ahead as opening hours may vary.

Hotel Bruny   PUB FARE **$$**
(Main Rd, Alonnah; mains $17-28; ☺lunch & dinner) An unassuming pub in Alonnah with outdoor water-view seating to help you unwind, plus a reasonable menu heavy on local seafood.

Penguin Café CAFE **$**
(710 Main Rd, Adventure Bay; breakfast mains $6-12, lunch & dinner mains $13-20; ☺breakfast, lunch & dinner Tue-Sun) Next to the Adventure Bay store, Penguin Café serves up rustic fare including burgers and pasta in a cosy wood-lined room. Coffee and cake is a more casual option, and wine and beer is available to enjoy on the outside tables.

Shopping
South Bruny has three general stores, open 9am to 5pm daily, all with Eftpos facilities, and all selling petrol, takeaway food and limited provisions. The largest is at **Adventure Bay** (712 Main Rd). The store at **Alonnah** (3 William Carte Dr) is also the post office. The third store, at **Lunawanna** (10 Cloudy Bay Rd), does a fine range of gourmet pies. There are no stores on North Bruny.

❶ Information
INTERNET ACCESS At the Adventure Bay general store or at the **Online Access Centre** (School Rd, Alonnah; per hr $5; ☺9am-noon & 1-4pm Mon-Wed, 1-3pm Thu, 6-9pm Fri) at Alonnah School (signposted).

TOURIST INFORMATION The Bruny D'Entrecasteaux visitor centre (p104) by the ferry terminal in Kettering can help with accommodation bookings; books and information on walks; camping; and driving tours. You can also buy passes for South Bruny National Park here. Online, check out www.brunyisland.net.au and www.brunyisland.com. Both offer information and online booking of accommodation.

❶ Getting There & Away
CAR Access to the island is via **car ferry** (☑6272 3277) from Kettering across to Roberts Point on the north of the island. There are at least 10 services daily, taking 20 minutes one way. The first ferry from Kettering is at 6.35am (7.45am on Sunday); the last is at 6.30pm

(7.30pm on Friday). The first ferry from Bruny is at 7am (8.25am on Sunday); the last is at 7pm (7.50pm on Friday). The timetable may vary, so double-check departure times. Return fares: cars $28 ($30 on public holidays and public-holiday weekends), motorcycles $12, bicycles $4 and foot passengers free.

Note that around summer weekends and Christmas and Easter there are often significant queues to access the ferry, despite the addition of more sailings. If you're travelling at these times, it's not really worth considering Bruny Island as a day trip as you're likely to spend a significant time waiting to catch the ferry from either end.

❶ Getting Around
You'll need your own wheels to get around – there are no buses. A bicycle is a great option, but be prepared for long rides between destinations. Bruny has some narrow, winding gravel roads, the slippery, logging truck–infested road over Mt Mangana being the prime case in point. Not all car-rental companies are cool with this concept.

Woodbridge
POP 250

Established in 1874 as Peppermint Bay (after the area's peppermint gums), Woodbridge was eventually renamed by a landowner nostalgic for his old home in England. It's a quiet village sitting squarely on the tourist trail thanks to the sexy Peppermint Bay development, which has consumed the old Woodbridge pub.

◉ Sights
About 3km south of Peppermint Bay is another stop for foodies. **Grandvewe Cheeses** (www.grandvewe.com.au; 59 Devlyns Rd, Birchs Bay; tastings free; ☺10am-5pm Sep-Jun, to 4pm Jul-Aug) is a farm churning out organic cheese from both sheep's and cow's milk. Sample some tasty produce, snack on a cheese platter (the pecorino is perfection) or quaff some Pinot Noir from the owners' nearby Grandvewe Vineyard.

A little further south is **Fleurtys** (www. fleurtys.com.au; 3866 Channel Hwy, Birchs Bay; ☺11am-4pm Wed-Sun), a cool little glass-fronted providore in the trees where you can take a bushwalk, inspect the essential-oil distillery and stock up on homemade jam, vinegar, honey, chutney, herbs, fudge and oils. The cafe here is great for lunch too (mains $12 to $20).

Hartzview Vineyard (☎6295 1623; www.hartzview.com.au; 70 Dillons Rd, Gardners Bay; ⏰10am-5pm; tastings $2 refunded with purchase) is 7km up the hill from Woodbridge, off the road to Gardners Bay. For your palate's pleasure are a range of fortified wines, fruit liqueurs, a peppery Pinot Noir and a mellifluous mead. Lunch is also a goer (gourmet pies, focaccia, smoked quiches, cheese platters; mains $14 to $18), and there's accommodation here, as well.

🛏 Sleeping & Eating

TOP
CHOICE **Woodbridge Hill Hideaway** APARTMENTS **$$**
(☎6295 1518; www.woodbridgehillhideaway.com.au; 369 Woodbridge Hill Rd; d $160-200, extra adult/child $40/20; 🐾🐕🏊) These flash self-contained cabins are really something special, with spectacular views of D'Entrecasteaux Channel and Bruny Island, and a design aesthetic best described as rustic, luxury chic. Local artwork, shimmering slabs of recycled timber, and granite bathrooms all add up to one of Tasmania's best. Leather furniture and romantic spa baths further enhance the experience. There's also a heated indoor swimming pool.

🌿 **Peppermint Ridge Retreat** RENTAL HOUSE **$$**
(☎6267 4192; www.peppermintridge.com.au; 290 Woodbridge Hill Rd; d $160-220, extra person $35) Two amazing handmade straw-bale-and-stone studios, complete with composting toilets, recycled timbers, spa baths, huge lofty spaces and brilliant D'Entrecasteaux Channel and Bruny Island views. Each sleeps five; breakfast supplies included.

Hartzview Vineyard RENTAL HOUSE **$$**
(☎6295 1623; www.hartzview.com.au; 70 Dillons Rd, Gardners Bay; d $160-200, extra adult/child $40/20) This secluded hilltop vineyard offers a fully equipped three-bedroom house endowed with a spa, antiques, a log fire, breakfast provisions and fine views over Gardners Bay. Dinners by arrangement.

Old Woodbridge Rectory B&B **$$**
(☎6267 4742; www.oldwoodbridgerectory.com.au; 15 Woodbridge Hill Rd; d $130-150) At the start of the Gardners Bay road is this friendly place with flower-filled gardens and two large ensuite rooms in a 1905 rectory.

Telopea MOTEL **$$**
(☎6267 4565; www.telopea-accommodation.com.au; 144 Pullens Rd; d $130, extra person $30) A

rural property with two wheelchair-accessible self-contained brick units on offer. Pullens Rd intersects with the Channel Hwy on the northern outskirts of Woodbridge. Telopa makes a good base for exploring the surrounding southeast area.

Peppermint Bay MODERN AUSTRALIAN **$$**
(☎6267 4088; www.peppermintbay.com.au; 3435 Channel Hwy; lunch daily, dinner Thu-Sat) On a mesmeric D'Entrecasteaux Channel inlet, Peppermint Bay houses a providore, an art gallery, the upmarket 'Stackings' Dining Room (mains $27 to $36), and the casual Local Bar (mains $18 to $23). The emphasis is on local produce, with seafood, fruits, meats, cheeses and other foodstuffs from just down the road. Bookings advised.

❶ Getting There & Away

BOAT Peppermint Bay Cruises (☎1300 137 919; www.peppermintbay.com.au; Brooke St Pier, Hobart) runs a five-hour float down the D'Entrecasteaux Channel to the sassy Peppermint Bay development. Prices start at adult/child $118/68 including lunch on board; cruise only from $98/58.

BUS Hobart Coaches (☎13 22 01) Four weekday services; the trip from Hobart takes one hour and costs $10.

Cygnet

POP 930

Groovy Cygnet was originally named Port de Cygne Noir (Port of the Black Swan) by Bruni d'Entrecasteaux (swans proliferate on the bay). Youthfully reincarnated as Cygnet (a baby swan), the town has evolved into a dreadlocked, artsy enclave, while still functioning as a major fruit-producing centre. Weathered farmers and banjo-carrying hippies chat amiably in the main street and prop up the bars of the town's three pubs. To the south, **Randalls Bay** and **Verona Sands** beaches aren't far away.

The **Cygnet Living History Museum** (37 Mary St; admission by donation; ⏰10am-3pm Tue & Wed, 12.30-3pm Fri & Sat) is a quaint history room next to the church on the main street, stuffed full of old photos, documents and curios.

Inside a converted Methodist church is the **Living History Museum of Aboriginal Cultural Heritage** (Nicholls Rivulet; adult/child $4.50/2; ⏰10.30am-2.30pm), out of town at the corner of Cross Rd and Nicholls Rivulet Rd in Nicholls Rivulet (5km from the turn-

DEEP-SOUTH FOODIE EXPERIENCES

The southeast is emerging as a real gourmet hotspot. Here are some of our favourite deep-south eating encounters. See www.huontrail.org.au to download handy seasonal food-trail brochures.

» Munch on the quintessential Tasmanian apple, fresh from a roadside stall between Huonville and Cygnet (p115).

» Visit Huonville's Ranelagh showgrounds in mid-March for the annual Taste of the Huon (www.tasteofthe huon.com) showcase of Huon Valley produce.

» Sip a late-afternoon Pinot Noir or two at Home Hill (p115), Hartzview (p111) or Panorama Vineyard (p113).

» Sniff out some peppery pecorino and smooth goat's-milk cheese at Grandvewe Cheeses (p110) south of Woodbridge.

» Get hot and bothered after a few oysters ('fuel for love') from Get Shucked Oyster Farm (p107) on Bruny Island.

» Wind down from a lazy lunch at the fabulous Peppermint Bay (p111) restaurant in Woodbridge.

» Melt into some of Tasmania's best food at the Red Velvet Lounge (p112) and the Lotus Eaters Café (p113) in surprising Cygnet.

off south of Cygnet). The small museum contains historical information and displays of southeast Tasmanian Aboriginal arts, crafts, artefacts and stories. It also has a garden and wetlands filled with plants significant to the local Melukerdee Aboriginal band.

January's ever-popular **Cygnet Folk Festival** (www.cygnetfolkfestival.org) is three days of words, music and dance, attracting talent like Jeff Lang and Monique Brumby. The warmer months also provide abundant fruit-picking work for backpackers.

🛏 Sleeping

Old Bank B&B TOP CHOICE   B&B $$$
(✆6295 0769; www.oldbank.com.au; 20 Mary St; d incl breakfast $225-250; 🛜) Cygnet's grand and stately former bank is now the town's best accommodation, with three spacious bedrooms dripping in natural wood, oriental carpets, and king-size beds with luxury linen. Bathrooms are especially lovely, with gleaming art-deco touches and wooden vanities crafted from recycled timber. Downstairs, breakfast and early-evening drinks are served in the Orangery, a modern conservatory. Evening meals are available by arrangement.

Cherryview   RENTAL HOUSE $$
(✆6295 0569; www.cherryview.com.au; 90 Supplice Rd; d $160) This self-contained cottage on 25 quiet acres is decked out with cosy wooden furniture and enjoys misty morning views over nearby cherry orchards. Oriental rugs, wooden floors and a king-size bed make it ideal for a romantic getaway. The bright lights of downtown Cygnet are just three minutes' drive away.

Commercial Hotel   PUB $
(✆6295 1296; 2 Mary St; s/d with shared bathroom $65/85) Upstairs at the rambling old Commercial are decent pub rooms, all recently redecorated with flat-screen TVs, fridges and new beds. Downstairs a gregarious gaggle of laconic locals occupy the bar and dive into robust seafood spreads.

Cygnet Art Hotel   PUB $$
(✆6295 1267; www.cygnethotel.com.au; 77 Mary St; r $110; 🛜) This big, red-brick heritage pub on the upper slopes of Cygnet's main drag has reinvented itself as the Cygnet Art Hotel. Rooms are heritage chic, and downstairs you can grab a cold Cascade or glass of wine in the Piano Bar & Lounge before adjourning to the more upmarket Black Swan Restaurant. Live jazz often permeates the friendly surroundings on summer afternoons.

Cygnet Holiday Park   CAMPGROUND $
(✆6295 1267; contact@cygnettophotel.com.au; 3 Mary St; unpowered/powered sites $15/25) A bogbasic camping ground accessed via the side road next to the Cygnet RSL.

🍴 Eating

Red Velvet Lounge TOP CHOICE   CAFE $$
(www.theredvelveetlounge.com.au; 24 Mary St; breakfast & lunch mains $8-25, dinner mains $27-30; ⊙breakfast & lunch daily, dinner Fri & Sat) This funky restaurant and coffee house serves deliciously healthy meals showcasing local Huon Valley produce to a diverse clientele. Try the free-range-pork chorizo or

the comforting slow-cooked chicken with parsnips and peas. On Friday and Saturday nights from 5pm, find the secret door – it's down the side, OK – and secure gourmet wood-fired pizzas ($17.50).

Lotus Eaters Café CAFE $
(10 Mary St; light meals $10-15; ☺breakfast & lunch Thu-Mon) What's in the water in Cygnet? Just a few doors along from the excellent Red Velvet Lounge is this equally fine cafe. Rustic decor belies a real culinary savvy with great eggy breakfasts, a rigorous focus on seasonal, organic, free-range and local, and superlative homemade cakes. Other standouts on the menu are hearty soups and gourmet pies and tarts.

Commercial Hotel PUB $$
(2 Mary St; mains $10-28; ☺lunch & dinner) Our favourite Cygnet pub has turned its dining room into an all-day cafe, serving up a respectable range of light meals (focaccia, salads, pasta), and top-notch coffee. If you're really hungry, treat yourself to a slap-up steak, seafood or schnitzel spread in the bar.

School House Coffee Shop CAFE $
(23a Mary St; meals $8-16; ☺breakfast & lunch Tue-Sun) Cute coffee shop with geranium-filled window boxes, serving hefty homemade pies, Turkish bread sandwiches, pasta, soups, all-day breakfasts and tempting cakes.

❶ Getting There & Away

Metro Tasmania (☎13 22 01) buses travel three times a day Monday to Friday, departing Hobart at 9am, 4.10pm and 5.10pm ($10, one hour).

Huonville & Around

The biggest town in the southeast, agrarian Huonville sits on the banks of the Huon River 35km south of Hobart, not far from some lovely vineyards and small villages. Having made its name as Tasmania's apple-growing powerhouse, it remains a functional, working town – low on charm but with all the services you need.

The Huon and Kermandie Rivers were named after Huon d'Kermandec, second in command to explorer Bruni d'Entrecasteaux. Prior to that, the area was known by Tasmanian Aborigines as Tahune-Linah. The region was originally steeped in tall forests, and timber-milling quickly became a major industry, focusing on the coveted softwood Huon pine. The initial plundering of Huon pine groves nearly wiped the tree out, as it's extremely slow-growing. Today, only immature trees survive along the river. Once the forest was levelled, apple trees were planted and the orchard industry blossomed – it's still the region's primary money-spinner.

The Huon Hwy traces the Huon River south, passing the settlements of Franklin, Castle Forbes Bay and Port Huon. These were once important shipping ports for apples, but nowadays the old wharves and packing sheds are decaying like old fruit.

Strung-out Franklin is the oldest town in the Huon Valley. The wide, reedy riverscape here is one of Australia's best rowing courses.

WORTH A TRIP

DETOUR: CYGNET COAST ROAD

If you're not in a hurry, don't miss the scenic coast road (the C639) between Cradoc and Cygnet. The direct route along the Channel Hwy (the B68) between these two towns is about 7km (this is the route for **roadside apple stalls**), but the coastal route is a meandering 27km, past Petcheys Bay and Glaziers Bay.

The C639 heads south from Cygnet's main street to Lymington. In January and February you can pick fruit at one of the **blueberry farms** along the way.

One kilometre from the Cradoc junction is the impressive Panorama Vineyard (www.panoramavineyard.com.au; 1848 Cygnet Coast Rd, Cradoc; tastings free; ☺10am-5pm Wed-Mon), where you can stick your nose into acclaimed Pinot Noir, plus Chardonnay, Merlot and Riesling.

A spectacular place to stay is Riverside (☎6295 1952; www.huonriverside.com.au; 35 Graces Rd, Glaziers Bay; d $250, extra adult/child $55/33), a deluxe contemporary abode (perfect for two couples) with amazing Huon views from the wide verandahs. Fresh flowers, quality linen and homemade breakfast provisions are all on tap. There's a minimum two-night stay, so look forward to slowing right down.

⊙ Sights & Activities

Home Hill VINEYARD
(☎6264 1200; www.homehillwines.com.au; 38 Nairn St, Ranleagh; tastings free; ⊙10am-5pm) In nearby Ranelagh (3km west of Huonville) is this superstylish winery, producer of award-winning Pinot Noir, Chardonnay and dessert wines. There's also an excellent restaurant here.

Huon Apple & Heritage Museum MUSEUM
(www.applemuseum.huonvalley.biz; 2064 Main Rd, Grove; adult/child $6/3; ⊙8.30am-5.30pm) At Grove, 6km north of Huonville, this museum has displays on almost 400 varieties of apples and on 19th-century orchard life. Lots of yummy produce – fudge, jams, juice – is for sale in the museum's Apple Blossom's gift shop, and the adjacent 'Starving Artist' gallery showcases work from creative locals.

Huon River Jet Boats BOATING
(☎6264 1838; www.huonjet.com; The Esplanade, Huonville; adult/child $69/47; ⊙9am-5pm Sep-May) Take a frenetic, 35-minute jet-boat ride through the local rapids. Bookings recommended.

Huon Valley Horsetrekking HORSE RIDING
(☎6266 0343; www.horsehavenfarmstay.com; 179 Judds Creek Rd) About 13km from Huonville at Judbury, horse treks are available; a two-hour ride costs $90 per person, including a picnic, and a half-day outing including lunch is $170 per person. There's also a lovely cottage for rent here (doubles $130) and the newly opened and cosy 'Love Nest' (doubles $100). Backpackers can kip in the main house for $25. A cooked farm breakfast is $15.

Wooden Boat Centre MUSEUM
(www.woodenboatcentre.com; Huon Hwy, Franklin; adult/child $6/4.50; ⊙9.30am-5pm) This salty spot is part of the School of Wooden Boatbuilding, a unique institution running accredited 12-month courses in traditional techniques using Tasmania's timbers. Stick your head in the door to learn about boat-building, watch boats being cobbled together and hear a sea shanty or two.

🛏 Sleeping

Huon Bush Retreats CABINS $$
(☎6264 2233; www.huonbushretreats. com; 300 Browns Rd, Ranelagh; d tepees $135, d cabins from $275, camp sites $30) This wildlife-friendly retreat is on a habitat reserve on not-miserable Mt Misery. On site are modern, self-contained cabins, a larger disabled-access cabin, luxury tepees, tent and campervan sites, plus walking tracks and barbecue shelters. Meals by arrangement. Check the website for directions: it's 10km from Huonville and well signposted.

Whispering Spirit Holiday Cottages RENTAL HOUSE $$
(☎6266 3341; www.whisperingspirit.com.au; 253 Swamp Rd, Franklin; d $95-140) We're not convinced a spirit can actually whisper, but we get what these guys are trying to say. The homey self-contained cottage and fantastic two-bedroom, crimson straw-bale unit definitely have soul! Cheaper rates for longer stays. Miniature ponies on site for everyone's inner child.

Huon Franklin Cottage B&B B&B $$
(☎6266 3040; www.huonfranklincottage.com.au; 3554 Huon Hwy, Franklin; d $135) This mustard-yellow house, set high above the road to catch the river views, gets good feedback from readers. Two cottagey B&B rooms plus an outdoor spa are offered at affordable rates. Dinner by arrangement. The owners also have the 'Cottage on Main' accommodation in the middle of town, sleeping six (doubles $140).

Camellia Cottage RENTAL HOUSE $$
(☎6297 1528; www.camelliacottagebandb.com; 119 Crowthers Rd, Castle Forbes Bay; d $110, extra person $25) Charming 1882 farm cottage with an open fire, nestled into flower-crowded gardens. The cottage sleeps three and has limited cooking facilities; breakfast provisions are included (juice, breads, jams, free-range eggs).

Donalea B&B B&B $$
(☎6297 1021; www.donalea.com.au; 9 Crowthers Rd, Castle Forbes Bay; d $120-150, extra person $30) A B&B with welcoming hosts, chill-the-hell-out views and petal-filled garden. Donalea has two bright rooms (one with spa), a spacious four-berth apartment, and a guest lounge with roaring log fire.

✕ Eating

Franklin Woodfired Pizza PIZZA $
(Huon Hwy, Franklin; pizzas $10-20; ⊙dinner daily, lunch Sun) This tiny tin shack bakes fantastic takeaway pizzas inside a kooky corrugated-iron oven. Try the tiger-prawn one with pineapple, chilli jam, pineapple and jalapeños.

Home Hill Winery Restaurant   WINERY $$
(www.homehillwines.com.au; 38 Nairn St, Ranleigh; mains $26-33; ☺lunch daily, dinner Fri & Sat) Home Hill vineyard has a fab restaurant in a slick-looking rammed-earth building with pasture views. The seasonal menu offers Tassie produce: Bothwell goat's cheese, Huon Valley mushrooms, King Island cream. Morning and afternoon tea, too.

Aqua Grill   SEAFOOD $
(3419 Huon Hwy, Franklin; meals $7-20; ☺lunch & dinner) Excellent takeaway or dine-in fish and chips and other marine snacks (try the curried-scallop crepe with white wine and cream sauce). The sweet-potato cakes are also mighty fine, and there's a well-chosen selection of beer and wine.

Petty Sessions   CAFE $$
(3445 Huon Hwy, Franklin; mains $22-34; ☺lunch & dinner) A picket fence and picture-perfect gardens enshroud this likeable cafe, inside an 1860 courthouse. Head for the deck and order classic cafe fare (salads, BLTs, tandoori chicken burgers and seafood fettucine), or try the house special: abalone chowder.

DS Coffee House & Internet Lounge   CAFE $
(34 Main Rd, Huonville; light meals $8-15; ☺breakfast & lunch; @☎) Hands down Huonville's most interesting cafe, DS has a funky collection of retro furniture that feels like your first student flat at uni. All-day breakfasts, sourdough sandwiches, daily soup specials and Huonville's best coffee all feature. It's also a handy internet lounge with PCs for hire and a wi-fi network for netbook travellers.

Two Birds   CAFE $
(4 Wilmot St, Huonville; mains $10-18; ☺breakfast & lunch) A welcoming little cafe with funky Indian decor. Eggs loads of ways for brekkie segue tastily to 'fritters of the day' and superior burgers on toasted Turkish bread. Everything's available for takeaway if you're pushing on further south.

❶ Information

DS Coffee House & Internet Lounge (34 Main Rd, Huonville; internet & wi-fi per 10 min $1; @☎) Wi-fi access.

Huon Valley Environment Centre (www.huon. org; 3/17 Wilmot St; ☺9.30am-4.30pm Tue-Fri) Excellent resource for anyone interested in Tasmanian environmental issues.

FAST FOOD

All along the Huon Valley roadsides, particularly the B68 between Huonville and Cygnet, you can pull over and buy farm-fresh produce from makeshift apple carts. These usually take the form of tin sheds out the front of farms, stocked with bags of whatever is in season: pears, apricots, peaches, blueberries, blackberries, raspberries, boysenberries, strawberries, potatoes, peas, beans and, of course, apples. It's an honesty system – grab your bag, drop some coins in the box and drive off brimming with vitamin C.

Huon visitor centre (☑6264 1838; www. huonjet.com/huonvisitorcentre.html; The Esplanade; ☺9am-5pm) Tourist information by the river on the road to Cygnet (also the Huon Jet office). Also see www.huontrail.org for lots of excellent touring information.

Parks & Wildlife Service (www.parks.tas.gov. au; 22 Main Rd; ☺9am-4.30pm Mon-Fri) Main street office.

❶ Getting There & Away

Tassielink (☑1300 300 520; www.tassielink. com.au) Runs regular Huon Valley services from Hobart to Dover, stopping at Huonville ($9.90, 50 minutes), Franklin ($9.90, one hour) and Castle Forbes Bay ($13, 70 minutes).

Geeveston
POP 830

A rugged timber town, Geeveston, 31km south of Huonville, is emerging as a low-key tourist centre, offering limited accommodation close to the Hartz Mountains and Tahune Forest AirWalk.

Geeveston was founded in the mid-19th century by the Geeves family, whose descendants still have fingers in lots of local pies. In the 1980s the town was the epicentre of an intense battle over logging the Farmhouse Creek forests. At the height of the controversy, some conservationists spent weeks living in the tops of 80m-tall eucalyptuses to prevent them being felled. The conservation movement ultimately won: Farmhouse Creek is now protected from logging.

There's a multicard ATM inside the (⊙7am-late), at the corner of School and Arve Rds.

◉ Sights

Forest & Heritage Centre   MUSEUM
(15 Church St; ⊙9am-5pm) In the town centre, this wood-lined building houses interesting displays showcasing the forestry heritage of the area. It presents a pro-forestry viewpoint, in contrast to the Huon Valley Environment Centre in Huonville, so you can consider both sides of the debate. The centre also sells Tahune Forest AirWalk tickets.

Pick up the *Geeveston Circuit Platypus Walk* brochure so you can (hopefully) spy the iconic, but shy, creatures on a pleasant stroll around town.

Southern Design Centre   ART GALLERY
(www.southerndesigncentre.com; 11 School Rd; ⊙10am-5pm) A good place to browse for local crafts (ceramics, paintings, knits) and timber furniture.

🛏 Sleeping & Eating

Cambridge House   B&B $$
(☑6297 1561; www.cambridgehouse.com.au; cnr School Rd & Huon Hwy; d $140, with shared facilities $110) A photogenic 1930s B&B offering upstairs accommodation in three bedrooms with shared facilities (ideal for families), or a downstairs en-suite room. Baltic pine ceilings and the timber staircase are wonders. Check out the friendly platypus at the bottom of the garden.

Bears Went Over the Mountain   B&B $$
(☑6297 0110; www.bearsoverthemountain.com; 2 Church St; d $130-200; @🖥) Right in the middle of town, Bears has four rooms decorated in a whimsical bear theme (with the odd stuffed tiger) – kids will be in heaven. Complimentary port for cold southern nights.

Contented Bear   CAFE $$
(6 Church St; lunch mains $11-18, dinner mains $25-35; ⊙lunch & dinner; @🖥) A rustic cafe run by the Bears Went Over the Mountain owners. Try a homemade scallop mornay pie for lunch; for dinner it's gotta be the Tassie salmon with garlic mash or the prawn and scallop salad. Wi-fi and internet access are available.

❶ Getting There & Away

Tassielink (☑1300 300 520; www.tassielink.com.au) The 1½-hour trip from Hobart costs $13.

Arve Road & Tahune Forest Reserve

The sealed Arve Rd, constructed to extract timber from the local forests, trucks west from Geeveston through rugged, tall-timber country to the Hartz Mountains, the Tahune Forest Reserve and the Tahune Forest AirWalk.

Pick up a map from the Geeveston Forest & Heritage Centre detailing some easy short walks along the Arve Rd:

Arve River Picnic Area Has picnic tables and a ferny forest walk (10 minutes round trip); 12km from Geeveston.

Big Tree Lookout A sub-five-minute walk leading to a timber platform beside a giant 87m-high swamp gum; turn-off is 14km from Geeveston.

Keogh's Creek Walk Fifteen-minute streamside circuit, 14km from Geeveston.

West Creek Lookout Provides views from a bridge extending out from the top of an old tree stump; 21km from Geeveston.

About 29km west of Geeveston is the **Tahune Forest Reserve**, its name derived from Tahune-Linah, the Aboriginal name for the area around the Huon and Kermandie Rivers. Here you'll find the hugely successful Tahune Forest AirWalk (☑1300 720 507; www.adventureforests.com.au; adult/child $24/12; ⊙9am-5pm), 600m of see-through steel-mesh walkways suspended 20m above the forest floor. One 24m cantilevered section is designed to sway disconcertingly with approaching footsteps. Vertigo? There are a couple of ground-level walks here, too, including a 20-minute riverside stroll through stands of young Huon pine. Phone bookings are recommended.

The AirWalk is accessible for people with disabilities, and there is a cafe (mains $8-18; ⊙lunch) and gift shop here too. There are plenty of picnic spots around the reserve, and limited unpowered campervan spots (no tents). There's a free (unofficial) camp site at the Arve River Picnic Ground about halfway to the AirWalk.

You can assess the Tahune forest from even higher up with the Tahune Eagle Glide (☑0419 311 198; www.cablehanggliding.com.au; adult/child $33/22; ⊙9am-5pm). Wannabe eagles are strapped into a hang-glider, which in turn is latched to a 220m cable 30m above the Huon River and forest. You get two crossings for the price. Eagle Glide is 400m from the AirWalk car park.

Hartz Mountains National Park

If you prefer your wilderness a little less pre-packaged than the Tahune Forest Reserve, head for the Hartz Mountains National Park (www.parks.tas.gov.au). A century ago, the Hartz plateau was a logging hot spot, and stocks of small varnished gums were harvested for eucalyptus oil, which was distilled in Hobart for medicinal applications. Eventually the area was declared a national park, and in 1989 became part of the Tasmanian Wilderness World Heritage Area.

The 65-sq-km Hartz Mountains National Park is only 84km from Hobart, within striking distance for weekend walkers and day-trippers. The park is renowned for its jagged peaks, glacial tarns, gorges and wonderful alpine moorlands, where fragile cushion-plant communities grow in the cold, misty airs. Rapid weather changes bluster through, and even day walkers should bring waterproofs and warm clothing.

There are some great hikes and isolated, sit-and-ponder-your-existence viewpoints in the park. **Waratah Lookout**, 24km from Geeveston, is an easy five-minute shuffle from the road. Other well-surfaced short walks include **Arve Falls** (20 minutes return) and **Lake Osborne** (40 minutes return). The steeper **Lake Esperance** walk (two hours return) takes you through beautiful high country. You'll need to be fairly fit and experienced to tackle the steep, rougher track that leads to **Hartz Peak** (five hours return), which is poorly marked beyond **Hartz Pass** (3½ hours return).

There's no camping within the park – just basic day facilities, including toilets, shelters, picnic tables and barbecues. Download a park fact sheet from www.parks.tas.gov.au.

Dover

POP 570

Sleepy Dover – a Port Esperance fishing town with a pub, a beach and a pier to dangle a line from – is a chilled-out spot to while away a few deep-south days. Dover was originally called Port Esperance after a ship in Bruni d'Entrecasteaux's fleet, but that moniker now only applies to the bay. The bay's three small islands are called Faith, Hope and Charity.

In the 19th century this was timber territory. Huon pine and local hardwoods were milled and shipped from here (and also nearby Strathblane and Raminea) to China, India and Germany for use as railway sleepers. Today the major industries are fruit growing and fish farming, with Atlantic salmon exported throughout Asia.

There's not much by way of attractions in Dover itself, but if you're heading further south, buy petrol and food supplies here.

🛏 Sleeping

TOP CHOICE **Peninsula** RENTAL HOUSE **$$$**
(☑1800 353 983; www.peninsulatas.com.au; Blubber Head Rd; d $440, extra person $75; 🛜) Proudly sited on a private peninsula, this stately 19th-century farmhouse is now a thoroughly 21st-century luxury retreat. Asian-chic design infuses the three bedrooms, and the huge open-plan living area and kitchen is packed with elegant furnishings. It's a perfect retreat for a few couples and is equipped with enough fine Tassie wine and food to last them a couple of days. At dusk, the local wildlife posse – pademelons and other wallabies, echidna – patrol the grounds. Up to six adults can be accommodated, but sorry, no kids.

Driftwood Holiday Cottages RENTAL HOUSE **$$$**
(☑1800 353 983; www.driftwoodcottages.com.au; 51 Bayview Rd; d $185-320) Modern, self-contained studio-style units huddle by the beach road, and further up the hill are two brand-new sleek and modern studio units. Sit on your verandah, sip something chilly and watch fishers rowing out to their boats on Port Esperance. Driftwood has a range of other properties in the area, including the open-plan, and very private, Tides Reach, and Beach Front, a heritage cottage just metres from the Dover sand.

Far South Wilderness Lodge & Backpackers CABINS **$**
(☑6298 1922; www.farsouthwilderness.com.au; Narrows Rd, Strathblane; dm/d/f $30/80/100) On the Esperance River 5km south of Dover, Far South provides some of Tasmania's best budget accommodation, with a bushy waterfront setting, cosy lounge piled high with *National Geographic* mags, quality accommodation and a strong environmental focus. Has mountain bikes for rent ($15 per day).

Smuggler's Rest MOTEL **$$**
(☑6298 1396; www.smugglersrest.info; Station Rd; d $85-125) Externally this terracotta place channels downtown Santa Fe, and inside are tidy self-contained studios and two-bedroom units. The owners have bikes, fishing rods and old golf clubs for guest use.

Dover Beachside Tourist Park CAMPGROUND **$**
(☑6298 1301; www.dovercaravanpark.com.au; 27 Kent Beach Rd; unpowered/powered sites $20/28, cabins from $90; 🖥) Opposite a sandy beach, this proudly maintained park features grassy expanses, spotless cabins and a bookshelf full of beachy, trashy novels.

✖ Eating & Drinking

Post Office 6985 MODERN AUSTRALIAN **$$**
(Main Rd; mains $13-30; ⊘dinner Thu-Sun) This is a surprise. Leonard Cohen and alt-country on the stereo, cool decor and lots of up-to-date music and food magazines. The menu featuring local seafood and wood-fired pizzas – try the scallop, caramelised onion and pancetta one – will probably have you asking your accommodation if you can stay an extra night. A sterling beer and wine list validates the urge even more.

St Imre WINERY **$$**
(☑6298 1781; ww.stimrevineyard.com.au; 6900 Huon Hwy; 3-course dinners $35; ⊘tastings 10am-5pm Sat & Sun, dinner Sat) Specialising in Pinot Noir, Chardonnay and the robust and rustic 'Tiger Blood', this compact hillside vineyard also offers weekly three-course dinners on Saturday, usually reflecting the owners' Hungarian heritage. Central European treats include slow-roasted duck with potato salad, and chicken and dumplings in a creamy paprika sauce. You'll need to book by early Saturday afternoon at the latest. Terrific woodwork, including stunning furniture, is also for sale.

Gingerbreadhouse Bakery BAKERY **$**
(Main Rd; items $4-13; ⊘breakfast & lunch, reduced hr outside summer) On the main bend as you curve down into town, this small German-style bakery dishes out cooked breakfasts, stuffed croissants, homemade pies and tasty cakes, all made on site.

Self-caterers can hit the fully stocked **Dover Grocer & Newsagency** (Main Rd) for beaut deli produce, Tassie wines, and fresh fruit and vegies.

ℹ Information

The **Online Access Centre** (Old School, Main Rd; ⊘10am-2pm Mon-Fri, 11am-2pm Sat & Sun) is near the Post Office 6985 restaurant. There's a network of 66 of these community-run places around Tassie. Locals (and visitors) can get online for around $5 per hour

There is a multicard ATM outside the Southgate Shopping Centre.

ℹ Getting There & Away

The **Tassielink** (www.tassielink.com.au) trip from Hobart takes 1¾ hours and costs $20. There are three services each weekday from Hobart, except from December through to March, when an extra service runs every Monday, Wednesday and Friday (en route further south to Cockle Creek).

Southport

POP 300

Originally Southport was called Baie des Moules (Bay of Mussels), one of several names it's had over the years. Many travellers don't take the 2km detour off the main road to visit the town, but it's a worthy diversion if only to stay in the B&Bs here, which make good use of the waterside slopes. Unfortunately, public transport won't get you here.

Known as **Burying Ground Point,** the bluff south of town was once a convict cemetery; it's now a public reserve. There's also a memorial to the 1835 shipwreck of the *King George III* in which 35 people bubbled below.

🛏 Sleeping & Eating

Jetty House B&B **$$**
(☑6298 3139; www.southportjettyhouse.com; Main Rd; s/d incl breakfast $100/140, extra person $25; 🖥) Tailor-made for relaxation (or post–South Coast Track recovery), this rustic, family-run guesthouse down near the wharf is a rambling, verandah-encircled homestead built in 1875. Rates include full cooked breakfast and afternoon tea, and the friendly feline attention of Pushkin. Dinner by arrangement. Minimum two nights, with cheaper rates for longer stays.

Southern Forest B&B B&B **$$**
(☑6298 3306; www.southernforest.com.au; 30 Jager Rd; s/d/tr incl breakfast $105/130/180, extra person $30) Up the hill opposite Southport Tavern is this hospitable B&B in native bush with plenty of warm timber and not a hint of twee floral excess. Accommodation is in

a wing sleeping six (three bedrooms, two bathrooms and lounge) – ideal for families and groups. No kitchen, but breakfast is included. There is also a two-bedroom cottage (double $170) in a private, forest-clad setting.

Southport Hotel & Caravan Park   CAMPGROUND $

(☑6298 3144; www.southportcaravanpark.com.au; Main Rd; unpowered/powered sites $18/22, cabins/motel d $75/130) A sprawling, faux-colonial pub, general store and caravan park. The weary can bunk down for the night in the caravan park or adjacent motel units; the hungry can nosh up in the dining room (mains $18 to $25; ☺dinner Wed-Mon) or with takeaways from the store (open 8am to 6pm).

Hastings Caves & Thermal Springs

Signposted 10km inland from the Huon Hwy, the excellent Hastings Caves & Thermal Springs facility attracts visitors to the once-thriving logging port of Hastings, 21km south of Dover. The only way to explore the caves (which are within the Hastings Caves State Reserve) is via guided tour. Buy tickets at the Hastings visitor centre (☑6298 3209; www.parks.tas.gov.au; adult/child/family $24/12/60; ☺9am-5pm Mar, Apr & Sep-Dec, 9am-6pm Jan & Feb, 10am-4pm May-Aug). Tours leave on the hour, the first an hour after the visitor centre opens, the last an hour before it closes. Admission includes a 45-minute tour of the amazing dolomite Newdegate Cave, plus entry to the **thermal swimming pool** behind the visitor centre, filled with 28°C water from thermal springs (pool-only admission adult/child/family $5/2.50/12). The wheelchair-accessible **Hot Springs Trail** does a big loop from the pool area, taking 20 minutes to navigate (note that the pool is also wheelchair-accessible).

There's a decent cafe (light meals $8-16; ☺breakfast & lunch) at the visitor centre, which also sells barbecue and picnic hampers.

From the visitor centre, the cave entrance is a further 5km drive. No public transport runs out this way.

Lune River

A few kilometres southwest of Hastings is the diminutive enclave of Lune River. Here, Australia's southernmost railway, the Ida Bay Railway (www.idabayrailway.com.au; 328 Lune River Rd; adult/child/family $25/12/60; ☺9am-5pm, closed Fri Feb–mid-Dec) tracks a scenic 14km, 1½-hour narrow-gauge course through native bush to Deep Hole Bay. Take a picnic lunch and explore the beach, then catch a later train back to Lune River. Trains depart Lune River at

FRENCH CONNECTIONS

Less than a decade ago, it seemed that the pristine Tasmanian south was about to change for the worse. In 2004 the Tasmanian government gave private landowners permission to log the forests of the northeast peninsula of Recherche Bay – a decision that stirred up controversy in Tasmania and as far away as France.

In 1792 two French ships under the command of explorer Bruni d'Entrecasteaux, *La Recherche* and *L'Espérance*, anchored in a harbour near Tasmania's southernmost point and called it Recherche Bay. More than a decade before British settlers arrived in Tasmania, the French met the Lyluquonny Aborigines here and were carrying out the first significant scientific studies on the continent. There are two heritage sites at Recherche Bay with protected status (relics of the French observatory and garden, not accessible to the public), but the explorers' journals record them venturing far into the bush. With the government's announcement, historians, scientists and conservationists became concerned that the area earmarked for clearfelling was home to yet more sites of historic interest to both Australia and France. Needless to say, tensions between the anti- and pro-logging groups escalated – the prospect of the kinds of protests that took place in Tasmania when the Franklin River was under threat in the mid-1980s loomed large.

Fortunately, in 2006 the landowners agreed to sell the northeast peninsula to the Tasmanian Land Conservancy, and it's now protected as a significant site. Read more at www.recherchebay.org and www.tasland.org.au.

9.30am, 11.30am, 1.30pm and 3.30pm during summer, and 10am, noon and 2pm during winter. There's a cafe (light meals $4-10; ☺breakfast & lunch) at the Lune River end of the line serving cakes, sandwiches, burgers and bacon and eggs.

Cockle Creek

Australia's most southerly drive is the 19km gravel stretch from Ida Bay past the soft-lulling waves of Recherche Bay to Cockle Creek. A grand grid of streets was once planned for Cockle Creek, but dwindling coal seams and whale numbers poured cold water on that idea.

The area features craggy, clouded mountains, sigh-inducing beaches, and (best of all) hardly any people – perfect for camping and bushwalking. The challenging **South Coast Track** starts (or ends) here, taking you through to Melaleuca in the Southwest National Park. Combined with the **Port Davey Track** you can walk all the way to Port Davey in the southwest. Shorter walks from Cockle Creek include ambles along the shoreline to the lighthouse at **Fishers Point** (two hours return), and a section of the South Coast Track to **South Cape Bay** (four hours return). National park entry fees (see p295) apply to all these walks; self-register at Cockle Creek.

There are some brilliant free **campgrounds** along Recherche Bay, including at Gilhams Beach, just before Catamaran. You can also camp for free at Cockle Creek itself, but national park fees apply as soon as you cross the bridge. Bring all your own provisions, including fuel or gas stoves. There are pit toilets (no showers) and some tank water (boil before drinking).

🛈 Getting There & Away

Tassielink (☎1300 300 520; www.tassielink. com.au) buses arrive at and depart from the Cockle Creek ranger station. The service runs via Huonville and Geeveston on Monday, Wednesday and Friday in November and March – departing Hobart at 8am. From December to February departures are Monday through Friday. The 3½-hour trip from Hobart costs $73, returning to Hobart on the same days.

Journeys

Walk on the Wild Side »
A Festive Air »
Tasting Tasmania »
Drinking Down South »

Rainforest stream in the Blue Tier (p168)

Walk on the Wild Side

Take to the forests and beaches of Tasmania to discover the wild heart of the island. Bushwalk with just a bivouac and a backpack, or treat yourself Tassie-style and take it easier with a guided walk along one of the planet's most stunning coasts.

The Overland Track

1 Traversing the Cradle Mountain–Lake St Clair National Park, the six-to-eight day Overland Track (p265) is a challenging procession of craggy peaks, tarn shelves, eucalypt forests and ice-cold lakes. All round, a pretty great way to spend a week, we reckon.

Bay of Fires Walk

2 Here's walking in Tasmania with a luxury twist. This four-day/three-night guided encounter (p167) combines the pristine bays and coves of the northeast with ecolodge accommodation, and fine food and wine.

South Coast Track

3 Spend a week negotiating the legendary South Coast Track (p274) through the Southwest National Park from Melaleuca to Cockle Creek, and you'll have completed an iconic once-in-a-lifetime experience covering a pristine 85km.

Tasmanian Wildlife

4 Learn about the excellent work being undertaken to protect the future of the Tasmanian devil (p300). While you're discovering Tassie's wildlife icon, don't overlook the variety of marine life populating the state's cool-water coastline.

Tarkine Wilderness

5 Ancient rainforest, rugged button-grass plains and windy wild beaches combine in the Tarkine (p238), the most diverse wilderness in Tasmania. Come prepared for isolation and capricious weather, and leave with memories of a special and remote habitat.

Clockwise from top left
1. Bushwalking on Overland Track **2.** Bay of Fires Walk
3. Views across Overland Track **4.** Tasmanian devil.

A Festive Air

Tasmania's more obvious attractions to visitors are well-known – astounding natural scenery and wilderness, quirky local wildlife, and a melancholy history that's inextricably linked with the development of Australia. Less well-known are the ongoing opportunities for visitors to get involved and experience a wide range of local festivals and events.

From the celebration of food, wine and a salty maritime heritage, through to eclectic and challenging music and art, Tasmania's festival calendar bubbles along nicely throughout the year. Tasmanians are passionate supporters of whatever is happening, so events are a great opportunity to get the local perspective. Here's our pick of the island's best ways to let your hair down.

ANDREW WATSON/LONELY PLANET IMAGES ©

JOHN SONES/LONELY PLANET IMAGES ©

TOP FESTIVALS

» **Ten Days on the Island** (March; p62) Music, culture and the arts across Tasmania

» **The Taste** (December; p61) Discover why mainland chefs get so excited

» **MONA FOMA** (January; p61) Eclectic and challenging music and arts

» **Festivale** (February; p184) Launceston's chance to shine with food, arts and entertainment

» **Cygnet Folk Festival** (January; p112) Funky, arty music festival with great catering

» **Australian Wooden Boat Festival** (February; p61) Showcasing Hobart's boat-building history

» **Lumina** (April-August; p62) Brightening winter with food, wine and culture

Clockwise from top left
1. & 2. Australian Wooden Boat Festival, Hobart
3. Celebrating Tasmania's food and wine at The Taste festival, Hobart

Tasting Tasmania

Welcome to Australia's finest food destination. Fire up your creativity with cooking classes, or graze at farm gates and visit artisan producers for the finest ingredients. Seek tasty inspiration at food festivals before tying it all together with local seafood.

Cooking Schools

1 Get busy preparing dishes crafted from Tasmania's fine local produce. The Agrarian Kitchen (p81) near Hobart has its own organic farm, while in the north near Hadspen, the Red Feather Inn (p198) combines luxury accommodation with a Slow-Food emphasis.

From the Farmer's Gate

2 Tasmanians are proud of their excellent produce (p291), including organic cheeses, leatherwood honey, and mouthwatering chocolate. Explore the foodie scene with Hobart's Herbaceous Tours (p58).

Fine Dining

3 Esteemed Australian chefs really rate Tasmanian meat, seafood and produce, and local chefs are also getting in on the act at fine-dining establishments across the island. See p291 for the best of the best.

Festival Frenzy

4 When your gourmet scene is as good as Tasmania's, it would be wrong not to occasionally blow your own trumpet. Devour the Hobart action of The Taste (p61) or head to the Taste of the Huon festival (p112).

Tassie's Briny Bounty

5 Tasmania's pristine waters produce some of Australia's finest seafood. For oysters, head to Bruny Island's Get Shucked (p107) and the Freycinet Marine Farm (p151), or dine with Hobart's seagulls at Flippers Fish Punt (p70).

Clockwise from top left

1. A glass of Tasmania's finest red **2.** Oysters at Fish Frenzy (p70), Hobart **3.** Picking fresh raspberries

Drinking Down South

There's simply no excuse to be a thirsty traveller in Tasmania. Peppy, cool-climate wines from around the state dot menus from cosmopolitan cafes to fine-dining establishments. Tasmania's gourmet food scene is also inspiring producers of fine whisky and rather excellent beers.

Small is Good

1 One chilled brew at a time, Tasmania's craft-beer scene (p293) is alive and kicking. Beers range from Moorilla's hip pilsner and hefeweizen to the real ales crafted at the Two Metre Tall brewery.

A Cascade of History

2 Hobart's gothic-looking Cascade Brewery (p52) has been bubbling beer since 1832, including globally acclaimed stouts, ales and lagers. Head to South Hobart (booking advised) to take a tour of the working brewery.

Top Drops in Tassie

3 Go vineyard hopping for cool-climate wines in the Tamar Valley (p191) and the nearby Pipers River region (p197). Book lunch at one of the excellent vineyard restaurants, then fill the car boot with Pinot Noirs, Rieslings and a few bottles of bubbles.

Southern Wine Touring

4 Take a Hobart day trip to the Coal River Valley (p80), including lunch at the scenic Meadowbank Estate. If you're heading further south, say g'day to the friendly winemakers at Bruny Island Premium Wines (p107) and Dover's St Imre Vineyard (p118).

Make Mine a Double

5 Much of Tasmania's midland landscape resembles the rugged Scottish highlands, so a fine whisky scene is no surprise. Start your single malt sojourn at Hobart's Lark Distillery (p50), before further sampling at Bothwell's Nant Distillery (p136) and Hellyers Road Whisky Distillery (p224) in Burnie.

Clockwise from top left
1. Cascade Brewery, South Hobart 2. Freycinet Vineyard (p147), near Bicheno

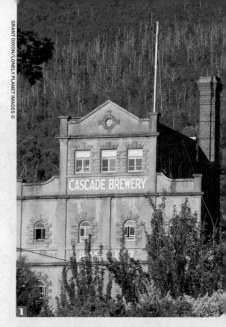

Midlands & Lake Country

Includes »

Midland (Heritage)
Highway.............131
Oatlands 131
Ross 132
Campbell Town......134
Lake Country 136
Bothwell 136
The Lakes 137
Derwent Valley 138
Hamilton 138
Tarraleah...........139

Best Places to Eat

» Companion Bakery (p131)

» Man O'Ross Hotel (p134)

» Red Bridge Café
& Providore (p135)

» Zeps (p135)

» Elm Corner Café (p137)

Best Places to Stay

» Stone Cottage (p133)

» Fox Hunters Return (p135)

» Priory Country Lodge
(p137)

» Over the Back (p139)

» Tarraleah Lodge (p140)

Why Go?

Baked, straw-coloured plains, hawthorn hedgerows, fertile river valleys lined with willows and poplars, roadside mansions: Tasmania's Midlands have a distinct English-countryside feel. Coach stations, garrison towns, stone villages and pastoral properties sprang from the dirt as convict gangs hammered out the road between Hobart and Launceston. But the course of the Midland Hwy (aka the Heritage Hwy) has veered from its original route. Many old towns are now bypassed, so make a few meandering detours to explore their Georgian main streets, rose-filled gardens, antique shops and country pubs.

The underpopulated and undertouristed Lake Country atop Tasmania's Central Plateau features subalpine moorlands and trout-filled lakes. On the southern fringe of the highlands is the fertile Derwent Valley, a fecund fold studded with vineyards, hop fields, orchards and old oast houses. If you consulted a dictionary for the definition of 'sleepy backwater', you'd probably find a concise list of Derwent Valley towns.

When to Go?

The Midlands and Lake Country is definitely at its best from November to March, with warmer and more settled weather. Through the winter months, snow is a relatively common occurrence, especially around the Lake Country. Conversely, if you're keen on the heritage architecture of Ross and Oatlands, consider travelling outside of the peak November-to-March period. Accommodation owners offer substantial discounts, and a good glass of local single malt whisky might be just the ticket in a cosy B&B on a cool night.

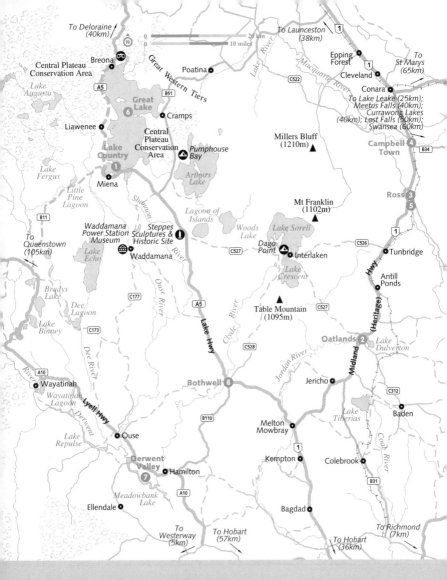

Midlands & Lake Country Highlights

1 Arcing a fly across a highland stream and snaring a trout in the **Lake Country** (p136)

2 Ascending the multiple levels of Oatlands' fascinating **Callington Mill** (p131)

3 Trying to find the carving of Jorgen Jorgenson, former king of Iceland, on the **Ross Bridge** (p132)

4 Reading the heinous convict histories in the red bricks along the main street of **Campbell Town** (p134)

5 Questioning your moral direction at the **Four Corners of Ross** (p133)

6 Watching the mist descend on **Great Lake** (p137) in winter

7 Touring through the hop fields, hedgerows and hamlets of the **Derwent Valley** (p138)

8 Attempting to make par on the heritage **Ratho** golf course (p136)

MIDLAND (HERITAGE) HWY

History

Hobart was founded in 1804 and Launceston in 1805. By 1807, the need for a land link between the two settlements prompted surveyor Charles Grimes to map an appropriate route. The road was constructed by convict gangs, and by 1821 was suitable for horses and carriages. Two years later a mail cart operated between the two towns, which became the first coach service (it sometimes carried passengers). The main towns on this road were established in the 1820s as garrisons for prisoners and guards, protecting travellers from the menace of bushrangers.

❶ Getting Around

Redline Coaches (☑1300 360 000; www.tasredline.com.au) powers along the Midland Hwy two to four times daily; you can jump off at any of the main towns – Kempton, Oatlands, Ross or Campbell Town – except on express services. The Hobart to Launceston one-way fare is $38.80 (about 2½ hours). For info on individual towns, see the relevant Getting There & Away sections.

Oatlands

POP 550

Oatlands contains Australia's largest collection of Georgian architecture. On the stately main street alone (which feels like a film set) there are 87 historic buildings, many of which are now galleries and craft shops.

The town's site was chosen in 1821 as one of four military posts on the Hobart–George Town route, but it was slow to develop. In 1832 an optimistic town surveyor marked out 50 miles (80km) of streets on the assumption Oatlands would become the Midlands capital. Many folks made the town home in the 1830s, erecting solid buildings with the help of former convicts and soldiers who were skilled carpenters and stonemasons.

◉ Sights & Activities

TOP CHOICE **Callington Mill**   LANDMARK
(Mill Lane; www.callingtonmill.org; adult/child/family $10/6/20; ⊘guided tours hourly 10am-4pm) Visible throughout the town, the Callington Mill was built in 1837 and ground flour until 1891. After years of neglect it's been fully restored and was reopened in 2010. It's a fascinating piece of engineering, all fully explained on guided tours leaving on the hour from the adjacent visitor

information centre. The mill is also back to producing high-grade, organic flour, an essential component of the baked goodies across the road at the Companion Bakery.

FREE **History Room**   MUSEUM
(⊘9am-5pm) At the northern end of town is an old garage full of photos, relics and old knick-knacks. While you're here, pick up the free handouts *Welcome to Historic Oatlands,* which includes self-guided tour directions, and *Lake Dulverton Walkway Guide,* for explorations around the lake. It's volunteer-run so hours may vary.

🛏 Sleeping

There's free camping (three-night maximum) for caravans and campervans in the picnic area beside Lake Dulverton, at the northern end of the Esplanade. There are toilets and barbecues here.

Oatlands Lodge   B&B $$
(☑6254 1444; oatlandslodge@bigpond.com; 92 High St; s/d incl breakfast $90/120) Warm and inviting in two-storey, hen-pecked sandstone splendour, Oatlands Lodge is the cream of the town's accommodation. Rates include a huge breakfast spread and lots of conversation with the friendly owners.

Blossom's Cottage   B&B $$
(☑6254 1516; www.blossomscottageoatlands.com.au; 116 High St; d incl breakfast $110) In a self-contained garden studio, Blossom's is bright and cheerful, with a cast-iron bed, blackwood timber floors, leadlight windows and a small kitchenette. Great value.

Waverley Cottages   RENTAL HOUSE $$
(☑6254 1264, 0408 125 049; www.waverleycottages.com; d $180, extra person $25) This is a fully equipped, thoroughly colonial collection of cottages: Amelia Cottage (104 High St), opposite the Midlands Hotel; Forget-me-not Cottage (17 Dulverton St), directly behind Amelia; and Waverley Cottage and Waverley Croft, both 7km west of town.

🍴 Eating

TOP CHOICE **Companion Bakery**   BAKERY $
(106 High St; www.companionbakery.com.au; snacks & light meals $6-15; ⊘9am-5pm Wed-Sun) Woodfired. Organic. Seriously good coffee. What's not to like about the Companion Bakery? As well as quite probably Tasmania's best sourdough sandwiches, other sustenance, for before or after exploring Oatlands' heritage

vibe, includes Moroccan lamb rolls, superlative pastries and quiche.

Kentish Hotel
PUB $$

(60 High St; mains $16-25; ⊘lunch & dinner) Our pick for evening dining in Oatlands. Favourites include steak, fish and chips, seafood crepes, smoked-salmon salad and daily specials. There are usually a few sly locals sipping frothies at the bar from opening time, and the **bakery** (baked goods $3-8; ⊘breakfast & lunch) next door sells pies, pasties, rolls, pizza and coffee.

Cassaveen
CAFE $

(44 High St; light meals $10-15; ⊘9am-5pm Mon-Fri, 10am-4pm Sat & Sun) Part of the Cassaveen knitwear centre at the southern end of town, this sunny garden cafe has *panini*, baguettes and gourmet pies. There are regular soup and salad specials, and a twice-weekly 'High Tea' ($20) on Sunday and Wednesday from 1pm to 4pm.

Stables
CAFE $

(High St; light meals $10-14; ⊘breakfast & lunch) This low-key cafe offers hearty and good-value dishes, including eggs Benedict and a fine beef burger to set you up for the next part of your journey. Despite the surrounding English-style ambience, a fine selection of stubby holders reminds you that you're definitely in Australia.

❶ Information
BP Service Station (52 High St; ⊘8am-8pm) Multicard ATM.

Oatlands visitor centre (☑6254 1212; www. southernmidlands.tas.gov.au; Mill Lane; ⊘9am-5pm) Proffers general info, handles accommodation bookings and runs regular guided tours of the town's attractions (adult/child from $8/5). Recently relocated to a spot near Callington Mill.

❶ Getting There & Away
Redline Coaches (☑1300 360 000; www.tasredline.com.au) Buses to Hobart ($20.30, 1¼ hours) and Launceston ($23.10, 1¼ hours) arrive at and depart from Oatlands Roadhouse at 47 High St.

Ross
POP 300

Another tidy (nay, immaculate) Midlands town is Ross, 120km north of Hobart. Established in 1812 to protect Hobart–Launceston travellers from bushrangers, Ross became an important coach-staging post at the centre of Tasmania's burgeoning wool industry, and, before the famous Ross Bridge was built in 1836, a fording point across the Macquarie River.

These days Ross' elm-lined streets are awash in colonial charm and history, but strict rules on development restrain the possibility of overcommercialisation. Soak up the ambience on two feet or two wheels and assess the heritage architecture. Check out the craft and antiques stores, and scoff down a Devonshire tea at one of the town's cafes. Lots of accommodation options keeps things competitive, especially in the good-value shoulder seasons outside of summer.

◎ Sights
Ross Bridge LANDMARK
TOP CHOICE The oft-photographed 1836 Ross Bridge is the third-oldest bridge in Australia.

WORTH A TRIP

DETOUR: KEMPTON

Pipsqueak Kempton, about 50km north of Hobart, was founded in 1838, making it one of the state's earliest settlements. Originally known as Green Ponds, it's notable for its antiques stores and breezy bucolic surrounds, and as the one-time residence of notorious rabble-rouser Anthony Fenn Kemp.

Kemp was a charismatic character: one-half egotistical bankrupt with scant moral fibre, one-half progressive patriot who was critical in Tasmania's evolution from convict dump to independent colony. Fleeing debts in England, he became a dedicated pastoralist, merchant and political sabre-rattler. Never far from controversy, he made as many friends as enemies, and left behind more than a dozen children – a fact that has seen him dubbed the 'Father of Tasmania'. For a critical (and comical) look at Kemp's exploits, read Nicholas Shakespeare's excellent *In Tasmania*.

In Kempton, the hospitable **Wilmot Arms Inn** (☑6259 1272; www.wilmotarms.com.au; 120 Main Rd; d incl breakfast $140) is a former coaching inn with authentically aged B&B rooms and a flower-filled garden.

Its graceful arches were designed by colonial architect John Lee Archer, and it was built by two convict stonemasons, Colbeck and Herbert, who were granted pardons for their efforts. Herbert chiselled out the 186 intricate carvings decorating the arches, which include Celtic symbols, animals and the faces of notable people (including Governor Arthur and Anglo-Danish convict Jorgen Jorgenson, the farcical ex-king of Iceland). At night the bridge is lit up, and the carvings shimmer with spooky shadows.

FREE **Ross Female Factory** HISTORIC BUILDING
(⊙9am-5pm) Off Bond St, this was one of Tasmania's two female convict prisons (the other was in Hobart). Only one building remains, but archaeological excavations among the sunburnt grass are under way, and descriptive signs and stories provide insight into these women's lives. Pick up a copy of the *Ross Female Factory* brochure from the visitor centre, then walk along the track near the Uniting Church at the top of Church St to get here. Nearby is the wind-blown **Old Ross Burial Ground**, with headstones carved by the same stonemasons who worked on the bridge.

Four Corners of Ross LANDMARK
The crossroads in the middle of town is the Four Corners of Ross, potentially leading your soul in one of four directions: temptation (represented by the Man O'Ross Hotel), salvation (the Catholic church), recreation (the town hall) or damnation (the old jail).

Tasmanian Wool Centre MUSEUM
(www.taswoolcentre.com.au; Church St; admission by donation; ⊙9am-5pm) This centre houses a wool exhibition, museum and craft shop. The museum focuses on convict times and the Australian wool industry; there are hands-on bales of wool and a woolly audiovisual display.

Other notable historic edifices include the 1832 **Scotch Thistle Inn** (Church St), now a private residence; the 1830 **Barracks** (Bridge St), restored by the National Trust and also a private residence; the **Uniting Church** (Church St), dating from 1885; **St John's Anglican Church** at the corner of Church and Badajos Sts, constructed in 1868; and the **Post Office** (26 Church St), opened in 1896 and still operating.

🛏 Sleeping

Stone Cottage RENTAL HOUSE **$**
(☑6381 5444; skummreow@hotmail.com; Church St; d $90, extra adult/child $20/10) One of the town's best options for families, with a truckload of kids' toys and DVDs and an expansive garden with well-established fruit trees. The country kitchen with a long wooden table is just perfect for lazy lunches and dinners. Stone Cottage sleeps up to seven.

Country Style Cabin RENTAL HOUSE **$**
(☑6381 5453; www.rossaccommodationcabin.com.au; 13-17 Bridge St; d incl breakfast $99) At last, a modern alternative to the heritage styling of most accommodation options in Ross. Enjoying a rural outlook with Bluey the miniature horse as a neighbour, this cosy wood-lined cottage has a modern bathroom and an open-plan lounge with a flat-screen TV and loads of magazines. Check in at the T-Spot Café & Teahouse.

Ross Motel MOTEL **$$**
(☑6381 5224; www.rossmotel.com.au; 2 High St; d/f incl breakfast from $135/160; 🐾) The independently owned Ross Motel offers spick-and-span Georgian-style cottage units, each with microwave, fridge, TV and DVD player (prices include breakfast provisions). Family units sleep four.

Ross B&B B&B **$$**
(☑6381 5354; www.rossaccommodation.com.au; 12 Church St; d $130-145) Choose from two en-suite rooms in a 1927 abode, or a two-bedroom retreat in a separate wing, among plenty of peachy colours and a garden setting with warbling birds. This organisation also manages five carefully restored, self-contained **cottages** (d $145-180; 🐾) dotted around Ross. See the website for full details.

Ross Bakery Inn B&B **$$**
(☑6381 5246; www.rossbakery.com.au; 15 Church St; s/d incl breakfast $80/150; 🐾) Wake up to breakfast fresh from a 100-year-old wood-fired oven when you stay in this 1830s coaching house, adjacent to the Ross Village Bakery. Small, cosy rooms are enhanced by a guest lounge with an open fire and complimentary bakery treats.

Ross Caravan Park CAMPGROUND **$**
(☑6381 5224; www.rossmotel.com.au; Bridge St; unpowered/powered sites $20/26, cabins s/d $50/60; 🐾) An appealing patch of green near Ross Bridge on the banks of the fish-filled Macquarie River. Utilitarian, barracks-style cabins sleep two to four people, have cook-

ing facilities and offer the cheapest accommodation in town. Bathrooms are shared, and you'll need your own linen. Reception is at the Ross Motel.

Eating & Drinking

Man O'Ross Hotel   PUB FARE **$$**
(35 Church St; mains $15-20; ⊙lunch & dinner; 🛜) Dinner options in Ross are thin on the ground, but the town's heritage pub offers a surprisingly diverse menu, including goodies like Tasmanian salt-crusted lamb and robust Indian curries. Definitely a cut above most pub meals in Tasmania.

Ross General Store, Bakery & Tearooms   CAFE **$**
(31 Church St; light meals $4-10; ⊙breakfast & lunch) This jack-of-all-trades store has an olden-days vibe, an open fire and a fuss-free menu of breakfast, soups, homemade cakes and sandwiches. The scallop pies are among Tassie's best.

Ross Village Bakery   BAKERY **$**
(15 Church St; items $8-14; ⊙breakfast & lunch; 🛜) Overdose on savoury carbs, including wood-fired pizzas and pies, and more virtuous soups and salads of all denominations. Coffee and cake is another good reason to linger awhile.

T Spot Café & Teahouse   CAFE **$**
(13-17 Bridge St; snacks $4-8; ⊙breakfast & lunch) Yummy cakes – including gluten-free options – and over 50 teas are reasons aplenty to stop here. The friendly owners, recent arrivals from the Hunter Valley, also hire bikes and operate the nearby Country Style Cabin accommodation.

❶ Information

Most accommodation offers wi-fi. If you're not staying the night, there's **WI-FI** access at the Man O'Ross Hotel and the Ross Village Bakery.

There are no ATMs or banking facilities in town.

Ross visitor centre (☑6381 5466; www.visitross.com.au; Church St; ⊙9am-5pm) Inside the Tasmanian Wool Centre. If you've got a group of eight or more, the centre runs guided **town tours** (adult/child $6/4). Bookings essential.

❶ Getting There & Around

BUS Redline Coaches (☑1300 360 000; www.tasredline.com.au) depart from Ross Newsagency at 38 Church St for Hobart ($28.70, 1½ hours) and Launceston ($13.20, one hour).

BICYCLE Hire bikes at the T Spot Café & Teahouse (single/tandem per hour $10/20); they're a great way to explore the town's sleepy streets.

Campbell Town

POP 900

Campbell Town, 12km north of Ross, is another former garrison settlement. Unlike in Oatlands and Ross, the Midlands Hwy still trucks right on through town. The local catch cry 'Campbell Town is reaching out to you!' overstates things just a little – the vibe here is more introspective and agrarian – but the town does make a handy stop between Hobart and Launceston (or between Cradle Mountain and the east coast). Along the main drag are a couple of hotels, a supermarket, a pharmacy, a bank, a post office and general shops.

The first white settlers here were Irish timber workers who spoke Gaelic and had a particularly debauched reputation. Today, Campbell Town is ground zero for Tassie's cattle- and sheep-farming industries. In late May or early June every year, the showgrounds behind the high school host the annual **Campbell Town Show** (www.campbelltownshow.com.au), aka the Midlands Agricultural Show. Running strong since 1839, it's the oldest show in Australia.

◉ Sights & Activities

FREE **Heritage Highway Museum**   MUSEUM
(☑6381 1353; 103 High St; ⊙10am-3pm Mon-Fri) The curio-strewn museum features histories of figures like John Batman and Martin Cash (a local bushranger), and artefacts like a 1930s film projector, old toys, coins and books. The museum is volunteer-run and has unpredictable opening hours, including on occasional weekends.

Red Bridge   LANDMARK
The bridge across the Elizabeth River here was completed in 1838, making it almost as venerable as the Ross Bridge. Locals call it the Red Bridge because it was convict-built from more than 1.5 million red bricks baked on site. There's a comprehensive booklet on the bridge available at the visitor centre.

Campbell Town also has a crop of buildings in the over-100-year-old category, mostly along High and Bridge Sts. Highlights include the 1835 **St Luke's Church of England** (High St); the 1840 **Campbell Town Inn** (100 High St); the 1834 **Fox Hunters Re-**

DETOUR: LAKE LEAKE

The secondary B34 road from Campbell Town heads east through the excellent fishing and bushwalking area around Lake Leake (33km from Campbell Town) to Swansea (69km) on the east coast. Redline buses ply this route once a day from Monday to Friday and can drop you at the Lake Leake turn-off, 4km from the lake.

The shimmering surface of Lake Leake itself is punctuated by ghostly tree stumps, and is encircled by holiday shacks. For passers-by there's a **camping area** (unpowered/powered sites $5/8) and a rough-and-tumble, shingle-covered pub, the **Lake Leake Hotel** (☑6381 1329; www.lakeleakechalet.com.au; 340 Lake Leake Rd; s/d $40/75). The hotel offers lunch and dinner daily (mains $16 to $20) and basic accommodation.

Explore further east to the **Meetus Falls** and **Lost Falls** forest reserves. Meetus Falls is the pick of the two: it's 10km from the signposted turn-off and has a sheltered picnic area, barbecues and toilets.

If you're into trout fishing, **Currawong Lakes** (☑6381 1148; www.troutfishtasmania.com.au; 1204 Long Marsh Rd, Lake Leake; d $185) is the place for you. It's a private trout fishery 12km west of the Lake Leake turn-off along an unsealed road. The property is home to trout-filled lakes, a handful of good-quality self-contained cabins, and plenty of peace and quiet. Fly fishers can fish for a full day for $150, with no licence required. Equipment hire (rod, waders, flies) costs $5.

turn (132 High St); **The Grange** (High St), an impossible-to-miss 1847 mansion, now a conference centre; and the 1878 **Old School** (Hamilton St), in the current school's grounds. Be sure to look down as you wander along High St. Rows of **red bricks** set into the footpath detail the crimes, sentences and arrival dates of convicts like Ephram Brain and English Corney, sent to Van Diemen's Land for crimes as various as stealing potatoes, bigamy and murder.

🛏 Sleeping & Eating

Fox Hunters Return   B&B $$
(☑6381 1602; www.foxhunters.com.au; 132 High St; d $139-159) On the left as you enter town from Hobart is this pukka establishment, built with convict labour in 1833 as a coaching inn and now offering spacious rooms, each with private bathroom and sitting area. The self-contained stand-alone 'Stables' cottage sleeps up four ($259). The cellar under the main building housed convicts during the construction of the neighbouring Red Bridge. At the time of writing it was being converted into a bookshop – the 'Book Cellar' – specialising in heritage tomes. It's open Thursday to Sunday or by prior arrangement.

St Andrews Inn   B&B $$
(☑6391 5525; Midland Hwy, Cleveland; s/d incl breakfast $90/140) Convict-built in 1845, this National Trust–classified roadside coaching inn is 16km north of Campbell Town at Cleveland. Upstairs are two large en-suite B&B

rooms (with TV and complimentary port); downstairs is a bubbly little cafe (meals $9 to $16) open for breakfast and lunch Tuesday to Sunday and for dinner by arrangement.

Red Bridge Café & Providore   ⌂TOP CHOICE   CAFE $
(137 High St; www.redbridgecafe.com.au; light meals $10-15; ⊙breakfast & lunch; 🕸) At the southern end of town near the eponymous Red Bridge, a couple of urban refugees from the mainland have transformed a former brewery into a funky space incorporating a huge dining room with shared wooden tables and a providore packed with the best of Tasmanian food, wine and beer. Shared platters ($15 to $45) and gourmet pies make this an essential stop either north or south. Wi-fi is available for customers.

Zeps   CAFE $$
(☑6381 1344; 92 High St; mains $10-25; ⊙breakfast, lunch & dinner; @) A top refuelling spot is the hyperactive Zeps, serving brekky, *panini*, pasta, fat pies and good coffee throughout the day, plus pizza and more substantial mains in the evening. It's a handy evening destination if you're staying in Ross and have already eaten at the Man O'Ross pub.

ⓘ Information

Campbell Town visitor centre (☑6381 1353; www.campbelltowntasmania.com; 103 High St; ⊙10am-3pm Mon-Fri, occasional weekends; @) Pick up a free brochure here detailing a self-guided Campbell Town tour. The centre is beside the post office in the old courthouse, a 1905 building still used occasionally for judicial proceedings. Also here is the Heritage Highway Museum. The centre is volunteer-run so hours may vary.

❶ Getting There & Away

Redline Coaches (☑1300 360 000; www. tasredline.com.au) Buses to Campbell Town chug up to the milk bar at 107 High St, next to the police station, and head to Hobart ($28.70, 1¾ hours) and Launceston ($13.20, one hour).

LAKE COUNTRY

The people-free Lake Country on Tasmania's Central Plateau is spiked with steep mountains and perforated with glacial lakes, waterfalls, abundant wildlife and unusual flora, including the ancient pencil pine. The plateau's northwestern sector, roughly one-third of its total area, is part of the Tasmanian Wilderness World Heritage Area. The region is also known for its world-class trout fishing and for its socially divisive hydroelectric schemes, which have seen the damming of rivers, the creation of artificial lakes, the building of power stations (both above and below ground), and the construction of massive pipelines arcing over rough terrain like giant metal worms. If you want to see the developments firsthand, check out the active Tungatinah, Tarraleah and Liapootah power stations on the extensive Derwent scheme between Queenstown and Hobart.

On the western edge of the Central Plateau is the Walls of Jerusalem National Park, a perennial fave of mountaineers, bushwalkers and cross-country skiers. Experienced bushwalkers can walk across the Central Plateau into 'The Walls', and also into Cradle Mountain–Lake St Clair National Park.

Bothwell

POP 340

Encircling a village green, Bothwell is a low-key historic town 74km north of Hobart in the Clyde River valley. Bothwell is best known for its proximity to Trout Heaven, but the town also lays claim to Australia's oldest golf course, known as Ratho.

◉ Sights

Nant Distillery   DISTILLERY

(☑6259 5790; www.nantdistillery.com.au; Clyde River, Bothwell; tastings & tours $30; ◷9am-5pm) The final component of Bothwell's mini-Scotland ambience is this distillery, where a quite superb single malt whisky is crafted in an 1820s flour mill. The modern art and cutting-edge architecture of Nant's tasting room contrasts beautifully with older structures, including the estate's original convict-built homestead. Bookings for tours are essential. If you're a big single malt aficionado, sign up for Nant's masterclass ($65), which includes four different single malts matched with Tasmanian cheeses. Nant Distillery also offers luxury accommodation in the adjacent **Nant Highland Lodge** (d incl all meals from $240).

Ratho   GOLF COURSE

(☑0409-595 702; www.rathogolf.com; Highland Lakes Rd; greens fees $15, club hire $18; ◷8am-dusk) This course was rolled out of the dust in 1822 by the Scottish settlers who built Bothwell. Have a chat to course professional Ross Baker, who also crafts handmade clubs perfect for negotiating Ratho's heritage links.

Australasian Golf Museum   MUSEUM

(www.ausgolfmuseum.com; Market Pl; adult/child $4/2; ◷10am-4pm Sep-May, 11am-3pm Jun-Aug) In the same building as the visitor centre, this museum celebrates golf achievements Down Under. There's a miniature putting green where you can try out old-style clubs, and a stupendous selection of collectable golf-themed Jim Beam bourbon decanters (sadly, empty).

Thorpe Farm   FARM

(☑6259 5678) Bothwell is also home to Thorpe Farm, which produces sensational goat's-milk cheese under the label Tasmanian Highland Cheese (often available at the visitor centre, the Fat Doe Bakery and select Hobart delicatessens). The farm also makes wasabi and stone-ground flour. Visits are by appointment; also call ahead for directions.

Standout National Trust–acknowledged buildings in Bothwell include an old **Bootmaker's Shop** (High St, ◷ by appointment), the 1820s **Thorpe Mill** (Dennistoun Rd), the **Castle Hotel** (14 Patrick St), first licensed in 1821, and the endearing 1831 **St Luke's Church** (Dennistoun Rd).

🛏 Sleeping & Eating

TOP CHOICE 🛏 **Elm Corner** RENTAL HOUSE **$$**
(☑6259 4028; www.elm-corner.webs.com;
20 Alexander St; d incl breakfast $120) Cosy as
can be, Elm Corner is a restored brick-lined
1830s cottage surrounded by gardens and
occasionally clucking hens. It's adjacent to
the rather excellent **Elm Corner Café** (light
meals $6-13; ⊙breakfast & lunch daily, dinner Fri;
🛜), where two energetic foodies are hard at
work making their Tassie dream come true.
Interesting meals include Spanish baked
eggs with chorizo and pesto, and additional
reasons to linger include great coffee, free
wi-fi, and a terrific vintage shop with poi-
gnant reminders from most people's child-
hoods. On Friday night there's beer and wine
along with regular themed dinners, from
Pakistani to pizza.

Priory Country Lodge BOUTIQUE HOTEL **$$$**
(☑6259 4012; www.thepriorycountrylodge.com.au;
2 Wentworth St; d incl breakfast $400-500; 🛜) A
sister property to the Islington in Hobart,
the Priory fills an 1848 Tudor mansion with
four luxurious rooms and elegant shared
spaces including an antiques-filled library.
Despite the heritage touches, the luxury is
dialled up to 21st-century levels, with spark
ling marble bathrooms and king-size beds.
Golf, whisky tasting and clay pigeon shooting
can all be arranged.

Bothwell Grange B&B **$$**
(☑6259 5556; 15 Alexander St; s/d incl breakfast
$95/105) A highway hotel built in 1836, the
once-grandiose Grange has a snug Geor-
gian atmosphere and comfortable B&B ac-
commodation. There are six rooms, all with
bathrooms, antique beds and timber ceil-
ings. Evening meals are by arrangement.
Mind your head – the doorways were built
for diminutive 19th-century bumpkins.
Caution: must like teddy bears.

ℹ Information

Bothwell visitor centre (☑6259 4033; www.
bothwell.com.au; Market Pl; ⊙10am-4pm
Sep-May, 11am-3pm Jun-Aug) Pick up the free
leaflet *Let's Browse in Bothwell* and check out
the wee map, marked with locations of historic
buildings.

ℹ Getting There & Away

Metro Tasmania (☑132 201; www.metrotas.
com.au) Runs bus 140 from Hobart to Bothwell
(one way adult/child $12/6, 1½ hours, 4pm
weekdays) from stop F on Elizabeth St.

The Lakes

Levelling out at 1050m above sea level on
the Central Plateau, **Great Lake** is the larg-
est natural freshwater lake in Australia. The
first European to dip his toe here was John
Beaumont in 1817; his servant circumnavi-
gated the lake in three days. In 1870 brown
trout were released into the lake and it
soon became a fishing fantasia. Rainbow
trout were added in 1910 and also thrived.
Attempts were made to introduce salmon,
but this recalcitrant species refused to mul-
tiply. Trout have now penetrated most of the
streams across the plateau. Some of the best
fishing is in the smaller streams and lakes
west of Great Lake.

In the seminal days of hydroelectric am-
bition, a small Great Lake dam was con-
structed to raise water levels near Miena.
Great Lake is linked to nearby Arthurs Lake
by canals, and a pumping station supplies
water to the Poatina power station on its
northeastern shore.

☆ Activities

There's brilliant **fishing** right across the
Central Plateau, with good access to most
of the larger lakes. Great Lake, Lake Sorell,
Arthurs Lake and Little Pine Lagoon are all
popular haunts. The plateau itself actually
contains thousands of lakes; many are tiny,
but most still contain trout. Note that the
region is prone to snowfalls during winter.

A long list of regulations apply to fish-
ing in the area, aimed at ensuring fish con-
tinue to breed and stocks aren't depleted.
On some parts of Great Lake, for instance,
you can use only artificial lures, and you're
not allowed to fish in streams flowing into
the lake. On the Central Plateau, some wa-
ters are reserved for fly fishing. Bag, size
and seasonal limits apply to all areas. The
Inland Fisheries Service (www.ifs.tas.gov.au)
website offers priceless advice. See p30 for
more fishy business.

🛏 Sleeping & Eating

Great Lake Hotel HOTEL **$$**
(☑6259 8163; www.greatlakehotel.com.au; Swan
Bay, Miena; dm $20-45, d/f from $105/150, mains
$14-30) From Miena, take the turn-off to
Bronte Park and you'll soon come across this
small-town pub, offering accommodation
from bog-basic anglers' cabins with shared
facilities to self-contained motel-style units.
The meat-based meals in the bar (open

SHOUT ABOUT TROUT

Catching a trout in Tasmania should be as easy as getting your feet wet – most of the state's rivers and lakes have been stocked with brown and rainbow species – but you still need to be in the right place at the right time. There are also restrictions on the types of tackle permitted in various areas in different seasons.

Live bait (impaling a grasshopper, grub or worm on a hook) is tried and true, but bait fishing is banned in most inland Tasmanian waters – it's too effective to give the fish a sporting chance! Artificial lures are more acceptable, coming in myriad shapes, sizes, weights and colours. Depending on the season, a 'Cobra' wobbler or Devon-type 'spinner' might work for you in lakes, while your preferred stream lure might be a 'Celta'. Other winners include claret dabblers, brown bead-head buggers and yum-yum emergers.

The most artful form of trout fishing is of course fly fishing, which often involves wading through rivers and lakes in the early morning. Fly fiends tie their own flies, but a huge variety is available in fishing shops. In Hobart try Spot On Fishing Tackle (p75). Many areas in Tasmania are dedicated fly-fishing reserves.

When fishing in the Lake Country, prepare for Tasmania's riotously changeable weather: bring warm, waterproof clothing, even in summer. Engaging a professional guide for lessons or a guided trip is a stellar idea: try **Fish-Wild Tasmania** (www.fishwildtasmania.com), **Rod & Fly Tasmania** (www.rodandfly.com.au) or **Trout Guides & Lodges Tasmania** (www.troutguidestasmania.com.au).

lunch and dinner) will reduce vegetarians to tears. 'Go bush or go home!' is their motto, and we can only agree.

Central Highlands Lodge HOTEL $$
(☑6259 8179; www.centralhighlandslodge.com.au; Haddens Bay, Miena; d $125-165, mains $19-25) On the southern outskirts of Miena, this jaunty, rough-sawn timber lodge offers clean, comfortable cabins. The lodge restaurant (☺lunch and dinner) is a great place to rejuvenate with a cold beer and a hot meal – venison hot pot, trout, salmon and quail all have that authentic tinge of the adjacent wilderness.

Campers can try the basic camping ground at Dago Point (camping per adult/child $4/2), beside Lake Sorell. A better bet for families is the camping ground on Arthurs Lake at Pumphouse Bay (camping per adult/child $4/2), which has better facilities, including hot showers. Campers self-register at both sites, and fee payments rely on an honour system. Bring all your supplies. It's recommended that you boil tap water.

❶ Information

For lake and bushwalking info, try the sporadically staffed **Parks & Wildlife Service Ranger Station** (☑6259 8148; www.parks.tas.gov.au) at Liawenee, 10km north of Miena on the western side of Great Lake.

Public transport services to the area are nonexistent.

DERWENT VALLEY

Lake St Clair is the head of the Derwent River, which flows southeast towards Hobart through the fertile Derwent Valley. (New Norfolk, the valley's lynchpin town, is covered in the Hobart & Around chapter, see p44.) The Lyell Hwy largely mimics the flow of the Derwent River to the Central Plateau, continuing past Derwent Bridge west to Queenstown.

Hamilton

POP 150

National Trust–classified Hamilton was planned with great expectations, but it never evolved beyond a small, soporific village. Historic sandstone buildings adorn the main street, with photo-worthy views of mountain ranges and peaks to the west. The Lyell Hwy rolls through town and is called Franklin Pl along this short stretch.

Hamilton was settled in 1808, when New Norfolk was established, and was a mid-19th-century boomtown. By 1835 it had 800 residents, well watered by 11 hotels and two breweries. Grids of streets were surveyed, but the dry local soils defeated many farmers. The town stagnated, and several buildings were eventually removed. Quite recently there's been a lonesome sense of abandon to the place, but the local pub has now reopened to bring some low-key energy back to Hamilton's streets.

Hamilton's history is documented in the **Hamilton Heritage Centre** (Cumberland St; adult/child $1/50c; ◷9am-5pm), set up in an 1840 Warder's Cottage. It is a DIY arrangement: keys are available from the adjacent council chambers.

Take a fascinating tour of the locally owned, 300-hectare working **Curringa Farm** (www.curringafarm.com; 5831 Lyell Hwy; 45min tours per person $55; ◷Sep-Apr), 3km west of Hamilton. The owners aim to strike a balance between business and sustainability, an approach applied to the 3000 sheep, poppies, oats and cabbage seed farmed here.

🛏 Sleeping

TOP CHOICE **Over the Back**   RENTAL HOUSE **$$**
(☑6286 3333; www.curringafarm.com. au; 5831 Lyell Hwy; d $195) You feel a long way from anywhere at Over the Back, but that's the appeal. About 3km west of Hamilton, three different and equally secluded accommodation options are dotted around a 300-hectare farm. Choose from the romantic one-bedroom Seaglenest Studio, or the larger two-bedroom Wedgetail Wings or Over the Back cottages. The owners are active in preserving local ecosystems, and run tours of their property, Curringa Farm.

Cherry Villa   B&B **$$**
(☑6286 3418; 38 Arthur St; d incl breakfast $120, extra person $40) The 1834 Cherry Villa offers two attractive rooms amid buzzy-bee rose gardens. Straight out of an architectural textbook, it's a classically symmetrical Georgian house, with twin dormer windows and chimneys. Dinners by arrangement.

Olde School House   B&B **$$**
(☑6286 3292; www.hamiltonschoolhouse.com; 39 Franklin Pl; d $150, extra adult/child $50/30, breakfast $7.50-15; 🐾) Pay attention, class! This educational edifice was built in 1856 and served as the school until 1935. The library now operates as a traditional bed and breakfast, while adjacent Rose Cottage is a two-bedroom self-contained option sleeping up to five – a good choice for families.

🍴 Eating & Drinking

Jackson's Emporium   CAFE **$**
(☑6286 3232; www.jacksonsemporium.com.au; 13 Franklin Pl; mains $10-24; ◷breakfast, lunch & dinner; 🍴) Ramshackle Jackson's (an emporium since the 1850s) cleverly caters to visitors staying in Hamilton's self-contained

accommodation, proffering a range of chef-prepared frozen meals (spaghetti Bolognese, beef stroganoff, Thai chicken), desserts, wine and beer. Internet access is also available, along with a collection of furniture and crafts conjured up from Huon pine. The entrepreneurial owners also keep busy by offering massage treatments ($30 to $50). Ask about their three heritage-accommodation options – McCauley's, Kelleher's and Arcadia (doubles $90 to $205). Accommodation can be booked either on a per-room basis, or for entire properties.

Hamilton Inn   PUB **$$**
(☑6286 3204; www.hamiltoninn.com.au; 10 Tarleton St; mains $18-30; ◷lunch & dinner; 🐾) Built by convicts way back in 1826, the Hamilton Inn dishes up the best restaurant food around these parts, followed by the opportunity to kip down in restored heritage rooms (doubles from $90) upstairs. At the very least, stop by for a cold and foaming Cascade brew at the sunny table out the front. There's wi-fi available for laptop luggers.

Hamilton Café & Bakehouse   CAFE **$**
(32 Franklin Pl; mains $10-15; ◷breakfast & lunch) More proof you're never far from superb gourmet pies and other tasty baked goodies anywhere in Tasmania.

❶ Getting There & Away

Tassielink (☑1300 300 520; www.tassielink. com.au) departs Hobart for Strahan via Hamilton ($14.10, 1¼ hours), Tarraleah and Lake St Clair at 10.15 Tuesday and Thursday, 4pm Friday and 9.15am Sunday. Buses stop at Hamilton Newsagency.

Tarraleah

POP 10

Halfway between Hobart and Queenstown, **Tarraleah** (☑6289 3222; www.tarraleah.com) is a surreal place. It was built in the 1920s and '30s as a residential village for hydroelectric workers, and at its peak it had a population of hundreds, complete with police station, town hall, shops, church, golf course and 100 houses. Once the hydro work dried up, the village declined and the population plummeted. Hydro sold off most of the houses for removal in the 1990s, and then put the remainder of the village up for sale.

In 2002, Tarraleah (pronounced 'Tarra-lee-uh') was purchased by a family from Queensland ('The Family that Bought a Town', as the tabloids tagged them). They poured buckets of cash into the place but recently sold the whole shebang to private interests who've spent further millions. Comfortable accommodation provides a backdrop to a variety of wilderness activities. It still feels like a ghost town if you visit outside peak season, but there's a full range of accommodation here (bookings via www. tarraleah.com), including **camp sites** (sites $15-26), rooms in the **Scholars House** (d from $130), self-contained one- to three-bedroom **cottages** (d from $190) and ritzy rooms in the luxury art-deco **Tarraleah Lodge** (☑6289 1199; www.tarraleahlodge.com; Wild River Rd; d incl all meals from $1000).

On the food front there's a pub called the **Highlander Arms** (mains $22-30; ☺dinner), the casual **Teez Café** (light meals $7-18; ☺breakfast & lunch), and **Wildside Restaurant** (4-course degustation menus $100; ☺dinner) in Tarraleah Lodge (bookings essential). Whisky buffs will love diving into the Lodge's stellar selection of more than 100 single malts.

Activities include mountain biking, bushwalking, golf, birdwatching, fishing, kayaking and squash. Less active types can submit to the pleasures of the Lodge's intimate cliff-top spa, or one-on-one cooking lessons focusing on the best of local produce.

Hobart–Strahan **Tassielink** (☑1300 300 520; www.tassielink.com.au) buses stop here on request daily (except Monday and Wednesday). The two-hour jaunt from Hobart costs $26; from Strahan it's 3½ hours and $43. Buses leave Hobart at 8.15am on Tuesday and Thursday and 4pm on Friday. From Strahan, departures are at 7.30am on Tuesday and Thursday and 4.30pm on Friday.

The East Coast

Includes »

Maria Island National
Park 144

Swansea. 146

Freycinet National
Park 150

Bicheno 157

Douglas–Apsley National
Park 161

St Helens. 163

Bay of Fires 166

Binalong Bay. 167

Weldborough. 168

Mt William National
Park 169

Scottsdale 171

Bridport 172

Flinders Island 173

Best Places to Eat

» Piermont Restaurant (p149)

» Ripple (p166)

» Passinis (p160)

» Freycinet Marine Farm
(p151)

Best Places to Stay

» Saffire (p153)

» Rocky Hills Retreat (p147)

» Aurora Beach Cottage
(p159)

» Point Break (p167)

Why Go?

White-blonde sand, ice-blue water, wide blue sky and sunshine. Now, strip off and plunge in. Don't think too long or it might just take your breath away.

Tasmania's east and northeast is salt tousled and refreshing. It's a land of quiet bays and sandy shores, punctuated by granite hills and headlands splashed with flaming orange lichen. The whole coast is fringed with eucalypt or pasture green, national parks for wildlife spotting or adventuring, and agricultural country for fabulous food and wine.

If you want to be active, hike, bike, kayak, surf, dive or fish here – then set up your beachside camp and chill. If luxury is more your thing you'll find that here too, with fancy lodges and beachhouses, and top-notch places to dine. It's not all high adventure or highbrow either: if you're after buckets-and-spades family fun, Tasmania's east and northeast are perfect for sun-soaked beach holidays. See www.northeast tasmania.com.au for more.

When to Go

Picture-postcard shots of the east coast make you think tropical: palm trees, bikinis and suntans. The truth is, those crystal-clear photographers' dream days are often in winter, so be open minded about when you visit.

The whole coast comes alive in summer. There's a relaxed, vacation vibe, but the most popular spots do get packed and accommodation prices surge. In the dead of winter (June to August) you'll find these parts in the doldrums. In autumn (March to April) the sea's at its warmest, and you might have a beach all to yourself.

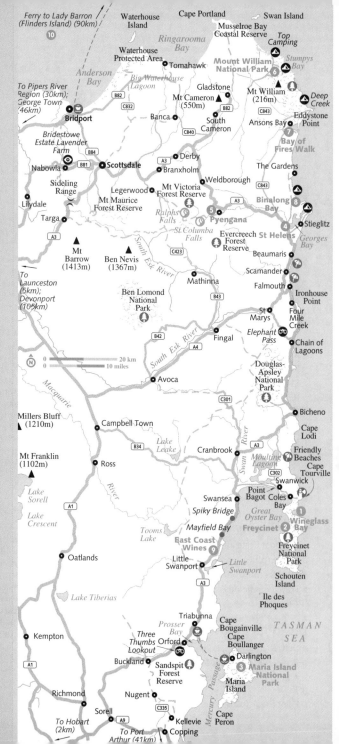

The East Coast Highlights

1 Whooping with exhilaration as you brave the ice-blue waters of gorgeous **Wineglass Bay** (p154)

2 Swooping over the Freycinet coastline on a **scenic flight** (p153)

3 Having close encounters with wildlife at **Maria Island National Park** (p144)

4 Luring in a deep-sea monster – or at least catching your dinner – at **St Helens** (p164)

5 Sampling heavenly ice creams produced by the happy cows of **Pyengana** (p168)

6 Dreaming under the whispering she-oaks when you camp at **Mt William National Park** (p169)

7 Floating your boat on the mirror-calm Ansons River lagoon with the **Bay of Fires Walk** (p167)

8 Being a water baby (or beach babe) at **Binalong Bay** (p167)

9 Feasting on fresh **seafood**, and quaffing fine **East Coast wines**

10 Beachcombing for Killiecrankie diamonds on **Flinders Island** (p173)

Orford

POP 500

The seaside village of Orford was once a seaport for the east coast whaling fleet, and the convict and military settlement on Maria Island, just across Mercury Passage. Today, Orford is a holiday village where Hobartians have their seaside 'shacks' and spend summer holidays on the beach.

The Prosser River flows through **Paradise Gorge** as it approaches town: often mirror-calm with perfect reflections. On the north side of the river is a convict-built road that once reached Hobart. It's now a riverside **walking track**. Another coastal track of about 5km leads from Raspins Beach, along Shelly Beach and around Luther Point cliffs, to beautiful **Spring Beach**, which has crystal-clear water and, in the right conditions, surfing. The walk passes a convict-era **quarry**, which provided the sandstone for buildings in Melbourne and Hobart.

The Prosser River is a good fishing and boating spot. There's also diving in the clear waters offshore. The recently sunk **Troy D** has provided an artificial reef near Orford that's already attracted plenty of sea life. East Coast Cruises (26257 1300; www.east coastcruises.com.au) can take you there and to dive sites around Maria Island.

Just off the highway opposite the service station is Darlington Vineyard (63 Holkham Crt; 10am-5pm daily Jan-Feb, Fri-Mon Mar-Nov), which produces an award-winning Riesling and is open for tastings and cellar-door sales.

Sleeping & Eating

Sanda House B&B $$
(26257 1527; www.orfordsandahouse.com.au; 33 Walpole St; d $125-145) A colonial B&B in Orford's oldest house, a pretty 1840s stone cottage surrounded by lovingly tended gardens on the south side of the river. Continental breakfasts are served fireside in the dining room.

Prosser Holiday Units RENTAL HOUSE $$
(26257 1427; cnr Tasman Hwy & Charles St; d $105-130) These family-friendly, self-contained units are just off the highway on the edge of the Prosser River. The two-storey units and a separate holiday house have views of the water, and accommodate up to five. Extra adult/child $20/10.

Blue Waters Motor Inn MOTEL $$
(26257 1102; 28 Tasman Hwy; d $85-115, mains $18-29; lunch except Tue & dinner) This place is more pub-and-gaming than accommodation oriented. It does have several different types of motel rooms, which are clean but unremarkable (extra person $25). The recently revamped dining room has wide river views and does big, better-than-pub meals.

Scorchers on the River CAFE $$
(26257 1033; 1 Esplanade; mains $12-25; 11am-9pm Fri & Sat, 11am-8pm Sun-Tue & Thu) Scorchers is known for superior eat-in or takeaway wood-fired pizzas, served all day, of which the garlic-prawn and Spring Bay seafood number is tops. There's also good lasagne and salads.

Gateway Café CAFE $
(26257 1539; 1 Charles St; lunch mains $7.50-20, dinner mains $20-25; breakfast & lunch, dinner Wed-Sat, varies in winter) This cafe does great breakfasts (until 11am), and then serves meals you'll definitely want to make a stop for right through the day. Try its toasted sandwiches, chicken wraps or yummy salt-and-pepper squid.

Getting There & Away

Tassielink (1300 300 520; www.tassielink.com.au) coaches stop here en route to Swansea and Bicheno, and go to Hobart ($17, 1½ hours).

Triabunna

POP 900

Triabunna, 8km north of Orford, is set on an inlet of Spring Bay that shelters a small cray- and scallop-fishing fleet. There's a pub and a good visitor centre (26257 4772; cnr Esplanade & Charles St; 9am-5pm Oct-Apr, 10am-4pm May-Sep), but not much else of great interest to tourists, except that this is the jumping-off point for beautiful Maria Island.

East Coast Cruises (26257 1300; www.eastcoastcruises.com.au) which operates the Maria Island Ferry, does three-hour ecotours (adult/concession/child $95/85/65) daily at 10.30am, visiting the Ile des Phoques seal colony and Maria Island's soaring Fossil Cliffs. Passengers can be dropped on the island after the tour.

Sleeping & Eating

Tandara Motor Inn MOTEL $$
(26257 3333; Tasman Hwy; d $125, extra person $10;) Recently refurbished, this is now

a decent place to stay with bright, well-decorated motel rooms. It offers free use of the on-site tennis courts.

Triabunna Cabin & Caravan Park
CARAVAN PARK $

(☎6257 3575; www.mariagateway.com; 4 Vicary St; unpowered/powered sites $23/26, on-site vans $60-88, cabins $77-120; ☎) This small, cheek-by-jowl compound opposite the sports fields has all the usual caravan-park facilities, as well as a backpackers with dorm ($25) and double rooms ($70).

Spring Bay Hotel
PUB $

(☎6257 3115; 1 Charles St; s/d $40/70) Often filled with salty characters from the local fishing fleet. Rooms have shared facilities and a continental breakfast is included. Reasonable pub food is served nightly except Sunday.

Gallery Artspaces Café
CAFE $

(7 Vicary St; meals $7-15 ⏱10am-4pm May-Nov, 9am-5pm Dec-Apr) Light lunches, snacks and great coffees are produced by the Austrian owner here among the art pieces of the gallery. Try the traditional Austrian *gugelhupf*.

❶ Getting There & Away

Tassielink (☎1300 300 520; www.tassielink.com.au) coaches stop at the visitor centre and travel from Hobart to Triabunna ($20, 1¾ hours).

Maria Island National Park

Beautiful Maria (pronounced ma-*rye*-ah) Island, with its high craggy peaks, rises up like a fairytale castle across the waters of Mercury Passage, which separates it from the mainland. It's a peaceful haven, blissfully free of cars, that's a top spot for walking, wildlife watching, biking, camping – and soaking in the peace.

Maria has gorgeous natural scenery: soaring cliffs, fern-draped forests, white-blonde

Maria Island

beaches and azure seas. Forester kangaroos, wombats and wallabies wander about, and there's bountiful bird life, including the grey-plumed Cape Barren goose. Below the water there's also lots to see, with good snorkelling and diving in the clear, shallow waters of the marine reserve.

Maria became a national park, as much for its history as for its natural assets, in 1972 and is now also a Unesco World Heritage Site.

History

Maria Island has seen various incarnations as a penal settlement, an industrial site and a farming community. The island was originally home to the Oyster Bay community of Tasmanian Aborigines, who called it Toarra Marra Monah. They lived primarily on shell-fish, and made the crossing to the mainland in bark canoes.

Dutch explorer Abel Tasman landed here in 1642, and named the island in honour of Anthony Van Diemen's wife. The island became Tasmania's second penal settlement in 1821 and, for the next 10 years, the convicts were set to work to develop it. Many of the surviving buildings such as the Commissariat Store (1825) and the Penitentiary (1830) are from this era. By the early 1830s Maria Island was becoming too expensive to be viable, so the convicts were shipped back to settlements on the Tasmanian mainland. For the next 10 years, the island was the domain of whalers, farmers and smugglers.

In 1842 Darlington reopened as a probation station and a road was built to a second settlement at Long Point (Point Lesueur). At one stage there were some 600 convicts on Maria, but when convict transportation to Tasmania slowed, convict numbers dwindled and Darlington was again closed in 1850.

Then, with the arrival of enterprising Italian businessman Diego Bernacchi in 1884, Maria Island began a new era. Darlington's buildings were renovated and structures like the Coffee Palace were added (1888). The town of 260 was renamed San Diego. Over the next 40 years a cement factory and wine and silk-growing industries were developed. This industrial era ended with the advent of the Great Depression in the 1940s and the island reverted to farming.

In the 1960s the government bought the properties on the island, and reintroduced animals like Forester kangaroos, Bennett's

wallabies and Cape Barren geese that had been wiped out since European occupation.

◎ Sights & Activities

Darlington   HISTORIC BUILDINGS

The township of Darlington is where you'll start your time on the island. Close to the jetty where boats arrive is the historic **Commissariat Store**, where there's a national parks visitor centre. Through an avenue of gnarled macrocarpa, there's the **Penitentiary**, which once housed convicts (and is now bunkhouse-style accommodation) as well as the restored **Coffee Palace** and **Mess Hall**.

Painted Cliffs   LANDMARK

From Darlington it's a two-hour-return walk to the Painted Cliffs at the southern end of Hopground Beach. From here you can clamber along the sculpted sandstone cliffs, stained with iron oxide in a kaleidoscope of colours. It's best to visit at low tide – ask when that is in the Commissariat Store – and the afternoon sun paints the cliffs a fiery orange.

Circuit Walk   WALKING

From Darlington, there's a two- to three-hour-return walk to **Cape Boullanger**, the **Fossil Cliffs** and the old brickworks. If you have more time (allow four hours return from Darlington), climb **Bishop & Clerk** (599m) and marvel at the soaring bird's-eye views while you eat your packed lunch on the exposed, rocky slabs at the top. **Mt Maria** (711m) is the island's highest point. It's a seven-hour-return hike through the eucalypt forests from Darlington. There are good views over the island's isthmus from the summit.

Bike Hire   CYCLING

Maria is a fantastic place to cycle. You can hire bicycles on the island for $15 per day. Ask at the **ranger station** (☑6257 1420), where staff can also give advice on where to cycle. The Maria Island Ferry also does bike hire for $20 per day.

Marine Reserve   SCUBA DIVING, SNORKELLING

The seas around Maria, from Return Point to Bishop & Clerk, are a marine reserve so there's no fishing allowed, including in the Darlington area. The reserve encompasses the giant kelp forests and caves around **Fossil Bay**, and has excellent scuba diving and snorkelling. Two good spots for snorkelling are under the ferry pier and at the Painted Cliffs. You'll need a wetsuit if you plan to stay in long.

Bird & Animal Spotting   WILDLIFE WATCHING

Birdwatchers will love the abundant bird life on Maria Island. If you're lucky, you might spot the endangered forty-spotted pardalote or the aptly named swift parrot; and you'll certainly see Cape Barren geese. In and around Darlington, you can get up close to grazing wombats and wallabies. Keep an eye out for echidnas when on forest walks.

Tours

Maria Island Walk   WALKING

(☑6227 8800; www.mariaislandwalk.com.au) If you like the idea of a multi-day bushwalk but don't much fancy a soggy tent and noodles from the camp stove at dinner, then this guided walk might be your thing. Between mid-October and the end of April, this four-day walk takes a gentle, guided wander through the most lovely parts of Maria. The first two nights are spent under canvas at secluded bush camps, and the third at the historic former home of Diego Bernacchi in Darlington. There's amazing food and fine Tasmanian wines to go with it. The walk costs $2150, including all meals, accommodation and transport from Hobart.

East Coast Cruises   CRUISES

(☑6257 1300; www.eastcoastcruises.com.au) Get up close to seals at Iles des Phoques seal colony just north of Maria, then see the soaring Fossil Cliffs and Painted Cliffs from the water on a half-day cruise ($95/65 per adult/child). A full-day cruise also allows you to spend the afternoon on Maria ($145/95). The same crew can take you diving around Maria (and further afield). A day trip with two dives and lunch costs $135 per person. Diving equipment is additional.

🛏 Sleeping

Campgrounds   CAMPGROUND $

There's camping at Darlington ($13 for two people, $5 per extra person), French's Farm (free) and Encampment Cove (free). Bookings are essential (and made via Penitentiary Accommodation, see below). Gas BBQs are provided close to the Darlington site only, so camping stoves are needed. Fires are allowed in designated fireplaces but are often banned over summer. French's Farm and Encampment Cove have limited tank water supplies – it's a good idea to take your own.

Penitentiary Accommodation Units   HOSTEL $

(☑6257 1420; email reservations: maria.island@parks.tas.gov.au; dm $15, d $44, 6-bed r $84) The brick rooms of the penitentiary that once housed the island's convicts are now a good, simple place to stay – if you don't mind the ghosts. There are six bunks in each room, a table and a wood heater, and shared bathrooms with coin-operated hot showers nearby. There's no linen provided, and no electricity. The Penitentiary is often fully booked over summer, so plan well ahead.

ℹ️ Information

The island has no shops: bring all your food and gear with you. For further information on Maria see www.parks.tas.gov.au.

Visitor reception/information (☺daylight hr) In the Commissariat Store. Buy park passes and get walking information here.

Public telephone Outside the Darlington rangers' station. For an emergency within office hours call 6257 1420; outside office hours call 000.

ℹ️ Getting There & Away

Maria Island Ferry (www.mariaislandferry.com.au) has a daily service from October to April between Triabunna and Darlington, with reduced services in other months and sailings by appointment only in July (see the website for exact timings). It costs $50/25/37 per adult/child 2-5 yr/child 6-16 yr. Bikes and kayaks cost $10/20.

East Coast Cruises (☑6257 1300; www.eastcoastcruises.com.au) has a charter water-taxi service ($450 return for up to 11 people, luggage and bikes included).

You can also land on the grass airstrip near Darlington by light plane. Talk to **Par Avion** (☑6248 5390; www.paravion.com.au), who visit Maria on a fly-cruise package.

Swansea

POP 580

Swansea lies on the western shore of beautiful Great Oyster Bay, and has sweeping views of the Freycinet Peninsula over often-calm waters. Founded in 1820 and originally known as Great Swanport, Swansea also has some historic streetscapes and a miniature museum.

Swansea has thrived on Tasmania's growth in tourism, though it retains its laid-back seaside-town feel. It has plenty of services for visitors, good beaches and some wonderful wineries and restaurants on its doorstep. There are lovely places to stay here, but they get busy in summer; book ahead.

◉ Sights & Activities

Bark Mill Museum Swansea   MUSEUM
(96 Tasman Hwy; adult/child/family $10/6/23; ☺6am-4pm) This display explains the processing of black wattle bark to obtain tannin for tanning leathers. The mill was one of the few industries that operated in Swansea through the Great Depression, and helped keep the town alive. There's also a display on early French exploration of Tasmania's east coast.

Jetty   MONUMENT
When Swansea's old wooden jetty began to succumb to rot, ingenious townspeople came up with a solution: a new one made of milk bottles. The jetty used over a million compressed plastic milk bottles – and is guaranteed to outlast its predecessor.

Heritage Centre   MUSEUM
(Franklin St; admission fee; ☺daily) Located in Swansea's original schoolhouse, this was closed for renovation at the time of writing (and the price of admission is as yet unconfirmed). It should re-open mid-2011 housing a visitor information centre, a gallery, and a museum collection of Aboriginal artefacts, convict paraphernalia and war memorabilia.

Duncombes Lookout   LANDMARK
Three kilometres south of town, this spot provides panoramic views of Oyster Bay and the Freycinet Peninsula. A further 4km south is **Spiky Bridge**, which was built by convicts in 1843 using thousands of local fieldstones but no mortar. The nearby beach and headland are popular for picnics and fishing.

Loon.tite.ter.mair.re.le.hoin.er Walk   WALKING
This 30- to 50-minute stroll between Waterloo Beach and the Esplanade passes through the rookeries of mutton birds (short-tailed shearwaters) that burrow here in the breeding season (September to April). The adults return at dusk in a flurry of wings from feeding at sea. The walk is named for the Tasmanian Aboriginal community that lived in this area.

Milton Winery   WINE TASTING
(www.miltonvineyard.com.au; off Tasman Hwy; ☺10am-5pm) Milton is 13km north of Swansea, and has tastings in an attractive pavilion overlooking a lake and the vineyards. You can buy one of their cheese platters or picnic by the lake. Try the sparkling rosé.

Spring Vale Vineyards   WINE TASTING
(www.springvalewines.com; 130 Spring Vale Rd; ☺11am-4pm) This vineyard is at Cranbrook, about 15km north of town. The cellar door is housed in an 1842 stables. Try the wonderful Pinot Gris, one of Tassie's hottest wines.

Craigie Knowe Vineyard   WINE TASTING
(80 Glen Gala Rd; ☺9am-5pm Sat & Sun) This little vineyard produces outstanding Cabernet Sauvignon and Pinot Noir. Opening hours can vary, so call first.

Coombend Estate   WINE TASTING
(www.coombend.com.au; off Tasman Hwy; ☺10am-5pm Wed-Sun) Further north, just past the Great Oyster Bay lookout, is Tasmania's largest vineyard – Coombend Estate, with 3000 acres of vines. There are tastings and cellar-door sales and you can also try and buy the olive oil.

Freycinet Vineyard   WINE TASTING
(www.freycinetvineyard.com.au; off Tasman Hwy; ☺10am-4.30pm May-Sep, 9.30am-5pm Oct-Apr) Continue up the same driveway from Coombend to where winemaker Claudio Radenti makes an exquisite Radenti sparkling. The tasting room also serves great coffee.

🛏 Sleeping

TOP CHOICE **Rocky Hills Retreat**   RENTAL HOUSE **$$$**
(📞1300 361 136, 0428 250 399; rocky hillsretreat.com.au; Tasman Hwy; d $400-500; 🐾) This hideaway in the hills overlooking Oyster Bay bills itself as a place for contemplation and retreat. It's up a 2km driveway on a large bush property so there's no one else around. The architecture is masterful and the setting gives you jaw-dropping panoramas over ocean and bush. Bring a loved one here for a few days: the fridge is deliciously stocked, so there's really no need to leave.

Piermont Retreat   RESORT **$$$**
(📞6257 8131; www.piermont.com.au; Tasman Hwy; d $235-315; ⛵) Piermont is the perfect spot for a romantic hideaway holiday. Set in gardens and bushland on the shores of Great Oyster Bay are 12 beautiful stone and rammed-earth cottages, with fireplaces and spas, close to a secluded beach. There's a pool, a tennis court, bikes for hire, and sea-kayaks for guests to use. The restaurant has been getting some rave reviews.

Swansea

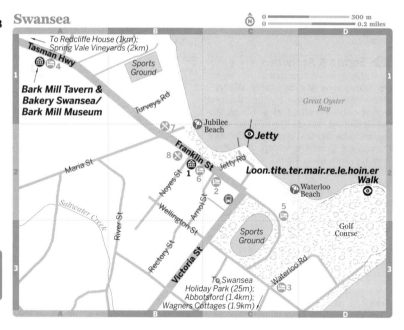

Avalon Coastal Retreat   RENTAL HOUSE **$$$**
(☑1300 36 11 36; www.avaloncoastalretreat.com.
au; Tasman Hwy, Rocky Hills; house sleeping 6
adults $800-900) This is the kind of place that
makes you feel you're in a movie about the
lives of the rich and famous. All glass and
steel and endless ocean views, this is pos-
sibly the most luxurious beach house in
Tasmania. The kitchen and cellar are well
stocked, and the beach is nearby – though
you'll hardly want to leave the house. It's
14km south of Swansea.

Tubby and Padman   B&B **$$**
(☑6257 8901; www.tubbyandpadman.com.au; 20
Franklin St; d $155-245; @) This snug Georgian
cottage on Swansea's main street was once
Swansea's department store, and is now
a classy B&B. The thoughtfully decorated
suites have spas and log fires, and come with
breakfast provisions. There are also two stylish self-contained apartments that sleep
four to five guests.

Wagners Cottages   COTTAGES **$$**
(☑6257 8494; www.wagnerscottages.com.au; Tas-
man Hwy; d $180-290) Wagners has five stone
cottages set in lush gardens a couple of kilo-
metres south of town. Each has a deep spa
bath, and there are open fires, fresh flowers,
a movie library and complimentary port.

Breakfasts feature fresh eggs from Wagners'
hens and just-out-of-the-oven bread.

Abbotsford   B&B **$$**
(☑6257 9092; www.swanseabedandbreakfast.com.
au; 50 Gordon St; d $155-$195) This delightful
stone house has been lovingly refurbished
by its Scottish owners, and is one of the
nicest places to stay in Swansea. There are
three double bedrooms with a shared bathroom and guest lounge, so it's perfectly suited to couples or families travelling together.
The owners put up the No Vacancy sign as
soon as one of the rooms is occupied so if
you're first in, you'll have the whole house to
yourself. Breakfasts are divine.

Redcliffe House   B&B **$$**
(☑6257 8557; www.redcliffehouse.com.au; 13569
Tasman Hwy; s $110, d $120-170) This restored
heritage farmhouse, built in 1835, is just
north of town. The rooms are beautifully dec-
orated and a guest lounge is equipped with
books and a decanter of port. It has an excel-
lent DVD library, and there's also a self-con-
tained apartment with breakfast provisions
supplied.

Schouten House   B&B **$$**
(☑6257 8564; www.schoutenhouse.com.au; 1 Wa-
terloo Rd; d $145-180) This convict-built brick-
and-sandstone mansion was presented as a

Swansea

◎ **Top Sights**

Bark Mill Tavern & Bakery
Swansea/Bark Mill Museum A1
Jetty..C2
Loon.tite.ter.mair.re.le.hoin.er
Walk D2

◎ **Sights**

1 Heritage Centre....................................B2

🛏 **Sleeping**

2 Freycinet Waters..................................C2
3 Schouten House C3
4 Swansea Backpackers........................ A1
5 Swansea Waterloo Inn C2
6 Tubby & Padman B2

🍴 **Eating**

7 Banc...B2
8 Trellis B2

wedding gift to a Swansea couple in 1844. Its huge rooms now house this atmospheric, antique-filled B&B. You can't go past the pancakes with bacon and maple syrup for breakfast.

Swansea Beach Chalets   CABINS **$$**
(☑6257 8177; www.swanseabeachchalets.com. au; 27 Shaw St; d $180-240; 🖥🏊) There are smart new chalets here just steps from Jubilee Beach: some have 180-degree water vistas, and some have spas. There's a BBQ pavilion, a games room, and a playground for kids.

Swansea Backpackers   HOSTEL **$**
(☑6257 8650; www.swanseabackpackers.com. au; 98 Tasman Hwy; dm $28-38, d 75-85; @) The new-ish backpackers next door to the Swansea Bark Mill has smart and spacious public areas and a shiny stainless-steel kitchen. The rooms surround a shady deck and are clean and peaceful.

Swansea Holiday Park   CARAVAN PARK **$**
(☑6257 8148; www.swansea-holiday.com.au; 2 Bridge St; powered sites d $25-35, cabins d $100-120; 🖥🏊) A neat, family-friendly park close to Schouten Beach. There's a games room and a playground for kids, a camp kitchen and BBQs.

Freycinet Waters   B&B **$$**
(☑6257 8080; www.freycinetwaters.com.au; 16 Franklin St; s $120-140, d $130-160) This brightly decorated B&B has friendly owners and a seaside ambience. There's

a sunny breakfast room with water views and also a self-contained apartment, with its own deck and entrance.

Swansea Waterloo Inn   MOTEL **$$**
(☑6257 8577; 1a Franklin St; d $77-150) You can't miss this red-brick block on the beach side as the road bends through Swansea. It's aesthetically uninspiring, but some of the rooms have close-up sea views.

🍴 Eating

TOP
CHOICE ⟩ **Piermont**
Restaurant   MODERN AUSTRALIAN **$$$**
(☑6257 8131; www.piermont.com.au; Tasman Hwy; mains $32-35; ⊘dinner Thu-Tue, closed Aug) There are gorgeous vistas over Great Oyster Bay from this dining room, but you will be more interested in what's on your plate. This much-talked-about and much-awarded restaurant works magic with all that's local and fresh. As well as an innovative à la carte menu, there's a fabulous five-course degustation menu ($100 with wine, $75 without).

Banc   MODERN AUSTRALIAN **$$$**
(☑6257 8896; cnr Franklin & Maria Sts; lunch mains $10-28, dinner mains $28-36; ⊘lunch Sun & Mon, dinner Wed-Sun) Banc is undoubtedly one of Tasmania's top restaurants. Using the freshest east-coast produce, it serves up wonderful dishes like venison steaks, slow-roasted suckling pig, and abalone confit with fresh lime mirin. Lazy late breakfasts are served Sunday and Monday.

Trellis   CAFE **$**
(26 Franklin St; mains $7-16; ⊘breakfast & lunch; 🛜) This trendy little eatery in the main street serves excellent breakfasts and cafe lunches. It also does a killer coffee and has comfy sink-into couches. Out the back there's a boutique wine store that sells some of the fine east-coast drops.

Kate's Berry Farm   CAFE **$**
(12 Addison St; teas & desserts $4-10.50; ⊘9.30am-4.30pm Nov-Apr, closed Wed-Thu May-Oct) Sit under the wisteria-draped pergola and absorb sweeping views over Great Oyster Bay while you indulge in Kate's berries. She does them in a range of ice creams, jams and sauces, and in handmade berry chocolate. The Belgian waffles with berry compote are to die for. Great coffees too. It's just south of Swansea, signposted off the Tasman Hwy.

Kabuki by the Sea JAPANESE $$
(☑6257 8588; Tasman Hwy; mains $22-26; ☺lunch daily, dinner daily Dec-Apr, Fri & Sat May-Nov) The smiling Japanese clientele here is a good sign that Kabuki is serving its Japanese food just right. Try the marinated *una ju* (eel) or the baby east-coast abalone. Incongruously, good Devonshire teas are also available. There's accommodation here too that styles itself on a Japanese ryokan. It's 12km south of Swansea.

Bark Mill Tavern & Bakery
Swansea PUB-BAKERY $$
(www.barkmilltavern.com.au; 96 Tasman Hwy; lunch mains $7-30, dinner mains $18-30; ☺bakery 6am-4pm daily, tavern lunch & dinner) There are two good dining options at the Swansea Bark Mill. The bakery does cooked breakfasts until 11am, and serves light meals and sweet temptations as well as great coffee all day. There's a playground attached for kids. At the tavern you'll find large servings of pub fare as well as excellent wood-fired pizzas and takeaways.

ℹ Information

Swansea has been having troubles with water quality for some time, though a dam has been built to deliver better water. Check when you visit whether water still needs to be boiled before drinking.

ATM (cnr Victoria & Franklin Sts; ☺7am-7pm) In Swansea Corner Store.

Online Access Centre (☑6257 8806; Franklin St; ☺variable times most weekdays) Adjacent to the town's primary school, call to check opening times.

ℹ Getting There & Away

Tassielink (www.tassielink.com.au) has buses to/from Hobart ($29, 2¼ hours) that stop at Swansea Corner Store (cnr Franklin & Victoria Sts).

For cyclists travelling between Swansea and Coles Bay, there's an informal **boat service** (☑6257 0239) between Point Bagot and Swanwick, costing $20 per person, saving approximately 46km of riding. The boat runs on request in both directions (October to April), weather permitting.

Coles Bay & Freycinet National Park

POP 150

The township of Coles Bay is set on a sweep of sand and clear sea at the foot of the dramatic orange-granite peaks of the

Hazards. It's a laid-back, salt-tousled holiday town with plenty of accommodation (though book well ahead in summer), and some fun, active tour options. The gorgeous Freycinet National Park is the reason that most people come here. It's a wild domain of sugar-white beaches and waters that are Bombay Sapphire clear. In the coastal heathland and forests, wildflowers and native birds and animals are abundant. The park encompasses the whole of the peninsula south of Coles Bay, including Schouten Island to the south, and a stretch of coastal bushland around Friendly Beaches further north.

The thing that most people come here to see is the heart-stoppingly perfect curve and ice-blue waters of Wineglass Bay. A dip in the (decidedly cool) sea here necessitates a walk of about three hours return on steep tracks with sublime views.

History

The first inhabitants of the Coles Bay area and the Freycinet Peninsula were the Oyster Bay community of Tasmanian Aborigines. Their diet was rich in the abundant shellfish of the bay, and there are shell middens as evidence of this all over the peninsula.

Dutch explorer Abel Tasman visited in 1642 and named Schouten Island. In 1802, Baudin's French expedition explored and named the Freycinet Peninsula, as well as having encounters with Aboriginals. When other expeditions noted the presence of seals, sealers arrived from Sydney and quickly plundered them.

A whale 'fishery' was established at Parsons Cove by Coles Bay in 1824 – the area is still known as the Fisheries. Here southern right whales that were hunted on their migration down the peninsula were processed; the sparkling waters and blonde sands soon became polluted with rotting whale remains. The station was closed by the 1840s, when most of the whales had gone.

Coles Bay was named after Silas Cole, who arrived in the 1830s and burnt shells from Aboriginal middens to produce lime for the mortar to build Swansea. Since the early field naturalists' expeditions here, in the late 1800s, the bay has been a popular holiday spot. In the 1920s the first holiday homes were built and the area has been a much-loved holiday idyll ever since.

In the early days of the colony both the Freycinet Peninsula and Schouten Island were farmed, but in 1906 both became game reserves. In 1916 Freycinet shared the honours with Mt Field in becoming Tasmania's first national park; Schouten Island was added in 1977. Friendly Beaches (north of Coles Bay) was added to the park in 1992.

⊙ Sights & Activities

For all national park walks, remember to get a parks pass (p295) and, for longer walks, to sign in (and out) at the car-park registration booth.

Wineglass Bay Walk   WALKING
This route is deservedly one of the most popular in Tasmania. You can make the steep climb to the **Wineglass Bay Lookout** to get superb views over the bay and peninsula (1½ hours return), but if you want to hear the squeak of those white sands beneath your feet, you're in for a longer walk. The steep descent from the lookout to the bay takes at least another 30 minutes, making the out-and-back trip from the car park 2½ to three hours.

Freycinet Peninsula Circuit   WALKING
This is a two- to three- day, 31km trek around the peninsula, from Hazards Beach south to Cooks Beach (there's an optional extension to beautiful Bryans Beach at the south end of the circuit), then across the peninsula over a heathland plateau before descending to the water at Wineglass Bay. Buy the *Freycinet National Park Map and Notes* at the national park visitor centre ($9.95) and see details online at www.parks.tas.gov.au or in Lonely Planet's *Walking in Australia*.

Freycinet Marine Farm   OYSTER TASTING
(1784 Coles Bay Rd; plates $14-25; ⊙9am-5pm daily Sep-May, honesty system Jun-Aug) Just off the Coles Bay road is Freycinet Marine Farm, which grows huge, succulent oysters ($14 a dozen) in the tidal waters of Moulting Lagoon. It now has a sales room where you can try and buy its wares, including freshly shucked oysters, mussels, rock lobsters and abalone. Sit out on the deck here, BYO wine (or buy here) and enjoy a seafood picnic, as fresh as it gets. In winter you put your money in the box and help yourself from the fridge.

Coles Bay Gear Hire   FISHING, BOATING
(☑0419 255 604; Garnet Ave boat ramp) This outfit hires dinghies with outboards and all safety equipment ($100/120 per two/three hours). It also rents fishing equipment (with boats or without) and can ad-

vise on good shore-based fishing spots. The friendly owner even guts and fillets your fish for you when you return. Snorkelling equipment and Canadian canoes ($55/65 per two/three hours for two people) also available for hire.

Honeymoon Bay   BAY
Gorgeous, tiny Honeymoon Bay – a short walk from Freycinet Lodge – is most beautiful at sunset when the orange rocks and east-coast lichen are lit a deep umber.

Friendly Beaches   BEACH
This magnificent ocean beach is signposted from the main road about 26km north of Coles Bay. A five-minute walk leads from the car park to a vantage point for uninterrupted views of tumbling surf and an endless stretch of sand.

Moulting Lagoon   LAGOON
The estuary of the Swan River (which the road to Coles Bay from the turn-off skirts around) is an important waterbird breeding ground. It's home to black swans, wild ducks and oyster farming.

Sleepy Bay   BAY
A beautiful granite-framed cove 10 minutes from the Cape Tourville Rd.

Cape Tourville   LANDMARK
There's an easy 20-minute circuit here for inspiring panoramas of the peninsula's eastern coastline. It's suitable for some wheelchair users and prams. You'll also see **Cape Tourville Lighthouse** and can gaze towards the northeast coast of Tasmania. It's spectacular at sunrise.

Bluestone Bay and Whitewater Wall   LANDMARK
There's challenging climbing, views and a quiet camp site at Whitewater Wall. You may need a 4WD to reach it, but many 2WDs make it in...not your hire car! Take your camera for the short walk to Bluestone Bay.

Mt Amos   WALKING
A superb walk, if you're fit, is the trek to see the spectacular views from this summit (three hours return), though it's dangerously slippery in wet weather.

⌂ Tours

Freycinet Experience   WALKING
(☑6223 7565, 1800 506 003; www.freycinet. com.au) For those who prefer to experience their wilderness in more comfort, Freycinet Experience offers a four-day, fully catered

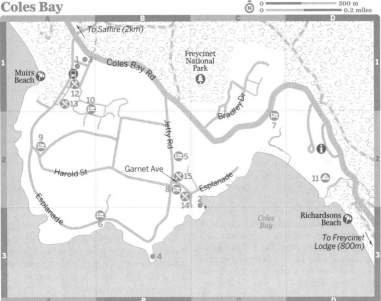

traverse of the entire length of the peninsula ($2175). Walkers return each evening to the peacefully secluded, environmentally sensitive Friendly Beaches Lodge to enjoy splendid meals, local wine and comfortable beds. The walk covers a total of 37km, with departures between November and May.

Freycinet Adventures KAYAKING
(☑6257 0500; www.freycinetadventures.com.au; 2 Freycinet Dr) Coles Bay is often sheltered from the wind and is a great spot for sea-kayaking. Freycinet Adventures offers three-hour tours ($95) twice daily (morning and twilight – times vary seasonally) that allow you to get a glimpse of the peninsula from the water. Kayak hire is available for experienced paddlers ($55 per person per day including safety gear).

Wineglass Bay Cruises CRUISES
(☑6257 0355; www.wineglassbaycruises.com. au) This company offers a four-hour cruise from the Esplanade jetty to Wineglass Bay (adult/child $110/75) including champagne, oysters and nibbles. You're likely to see dolphins, sea eagles, seals, penguins and perhaps even migrating whales in the right season. It's a superb way to experience the peninsula. Departure times vary through the year (9am midsummer, 10am

shoulder season; no cruises June to August). Reserve several days in advance for this popular tour.

All4Adventure QUAD BIKING
(☑6257 0018; www.all4adventure.com.au; Coles Bay Esplanade) Get off the beaten track into parts of the national park few others access. Two-hour quad-bike tours (with 30 minutes' training beforehand) depart daily at 1pm and 4.30pm (the latter only during daylight saving), costing $115. Half-day tours to Friendly Beaches and lovely Bluestone Bay depart at 8am and cost $195. A driver's licence is essential. It also has ATV passenger vehicles for adults or kids ($65 per two hours, $105 per half day). Family discounts available.

Long Lunch Tour Co. FOOD & WINE
(☑6257 0159, 0409 225 841; www.longlunchtourco. com.au) Now this is a great idea! Foodie Brad Bowden will take you on a gastronomical adventure of the east coast. You might do a slow degustation of top wines and tempting morsels...and finish it off with a bounty of berries ($130), take a quicky afternoon wine-and-nibbles tour ($65), or travel all the way from Hobart, stopping to wine and dine along the way ($220).

Coles Bay

Activities, Courses & Tours
1 All4Adventure A1
2 Coles Bay Gear Hire C2
3 Freycinet Adventures.......................... A1
4 Wineglass Bay Cruises........................ B3

😴 Sleeping
5 Coles Bay Retreat................................ B2
6 Freycinet Getaway............................... B3
7 Freycinet Haven................................... C2
8 Freycinet Rentals................................ B2
9 Hubie's Hideaway A2
   Iluka Backpackers .... (see 10)
10 Iluka Holiday Centre........................... A1
11 Richardsons Beach.............................. D2

⊗ Eating
12 Freycinet Bakery & Café A1
13 Iluka Tavern A1
14 Madge Malloys B2
15 Seafood Muchies B2

Freycinet Air   SCENIC FLIGHTS
(☑6375 1694; www.freycinetair.com.au) Thirty-minute scenic flights over the peninsula are available for $95 per person and longer flights as far afield as Maria Island are also on offer. The airfield is close to Friendly Beaches, signposted off the main road.

🛏 Sleeping

Saffire   RESORT $$$
(☑6256 7888; www.saffire-freycinet.com.au; 2352 Coles Bay Rd; d incl breakfast & lunch $1450-2450, extra adult/child $150/100) Eagerly awaited for years, Saffire promised to be an architectural and gastronomical marvel that would set the bar for top-notch Tasmanian hospitality. It pretty much lives up to the hype. There are 20 luxurious suites here 'where the cerulean sky collides with the azure ocean'. You have the run of the amazing main building – curvaceous like a sea creature – which houses the swanky restaurant, self-serve bar, DVD and book library, art gallery and spa. And then you can take in the great outdoors, with a menu of activity options, all included in the price.

Eagle Peaks   APARTMENTS $$
(☑6257 0444; www.eaglepeaks.com.au; 11-13 Oyster Bay Court; d $215-350) There are two beautiful new timber and rammed-earth studios here, just south of Coles Bay, which the friendly owners have decorated with great thought and style. Each unit has its own kitchenette, timber deck and comfortable king-size beds. It also rents the immaculate Beach house (double $235 to $370, extra adult $40), sleeping four. All guests have access to BBQs, and you can eat outside while you take in the views. It's only five minutes to Sandpiper Beach.

Freycinet Eco Retreat   APARTMENTS $$$
(☑6257 0300, 0408 504 414; www.mtpaul.com; d $250-350) To really get away from it all at Freycinet, retreat up to Mount Paul, where two carefully crafted eco-lodges offer wonderful panoramas of the peninsula and only the wildlife for neighbours. This is a magically peaceful spot – you'll want to stay for days. It also has a standing camp with bathroom and dining-room facilities for groups of eight or more. It's gay friendly, wheelchair accessible and eco-certified. Minimum two- night stay.

Edge of the Bay   RESORT $$$
(☑6257 0102; www.edgeofthebay.com.au; 2308 Main Rd; d $208-348, cottages d $180-265; 🐾) This peaceful, small resort is right on the beach, 4km north of Coles Bay. It has smartly decorated waterside suites, and cottages sleeping up to five. There are mountain bikes, dinghies and two artificial-grass tennis courts for guests' use. There's also an excellent restaurant on site.

Freycinet Lodge   RESORT $$$
(☑6257 0101; www.freycinetlodge.com.au; d $221-525, extra adult/child $62/31) Freycinet Lodge is in a gorgeous location right in the national park, just steps from Richardsons Beach. While staff are making an effort to keep doing the place up, it simply isn't the beachside holiday nirvana it once was. Many of its cabins have been recently refurbished, though, some with enormous spas, and several also have disabled access. There are guided activities, bikes and tennis gear for hire, and two restaurants on site.

Richardsons Beach CAMPGROUND, CARAVAN PARK $
(☑6256 7004; freycinet@parks.tas.gov.au; unpowered sites for 2/family $13/16, extra adult/child $5/2.50, powered sites $16/22, extra adult/child $7/3.50) There are pretty beachside camping spots with toilets and running water all along Richardsons Beach. Camping here is popular, especially during the summer holiday period. Between December and after Easter, allocation of sites is by a ballot system. Applications must be made on a form downloadable from the **Parks & Wildlife Service** (www.parks.tas.gov.au) website or by

WINEGLASS BAY

The hype surrounding Wineglass Bay is quite remarkable. You've no doubt seen the iconic images of this perfect arc with its stunning clear waters and pure white sand. It's been voted one of the top 10 beaches in the world (by US-based magazine *Outside*). Visiting Wineglass will be no lazy beach day, however: to get here you have to walk – and to get away from the bay-admiring crowds, you'll need to walk further.

To frolic on the sand and/or swim in the bay's pristine waters is at least a half-day expedition on foot and you'll need to climb 800 steep steps each way. If you only go to the viewpoint over the bay from the Hazards, Freycinet's distinctive range of granite hills, you'll likely share your Wineglass Bay experience with a horde of other camera-clickers: some of the 250,000 that come here annually. To get away from the crowds, visit early, and walk right down to the bay and return via the shady Isthmus Track, then follow the coastal track along the west side of the peninsula back to the car park (about four hours). Take water, food and sun protection – and whatever you do, swim!

Don't despair if this sort of physical exertion is beyond you. You can swoop over the bay instead on a scenic flight, or cruise in by boat.

calling the **visitor centre** (☑6256 7004), and must be submitted by 31 July. There's sometimes the odd tent spot left over, even during the peak season, so it's worth calling to see if they can squeeze you in. Outside the bal-lot period, bookings can be made in advance for these sites at the visitor centre. National park entry fees apply.

Iluka Holiday Centre CARAVAN PARK $
(☑6257 0115, 1800 786 512; www.ilukaholiday centre.com.au; Coles Bay Esplanade; unpowered/powered sites for 2 $25-30/35, on-site vans $65-75; ☞) Iluka is a big, friendly park that's a favourite with local holidaymakers, so book ahead. There's a shop, bakery and pub-bistro adjacent. There are also cabins and units (doubles $100 to $180, additional adult/child $20/15). Iluka Backpackers has six four-bed dorms ($30 per person) and just one double ($72), as well as a large kitchen. Discounts for YHA members.

Coles Bay Youth Hostel HOSTEL $
(dm $12-15, r $55-70, 2-person minimum booking) Right on the waterfront at Parson's Cove, this rustic, unstaffed hostel has two basic five-person cabins and a kitchen area with fridge and stove. There are pit toilets and only cold water on tap. Entire cabins can be rented for $55 ($70 for non-YHA members) via a ballot system from mid-December to mid-February and at Easter (call before mid-September to register for the summer ballot, and by mid-January for the Easter ballot). Book through Tasmania's YHA head office (www.yha.com.au). Keys and bed linen are obtained from the Iluka Holiday Centre.

Freycinet Rentals RENTAL HOUSE $$
(☑6257 0320; www.freycinetrentals.com; 5 Garnet Ave, Coles Bay) This is your hub for renting (mostly older-style) holiday cottages and beach 'shacks' in and around Coles Bay. Prices vary considerably from summer to winter and minimum stays apply for long weekends and Christmas holidays. The modern Freycinet Beach Apartments (doubles for two nights $440 to $600, extra person $25) at Swanwick are our favourites. There are also plenty of private holiday houses for rent around Coles Bay. Here're our pick:

Coles Bay Retreat RENTAL HOUSE $$$
(☑0418 132 538, 8660 2446; www.colesbay retreat.com; 29 Jetty Rd; d $240, extra person $35) A contemporary, well-appointed three-bedroom house with close-up Hazards views. There's also a one-bedroom cottage sleeping up to three (doubles $120, extra person $15).

Freycinet Haven RENTAL HOUSE $$
(0419 139 927, 6225 1761; www.freycinethaven. com.au; 91 Freycinet Dr; d $200-275, extra person $25) This is about as close as holiday houses get to the national park. This stylishly furnished new four-bedroom house is set peacefully among trees. There's a deck with BBQ out front; the house sleeps up to eight.

Freycinet Getaway RENTAL HOUSE $$
(☑0417 609 151; www.freycinetgetaway.com; 97 Coles Bay Esplanade; d $135-230) Freycinet Getaway has the funky Cove Beach Apartments; two separate spaces – upstairs and downstairs – in a large wooden

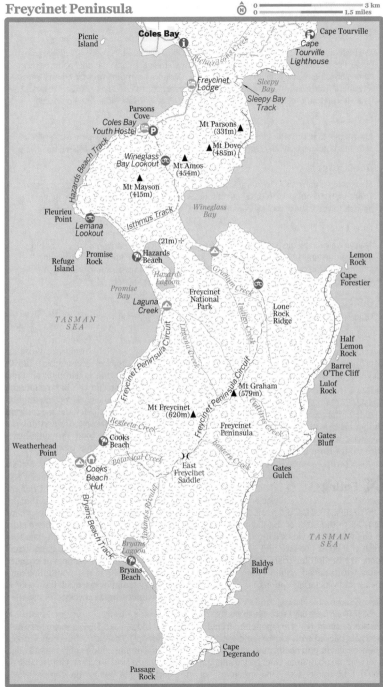

LOCAL KNOWLEDGE

TIM WARREN: OUTDOOR GUIDE

I've been coming to the east coast since I was a kid. Now as a bushwalking and kayaking guide, I spend a lot of time in nature here. Because the east-coast national parks here are so heavily visited, sustainable practices in the outdoors are more important than almost anywhere. There's so much bush and so many beaches, and not many rangers to oversee it...so it's up to the visitor to know how to be sustainably responsible in the outdoors.

Must do

Always talk to park staff before you go on a bushwalk. On the east coast, there are a lot of seasonal changes that affect where it's best to go – sustainably – at a certain time of year.

Don't forget

Always scrub your boots with water before entering a national park on the east coast. There's a big problem with the root-rot fungus *Phytophthora cinnamomi* that can devastate vegetation, and it's transmitted very easily by contaminated soil on boots.

Don't walk there

Always walk below the high-tide mark on beaches. Several endangered species of birds nest – almost invisibly – among seaweed just above the high-tide mark. You wouldn't know if you trod on one. And stick to tracks. It's easy to trample around on things. Walking on mosses and small plants can have a really big impact.

Biggest no-no

Feeding wildlife or throwing food scraps into the bush. It can kill an animal.

beachhouse, decorated in better-than-beachhouse style. Apartment 2 has great views of the Hazards.

Hubie's Hideaway RENTAL HOUSE **$$**
(☑0427 570 344; 33 Coles Bay Esplanade; d $120-160, extra adult/child $25/15) At this cute timber cabin with its jasmine-fringed timber deck, you'll fall asleep to the sound of the sea. It's close to the shops and bakery and sleeps up to seven.

✖ Eating

Edge MODERN AUSTRALIAN **$$**
(☑6257 0102; 2308 Main Rd; mains $28-32; ☺dinner) Get to the Edge of the Bay resort early to enjoy the water views. The chefs serve up fresh east-coast produce and plenty of seafood. Try the lobster pasta, or stripy trumpeter with seafood risotto. There are also meaty and vegetarian options.

Iluka Tavern PUB **$$**
(☑6257 0429; Coles Bay Esplanade; mains $18-29; ☺lunch & dinner; 🛜) This popular, friendly pub gets packed with tourists and locals. It offers excellent pub nosh: among the reef 'n' beef and the ubiquitous chicken parmigiana you'll find things like Thai green prawn curry and seafood linguine.

Bay MODERN AUSTRALIAN **$$$**
(☑6257 0101; Freycinet Lodge; mains $25-38; ☺dinner) At night the Lodge puts on Freycinet's finest dining in the Bay restaurant. There are delicacies like slow-cooked rabbit and tender local lamb. Try the magnificent seafood platter for two, with everything out of the bay. There's a good Tasmania-heavy wine list to boot. Bookings essential.

Madge Malloys SEAFOOD **$$$**
(☑6257 0399; 7 Garnet Ave, Coles Bay; mains $32-35; ☺dinner Tue-Sat) The blackboard out the front says 'Gone fishing, see you tonight: Chef', and that's exactly how it works here. The menu depends on what Mother Nature provides to the fishing boat each day. That might mean steam-baked bastard trumpeter, wrasse with crab stuffing, or poached calamari that melts in the mouth. Bookings and hungry tummies essential. It's closed in dead of winter: ring to check.

Richardsons Bistro MODERN AUSTRALIAN **$$**
(Freycinet Lodge; mains $18-24; ☺from 10am daily, dinner Nov-Apr) There's nothing fancy about this casual dining option at Freycinet Lodge, but the bistro food is decent. Grab a table on the deck outside to enjoy the glorious view.

Seafood Munchies　　FISH AND CHIPS $$

(6 Garnet Ave; meals $6-28; ⊘lunch & dinner Nov-
Apr, lunch May-Oct) You can sit on the deck
here or grab a quick takeaway. It serves
good fish and chips, an excellent spaghetti
marinara and even Cape Grim scotch fillet.

Freycinet Bakery & Café　　BAKERY $

(Shop 2, Coles Bay Esplanade; meals $4-20; ⊘8am-
4pm; @) This bakery has fuelled many a
Freycinet walking epic. Pick up pies, cakes
and sandwiches here or enjoy a lazy all-day
breakfast outside.

❶ Information

Coles Bay lies 31km from the Tasman Hwy
turn-off. Travel this stretch particularly slowly
between dusk and dawn to avoid hitting the
abundant wildlife.

Internet access is available at the Freycinet
Bakery & Café and there's free wireless in the
pub. See www.freycinetcolesbay.com for more
information on the area.

ATM In Iluka Supermarket.

Illuka Supermarket (The Esplanade; ⊘8am-
6pm Mar-Nov, 7am-7pm Dec-Feb) The general
store and newsagency; sells petrol and essen-
tials like fishing rods, tackle and bait, buckets
and spades.

Freycinet Adventures (www.freycinet
adventures.com; 2 Freycinet Dr) Hires camping
equipment.

Freycinet visitor centre (🗋6256 7000;
www.parks.tas.gov.au; ⊘9am-4pm May-Oct,
8am-5pm Nov-Apr) At the park entrance; get
your parks pass here. Enquire also about free
ranger-led activities December to February.
Park information is online at www.parks.tas.
gov.au

❶ Getting There & Away

Bicheno Coaches (www.freycinetconnections.
com.au) runs a Bicheno–Coles Bay–national park
walking tracks service, connecting with Tassielink
east-coast services at the Coles Bay turn-off.

Coles Bay turn-off–Coles Bay ($9, 30 minutes)

Bicheno–Wineglass Bay walking track ($15, 50
minutes)

In Coles Bay, buses depart from in front of the
Iluka Tavern and shops. Bicheno Coaches also
run day tours including visits to Sleepy Bay
and Cape Tourville Lighthouse: pre-booking
essential.

❶ Getting Around

It's 7km from Coles Bay to the national park
walking tracks car park. Bicheno Coaches does
the 10-minute trip three times each weekday and

once on Saturday and Sunday (one way/return
$6/10); bookings essential:

Bicheno

POP 750

Bicheno is blessed with idyllic coastal
scenery that makes it a hit with seaside
holidaymakers. The Gulch, Bicheno's curvaceous natural harbour, is filled with water
of the clearest blue, its foreshore is edged
with granite and fine white beaches, and
the whole town is fringed with the startling
green of eucalypts under an often deep-blue
sky. The fishing boats that shelter in the
harbour are this town's mainstay – as are
the tourists in the summer holiday season.

European settlement began here when
whalers and sealers came to the Gulch as
early as 1803. The town became known as
Waubs Bay Harbour, after an Aboriginal
woman, Waubedebar, rescued two drown-
ing men when their boat was wrecked offshore. After her death in 1832, the settlement bore her name until the 1840s when
it was renamed to honour James Ebenezer
Bicheno, once colonial secretary of Van
Diemen's Land. In 1854 Bicheno became a
coal-mining port, but mining fortunes
declined after the discovery of gold in
Victoria, so the town evolved into a quiet
fishing port and eventually the seaside holiday spot it is today.

---

❶ **CAMPING AT
FREYCINET**

There are walkers' campgrounds at
Wineglass Bay, Hazards Beach (two to
three hours' walk from car park), Cooks
Beach (4½ hours) and Bryans Beach
(5½ hours). Further north, there are
two basic camp sites with pit toilets at
Friendly Beaches. These camp sites are
free, but national park entry fees apply.
The park is a fuel-stove-only area and
campfires are not permitted. There's
limited water availability at camp sites:
check with a ranger before departing.
There's free bush camping outside the
national park at the River & Rocks site
at Moulting Lagoon. Drive 8km north of
Coles Bay, turn left onto the unsealed
River & Rocks Rd, then left at the T-
junction. Bring your own water.

Bicheno

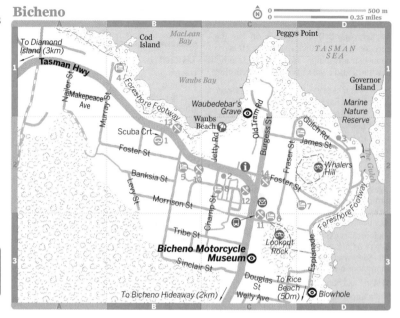

Bicheno's style is more fish and chips (and buckets and spades) than upmarket Swansea, but it's still a hugely popular holiday spot. Book ahead if you intend to stay overnight in summer.

◉ Sights & Activities

TOP CHOICE Bicheno Motorcycle Museum
MUSEUM

(33 Burgess St; adult/child under 16 $9/free; ⊙9am-5pm Mon-Fri, to 4pm Sat & Sun) Andrew Quin got his first Honda at four years old, and since then he's been hooked on motorbikes. You don't have to be an aficionado, though, to visit his wonderful little museum out the back of his bike-repair shop. It's all shiny chrome and enamel under the bright lights here, with 60 immaculately restored bikes on display, including the rare Noriel 4 Café Racer – the only one of its kind in the world.

Bicheno Dive Centre
DIVING

(☏6375 1138; www.bichenodive.com.au; 2 Scuba Crt; ⊙9am-5pm) The clear waters off Bicheno are known for their excellent temperate water diving. This crew visits dive sites mainly in the Governor Island Marine Reserve. One-day charters including all equipment and one/two boat dives cost $120/160. There is also budget accommodation in a basic self-contained unit available to divers.

East Coast Natureworld
WILDLIFE PARK

(☏6375 1311; www.natureworld.com.au; adult/child/family $18.50/9.75/50; ⊙9am-5pm) About 7km north of Bicheno, this wildlife park is a place both kids and adults can enjoy. It's a varied menagerie of native and non-native wildlife including Tasmanian devils, wallabies, quolls, snakes, wombats and enormous roos. There are devil feedings daily at 3.30pm, and a devil house where you can get up close to these creatures. Other animals are fed at 10am. The tea-rooms serve Devonshire teas and the like.

Foreshore Footway
WALKING

This 3km route extends from Redbill Point to the **Blowhole**, right around the **Gulch**, and wandering its length is the best way to see Bicheno's pretty coastline. When the seas are rolling in just right, huge columns of foamy seawater spurt spectacularly into the air through the granite rock formations at the Blowhole. Don't get too close: even on calm days you can be unexpectedly drenched. You can return along paths through the she-oaks at **Whalers Hill**, which has panoramic views over town. In whaling days, passing sea giants were spotted from here.

Beaches
SWIMMING, SURFING

Waubs Beach and Rice Beach are fairly safe ocean beaches for swimming on calm days.

Bicheno

⊚ Top Sights
  Bicheno Motorcycle Museum............C3

◎ Sights
  Bicheno Penguin Tours...............(see 2)

Activities, Courses & Tours
  1 Bicheno Dive Centre...........................B2
  2 East Coast Surf (Penguin Tours
    Bookings & Departure
    Point)...C2
  3 Glass-Bottom Boat Departure
    Point D2

⊜ Sleeping
  4 Anchlia Waterfront Cottage................ B1
  5 Beachfront at Bicheno........................B2
  6 Bicheno Backpackers C3
  7 Bicheno by the Bay..............................D2
  8 Bicheno East Coast Holiday
    Park..C2
  9 Windows on Bicheno...........................D2

⊗ Eating
  10 Beachfront Tavern...............................B2
  11 Blue Edge Bakery................................C3
    Delmare's..(see 5)
  12 Passinis...C2
  13 Sea Life Centre Restaurant................B2
  14 Sir Loin Breier.....................................C2

Redbill Point often has good surfing breaks: there's usually a **surf carnival** here in January. For surfboard, boogie-board and kayak hire, talk to the friendly people at Bicheno Backpackers.

☞ Tours

Bicheno Penguin Tours   PENGUIN SPOTTING
(☑6375 1333; www.bichenopenguintours.com.au; East Coast Surf; adult/child $25/15) Bicheno is one of the top spots in Tassie to view penguins: see them on these nightly tours at dusk as they head back to their burrows. The one-hour tour with an expert guide will take you as close to the little birds as you can get anywhere. This is a wonderful and pure nature experience: no grandstands or souvenirs. Departure times for the tours vary year-round, dependent on when dusk falls. Enquire at East Coast Surf. No photography allowed.

Glass-bottom Boat   BOAT
(☑6375 1294, 0407 812 217; adult/child $20/5) This 40-minute trip will show you some of Bicheno's underwater wonders. Tours leave from the Gulch at 10am, noon and 2pm in summer, weather permitting (bookings advised in January).

Go Fish   FISHING CHARTERS
(☑6375 1581, 0419 750 757) If you find the most interesting fish the one wriggling on the end of a fishing line, then these guys can help you catch it. They take three-hour charters with all fishing gear included, costing from $90 per person. Fish are cleaned for you before you leave the boat.

🛏 Sleeping

Windows on Bicheno   B&B $$$
(☑6375 2010; www.windowsonbicheno.com.au; 13 James St; d $250-450) This fantastic new B&B has just two luxurious, stylish suites, furnished and managed with absolute attention to detail. Spot whales from the balcony, relax on the comfy leather sofas, or wallow in your deep spa bath for two. As well as being a bit of a style goddess, your host cooks amazing three-course breakfasts.

Diamond Island   RESORT $$$
(☑6375 0100; www.diamondisland.com.au; 69 Tasman Hwy; d $250-510; ☎⊠) About 2km north of Bicheno, this complex of 27 sun-soaked apartments surrounded by green lawns has wonderful views north along the coast. Recently renovated and stylishly furnished with luxury linens, spa baths and DVD players, the resort has a solar-heated pool and private beach access. You can wander over to Diamond Island when the tide is low. There's also a good restaurant on site. Free penguin tours for guests.

Aurora Beach Cottage   RENTAL HOUSE $$$
(☑6375 1774; www.aurorabeachcottage.com.au; 207 Champ St, Seymour, via Bicheno; d from $230) For somewhere totally secluded and away from it all, gorgeous Aurora Beach Cottage has to be the pick. This timber and stone cottage is 18km north of Bicheno in a beautifully quiet spot, right on the beach. You can sit out on the deck and watch the waves, or stroll on the sand for miles. Breakfast provisions on request. It doesn't take children under 12.

Anchlia Waterfront Cottage   COTTAGE $$
(☑6375 1005; www.anchliawaterfront.com.au; 2 Murray St; d $130-240, extra person $30) Anchlia is one large house, divided into two separate self-contained cottages, set among the gum trees right by the sea. You can sometimes watch penguins gambol in the garden.

Bicheno Hideaway CABINS $$
(6375 1312; www.bichenohideaway.com; 179 Harveys Farm Rd; d $135-180, extra person $25) These architecturally interesting chalets are set in wildlife-rich bushland, close to the sea and with glorious views. Minimum stays of two or three nights, depending on the cabin. Not for children under 10.

Beachfront at Bicheno HOTEL $$
(6375 1111; www.beachfrontbicheno.com.au; Tasman Hwy; d $95-160; @) This recently renovated property has several grades of room, but the sea-view ones are the pick. There's a playground and a BBQ area, as well as a pub with a bistro and a good à la carte restaurant with views over the bay.

Bicheno by the Bay CABINS $$
(6375 1171; www.bichenobythebay.com.au; cnr Foster & Fraser Sts; 1-bedroom units $140-175, 2-bedroom units $170-210;) There are 20 cabins in a bushland setting here, some sleeping up to 10. The sea-view cabins are best. Facilities include an outdoor heated pool, a tennis court, a communal fire pit and a kids' pirate-boat playground.

Sandpiper Ocean Cottages COTTAGES $$
(6375 1122; www.sandpipercottages.com.au; Tasman Hwy; d $140-300, extra adult/child $45) These simple, secluded cottages and the smart Beachhouse are 8km north of Bicheno on Denison Beach. All have BBQs and decks for admiring the views.

Bicheno East Coast Holiday Park CARAVAN PARK $
(6375 1999; www.bichenoholidaypark.com.au; 4 Champ St; powered sites $33, d unit $95-105, d cabins $118-138) This neat, friendly park with plenty of green grass is centrally located and has BBQ, camp kitchen, laundry facilities and kids' playground. It also does showers for non-stayers ($5). Cabins sleep up to seven (extra person $15 to $25).

Bicheno Backpackers HOSTEL $
(6375 1651; www.bichenobackpackers.com; 11 Morrison St; dm $27-29, d $65-75) This friendly backpackers stretches across two mural-painted buildings. The double rooms are quite plush (the sea-view one's the pick) and there's a good communal kitchen. It's the fun equipment for rent here that's the highlight, though. It has bikes, kayaks, surfboards, boogie boards and fishing rods. There's also free luggage storage, and the friendly owners can help with bookings.

 Eating

TOP CHOICE **Passinis** ITALIAN $$
(6375 1076; 70 Burgess St; mains $10-25; breakfast & lunch, dinner Mon-Sat) This is a truly fantastic place to eat and any stop in Bicheno should include a call-in here. It does staples like antipasto plates, focaccias and lasagne – but oh, *so much* better than most. Then there are fancy dishes like chargrilled polenta with marinated quail and scallop ravioli in lemongrass butter. The pastas and gnocchi are homemade, the coffees are richly delicious, and if you haven't had enough, you can do a bit of shopping in the gourmet providore. It has a takeaway menu too.

Facets MODERN AUSTRALIAN $$
(6375 0100; 69 Tasman Hwy; mains $25-34; lunch Nov-Easter, dinner nightly) This breezy restaurant at Diamond Island has a smart, nautical feel and serves up equally sophisticated fare. Have an aperitif on the deck outside so you can absorb the views, then come in for a menu that's a feast of fresh seafood. If you have dinner here you can do Diamond Island's exclusive penguin tour for free. Bookings advised.

Sir Loin Breier DELI $$
(57 Burgess St; 9am-5pm Mon-Sat) This superior butcher's shop has an amazing range of deli items: stock up here for picnics. The shop brims with cooked local crayfish, smoked trout, oysters, gourmet pies, cheeses and smoked-quail sausages. Divine.

Blue Edge Bakery BAKERY $
(55 Burgess St; meals $2.50-15; 6am-4.30pm) Blue Edge does good sandwiches, pies, cakes and salads, and you can enjoy the aromas of the freshly made breads, all baked on the premises. The chicken and camembert pie is excellent.

Beachfront at Bicheno MODERN AUSTRALIAN $$
(6375 1111; Tasman Hwy) Delmare's (mains $22 to $35; open dinner Thursday to Saturday October to April) has a seafood-heavy à la carte menu; while the Beachfront Tavern (mains $22 to $35; open lunch and dinner) serves standard pub fare.

Sea Life Centre Restaurant SEAFOOD $$
(6375 1121; 1 Tasman Hwy; meals $15-30; lunch & dinner, closed Aug) The best thing about the restaurant here are the views over the startlingly blue waters of the Gulch. The crayfish and seafood chowder are recommended by locals.

ℹ Information

ATM Outside the pharmacy on Burgess St, and by the newsagency on the town's main strip.

Bicheno visitor centre (☑6375 1500; 49B Foster St; ☺9am-5pm Mon-Fri, 9am-1pm Sat, 11am-4pm Sun, hr vary winter)

Online Access Centre (The Oval, Burgess St; ☺9.30am-12.30pm Mon, 10am-2pm Tue-Thu, noon-4pm Fri) Behind the public loos at the oval.

ℹ Getting There & Away

Calows Coaches (www.calowscoaches.com) and **Tassielink** (www.tassielink.com.au) serve the town.

Tassielink: Hobart–Bicheno ($36, three to four hours)

Calows: Launceston–Bicheno ($34, 3½ hours)

Bicheno Coach Service (☑6257 0293, 0419 570 293) runs between Bicheno and Coles Bay, departing from Blue Edge Bakery:

Bicheno–Coles Bay ($11.50, 50 minutes)

Douglas-Apsley National Park

This stretch of intact dry eucalypt forest is the kind of environment that existed over much of the east coast before European settlement. The area was declared a national park in 1989 after a public campaign expressed concern over woodchipping of local forests.

Douglas-Apsley is often overlooked, but it's a wonderful park, cut through at one end by a river gorge that has deep, inviting swimming holes, and plenty to explore. There are rocky peaks, waterfalls and abundant bird and animal life – and best of all, you won't encounter the midsummer hordes that you do at Freycinet.

Access to the park is by gravel roads. To reach the southern end, turn west off the highway 4km north of Bicheno and follow the signposted road for 7km to the car park. A basic camping ground with a pit toilet is provided, and you can throw yourself into the **Apsley Waterhole** for refreshment.

At the time of writing, access to the northern end of the park was restricted due to dangerous road conditions on the forestry E-road that leaves the highway at Thompsons **Marshes**. You can still walk the Leeaberra **Track** (see below), but you need to leave your vehicle beside the highway and walk the 5.5km along the E road to the start of the track. For up-to-date information on the road situation, call local parks rangers on ☑6256 7070, or visit www.parks.tas.gov.au.

National park entry fees apply. Open fires are not permitted here from October to April, when cooking is only allowed on fuel stoves.

Bushwalking

There's an easy 10-minute stroll along a wheelchair-standard track leading to the **Apsley Lookout**, where you can get a great view over the river. A three- to four-hour return walk leads to **Apsley Gorge**.

At the park's northern end is the walk to **Heritage and Leeaberra Falls**, which takes five to seven hours return (plus the walk in from the road). There's camping near the falls.

For experienced walkers, the major walk is the three-day **Leeaberra Track**. The walk must be done from north to south to prevent the spread of the *Phytophthora* plant disease present in the south. There can be little adequate drinking water on this walk, so you may need to carry your own. Check with Parks & Wildlife before you undertake it. Water from the Apsley River needs to be boiled for three minutes before drinking it.

WORTH A TRIP

IRON HOUSE BREWERY

Has all this adventuring left you thirsty? Then your thirst may need quenching at **Ironhouse Point** (☑6372 2228; www.ironhouse.com.au). This hidden secret, just off the Tasman Hwy 38kms north of Bicheno, is Tasmania's newest microbrewery and produces six flavoursome boutique brews. You can sample them for free at the Brew Haus Café Bar, (accompanying tasting plates cost $10). If you visit on a Saturday (11.30am) you can join a tour of the brewery ($15 including tasting plate). The cool, white **Brew House** (mains $10-28; ☺lunch & dinner daily, breakfast Sat & Sun) has vast windows overlooking the sea. There's also fine dining at **Le Blanc restaurant** (mains $32; ☺lunch Sat & Sun, dinner Tue-Sun). There's accommodation here too (doubles $160 to $200), but it's really the eating and drinking that are the hit.

WARNING

Cyclists riding **Elephant Pass** must be careful. The road is steep, narrow and winding, and it's difficult for vehicles to negotiate their way around bicycles.

St Marys

POP 800

St Marys is a peaceful little town in the Mt Nicholas range, surrounded by forests and cattle farms. Visit for the quiet, small-town atmosphere and the craggy heights around town, which you can climb for breathtaking views over the area.

e.scApe Tasmanian Wilderness Café & Gallery (☏6372 2444; Main Rd) has information leaflets and can give walking advice. It also serves cafe meals, has internet access and offers a laundry with dryers for campers to use.

The top of **South Sister** (832m), towering over German Town Rd, 6km north of town, is a 10-minute walk from the car park. To get to **St Patricks Head** (683m) turn down Irishtown Rd, just east of town. This long, steep, 90-minute (one-way) climb with some cables and a ladder is a true challenge, but the top is a spectacular vantage point for views right along the coast.

You can also have horseback adventures at St Marys. **Mariton House** (☏6372 2059; www.maritonhouse.com) is close to town, just off the A4 Esk Hwy from St Marys Pass. It offers a variety of trail rides and can organise east-coast beach rides. There's also B&B accommodation available here.

🛏 Sleeping & Eating

Addlestone House   B&B **$$**
(☏6372 2783; www.addlestonehouse.com.au; 19 Gray Rd; s 110, d $140; 🖧) This immaculate B&B is as good as they get. The rooms are beautifully decorated, there's a cosy guest lounge, and the host is charming. Highly recommended: the top place to stay in these parts.

St Marys Seaview Farm   B&B **$**
(☏6372 2341; www.seaviewfarm.com.au; Germantown Rd; dm $40, d with shared bathroom $75, d units $95-110) Yes, 'Seaview' is right: the coastal panoramas from here are unbelievable. This beef and blueberry farm is a quiet hilltop retreat – the kind of place you'll want to

stop and stay for a while. You'll find Seaview Farm at the end of a dirt track 8km from St Marys – Germantown Rd opposite St Marys Hotel. Bring all your own food and leave the kids (under 12) at home.

St Marys Hotel   PUB **$**
(☏6372 2181; Main Rd; s/d $45/70) There's accommodation upstairs at this corner pub: ask for one of the handsome newly renovated rooms. It also does good dinners ($10 to $26) in the restaurant nightly. Try the great homemade pies.

FREE **St Marys Recreation Ground**   CARAVAN PARK, CAMPGROUND
(Harefield Rd) There are free caravan and tent camping sites as well as hot and cold showers next to the peaceful, green oval here. It's a right turn after the rivulet off Grey Rd (A4) heading out of town towards Elephant Pass.

Purple Possum Wholefoods   CAFE **$**
(5 Story St; light meals $5.50-12.95; ◷9am-6pm Mon-Fri, to 2pm Sat) An unexpected find in a little country town, this place has wonderful homemade soups, vegetarian wraps, fabulous coffee and cakes to die for. You can't go past the rhubarb cake.

Mt Elephant Fudge   ICE CREAM **$**
(7 Story St; fudge from $3; ◷10am-5pm Mon-Fri) Don't miss this new place, right next to Purple Possum. There's fudge in 10 different flavours, handmade chocolates, Belgian hot chocolate, smoothies, sundaes and cheesecake. Sound tempting?

Mt Elephant Pancake Barn   CAFE **$$**
(www.mountelephantpancakes.com.au; Mt Elephant Pass; pancakes $7.90-20.90; ◷8am-5.30pm, reduced hr winter) This place, 9km south of town off the highway to Bicheno, is a bit of an institution, but it may just be a tad overrated and over-priced. Cash payment only.

❶ Getting There & Away

The **Calows Coaches** (www.calowscoaches. com) Launceston–St Helens service stops at St Marys. (Redline and Tassielink buses from Hobart connect with this service at Epping or Conara on the Midlands Hwy):

Launceston–St Marys ($31, two hours)

St Marys–St Helens ($6.50, 40 minutes)

Broadby's also stops here on its postal run from St Helens; see p166.

Scamander & Beaumaris

POP 990 (COMBINED)

Low-key Scamander and Beaumaris probably aren't much of an attraction in themselves, but they do have beautiful, long white-sand beaches where the surf rolls in and you feel like you can wander forever. There are good surfing spots around Four Mile Creek. Fishers can toss in a line for bream from the old bridge over the Scamander River, or try catching trout further upstream. Shelley Point, just north of town, has rock pools to explore and shells to collect.

🛏 Sleeping & Eating

Pelican Sands APARTMENTS $$
(☑6372 5231; www.pelicansandsscamander.com.au; 157 Scamander Ave; unit d $100-160, f $160-230; 🖳) If you want to stay on the waterfront, you can't get closer to the beach than this. Most units have been recently renovated and are top notch. There's also a brand new restaurant, Wise & Tilly (mains $19 to $37) on site here, which promises to be excellent.

Scamander Beach Resort Hotel HOTEL $$
(☑6372 5255; www.scamanderbeach.com.au; Tasman Hwy; d $110; 🖳) Though it's Soviet blocish from the outside, this hotel has a lovely lounge interior and the newly renovated rooms are really decent – most have great sea views. The highlight, though, is the excellent Asian-influenced Five Spice restaurant

(mains $22 to $29; open for dinner), and the pub here does lunches (mains $20 to $26).

Scamander Tourist Park CARAVAN PARK $$
(☑6372 5121; Scamander Ave; unpowered/powered sites d $20/30, extra adult/child $10/5, on-site vans $60, cabins $85-200, extra adult/child $20/10) There are shady sites at this simple park and it's close to the beach. Pets are allowed in the camping and caravan area, and there's a camp kitchen, a laundry and a playground.

Eureka Farm CAFE $
(www.eurekafarm.net, 89 Upper Scamander Rd; breakfast & light meals $8-15; ⊙8am-6pm Oct-Jun, 10am-4pm Jul-Sep) A couple of kilometres south of Scamander is a sign for this fruitlover's paradise, and it's worth the short detour. Try a smoked-salmon omelette for breakfast, or get stuck into the all-day fruit wonders: berry crepes, the fruitiest ice creams, smoothies, summer puddings or the amazing choc-raspberry pavlova.

St Helens

POP 2000

Set on the wide and protected sweep of Georges Bay, St Helens began life as a whaling and sealing settlement in the 1830s. Soon the 'swanners' came to plunder here, harvesting the bay's black swans for their downy underfeathers. By the 1850s, the town was a permanent farming settlement, which swelled in 1874 when tin was

---

FINGAL VALLEY

To get off the east-coast tourist route, head west from St Marys on the A4 and drive through beautiful, rolling country to Fingal, Mathinna and the Evercreech Forest Reserve.

Sleepy **Fingal**, 21km west of St Marys, was one of the larger agricultural settlements from the early days of the colony and has fine 19th-century buildings in the main street. It holds the quirky annual **Fingal Valley Festival** in March, including World Roof Bolting and World Coal Shovelling Championships.

For amazing tree-scapes, visit **Evercreech Forest Reserve**, 34km north of Fingal, near Mathinna. A 20-minute circuit walk through blackwood and myrtle takes you to the White Knights, a group of the world's tallest white gums (*Eucalyptus viminalis*); the loftiest branches reach 91m. You can also visit **Mathinna Falls** (follow signs from the Mathinna junction on the B43), a spectacular 80m-high, four-tier waterfall. There's a 30-minute return stroll to the base.

The 1844 Fingal Hotel (☑6374 2121; 4 Talbot St, Fingal; s with/without bathroom $50/40, d with/without bathroom $70/60) has no-frills rooms and serves lunch and dinner daily. For the best coffee in these parts, try the Hayshed Café (31-33 Talbot St, Fingal; mains $5-18; ⊙8am-4pm Mon-Fri), which also does light meals and sweet treats.

There's camping at the Griffith Camping Area (signposted off the C423 just after you turn off for Mathinna Falls), and free camping in town with toilets and power just past the post office on Talbot St.

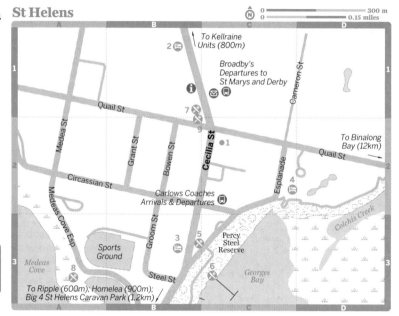

discovered. St Helens has long been an important Tasmanian fishing port and today harbours the state's largest fishing fleet. All that fish means there's plenty of excitement for anglers: charter boats will take you out to where the big game fish swim. For landlubbers this sweet little town is a lively holiday spot. There are plenty of places to eat and stay, and good beaches nearby.

◉ Sights & Activities

Fishing

If you are at all into the sport of fishing, then St Helens – Tasmania's game-fishing capital – is the place to collect stories about the big one that didn't get away. The following operators offer game-fishing charters:

Professional Charters (☑6376 3083, 0419 383 362; www.gamefish.net.au)

Gone Fishing Charters (☑6376 1553, 0419 353 041; www.breamfishing.com.au)

Zulu Fishing Charterz (☑0438 279 164, 0409 705 605)

Keen Angler (☑0409 964 847)

Swimming & Watersports

Because it's set on a muddy, tidal bay, St Helens' beaches aren't tops for swimming. The beaches at **Stieglitz** (7km away at St Helens

Point) and at **Humbug Point** are better options, though check surf conditions as there can be rips.

The calm waters of Georges Bay are excellent for water sports. **East Lines** (☑6376 1720; 28 Cecilia St; ⊙9am-5pm Mon-Fri, 10am-2pm Sat & Sun summer) hires equipment (surfboards, wetsuits, snorkelling gear and fishing rods) and also has bikes for rent ($5/15/25 per hour/four hours/day).

Walking

Both sides of the entrance to Georges Bay are state reserves and have some gentle walking tracks. A good track circles around **St Helens Point** (one hour return; take St Helens Point Rd out). Also on St Helens Point are the spectacular **Peron Dunes**.

On the north side of Georges Bay, off Binalong Bay Rd, is the Humbug Point Recreation Area. Skeleton Bay (10km north) and Dora Point (11km north) offer hours of walking on well-marked tracks. Ask at the St Helens visitor centre for their walking map and track notes.

☞ Tours

Johno's 'Quicky' 4WD Tas Tours   OFF-ROAD
(☑6376 3604, 0418 132 155; www.johnos4wdtours.com.au) Venture up dry riverbeds, make wet river crossings and climb steep hills around

St Helens

Activities, Courses & Tours
1 East Lines...................................C2

Sleeping
2 Artnor Lodge B1
3 St Helens Backpackers.....................B3
4 Tidal Waters Resort......................C2

Eating
5 Bayside Inn Bistro..............................B3
6 Blue Shed.......................................C3
7 Breakers......................................B1
8 Salty Seas A3
9 Village Store & More.........................B2

St Helens for sublime views on one of Johno's 'quickies' (1½ hours, $35). Half-day tours ($85) discover the Bay of Fires or Pyengana, taking in secret spots along the way, and full-day excursions visit both coast and rainforest ($145).

Green Island Cycle Tours BICYCLE
(☑6376 3038; www.cycling-tasmania.com; 3 Simeon Pl) Wish you could mosey along the east coast by bike, with all logistics taken care of? That's exactly what this gang will let you do. It offers four-day ($750 to $1350) St Helens–Hobart and 11-day ($1790 to $3580) Launceston–Hobart trips including all accommodation in varying levels of luxury, breakfasts and lunches. You'll be picked up from the airport and provided with the sagwag, which also transports all your gear as you ride. Bike hire is extra.

🛏 Sleeping

Camping CAMPGROUND
There are free camping sites in bushland north of St Helens at Humbug Point Nature Recreation Area. The turn-off is 7km out of town, en route to Binalong Bay. The camping area is a further 5km through the reserve, at Dora Point.

Bed in the Treetops B&B B&B $$$
(☑6376 1318; www.bedinthetreetops.com.au; 701 Binalong Bay Rd; s $200-230, d $250-310) Some 7km out of St Helens en route to Binalong Bay, you drive up and up through the trees to reach this secluded, stylish wooden home. There are two luxurious apartments here, immaculately furnished and with spas and views. Rates include afternoon tea or pre-dinner drinks and a full breakfast. Extra person $75.

Tidal Waters Resort RESORT $$$
(☑6376 1999, 1800 833 980; www.tidalwaters.com. au; 1 Quail St; d $165-260, extra person $40; @≋) On the tidal lagoon at Georges Bay, this large complex has 60 rather generic rooms (some with disabled facilities) and echoingly large public areas. There's an à la carte restaurant (mains $17 to $36; open for dinner) and a deck for casual lunches (mains $10 to $20) in summer right on the water's edge.

Artnor Lodge MOTEL $$
(☑6376 1234; 71 Cecilia St; d $105) Just back off St Helen's leafy main street, this neat and peaceful little complex has off-street parking, clean rooms and shared laundry-kitchen facilities.

Homelea APARTMENTS $$
(☑6376 1601; www.homeleasthelens.com.au; 16 & 22 Tasman Hwy; cottage d $160-189, unit d $95-155; ☎) Just over the road from the water, Homelea is a neat, brightly painted complex with comfortable units, some recently renovated. There's plenty of space for kids to tear about and a playground where they can burn energy. There's also a spa cottage. Extra adult/child $20/15.

St Helens Backpackers HOSTEL $$
(☑6376 2017; www.sthelensbackpackers.com.au; 9 Cecilia St; dm $25-30, d 50-75) This is a hostel of the very nicest variety: it's spick and span, peaceful and spacious. The newly renovated 'flashpacker' section has dorms and doubles with fancy bathrooms attached. Hang out on the spacious deck and BBQ or shoot the breeze. It also hires out bikes ($20) and arranges camping trips to the Bay of Fires with all camping gear included.

Kellraine Units APARTMENTS $
(☑6376 1169; 72 Tully St; d $70, extra adult/child 40/20) On the way out of town to the north, these clean, self-contained units (one with wheelchair access) are good value. The friendly owners tend a good video library, too.

Big 4 St Helens Caravan Park CARAVAN PARK $$
(☑6376 1290; st-helens-caravan-park.tas.big4. com.au; 2 Penelope St; unpowered/powered sites d $28-38/$30-40, cabins & villas d $80-200; @☎) This park is in a green setting south of town and has family-friendly amenities including a games room, a jumping pillow and a playground. There's a good camp kitchen and laundry facilities too. Extra person $15 in cabins and villas.

✕ Eating

Blue Shed Restaurant SEAFOOD **$$**
(☑6376 1170; www.blueshedrestaurant.com.au;
Marina Pde; mains $18-35; ⊙lunch & dinner) This
commendable eatery does the best seafood
in St Helens. Start with a spicy oyster shoot-
er, and then try its signature crispy squid,
or opt for grilled rock lobster with herb
and mascarpone butter. It also does pizzas,
chicken and beef. There's a takeaway outlet
on the side.

Ripple MODERN AUSTRALIAN **$$**
(☑6376 2444; 2 Tasman Hwy; mains $7-30; ⊙lunch
Thu-Sun, dinner Tue-Sun) Ask locals their favourite spot to eat and they might well tell you
it's here. The young couple that run the place
have a talent for shaping the freshest of
local produce – and plenty of seafood – into
meals you'll want to linger over. The tender
pork belly with potato and chilli dumplings
is divine.

Village Store & More CAFE, DELI **$**
(55 Cecilia St; meals $8-15; ⊙breakfast & lunch)
This great little eatery serves what it calls
'peasant food' on big wooden tables among
funky decor. There are wood-fired organic
breads, gourmet Tassie titbits to take away,
scrumptious breakfasts and lunch items like
focaccias, rotis and homemade meat pies.
Try the salmon Mardi Gras: 'like a party in
your mouth'.

Breakers CAFE **$**
(57a Cecilia St; meals $6-15; ⊙8am-4pm Mon-Fri,
to 3pm Sat) Eat outside under the umbrellas
here, just off the main street, or take away
good, simple fare including sandwiches,
salads and meaty or vego mains. It does
fantastic homemade jam and cinnamon do-
nuts. There's 10% off for seniors and it's pet
friendly too.

Salty Seas SEAFOOD **$$**
(18 Medeas Cove Esplanade; mussels/crayfish per
kg $7/50; ⊙daily) Crayfish are the speciality
here – you can choose them right out of the
tanks – but there are also oysters, mussels
and fish fresh off the boat. Feast on this ma-
rine abundance on the deck overlooking a
bird sanctuary.

Bayside Inn Bistro PUB **$$**
(2 Cecilia St; mains $15-30; ⊙breakfast summer,
lunch & dinner) A big, crowd-pleasing menu
is on offer here, with lots of the expected meat
and fish dishes (roast of the day, schnitzel,
steak, and fish and chips), but also crayfish
(in season) and a few veg options.

ℹ Information

ATMs and the **post office** are on Cecilia St.
Online Access Centre (61 Cecilia St; ⊙9am-
5pm Mon-Fri, 10am-noon Sat & Sun; 🛜)
Service Tasmania (61 Cecilia St; ⊙8.30am-
4.30pm Mon-Fri) Has national parks passes.
St Helens visitor centre (☑6376 1744; 61
Cecilia St; ⊙9am-5pm) Is just off the main
street behind the library. It also houses the
town's History Room.

ℹ Getting There & Away

Broadby's (☑6376 3488) makes a weekday
postal run – with an informal lift-share system –
between St Helens and St Marys. This departs
from behind St Helens post office at 7am and
leaves St Marys post office at 8am. The contribution is $7 for petrol money each way. The St
Helens– Derby– Winnaleah– St Helens run departs from the same spot at 9.45am weekdays,
costing $15 each way. It meets the **Sainty's**
bus from Scottsdale (see p171) in Winnaleah or
Derby. There's a $5 charge to transport bikes.

Calows Coaches (www.calowscoaches.com; 2
Circassian St, St Helens) runs from Launceston
to St Helens ($32, three hours).

Tassielink (www.tassielink.com.au) and
Redline (www.tasredline.com.au) connect with
Calows Coaches at Epping Forest or Conara on
the Midlands Hwy (Hobart to St Helens $51, four
hours).

Bay of Fires

The Bay of Fires is a 29km sweep of powder-
white sand and crystal-clear seas that's been
called one of the most beautiful beaches in
the world. To think of the Bay of Fires as just
one beach, though, is really a mistake The
Bay of Fires is made up of a string of superb
beaches, punctuated by lagoons and rocky
headlands, and backed by coastal heath
and bush. There are gulches full of crayfish
and abalone, and there's great recreational
diving in the bay's clear waters. The ocean
beaches provide some good surfing but are
prone to rips. Check conditions with locals
before swimming, or plunge into one of the
tiny rock-protected coves.

There's no road that runs the length of
the bay. The C850 heads out of St Helens to
the gorgeous beachside holiday settlement
of **Binalong Bay**, which marks the southern
end of the Bay of Fires. The road (C848) continues north to holiday 'shacks' at the Gardens, but stops here. There are some beautiful bush-camping sites behind the beaches

all along this stretch; **Swimcart Beach** and **Cosy Corner** are the most popular and have pit toilets. **Seatons Cove** and **Sloop Beach** are generally quieter. Bring your own water and firewood: fires are allowed outside fire-ban periods.

The bay's northern end is reached via the gravel C843, which leads to **Ansons Bay** and then Mt William National Park. Pretty Ansons Bay is a quiet holiday village that's a popular fishing, boating and swimming spot: if you have kayaks, Ansons River Lagoon is perfect for sheltered paddling. Policemans Point has free camping spots. There are no petrol stations or shops at Ansons Bay, so fill up at either St Helens or Gladstone.

Eddystone Point, just north of Ansons Bay, marks the Bay of Fires' northern extremity. Since 1889 the imposing granite tower of Eddystone Point Lighthouse (37m) has warned ships off this rocky shoreline. The complex, which includes historic lighthouse keepers' cottages, is worth a visit. There's bush camping at nearby Deep Creek within Mt William National Park.

☞ Tours

TOP CHOICE Bay of Fires Walk   WALKING
(✆6392 2211; www.bayoffires.com.au; Oct, Nov, Dec & Apr $2050, Jan-Mar $2150) From November to May the Bay of Fires Walk can take you on a four-day, three-night adventure in this glorious wave-washed domain. A maximum of 10 guests beachcomb the coastline, expertly led by knowledgeable and personable guides. The first night is spent at a secluded tented beach camp, the next two at the sublime Bay of Fires Lodge, which is both architecturally innovative and environmentally sound. Based here for day three, you can opt to kayak on peaceful Ansons River or just laze at the lodge, working up an appetite for dinner. Fine wines and dining accompany this relaxed, beachside journey that takes you a million miles away from it all.

Binalong Bay

POP 200

Set on a sheltered gulch, and drenched in picture-perfect views of sea and sand, Binalong Bay is the only permanent settlement on the Bay of Fires. It was first used by fishermen and farmers around 1900, and only by the 1940s were there any permanent residents. Now, this quiet spot is growing in popularity as a beachside holiday idyll. There's not much here – no shops, just some holiday cottages, and a wonderful white-sand beach, but it is precisely this quiet, low-key atmosphere that most people come for. At the time of writing, the famed Angasi restaurant here had just closed down – but rumour had it that there was another eatery planned for the same location: ask before you go.

Swimming, snorkelling and surfing draw water babies to Binalong. There's good surf in and around the bay, and great swimming on calm days. Snorkellers head to **Binalong Gulch**, where they can pick up abalone (with a licence). This is one of the best spots in Tasmania for diving: the elusive weedy sea dragon is often spotted here. **Bay of Fires Dive** (✆6376 8335, 0419 372 342; www.bayoffiresdive.com.au; 291 Gardens Rd) rents out scuba equipment and does boat dives and subaqua training. You can also hire snorkelling gear and wetsuits here.

🛏 Sleeping

Point Break   RENTAL HOUSE $$$
(✆6331 1224; www.pointbreakbinalong.com; 20 Beven Heights; d 200-220, extra person $40) Surely the coolest beachhouse at Binalong Bay. All timber floors, high ceilings and bright, nautical white, this beautifully furnished house is a place to chill with friends after a day in the surf. It has every possible mod con, and sleeps up to eight.

Bay of Fires Character
Cottages   COTTAGES $$
(✆6376 8262; www.bayoffirescottages.com.au; 64-74 Main Rd; d $160-220, extra person $30-50) These well-kitted-out cottages have a million-dollar location overlooking the bay. All have mesmerising views, in which you can absorb yourself as you hang out and have a BBQ on the deck. There are full kitchen and laundry facilities in each.

Bay of Fires Bed and Breakfast   B&B $$
(✆6376 8332, 0407 300 766; www.bayoffires bedandbreakfast.com.au, 16 Bevan Heights; d 130, d 2 nights $220, extra person $50) Your hosts, Des and Violet, have converted the ground floor of their house into two immaculately neat B&B rooms. There's an en-suite bathroom, laundry facilities, and a covered deck for BBQs. Their slap-up breakfast is served on the upstairs deck with sea views.

Angasi Apartment   RENTAL HOUSE $$
(✆6376 8222; www.angasi.com.au; Main Rd; d $160, extra person $50) From the outside this looks

WORTH A TRIP

THE GREEN FIELDS OF PYENGANA

About 26km west of St Helens the turn-off to tiny Pyengana (pie-en-*ga*-na) leads to an impossibly emerald-green valley with three great attractions you simply shouldn't miss.

'Pyengana' is derived from an Aboriginal word describing the meeting of two rivers and it's these, together with the high rainfall here, that make ideal dairy pasture. In the 1890s, European pioneers recognised this and brought in dairy cattle, which thrived on the lush grass. Exporting milk from this isolated valley was impractical, but once converted into cheese and butter the produce could survive the slow journey to market.

Today, cheddar cheese is still produced using century-old methods at the **Pyengana Dairy Company** (St Columba Falls Rd; ◷9am-5pm Sep-May, 10am-4pm Jun-Aug), but these days the milking process is robotic – and if you visit you get to watch it. You can also taste and purchase cheddars in kaleidoscopic flavours, then take a seat in the **Holy Cow! Café** (meals $8-35) for dairy delights like ploughman's lunch, cheese on toast, milkshakes and heavenly, rich ice creams. Try the pepperberry version, flavoured with berries from the nearby Blue Tier plateau.

Pyengana **Pub in the Paddock** (☑6373 6121; St Columba Falls Rd; s/d/tw $55/75/80; mains $12-25; ◷lunch & dinner) is world famous for Priscilla, Princess of the Paddock, the beer-imbibing pig, but it's worth a visit just as much for its old-world country atmosphere and great home-cooked meals. It's also a lovely place to stay: rooms are prettily decorated and peaceful. You'll wake up to views of the cow pastures and thoroughly country sounds.

Further down the valley there's also **St Columba Falls**. They take a spectacular 90m plunge off the hillside and are particularly impressive after rain. An easy 20-minute walk from the car park (where there are loos and picnic tables) leads to a platform at their base. If you loved this you'll also appreciate **Ralphs Falls** (take the turn-off to the right signed shortly before St Columba Falls.) There's a 20-minute return walk or a 50-minute circuit taking in the falls and sweeping views across astoundingly green farmland. Note: it's not recommended to continue on the rough road past Ralphs Falls to Ringarooma unless you have a 4WD with good clearance.

like a humble little fisherman's cottage, but inside it's been funkily modernised to make it a cool beachside apartment: perfect for romantic escapes. The sound of the sea will shush you to sleep. Extra person $50.

Bay of Fires Retreat RENTAL HOUSE **$$$** (☑0419 319 131; Jeanneret Beach; up to 6 people $250-350) Thirty minutes' stroll along the beach from Binalong Bay, this breezy, private beachhouse sleeps up to six in classy surroundings with Tasmanian art on the walls.

Weldborough

POP 50

As the Tasman Hwy approaches the Weldborough Pass, an arabesque cutting that is famously popular with motorcyclists, it follows a high ridge with vistas of surrounding forests and mountains. Near the top, stop at the **Weldborough Pass Rainforest Walk** for a 15-minute interpretative circuit through moss-covered myrtle rainforest.

Tiny Weldborough is almost a ghost town today, compared with the bustling settle-

ment it must have been in the midst of the tin rush here in the late 1800s. In mining days Weldborough had 800 inhabitants, mostly Chinese, and there are still remains of their culture here.

In a quiet, forest setting the characterful **Weldborough Hotel** (☑6354 2223; www. Tasman Hwy; unpowered/powered sites for 2 $5/20, dm $15, s $50, d $70-85, f $100-120; meals $5-28; ◷lunch, dinner Mon-Sat, dinner by booking in winter) is a favourite spot with cyclists and makes a wonderful lunchtime or overnight stop for anyone. It serves excellent food and has comfortable rooms in a welcoming, country-hotel atmosphere. If you're a beer appreciator, you shouldn't miss this place: it's now the cellar door for every microbrewery beer in Tasmania. There's camping with hot showers, laundry and BBQ in an attractive setting out back.

You could also base yourself in Welborough for a day or two to do some hiking or mountain biking in the gorgeous **Blue Tier**. There are beautiful rainforest walks and overgrown mining ruins here. The mountain bike trails are developing an enviable reputation amongst bikers in the know. Purchase a map and get info on the Tier at the St Helens visitor centre or the Forest Eco-Centre in Scottsdale.

Mt William National Park

Beautiful Mt William in Tasmania's far northeast corner is one of the state's most gloriously unvisited national parks. It's the kind of place to come and camp for a few days, stroll the beaches, fish, swim or surf, and let the wildlife come to you. It's a land of shimmering turquoise waters, dazzling white beaches, coastal woodlands and heath that's abundant with native animals, birds and flowers. The area was declared a national park in 1973 to protect the endangered Forester kangaroo, which now flourishes here.

The high point of the park is 216m Mt William. It's an easy, gradual climb (two hours return) and affords wide views of the coastline and the islands of the Furneaux Group. These were the high points of the Bassian Plane that formed the land bridge linking Tasmania to what's now the mainland, via which the first inhabitants crossed to Tasmania. Aboriginal habitation of the area is illustrated by the **large shell midden** at Musselroe Point, and many others across the region. To the south, the lighthouse at Eddystone Point is clearly visible, its night-time beam a beacon to ships entering dangerous Banks Strait, between the Furneaux Group and mainland Tasmania.

There's idyllic beachside camping (d $13, extra adult/child $5/2.50, family $16) under the she-oaks at Stumpys Bay, at Top Camp near Musselroe Bay and also beside lovely tannin-stained Deep Creek in the park's south. Campground 4 at Stumpys has a shelter, picnic tables and gas BBQs that are free to use. All the sites have pit toilets but no drinking water. Fires are allowed in designated fire spots, but bring your own firewood and beware of fire restrictions. National park entry fees apply. You can register and pay at the kiosk on the northern access road or, if approaching from the south, buy a pass from Service Tasmania ([icon]1300 135 513; 23 Quail St; ⊙8.30am-4.30pm Mon-Fri) in St Helens.

ⓘ Getting There & Around

The northern end of Mt William is 17km from Gladstone and the southern end is around 60km from St Helens. From Bridport, take the road towards Tomahawk and continue to Gladstone. The nearest petrol stops to the park are in Gladstone or St Helens. There's no petrol station at Ansons Bay. Be careful driving at night as there's always wildlife on the road.

Derby

POP 170

Today little Derby (pronounced *dur*-bee) is a quiet, attractive town set in the valley of the peaceful Ringarooma River. If you're driving from the north, check out the gigantic trout mural splashed across the riverside cliffs as you cross the bridge into Derby.

One hundred years ago Derby was a thriving mining centre, which began when tin was discovered here in 1874. The northeast's

---

THE TRAIL OF THE TIN DRAGON

Tin was discovered in Tasmania's northeast in the late 1800s, attracting thousands of miners. Many came from the goldfields of Victoria, and many were Chinese. At its peak, the Chinese community in and around Derby, Weldborough and Moorina numbered a thousand people. There's currently a project under way to document this Chinese mining heritage on a route called the **Trail of the Tin Dragon**.

The route is still under development but when it's complete it will run between Launceston and St Helens, its centrepiece being the new **Tin Centre** (see p170) in Derby.

At Moorina, visitors can see a **Burning Tower**, inscribed with Chinese characters where paper offerings were burnt for good fortune, and at Branxholm there is the **Red Bridge**, inscribed with Chinese text. Chinese miners congregated for recreation at Weldborough, where there was once a **Daoist temple** (or 'joss house'), now in the Queen Victoria Museum & Art Gallery in Launceston; see p178. There are also Chinese mining artefacts on display in the St Helens visitor centre. Ask at the Scottsdale or St Helens visitor centres whether a map of the trail is yet available, or visit: www.trailofthetin dragon.com.

tin rush attracted thousands and several mines operated in Derby and its surrounds. At its boom-time height, it numbered 3000 souls. In 1929, after heavy rains, a mining dam burst in Derby and 14 people died in the resulting flood. The mines closed for five years after this tragedy; they reopened in 1935 but closed again after WWII, causing an exodus. Today, Derby sells itself on this mining history and has an appealing streetscape that's a pleasure to wander and browse.

⊙ Sights & Activities

Tin Centre MUSEUM
(☑6354 1062; www.trailofthetindragon.com; adult/child/family $12/6/30; ⊙9am-5pm) Derby's tin-mining heritage is on display in this architecturally striking building by the Ringarooma River. The centrepiece is its multimedia presentation 'Life, the Universe and Tin', documenting the life and times of miners and mining in the northeast's tin-mining boom days.

Derby History Room HISTORIC BUILDING
(admission by donation) In the historic Old Schoolhouse building adjacent to the Tin Centre, there's a display on the social history of Derby, as opposed to its mining past. Opening hours vary as it's staffed by volunteers: the Tin Centre can tell you when it's open.

⚐ Festivals & Events

Derby River Derby RIVERBOAT RACE
Derby gets as many as 10,000 visitors in late October for its annual Derby River Derby. Around 500 competitors in all sorts of inflatable craft, with the emphasis on the distinctly homemade, race down a 5km river course. The primary goal in this good-humoured contest is not so much to reach the finish line but to sabotage your neighbours' vessels and be the last one still floating. As a free-for-all spectacle, it's hard to beat.

⚏ Sleeping & Eating

There's not much accommodation in Derby. Free short-term camping is allowed in Derby Park by the Ringarooma River, including caravan spots, but there are but no powered sites. Facilities include toilet blocks, a kids' playground, gas BBQs, picnic tables and a tennis court nearby. Washing is *au naturel:* you can swim in the river.

Tin Dragon Trail Cottages COTTAGES $$$
(☑6354 6210, 0407 501 137; www.tindragontrail cottages.com.au; 3 Cox's Lane, Branxholm; d $200-

250) These sweet, neat – and sustainably built – cottages are set close to the Ringarooma River on a property that has an interesting story to tell from the Chinese mining past (see also p169). They're perfect as a cosy base from which to explore the area. Two interpretative walks here follow some of the original (now dry) mining races built by Chinese miners.

Cloverlea Gardens Bed & Breakfast B&B $$
(☑6354 6370; 27 Legerwood Lane, Branxholm; d $88-110) The Gardens' pretty Camelia Cottage at Branxholm is the best accommodation option near Derby. The glorious gardens here are reason enough to visit, and the cute, cosy cottage (that comes with breakfast provisions) is a peaceful spot to stay.

Cobbler's Cottage RENTAL HOUSE $$
(☑6354 2145; 63 Main St, Derby; d $140, extra person $20) This old timber miner's cottage in the main street is pretty low key, but if you don't mind a basic overnight stop, it's a good self-contained option. It's run by Federal Tavern, just up the street.

Berries Café CAFE $
(☑6354 2520; 72 Main St; meals $5-15; ⊙10am-5pm summer, reduced hr winter) This welcoming cafe is housed in a pretty mining-era weatherboard cottage where you can sit on the verandah in summer or beside the log fire in winter. Try the smoked salmon and King Island brie quiche, homemade with free-range eggs, or the great pavlovas with home-grown berries.

The old mining-era pubs in the area offer budget accommodation and pub meals:

Dorset Hotel PUB $
(☑6354 2360; Main St; s/d $45/70) This creaky old pub in Derby offers very basic rooms, and does decent pizzas of an evening.

Imperial Hotel PUB $
(☑6354 6121; Stoke St; s/d $35/60; ⊙lunch & dinner Wed-Mon) This attractive old building in nearby Branxholm dates from 1907.

Winnaleah Hotel PUB $
(☑6354 2331; Main St; s $50, d with/without bathroom $75/55; ⊙lunch & dinner) Winnaleah's pub offers basic pub rooms, all-day dinner and counter meals of an evening.

ⓘ Getting There & Away

Sainty's North East Bus Services (☑0437 469 186, 0400 791 076) run the Launceston to Derby service ($21, 2½ hours) via Scottsdale .

Scottsdale & Around

POP 2000

Scottsdale was planted on the rich agricultural landscape of Tasmania's northeast in the 1850s, and the main street is lined with some fine heritage buildings. It's a bustling, pocket-sized town that looks out to the rolling hills that surround it. Poppies and potatoes are the big thing here, and Scottsdale has long been a hub for forestry operations as well. Learn about the northeast forests at the town's Forest EcoCentre, and, if you visit in midsummer, take in the amazing sight of endless purple fields of lavender in bloom at Nabowla, nearby.

◎ Sights & Activities

Bridestowe Estate Lavender Farm   FARM
(☑6352 8182; www.bridestowelavender.com.au; 296 Gillespies Rd; ⊙9am-5pm daily Nov-Apr, 10am-4pm Mon-Fri May-Oct) Near Nabowla, 22km west of Scottsdale, is the turn-off to the largest lavender farm in the southern hemisphere. The fragrant, deep-purple display here in the flowering season (mid-December to late January) is unforgettable. The farm produces lavender oil for the perfume industry, and you can take a tour of the operation, including the farm and distillery in the flowering season (adult/child under 16 $7/free). There's also a cafe and gift shop that sells all things lavender, from drawer scenters to fudge to ice cream.

Sideling   LANDMARK
The road from Scottsdale to Launceston crosses a pass called the Sideling (about 15km south of Scottsdale). Outfitted with toilets, picnic tables and outstanding views as far as Flinders Island on a clear day, it makes a great respite from the winding road.

⊨ Sleeping & Eating

Willow Lodge   B&B **$$**
(☑6352 2552; www.willowlodge.net.au; 119 King St; s $90, d $125, extra person $30; ☞) One of the nicest places to stay in the northeast, this wonderful B&B in a Federation home is presented with absolute attention to detail. The bright, colourful rooms look over lovely gardens. The owners spoil guests with after-dinner liqueurs, which you can enjoy in the outside hot tub.

Bella Villa   RENTAL HOUSE **$$**
(☑0428 137 286; 83 King St; units $150-180, extra person $20) There are two spacious units here:

one has two bedrooms sleeping up to five, the other has one bedroom and sleeps three. They're neat, modern and quite stylish: both have full kitchens. Outdoor pets welcome.

Beulah   B&B **$$**
(☑6352 3723; 9 King St; s $110-120, d $130-145; ☞) This elegantly decorated 1878 home has three rooms decked out in heritage style. To be completely spoilt, pick the spa and sauna suite with an open fireplace. There's also a cosy guest lounge, where you can enjoy complimentary port or sherry by the fire.

Anabel's of Scottsdale   APARTMENTS **$$**
(☑6352 3277; www.vision.net.au/~anabels; 46 King St; s/d $110/130, extra adult $15) Anabel's is a National Trust–classified home with accommodation in spacious, modern motel-style units (some with cooking facilities) overlooking a woodland garden.

Lords Hotel   PUB **$**
(☑6352 2319; 2 King St; s/d $40/60, extra person $15; ⊙lunch & dinner) Lord's has been a Scottsdale landmark since 1911 and is still known for better-than-counter pub meals (mains $16 to $25) like its signature chicken Oscar, as well as good roasts and steaks. There's recently refurbished accommodation with shared facilities.

Steakout   CAFE **$**
(15 King St; mains $6-24; ⊙breakfast, lunch & dinner Mon-Sat) This little cafe-restaurant is a local favourite. It does breakfast until 11am and bistro meals all day. There are steaks and hamburgers, good seafood, and good vegetarian options. Scrumptious cakes and coffee too.

Cottage Bakery   BAKERY **$**
(9 Victoria St; ⊙6am-5.30pm Mon-Fri) Pop into this famously good bakery to pick up picnic fodder. It also does fine pies.

❶ Information

ATMs are located along King St, the main road through town. The architecturally innovative **Forest EcoCentre** (King St; ⊙9am-5pm), run by Forestry Tasmania, houses an interactive forest interpretation centre (and also a cafe and gift shop selling local handicrafts). **Scottsdale visitor centre** (☑6352 6520; www.northeast tasmania.com.au) is in the same building.

❶ Getting There & Away

Sainty's North East Bus Services (0437 469 186, 0400 791 076) runs from Launceston to Scottsdale ($12, one hour). In Scottsdale services depart from Rose's Newsagency, King St.

LEGERWOOD CHAINSAW SCULPTURES

When the small community of Legerwood was forced to lop gigantic trees in its main street, planted to commemorate its WWI soldiers, it came up with a novel idea. It commissioned chainsaw sculptor Eddie Freeman to carve figures of the soldiers (and other significant local personages) from the tree stumps that remained. It's really worth the detour off the A3 to St Helens, 24kms south of Scottsdale. Take the C423, signed to Legerwood and Ringarooma. In Scottsdale, Children's Reserve Park has carvings by the same artist.

Bridport

POP 1235

This well-entrenched holiday resort is on the shore of Anderson Bay. Just 85km from Launceston, it's popular with leisure-seeking Tasmanians. Bridport has safe swimming beaches and its sheltered waters are also ideal for waterskiing. Sea, lake and river fishing are also attractions here, and there's trout fishing in nearby lakes and dams. Golfers come from across the globe to play on the two world-class courses nearby. Bridport is also the launching point for the boat to Flinders Island.

Sights & Activities

Barnbougle Dunes   GOLF
(6356 0094; www.barnbougledunes.com; 425 Waterhouse Rd) Who would have thought Australia's current top-ranked public golf course would be in this remote location, 5km east of Bridport? It's a challenging par-71 links, in rolling sand dunes right on the edge of Bass Strait. Green fees for nine holes/18 holes/all day are $70/98/130; golf-set hire is from $55.

Lost Farm   GOLF
(6356 1124; www.lostfarm.com.au; 425 Waterhouse Rd) All sorts of superlatives have been applied to the Lost Farm even before it opened (in October 2010) and it promises to be a formidable rival for Barnbougle (on the same property but managed separately). Like Barnbougle, the course meanders over a wild coastal dunescape, often just metres from

the ocean. A day spa offers massages and treatments to soothe away the golfing aches.

FREE **Bridport Wildflower Reserve**   NATURE RESERVE
(Richard St) The Bridport area is renowned for its native orchids, which flower from September to December. In this reserve, 2kms past the caravan park, you might spot endangered flora like the juniper wattle *(Acacia ulicifolia)*, some of the 49 bird species, or the threatened eastern barred bandicoot, spotted-tail quoll or wedge-tailed eagle.

Tours

Kookaburra Ridge Quad Bike Tours   QUAD BIKING
(6356 1391, 0409 656 213; www.kookaburraridgequadbiketours.com; 238 Boddingtons Rd) Just the thing for the hoon in everyone: quad bike tours over the pastures, gullies and hidden bush tracks outside Bridport. They include instruction in the one-hour tours, which cost $40 per adult. You don't need a licence, but you must be over 16 to drive. Under 16s travel half price as passengers: no under eights.

Sleeping & Eating

Barnbougle Dunes   COTTAGES **$$**
(6356 0094; www.barnbougledunes.com; 425 Waterhouse Rd, d $150-210, extra person $20) There is a row of attractive self-contained timber cottages and villas right on the golf course here. Designed for golfing groups, they sleep four or eight – and each has an expansive verandah where you can relax and have a yarn after a long day's play. From Barnbougle's lively clubhouse you can absorb beach-and-ocean panoramas. Lunch on the deck, try a Tasmania drop in the bar, or fuel your golf-induced appetite on a hearty dinner (mains $22 to $35).

Lost Farm   HOTEL **$$**
(6356 1124; www.lostfarm.com.au; 425 Waterhouse Rd, d $170, extra person $20) There are 50 first-class lodge rooms perched on the oceanside dunes here. They're brand new and feature up-to-the-minute extras like Ipod docks and acres of flat-screen TV. Each has views of sparkling Bass Strait, and it's only a short wander from the restaurant and the first tee. **Dunetop Lost Farm Restaurant** (mains $30; ⊙breakfast & dinner) and bar has fantastic vistas of the course, and a classy but casual feel.

Bridport Bay Inn
MOTEL $$
(☎6356 1238; 105 Main St; d $95-105, villa d $120-135, extra person $15; mains $18-30; ☺lunch & dinner) There are older-style motel units and smart new villas here. The restaurant serves a satisfying menu including good, fresh, locally caught fish and seafood, roasts, and delicious wood-fired pizzas.

Bridport Resort
RESORT $$
(☎6356 1789; www.bridport-resort.com.au; 35 Main St; 1-/2-/3-bedroom villas $160/230/280; ☎☒) A low-key little complex set in bushland right by the sea, this place has a range of neat, recently renovated cabins and Joseph's restaurant (mains $22 to $45; open for dinner Tuesday to Saturday), which is popular with locals. Kids love the resort's play areas, games room and heated indoor saltwater pool and spa.

Platypus Park Country Retreat
RENTAL HOUSE $$
(☎6356 1873; www.platypuspark.com.au; Ada St; d $120-190) In a quiet spot beside the Brid River, Platypus Park has a range of appealing self-contained cottages and units, overseen by the friendly owners, who are fifth-generation Tasmanians and can tell you all about the area. There's trout fishing in well-stocked dams nearby.

Bridport Seaside Lodge Backpackers
HOSTEL $
(☎6356 1585; www.bridportseasidelodge.com; 47 Main St; dm/tw/d $25/28/50, en suite d $80-95) There are great water views from this friendly hostel that feels more like a beachhouse than a backpackers. You can hire bikes and canoes too, or BBQ on the expansive deck.

Bridport Caravan Park
CARAVAN PARK $
(☎6356 1227; Bentley St; unpowered/powered sites $18/25) Strung out for 1.3km of foreshore, this must be Tasmania's longest caravan park. There are BBQs, a kids' playground and a tennis court nearby. It fills up quickly in summer.

Bridport Café
CAFE $
(89 Main St; mains $9-17; ☺9am-4pm) The food is both scrumptious and healthy here. It serves an imaginative cafe menu of salads, homemade soups, good vegetarian fare, coffee and cakes. Great all-day breakfasts too.

❶ Getting There & Away

Stan's Coaches (☎0409 561 662) runs from Scottsdale to Bridport ($5, 40 minutes). The service connects with **Sainty's Northeast Coach Services** (see p170) and does door-to-door pickups/drop-offs on request. Booking essential.

See p175 for details of the weekly **Bridport–Flinders Island ferry**.

Flinders Island

'Mountains in the Sea' is how Flinders Island describes itself – and that's exactly what Flinders and the other 51 islands of the Furneaux Group are. Scattered into Bass Strait off the Tasmanian mainland's eastern tip, they're all that remains here of the land bridge that connected Tasmania with mainland Australia 10,000 years ago.

Flinders had a lawless early history as the domain of sealers. These pirates kidnapped Aboriginal women to take as 'wives', lured ships with lanterns onto the island's rocks, and slaughtered thousands of seals. Flinders is also known, tragically, for its role in the dismal treatment of Tasmania's first inhabitants. Between 1829 and 1834, 135 indigenous people were transported to Wybalenna to be 'civilised and educated'. After 14 years, only 47 survived. See p282 for more.

Today, sparsely populated (just 900 souls spread over 1400 sq km) and naturally gorgeous, Flinders is a rural community that lives mostly from fishing and agriculture. For the visitor, Flinders feels refreshingly remote. There's great bushwalking, wildlife spotting, fishing, kayaking, snorkelling and diving; and safe swimming in its curvaceous, blonde bays. Or you can spend leisurely hours combing the beaches for elusive Killikrankie diamonds and paper nautilus shells.

◉ Sights

Wybalenna Historic Site HISTORIC SITE
A few piles of bricks, the chapel and cemetery are all that remain of this settlement to 'care for' Aboriginal people. Eighty-seven people died here from poor food, disease and despair. You can feel the profound sadness on the wind.

Furneaux Museum MUSEUM
(☎6359 2010; 8 Fowlers Rd, Emita; adult/child $4/free; ☺1-5pm daily late Dec-Jan, 1-4pm Sat & Sun Feb-Nov) The Furneaux Museum lies in grounds strewn with whalebones, blubber pots and rusty wrecks. It displays Aboriginal artefacts (including beautiful shell necklaces), sealing, sailing and mutton-bird industry relics.

Mt Tanner LANDMARK

Drive to the top of Mt Tanner (331m) to see the island laid out spectacularly like a treasure map below. (Turn your back to the ugly communications tower here, though.)

Unavale Vineyard VINEYARD

(☑6359 3632; www.unavale.com.au; 10 Badger Corner Rd) The island's only vineyard produces a fine Sauvignon Blanc. Everything is done on site, right down to the labels. The vineyard welcomes visitors to taste at the cellar door – call first to make sure someone is around.

Activities

There's great **walking** on Flinders. The highlight is a well-signposted (five- to six- hour- return) track to the peak of **Mt Strzelecki** (756m) for awe-inspiring views. At Trousers Point itself, there's also a magnificent 3.4km coastal circuit walk. Ask at the visitor centre about the **Flinders Island Ecology Trail**, which details walks ranging from 20 to 60 minutes. There's also *A Walking Guide to Flinders Island and Cape Barren Island* by Doreen Lovegrove and Steve Summers, and *Walks of Flinders Island* by Ken Martin.

It's easy to find your own private beach for **swimming**. A local secret is the **Docks** below Mt Killiecranke, where granite boulders protect white-sand coves. Trousers Point Beach is the classic Flinders swimming spot, with picnic tables, BBQs, toilets and **free camping** under the she-oaks.

Fishing possibilities around Flinders abound. Bring your own gear, or go on a charter. Several operators arrange trips, including **Flinders Island Adventures** (☑6359 4507; www.flindersisland.com.au), which also does land-based tours. There's also great diving in the clear waters here: talk to **Flinders Island Dive** (☑6359 8429).

The elusive Killiecrankie 'diamond' is actually semiprecious topaz. **Whitemark Shop** (Lagoon Rd) hires shovels ($2) and sieves ($2), and can advise where to fossick.

If you're interested in rock on a larger scale, the granite faces of Mt Killiecrankie (319m) offer challenging **rock climbing**. There's also a climbable 200m granite wall on Mt Strzelecki.

To swoop over it all, take a joy flight with **Flinders Island Aviation** (☑6359 3641; www.flindersislandaviation.com).

Sleeping

Green Valley Homestead RENTAL HOUSE $$

(☑6359 6509; www.flinderislandaccommodation.com.au; Butterfactory Rd, Whitemark; d $150, extra person $25) Two faultlessly pretty properties, the swish Green Valley Homestead, close to Whitemark (sleeps six); and Echo Hills Retreat (doubles $120, extra person $20, sleeps eight), are set in rural paddocks with views and peace.

Vistas on Trousers Point BOUTIQUE HOTEL $$$

(☑6359 4586; www.healingdreams.com.au; 855 Trousers Point Rd; s/d $160/260) At the foot of the Strzelecki Peaks, by Trousers Point Beach, this eclectic lodge offers healing treatments and home-grown organic food. Do yoga in the yurt, grab a bike, soak in the spa or the ocean, absorb the peace.

Lemana RENTAL HOUSE $$

(☑6359 6507; www.lemana.com.au; Port Davies Rd, Emita; d $180, extra person $35) A handsome new beachhouse, sleeping up to six, beautifully equipped and only minutes' stroll from Emita Beach. No kids under 12.

Interstate Hotel PUB $

(☑6359 2114; Patrick St, Whitemark; s $50-70, d $90-110) Clean, comfortable rooms above this Federation pub, some with shared facilities. A big breakfast is included.

Furneaux Tavern PUB $$

(☑6359 3521; Franklin Pde, Lady Barron; d 120, extra person $30; ☎) Timber-panelled motel cabins with wraparound decks, set in native gardens.

Flinders Island Cabin Park CABINS, CAMPGROUND $

(☑6359 2188; www.flindersislandcp.com.au; 1 Bluff Rd, Whitemark; d $20, backpacker cabin s $40, d $90-105, extra person $20) Backpacker accommodation and recently renovated cabins, car and campervan hire ($50 to $110 per day). Free use of bikes for guests (or $25 per day for non-stayers); kayaks coming soon!

Lady Barron Holiday Home RENTAL HOUSE $$

(☑6359 3555; www.ladybarron.com; 31 Franklin Pde; d $110, extra person $20) A homely, renovated 1940s place with three bedrooms (sleeping six).

Camping CAMPGROUND

There is free camping at several spots around the island. North East River, Killiecrankie and Trousers Point are best.

✗ Eating

Fresh fish and seafood are bountiful on Flinders. It's also known for its tender lamb, game and organic vegies. You can find some of these island goodies at:

Vistas Café & Chappells Restaurant
MODERN AUSTRALIAN **$$**

(Vistas on Trousers Point, 855 Trousers Point Rd; mains $29; ☺lunch & dinner midsummer, Wed-Sun rest of yr) Fine dining with views.

Shearwater Restaurant
MODERN AUSTRALIAN **$$**

(Furneaux Tavern, Franklin Pde, Lady Barron; mains $10-33; ☺lunch & dinner 6-7.30pm) Excellent bistro food; don't be late.

Flinders Island Bakery
BAKERY **$**

(Lagoon Rd, Whitemark; sandwiches & pies $4.50-7.50; ☺7am-5pm Mon-Fri, some Sat) Divine wallaby and red-wine pie.

Freckles Café
CAFE **$$**

(Lagoon Rd, Whitemark; mains $10-15; ☺7am-5pm Mon-Fri & weekends in summer) Trendy, friendly cafe serving fine coffees.

JJs on the Bay
CAFE **$**

(☎6359 8499; 527 Killiecrankie Rd, Killiecrankie; mains $8.50-14.50; ☺10am-4pm Thu-Sun summer) Art gallery–cafe close to the beach. Ring to check opening times.

Interstate Hotel
PUB **$$**

(Patrick St, Whitemark; lunch $12.50-16, dinner $18-30; ☺lunch Mon-Fri, dinner 6-7.30pm Mon-Sat) Decent pub grub – get chatting with locals.

ℹ Information

There are no **ATMs**, but most businesses have Eftpos facilities for cash withdrawals.

Online Access Centre (2 Davies St, Whitemark; ☺10am-1pm & 2-5pm Wed-Fri) At the library.

Post office (7 Patrick St, Whitemark; ☺9am-5pm Mon-Fri)

Service Tasmania (☎6359 2201; 2 Lagoon Rd, Whitemark; ☺10am-4pm Mon-Fri) Walking track advice and national park passes.

Visitor centre (☎6359 5002; www.visit flindersisland.com.au; 4 Davies St, Whitemark; ☺9am-4.30pm Mon-Fri)

ℹ Getting There & Away

Sharp Airlines (www.sharpairlines.com.au) covers the following routes:

Melbourne (Essendon)–Flinders ($212)

Launceston–Flinders ($157)

Flinders Island Travel (☎1800 674 719; www.flindersislandtravel.com.au) has package deals (flights, accommodation and car rental).

Furneaux Freight (www.furneauxfreight.com.au; Main St, Bridport) operates a Bridport–Lady Barron car ferry on the high tide on Monday (cars $400 return, extra passenger adult/child $100/55 return). The trip takes eight to nine hours. Advance bookings essential.

ℹ Getting Around

Many roads are unsealed – take great care when driving. Don't drive after dusk unless essential, to avoid killing native wildlife.

Flinders Island Car Hire (☎6359 2168, www.ficr.com.au) has vehicles for $70 to $77 per day. **Flinders Island Cabin Park** also rents vehicles.

There's a **taxi & airport shuttle bus** (☎6359 3664).

THE EAST COAST FLINDERS ISLAND

Launceston & Around

Includes »

Launceston 178
Tamar Valley 191
Legana & Rosevears . 192
Beauty Point 194
Narawntapu
National Park 195
George Town 195
Low Head 196
Lilydale 197
Hadspen & Carrick . . 198
Westbury 199
Liffey Valley 200
Longford 200
Evandale 201
Ben Lomond National
Park 203

Best Places to Eat

» Stillwater (p187)
» Black Cow (p187)
» Pierre's (p187)
» Strathlynn (p192)
» tant pour tant (p187)

Best Places to Stay

» Red Feather Inn (p198)
» Charles (p185)
» Two Four Two (p185)
» Wesleyan Chapel (p202)
» Quamby Estate (p199)

Why Go?

It's hard to imagine a pocket-sized city more lovely than Launceston. Large enough to feel sophisticated, but petite enough for small-town friendliness, Launceston melds historic and contemporary, urbane with country character, and has lively epicurian and arts scenes to boot. It's a city that's refreshingly natural: green parks burgeon with European trees and the wide Tamar River carries the sea breeze. Amazing Cataract Gorge, surrounded by forest and parkland, brings the wilds into the heart of town.

Launceston is cradled by rolling hills, with craggy – sometimes snow-sprinkled – peaks on its horizons. Just outside the city, the gently beautiful Tamar Valley unfolds. Vine-covered hillsides and fertile soils nurture famously top-notch produce that can be sampled at cellar doors and winery-restaurants.

To discover a land of stately homes and historic towns, head south and west of Launceston. Go north to see penguins, lighthouses and the earliest European settlement in Tasmania.

When to Go

Summer sees Launceston come alive with flowering parks and gardens, festivals, and long, still evenings for strolling by the waterfront. March is vintage time, when the vineyards of the Tamar Valley buzz with activity – and then turn gorgeously golden for autumn. Launceston winters are crisp. There's the delight of frosted peaks nearby for snow play and a spot of skiing. Spring in October is a return to budding green. Cataract Gorge gets pumping with white water and is a magnet for kayaking daredevils.

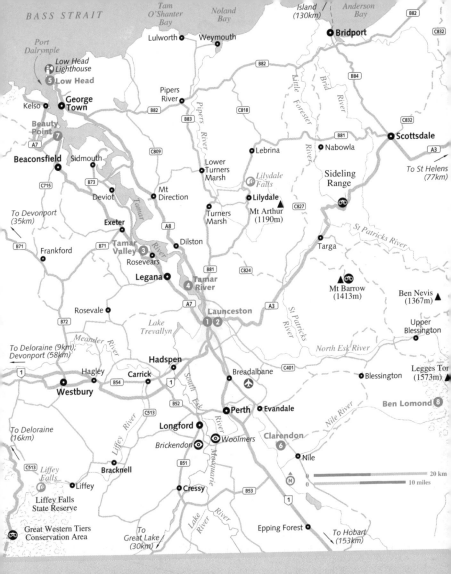

Launceston & Around Highlights

1 Marvelling at the wilds in the city in Launceston's **Cataract Gorge** (p178)

2 Sampling Launceston's **epicurian delights** at one of the city's top-notch restaurants, providores and patisseries (p187)

3 Quaffing fine wines at the many **vineyard cellar doors** of the Tamar Valley (p191)

4 Cruising the **Tamar River** on the *Tamar Odyssey* or the *Lady Launceston* (p181)

5 Spotting the world's tiniest penguins come home from sea at dusk at **Low Head** (p196)

6 Pretending you're on the set of *Gone with The Wind* at Tasmania's grandest colonial home, **Clarendon** (p201)

7 Getting friendly with the sea critters at Beauty Point's **Seahorse World** (p194)

8 Swooping down the ski slopes – or hopping on a mountain bike – at lofty **Ben Lomond** (p203)

Launceston

POP 103,000

Launceston is Tasmania's second city, and has always upheld a hearty rivalry with Hobart in the south. Launcestonians will argue their city is more elegant; their parks and gardens more beautiful, the surrounding hills more verdant – and even their food scene just downright tastier. And on many of these points it's hard to argue.

It might have something to do with the recent rebuilding of arts and museum precincts, with an influx of art students and creative types. Art design is big here, and there's a new respect for the city's fabulous colonial architecture.

Or perhaps it's the recent success of its food and wine scene that's transformed the city. Launceston punches well above its weight in terms of epicurean excellence, and the ambrosial wines of the Tamar Valley garner international respect.

Launceston's also become a sporty, outdoor city of late. Get up early any day of the week, and you'll see squads of road bikers, rowers on the river, swimmers funnelling into Tasmania's best pool, and joggers revelling in the jewel of this place: the amazing wilds-in-the-city of Cataract Gorge.

History

Bass and Flinders were the first Europeans to sight Launceston's Tamar River when they sailed in here on their 1798 voyage of discovery. The first settlement was established in 1804, when the British, intent on beating the French in claiming this island, built a military post at what's known as George Town today. Not long after, an expedition scouted south and found the present-day site of Launceston, naming it for the English seaside town in Cornwall – although this Tasmanian version came to be pronounced *Lon-ses-ton*. Early Launceston was both a port and a military headquarters. By 1827 it already had a population of 2000, and was shipping wool and wheat from the surrounding districts. By the 1850s the town was Tasmania's second major centre and was proclaimed a municipality. In 1871 tin was discovered at Mt Bischoff, which further cemented Launceston's fortunes as a trading hub and a decade later it opened its own stock exchange. In the 20th century it has been an important service town for the rich agricultural region that surrounds it.

Sights

Cataract Gorge PARK
(Map p180; www.launcestoncataractgorge.com.au; ⊙9am-dusk) Ten minutes' wander west of the city centre, edging the residential suburb of Trevallyn, is the magnificent Cataract Gorge. It's amazing to have such a wild area cut right into the core of the city: the bushland, cliffs and tumbling waters of the South Esk River feel a million miles away from town.

Two walking tracks straddle the gorge, leading from Kings Bridge up to the Cliff Grounds Reserve and First Basin, where there's an outdoor **swimming pool** (admission free; ⊙Nov-Mar), picnic spots and fine dining at the Gorge Restaurant (p188) with sociable peacocks loitering outside. There's also a kiosk that serves snacks and afternoon tea. Trails lead from here up to the Cataract and Eagle Eyrie Lookouts. The gorge walk takes about 30 minutes; the northern trail is the easier, while the southern Zig Zag Track has some steep climbs as it passes along the cliff tops. The whole scene is impressively floodlit at night. You can also access First Basin from the main car park by following the signs from York St to Hillside Crescent, Brougham St, then Basin Rd. The **Basin Café** (☑6331 5222; ⊙breakfast, lunch & afternoon tea) has wide views over the river and greenery from fold-back windows and is just the spot for a lazy, late weekend breakfast.

At First Basin, the world's longest single-span **chairlift** (adult/child one way $12/8, return $15/10; ⊙9am-dusk) makes the 10-minute crossing over the parkland and river (you can board at either end). Just upstream is the Alexandra Suspension Bridge. Another walking track (45 minutes one way) leads further up the gorge to Second Basin and further still to Duck Reach, the earliest municipal hydroelectric power station in Australia (established in 1895).

FREE Queen Victoria Museum & Art Gallery MUSEUM
Launceston's wonderful museums are on two sites – at the **Inveresk railyards** (Map p180; ☑6323 3777; www.qvmag.tas.gov.au; 2 Invermay Rd; ⊙10am-5pm) and at **Royal Park** (Map p182; 2 Wellington St). The stylishly renovated industrial warehouses at Inveresk contain natural and social history and technology-focused collections. While admission is free, expect to pay an entrance fee to view any of the touring exhibitions. Inveresk is also home to Launceston's **Planetarium** (adult/child $5/3;

show times 2pm & 4pm Tue-Fri, 2pm & 3pm Sat), which has spectacular shows on the heavens.

At the time of writing, the museum's 1890s Royal Park building was undergoing a meticulous renovation to reveal its original Victorian architectural glory. It was expected to re-open in late 2011, housing arts and decorative arts collections – with an especially fine display of colonial paintings. The park itself is another of Launceston's handsome public spaces. Paths linking the Cataract Gorge Reserve, Ritchie's Mill and Launceston Seaport start here.

City Park   PARK

(Map p182) Wonderful, green City Park has enormous oaks and plane trees, an elegant fountain, a glass conservatory with changing plant displays, a Victorian bandstand and a playground and minitrain for kids. A glass-walled enclosure of **Japanese macaques** (8am-4pm Apr-Sep, to 4.30pm Oct-Mar), a gift from Japanese sister-city Ikeda, will fascinate little ones for hours.

Design Centre of Tasmania   ART GALLERY

(Map p182; 6331 5505; www.designcentre.com.au; cnr Brisbane & Tamar Sts; 9.30am-5.30pm Mon-Fri, 10am-4pm Sat winter, 10am-2pm Sat summer) On the fringes of City Park, the excellent **Wood Design Collection** (adult/child $5/free) showcases local creations in wood, with more sassafras, Huon pine and myrtle than you can shake a stick at. There's also top-notch craftwork for sale – great for classy Tassie gifts.

Boag's Centre for Beer Lovers   BREWERY

(Map p182; 6332 6300; www.boags.com.au; 39 William St; tours at 10am, 11am & 2pm Mon-Thu, 11am & 1pm Fri, tastings 1pm & 2pm Sat summer, 11am & 2pm Sat winter) Boag's beer (imbibed by northern Tasmanian beer-lovers – southerners are loyal to Hobart's Cascade) has been brewed on William St since 1881. You can see this alchemy in action on a variety of tours, ranging from one hour ($18/14 per adult/child) to 90 minutes ($25/22) taking in the brewery and a tasting (with soft drinks for kids). You can taste the full Boag's range on Saturday ($15 per adult). The on-site museum sheds further light on brewing history.

National Automobile Museum of Tasmania   MUSEUM

(Map p180; 6334 8888; www.namt.com.au; 86 Cimitiere St; adult/child $11/6; 9am-5pm Sep-May, 10am-4pm Jun-Aug) Revheads get all revved up over the display here: one of Australia's best presentations of classic and historic cars and motorbikes. The racy '69 Corvette Stingray is so fast, it'll burn tyre tracks into your retinas.

Old Umbrella Shop   HISTORIC BUILDING

(Map p182; 6331 9248; 60 George St; 9am-5pm Mon-Fri, to noon Sat) Launcestonians once kept dry under the umbrellas made here. Now the shop stands as a rare example of an intact early-20th-century store, complete with its original till, and blackwood display cases offering gifts and knick-knacks and, of course, a large range of brollies for sale.

Princes Sq   PARK

(Map p182; btwn Charles & St John Sts) Leafy Princes Sq was once the site of military drills, public hangings and rowdy political meetings. It's graced by a bronze fountain purchased at the Paris Exhibition of 1855. There's also a statue of Dr William Russ Pugh, the first surgeon in the southern hemisphere to use general anaesthetic.

Tasmania Zoo   ZOO

(6396 6100; www.tasmaniazoo.com.au; 1166 Ecclestone Rd, Riverside; adult/child $18/8; 8.30am-5.30pm Oct-Mar, 9am-4pm Apr-Sep) There's a veritable menagerie of feathers, fur and fins here at Tasmania's biggest wildlife park. Over 80 species – native and non native – put in an appearance. They're particularly proud of their Tasmanian devils, which you can watch snarling over a meaty meal (10.30am, 1pm and 3pm). To get to the zoo, take West Tamar Rd (A7) out of Launceston and turn onto Ecclestone Rd (C734) just north of Riverside. The zoo is about 9km from central Launceston. It also has a shuttle bus that picks up visitors from Launceston accommodation ($25/20 per adult/child for a return trip, including park entry).

Franklin House   HISTORIC BUILDING

(6344 7824; 413 Hobart Rd, Franklin Village; adult/child/family $8/free/16; 9am-5pm summer, to 4pm winter Mon-Sat, 12-4pm Sun) Just south of the city, Franklin House is one of Launceston's most attractive Georgian homes. Built in 1838, it's now beautifully restored, furnished and managed by the National Trust. Franklin Village–bound Metro buses 40 and 50 from the city stop here.

Tamar Island Wetlands   NATURE RESERVE

(6327 3964; West Tamar Hwy; adult/child/family $3/2/6; 10am-4pm Apr-Sep, 9am-5pm Oct-Mar) A 10-minute drive north of the city, this wetland reserve has a 2km wheelchair-friendly boardwalk running through it,

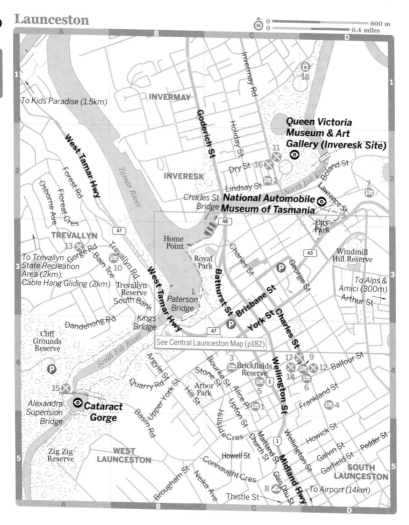

strategically placed to admire all the bird life. The island has BBQs and is perfect for picnicking, kite flying and watching passing boats and waterbirds.

Trevallyn State Recreation Area PARK
(⊙8am-dusk) Artificial Lake Trevallyn on the South Esk River above Cataract Gorge is a favourite spot with the locals for water sports. You can take a picnic and have a splash in the shallows on a warm day. To get here, follow Paterson St west (after crossing Kings Bridge it becomes Trevallyn Rd and then Gorge Rd), then turn right into Bald Hill Rd, left into Veulalee Ave and veer left into Reatta Rd to the reserve.

🏃 Activities

Mountain Bike Tasmania CYCLING
(Map p182; ☎6334 0988; www.mountainbike tasmania.com.au; 120 Charles St; bike hire per day $30; ⊙9am-5.30pm Mon-Fri, to 4pm Sat, 11am-3pm Sun) Get on two wheels and get off the beaten track with Mountain Bike Tasmania. Located in the Mountain Designs store, it offers guided riding tours by the North Esk River ($90) and through the Trevallyn Reserve ($100), as well as a thrilling descent of

Launceston

◎ Top Sights

Cataract Gorge..............................A4
National Automobile Museum of
  Tasmania...................................D2
Queen Victoria Museum & Art
  Gallery (Inveresk Site)..............C2

🛏 Sleeping

1 Alice's Cottages & Spa
  Hideaways.................................C4
2 Arthouse Backpacker Hostel..............C2
3 Auldington..................................C4
4 Charles.....................................D4
5 Launceston Backpackers...................C4
6 Sportsmans Hall Hotel....................D4
7 Thyme Cottage.............................D2
8 Treasure Island Caravan Park..........C5
9 Two Four Two..............................D4
10 Werona....................................B3

🍴 Eating

11 Blue Café Bar..............................C2
12 Burger Got Soul..........................D4
13 Café Culture..............................A3
14 Elaia......................................C4
15 Gorge Restaurant........................A4
16 Me Wah....................................C2
  Pasta Merchant..........................(see 6)
  Sportys Restaurant.....................(see 6)
17 tant pour tant............................C4

🛍 Shopping

18 Esk Market.................................D1

Ben Lomond ($175) – a downhill adrenaline rush losing 1050m in altitude as fast as you can say 'Marzocchi shocks'. For experienced riders there are also day trips to the Blue Tier ($250).

Tasmanian Expeditions   ROCK CLIMBING
(☑6331 9000, 1300 666 856; www.tasmanian expeditions.com.au; departures 8.30am yr round on request) Let the good outdoor crew at Tasmanian Expeditions show you some adventure on the dolerite crags of Cataract Gorge. It offers half-day ($170 per person, $120 for two or more people) and full-day ($200, minimum two people) climbs. You need no previous climbing experience and it provides all the gear. Bookings preferred.

Cable Hang Gliding   HANG-GLIDING
(☑0419 311 198; www.cablehanggliding.com. au; Reatta Rd; adult/child $20/15, tandems $30; ⊙10am-5pm daily Dec-Apr, Sat & Sun May-Nov

& school holidays) Who hasn't looked at a bird and marvelled at its swooping, soaring flight? You can do the same with a spot of cable hang-gliding. You'll hurtle over the edge of a cliff and glide down a 200m-long cable, suspended under wide wings. It's great stomach-in-your-mouth fun. Head west along Paterson St and from King's Bridge follow the signs.

Launceston Aquatic   SWIMMING
(Map p182; ☑6323 3636; www.launcestonaquatic. com.au; 18a Hight St; adult/child $6/5; ⊙6am-8pm Mon-Fri, 8am-6pm Sat & Sun) Lofty Windmill Hill, with its green lawns and panoramas over the city, is home to Launceston's superb new aquatic centre. There are several pools indoors and out, a watery playground for kids, and the really quite salubrious Cube Aqua cafe.

Kids Paradise   PLAY CENTRE
(☑6334 0055; www.kidsparadise.net.au; 32 Elouera St; adult/toddler/child/family $12/$5/$9/$15; ⊙9am-4pm school holidays, 9am-4pm Tue-Sun school terms) On rainy days this is the place to let the little ones loose. There are three floors offering rapturous fun here: a pirate playground, interactive rooms, giant inflatables for bouncing all over, and an array of Wiis, Xboxes and Playstations for little video-game addicts.

To get here from Launceston city centre, follow West Tamar Rd (A7) 5km north. As you approach the suburb of Riverside, turn left into Pomona Rd. Travel right around the roundabout and double back the way you came. Turn right onto the A7, back in the direction of Launceston and then take the exit onto Elouera St.

👉 Tours

Tamar River Cruises   CRUISES
(Map p182; ☑6334 9900; www.tamarrivercruises. com.au; Home Point Pde) To appreciate Launceston from the water, hop on board the 1890s-style *Lady Launceston* for a 50-minute exploration of Cataract Gorge and the Launceston riverfront ($25/12 per adult/child). If you're up for more extended cruising, board the *Tamar Odyssey* for the Batman Bridge luncheon cruise ($115/60 per adult/child). There's also an extended afternoon cruise and an evening voyage with dinner on Saturday night in summer (November to March).

Launceston Historic Walk   WALKING
(☑6331 2213; adult/child/family $15/10/40; ⊙10am Tue-Sat, 4pm Mon) Get your historical

Central Launceston

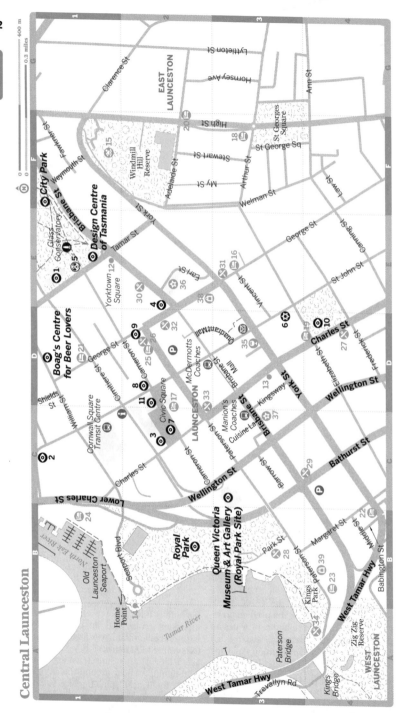

400 m
0.2 miles
0

EAST LAUNCESTON

Lyttleton St

Hornsey Ave

Ann St

Clarence St

St Georges Square

St George Sq

High St 20

18

Stewart St

Arthur St

Adelaide St

My St

Welman St

Windmill Hill Reserve

15

Fawkner St

Weymouth St

City Park

Brisbane St

Glass Conservatory

Design Centre of Tasmania

Tamar St

George St

William St

Law St

Canning St

St John St

Earl St

16

31

5

1

36

38

30

4

Yorktown Square 12

Vincent St

6

19

10

Charles St

27

Boag's Centre for Beer Lovers

21

George St

Cameron St

9

25

26

32

Quadrant Mall

35

McDermotts Coaches

Brisbane St

Mall

P

Shields St

Cornwall Square Transit Centre

8

11

17

Civic Square

7

33

13

Kingsway

York St

Wellington St

2

3

Charles St

Paterson St

Manion's Coaches

Cuisine La

37

Frederick St

Elizabeth St

Bathurst St

29

Charles St

Lower Charles St

Wellington St

Royal Park

Queen Victoria Museum & Art Gallery (Royal Park Site)

Barrow St

Margaret St

Middle St

22

West Tamar Hwy

Babington St

North Esk River

Old Launceston Seaport

Seaport Blvd

24

Home Point

16

Tamar River

Park St

28

Kings Park Pl

23

39

34

Paterson Bridge

Kings Bridge

Zig Zig Reserve

WEST LAUNCESTON

West Tamar Hwy

Trevallyn Rd

◉ **Top Sights**
Boag's Centre for Beer Lovers D1
City Park...F1
Design Centre of Tasmania E1
Queen Victoria Museum & Art
  Gallery (Royal Park Site)...................C3
Royal Park B2

◉ **Sights**
1 Albert Hall E1
2 Custom House C1
3 Henty House C2
4 Holyman House E2
5 Japanese Macaque Enclosure..............E1
6 Launceston Synagogue D3
7 Macquarie House C2
8 Old Post Office D2
9 Old Umbrella Shop D2
10 Princes Sq D4
11 Town Hall..D2

Activities, Courses & Tours
12 Ghost Tours E1
13 Mountain Bike Tasmania D3
14 Tamar River Cruises............................A2
15 Launceston Aquatic F1

◉ **Sleeping**
16 41 On York E3
17 Airlie on the Square.............................D2
18 Ashton Gate F3
19 Hotel Tasmania.....................................D4
20 Kurrajong House....................................F2

21 Lloyds Hotel Backpackers.....................D1
22 Old Bakery Inn.......................................B4
23 Penny Royal Hotel &
  Apartments...B4
24 Peppers Seaport Hotel B1
25 Quest Launceston Serviced
  Apartments...D2

◉ **Eating**
26 Black Cow D2
27 Fresh D4
28 Hallam's Waterfront.............................B3
29 Irish Murphy's.......................................C4
Mud ....(see 24)
30 Novaros..E2
31 Pickled Evenings E3
32 Pierre's..D2
33 Star of Siam...D2
34 Stillwater..A4

◉ **Drinking**
35 Hotel New York......................................D3
Royal Oak Hotel...........................(see 12)

◉ **Entertainment**
36 Princess Theatre E2
37 Village Cinemas.....................................C3

◉ **Shopping**
Mill Providore & Gallery ....(see 34)
Mountain Designs ....(see 13)
38 Paddy Pallin E2
39 Pinot Shop B4

bearings with a 1½-hour walking journey through the Georgian, Victorian and modern architecture of the city. Walks depart the '1842' building, on the corner of St John and Cimitiere Sts.

Valleybrook Wine Tours   WINERY
(☏6334 0586; www.valleybrook.com.au) These wine specialists offer full-day tours visiting six Tamar Valley cellar doors. You can choose from a lunch-inclusive tour ($140), or morning/afternoon tours ($90) visiting four wineries. It offers a pick-up/drop-off service to your accommodation.

Walks on the Wildside   WALKING
(☏6331 0916; www.walksonthewildside.com.au) This operation offers small-group day trips to Cradle Mountain ($120) and Bay of Fires ($125); and a Tamar Coast trip with a walk

at Narawntapu National Park ($99) followed by a winery and organic-farm visit.

Pepper Bush Adventures   FOOD & WINE
(☏6352 2263; www.pepperbush.com.au; per person from $390) This crew runs premium 4WD tours to give you a taste of the Tasmanian back country in style. Bushman Craig Williams will teach you some bushcrafts, then prepare a four-course gourmet campfire bushtucker dinner, after which you go spotting night-time wildlife. It also offers Tamar Valley wine tours ($375) with tastings at seven wineries and lunch.

Ghost Tours   GHOSTS
(☏0421 819 373; www.launcestoncityghost tours.com; adult/child under 11 yr/child 12-16 yr $25/5/15) Just after sunset, get spooked on a 90-minute wander around the city's back alleys. You'll hear spine-tingling stories of

DON'T MISS

LAUNCESTON ARCHITECTURE

Launceston has a fascinating architectural heritage. Wander Trevallyn and Windmill Hill to stickybeak at some beautifully crafted private homes, and keep your eyes open in the city for these notable public edifices:

» **Albert Hall**
(Map p182;cnr Tamar & Cimitiere Sts) A Launceston landmark, built in 1891 in classical Victorian style.

» **Town Hall**
(Map p182; St John St) Erected in 1864 with soaring neoclassical columns.

» **Custom House**
(Map p182; Esplanade) A magnificent 1885 neoclassical colonnade reflecting Launceston's 19th-century prosperity.

» **Old Post Office**
(Map p182; cnr Cameron & St John Sts) Ornate 1880s high Victorian style with an unique round clock tower added in the early 20th Century.

» **Macquarie House**
(Map p182; Civic Sq) This plain 1830s Georgian warehouse is one of the city's oldest buildings.

» **Launceston Synagogue**
(Map p182; 126 St John St) Built 1844; a rare example of architecture in Egyptian revival style.

» **Holyman House**
(Map p182; cnr Brisbane & George Sts) Built 1936 and a fine example of interwar art deco.

» **Henty House**
(Map p182;Civic Sq) Tasmania's finest example of raw concrete architecture; built in 1983.

Launceston City Council (✆6323 3000; Town Hall, St John St) publishes a map of three **Launceston heritage walks**, taking in these landmarks and more: pick one up from the Town Hall.

ghoulish spectres and severed heads. Tours depart from the **Royal Oak Hotel** (Map p182; ✆6331 5346; 14 Brisbane St) – where Cyril is the resident ghost – at dusk. Bookings essential; departure time varies throughout the year.

Coach Tram Tour Company CITY
(✆0419 004 802; coachtramtour@bigpond.com.au) Two-and-a-half-hour bus-based tours of the city's key attractions depart at 10am daily ($40/20 per adult/child). Tamar Valley tours depart at 1.30pm ($65/33 per adult/child), and there's a Sunday Special trip to the Evandale Markets and Clarendon Homestead in summer that departs at 10am ($55/25 per adult/child).

✯✯ Festivals & Events

Festivale FOOD & WINE
(www.festivale.com.au) Three days in February that celebrate eating, drinking, arts and en-

tertainment, staged in City Park. There are Tasmanian food and wine stalls, dancing, theatre and bands.

Launceston Cup HORSE RACING
(www.tsrc.com.au) Also in February, horses work up a sweat on the track and well-dressed fillies look on.

Australian Three Peaks Race SAILING & RUNNING
(www.threepeaks.org.au) A four-day nonstop nautical rush in March to sail from Beauty Point (north of Launceston) to Hobart, pausing for runners to jump ashore and scale three mountains along the way.

Royal Launceston Show AGRICULTURAL SHOW
(www.launcestonshowground.com.au) In October – think candy floss and bumper cars, with pedigree livestock thrown in for good measure.

📭 Sleeping

Charles
TOP CHOICE
HOTEL $$$

(Map p180; ✆6337 4100; www.hotel charles.com.au; 287 Charles St; d $139-430, extra person $40; ❄️🛜) It's hard to believe Launceston's newest and hippest hotel was once a dreary hospital. The Charles is all light and bright now, with snappy decor, intelligent service and a stylish restaurant ($8-33; ☺breakfast, lunch & dinner,). The cheaper rooms are a squeeze; pay a bit more for a palatial studio. All rooms have kitchenettes, free (plug-in) internet, flat-screen TVs and iPod docks. There's (metered) wi-fi in the lobby.

Two Four Two
APARTMENTS $$$

(Map p180; ✆6331 9242; www.twofourtwo.com. au; 242 Charles St; d incl breakfast $205-230, extra adult/child $50/25; ❄️🛜) Now *this* is a cool renovation! Alan the furniture maker has channelled his craft into four self-contained townhouses, each with blackwood, myrtle or Tasmanian-oak detailing. Flat-screen TVs, stainless-steel kitchens, coffee machines and spa baths complete the experience.

Ashton Gate
B&B $$

(Map p182; ✆6331 6180; www.ashtongate.com. au; 32 High St; s $115, d $140-200, cottage d $200, extra person $30; 🛜) This thoroughly welcoming Victorian B&B exudes a sense of home, and each en-suite room is stylishly decorated with immaculate period taste – no doilies here. There's also a self-contained cottage in the old servants' quarters. A delicious cooked breakfast will set you up for the day.

Alice's Cottages & Spa Hideaways
COTTAGES $$

(Map p180; ✆6334 2231; www.alicescottages. com.au; 129 Balfour St; d $150-210) Alice's bills itself as the place for 'wickedly wonderful romantic retreats' – and why not indeed? It has several sumptuously decorated B&B cottages, including Camelot and The Boudoir, where you can enjoy spas, four-poster beds, open fires and self-contained privacy. Flouncy Aphrodite's villa – dedicated to the goddess of love – takes the cake.

Werona
B&B $$

(Map p180; ✆6334 2272; www.werona.com; 33 Trevallyn Rd; d $120-230; 🛜) This opulent B&B is in a Queen Anne Federation home with unsurpassed views. There are amazing decorative mouldings, *trompe l'oeil* murals and beautiful leadlighting. The Joan suite is top-of-the-line here, with a fairy-tale four-poster bed and spa en suite. On the ground level there's a billiards table and a guest lounge, and a pretty garden out back.

Peppers Seaport Hotel
HOTEL $$$

(Map p182; ✆6345 3333; www.peppers.com.au/ seaport/; 28 Seaport Blvd; d $169-400; ❄️🛜) Right on the waterfront in the smart new Seaport development, this glam hotel is big on design in natural timbers and muted tones. The adjacent Urban Mud day spa offers all manner of massages and beauty treatments, and when you've worked up an appetite you can hang out at the Mud bar (see p187) on the ground floor.

Thyme Cottage
RENTAL HOUSE $$

(Map p180; ✆6331 1906; www.thymecottage. com.au; 31 Cimitiere St; d $150, extra adult/child $30/20) A delightful 1880s cottage providing self-contained heritage accommodation. With cottage furniture and antiques, it exudes warmth and charm. Modern facilities and light breakfast supplies provided. Sleeps up to seven in three bedrooms.

Auldington
HOTEL $$$

(Map p180; ✆6331 2050; www.auldington.com.au; 110 Frederick St; d from $242, extra person $48; 🛜) This small private hotel has a historic exterior complete with lacy wrought-iron balconies that belies the funkily modern fit out inside. Right in the middle of town yet in a quiet spot, it has a wheelchair-friendly suite and the kind of cheerful, personal service that you don't get in the larger hotels.

LAUNCESTON & AROUND FOR CHILDREN

» Squealing with delight at City Park's **Japanese macaques** (p179)

» Floating through the air on the **Cataract Gorge chairlift** (p178)

» Burning energy with hours of creative play at **Kids Paradise** (p181)

» Being entranced by the weird and wonderful critters at **Seahorse World** (p194)

» Getting hands-on with the past at **Beaconsfield Mine & Heritage Centre** (p193)

Arthouse Backpacker Hostel HOSTEL $

(Map p180; ☎6333 0222; www.arthouse hostel.com.au; 20 Lindsay St; 4-/6-/8-bed dm $27/25/23, s/d $55/65; @) Housed in the original Esplanade Hotel, built in 1881, the Arthouse has spacious, airy dorms, a welcoming shared sitting room with a huge plasma TV, a wide upstairs verandah for shooting the breeze and a courtyard with BBQ out back. You can also hire bikes or camping equipment and there's storage for your gear. It's even set up for disabled travellers and is also Australia's first carbon-neutral backpackers.

Airlie on the Square B&B $$

(Map p182; ☎6334 0577; www.airlielodge.com. au; Civic Sq; s/d $110/130-140, extra person $30; ☎) Airlie is truly a rose among thorns. It's housed in the last of the beautiful old buildings on Civic Sq – the others were demolished to make way for 1970s and '80s concrete. Wonderfully peaceful Airlie has been thoughtfully decorated and the friendly owner serves scrumptious breakfasts. A real haven in the city's heart.

41 on York APARTMENT $$$

(Map p182; ☎6344 9989; www.41onyork.com. au; Apt 5/41 York St; d $290, extra person $30, 6 people $410; ❄☎) If you crave a bit of private luxury for your Launceston stay, this swanky downtown apartment might fit the bill. There are acres of space here: three bedrooms, three bathrooms, a gorgeous Huon-pine kitchen (stocked with Tasmanian wines and provisions), a deck with BBQ for outdoor dining, and fluffy bathrobes and slippers if you don't feel like getting dressed.

Kurrajong House B&B $$

(Map p182; ☎6331 6655; www.kurrajonghouse. com.au; cnr High & Adelaide Sts; d $130-170; ☎) You'll love the just-like-home-but-smarter feel of this welcoming B&B. Rooms are quite sophisticated and adults-only: kids under 16 aren't allowed. Outside there's a scented rose garden and a tranquil courtyard. Hearty cooked breakfasts are served in the bright and breezy conservatory.

Quest Launceston Serviced Apartments APARTMENTS $$

(Map p182; ☎6333 3555; www.questlaunceston. com.au; 16 Paterson St; d $153-199; ❄@) Set in the beautifully restored Murray Building in the heart of town, these apartments are everything you could want in an upmarket home-away-from-home: spacious, comfort-able, fully self-contained and decorated with style. They also have facilities for disabled travellers.

Launceston Backpackers HOSTEL $

(Map p180; ☎6334 2327; www.launcestonback packers.com.au; 103 Canning St; 4-/6-bed dm $23/22, tw/tr $28/25, s $52, d $60-70; @☎) The insides of a large Federation house have been gutted to make way for the cavernous interiors of this hostel. It's in a leafy, green location looking over Brickfields Reserve, but it's not the most inspiring hostel you'll ever visit. Rooms are clean and fresh, though, and the friendly staff will book bus tickets and wine tours. Walks on the Wildside, offering a selection of walking day trips (see p183) operates out of here.

Sportsmans Hall Hotel PUB $

(Map p180; ☎6331 3968; cnr Charles & Balfour Sts; s/d from $50/75) In the most salubrious part of Charles St, 'Sportys' is a bit of a local institution. It's been done up recently and the rooms are really decent; three have en suites and others have their own private bathrooms down the hallway. Whatever you do, don't get one of the rooms that are located just above the bar – if you intend to get any sleep, that is.

Hotel Tasmania PUB $

(Map p182; ☎6331 7355; www.hoteltasmania.com; 191 Charles St; incl breakfast s $65, d $85, tr $120) The en-suite rooms here are more motel spick-and-span than pub-grunge. Beware Wednesday night when the bar goes off and you may struggle to sleep over the revelry. It's quieter after 11pm weeknights.

Old Bakery Inn HOTEL $$

(Map p182; ☎1800 641 264, 6331 7900; www. oldbakeryinn.com.au; cnr York & Margaret Sts; d $110-145) You can almost smell freshly baked bread aromas coming from the ovens, which are still a feature of this 130-year-old building. Rooms have minibars and electric blankets. As much as you might like to wake to the smell of fresh croissants, note that rates don't include breakfast.

Penny Royal Hotel & Apartments HOTEL $$

(Map p182; ☎1800 060 954, 6331 6699; 147 Paterson St; d $120-198, extra adult/child $30/15; ☎) Originally a coaching inn in Tasmania's Midlands, this hotel was moved to its present location brick by painstaking brick. Rooms have been done up but retain the wooden beams and old-world feel.

Lloyds Hotel Backpackers
HOSTEL $

(Map p182; ☑1300 858 861; www.backpackers-accommodation.com.au; 23 George St; dm $32, s/d/f $58/75/128) Lloyds stakes a claim as Launceston's happening-est pub. Downstairs the place goes nuts, but, above, things remain relatively calm, with clean en-suite rooms, kitchen and capacious communal areas.

Treasure Island Caravan Park
CARAVAN PARK $

(Map p180; ☑6344 2600; treasureisland launceston@netspace.net.au; 94 Glen Dhu St; sites $22-30, on-site vans $58, cabins $85-95) Just 2.5km from the city, there are camping and caravan spots here. Unfortunately there's road noise – but it's quieter at night. Facilities include a kids' playground, a campers' kitchen and a laundry.

✕ Eating

TOP CHOICE

Stillwater
MODERN AUSTRALIAN $$$

(Map p182; ☑6331 4153; www.stillwater. net.au; Ritchie's Mill, 2 Bridge Rd; breakfast $8-21, lunch $15-29, dinner $34-39; ☺breakfast & lunch daily, dinner Mon-Sat;) Set in the stylishly renovated Ritchie's Flour Mill (c 1840s) beside the Tamar, Stillwater does laid-back breakfasts, relaxed lunches – and then puts on the ritz for dinner. This is one Launceston restaurant you shouldn't miss. There are delectable seafood, meaty and vegie mains and the emphasis is on locally sourced produce, with an extensive wine cellar to match. It also has a wine-bar menu offering tasty titbits.

Black Cow
STEAKHOUSE $$$

(Map p182; ☑6331 9333; www.blackcowbistro.com. au; 70 George St; mains $30-40; ☺dinner) This high-class bistro-steakhouse specialises in Tasmanian free-range, grass-fed, artificial-hormone-free beef. It offers six different melt-in-the-mouth cuts and claims to be the best steakhouse in Tassie, which, judging by the restaurant's runaway success, can't be too far wrong. Try the tender eye fillet with Black Cow butter or the very special truffle Béarnaise sauce.

Pierre's
MODERN AUSTRALIAN, FRENCH $$

(Map p182; ☑6331 6835; www.pierres.net.au; 88 George St; lunch mains $18-25, dinner mains $20-35; ☺breakfast, lunch & dinner Mon-Sat, dinner Tue-Sat) Pierre's is a Launceston institution and rightly so. Now coolly done up in dark leather with low lighting, it still offers its long-time classics like steak tartare and fries, escargot and – some say – the best coffee in

Launceston. This is a stylish place with an atmosphere that is relaxed and welcoming. Bookings recommended.

Novaros
ITALIAN $$$

(Map p182; ☑6334 5589; 28 Brisbane St; mains $30-40; ☺dinner Mon-Sat) Set in an unassuming terrace house, Novaros doesn't look like much from the outside – but locals will tell you that you simply have to eat here. The restaurant has been serving ambrosial Italian food for years, and is known for excellent service and a down-to-earth atmosphere as much as for the food. Make sure to book well ahead as it gets packed – even on weeknights.

Me Wah
CHINESE $$$

(Map p180; ☑6331 1308; www.mewah.com.au; 39-41 Invermay Rd; mains $21-90; ☺lunch & dinner Tue-Sun) This is hands-down Launceston's best Chinese restaurant. It serves old favourites as well as innovative dishes heavily influenced by fresh Tasmanian seafood. The abalone with shiitake mushrooms in oyster sauce ($90) may blow your budget – but might also just blow your mind.

Mud
MODERN AUSTRALIAN $$

(Map p182; www.mudbar.com.au; 28 Seaport Blvd; lunch mains $15-30, dinner mains $16-40; ☺breakfast Sat & Sun, lunch & dinner) You can hang out on the cool leather sofas or at the bar here, then migrate to the tables for sophisticated fare from the tempting, Italian-influenced menu. There is a bar-snack menu from midday and it serves up lazy breakfasts on weekends. Trendy and relaxed – with food that's consistently great.

tant pour tant
PATISSERIE $

(Map p180; www.tantpourtant.com.au; 226 Charles St; items $5-13; ☺7.30am-5pm Mon-Fri, 8.30am-3pm Sat & Sun) Your eyes will surely be bigger than your stomach at this wonderful French patisserie. As well as artisan and organic breads, it serves a jaw-dropping range of croissants, cakes and pastries, and does breakfasts and light lunches too. You'll feel like you're in Paris, savouring your coffee and petit fours at a streetside table.

Blue Café Bar
CAFE $$

(Map p180; www.bluecafebar.com.au; Inveresk Railyards; lunch mains $15-30, dinner mains $20-35; ☺breakfast & lunch daily, dinner Tue-Sat) This stylish eatery serves awesome coffee and scrumptious local/organic produce to an arty, young crowd. On Wednesday night it does $14 pizzas from the wood-fired oven. Closed evenings in midwinter.

Elaia
MEDITERRANEAN $$
(Map p180; ☑6331 3307; www.elaia.com.au; 240 Charles St; dinner mains $15-30; ☺breakfast, lunch & dinner; ☎) You'll love the Mediterranean atmosphere in this great spot on Charles St. It does inventive pizzas, delicious pastas and risottos, steaks and good salads. Occupy the soft leather wall benches for all-day breakfast or coffee and cake – and use the wireless internet for free.

Fresh
CAFE $$
(Map p182; 178 Charles St; mains $8-16; ☺breakfast & lunch daily, dinner Fri; ♬) Retroarty Fresh offers an all-vegetarian/vegan menu that's both deliciously tempting and environmentally aware. It does energising breakfasts; linger over lunches and coffees and cakes in between. The food's organic as much as possible and the staff work hard to recycle waste, as well as supporting green community issues.

Pasta Merchant
ITALIAN $
(Map p182; ☑6334 7077; 248b Charles St; mains $8-12; ☺) The popularity of this little eatery says it all. There's wonderful fresh pasta with lashings of mouthwatering sauces: try the unbeatable spinach and ricotta ravioli with homemade pesto. It also serves *panini*, pizza, and real gelati in 12 flavours. You can buy pasta and sauces to take away for around $12 per kilo.

Café Culture
CAFE $$
(Map p180; 1-3 Osborne Ave; mains $14-24; ☺breakfast & lunch, dinner Fri) This little foodie enclave on the hill at Trevallyn serves organic produce as much as possible. There's fair-trade coffee, delicious breakfasts and huge meals. Next door, the **Trevallyn Deli Grocer** offers everything you need for a gourmet picnic hamper, or to stock your holiday pantry in style.

Burger Got Soul
BURGERS $
(Map p180; 243 Charles St; burgers $10-14; ☺lunch & dinner) Best burgers in Launceston, served in a funky atmosphere. It's healthy too: good, lean meat, the freshest bread and crunchy salads. There's soul veggie burgers for non meat-eaters.

Hallam's Waterfront
SEAFOOD $$
(Map p182; ☑6334 0554; www.hallamswaterfront. com.au; 13 Park St; mains $23-37; ☺lunch & dinner) This place has a nautical ambience, friendly

service and superfresh seafood, particularly crayfish. The hot-and-cold seafood platter ($85 for two people) gets a thumbs up. There's a takeaway area attached, catering to fish-and-chip lovers.

Gorge Restaurant
MODERN AUSTRALIAN $$
(Map p180; ☑6331 3330; Cataract Gorge cliff grounds; lunch mains $15-18, dinner mains $28-33; ☺lunch Tue-Sun, dinner Tue-Sat) It's worth eating here for the setting alone, especially when you can sit outside in summer and watch the peacocks strut. Enjoy the walk through the gorge to get here.

Sportys Restaurant
PUB FARE $$
(Map p182; cnr Charles & Balfour Sts; mains $18-33; ☺breakfast, lunch & dinner Tue-Sun) This restaurant in the Sportsman's Hall Hotel does great bistro fare: hearty staples like thick beef sausages with creamy mashed potato. Leave room for wicked desserts.

Pickled Evenings
INDIAN $$
(Map p182; ☑6331 0110; 135 George St; mains $18-24; ☺dinner Tue-Sun) The heady aromas that greet you at the door confirm this'll be the best Indian food you've had in ages. There are good vegetarian choices – and it also does takeaways.

Star of Siam
THAI $$
(Map p182; cnr Paterson & Charles Sts; mains $17-23; lunch Tue-Fri, dinner daily) Launceston's best Thai eatery does excellent, value-for-money Thai staples, as well as at least 10 chef's specials, which you won't sample anywhere else.

Irish Murphy's
PUB FARE $$
(Map p182; cnr Brisbane & Bathurst Sts; mains $8-28; ☺lunch Fri, dinner daily) This popular pub offers a better-than-average take on the humble counter meal. The menu offers excellent Irish (and Aussie) fare: don't miss the beef and Guinness pie.

Drinking & Entertainment

Royal Oak Hotel
PUB
(Map p182; 14 Brisbane St; ☺12pm-late) Launceston's friendliest and most laid-back pub. There are lots of brilliant beers on tap, open-mic nights (last Wednesday of the month) and live music Wednesday to Sunday.

Hotel New York
PUB
(Map p182; www.hotelnewyork.net.au; 122 York St; nightclub $5-7; ☺3pm-midnight Mon-Wed, 2pm-5.30am Thu-Sat) This pub hosts a steady

KIM SEAGRAM: RESTAURATEUR

A food culture follows good wine: it just goes hand in hand. That's how the local restaurant industry began. The wine styles that are grown here complement the amazing fresh produce that's available: sparkling wine and oysters, Sauvignon Blanc and crayfish, Pinot Noir and rabbit...they're a marriage made in heaven. Then came the coffee culture, following the Italian model, and once you've got your coffee organised, you get your breads sorted. We've got a few wood-fired bread ovens from the late 1800s still around here. And the climate here suits a food culture too: we grow olives, make olive oil...and produce all sorts of wonderful fruit and veg. How could this not be foodie heaven?

Top food experience
The cooking school at the Red Feather Inn at Hadspen (p198), where you learn to treat quality produce with the respect it deserves, and then get to eat the amazing results.

Best cafe
Blue Café Bar (p187) at the Inveresk Railyards precinct for brilliant coffees and arty ambience.

Best-kept secret
Koukla's at Exeter (p193) for fresh, seasonal, yummy Greek food – and beautiful river views.

Top drop
The Arras sparkling from Bay of Fires Wines (p197).

Must try
The first fresh cherries of the season....exquisite.

---

stream of local and interstate acoustic and full-blown rock acts, plus DJs in Reality nightclub out the back (Thursday to Saturday from 11pm).

Tonic Bar   BAR
(Country Club Av, Prospect Vale; ☺5pm-late Mon-Sat, 2pm-late Sun) This glamorously decorated venue at Country Club (8km out of town) is one of Launceston's shiniest places to see and be seen. There are cocktail specials on Friday evening and live music Friday and Saturday. Bar snacks also available.

Irish Murphy's   PUB
(Map p182; cnr Brisbane & Bathurst Sts; admission free; ☺noon-midnight Sun-Wed, to 2am Thu-Sat) This low-lit watering hole stuffed full of Emerald Isle predictabilia, has live music every night (usually free), including Sunday-arvo jam sessions.

Princess Theatre   THEATRE
(Map p182; ☎6323 3666; 57 Brisbane St) Built in 1911 and including the smaller Earl Arts Centre, this theatre stages an eclectic mix of drama, dance and comedy, drawing acts from across Tasmania and the mainland.

Village Cinemas   CINEMA
(Map p182; ☎1300 555 400; 163 Brisbane St; adult/child/concession $16/11/13) Big-budget flicks and Hollywood blockbusters offer cinematic escapism.

🛍 Shopping

TOP CHOICE **Alps & Amici**   FOOD
(www.alpsandamici.com; cnr Abbott & Arthur Sts) Esteemed chef Daniel Alps has set up this smart providore where you can buy his restaurant-quality meals to take away: classy cakes, cheeses, meats and seafood, the freshest fruit and veg, and Tasmanian beer and wine.

Mill Providore & Gallery   FOOD
(Map p182; Ritchie's Mill, 2 Bridge Rd) Above Stillwater Restaurant in the Ritchie's Mill complex, you'll find this treasure trove of everything for the home, kitchen, stomach and soul! There's a brilliant delicatessen and chocolatier for picnic goodies, and a browse-worthy gallery upstairs.

Pinot Shop   WINE
(Map p182; 135 Paterson St) This boutique bottle shop specialises in Pinot Noirs and

fine wines – particularly of the Tasmanian variety. It also does premium international and 'big-island' (i.e. Australian mainland) vintages. Tastings of selected wines available – and it can freight wine Australia-wide.

Paddy Pallin
OUTDOOR GEAR

(Map p182; 110 George St; ⊙9am-5.30pm Mon-Fri, to 4pm Sat, 10am-2pm Sun) Sells (and hires out) all the gear you need for a camping adventure.

Mountain Designs
OUTDOOR GEAR

(Map p182; 120 Charles St; ⊙9am-5.30pm Mon-Fri, to 4pm Sat, 11am-3pm Sun) Also does gear sales and hire, fuel sales, mountain-bike hire and park passes.

Esk Market
BRIC-A-BRAC

(Map p180; ⊙9am-2pm Sun) These markets are held every weekend near Launceston showground just past Aurora Stadium (off Forster St) and sell crafts, pre-loved clothes and books, and local fresh produce.

ⓘ Information

ATMs At most city-centre banks, mainly on St John or Brisbane Sts.

Cyber King Internet Lounge (113 George St; ⊙9.30am-7pm Mon-Fri, to 4.30pm Sat & Sun)

Launceston General Hospital (☑6348 7111; 287-289 Charles St)

Main post office (111 John St; ⊙9am-5pm Mon-Fri, 9.30am-1pm Sat)

St Vincent's Hospital (5 Frederick St)

Visitor centre (☑1800 651 827, 6336 3133; www.visitlauncestontamar.com.au; cnr St John & Cimitiere Sts; ⊙9am-5pm Mon-Fri, to 3pm Sat, to noon Sun & public holidays)

ⓘ Getting There & Away
Air

There are regular flights between Launceston, Melbourne and Sydney, connecting with other Australian cities:

Qantas (www.qantas.com.au)

Jetstar (ww.jetstar.com)

Virgin Blue (www.virginblue.com.au)

For details of the daily flights from Launceston to Flinders Island see p175.

Bus

Redline Coaches (www.tasredline.com.au) and **TassieLink** (www.tassielink.com.au) operate out of Launceston. The depot for services is at **Cornwall Square Transit Centre** (cnr St John & Cimitiere Sts), behind the visitor centre.

Redline runs buses to:

Burnie ($40, two hours 20 minutes)
Deloraine ($15, 45 minutes)
Devonport ($25, 1½ hours)
Hobart ($40, 2½ hours)
Stanley ($60, four hours).

Callows Coaches (www.calowscoaches.com) service the east coast from Launceston:

Bicheno ($35, 2½ hours)
St Helens ($35, 2¾ hours)

Tassielink (www.tassielink.com.au) runs services to:

Devonport ($25, 1¼ hours)
Hobart ($35, 2½ hours)
Sheffield ($30, two hours)
Gowrie Park ($30, 2¼ hours)
Cradle Mountain ($60, three hours)
Tullah ($55, 4¾ hours)
Rosebery ($55, five hours),
Zeehan ($65, 5½ hours)
Queenstown ($75, six hours)
Strahan ($82, seven hours)

Sainty's Coaches (www.saintyscoaches.com. au), in association with **Maxwells**, runs a variety of bushwalker services on demand including to Cradle Mountain and Lake St Claire. See p269 for further details.

Manions' Coaches (www.manionscoaches. com.au) services the West Tamar region from Launceston. For details see p192.

Car

Many of the major car-rental firms have desks at the airport or in town:

Europcar (☑13 13 90, 6331 8200; 112 George St)

Thrifty (☑6333 0911, 1300 367 227; 151 St John St)

Lo-Cost Auto Rent (☑1300 883 728; www. rentforless.com.au; 80 Tamar St)

ⓘ Getting Around
To/From the Airport

Launceston airport is 15km south of the city. A shuttle bus runs a door-to-door airport service costing $14/7 per adult/child. A taxi to the city costs about $35.

Bicycle

Arthouse Backpacker Hostel (see p190) rents out bikes on an hourly and daily basis, as does **Mountain Designs** (see p190).

Bus

Metro (www.metrotas.com.au) buses have a Day Rover pass (adult/concession $5/3) for unlimited travel after 9am. Buses depart from the two blocks of St John St between Paterson and York Sts. Many routes don't operate in the evening or on Sunday.

There's also a **Free Tiger Bus** provided by Launceston City Council that plies Launceston from Invaresk to Princes Park, Windmill Hill and back to Invaresk Monday to Friday every 30 minutes between 10am and 3.30pm.

TAMAR VALLEY

Funnelling north from its higher reaches around Launceston to its ocean mouth on Bass Strait, the Tamar River and the valley that cradles it are among Tasmania's greatest natural beauty spots. This wide, tidal stretch of water is often glassy-calm. Fringed with deep-green reeds and framed with emerald hills, it can be picture-postcard perfect.

From Launceston the Tamar River stretches 64km, separating the east and west Tamar districts. On the east side is the river's ocean port, Bell Bay near George Town. The Batman Bridge unites the Tamar's two banks near Deviot.

The hillsides of the Tamar Valley and the nearby Pipers River region are covered with a maze of vines. This is Tasmania's key wine-producing area, and the premium wines created here have achieved international recognition. Many of the wineries come under the banner of the Tamar Valley Wine Route (www.tamarvalleywines.com.au) and you can visit cellar doors for tastings and sales. Pick up the excellent self-drive guide to the route from Launceston's visitor centre, or go on a guided tour (see p183).

There's been conflict in the valley in recent years over the proposed construction of a giant pulp mill by Gunns Ltd at Long Reach. At the time of writing the project

Tamar Valley

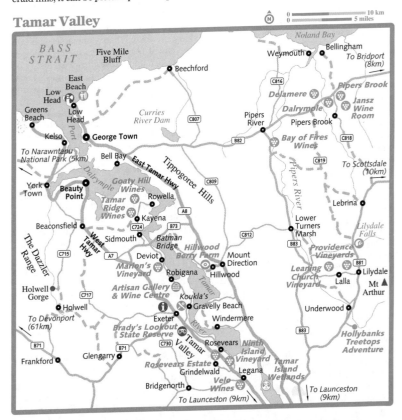

was still not certain to go ahead and public opinion remained divided (see p296).

❶ Getting There & Around

The drive (or bike ride) north along the Tamar River is an absolute gem of an experience. On the west bank, you can avoid most of the highway and follow quiet roads through small settlements. On the eastern shore, follow the hilly minor roads inland through stunning landscape to Lilydale. You can cross the lower reaches of the Tamar River via Batman Bridge.

On weekdays **Manions' Coaches** (www.manionscoaches.com.au; 72 Shore St, Beaconsfield) services the West Tamar Valley from Launceston:

Legana ($4)

Grindelwald/Rosevears ($7)

Exeter and Gravelly Beach ($8)

Beaconsfield ($10)

Beauty Point ($10)

In Launceston, buses leave from 168 Brisbane St opposite the Village cinemas. Southbound the bus stop is in Beaconsfield's main street (Weld St) near the IGA Supermarket.

Lee's coaches (www.leescoaches.com) services the East Tamar from Launceston's Cornwall Square Transit Centre, with stops at Hillwood ($10) and George Town/Low Head ($12).

Legana & Rosevears

POP 2150

First stop on the West Tamar Hwy (A7) north of Launceston must be **Velo Wines** (⊙10am-5pm) at Legana. This boutique winery was founded by former cycling Olympian and Tour de France rider Michael Wilson – hence the name (French for bicycle). Try the award-winning reserve Chardonnay, the cool-climate Shiraz and the fine Pinot Gris. The cafe here serves titbits ($10 to $35) to savour with the wines.

Head north to **Grindelwald**, a residential suburb and resort rendered in a rather kitsch, faux-Swiss-village style. The **Tamar Valley Resort** here has accommodation (see Sleeping), a restaurant, some slightly twee shops and an activity centre – which kids will love – with water bikes, boats, canoes, pedal carts, a playground with a giant jumping pillow, minigolf, full-sized golf and tennis courts.

Further down Waldhorn Dr is **Rosevears Vineyard** (1A Waldhorn Dr; mains $22-22; ⊙breakfast & lunch daily 10am-5pm), producer of some of Tasmania's finest sparkling wines and Pinots. There are

free wine tastings, cellar door sales, and a terrace where you can sip coffee and soak in the views. The restaurant pairs classy food with the produce of the vineyard. There's also on-site accommodation in studio apartments (see Sleeping).

To keep on the wine trail, get off the main highway (A7) onto narrow Rosevears Dr that follows the waterside past moored yachts and swaying reed-beds to the pretty riverside settlement of Rosevears. Even if you're no wine buff, you should drop into glorious **Ninth Island Vineyard** (95 Rosevears Dr; ⊙10am-5pm). The vines and views are achingly beautiful – especially when they turn golden in autumn. Go inside to taste the vino or pop into the popular **Strathlynn** (✆6330 2388; mains $25-35; ⊙lunch) restaurant – great for a long, lazy lunch. There's seasonal, regional food here and the menu is different each day.

Along the scenic riverbank drive, you'll come across **Rosevears Waterfront Tavern** (215 Rosevears Dr; mains $20-25; ⊙lunch & dinner). One of Tasmania's oldest pubs, it was opened in 1831 and must have some of the best pub views anywhere. There's upmarket pub fare here and it serves snacks in the laid-back beer garden under cascading wisteria.

From here, you can follow Brady's Lookout Rd (off Rosevears Dr if you're travelling north) and follow the signs to the nearby **Brady's Lookout State Reserve**. The well-known bushranger Brady used this rocky outcrop to spy on travellers on the road below, so the views are spectacular.

🛏 Sleeping

Rosevears Vineyard   APARTMENTS **$$$**
(✆6330 0300; www.rosevears.com.au; 1A Waldhorn Dr; d $250-350) There are 16 villas on the hillside here overlooking the river. There's floor-to-ceiling glass to highlight the spectacular views. The larger versions have kitchenettes, balconies and spas.

Viewenmore Villa   RENTAL HOUSE **$$**
(✆0421 422 779, www.viewenmorevilla.com.au; 321 Rosevears Dr; d $130-150, extra person $20, 2-night minimum stay) This immaculate little octagonal villa is just past Rosevears Hotel, heading north. There are sensational views and it's pin-neat and comfortable. Hang out on the deck here for a BBQ or to enjoy the day's wine buys.

Tamar Valley Resort   RESORT **$$**
(✆6330 0400; www.tamarvalleyresort.com.au; 7 Waldhorn Dr; hotel ste/d $75/140, chalets $120-

230, apt $150-250, extra person $25; 🛜🎦) There are plain hotel rooms and some quite luxurious chalets and apartments here. The alpine theme is carried right through the hotel with the giant flower canvases on its walls.

Conmel Cottage RENTAL HOUSE $$
(📞6330 1466; www.conmelcottage.com.au; 125 Rosevears Dr; s/d $130/140). This cute, country cottage is neat and wood lined. Breakfast provisions are supplied for you to cook and there's a vegie garden and orchard with fruit and nut trees to raid.

Launceston Holiday Park CARAVAN PARK $
(📞6330 1714; www.islandcabins.com.au; 711 West Tamar Hwy; sites d $25-30, cabins d $115-125; @) This park has camping under the trees, grassy caravan spots and a range of cabins, from basic stuffy budget versions to deluxe spa units. There's a guest laundry, BBQ and games room. Beware highway noise.

Exeter

POP 400

This is predominantly an orchard and mixed farming area. The local **Tamar visitor centre** (📞6394 4454; www.visitlauncestontamar; 81 West Tamar Hwy; ⊙8.30am-5pm) will inform you of local highlights.

The **Exeter Hotel** (Main Rd) serves counter meals Wednesday to Saturday, but a better food option is the **Exeter Bakery** (Main Rd; ⊙7am-5pm). Its century-old wood-fired oven produces all manner of pies – from seafood to tender wallaby. It also offers cakes, bread and slices, and filled rolls to take away.

South of Exeter, Gravelly Beach Rd will take you to wonderful **Koukla's** (📞6394 4013; 285 Gravelly Beach Rd; mains $18-25; ⊙lunch Wed-Sun, dinner Fri & Sat), a BYO cafe-restaurant serving huge portions of sensational Greek-influenced cuisine. Try the amazing *kleftiko* – slow-baked lemon lamb with roasted vegetables – or the Greek custard pie. The same road will take you to Robigana (derived from the Aboriginal word for swans), where the road crosses the Supply River. From here there's a marked walking track (one hour return) beside the Tamar River to **Paper Beach**. Further along, the **Artisan Gallery & Wine Centre** (📞6394 4595; www.artisangallery.com.au; 32 Deviot Rd, Robigana; ⊙10am-5pm Sep-May, by appointment only Jun-Aug) showcases crafts of well-known and local artisans. There are glass, ceramics, jewellery, paintings, and all sorts of creations in wood. It also has a strong collection of Tasmanian wines.

Batman Bridge

Opened in 1968 as one of the world's first cable-stayed truss bridges, the Batman Bridge has an eye-catching design that resulted not so much from creative inspiration as from foundation problems. The Tamar's eastern shore offered poor support for a large bridge, so it holds up just a minor part of the span. Most of the bridge is actually supported by the 100m-tall west tower that leans out over the river. There are good views from the east side.

Passing underneath the bridge on the western bank is a gravel road leading to **Sidmouth**. Here the long-worshipped local institution is Auld Kirk ('old church'), built in 1843 from 'freestone' by convict and free labour. Proceed north on the C724 to the Auburn Rd junction at Kayena. Turning left on Auburn Rd and travelling for about half a kilometre leads you to **Tamar Ridge Wines** (Auburn Rd, Kayena; ⊙10am-5pm, to 4pm Jun-Aug), which offers tastings and cellar-door sales as well as gourmet nibbles and wine-related paraphernalia in its gift shop. Slightly further on the same route is wonderful **Goaty Hill Wines** (530 Auburn Rd, Kayena; ⊙10am-5pm, by appointment Jun & Jul), best known for top-notch Riesling and Pinot Noir.

Beaconsfield & Around

POP 1015

This little town set in apple-growing country has had two great moments in the spotlight. The first was when gold was discovered here in 1877 and the second was when a mining accident killed one miner and kept two trapped deep underground – and under unwavering national attention – for two weeks in 2006. This incident kept the mine closed for some time and Beaconsfield in the doldrums, but now the excitement's died down, this slightly shabby town has gone back to what it always was: a quiet rural backwater, presiding over historically one of the richest small goldmines in Australia.

Most visitors come to Beaconsfield to see the **Beaconsfield Mine & Heritage Centre** (www.beaconsfieldheritage.com.au; West St; adult/child/family $11/4/28; ⊙9.30am-4.30pm). To tell the history of what was once Australia's biggest goldmine, the museum has hands-on interactive exhibits, including old mining machinery, a waterwheel, a mine-rescue exhibition, and a fascinating new interactive high-tech mine hologram that seems to take you right down the mine. You can see the working mine headshaft right behind the museum and, wherever you walk in Beaconfield, you can imagine the miners hard at work in the ground right beneath your feet. Note: you can get a three-attraction Tamar Triple Pass to Beaconsfield's Mine & Heritage Centre, and to Platypus House and Seahorse World in Beauty Point for $43 per adult and $115 for a family (children under four go free).

If you want to stay in town, **Beaconsfield Backpackers** is the pick. Set in the attractive **Exchange Hotel** (☑6383 1113; 141 Weld St; dm/s/d $25/40/60; ☺lunch & dinner Mon-Sat), this friendly place is often frequented by seasonal fruit-picking travellers. All the clean rooms have TVs and there's a communal kitchen–sitting room and laundry facilities. Downstairs the pub does decent counter meals and also serves Tassie's favourite Valhalla ice cream.

Nine kilometres south of Beaconsfield is **Holwell Gorge** reserve, with giant trees and three waterfalls. The walking track linking the southern and northern gorge entrances takes around two hours one way.

Beauty Point

POP 1500

Though the surrounding landscape is certainly bonny, the town's name actually derives from pulchritude of the bovine variety: a now-immortalised bullock called Beauty.

The main attractions here are two nature-based displays in wharf sheds down on the water. At **Seahorse World** (☑6383 4111; www.seahorseworld.com.au; Beauty Point Wharf; adult/child/family $20/10/50; ☺9.30am-4.30pm Sep-Apr, 10am-3pm May-Aug) you can view specimens of these astounding sea creatures from around the world – from Tasmania's own weedy sea dragons to the strange pot-bellied seahorse *(Hippocampus abdominalis),* in various stages of development from the tiniest shrimpy critters to portly full grown. There are also some diminutive local sharks and giant cuttlefish in tanks and a hermit-crab touch pool for kids.

In the wharf shed opposite, **Platypus House** (☑6383 4884; www.platypushouse.com.au; Inspection Head Wharf; adult/child/family $20/10/50; ☺9.30am-3.30pm) has the world's only two monotremes: the platypus and the echidna. Here, platypus gambol in their glass-sided tanks and transparent 'burrows', and in the echidna room you can walk among these trundling creatures as cheerful guides interpret.

For information on a three-attraction pass to the above spots, combined with Beaconsfield's Mine & Heritage Centre, see p193.

🛏 🍴 Sleeping & Eating

TOP CHOICE **Tamar Cove** HOTEL **$$**
(☑6383 4375; www.tamarcove.com; 4421 Main Rd; d from $120-150; mains $20-35; ☺breakfast, lunch & dinner; 🛜❄) What an appealing little enclave you'll find here! Stylishly done-up rooms front a well-manicured landscape with a solar-heated pool to dip in. The restaurant gets rave reviews. You can't go past the signature seafood chowder. Yum!

Beauty Point Cottages B&B **$$**
(☑6383 4556; www.beautypointcottages.com.au; 14 Flinders St; d $185-195) You can stay in the historic homestead here, or in a self-contained spa cottage. Great decoration with attention to detail makes it look good inside, but even better is looking outdoors – the river views are sensational.

Pomona Spa Cottages RENTAL HOUSE **$$$**
(☑6383 4073; www.pomonaspacottages.com.au; 77 Flinders St; d $200-250, extra person $40) There are three spa cottages in the grounds of this heritage homestead, masterfully built in the same genre as the old home itself and so comfortably kitted out you could move right in. There are decks with rotundas and, naturally, great views.

Beauty Point Tourist Park CARAVAN PARK **$**
(☑6383 4536; www.beautypointtouristpark.com.au; Redbill Point; powered sites $30, on-site vans d $90, cabins $100-200; 🛜) There's tranquil camping on the grass by the water here, comfortable vans and well-equipped cabins. A tennis court and river swimming will keep you busy.

Carbone's Café CAFE **$$**
(☑6383 4099; 225 Flinders St; mains $10-20; ☺breakfast & lunch Tue-Sun) On sunny days at Carbone's the windows wrap right back and the water feels so close you could touch it. The menu tempts with fresh local fare – we liked the lamb souvlakis – and the chai lattes are just about perfect too.

Narawntapu National Park

Located 25km east of Devonport (12km off the B71), Narawntapu National Park is a reserve of coastal heath, dunes and bushland that's astoundingly abundant in wildlife. Visit just on dusk and you'll see Forester kangaroos, foraging wombats, wallabies and pademelons.

The park can be accessed at two points near the small coastal settlement of Greens Beach via the C721 and C741. However, the main entrance, where there's a **ranger station and information centre** (☑6428 6277; ⊙9am-4pm Dec-April, 9 to 3pm May-Nov) is off the B71 near Port Sorell. Discovery rangers provide **guided walks** and activities from here in summer. If you're entering the park from the Greens Beach side, you can buy your parks pass from the Greens Beach shop, or self-register on entry.

Horse riding is allowed and the park has corrals and a 26km trail; bookings with the ranger are required. **Bakers Beach** is the safest swimming area and waterskiing is permitted here in summer.

There are some engaging walking trails in the park. You can hike round **Badger Head** in around six to eight hours (via Copper Cove), while the **Archers Knob** (114m high) walk (around two hours return) has good views of Bakers Beach. The one-hour **Springlawn Nature Trail** includes a boardwalk over wetlands to a bird hide. The beach from Griffiths Point to Bakers Point is good for beachcombing and sunset-watching.

The park has four **camp sites**. Caravans can drive to **Springlawn Beach** (powered sites d/family $16/22) and there are unpowered sites at **Koybaa**, **Bakers Point** and **The Horseyard** (d/family $13/16), which has a corral for horses. There are tables and toilets at all sites. Firewood is sometimes provided but there's not always reliable water, so check with rangers before setting off or bring your own.

George Town

POP 5550

George Town sits sentinel on the Tamar River's eastern shore, close to where it empties into Bass Strait. The town was founded in 1804 by Lieutenant Colonel Paterson, as part of the British attempt to stave off settlement by the French, who had been reconnoitring the area. The town's older buildings date from the 1830s and 1840s, when it prospered as the port linking Tasmania with Victoria. Though today it's perhaps not the most appealing of towns, it's still got a historic maritime feel and a couple of attractions worth visiting.

◎ Sights

Bass & Flinders Centre   MUSEUM
(8 Elizabeth St; adult/child/family $10/4/24; ⊙10am-4pm) Undoubtedly the highlight of a visit to George Town, even for committed landlubbers, this small museum houses a replica of the *Norfolk,* the little yacht used by Bass and Flinders for their 1897 circumnavigation of Van Diemen's Land. Built for a historic re-enactment of the voyage in 1998, the red-sailed replica *Norfolk* now rests here, together with other historic wooden vessels.

George Town Heritage Trail HISTORIC BUILDINGS
Ask at the visitor centre for a map detailing this trail, which takes you on foot through the town's history, starting at the **Old Watch House** (1843) on Macquarie St, which houses a small museum.

Mt George   LOOKOUT
Just outside town there's this panoramic viewpoint, which (now among modern communications towers) retains the semaphore equipment once used to relay signals via Mt Direction to Launceston. There's a wheelchair-accessible pathway from the car park to near the mountain top. Travelling into George Town, turn right off the highway into Mt George Rd just before town.

Hillwood Berry Farm   FARM
(www.hillwoodberryfarm.com.au; 105 Hillwood Rd, Hillwood; ⊙9am-5pm daily Oct-Jun, 10am-4pm Wed-Sun Jun-Sep) Hillwood burgeons with berries in summer. You can pick your own strawberries, raspberries, loganberries, black- and redcurrants and blueberries too. Then make a bee-line to the cafe for one of its famous berry sundaes or a slice of berry-swirl cheesecake. It also serves light meals ($8 to 15) and good coffees. It's just off the East Tamar Hwy, 22km south of George Town.

☞ Tours

Seal & Sea Adventure Tours SEAL WATCHING
(☑6382 3452, 0419 357 028; www.sealandsea. com) Cruise out to the Australian fur-seal colony at Tenth Island, with an enthusiastic and knowledgeable guide at the helm.

Trips cost $121 per person for two people and $100 per person for groups of three or more. River trips, fishing, diving, charters to Flinders Island and PADI instruction are also available.

Freedom Flight   SCENIC FLIGHTS
(☑6382 4700; www.freedomflight.com.au) North of town at the airport (heading towards Low Head, turn right down North St for about 2km) you can take ultralight-plane flights over the hills with Freedom Flight. These cost from $95 per person for 30 minutes. You can even have a go at the controls. Book well ahead.

Sleeping & Eating

York Cove   HOTEL/APARTMENTS $$$
(☑6382 9900; www.yorkcove.com.au; 2 Ferry Blvd; d $200-300; mains $15 to $32; ⊘breakfast, lunch & dinner; ⊛⊠) This swish waterfront resort is making waves on the Tamar. There are upmarket hotel rooms and apartments here, and the funky bar-restaurant does contemporary cafe food and excellent coffees.

Charles Robbins   GUESTHOUSE $$$
(☑6382 4448; www.thecharlesrobbins.com.au; 3 Esplanade North; d $260-380, extra person $76; ⊛) Done up in a modern style with leather sofas and glass, these waterfront spa suites are George Town's take on luxury. There is a sauna, and one suite is equipped with disabled facilities.

Pier Hotel Motel   PUB, MOTEL $$
(☑6382 1300; www.pierhotel.com.au; 5 Elizabeth St; d $155-180; ⊛) There are clean-and-tidy motel rooms here, but the star attraction is the popular **bistro** (mains $6-30; ⊘breakfast, lunch & dinner). It serves excellent pizzas, porterhouse steaks, snacks and salads. Fold-back doors open onto the water in warm weather. The stylish new **Pier House** (www.pierhouse.com.au; d $350, extra person $25; ⊛) is also run by the Pier Hotel Motel.

George Town Heritage Hotel   PUB $$
(☑6382 2655; 75 Macquarie St; d $80; ⊛) Built in 1845, this historic pub with ornate wrought-iron balconies offers basic but comfortable accommodation with en suites, and includes a decent bistro (mains $15 to $24).

Signature Café   CAFE $
(48 Macquarie St; mains $8-12; ⊘8am-5pm Mon-Fri) This is a cheerful place with a good range of light meals such as focaccias and salads.

ⓘ Information

ATM At the Commonwealth Bank (Macquarie St)

Post office (Macquarie St)

Visitor centre (☑6382 1700; Main Rd; ⊘9am-5pm) On the main road as you enter from the south.

ⓘ Getting There & Away

Lee's Coaches (www.leescoaches.com) services George Town and Low Head from Launceston, stopping at the **Shell service station** and in the main street of town. Coaches stop at:

Hillwood Berry Farm ($10, 30 minutes)

George Town ($12, 55 minutes)

Low Head ($12, 1¼ hours – stopping at the pilot station)

Low Head

POP 465

Low Head and George Town are barely divided – you won't notice leaving one before arriving in the other. Low Head's in a spectacular setting, though, looking out over the swirling – and treacherous – waters of the Tamar as it empties into the sea.

The historic **Low Head Pilot Station** was established in 1805, with the current buildings erected between 1835 and 1962. The Tamar pilot boats are still based here. The **Pilot Station Maritime Museum** (☑6382 2826; Low Head Rd; adult/child $5/3; ⊘10am-4pm) has a great display of maritime clutter – from whalebones to diving bells to shipwreck flotsam and jetsam. Even landlubbers will love it

At the head itself visit the 1888 **lighthouse** (⊘grounds open to 6pm) to get a perspective over the great torrent of the Tamar as it spills into the strait. Bring earmuffs if you plan to be here on a Sunday at noon: this is when the **foghorn** sounds with an earsplitting bellow.

Little penguins live around the lighthouse and you can view them with **Low Head Penguin Tours** (☑0418 361 860; www.penguintours.lowhead.com.au). Tours cost $16/$10 per adult/child and take place nightly from dusk, departing from a signposted spot beside the main road just south of the lighthouse. You need to pay cash at the kiosk here.

MANNA OR MADNESS? GEORGE TOWN & THE PULP MILL

It's been said you can gauge Tasmania's political climate by the messages on its bumper stickers, and while the West Tamar appears – from the stickers and placards at least – to be vociferously anti-mill, in George Town it's another story. George Town would be the closest town to the proposed $2 billion Gunns pulp mill and hopes to benefit from mill-related jobs and rising house prices. For this quiet town it seems like a boon. But ask people here about the pulp mill and– if they'll talk to you about it at all – the mood is not so clear. Sure, people would like to see new opportunities and investment in town, but it seems the bulk of mill-construction jobs would be filled by imported contractors. There are concerns about dangerous construction traffic and ongoing log-truck traffic on local roads. The issue of pollution has people worried too. So although the most widespread bumper sticker you might see in George Town is the seemingly pro-mill–judgement 'Greens Tell Lies', dig a little deeper here and you'll find a town that's uneasy about the megamill that may be built on its doorstep. See p294 for the latest on the situation.

There's good surf at **East Beach** on Bass Strait and safe swimming at most beaches around the head.

Sleeping & Eating

Pilot Station   COTTAGES **$$**
(6382 2826; Low Head Rd; d from $120, extra room $20) Low Head's historic precinct offers a range of pleasant, older-style, fully self-contained, waterfront colonial cottages for up to eight people. The place was in the process of a complete refurbishment at the time of writing – so it might get more expensive.

Low Head Tourist Park   CARAVAN PARK **$$**
(6382 1573; www.lowheadtouristpark.com.au; 136 Low Head Rd; sites $22-28, cabins $80, cottages $95) This river's-edge park has comfortable timber-lined cabins as well as caravan and camping spots – water views included.

Coxwain's Cottage Café   CAFE **$$**
(Low Head Rd; Pilot Station; mains $10-20; 9am-5pm) There's a great range of platters for two to share, plus pizzas, salads and hearty soups in winter – and fine espresso coffee. You can sit in the cafe overlooking the water, or in the adjacent marquee.

Pipers River Region

This region's most famous vineyard is **Pipers Brook** (6382 7527; 1216 Pipers Brook Rd; 10am-5pm) where you can try Pipers Brook, Ninth Island and Krieglinger wines in an architecturally innovative building that also houses the **Winery Café** (mains from $14-25; lunch), which serves a changing menu of light snacks and a delectable tasting plate.

Also within the Pipers Brook estate, but signposted up a different drive, you can visit the separately run **Jansz Wine Room** (6382 7066; 1216B Pipers Brook Rd; 10am-4.30pm), where you can taste fine sparkling wine, including a delightful pink fizzy rosé. Self-guided tours clarify some of the '*méthode Tasmanoise*' wine production. You can enjoy cheese platters with the sparkly, and take a spell on the lakeside terrace contemplating the vines.

Some 15km away, south of Pipers River, **Bay of Fires Wines** (6382 7622; 40 Baxters Rd, Pipers River; 10am-5pm, 11am-4pm Jun-Aug) is the home of prestigious Arras sparkling and a fine Tigress Riesling. Other local vineyards worth a visit include the friendly **Delamere** (6382 7190; 4238 Bridport Rd, or B82 Hwy, Pipers Brook; 10am-5pm), which offers a superb nonvintage rosé and Pinot Noir varieties; and **Dalrymple** (/fax 6382 7222; 1337 Pipers Brook Rd; 10.30am-4.30pm Fri-Sun) for good French-style Pinot Noir and award-winning Sauvignon Blanc.

Lilydale

POP 345

Quiet Lilydale is little more than a main street with a few stores and services – and some brightly painted utility poles. You can stock up for a picnic at National Trust–listed **Bardenhagen's General Store** (Main Rd; 7am-7pm Mon-Fri, 7.30am-6pm Sat) and then take a walk to **Lilydale Falls**, 3km north of town. If you're feeling energetic, you could tackle **Mt Arthur** (five to seven hours return), which towers dramatically above Lilydale.

Two kilometres out of town up the Lalla Rd is Tasmania's oldest working vineyard,

Providence Vineyards (www.providence-vineyards.com.au; 236 Lalla Rd; ⊙10am-5pm Thu-Mon Sep-15 Jun), which has a fine Chardonnay and Pinot, and also sells wines from other boutique vineyards. It does free shipping for a dozen anywhere in Australia.

And don't miss funky new Leaning Church Vineyard (☑6395 4447; www.leaning church.com.au; 76 Brooks Rd, Lalla; ⊙10am-5pm Thu-Mon Sep-May, Sat & Sun only Jun-Aug), where you can try excellent sparkling wine and Pinots and linger over a grazing platter ($35 for two) in its eatery. There's eye-fillet steak barbies every Sunday ($25 per person).

High adventure can be had at Hollybank Treetops Adventure (☑6395 1390; www. treetopsadventure.com.au; adult/child $100/75; ⊙9am-5pm) about 6km south of Lilydale. Harnessed to a cable-mounted swing-seat, you can skim through the treetops at stomach-churning heights, in the care of an experienced guide who will provide interpretation on the surrounding forest. There are short walks and forest picnic spots for nonadventurers.

🛏 Sleeping & Eating

Camping is possible for $6 per unpowered site at Lilydale Falls Reserve. Pay the $50 deposit at Lilydale Newsagency (☑6395 1156; Main Rd) to get a key to the amenities block for hot showers. Your deposit is refunded on return of the key (two-night-stay limit).

Cherry Top & Eagle Park   RENTAL HOUSE $$$
(☑6395 1167; cherrytop@bigpond.com; 81 Lalla Rd; d from $200, ▪) This is a place you can pause for a while. Relax in a neat cottage on a farm that grows most of its own food. Share a yarn around the fire pit, be guided on a farm walk, and enjoy fresh produce for your breakfast. Take the C822 out of Lilydale and follow the signs.

Yummies   CAFE $
(Main Rd; mains $6.95-14; ⊙breakfast, lunch & dinner) This little eatery in the Lilydale Newsagency does hearty cooked breakfasts, and meals and snacks all day. The pizzas, steak sandwiches, hamburgers and vegie burgers and BLTs are all said to be very...well...yummy.

Lilydale Tavern   PUB $$
(☑6395 1230; Main Rd; s/d $80/90; ⊙bakery 9am-5pm, tavern dinner Fri & Sat) There are simple motel-style rooms here and a fabulous bakery-cafe offering light meals, cakes and pastries. People come from miles around to eat its famous pies.

Hadspen & Carrick

Ten kilometres southwest of Launceston, Hadspen is home to Entally Estate (www. entally.com.au; adult/child/family $10/8/25; ⊙10am-4pm). Built in 1819 by shipping entrepreneur Thomas Haydock Reibey, it is one of Tasmania's oldest – and loveliest – country homesteads and gives a vivid picture of the affluent rural life of that period. You can inspect the house, but better still, stroll under the magnificent English trees on the estate.

The attraction that's bringing those in the know to Hadspen these days, though, is the unreservedly gorgeous Red Feather Inn (see Sleeping & Eating). This magical boutique hotel looks like it's stepped right out of the pages of a chic magazine. Set in an 1842 coaching inn, it exudes style, down-to-earth hospitality and country peace. Not only can you stay quite luxuriously here, you can eat divinely...and learn to cook! Chef Lee Christmas is a leading slow-food advocate and will show you some tricks in the capacious country kitchen.

Just 4km from Hadspen, on the old highway to Deloraine, is Carrick. The village's most prominent feature is the 1846 four-storey Carrick Mill (67 Meander Valley Hwy), which still houses the mill's working water wheel. At the time of research the mill was closed for renovations, but was due to open mid-2011 as an upmarket pub-restaurant. Behind the mill is the crumbling 1860 ruin known as Archers Folly (Church St). Next door is the Tasmanian Copper & Metal Art Gallery (www.tascoppermetalart.com; 8 Church St; ⊙10am-4pm Mon-Fri), where there's an Aladdin's Cave of imaginative metalwork for sale.

🛏 Sleeping & Eating

TOP CHOICE Red Feather Inn   BOUTIQUE HOTEL $$$
(☑6393 6506, www.redfeatherinn.com. au; 42 Main St, Hadspen; incl breakfast d $300-450) This exquisite property really is the feather in the cap of Tasmanian tourism. It just feels perfect in every way: from the classy decor to the history-soaked ambience to the effortless hospitality. You can eat dinner here if you stay (three courses are $85

per person). Private classes can be arranged on request in the on-site cooking school, or you can join one of its regular courses.

Hawthorn Villa Stables   B&B $$
(☑6393 6150, www.hawthornvilla.com.au; cnr Meander Valley Hwy & Church St, Carrick; d $130-150) Encircled by the well-tended gardens here are four mud-brick cottages providing comfortable B&B accommodation with thoughtful touches like crisp white linen and extra-thick bath towels. All cottages have wood fires and generous breakfast provisions.

Carrick Inn   PUB $$
(☑6393 6143; Meander Valley Hwy, Carrick; mains $10-25; ☉lunch & dinner Wed-Sun) This inn has been in the hospitality business since 1833 and does better-than-average pub meals in the welcoming Sammy Cox Bistro, with plenty of meat and seafood.

Westbury

POP 1300

This languid country town, with its tree-lined streets and village green, has a feast of historic buildings and a decidedly English feel.

The most fun to be had here is at **Westbury Maze** (10 Meander Valley Rd; adult/child/family $7/5/24; ☉10am-5pm Sep-Jul, to 6pm Jan) where there is a kilometre of bamboozling paths among 3000 privet hedges. Make your way to the centre to climb a viewing platform and get a bird's-eye view of this gigantic maze.

Just down the road, **Pearn's Steam World** (65 Meander Valley Rd; adult/child $7/3; ☉9am-4pm Aug-Jun, 10am-3pm Jul-Sep) comprises two huge sheds filled with the world's largest collection of antique steam engines and relics. This place will appeal most to old-machinery enthusiasts. If that's not enough to oil your engines then head on over to the **Vintage Tractor Shed Museum** (5 Veterans Row; adult/child $3/free; ☉9.30am-4pm), which has 93 farm tractors from 1916 to 1952, as well as 600 scale models of tractors: in short, everything pertaining to these beasts of the field.

If you're more of the artistic persuasion, you shouldn't miss Westbury's **John Temple Gallery** (103 Meander Valley Rd; admission free; ☉10am-5pm), which exhibits inspiring photographs by this top Tasmanian photographer.

Between Carrick and Westbury is the village of Hagley, where **Quamby Estate** (see below) is the star attraction. The 1830s Anglo-Indian-style homestead has been converted to swanky accommodation. Twice round the challenging nine-hole golf course here commands a par 76.

🛏 Sleeping & Eating

Quamby Estate   BOUTIQUE HOTEL $$$
(☑6392 2211; www.quambyestate.com.au; 1145 Westwood Rd, Hagley; d 150-350; @) This classy country-house hotel has 10 stylish rooms – all uniquely furnished in a mix of antique and contemporary. Indoors there's a drawing room, a billiards room, and a **restaurant** (☉lunch Fri & Sun, dinner, bookings essential). Outside there are acres of green lawns, avenues of mature trees, and tennis and golf for the energetic.

Gingerbread Cottages   RENTAL HOUSES $$
(☑6393 1140; www.westburycottages.com.au; 52 William St; Westbury; d from $170-190, extra adult/child $30/20) It's worth staying in Westbury just for these little self-contained cottages. They're decked out with antiques, have a cosy, country feel and are cared for with absolute attention to detail. The friendly owners even bring you freshly baked cake for afternoon tea. Our favourite is sweet Apple Tree Cottage (c 1860).

Fitzpatricks Inn   INN $$
(☑6393 1153; www.fitzpatricksinn.com.au; 56 Meander Valley Hwy; d incl breakfast from $110) This grand 1833 building has been comprehensively refurbished but retains its old feel. There are eight rooms, four with en suites and four with shared bathrooms. There's also an à la carte **restaurant** (mains $29-33; ☉lunch & dinner Wed-Sun) and a bar menu for snacks.

Hobnobs Coffee Shop   CAFE $
(☑6393 2007; 47 William St; mains $9-15; ☉10am-5pm Wed-Sun) Set in an English cottage garden, this popular eatery-deli serves light meals and sweet treats throughout the day. The pork pies have a reputation so good, Hobnobs can't keep up with demand.

Westbury Hotel   PUB $$
(☑6393 1151; 107 Bass Hwy; mains $14-22; ☉lunch & dinner) Following renovations, this pub should be offering accommodation from May 2011. It also serves good meals: roasts, chicken kiev and a parmigiana that's up there with the best of them.

TALL POPPIES

As you travel Tasmania's agricultural heartlands, you may see fields of purple poppies. Nearly half of the legal global poppy crop is grown in Tasmania – an industry worth $100 million a year. The opiate alkaloids used in painkillers and other medicines are extracted at the sprawling Tasmanian Alkaloids plant near Westbury.

The growing and harvesting of poppies in Tasmania is strictly controlled by the state government and the Poppy Advisory and Control Board. Never try to enter a poppy field; it's illegal and most are protected by electric fences. Believe the warning signs on fences: the unrefined sap from opium poppies can kill.

Andy's Bakery BAKERY **$**
(☑6393 1846; 45 Meander Valley Hwy; ⊘24hr Fri-Sat; 7am-10pm Mon-Thu; reduced hrs winter; @ 🛜) There are camping spots for both tents ($4 per person) and camper-caravans ($6 per person) behind Andy's. Showers cost $6, and you can hang out inside until late (or all night Friday and Saturday) and use the free wireless internet.

LIFFEY VALLEY

This valley at the foot of the Great Western Tiers (Kooperona Niara or 'Mountains of the Spirits') is famously the spiritual home of conservationist and politician Dr Bob Brown. The natural centrepiece of Liffey Falls State Reserve (34km southwest of Carrick) is **Liffey Falls**. There are two approaches to the falls, which are actually four separate cascades. From the upstream car park (reached by a steep and winding road) it's a 45-minute return walk on a well-marked track. You can also follow the river upstream on foot to the Gulf Rd picnic area; allow two to three hours return. The area has some fine fishing.

Longford

POP 2830

Longford was founded in 1807 when free landholding farmers were moved to Van Diemen's Land from Norfolk Island. It's one of the few Tasmanian towns not established by convicts.

The town is spread out around Memorial Park and is known for architectural gems such as the bluestone **Anglican Church** (Goderich St), the **Town Hall** (Smith St), and the **library** and **Queens Arms Hotel**, both in Wellington St.

Longford's streets are also known for something quite different: their stint in the 1950s and '60s as an Australian Grand Prix track. The **Country Club Hotel** is a shrine to this racy past, with racing photos and paraphernalia all over the walls.

There are two wonderful historic estates nearby, both established by the Archer family in the colony's early days. Both **Woolmers** and **Brickendon** are now Unesco World Heritage Sites: and they're firmly on the must-see list when you're visiting these parts. Both properties offer accommodation and can be reached by following the signs from Wellington St in Longford.

The Longford area and nearby Cressy (13km to the south) are well known to trout-fishing enthusiasts. Feisty brown and rainbow trout inhabit the waterways here. The giant brown trout in particular are the stuff of legend.

There's an **Online Access Centre** (Wellington St; ⊘11am-5pm Mon-Thu, to 7pm Fri), just behind the library. There's a Commonwealth Bank ATM next to the service station on Marlborough St.

🔾 Sights & Activities

Woolmers HISTORIC SITE
(☑6391 2230; www.woolmers.com.au; Woolmers Lane; adult/child from $20/7; ⊘9.30-4.30 Oct-May, 10am-4pm Jun-Sep, tours 11.15am, 12.30, 2pm & 3.30pm) The homestead at Woolmers dates from 1819 and you'll feel like you've stepped back in time, wandering through the antique-filled rooms. There's also the **National Rose Garden** here – 2 hectares of headily scented blooms on the banks of the beautiful Macquarie River.

Brickendon HISTORIC SITE
(☑6391 1383; www.brickendon.com.au; Woolmers Lane; adult/child $12/5; ⊘9.30am-5pm Tue-Sun, closed Jul & Aug) Brickendon was settled in 1824 and the homestead is still lived in by the Archer family, so you can't visit that but you can spend time in the gorgeous old gardens and the farm village. Kiddies will love the animal feeding, and there's trout fishing in the river.

✨ Festivals & Events

Blessing of the Harvest Festival   HARVEST
Longford's Harvest Festival is in March, with a street parade and country-fair stalls.

Longford Revival Festival   CAR RACING
(www.longfordrevival.com.au) Held in early April, this is a tribute to the days of motor racing at Longford – featuring some of the original cars that raced here as well as newer speedsters. Speed demonstrations on the section of road known as the Flying Mile are the highlight.

Longford Garden Festival   GARDENS
A celebration of Longford's garden pride, held each November.

🛏 Sleeping & Eating

**Longford Boutique
Accommodation**   B&B **$$**
(☑6391 2126; www.longfordboutique.com; 6 Marlborough St; d $165-185; 🐾) Just off the main street, this National Trust–listed bank built in 1865 is now a boutique B&B. There are luxurious touches like port and chocolates, fluffy bathrobes, a cosy wood fire and a DVD library from which you can choose movies to view with surround sound in your room. There's afternoon tea on the verandah when you arrive.

Racecourse Inn   INN **$$**
(☑6391 2352; www.racecourseinn.com; 114 Marlborough St; d $65-210; 🐾) There's welcoming (and gay-friendly) hospitality in this restored Georgian inn. The rooms are antique decorated and the à la carte breakfasts are distinctly gourmet: think eggs Benedict, eggs with smoked salmon, and berries and fruits from the property. Guests can dine in the restaurant – bookings recommended.

Brickendon   RENTAL HOUSES **$$**
(☑6391 1383; www.brickendon.com.au; Woolmers Lane; $120-195, extra adult/child $40/25) Brickendon has two well-equipped, early-19th-century cottages (one each for 'coachman' and 'gardener' wannabes), furnished with antiques and family collectables, plus three much newer self-contained cottages with old-style trimmings.

Woolmers   RENTAL HOUSES **$$**
(☑6391 2230; www.woolmers.com.au; Woolmers Lane; d incl breakfast & estate tour from $164-178, extra adult/child $35/30,) Seven little estate cottages, once home to servants and free settlers, now house visitors to Woolmers. The

Gardeners Cottage is heartbreakingly beautiful. You can eat at the **Servants Kitchen Restaurant** (☉lunch & morning & afternoon tea) and if you're staying in the cottages the restaurant can provide two-/three-course ($28/32) dinner hampers to take away.

Country Club Hotel   PUB **$**
(☑6391 1155; 19 Wellington St; s/d $45/65) This busy pub is a shrine to Longford's car-racing days. Dine in the Chequered Flag **bistro** (mains $17-27; ☉lunch & dinner) here among the fast-car memorabilia.

**Longford Riverside Caravan
Park**   CARAVAN PARK **$**
(☑6391 1470; 2a Archer St; sites d $20-25, dm sleeping 2 $40, d $50-60; 🐾) Fish and kayak right from the green riverbanks here. There are cheap bunks, decent rooms and cabins, and the amenities block is wheelchair-accessible. Well-behaved dogs welcome. Kayaks available to hire for $10 per hour.

JJ's Bakery & Old Mill Cafe   BAKERY **$**
(52 Wellington St; mains $10-20; ☉7am-5.30pm Mon-Fri, to 5pm Sat & Sun) This place in the Old Emerald flour mill is always busy. It does great pizzas, bruschettas, pies, quiches and a fine chocolate-mud muffin. The rosette-adorned walls are evidence enough of the winning recipes.

Evandale

POP 1035

Walk down the main street in Evandale and you'll feel like you've stepped back a century, which is why the whole town is National Trust listed. It's such an attractive place you'll want to take time to wander its sweet, quiet streets, browse its galleries and market stalls and hang out in cafes. The highlight of the year here is February's National Penny Farthing Championships, when one-wheel warriors race the town's streets at alarming velocities.

⊙ Sights & Activities

Clarendon   HISTORIC BUILDING
(☑6398 6220; 234 Clarendon Station Rd; adult/child/family $10/free/20; ☉10am-4pm) South of town via Nile Rd is stately Clarendon. Built in 1838 in neo-classical style, it looks like it's stepped straight out of *Gone with the Wind* and was long the grandest house in the colony. The home is graced with antiques and set in seven park-like hectares on the South Esk River bank and you can tour both.

Evandale Market MARKET
(Falls Park; ⊘9am-1pm) is held each Sunday, and is an exuberant mix of happy locals selling fresh fruit and veg, kids' pony rides (and occasionally a mini train) as well as stalls selling crafts and bric-a-brac.

Water Tower HISTORIC BUILDING
As you enter town travelling from the airport to the north, there's a castle-like water tower which encloses a convict-dug tunnel designed to supply water to Launceston.

St Andrews Uniting Church CHURCH
This historic church on High St with its imposing Doric columns and a classical belltower opened for worship in 1840. It's a much-admired example of Greek revival architecture.

St Andrews Anglican CHURCH
Also on High St, the 'other' St Andrews, with its soaring spire, first opened in 1837. But faulty foundations meant it had to be rebuilt from the ground up not long after, and it was rededicated in 1872.

Brown's Village Store HISTORIC SHOP
This shop in Russel St still has the original Victorian wooden shop fit-out (and seemingly some of its wares).

✿✦ Festivals & Events

Evandale Village Fair & National Penny Farthing Championships PENNY FARTHING RACES
(www.evandalevillagefair.com; adult/child $7/free) The village fair in February is when the town comes out to play. There are penny farthing races at breakneck speed, a market and the occasional pipe-band parading the streets.

Glover Art Prize ART COMPETITION
(www.johnglover.com.au) During the March long weekend each year, the historic pavilion in Falls Park hosts an exhibition ($5 per adult, children free) of finalist works in the Glover Art Prize competition, Australia's richest. It's a feast of top contemporary art that's not to be missed.

⌂ Sleeping & Eating

TOP CHOICE **Wesleyan Chapel** RENTAL HOUSE $$
(☑6331 9337; 28 Russell St; d incl breakfast $115-125) Built in 1836, this tiny brick chapel has been used as a druids' hall, an RSL hall and a meeting place for scouts. Now, under the high ceiling, it's stylish accommodation for two.

Farthings Village Accommodation RENTAL HOUSE $$
(☑6391 8251; 16 Russell St; d $140, extra person $20) Sleeping up to four, this cute cottage has been lovingly restored in old-world style. The master bedroom has a king-size four-poster bed and the bathroom has a spa. Enquire at the Evandale General Store.

Grandma's House COTTAGE $$
(☑6391 8444; www.grandmashouse.com.au; 10 Rodgers Lane; d 170, extra person $35; @) This cottage is set in the leafy gardens of historic Marlborough House in the centre of Evandale and has four bedrooms sleeping up to seven. There's a verandah with a BBQ out the back, and you have the run of the extensive gardens. Reduced rates for stays of two nights or more.

Clarendon Arms Hotel PUB $
(☑6391 8181; 11 Russell St; s/d $45/80) This pub has decent budget rooms with shared facilities, and does lunch and dinner in its commendable restaurant daily; mains range from $12 to $27. There's also a $12 bar menu for lunch and dinner.

Prince of Wales Hotel PUB $$
(☑6391 8381; cnr High & Collins Sts; d $90, f $110) Evandale's other drinking hole offers basic pub-style accommodation; doubles and family rooms come with en-suite bathrooms.

Ingleside Bakery Café CAFE $$
(☑6391 8682; 4 Russell St; mains $15-22; ⊘breakfast & lunch) Sit in the beautiful walled courtyard or under the high ceiling inside these atmospheric former council chambers. Fresh baking smells waft from the wood oven, making the bakery wares quite irresistible. It does delectable pies and pasties ($6), a swagman's lunch for the hungry ($22) and all manner of sweet treats.

Muse Coffee Bar CAFE $
(☑6391 8552; 14 Russell St; mains $6-14; ⊘10am-5pm Sun-Thu, 6-8pm Fri & Sat) This cool little eatery does morning and afternoon teas and delicious lunches using plenty of fresh local produce. Try the Tasmanian smoked salmon on sourdough with figs. Friday and Saturday are pizza nights.

❶ Information

At the informative community **visitor centre** (☑6391 8128; 18 High St; ⊘9am-5pm Oct-Apr, 10am-4pm May-Sep) you can pick up the pamphlet *Evandale Heritage Walk* ($3), which will guide you around the town's historic features.

The history room here has a display on famous locals, including painter John Glover and highly decorated WWI soldier Harry Murray. Both are commemorated with statues on Russell St: Glover 18 stone and club footed and Murray hurling a grenade.

Ben Lomond National Park

This 165-sq-km park takes in the whole of the Ben Lomond massif: a craggy alpine plateau some 14km long by 6km wide. The plateau reaches heights of 1300m and its peaks are above 1500m. Legges Tor (1573m) is the second-highest peak in Tasmania and in fine weather affords amazing 360-degree views. A feature of the park is the tumbled landscape of dolerite columns (popular with rock climbers) and chunky scree slopes.

Ben Lomond has long been Tasmania's St Moritz – well, not quite, but when the snow does fall the lifts grind into action and there is skiing here. The park's also magnificent in the summer when alpine flowers run riot.

In summer, there's easy walking here. It's two hours each way to **Legges Tor** from Carr Villa, about halfway up the mountain. You can also climb to the top from the alpine village on the plateau, which takes about 30 minutes each way on marked tracks. (All walkers and cross-country skiers should register at the self-registration booth at the alpine village.) If you're happy to go off track, you can walk across the plateau in almost any direction. This is easy enough in fine weather but not recommended in less-than-complete visibility. Unless you're well equipped, walking south of the ski village isn't advised.

The snow can be fickle, but the Ben Lomond ski season is generally from early July to mid-September. Snow-making equipment will be on trial from 2011 so better snow should be guaranteed.

Full-day ski-lift passes cost $55/30 per adult/junior, while half-day passes cost $38/20. Under sixes and over 65s ride free! There are three T-bars and four Poma lifts. **Ben Lomond Snow Sports** (☑6390 6185; www.skibenlomond.com.au; ⊙from 9am in season) runs a kiosk selling takeaway fare and a shop doing ski, snowboard and toboggan rental, and associated gear. Skis, boots, poles, a day lift pass and a lesson cost $120/75/65 per adult/junior/child under six.

🛏 Sleeping & Eating

There's a **camping** area 1km along from the park entrance, which offers secluded, cleared, unpowered sites, flushing toilets, drinking water and a fantastic lookout.

Creek Inn   INN **$$**
(☑6390 6199; summer adult/child $20/10, winter adult child/$50/25) There's accommodation year-round here at Tasmania's highest pub. There are cosily heated en-suite rooms and – snow conditions permitting – you can ski right to the door. There's also a fully licensed **restaurant** (mains $15-30; ⊙10am-4pm summer, breakfast, lunch & dinner winter) where you can top up your skiing or hiking energy.

❶ Getting There & Away

In the ski season **McDermotts Coaches** (☑6394 3535) runs a limited service – only when there is actually skiable snow – departing from the back entrance of the Launceston Sport & Surf store (the Birchalls car park) at roughly 8.30am and leaving the mountain at about 4pm. Call to enquire when services are operating. Bookings at least a day in advance are essential.

Outside the ski season, driving is your only transport option. Note that the track up to the plateau is unsealed and includes Jacob's Ladder, a very steep climb with six dramatic hairpin bends and no safety barriers. During the snow season, chains are standard equipment. Don't forget antifreeze.

Devonport & the Northwest

Includes »

Devonport 205
Latrobe 212
Deloraine. 213
Sheffield 218
Ulverstone. 220
Penguin 221
Burnie 223
Wynyard & Around . .227
Rocky Cape
National Park 229
Stanley 230
Smithton & Around . .234
Corinna &
The Pieman River . . .240
King Island 241

Best Places to Eat

» Wild Café Restaurant (p223)

» Restaurant Red (p214)

» Deli Central (p221)

» Rialto Gallery Restaurant (p226)

Best Places to Stay

» @VDL (p231)

» Calstock (p214)

» Mole Creek Guesthouse (p216)

» Ulverstone River Retreat (p220)

Why Go?

If you designed a pirate's treasure map of a remote island's remotest corner, it might look something like this: a deep-forested, jagged-peaked interior where devils roam and eagles soar; a farmland patchwork scored through by gorges; mountain rivers; glow-worm-bejewelled caves. There'd be azure seas in white-sand coves; roaring beaches, islands, shipwrecks. And in the deep surrounding oceans you might write 'here be dragons'...except you'd make those dragons giant waves.

Imagine this, and you've conjured up some of the magic of Tasmania's northwest. There's much to captivate in this edge-of-the-world domain: from the epicurean to the creative to the wildest of natural. Come here to get arty or go bush – and meet the people who drink Cloud Juice, farm the wind, and breathe the cleanest air on earth.

When to Go

In spring and summer the northwest blooms: fields of purple poppies, multicoloured tulips, fragrant rainforest leatherwood. There's fresh crayfish, penguin-watching and festivals of music and craft, and you can camp beachside, ready for the perfect surf break.

Want to experience the full power of the Roaring Forties? Then consider visiting in winter. Locals batten down the hatches for the longest, darkest nights, when it's 999exhil-aratingly wild and wind-lashed. You'll get a warm welcome, but call ahead: some things close completely – or open less frequently – in winter.

Devonport

POP 25,122

Devonport is best known to visitors to Tasmania as the port of the *Spirit of Tasmania* I and II, the red-and-white ferries that connect the island-state with the mainland. They're quite an evocative sight when, after three deep burps of the horn, they cruise past the end of the main street to begin their voyage north. Devonport is a waterside city: it straddles the Mersey River and seascapes stretch out from it to either side. One of the landmarks in town is the Mersey Bluff Lighthouse, built in 1889 to warn ships off the rocky coastline and guide them safely into port, and the protected Mersey River mouth is still an important harbour for exporting agricultural produce from surrounding fertile lands.

Many visitors get off the ferry in Devonport, jump in their cars and scoot. This quiet port town is possibly not the most glamorous spot in the state, but take your time to ground your feet on Tasmanian soil here: walk along the Mersey and up to the lighthouse for unmissable views over the coastline and Bass Strait. The new Mersey Bluff development (under way at the time of writing), with its smart surf club, restaurants, swimming beach, free hot showers and playground, will also be worth visiting.

Sights & Activities

Tiagarra   MUSEUM
(Bluff Rd; adult/child $10/5; 9am-5pm Mon-Fri, 10am-4pm Sat) The absorbing displays here tell the story of Aboriginal culture in Tasmania from the time humans first crossed over the land bridge that's now under Bass Strait. There's a soberingly frank assessment of the decimation of Aboriginal society and culture at the time of European arrival. Outside, you can follow a trail around the headland to see Aboriginal rock carvings (petroglyphs), some more than 10,000 years old.

Devonport Maritime Museum   MUSEUM
(6 Gloucester Ave; adult/child/family $5/2/10; 10am-4.30pm Tue-Sun Oct-Mar, to 4pm Apr-Sep) This museum is in the former harbourmaster's residence (c 1920) and pilot station near the foreshore. It has an extensive collection of flags and other maritime paraphernalia, including a superb set of models from the ages of sail and steam to the present seagoing passenger ferries.

Don River Railway   MUSEUM
(www.donriverrailway.com.au; Forth Main Rd; adult/child/family $17/12/38; 9am-5pm) You don't have to be a trainspotter to love this collection of locomotives. Trainheads will go crazy over the brightly painted rolling stock. The entry price includes a half-hour ride in a diesel train (between 10am and 4pm), and you can hop on the puffing steam train on Sunday and public holidays. The railway is 4km west of town. Drive west out of Devonport on the Bass Hwy, then take the B19 exit towards Don, Devonport and Spreyton. Follow signs to the railway, which is 4.5km from the centre of Devonport.

Pandemonium   AMUSEMENT PARK
(62-64 North Fenton St; admission from $8; 10am-5.30pm Tue-Sun) This is the place in Devonport where kids can let off steam. It's an indoor play centre with a giant jungle gym, jumping castles and slides (for up to 11-year-olds), laser skirmish (eight-year-olds and up), rock climbing (six and up) and the hands-on scientific displays of the Imaginarium Science Centre. There's a cafe to collapse in when you're done. The park is also open on public- and school-holiday Mondays.

FREE Devonport Regional Gallery   ART GALLERY
(www.devonportgallery.com; 45-47 Stewart St; 10am-5pm Mon-Fri, noon-5pm Sat, 1-5pm Sun) This excellent gallery houses predominantly 20th-century Tasmanian paintings, contemporary art by local and mainland artists, plus ceramics and glasswork.

Home Hill   NOTABLE BUILDING
(77 Middle Rd; adult/under 18 yr $10/free; 1.30-4pm Tue-Thu Sat & Sun Sep-Jun, by appointment Jul & Aug) This was the residence of Joseph Lyons (Tasmania's only prime minister of Australia; 1932–39) and his wife, Dame Enid Lyons, and their 12 children.

Penguin-watching season runs from August to March. At Lillico Beach, off the Bass Hwy on the western edge of town, you can watch little penguins emerge from the sea and return to their burrows at dusk.

Tours

Murray's Day Out   SIGHTSEEING
(6424 5250; www.murraysdayout.com.au; day trips per person from $110) To be shown some of Tasmania by an entirely passionate and charming Tasmanian, consider taking one of these tours. Murray offers 'service with humour' in his comfortable van (seating up

Devonport & the Northwest Highlights

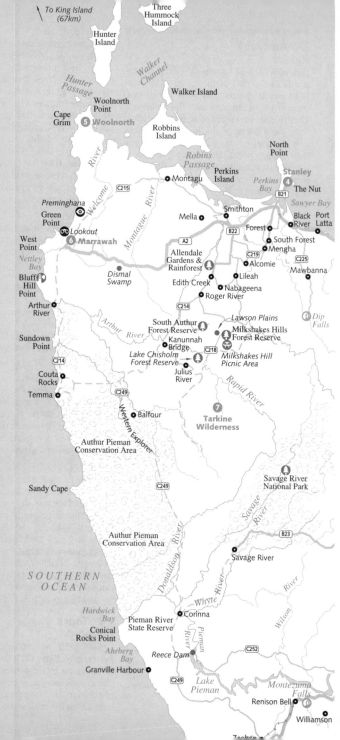

1 Marvelling at limestone cave formations, lit by constellations of glow worms, at **Mole Creek Karst National Park** (p215)

2 Walking through gnarled forests of pencil pines at gorgeous **Walls of Jerusalem National Park** (p216)

3 Getting to know northwest-coasters' creative sides at the **Makers' Workshop** (p223) in Burnie

4 Tucking into just-out-of-the-water crayfish at the fresh-seafood outlets in **Stanley** (p230)

5 Feeling the power of the Roaring Forties – and breathing the world's cleanest air – at **Woolnorth** (p234)

6 Watching Tasmanian devils tuck, snarling, into a meal on a **King's Run Wildlife Tour** at Marrawah (p237)

7 Delving deep into the **Tarkine Wilderness** to marvel at some of the last pristine temperate rainforest on earth (p238)

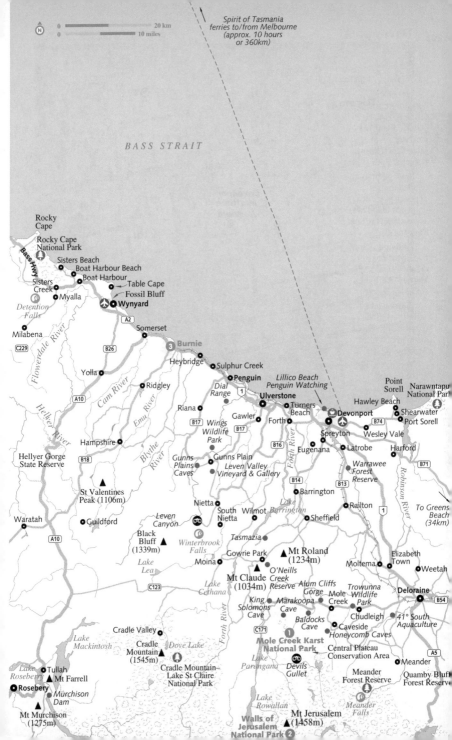

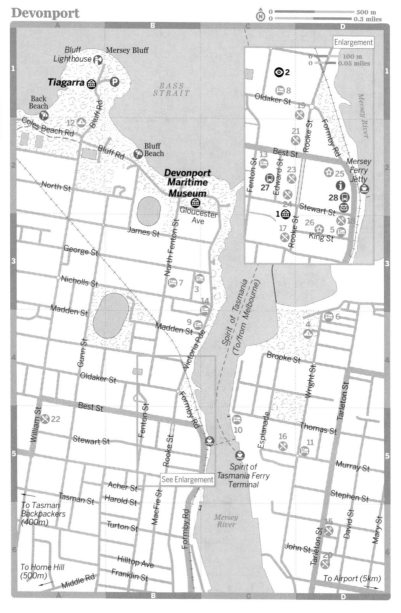

to seven). Go all the way west to Marrawah, drop in on Cradle Mountain or just tool around the back lanes near Devonport. Given the combination of the jovial Murray and the stunning scenery, you're bound to have a smile on your face at the end of the day.

Sleeping

Cameo Cottage   RENTAL HOUSE **$$**
(✆6427 0991, 0439 658 503; www.devonport bedandbreakfast.com; 27 Victoria Pde; d $140-160, extra adult/child $35/25) Tucked away in quiet backstreets, this two-bedroom cottage was

⊙ Top Sights

Devonport Maritime
  Museum B2
Tiagarra A1

⊙ Sights

1 Devonport Regional Gallery C2
2 Pandemonium C1

⊙ Sleeping

3 3 George St B3
4 Abel Tasman Caravan Park D4
5 Alexander Hotel D3
6 Alice Beside the Sea D4
7 Barclay Motor Inn B3
8 Birchmore of Devonport C1
9 Cameo Cottage B4
10 Edgewater C5
11 Hawleys Gingerbread
   House D5
12 Mersey Bluff Caravan Park A2
13 Quality Hotel Gateway C2
14 River View Lodge C3

⊙ Eating

15 All Things Nice D6
16 Barrie Martins Pizza C5
17 Bento C3
18 Central at the Formby D3
19 Dannebrog D1
20 Kit Kat Café D6
21 Molly Malone's D2
22 Renusha's A5
23 Stonies Fifties Café C2
24 Tapas Lounge Bar C2

Drinking

Formby Hotel .... (see 18)
Molly Malone's .... (see 21)

⊙ Entertainment

25 Cmax Cinema D2
26 Warehouse Nightclub D3

Transport

27 Redline Coaches Terminal C2
28 Tassielink Coaches
   Arrival/Departure Point D2

built in 1914 but is now beautifully redecorated. It's got a well-equipped kitchen, a cosy lounge, a laundry, and a quiet garden with BBQ facilities.

Quality Hotel Gateway　　HOTEL **$$$**
(☑6424 4922; www.gatewayinn.com.au; 16 Fenton St; d $170-300, mains $21-29; @☜) When we visited, this hotel was being renovated into a more contemporary style. For somewhere top notch to stay in Devonport, try its super-swanky deluxe spa rooms. You can also eat dinner at the restaurant here.

3 George St　　B&B **$$**
(☑0400 637 199; www.threegeorgestreet.com.au; 3 George St; s/d $120/140) This pleasant B&B is set in a pretty 1910 home just a street back from the Devonport waterfront. You'll receive a friendly welcome but also peace and privacy in your own well-furnished suite. There's a guest lounge and a kitchen to share, and a DVD library.

Birchmore of Devonport　　B&B **$$**
(☑6423 1336; www.bedsandbreakfasts.com.au/birchmore; 10 Oldaker St; s $145-160, d $170-190; ☜) This old Federation dame has spacious, well-appointed rooms and is just a minute away from the city centre. Cooked breakfast is served each morning in the conservatory.

Alice Beside the Sea　　APARTMENTS **$$**
(☑6427 8605; www.alicebesidethesea.com; 1 Wright St; d $115-190) Located close to the ferry terminals, this compact B&B offers comfortable, two-bedroom, self-contained accommodation across the road from the beach and close to supermarkets. It's pet-friendly too.

Edgewater　　MOTEL **$$**
(☑6427 8441; www.edgewater-devonport.com.au; 4 Thomas St; d $100-230; ☜) This motel has been snazzed up recently. and is now a good place to stay in East Devonport Some of the rooms have spas and pleasant water views, and there's a popular **bistro** (mains $10-25; ☺dinner Mon-Sat). It's just a hop and a skip away from where the *Spirit of Tasmania* docks.

River View Lodge　　B&B **$$**
(☑6424 7357; www.riverviewlodge.com.au; 18 Victoria Pde; d $100-145) This is a comfortable, homely guesthouse just across the road from the Mersey. Most rooms have en suites and there's a lounge with a fire to relax by.

Mersey Bluff Caravan Park　　CARAVAN PARK **$**
(☑6424 8655; www.merseybluff.com.au; 41 Bluff Rd; sites d $12-28, on-site vans d $90) In a seaside setting on Mersey Bluff, this pleasantly green park is just steps from the

beach. There's a campers' kitchen and BBQ facilities. Eco-cabins were in the pipeline at time of writing, and a playground was due to open nearby. The new waterfront precinct at Mersey Bluff, with its amazing new surf club and restaurants, is adjacent.

Tasman Backpackers   HOSTEL $
(☑6423 2335; www.tasmanbackpackers.com.au; 114 Tasman St; dm/tw/d $20/50/52; @) This hostel was once a sprawling nurses' quarters, but it's now a friendly place to stay with an international feel. The en-suite doubles all have TV-DVD and there are (free) movies in the lounge most nights. The hostel offers free ferry and bus station pick-ups, and can make tour and bus bookings. Staff also do placements for harvest and fruit-picking jobs.

Barclay Motor Inn   MOTEL $$
(☑6424 4722; www.barclaymotorinn.com.au; 112 North Fenton St; d $110-160, extra person $25; ☎⊛) This may not be your most architecturally rewarding stay in Tasmania, but the rooms are spick-and-span, there's a swimming pool and tennis court, and staff can help with travel info.

Alexander Hotel   PUB $
(☑6424 2252; 78 Formby Rd; dm/s/d $25/49/59) The rooms here are no great shakes, but it's a cheap and central place to stay. In the pub downstairs you're sure to get talking to locals.

Hawleys Gingerbread House   HOSTEL $
(☑6427 0477; www.gingerbreadhousehotel; 71 Wright St; dm $24, mains $15-30; ☎) Just 100m from the ferry, this basic backpacker hostel is housed in a rather ramshackle heritage home. The restaurant below serves hearty lunches and dinners (Wednesday to Sunday).

Abel Tasman Caravan Park   CARAVAN PARK $
(☑6427 8794; www.tigerresortstas.com.au; 6 Wright St; unpowered/powered sites $20/32, vans $50-65, cabins $89-145; ☎) Right by East Devonport Beach and only 800m from the *Spirit of Tasmania* dock, this friendly park has neat cabins, clean amenities, BBQ areas and a campers' kitchen.

✖️ Eating
At time of writing, the redevelopment at Mersey Bluff was about to provide two new restaurants on the Devonport dining scene in the smart new surf-club building. They'll surely be worth a visit.

Tapas Lounge Bar   TAPAS $$
(www.tapasloungebar.com; 97a Rooke St Mall; tapas $9.50; ⊙4.30pm-late Wed-Sun, lunch Sat & Sun) Everyone's talking about this cool new place upstairs in the Rooke St Mall. It's all done up in black leather and has funky music and, people say, the best eating in Devonport. The tempting tapas-style menu also has options for kids. After 9pm it morphs into a bar for over 25s with live music Friday to Sunday.

Renusha's   INDIAN, ITALIAN $$
(132 William St; mains $15-20; ⊙lunch Wed-Fri, dinner Tue-Sun) The gaudy decor here may be what first catches your attention, and you'll be glad it did: the food is sensational. It serves superb Indian food and fine Italian pasta too, and has earned a local reputation for being consistently great.

Stonies Fifties Café   CAFE $
(77 Rooke St; meals $8-18; ⊙breakfast & lunch Mon-Sat) You can eat hearty all-day breakfasts at this classic Devonport diner, or choose from a good range of burgers: the Chubby Cheeser is its renowned cheeseburger. The coffees here are the standout: they have 18 different types – all named after '50s music stars: say 'Little Richard' for an espresso.

Barrie Martins Pizza   ITALIAN $$
(13 Murray St; mains $10-24; ⊙from 4pm daily summer, Wed-Sun in winter) This place has a reputation for producing the best pizzas in Devonport, straight out of the wood oven, with traditional and inventive toppings. It also does pastas and salads and commendable coffees.

Dannebrog   STEAKHOUSE $$
(161 Rooke St; mains $16-35; ⊙lunch & dinner) There's nothing Scandinavian about this restaurant, but it's named after the Danish flag in honour of Tasmanian Crown Princess Mary of Denmark (see p87). If you're a committed carnivore you'll feel at home here amid the steaks, served with salad, chips and a sauce of your choice. They also run nearby B&B accommodation at River View Lodge.

Formby Hotel   PUB FARE $
(82 Formby Rd; mains $19-30, s/d $45/79; ⊙lunch & dinner) The refurbed dining room here offers bistro meals, including pizza, pastas, salads, steaks and seafood. There are excellent fresh juices and smoothies at the cafebar, and coffee and cakes between mealtimes. Upstairs are simple rooms, some with good river views: watch the *Spirit of Tasmania* voyage past your window.

Molly Malone's PUB FARE $

(6424 1898; 34 Best St; mains $9-27) Hungry for some down-home pub fare with an Irish twist? Then you can't go wrong at Molly's. There are the usual Irish suspects like Kilkenny stew and a fine Belfast beef-and-Guinness pie, as well as more local pub staples. There's also a basic **hostel** (dm/d with shared bathroom $20/30, d $50; @) upstairs, which can get noisy Friday to Sunday.

Bento JAPANESE $

(5 Rooke St; mains $3-18; ⊙lunch & dinner) Economically priced – finger food starts at $3 – this place offers lacquered bento-box meals, including a bento banquet ($17.50), which comes with unlimited miso and hot dishes, and Japanese-style ice cream.

All Things Nice BAKERY $

(175 Tarleton St; items $3-10; ⊙24hr) Located near the ferry terminal, this place offers bakery items, including gourmet chunky pies, (try Tasmania's iconic scallop pie for $5), cakes, sweets and a good strong cuppa.

Kit Kat Café CAFE $

(175 Tarleton St; ⊙breakfast, lunch & dinner) Just next door to All Things Nice, this welcoming cafe serves hungry arrivals off the ferry big bacon-and-egg breakfasts ($7), juicy burgers, fish and chips, sandwiches and wraps.

☕ Drinking & Entertainment

Central at The Formby BAR

(82 Formby Rd; ⊙3pm-midnight Wed, 3pm-1am Thu & Fri, 1pm-1am Sat, 1-9pm Sun) Locals regard this as Devonport's best bar. It's all done up in leather sofas and laid-back cool, and they fold the concertina windows open on to the river on warm nights. There are live bands Friday and Saturday; Sunday afternoon sees acoustic sessions and a more sophisticated crowd.

Molly Malone's BAR

(34 Best St) An expansive, wood-panelled Irish den that gets big, beer-guzzling crowds and has live music Friday and Saturday.

Warehouse Nightclub NIGHTCLUB

(18 King St; admission $6-10; ⊙10pm-late Thu-Sat) This is one of Devonport's few clubbing hang-outs and draws a young (possibly boisterous) crowd for live bands and Saturday-night DJs.

Cmax CINEMA

(6420 2111; 5-7 Best St; adult/child $12/9) The Cmax hosts mostly blockbusters but sometimes has live feeds from international events.

ℹ Information

Online Access Centre (21 Oldaker St; ⊙9.30am-5.30pm Mon-Thu, to 7pm Fri, to 1.30pm Sat, 11am-5pm Sun) In Devonport's library.

Post office (88 Formby Rd)

Rooke St Mall ATMs are located in and around the mall.

Visitor centre (6424 4466; www.devonport tasmania.travel; 92 Formby Rd; ⊙7.30am-5pm) Free baggage storage is available here.

ℹ Getting There & Away

Air

QantasLink (13 13 13) Regular flights to Melbourne.

Tasair (www.tasair.com.au) To Hobart and King Island.

Boat

Spirit of Tasmania (1800 634 906, 13 20 10; www.spiritoftasmania.com.au; ⊙telephone bookings 6.30am-9.30pm) ferries sail between Station Pier in Melbourne and the ferry terminal on the Esplanade in East Devonport. For details of services, see p320.

Bus

Redline Coaches (www.redlinecoaches.com.au) stop at 9 Edward St and the *Spirit of Tasmania* terminal. There's a Launceston to Devonport via Deloraine and Latrobe service ($24, 2½ hours).

Redline buses from Devonport:

Ulverstone ($7, 25 minutes)

Penguin ($8, 40 minutes)

Burnie ($11, one hour)

Stanley ($30, two hours)

Smithton ($33, 2½ hours)

Tassielink (www.tassielink.com.au) buses stop at the visitor centre and at the *Spirit of Tasmania*. Tassielink buses from Devonport:

Launceston ($24, 70 minutes)

Sheffield ($6, 40 minutes)

Gowrie Park ($10, 55 minutes)

Cradle Mountain ($41, two hours)

Queenstown ($54, four hours)

Strahan ($64, five hours)

Merseylink (www.merseylink.com.au) operates local buses between Devonport and Latrobe ($3.60, 25 minutes) from Devonport's Rooke St interchange.

Sainty's Coaches (6334 6456) does charter services in association with **Maxwells** for bushwalkers from Devonport. Prices are for groups of up to four (for five or more, the price is per person):

Cradle Mountain ($220, or $50 per person)

Walls of Jerusalem National Park ($220, or $55 per person)

Lake St Clair (via Great Lake; $320, or $80 per person)

Car

Avis (☏6427 9797; airport)

Bargain Car Rentals (☏0439 370 127)

Budget (☏6427 0650; airport)

Europcar (☏6427 0888; ferry terminal)

Hertz (☏6424 1013; 26 Oldaker St).

Thrifty (☏1800 030 730, 6427 9119; ferry terminal)

❶ Getting Around

BOAT A cross-Mersey **ferry** (one-way $2.50; ☺7.30am-6pm Mon-Sat) operates near a pontoon near the post office and the *Spirit of Tasmania* terminal. It runs on demand.

BUS & TAXI A **shuttle bus** (☏1300 659 878) runs between the airport and ferry terminal, the visitor centre and your accommodation ($15 per person). There's also a service to Launceston Airport ($50). Bookings are essential. A **taxi** (☏6424 1431) from the airport to the centre of town will cost approximately $20.

Latrobe

POP 2770

Ten kilometres south of Devonport on the Bass Hwy, Latrobe exudes an entirely different flavour from its larger neighbour. It's an attractive, historic town, with heritage buildings housing cafes and antique shops. Once a busy shipping port on the Mersey River, Latrobe was built on mining and agricultural fortunes, with 75 National Trust–registered buildings on the main street alone. There are beautiful riverside forest walks here, where you may spot platypuses. The town also has the distinction of being the home of that most Tasmanian of sports: competitive wood-chopping.

◎ Sights

Australian Axeman's Hall of Fame   MUSEUM
(www.axemanscomplex.com.au; 1 Bells Pde; adult/child/family $10/5/25; ☺9am-5pm) This complex honours the legendary axemen of the northwest who dominate the sport of competitive wood-chopping. There's a film on the history of wood-getting; displays on hauling, milling and of course chopping

wood; plus an examination of sustainable forestry. Included in the entry fee here is the **Platypus & Trout Experience**, which sheds light on the breeding life and habits of this shy monotreme – often spotted in the Mersey River just over the road. There are trout in display tanks, and you can get information on fishing in nearby waters, plus buy licences. There's also a cafe for light meals.

Warrawee Forest Reserve   NATURE RESERVE
(☺9am-dusk) In this beautiful slice of nature by the Mersey River, with several walking tracks – some wheelchair accessible – you have an excellent chance of seeing platypuses. Two-hour **platypus-spotting tours** (☏6426 1774; tours $10) are organised through the visitor centre, departing at dawn and dusk. Book ahead.

Sherwood Hall   HISTORIC BUILDING
(Bells Pde; adult/under 15 yr $2/free; ☺10am-2pm Tue & Thu, 1-4pm Sat, Sun & public holidays) Adjacent to Axeman's is this historic cottage built by a remarkable pioneer couple, ex-convict Thomas Johnson and his part-Aboriginal wife, Dolly Dalrymple Briggs.

Court House Museum   MUSEUM
(113 Gilbert St; adult/child $2/1; ☺1-4pm Tue-Fri) There's a rich photographic display of the area's history here, next to the post office in the centre of town.

House of Anvers   CHOCOLATE FACTORY
FREE (www.anvers-chocolate.com.au; 9025 Bass Hwy; ☺7am-7pm) House of Anvers is a chocolate factory and a museum of chocolate that creates a range of sweet treats: fudges, truffles, and the most amazing chocolate-orange slices. You can also come here for your breakfast *pain au chocolat,* washed down with what's surely one of the best hot chocolates known to humankind. House of Anvers is clearly signposted off the Bass Hwy approximately 3km past Latrobe in the direction of Devonport

★ Festivals & Events

Henley-on-the-Mersey Carnival   REGATTA
Held on Australia Day (26 January) at Bells Pde in Latrobe, site of the town's former docks.

Latrobe Chocolate Winterfest   CHOCOLATE
(chocolatewinterfest.com.au) This midwinter festival celebrates all things chocolate.

Latrobe Wheel Race   BICYCLE RACE
Annual bicycle race held on Boxing Day, attracting professional riders from around Australia.

🛏 Sleeping & Eating

Lucas' Hotel   PUB $$
(☎6426 1101; www.lucashotellatrobe.com.au; 46 Gilbert St; s/d $105/115, without bathroom $80/90, with spa $125/140) This excellently restored pub has comfortable, upmarket rooms. There's good food on offer in an elegant old-world **dining room** (mains $12-28; ☺breakfast, lunch & dinner). They also have a kids' menu and some wickedly good desserts.

Lucinda   B&B $$
(☎6426 2285; www.lucindabnb.com.au; 17 Forth St; s $95-120, d $110-145) Lucinda provides handsome accommodation in a National Trust-classified home, set in parklike grounds. A couple of its heritage rooms have spectacularly intricate moulded ceilings: see if you can spot the one red rose in the plasterwork as you lie in your four-poster bed.

Café Zeta   CAFE $$
(☎6426 3139; 20 Gilbert St; mains $6-24; ☺breakfast & lunch Wed-Mon) This stylish establishment serves beautifully presented cafe food – all freshly homemade to order. It does great pastas, fine spanakopita, brilliant chilli-and-coconut prawns and excellent coffees and cakes. Browse in the gift shop afterwards.

ℹ Information

Visitor centre (☎6421 4699; www.latrobe tasmania.com.au; 1 Bells Pde; ☺9am-5pm, reduced hr winter) At the Axeman's Hall of Fame.

Deloraine

POP 2500

You could hardly go wrong if you decided to establish a town in such beautiful rural surroundings as stretch out around Deloraine. At the foot of the Great Western Tiers, the town has wonderful views just about wherever you look. Wisely, they've made the streetscapes here pretty lovely, too. Georgian and Victorian buildings, ornate with wrought-iron tracery, crowd together along the main street that leads to green parkland on the banks of the Meander River. The town has an artsy, vibrant feel, with several cool little eateries, some bohemian boutiques and secondhand shops. The strong artistic community here celebrates annually with the Tasmanian Craft Fair, drawing tens of thousands of visitors in late October or early November: book accommodation ahead if you're visiting at this time.

◉ Sights & Activities

Deloraine Folk Museum & YARNS: Artwork in Silk   MUSEUM
(98 Emu Bay Rd; adult/child/family $8/2/18; ☺9.30-4pm) The centrepiece of the museum here is an exquisite four-panel, quilted and appliquéd depiction of the Meander Valley through a year of seasonal change. It's an astoundingly detailed piece of work that was a labour of love by 300 creative local men and women. Each of the four panels entailed 2500 hours of labour, and the whole project took three years to complete. It's now housed in a purpose-built auditorium, where you can witness a presentation explaining the work: it's fascinating and truly worth seeing. Also on display at the museum are slightly moth-eaten local history exhibits.

FREE **Ashgrove Farm Cheese**   DAIRY
(www.ashgrovecheese.com.au; 6173 Bass Hwy, Elizabeth Town; ☺7am-6pm summer, 7.30am-5.30pm winter) Journey 15km north of Deloraine to find this award-winning cheese factory. You can watch the cheeses being made and then sample the fine results in the tasting room–providore. The milk bar here serves pies and platters, and milkshakes and ice creams aplenty.

41° South Aquaculture   FARM
(☎6362 4130; www.41southtasmania.com; 323 Montana Rd; admission free, tours adult/child $10/5; ☺9am-5pm Nov-Mar, to 4pm Apr-Oct) You don't have to be a fish-lover to visit this interesting farm where salmon are reared in raised tanks and a wetland is used as a natural biofilter. This no-waste, no-chemical method of fish farming is the cleanest way of raising fish – and also makes for superb smoked salmon, which you can taste (free) and buy in the tasting room, or lunch on in the cafe. The farm is 6km out of town towards Mole Creek (signed down Montana Rd).

DON'T MISS

THE CHERRY SHED

Don't miss sweet treats on offer at this cherry **farm gate** (☺9.30am-5pm) at the corner of Gilbert St and Bass Hwy. You can sample and buy the plump red cherries in season, and there's a shop-cafe offering cherry wines and liqueurs, jams, pies and divine cherry ice cream all year round.

Walking

Dominating the southern skyline are the **Great Western Tiers** (their Aboriginal name is Kooparoona Niara, 'Mountain of the Spirits'). The **Meander Forest Reserve** is the most popular starting point for walks here. From the swing bridge over the Meander River – where there are bowers of man ferns and tall trees – you can walk to **Split Rock Falls**. This route takes about three hours return, or you can walk to **Meander Falls** – five to six hours return.

Other good walks on the Great Western Tiers include those to **Projection Bluff** (two hours return), **Quamby Bluff** (five hours return) and **Mother Cummings Peak** (three to five hours return). Ask at the visitor centre for walking information.

Festivals & Events

Tasmanian Craft Fair CRAFTS

(www.tascraftfair.com.au) This impressive four-day fair is held annually in early November. Up to 30,000 people visit hundreds of craft stalls around town, and there's talent aplenty on show.

Sleeping

Calstock BOUTIQUE HOTEL $$$

(☎6362 2642; www.peppers.com.au/calstock; Lake Hwy; d incl breakfast $325-495; 📶) Just south of Deloraine, parklike grounds surround a Georgian mansion housing a much-awarded boutique hotel. There are seven bedrooms (one wheelchair-accessible) and two suites decorated in French-provincial style, as well as grand lounges, gourmet breakfasts, and a three-course set-menu dinner ($90) by arrangement. Leave the kiddies (under 13) at home.

Bluestone Grainstore B&B $$

(☎6362 4722; www.bluestonegrainstore.com.au; 14 Parsonage St; d $150, extra person $50; 📶) A 150-year-old warehouse has been renovated with great style here: think whitewashed stone walls, crisp linen, leather bedheads, deep oval bathtubs…and a few funky touches like origami flowers. There's even a mini-movie theatre and films to choose from. Breakfasts draw on local produce – organic where possible.

Blake's Manor APARTMENTS $$

(☎6362 4724; www.blakesmanor.com; 18 West Goderich St; d $128-185, extra adult/child $50/30) Wow, what an amazing job has been done on these two self-contained suites, attached to Georgian Blake's Manor. They're wonderfully ornate in period style, with velvet drapes, plush antiques and Persian rugs – and yet both have kitchenettes and contemporary bathrooms. Breakfast provisions, port, cheese and nibbles are laid on.

Deloraine Hotel PUB $

(☎6362 2022; www.delorainehotel.com.au, Emu Bay Rd; s $40, d $80-120) This 1848 pub is veritably *draped* in wrought-iron lace, and its once pubbish interior recently had a cool, contemporary makeover. Hang out in the bar, dine on good pub grub (mains $16 to $26) and then stay the night. The basic rooms upstairs were just about to get the same spruce-up as downstairs when we visited.

Tierview Twin Cottages COTTAGES $$

(☎6362 2377; 125 Emu Bay Rd; d $115-135, extra person $20) Just off the main street, these five- and six-person cottages offer comfortable self-contained accommodation. One has an open fire, the other a spa bathroom. Book ahead and collect your keys from the Shell service station opposite.

Highview Lodge Youth Hostel HOSTEL $

(☎6362 2996; 8 Blake St; dm/d/f from $20/60/72) It's a steep climb to this hilltop YHA, but the reward is expansive views over the Great Western Tiers. With the wood heater roaring there's a cosy, homey atmosphere. Nonguests can use showers for $5.

Deloraine Apex Caravan Park CARAVAN PARK $

(☎6362 2345; West Pde; unpowered/powered sites d $21/25) This simple camp spot is at the bottom of the main street by the Meander River. Don't be alarmed if an almighty thundering disturbs your slumber here: the train tracks are adjacent.

Eating

TOP CHOICE **Restaurant Red** ITALIAN $$

(☎6362 3669; 81 Emu Bay Rd; mains $16-34; ⏰lunch & dinner) We'll go out on a limb and say this is the best place to eat in Deloraine. Set in the 1886 Bank of Australia building, the place looks classy, smells amazing, and the food tastes just as good. It's fantastic Italian-inspired fare: from wood-fired pizza to saltimbocca to veal scallopini – with a well-chosen wine list to match.

Deloraine Delicatessen & Gourmet Foods DELI & CAFE $

(36 Emu Bay Rd; mains $6-14; ⏰breakfast & lunch Mon-Sat) A fine place for late-morning baguettes, bagels and focaccias, with a vari-

ety of tasty fillings. Its coffee is pungently superb, and it does dairy- and gluten-free meals too.

Empire Hotel & Thai Restaurant THAI **$$** ([📞]6362 2082; 19 Emu Bay Rd; mains $19-29; [🕐]lunch & dinner) There's the usual Aussie bar here, and then – a surprising find in Deloraine – a really excellent Thai restaurant. Try the duck curry, its signature dish. Upstairs there's simple accommodation with shared facilities (from $75/100 for singles/doubles).

Christmas Hills Raspberry Farm Cafe CAFE **$$** (www.raspberryfarmcafe.com; Christmas Hills Rd, Elizabeth Town; meals $9.50-25; [🕐]7am-5pm) There are 16 acres of raspberries grown here, and you can see them in all their glory – before indulging in everything raspberry at the lakeside cafe. Think raspberry sundaes piled high with the ruby-coloured fruits, homemade raspberry ice cream, raspberry waffles, baked raspberry cheesecake, pavlovas, smoothies and even a shocking-pink raspberry latte. The farm is 8km north of Deloraine on the Bass Hwy.

ℹ️ Information

There are ATMs at **ANZ Bank** (54 Emu Bay Rd) and **Commonwealth Bank** (24 Emu Bay Rd).

Great Western Tiers visitor centre ([📞]6362 5280; 98-100 Emu Bay Rd; [🕐]9am-5pm) Shares premises with the Deloraine Folk Museum & YARNS: Artwork in Silk. Internet access is available ($4 per 15 minutes).

Online Access Centre (Emu Bay Rd; per 30min/hr $3/5; [🕐]10am-4pm Mon-Fri, 1-4pm Sun) Located down the steps behind the library.

Post office (10 Emu Bay Rd)

ℹ️ Getting There & Away

Redline Coaches ([📞]1300 360 000, 6336 1446; www.redlinecoaches.com.au) Buses to Launceston ($14, 45 minutes).

Tassielink ([📞]1300 300 520, 6230 8900; www. tassielink.com.au) Buses to Cradle Mountain ($59, three hours) and Strahan (with transfer in Queenstown; $82, 6½ hours).

Chudleigh

Make a beeline (sorry...) for Chudleigh's **Honey Farm** (www.thehoneyfarm.com.au; 39 Sorell St; [🕐]9am-5pm Sun-Fri, reduced hr winter), where you can get sticky fingers lingering over the free tastings of some of their more than 50 different types of honey, or sample some of the superb honey ice cream. In the shop you can browse through all things bees and honey – from beeswax boot polish to propolis supplements, honeycomb and bee cuddly toys. Less cuddly – but much more fascinating – are the 1000 bees you can watch hard at work in a glass-walled hive in the museum display corner.

Two kilometres west of Chudleigh is the **Trowunna Wildlife Park** (adult/child/family $18/9/50; [🕐]9am-5pm), which specialises in Tasmanian devils, wombats and koalas – as well as birds. There's an informative tour (starting at 11am, 1pm and 3pm in summer) during which you get to pat, feed or even hold the critters.

Mole Creek

POP 260

About 23km west of Deloraine and just around the bend from Chudleigh is pretty Mole Creek, a tiny rural town with beautiful mountain views and a couple of good places to stay and eat. It's also a great jumping-off point for spelunking and bushwalking.

◉ Sights & Activities

Mole Creek Karst National Park NATIONAL PARK ([📞]6363 5182 for tour bookings) The word 'karst' refers to the scenery characteristic of a limestone region, including caves and underground streams. The Mole Creek area contains over 300 known caves and sinkholes. The park itself is in a number of small segments, including the public caves which you can tour.

Public Caves

The name of the **Marakoopa Cave** derives from an Aboriginal word meaning 'handsome' – which it surely is – with delicate stalactites and stalagmites, glow-worms, sparkling crystals and reflective pools. Two tours are available here. The easy **Underground Rivers and Glow-Worms Tour** ([🕐]10am, noon, 2pm & 4pm Oct-May, no 4pm tour rest of yr) is for all ages. The **Great Cathedral and Glow-Worms Tour** ([🕐]11am, 1pm & 3pm) is more challenging. **Tours** ([🕐]10.30am, 11.30am, 12.30pm, 2.30pm, 3.30pm & 4.30pm Dec-Apr, 1st & last tours dropped rest of yr) of **King Solomons Cave** will show you lavish colours and formations in this more compact cave. All tours cost $16/8 for adults/children. The caves are a constant 9°C: wear warm clothes and good walking shoes. Entry to King Solomons Cave is payable only by credit card or Eftpos – no cash. If you don't have a card, cash payments for entry to both caves can be made at Marakoopa, 11km away. When you come back up into the light you can hang out at the picnic grounds or use the free BBQs.

Wild Caves

Cyclops, Honeycomb and Baldocks are among the better-known wild caves in the Mole Creek area that are without steps or ladders. If you're an experienced caver who wants to take on some vertical rope work, you'll need to make arrangements with a caving club. Alternatively, you can take one of the excursions offered by **Wild Cave Tours** (☑6367 8142; www.wildcavetours.com; 165 Fernlea Rd, Caveside; half-/full-day tours incl gear $95/190); they're not for children under 14. The guide is an environmental scientist and her love of the caves really shines through. She'll show you a host of endangered species, and knows of species yet to be described. Book ahead and bring spare clothing and a towel.

R Stephens Leatherwood Honey Factory   HONEY FACTORY
(25 Pioneer Dr; ⊙9am-4pm Mon-Fri Jan-Apr) Tasmania's wonderful Leatherwood honey is sold here. Ask nicely and they might give you a low-key tour of the honey-extraction plant.

Devils Gullet   LANDMARK
Those with transport should head for the Western Tiers. The only road that actually reaches the top of the plateau is the gravel road to Lake Mackenzie. Follow this road to Devils Gullet, where there's a 40-minute-return walk leading to a platform bolted to the top of a dramatic gorge: looking over the edge isn't for the faint-hearted.

Alum Cliffs Gorge   WALKING
A one-hour-return walk along a sloping spur takes you to an impressive lookout. Alum Cliffs (or Tulampanga, as it's known to its tribal custodians, the Pallittorre people) is a sacred celebration place where tribes met for corroborees.

🛏 Sleeping & Eating

Mole Creek Guest House   B&B **$$**
(☑6363 1399; 100 Pioneer Dr; s $115-145, d $125-170; ◉) This place is a real find. There are beautifully renovated, spacious rooms and a little private cinema upstairs. Downstairs, **Laurel Berry Restaurant** (lunch mains $10-17, dinner mains $22-26) serves really excellent food all day – from the hearty walkers' breakfasts to scrumptious homemade quiche at lunch to the fantastic steaks at dinner.

Blackwood Park Cottages   COTTAGES **$$**
(☑6363 1208; www.blackwoodparkcottages.com; 445 Mersey Hill Rd; d $125-165) There are two lovely self-contained cottages here, set among well-maintained gardens, with views to the surrounding mountains. There's handcrafted furniture and heated floors, and breakfast is homemade bread, muffins, real coffee and free-range eggs. It's well signed off a side road on the Deloraine side of Mole Creek.

Mole Creek Hotel   PUB **$$**
(☑6363 1102; www.molecreekhotel.com; Main Rd; s/d $50/100, mains $12-24) This pub was built in 1907 and has excellent rooms, some with good views, upstairs. The restaurant (open for lunch and dinner) does meaty meals, like lamb shanks in red wine and rosemary sauce. If you're tiger-curious, you should pop into the Tiger Bar here, where you can see a life-size model of the Tasmanian tiger, jaws dramatically agape, and a collage of tiger-sighting articles from the local paper. Ask about the bushwalker's transport run from here.

Mole Creek Caravan Park   CARAVAN PARK **$**
(☑6363 1150; cnr Mole Creek & Union Bridge Rds; unpowered/powered sites $17/20, extra person $3) This is a thin sliver of a park about 4km west of town beside Sassafras Stream, at the turn-off to the caves and Cradle Mountain.

❶ Information

The **Parks and Wildlife visitor centre** (☑6363 1487; internet per hour $4; ⊙9am-5pm Tue-Fri; ◉) can help with info on bushwalking in the area – particularly at the Walls of Jerusalem – and on visiting the nearby caves.

Walls of Jerusalem National Park

This compact park is one of Tasmania's most beautiful. It's a glacier-scoured landscape of spectacularly craggy dolerite peaks, alpine tarns, and forests of ancient pines. The park adjoins the lake-spangled wilderness of the Central Plateau and is part of the Tasmanian Wilderness World Heritage Area. Several walking tracks lead through it, and also join the park with hikes in the Cradle Mountain–Lake St Clair National Park.

The most popular walk here is the full-day trek to the 'Walls' themselves. A steep path leads up from the car park on Mersey Forest Rd to Trappers Hut (two hours return), Solomon's Jewels (four hours return), through Herod's Gate to Lake Salome (six to eight hours return), then Damascus Gate (nine hours return). If you plan to visit historic Dixon's Kingdom hut and the hauntingly beautiful pencil-pine forests that surround it (10 hours return from the car park) or climb to the top of Mt Jerusalem (12 hours return), it's better to camp overnight. There are tent platforms and a composting toilet at Wild Dog Creek. You'll need to be prepared for harsh weather conditions: it snows a substantial amount here, particularly – but not only – in winter. Walks across the park are described in *Cradle Mountain Lake St Clair and Walls of Jerusalem National Parks*, by John Chapman and John Siseman, and in Lonely Planet's *Walking in Australia*.

Tasmanian Expeditions (✆1300 666 856, 6331 9000; www.tas-ex.com) conducts a four-day Walls of Jerusalem trip ($1095) taking in the park's highlights as well as some of the more out-of-the-way spots.

ⓘ Getting There & Away
The park is reached from Mole Creek by taking the Mersey Forest Rd to Lake Rowallan. The last 11km is on well-maintained gravel roads.

BUS **Sainty's Coaches** (✆6334 6456)(in association with **Maxwells**) runs charter buses from Devonport to the Walls of Jerusalem ($220 for up to four people, $55 per person for five or more) and from Launceston ($300, $75 per person).

Gowrie Park
Situated at the foot of Mt Roland just 14km from Sheffield, Gowrie Park makes an excellent base for mountain walks or for a rural retreat. There are walks to the summits of Mts Roland (1234m), Vandyke (1084m) and Claude (1034m), and shorter walks in the cool, shady forests of the lower slopes, such as the pleasant meander through the bush at nearby O'Neills Creek Reserve. Bird lovers take note: there are 94 species in the Mt Roland area.

⊙ Sights
The sharp comb of rock that's the dramatic backdrop to the rural views here is Mt Roland. It looks spectacularly difficult but is easily climbed by confident walkers. Access is from the village of Claude Rd. Turn off at Kings Rd and head south for about 1.5km to the start of the track (about 6.5km, 3½ hours return). There's an easier track from near Gowrie Park. Turn off the main road near the sports ground and travel 2km to the trailhead (10km, four hours return).

🛏 Sleeping & Eating
Silver Ridge Wilderness Retreat CABINS $$
(✆6491 1727; www.silverridgeretreat.com.au; 46 Rysavy Rd; s $60, d $155-220, extra person $25; 🐾)
Right at the foot of Mt Roland, these cottages are about as peaceful as you can get, and have fantastic mountain views. You can soak in the heated indoor pool, climb mountains, watch the birds and the beasts, or go horse riding on Mustang Sally, Misty or Mac.

Gowrie Park Wilderness Village CABINS, CARAVAN PARK $$
(✆6491 1385; 1447 Claude Rd; powered sites $20, dm/d $20/92) There are neat but basic self-contained cabins here sleeping up to six, bunk rooms and caravan/camping sites. Tracks lead right from the grounds to nearby peaks. The highlight here, though, has to be **Weindorfers Restaurant** (mains $12-27; ⊙lunch Sat & Sun, dinner daily summer), which has a wonderful log-cabin ambience, especially when the fire is roaring, and serves hearty, post-bushwalking fare.

Lake Barrington & Around
Beautiful Lake Barrington (created by the Mersey-Forth hydroelectric scheme in 1969) stretches for 20km between steep, green banks. The lake's calm waters host an international-standard rowing course where world championships, national and state rowing events and waterskiing and canoeing competitions are held. The recreation area here has an **adventure playground**, BBQs, picnic spots, and an easy two-hour rainforest walk. There are boat ramps on both sides of the lake and camping at Kentish Park at the lake's northern end. The amazing 84m Devil's Gate Dam, which holds the waters back, is engineered to be one of the thinnest concrete dams in the world, and there are viewing areas where you can get quite close.

Close to the lake is Tasmazia (✆6491 1934; www.tasmazia.com.au; 500 Staverton Rd (C141); adult/child $17.50/10; ⊙10am-4pm Apr-Nov, 9am-5pm Dec-Mar). Kids love the whimsical complex of hedge mazes, the Village of Lower

Crackpot (a colourful miniature village) and a lavender farm. Look out for such waggish touches as Nancy the Witch, who appears to have crashed her broomstick, or the sword in the stone. If you can retrieve it, King Arthur–style, you win this whole fanciful kingdom for yourself. When you're famished from all the fun, you can retreat to the **pancake parlour** (pancakes $9-20; ⊘10am-4pm) to feast on sweet and savoury pancakes.

Lovers of fine food and wine should visit **Barringwood Park Vineyard** (www.barringwoodpark.com.au; 60 Gillams Rd, Lower Barrington; ⊘10am-5pm Wed-Sun, closed Aug), which has tastings and cellar-door sales of handcrafted cool-climate wines. You can savour a gourmet platter with your vino on the deck and be awe-inspired by glorious views over the Don River Valley towards Bass Strait.

On the western side of Lake Barrington just north of the village of Wilmot is another winery-distillery. At **Wilmot Hills Vineyard** (www.wilmothills.com; 407 Back Rd, Wilmot; ⊘10am-6pm Thu-Tue) you can try a fine Pinot Noir, the 'Highland White' (a Müller Thurgau and Gewürztraminer blend) and apple cider. But there's also a delicious range of spirits distilled here – calvados, kirsch, raspberry schnapps, grappa and *basilica* – and you get to peek in at winemaking and distilling operations.

For more active adventures, **Highland Trails Horse Riding** (☑6491 1533, 0417 145 497; 1030 Staverton Rd (C141); per hr $40) can take you on horseback into the foothills of nearby mountains on rides ranging from one hour to several days.

Places to stay nearby include **AAA Granary Accommodation** (☑6491 1689; www.granary.com.au; 575 Staverton Rd (C141); s $100-120, d $130-195, extra person $30; ◉), which has older-style timber cottages, some with panoramas of Mt Roland, and good facilities for children. On the same road, closer to Sheffield, is **Carinya Farm Holiday Retreat** (☑6491 1593; www.carinyafarm.com.au; 63 Staverton Rd (C141); d $99-130, extra person $20-28), which has pine-lined loft-bedroom chalets overlooking peaceful farmland and Mt Roland. There's a kids' cubby and friendly farm animals to view. Beautiful self-catering **Kentisbury Country House** (☑6491 2090; www.kentisburycountryhouse.com; 42 Luttrells Rd, Kentish Park; d $199, extra person $50) is close to Lake Barrington's western shore and set in magnificently green pasture land with sublime views. But surely the best panoramas of all are to be had at **Eagle's Nest Retreat** (☑6491 1511; www.eaglesnestretreat.com.au; d $520-620), two amazingly opulent holiday houses with wall-high glass framing incredible Mt Roland views.

Sheffield

POP 1020

The lovely 'Town of Murals' wasn't always the thriving rural hub it is today. In the 1980s Sheffield was a typical small Tasmanian town in the doldrums of rural decline. That was until some astute townsfolk came up with an idea that had been applied to the small town of Chemainus in Canada, with some surprisingly wonderful results. The plan was to paint a few large murals on walls around town, depicting scenes from the district's pioneer days. What started with these humble beginnings has been a roaring success: Sheffield is now a veritable outdoor art gallery, with over 50 fantastic large-scale murals, and an annual painting festival to produce more. People come from all over the world to wander its streets and appreciate what's now a collection of excellent artwork, and the influx of visitors has allowed the town to thrive way beyond those early mural-painting dreams.

◉ Sights & Activities

Kentish Museum – MUSEUM
(93 Main St; admission by donation; ⊘10am-noon & 1-4pm Mon & Wed, 10am-3pm Tue, Thu & Fri) Here there's all sorts of historic clutter on display: an early telephone exchange, old organs, military paraphernalia, and the world's first automatic petrol pump, invented by a local Sheffield boy.

Mural House ART GALLERY
(100 High St; adult/child $2/50c; ⊘1-5pm Tue, Thu, Sat & Sun) This odd little attraction contains interpretations of Indigenous art of various cultures in the form of internal wall murals. You may be better off with the outdoor art in town, but if you want to actually buy some art, you can do so here.

Redwater Creek Steam Rail TRAIN RIDING
(☑6491 1613; www.redwater.org.au; cnr Main & Spring Sts; adult/child $5/3) Departing from the original Sheffield train station at the eastern end of town, the steam rail offers rides on locomotives running on a narrow-gauge track from 11am to 4pm on the first weekend of each month, for two weeks in early January and on some public holidays – dependent on volunteer train-driver availability. Train

buffs will ooh and ahh at the rare A Krauss 10 locomotive here. There's also **Steam Fest**, a grand three-day occasion on the long weekend of March that's a true celebration of steam and bygone days, and a must (not just for trainspotters). The tractor-pulling competitions are a hoot!

👉 Tours

Mural Audio Tours   CITY

You can now grab a headset ($9) from the visitor centre and take a thoroughly informative audio tour of Sheffield's alfresco art. It's the perfect way to see the murals, and the interpretation is first-class. The tour takes about 90 minutes with strolling time between murals, but you can keep the headset all day. You'll hear all about the best-known paintings, like *Stillness and Warmth*, which features Gustav Weindorfer of Cradle Mountain fame (see p268); *Butlers Mail Coach 1910*, a huge, magnificent depiction of a coach and horses against the backdrop of Mt Roland; and *Cradle Mountain Beauty*, a wide panorama of Cradle Mountain in snow. Spot the park ranger carrying a bathtub to one of the Overland Track huts! The audio tour takes you to some 20 of the best of the murals in town and also leads you through the **Working Art Space** (⊙11am-3pm, reduced hr winter), where you can see local artists at work and buy some of their oeuvre.

🎉 Festivals & Events

Mural Fest   ARTS

(www.muralfest.com.au) Sheffield's celebration of outdoor art is held late March to early April each year. It's a massive paint-off; a theme is set and artists from all over Australia descend upon the town to compete for a cash prize and add another nine murals to the town's walls. The best thing is that you get to watch some incredibly skilled artists at work. If you visit at this time, book accommodation well ahead.

🛏 Sleeping

TOP CHOICE **Glencoe Farm**   B&B **$$**

(☑6492 3267; www.glencoeruralretreat. com.au; 1468 Sheffield Rd; d $175-185; 🐾) Just north of Sheffield on the B14 at Barrington, this gorgeous property, owned by celebrated French chef Remi Bancal, is making a great name for itself. You can stay in its romantic and eminently stylish rooms (no kids under 12), and you mustn't miss the superb three-course dinners ($60), available by prior arrangement. A **cafe** (mains $25; ⊙lunch

Thur-Sun), open to the public, offers fantastic French-Creole cooking.

Platypus Valley B&B   B&B **$$**

(☑6491 2260; www.platypusvalley.com.au; 10 Billing Rd; s $110-140, d $120-165, extra adult $80) Tucked away in green country just outside Sheffield, this beautiful spot is somewhere you're almost guaranteed to see platypuses gambolling. This is a beautiful timber home with attractive guest rooms, in an environment where the key ingredient is peace. The B&B is off the C141; take the turn-off onto the B141 about 1km outside town.

Sheffield Country Motor Inn   MOTEL **$$**

(☑6491 1800; www.sheffieldmotorinn.com.au; 49-53 Main St; motel s $90-110, d $95-125, extra person $25) There are neat and well-equipped motel rooms here, one with three bedrooms, set just off Main St. Some of the town's best murals are immediately adjacent.

Tanglewood   B&B **$$**

(☑6491 1854; www.tanglewoodtasmania.com; 25 High St; d $120-140, extra person $30) There are three large bedrooms here, all with delicious feather doonas, electric blankets and a great sense of old-world style. You can sip a port in front of the open fire in the guest lounge, or stroll the English gardens.

Kentish Hills Retreat   MOTEL **$$**

(☑6491 2484; www.kentishhills.com.au; 2 West Nook Rd; d $124-154, extra person $30; @) In a quiet location just west of town with superb views of Mt Roland, Kentish Hills has a range of accommodation, from double rooms to an apartment sleeping up to six. It's more motel than hotel in style, but there are good facilities, including spas, minibars, queen-size beds and a guests' laundry.

Sheffield Cabins   CABINS **$$**

(☑6491 2176; www.sheffieldcabins.com.au; 1 Pioneer Cres; d $90-95, extra adult/child $15/10) These are simple, clean, self-contained cabins close to the visitor centre: you can't beat what you get for the price. They're pet-friendly too.

Sheffield Pub   PUB **$**

(☑6491 1130; 38 Main St; s $50, d without/with bathroom $70/80) The no-frills rooms here have both private and shared bathrooms. The pub does decent food (lunch and dinner), and breakfast is included for guests.

There's free overnight **caravan and campervan parking** (with water and toilets – no showers) next to the recreation centre on

Albert St. You can use showers at the visitor centre (three minutes for $1).

✖ Eating

Skwiz Café Gallery CAFE $
(63 Main St; mains $6-10; ⊘breakfast & lunch) This friendly, arty cafe boasts of having the best coffees in Sheffield – and it may just be right. With its retro decor, funky music, and roaring wood stove on cold days, it's a great place to hang out, have a slap-up breakfast, lazy lunch, or coffees and cakes in between. There's a rollicking folk-singing night the last Friday of every month.

Highlander Restaurant CAFE $$
(www.highlanderrestaurant.com.au; 60 Main St; mains $6-25; ⊘breakfast, lunch & dinner Tue-Sun) This delightful place builds its menus on the best of local produce. By day here are all-day breakfasts, and it offers hearty cafe fare. By night there's a changing à la carte menu using whatever's in season. In winter you can savour truffle season here with truffle scrambled eggs, truffle-infused mashed potatoes and even truffle crème brûlée.

Bossimi's Bakery BAKERY $
(44 Main St; ⊘breakfast & lunch Mon-Fri) This bakery does the industry proud, with lots of speciality pastries, cakes and bread, and gets very busy when the coach tours come through.

Hotel Sheffield PUB $$
(38 Main St; mains $10-23; ⊘lunch & dinner) You can always try the pub, which offers good-value counter-meal options and has a lively local atmosphere.

WORTH A TRIP

SEVEN SHEDS BREWERY

In the small town of Railton, 12km northeast of Sheffield, brewer and beer connoisseur Willie Simpson has turned a passion for home brewing into one of the best boutique breweries in Tasmania. Seven Sheds (www.sevensheds. com; 22 Crockers St; ⊘11am-5pm Wed-Sun) was opened in 2008 as a brewery, meadery and hop gardens, and you can pop in here to taste its range of Kentish Ale, Melomel and a fabulous Dry Mead. You can also tour its microbrewing operation and have a yarn with the friendly (and exceptionally beer-knowledgeable) owners.

---

❶ Information

Commonwealth Bank ATM (Main St)

Newsagency (Main St) Acts as a Westpac agent; also has a multicard ATM.

Visitor centre (☑6491 1036; 5 Pioneer Cres; internet per 15 min $2; ⊘9am-5pm) Supplies information on the Kentish region, provides internet access and makes accommodation and tour bookings.

❶ Getting There & Away

Tassielink (www.tassielink.com.au) buses stop directly outside the visitor centre. Services from Sheffield:

Launceston ($30, two hours)
Devonport ($6, 40 minutes)
Cradle Mountain ($27, 70 minutes)
Strahan ($58, five hours)

Ulverstone
POP 9800

Quiet little Ulverstone sits around the mouth of the Leven River and has a pleasantly old-fashioned rural-town feel: you could be forgiven for thinking you have stepped back in time 30 years. The commanding feature in town (at the intersection of Reibey St and Alexandra Rd) is the vastly imposing Shrine of Remembrance, built in 1953 and incorporating an older WWI memorial.

You can see the natural side of Ulverstone with a peaceful river cruise (www.discover theleven.com; 2hr cruises adult/child $42/21, 5hr lunch cruises adult/child $98/49) on the Leven. Tours depart most days in summer; book at the visitor centre (☑6425 2839; 13 Alexandra Rd; ⊘9am-5pm).

⌷ Sleeping

TOP CHOICE Ulverstone River Retreat APARTMENTS $$
(☑6425 2999; www.ulverstoneriverretreat.com.au; 37 Lobster Creek Rd; d $130-165, extra person $25) Watch kingfishers from your front deck, fish and kayak the river, or just soak up the birdsong and peace. This gorgeous riverside spot offers a smart upstairs apartment and a separate villa, both with decks out front and BBQ facilities. There are kayaks and fishing gear to borrow, and there's river swimming when the tide's in. It's right next to Ulverstone golf course, about 4km from town.

Boscobel B&B $$
(☑6425 1727; www.boscobel.com.au; 27 South Rd; s $95-115, d $120-160; 🛱🖵) Boscobel has com-

fortable, old-fashioned accommodation in a National Trust–listed home that's reminiscent of a grandmother's house in the best possible sense. It's set in beautiful gardens and there's a heated indoor pool in summer, but you may opt instead to go swimming in your bathroom: the deluxe room has the biggest spa you've ever seen.

Beachway
MOTEL $$
(☑6425 2342; www.beachwayulverstone.com.au; 1 Heathcote St; d $100-120, extra adult/child $20/15, mains $14-30; @≋) This complex has motel-style rooms and one recently upgraded self-contained apartment. There's an outdoor heated pool, and a restaurant on site, serving breakfast and evening meals.

Big 4 Ulverstone Holiday Park
CARAVAN PARK $
(☑6425 2624; 57 Water St; sites d $32-40, 3-bunk cabins from $95; @) Set in grassy surroundings just behind East Beach, this park, close to the town centre, is friendly and has good facilities, including a campers' kitchen, playgrounds, jumping pillow and plenty of adjoining parkland to run free in.

Furners Hotel
PUB $
(☑6425 1488; 42 Reibey St; s/d $60/80, mains $10-21) Furners is set in an ornate Federation building with a wide verandah and liberal wrought-iron lace. The rooms upstairs are comfortable, if pubbish. The meals downstairs (lunch and dinner) are popular with locals and feature plenty of carnivorous fare from the wood-fired grill.

✕ Eating

Deli Central
CAFE $$
(48b Victoria St; meals $6-18; ☺8am-5pm Mon-Fri, to 12.30pm Sat) What a find – when you can find it (ask for the car park off Edward St, behind Thai Delight). Ulverstone's best food is here – like wonderful breakfasts of chewy French sourdough with poached free-range eggs and homemade relish, or roast-pumpkin-and-caramelised-onion tart for lunch. The food is organic and locally grown as far as possible. Stock up for picnics at the impressive deli counter.

Pedro's the Restaurant
SEAFOOD $$
(☑6425 6663; Wharf Rd; mains $24-29; ☺lunch & dinner) Grab a table right by the water at this eatery, perched on the banks of the Leven River, and savour tastes of the sea as the sun goes down. What a view! The paradise seafood platter for two ($119) is the most popular offering here. Make sure you arrive

with an empty stomach. The menu caters to both carnivores and vegetarians. **Pedro's Takeaway** (mains $4-12; ☺11am-7pm), for fish and chips, is next door.

Thai Delight
THAI $$
(☑6425 3055; 25 King Edward St; mains from $10; ☺dinner Tue-Sat) Locals rave about this place and you can tell why: the Thai chef in the kitchen whips up everything from scratch, to order, and it's perfectly, pungently spicy. If you can't tell your *tod mon gai* from your *peek gai tod*, the friendly servers will explain.

Lancaster House
CAFE $$
(1 Reibey St; mains $8-24; ☺breakfast & lunch Tue-Sun) This breezy little eatery with views over the Leven offers yummy breakfasts, bistro lunches, good coffees and homemade cakes.

Oliver's Bakery & Café
CAFE $
(41 Reibey St; sandwiches from $5.20; ☺6am-6pm) Oliver's has inventive focaccias, tasty savoury pies and all things sweet, including great apple cakes, lamingtons, caramel slices and custard tarts.

Retromania
CAFE $
(31 King Edward St; dishes $7-15; ☺breakfast & lunch Mon-Sat) There's fine Italian coffee, sandwiches and soups here. Try a 1950s meal: a hamburger with corn chips, or be adventurous with lamb's fry on toast for breakfast.

❶ Information

Free internet access is available at the **Online Access Centre** (15 King Edward St; ☺9.30am-6pm Mon-Fri) in the local library.

❶ Getting There & Away

Redline Coaches (www.redlinecoaches.com.au) arrive at and depart from Alexandra Rd, near the War Memorial clock, outside the IGA Supermarket. **Metro** (☑13 22 01, 6431 3822) operates local buses to Burnie ($5.50) from the corner of King Edward and Reibey Sts. Redline services from Ulverstone:

Burnie ($9, 30 minutes)

Devonport ($7, 20 minutes)

Penguin
POP 4040

Penguin feels like one of those pretty little English seaside towns where it's all ice cream, buckets and spades, and the occasional sneaky breeze as you brave it out on

WORTH A TRIP

THE ULVERSONE & PENGUIN HINTERLAND

The forested interior behind Ulverstone is perfect for off-the-beaten-track exploration. There's a circuit using the B17 from either Ulverstone or Penguin known as the **Coast to Canyon Circuit**. From Ulverstone, start by driving to Penguin along the picturesque coast road, then delve south to Riana. In the **Dial Range**, just behind Penguin, there are some good walking tracks, including the little-known **Penguin Cradle Trail**, an 80km, six-day journey for experienced walkers through rugged backblocks to Cradle Mountain. Ask for a route guide at Penguin's visitor centre.

From Riana, a scenic drive brings you to the **Woodhouse Lookout**, for views over the Leven Valley. More winding road leads to **Wings Wildlife Park** (☑6429 1151; www. wingswildlife.com.au; 137 Winduss St; adult/child $17/8; ☺10am-4pm), which has an eclectic collection of creatures, native and exotic, ranging from devils to camels, crab-eating macaque monkeys and even bison. There's a **camping ground** (sites d $10-14; dm from $15, cabins from $115) and a cafe for light meals.

Close by are **Gunns Plains Caves** (☑6429 1388; adult/child/family $12/6/35; ☺10am-4pm), filled with magical limestone formations and glow-worms. There are guided tours between 10am and 3.30pm that involve some clambering and ladder work.

Back on the B17, you can complete the circuit to Ulverstone or take the C127 and C125 to the Leven Canyon. On the C124 at Gunns Plains is **Leven Valley Vineyard & Gallery** (☑6429 1186; 321 Raymond Rd; ☺10am-5pm), a boutique vineyard where you can taste and buy wine and browse fine art. Signposted just off the road near the vineyard are lower and upper **Preston Falls**: all cascading water and primeval man ferns.

If you'd like to make a night of it, stay at gorgeous **St Marks Luxury Accommodation** (☑6429 1159; www.stmarksluxurystay.com; 1019 Gunns Plains Rd; d $150-180), a meticulously converted church set in emerald cow paddocks where the emphasis is on privacy and luxury.

Continue via Nietta to **Leven Canyon**. A 20-minute return walk leads to the sensational gorge-top lookout, a sky platform peering 300m down to the Leven River below. From the Leven Canyon picnic ground drive 1km down Loongana Rd to the car park for a 35-minute return walk to the canyon floor. Nearby day walks lead to **Winterbrook Falls** (four hours return) and **Black Bluff** (six hours return).

There's B&B accommodation and visits to gorgeous gardens (adults $5) at **Kaydale Lodge** (☑6429 1293; www.kaydalelodge.com.au; 250 Loongana Rd, Nietta; s/d $80/120). The tearoom here serves snacks, teas and home-cooked meals by arrangement.

the beach. But there's one very un-English thing about this place: penguins! The world's smallest penguin (*Eudyptula minor*) comes ashore here during its breeding season, and even if you don't see any of them in the feather, you can get acquainted with model penguins around town: perfect for photo ops.

Every Sunday, off Arnold St, the popular undercover **Penguin Market** (☺9am-3.30pm) takes place. There are browseworthy stalls here selling fresh local produce, art and crafts, gifts and collectables.

🛏 Sleeping & Eating

Madsen BOUTIQUE HOTEL **$$$**
(☑6437 2588; www.themadsen.com; 64 Main St; d $150-300; ☎) This boutique hotel is housed in a grand edifice right on the waterfront.

Some of the rooms have great views of Bass Strait, and the views of the interior aren't half-bad either. Decorated in good taste, with a touch of the antique and a good measure of contemporary cool, this is a particularly pleasurable place to stay. Book the new penthouse suite for the ultimate luxury.

Inglenook by the Sea B&B **$$**
(☑6435 4134; www.inglenook.com.au; 360 Preservation Dr; d $110-140, extra person $30; ☎) On the coast road towards Burnie, 5km from the centre of Penguin, is welcoming Inglenook. There are three rooms here, kitted out in crisply ironed linens. One room has lovely sea views, one a spa, and one a second bunk room attached for travelling families. The friendly hosts whip up a delicious and 'aggressively local' breakfast.

Wild Café Restaurant MODERN AUSTRALIAN $$
(6437 2000; 87 Main Rd; lunch mains $12-32, dinner mains $28-32; lunch & dinner Wed-Sun) Ask anyone in the know the best place to dine on the northwest coast, and they're bound to direct you here. You can sit in the window and gaze over the water while you enjoy top-notch contemporary Aussie cuisine. Try the house special: Thai-inspired char-grilled calamari...and leave room for the fantastic desserts.

Groovy Penguin Café CAFE $
(6437 2101; 74 Main Rd; mains $8-13; breakfast & lunch Wed-Sun;) This lesbian- and gay-friendly retro gallery-cafe sports melamine tables, crazy-coloured walls and a menu that's strong on organic. You can't go wrong with a zesty vegie burger, a huge, creamy smoothie or a potent coffee from the hands of some mightily skilled baristas. They also run a modest two-bedroom holiday **unit** (d $95, extra person $15) in the Penguin backstreets with great sea views: ask in the cafe.

Neptune Grand Hotel PUB $
(6437 2406; 84 Main Rd; s/d/tw without bathroom $39/49/49, mains $6-30) This friendly pub has basic accommodation: rooms have sinks, but facilities are shared. The dining room serves cheap staples and does chicken-parmigiana specials from $5.

Casablanca MODERN AUSTRALIAN $$$
(6437 1621; Preservation Dr; lunch mains $14-38, dinner mains $29-38, lunch & dinner Mon, Thu & Fri, dinner Sat, breakfast & lunch Sun) What a surprising find, set in the brick block of the Penguin Lifesaving Club overlooking Preservation Bay. The eclectic fine-dining menu is served with beautiful sea views.

Information

The **Online Access Centre** (125 Ironcliffe Rd; 9am-5pm Mon-Wed & Fri, 10am-12pm Sat) is on the grounds of the Penguin High School.

Staff at the friendly Penguin **visitor centre** (6437 1421; 78 Main Rd; 9am-4pm Oct-Mar, 9.30am-3.30pm Apr-Sep) will ply you with the local low-down, including details on the Penguin-to-Cradle walking trail that starts at Dial Range just outside town (see p222).

Getting There & Away

Metro (13 22 01, 6431 3822) runs regular local buses from Burnie to Penguin ($5.50, 15 mins). The main stop is at the (now defunct) Penguin Station on Crescent St. **Redline** (www.redlinecoaches.com.au) buses also go from Penguin to Burnie ($6.40, 15 mins) as part of their northwest-coast runs.

Burnie

POP 19,335

Try as you might, you can't exactly call Burnie an outrageously attractive town. It's certainly in a dramatic natural setting – tumbling down steep hillsides to the shores of Emu Bay – but Burnie has long been an industrial stronghold for paper-making, heavy-machinery manufacturing, agricultural services and shipping. Perhaps the biggest features in town are the shockingly gigantic piles of woodchips on the dockside.

Burnie's own paper mill closed recently, and the city has of late been reinventing itself as a City of Makers: referring both to its heavy manufacturing past and its present creative flair. The amazing new Makers' Workshop is Burnie's showcase tourist attraction and should be your first stop when you visit.

Sights & Activities

Makers' Workshop MUSEUM
(6430 5831; www.discoverburnie.net; 2 Bass Hwy, 9am-5pm) Part museum, part arts centre, this dramatic new structure dominates the western end of Burnie's main beach. Come here for tourist information (Burnie's visitor information centre is here) but also to get acquainted with this city's creative heart. You'll notice the life-size **paper people** in odd corners of the workshop's cavernous contemporary interior. These are the work of **Creative Paper** (tours adult/child $15/8), Burnie's handmade-paper producers, who shape raw materials as varied as rags, rainforest leaves, wombat droppings and apple cores into an array of creative products. There are also **makers' studios** stationed throughout the centre, where you can watch local makers at work on handicrafts from jewellery to violins, ceramics to glass, felt to papier mâché. In the shop you can buy some of the products produced, and there's a **cafe** (9am-4pm), which serves light meals and all-day breakfasts on Sunday.

Burnie Regional Art Gallery FREE ART GALLERY
(Burnie Arts & Function Centre, Wilmot St; 10am-4.30pm Mon-Fri, 1.30pm-4.30pm Sat & Sun) This art gallery has excellent exhibitions of contemporary Tasmanian artworks, includ-

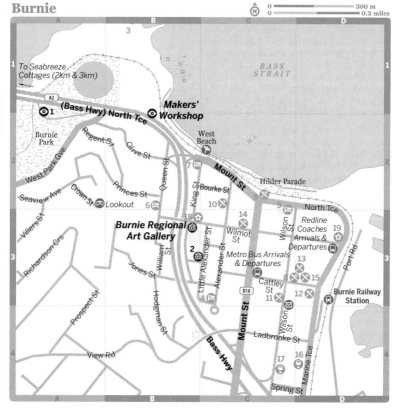

ing fine prints by some of Australia's most prominent artists.

Cheese Tasting Centre   CHEESE TASTING
(145 Old Surrey Rd; ⊙9am-5pm Mon-Fri, 10am-4pm Sat & Sun) Down Old Surrey Rd, on the way to Fern Glade, you'll find this cheesemaker and cheese-tasting centre. There's a range of creamy bries and camemberts, hard, crumbly cheddars and intense blue cheeses to try here. You can also have a ploughman's lunch in the cafe or buy picnic provisions. To reach the centre from Marine Terrace/Bass Hwy, turn south onto Mount St (B18) following signs for Upper Burnie and Queenstown. Turn left onto Old Surrey Rd (C112) and follow signs to the cheese centre.

Hellyers Road Whisky Distillery   WHISKY TASTING
(www.hellyersroaddistillery.com.au; 153 Old Surrey Rd; tours adult/under 16 yr $10/free; ⊙10am-4.30pm) About 1km further up Old Surrey Rd is Hellyers Rd, recognised as the home of Australia's best whiskies. You can tour the distillery here to see how its golden single-malt is made, and afterwards take a tasting of whisky, whisky cream or Southern Lights vodka, which is also made here (nips $2 to $4). The on-site cafe serves snacks and lunches. To get to the distillery, follow the directions above for the cheese factory. You reach the distillery shortly before the cheesery.

Pioneer Village Museum   MUSEUM
(Little Alexander St; adult/child $6/2.50; ⊙9am-3pm Mon-Fri) This absorbing museum is a re-creation of a 1900s village streetscape – including blacksmith, wash house, stagecoach depot and bootmaker – complete with appropriate soundtrack.

Burnie Park   PARK
(⊙car access sunrise-sunset) This park features rose-filled flower beds and the oldest build-

Burnie

◉ **Top Sights**
Burnie Regional Art Gallery B3
Makers' Workshop B2

◉ **Sights**
1 Burnie Inn A1
2 Pioneer Village Museum B3

Activities, Courses & Tours
3 Penguin Observation Centre B1

◎ **Sleeping**
4 Apartments Down Town C3
5 Beachfront Voyager Motor Inn C2
6 Duck House B2
Mrs Philpott's ....(see 6)
7 Regent Hotel B2

◎ **Eating**
8 Another Mother C3
9 Bayviews Restaurant C2
10 Curry Club C2
Fish Frenzy ....(see 9)
11 Fortuna Garden C3
Hot Mother Lounge ....(see 8)
Mallee Grill ....(see 7)
12 Merchant D3
13 Pickled Sisters Pantry D3
14 Rialto Gallery Restaurant C3
15 Rienos D3

◎ **Drinking**
16 Greens Hotel D4
17 Maginty's Bar C4

◉ **Entertainment**
18 Burnie Civic Centre B3
19 Metro Cinemas D3

ing in town, **Burnie Inn**. The National Trust-classified inn was built in 1847 and later moved to the park from its original location. You can admire it from the outside only. The adjacent oval is home to New Year's Day Burnie Athletics Carnival, and also the revered Burnie Dockers Aussie Rules football team.

Federation Walks & Art Deco Trail WALKING
Burnie has some impressive civic and domestic architecture that you can view on two Federation walking trails designed to showcase it. The city is also renowned for its art-deco buildings, and you can see these on a stroll round the city. Ask at the visitor information counter in the Makers' Workshop for interpretative maps of all three walks.

FREE **Penguin Observation Centre** WILDLIFE WATCHING
A boardwalk on Burnie's foreshore leads from Hilder Pde to the western end of West Beach, close to the Makers' Workshop, where there's a spot for watching penguins. From October to February you can take a **Penguin Interpretation Tour** (☏0437 436 803; tours-free) about one hour after dusk as the penguins emerge from the sea and waddle back to their burrows. Volunteer wildlife guides are present to talk about the penguins and their habits.

Just outside the city centre, the best places for nature and peace:

Emu Valley Rhododendron Garden GARDEN
(Breffny Rd; adult/child $5/3; ◷9am-5pm Aug-Apr) This serene garden, 8km south of Burnie (on the B18) via Mount St and then Cascade Rd, has 20,000 rhodos that flower in riotous colour.

Round Hill Lookout LOOKOUT
Round Hill is accessed by a side road off Stowport Rd, which departs the Bass Hwy on the eastern fringe of suburban Burnie.

Fern Glade NATURE RESERVE
Fern Glade is renowned as a top spot for platypus spotting at dawn and dusk. It's also east of the city centre: turn off the Bass Hwy on to Old Surrey Rd, just past the old Australian Paper Mill, then take Fern Glade Rd to the left.

Guide Falls WATERFALL
At West Ridgley, 19kms south of Burnie off the B18, these easily accessible falls are most spectacular in winter and spring.

Guide Falls Alpaca and Animal Park FARM
(309 West Ridgley Rd; adult/child $5/3; ◷9.30am-5pm) Next to Guide Falls is this alpaca stud with a herd of 80 alpacas and a host of other animals: great for kids.

🛏 Sleeping

TOP CHOICE **Seabreeze Cottages** RENTAL HOUSES **$$**
(☏6435 3424; www.seabreezecottages.com.au; s/d from $140/165, extra adult/child $40/20) These cottages just west of the city centre may just be Burnie's best. There's the cool, contemporary Beach House (243 Bass Hwy, Cooee), just a stroll across the road from the beach; West Park (14 Paraka St); and cute Number Six (6 Mollison St), both an easy 10-minute walk to town. All are kitted out with mod-

ern, chic decor, Number 6 with a juke box and all. We love them!

Duck House COTTAGES **$$**
(☑6431 1712; www.ozpal.com/duck; 26 Queen St; s/d $100/140, extra adult/child $30/20) Salvation Army stalwarts Bill and Winifred Duck lived here for 30 years and have been immortalised in this charming little two-bedroom cottage that bears their name. The decoration, predictably, has an emphasis on ducks. The sister property next door has the same rates: **Mrs Philpott's** (26 Queen St) sleeps up to seven, with leadlighting, a claw-foot bath, brass bedsteads and an unusual keyhole-shape entry.

Apartments Down Town APARTMENTS **$$**
(☑6432 3219; www.apartmentsdowntown.com.au; 52 Alexander St; d $145-190) Didn't we say Burnie was big on art deco? This 1937 building is deco through and through and has been thoroughly modernised to house spacious and well-equipped two- and three-bedroom serviced apartments. Beware: the apartments at the rear of the building may suffer highway noise.

Glen Osborne House B&B **$$**
(☑6431 9866; 9 Aileen Cres; s/d from $130/165) It may be set in the suburban hills in Burnie's south (off B18, or Mount St) but there's nothing suburban about this grand establishment. It provides high-standard hospitality in a lavish, National Trust–listed 1885 Victorian house with well-tended gardens. The rate includes a home-style cooked breakfast.

Beachfront Voyager Motor Inn MOTEL **$$**
(☑1800 355 090, 6431 4866; www.beachfront voyager.com.au; 9 North Tce; r $132-169; ☎) Right across the road from West Beach, this motel has several grades of room: opt for one of the recently renovated ones overlooking the water if you can. The on-site **Raindrops Restaurant** (mains $21-40; ☺dinner) is well frequented by Burnie-ites.

Burnie Oceanview CARAVAN PARK **$$**
(☑6431 1925; www.burniebeachaccommodation. com.au; 253 Bass Hwy, Cooee; sites $23-28, dm $25, vans d $50, extra person $20; @☒) Located 4km west of the city centre, this park has backpacker rooms, some grassy camping sites at the property's rear, vans with kitchenettes and a range of cabins (doubles from $92). The indoor heated pool is the best attraction here.

Regent Hotel PUB **$**
(☑6431 1933; 26 North Tce; s/d without bathroom $30/60) This is not a flashpackers by any means, but there are basic rooms above the pub here, and the communal lounge on the corner of the property has perhaps the best ocean panoramas in Burnie. Double rooms have showers but other facilities are shared. The **Mallee Grill** (mains $15-43; ☺lunch Sun-Fri, dinner daily) downstairs does particularly meaty pub fare.

Eating

Bayviews Restaurant MODERN AUSTRALIAN **$$**
(☑6431 7999; www.bayviewsrestaurant.com.au; 1st fl, 2 North Tce; mains $26-35; ☺breakfast Sat & Sun, lunch & dinner Thu-Tue) This upmarket establishment is right on the beach and serves a brief menu of excellent fine-dining dishes, from local free-range pork to the region's amazing grass-fed beef and great seafood. The wraparound views are sublime.

Rialto Gallery Restaurant ITALIAN **$$**
(☑6431 7718; 46 Wilmot St; mains $14-25; ☺lunch Mon-Fri, dinner Mon-Sat) It's no wonder that this restaurant is such a well-loved Burnie institution: it's been doing a roaring trade for 28 years with its mouthwatering Italian fare. Dishes include tortellini in butter and sage, meltingly delicious ravioli with a pungent four-cheese sauce and fine wood-oven pizzas.

Merchant CAFE, WINE BAR **$$**
(1 Cattley St; mains $7.50-18.50; ☺8am-5pm Mon-Wed, to late Thu-Sat) This is the cool new venue on the Burnie wining and dining scene. It produces huge serves of excellent bistro fare by day, then morphs into a wine bar by night. It has live music Friday and Saturday, and open-mic night Thursday from eight. It's done up in contemporary cool and is quite the place to seen. It also sells flowers.

Another Mother MODERN AUSTRALIAN **$**
(14 Cattley St; mains $9-15; ☺breakfast & lunch Tue-Sat; ☑) A cute, vibrant eatery with bright red walls, eclectic furniture and local photography for decoration, this eatery offers wholesome, predominantly vegetarian (and some meaty) dishes crafted from local produce – organic where possible. It serves an exceptional pumpkin-and-cashew burger with yoghurt and chilli. Its sister establishment is **Hot Mother Lounge** (70 Wilson St; ☺7am-3pm Mon-Fri), serving equally good wraps, bakes, soups and takeaways.

Rienos TAPAS **$**
(12 Cattley St; mains $9-12; ☺9.30am-5pm Mon & Tue, to late Wed-Sat) An amazing aroma of garlic greets you as you walk through the door of this tapas and wine bar. It does soups, salads,

bruschettas and fine antipasto platters with an emphasis on laid-back and shared eating. It's one of a few places in Burnie where you can order until late, when it's busy.

Grove Café
CAFE $
(63 West Park Grove; mains $9-15; ⊙breakfast Sat & Sun, lunch daily) Next to a garden centre and sharing its outdoor ambience, this little cafe serves light lunches and morning and afternoon teas. The coffee here is excellent, and the Grove is famous for its lemon meringue pie. It's at the West Park Nursery (drive up West Park Grove alongside Burnie Park, less than 1km from the city centre.)

Fish Frenzy
FISH & CHIPS $$
(2 North Tce; meals $10-27; ⊙11am-9pm) Downstairs from Bayviews Restaurant, this gourmet fish 'n' chippery does all the usual takes on this seaside favourite, and also offers healthy options such as grilled fish with Greek salad.

Pickled Sisters Pantry
CAFE $
(Rear 6 Cattley St; mains $9-15; ⊙breakfast & lunch Mon-Sat) Up a narrow alleyway off Cattley St, this place is tricky to find but worth hunting down. There's a providore with a tasting station, and the 'sisters' make yummy light meals to eat in or take away.

Fortuna Garden
CHINESE $$
(66 Wilson St; mains $10-23; ⊙lunch Mon-Fri, dinner daily; ⊘) This is a licensed and BYO Chinese restaurant serving great garlic prawns, Mongolian beef, and piles of stir-fry veg to keep vegetarians happy. Eat-in or takeaway.

Curry Club
INDIAN $$
(☑6431 5111; 8 Alexander St; mains $18-25; ⊙lunch Mon-Fri, dinner daily; ⊘) In a tandoori-red building close to Burnie's centre, this new restaurant looks a bit bare inside, but locals swear by the excellent curries it serves. Good vegetarian options here.

🍸 Drinking & Entertainment

Maginty's Bar
PUB
(139 Wilson St) This venue in the Bayside Hotel has live music Thursday to Saturday.

Greens Hotel
PUB, NIGHTCLUB
(27 Marine Tce) This pub transforms into a nightclub Friday and Saturday, when there's a line-up right down the street to get in.

Metro Cinemas
CINEMA
(☑6431 5000; www.metrocinemas.com.au; cnr Marine Tce & Wilmot St) This shiny cinema shows mainly first-release Hollywood flicks.

Burnie Civic Centre
THEATRE
(☑6431 5033; Wilmot St) This multifunctional complex sees everything from concert divas to comedy acts to readings. Entry via King St.

ℹ️ Information

North West Regional Hospital (☑6430 6666; Brickport Rd) A few minutes west of the city centre: take Brickport Rd off the Bass Hwy just east of Cooee.

Online Access Centre (30 Alexander St; ⊙9am-5pm Mon-Fri, 9.30am-noon Sat) This centre is in Burnie's library.

Visitor information centre (☑6430 5831; 2 Bass Hwy; ⊙9am-5pm) Located in the Makers' Workshop.

ℹ️ Getting There & Away

AIR Burnie/Wynyard airport (known as either Burnie or Wynyard airport) is at Wynyard, 20km northwest of Burnie.

BUS Redline Coaches (www.redlinecoaches.com.au) stop on Wilmot St opposite the Metro Cinemas. Useful routes from Burnie:

Launceston ($37, 2½ hours)

Smithton ($22, 1½ hours)

Metro (☑13 22 01, 6431 3822) has regular local buses to Penguin, Ulverstone and Wynyard ($5.50 each), departing from bus stops on Cattley St beside Harris Scarfe department store.

Wynyard & Around
POP 4200

Arranged around the wooded banks of the sinuous Inglis River, Wynyard is a quiet little town that's a service centre for all the agriculture that surrounds it. It's sheltered from westerly weather by prominent **Table Cape** and **Fossil Bluff** and has a pleasant, sedate air. On its doorstep are unpeopled beaches, wind-blasted lighthouses, and an amazing spring display of tulips – spread like a giant coloured bar code across the rich red soils of Table Cape.

👁️ Sights

An extinct volcano, right here in the verdant hills of Tasmania? Believe it or not, the rocky ramparts of Table Cape once encircled a lake of boiling lava. To visit the cape in its present, more benign, condition, take the minor road (C234) 4km northwest out of Wynyard, and drive to the lighthouse, which began its seaside vigil in 1888. You can now also climb the spiral stairs inside and walk around the light at the top on a Table Cape Lighthouse Tour (☎6442 3241; www.tablecapelight.com.au; adult/child $15/8). The 50-minute tours depart at 11am and 2pm and reveal sensational views over Bass Strait as well as some of the fascinating history of this place.

The volcanic, chocolate-red soils of the cape are extraordinarily fertile and it's just the spot to grow tulips. There's a mesmerising array of colour at Table Cape Tulip Farm (363 Lighthouse Rd; ⏰10am-4.30pm late Sep–mid-Oct) when the bulbs are in flower in October. A **Tulip Festival** is held usually on the first weekend of October, and is a fun family affair with food, song and dancing against the bright backdrop of the flowers. From March to August you can buy bulbs in the farm's shop.

Three kilometres west of the town centre is 275-million-year-old Fossil Bluff. It was created by an ancient tidewater glacier and is rich in **fossils**, including the remains of prehistoric whales and the oldest marsupial fossil found in Australia. The species was named *Wynyardia bassiana* in honour of the town. At low tide you can walk around the base of the bluff and fossick for some of the hundreds of different kinds of fossils preserved here. Ask at the visitor centre for the geological guide *Looking for Fossils*.

Adjacent to the Wynyard visitor centre is the Wonders of Wynyard (8 Exhibition Link; adult/child $7/4; ⏰9am-5pm), a veteran car collection owned and restored by a Wynyard local. There's a rotating collection of at least 15 ancient Ford cars and motorbikes, including the world's equal-oldest Ford.

🏃 Activities

Scuba Centre
SCUBA DIVING
(☎6442 2247; 62 Old Bass Hwy; ⏰8.30am-4.30pm Mon-Sat) The experienced diving guides at this centre can take you out on dives in Wynyard Bay and at beautiful Boat Harbour.

Noel Jago Walk
WALKING
South of Wynyard the hills of the Oldina State Forest Reserve offer this short (30- to 45-minute) nature walk beside Blackfish Creek, passing under man ferns and eucalyptuses. There are reputed to be platypuses in the creek.

🛏 Sleeping & Eating

Beach Retreat Tourist Park
CARAVAN PARK $
(☎6442 1998; 30b Old Bass Hwy; powered sites d $27, s/d $35/50, motel units/cabins $85/95) This has to be one of the prettiest caravan parks anywhere. It's in a peaceful spot right by the beach in grounds that are meticulously manicured and pleasingly green. The backpackers' accommodation is in simple double rooms – none of that dorm-sleeping nonsense. There's a well-equipped kitchen to share.

Waterfront
MOTEL $$
(☎6442 2351; www.waterfront.net.au; 1 Goldie St; s $95-135, d $115-165; 🐾) As motels go, this one is particularly satisfying. As the name implies, the place is slap-bang on the water and has clean, stylish rooms with extras like wi-fi. It's a pleasant and quiet place to stay.

Wharf Hotel
PUB $
(☎6442 2344; 10 Goldie St; s/d $49/75) The Wharf is slowly being upgraded throughout, and the clean and pleasant rooms upstairs are really decent. Some have baths (baths!) and look out over the peaceful Inglis River. Downstairs the bistro (⏰breakfast Sun, dinner daily) serves excellent steaks and seafood.

Ladybugs Licensed Café
CAFE $
(8 Inglis St; mains $9-16; ⏰breakfast, lunch & dinner Mon-Sat) Decked out in funky retro furniture, this wonderful little cafe serves a slap-up all-day breakfast, healthy lunches and snacks, and then pizzas in the evening. The cakes are reportedly the best in Wynyard. It also caters to gluten-free eaters.

Buckaneers for Seafood
SEAFOOD $$
(4 Inglis St; lunch mains $7-15, dinner mains $18-32; ⏰lunch & dinner) This is a hugely popular seafood emporium. Diners sit around the clinker-built sailing boat and chow down on fresh fish catches. Steaks, pasta and takeaways also available.

Wynyard Hotel
PUB FARE $
(1 Inglis St; mains $9-30; ⏰dinner Tue-Sat) The glass panel above the dining-room door says 'Dining Room and Cabaret', but you can no longer take in any high kicks here. There's solid pub fare, though, including that ubiquitous chicken parmigiana.

❶ Information

There are **ATMs** on Goldie St.

Online Access Centre (21 Saunders St; per hr $5; ⏰10am-5pm Mon-Fri) At the library, just behind the police station on Goldie St. There's also internet access at the visitor centre.

Visitor centre (📞6443 8330; www.wowtas.com.au; 8 Exhibition Link; ◷9am-5pm) Ask for the brochure *Scenic Walks of Wynyard and the Surrounding Districts* here if you're keen to get out and about on foot.

❶ Getting There & Away

AIR The Burnie/Wynyard airport (often listed as Burnie airport) is just one block from Wynyard's main street. **Rex** (www.regionalexpress.com.au) flies to Melbourne from Burnie/Wynyard four times a day.

BUS The **Burnie Airbus** (📞0439 322 466; adult $30) meets flights if pre-booked and does pick-up/drop-off where you want. **Metro** (📞6431 3822) buses from Burnie to Wynyard ($5.50) stop on Jackson St.

Boat Harbour Beach

POP 400

Picture-perfect Boat Harbour has the kind of blonde-sand beach and sapphire-blue waters that make you feel like you've taken a terribly wrong turn off the Bass Hwy and ended up somewhere in the Caribbean. Not to worry: no pirates here – apart from a particularly Jolly Roger on the beach, that is. You can take to the harbour's remarkable waters to swim and snorkel, discover the rock pools, or paddle in the shallows. The usually calm seas are perfect for kids, and it's a low-key, family-friendly place.

🛏 Sleeping

Paradise House RENTAL HOUSE $$$
(📞6435 7571; www.paradisehouse.com.au; 22 Azzure Beach Houses, 263 Port Rd; d $240, extra adult/child $30/20; 📶) This supersmart beach house is part of a new complex and has absolutely top-notch accommodation in three bedrooms. The trendy living areas have mod cons, including free wi-fi. Bikes, fishing gear, surfboards, boogie boards and all manner of beach gear come free.

Harbour Houses RENTAL HOUSES $$$
(📞6442 2135; www.harbourhouse.com.au; Esplanade; d $220, extra person $40) These perfect little waterfront cottages are open-plan, brightly decorated and liberally doused with a good dose of cool. We love the surfboard tables and rugs. Your deck hangs right over the beach. Superb!

Azzure Holiday Houses RENTAL HOUSES $$
(📞0400 142 222; www.azzurebeachhouses.com.au; 263 Port Rd; house sleeping up to 4/6 from $180/250; 📶) It's all contemporary style at the beach houses in this complex. There's every convenience you could imagine: DVD-CD players, wi-fi, air-conditioning, swanky kitchens, and walls hung with contemporary art. There's an on-site health spa in the pipeline too.

Harbourside B&B B&B $$
(📞0400 595 036/66; www.harboursidebnb.com.au; 237 Port Rd; d $160) This cute B&B is more a contemporary private apartment – with great water views – and breakfast is included. There are sensational vistas right from your bed, a spa and private decks.

Sunny Sands Holiday Unit RENTAL HOUSE $$
(📞6442 2578; www.sunnysands.com.au; 285 Port Rd; d $150-200) This well-thought-out self-contained unit has balconies to relax on and wide views of the sea.

Boat Harbour Beach Holiday Park CABIN $$
(📞0407 901 943; www.boatharbourbeachhp.com.au; 21 Moore St; d $100-120, extra adult/child $15/10) This funky new holiday cabin will one day be one of many on the site, but for now there's just one: a cute, self-contained mini–beach house.

Jolly Rogers SEAFOOD $$
(📞6445 1710; 1 Port Rd; mains $16-32; ◷breakfast, lunch & dinner) This laid-back beachside cafe serves real-hunger solutions: burgers, pastas and, of course, fish and seafood. Try the fabulous salt-and-pepper squid. There's also a fenced play area where you can stow the little ones. In summer there's also a **takeaway kiosk**, serving excellent fish and chips, attached.

❶ Getting There & Away

By bus, the daily **Redline Coaches** service from Burnie will drop you at the turn-off to Boat Harbour (3km) or Sisters Beach (8km) for $6. If driving from Wynyard, the best route from the cape is to follow C234 northwest; there are some great views of the cliffs and rocky coast along this road.

Rocky Cape National Park

This is Tasmania's smallest national park, stretching 12km along Bass Strait's shoreline. It was known to Aboriginal Tasmanians as

WORTH A TRIP

THE NORTHWEST BACKCOUNTRY

Head into the hills behind Rocky Cape (on C225) and you'll discover forests, waterfalls and timber-getting the way it used to be done. At **Water Wheel Creek Timber Heritage Experience** (☑6458 8144; www.waterwheel-creek.com.au; 1314 Mawbanna Rd; adult/child $15/5; ☺10am-5pm Jan-Apr, to 4pm Sun-Fri May-Dec) there's a timber-working museum, interpretative forest walks, a working timber tramway and a warm, wood-lined cafe. Further south you can visit **Dip Falls**, where a short, steep walk will get you to the cascades' base. About 1km from the car park, you'll find the **Big Tree**, its circumference a whopping 16m.

Tangdimmaa and has great significance to the Rar.rer.loi.he.ner people, who made their homes in the sea caves along the coastline here 8000 years before European occupation.

Inland, the park is made up of coastal heathland and rare *Banksia serrata* forests. The rolling green hills are splashed bright with wildflowers in the spring and summer months; those fond of flowers will be thrilled by the orchid-hunting here. The rocky quartzite coastline has abundant rock pools brimming with seaweed and brightly coloured anemones and starfish.

There's good swimming in the park at Sisters Beach, Forwards Beach and Anniversary Bay. **Sisters Beach** has an 8km stretch of bleached-blonde sand, picnic tables and a shelter. Close by is Sisters Beach village, reached via C233 from Boat Harbour.

On Rocky Cape itself, you can drive out to a stunted **lighthouse**, with the Nut (p231) floating distantly on the horizon.

🏃 Activities

There are some satisfying coastal walks at Rocky Cape, varying from short ambles to full days on foot. There's no drinking water in the park, so carry your own, and watch out for snakes, particularly in summer.

Walking

From Sisters Beach, the walk to **Wet Cave**, **Lee Archer Cave** and **Banksia Grove** takes 45 minutes (one way). To reach the start, follow the signs to the boat ramp. You can con-

tinue further along the coast to Anniversary Point (three hours return). It's also possible to follow the coast to Rocky Cape and return along the **Inland Track** (eight hours return).

From the western end of the park at Rocky Cape Rd (accessed from a separate entrance off the Bass Hwy, west of the turn-off to Sisters Beach), you can walk to two large Aboriginal caves, **South Cave** and **North Cave**, the latter off the road to the lighthouse. The caves are significant Aboriginal sites, so visitors are encouraged *not* to enter them. There's also a good circuit of the cape itself – allow 2½ hours.

🛏 Sleeping

Sisters Beach House RENTAL HOUSE **$$**
(☑8774 2305; www.sistersbeachhouse.com.au; Irby Blvd; d $200, extra person $20) This traditional Tassie beach 'shack' was built in 1969 but has been coolly done up inside in laid-back, eclectic beach-house style. It's just across the road from the white sands and clear waters of Sisters Beach.

Blue Bayou Beach House RENTAL HOUSE **$$**
(☑0407 871 394; Kenelm Ave; d $185, extra person $20) The theme in this bright and breezy beach house is of course, blue. There's an enormous deck out front, and sliding doors open up the house to sea breezes. It comes with bikes and boogie boards for guests to enjoy.

Stanley

POP 550

Get this far west in Tasmania and you begin to feel it: there's a whiff of something in the air that feels quite distinctly like the very end of the world. Little Stanley exudes more than a trace of this frontier, life-on-the-edge ambience. The town is a scatter of brightly painted cottages, sheltering in the lee of an ancient volcano, the Nut, that's been extinct for 13 million years. In Stanley's harbour bobs a fleet of fishing boats, piled high with cray pots and orange buoys, but beyond this shelter the ocean is often whipped into whitecaps. Stroll through town on a fine day and you may not feel that underlying edginess that comes from being on the world's rim; but when the Roaring Forties blast through, you'll feel it sure enough, and that's part of the excitement of being here.

Sights & Activities

The Nut   VOLCANO

This striking 152m-high volcanic rock formation can be seen for many kilometres around Stanley. It's a steep 20-minute climb to the top: worth it for the views. The best lookout is a five-minute walk to the south of the **chairlift** (☑6458 1286; adult/child $10/8; ⊙9.30am-5.30pm Oct-May, 10am-4pm Jun-Sep), and you can also take a 35-minute walk (2km) on a path around the top. From here, in summer, you can wait to view mysterious short-tailed shearwaters (also called mutton birds) as they return to their burrows at dusk after a day's foraging in the ocean.

Stanley Discovery Museum & Genealogy Centre   MUSEUM

(Church St; adult/child $3/50c; ⊙10am-4pm) To learn more about Stanley, visit this diminutive museum, filled with old Circular Head photos and artefacts, including marine curios. It also runs a genealogical service ($5, including museum entry).

Seaquarium   AQUARIUM

(Fisherman's Dock; adult/child $10/5; ⊙9am-5pm mid-Sep–mid-May, 11am-3pm Sat & Sun mid-Jun–mid-Sep) Providing a great display of marine life, Seaquarium is a fun and educational place to bring the kids. They'll squeal with delight at the touchy-feely tank.

Highfield   HISTORIC BUILDING

(Green Hills Rd; adult/child/family $10/5/25; ⊙10am-4pm) This homestead 2km north of town was built in 1835 for the chief agent of the Van Diemen's Land Company. It's a rare example of domestic architecture of the Regency period in Tasmania. You can tour the house and outbuildings, including stables, grain stores, workers' cottages and the chapel.

Van Diemen's Land Company Store   HISTORIC BUILDING

(16 Wharf Rd) This bluestone warehouse on the seafront dates from 1844, and while it once held bales of wool for export, it now houses an exclusive boutique hotel, @VDL.

Ford's Store   HISTORIC BUILDING

(15 Wharf St) Also near the wharf is this particularly fine old bluestone store, first used for grain storage and then as a bacon factory. It's believed to have been built in 1859 from stones brought here as ship's ballast. Today it's home to Stanley's on the Bay restaurant.

Plough Inn   HISTORIC BUILDING

(Church St) Next door to the Stanley Discovery Museum is this Georgian terrace that began life in 1854 as a hotel. It's now a private residence.

Lyons Cottage   HISTORIC BUILDING

(14 Alexander Tce; admission by donation; ⊙10am-4pm Nov-Apr, 11am-3pm May-Oct) The birthplace of prime minister Joseph Lyons (b 1879).

Stanley Hotel   HISTORIC BUILDING

(19 Church St) Formerly the Union Hotel, dating from 1849.

St James Presbyterian Church   HISTORIC BUILDING

(Fletcher St) This church was possibly Australia's first prefabricated building, transported to Stanley from England in 1885.

Festivals & Events

Dockside Festival   MUSIC, FOOD

On the weekend before the Melbourne Cup (the first Tuesday in November), Stanley hosts the Dockside Festival. This annual feast of food, entertainment and jazz music celebrates the culmination of the Melbourne-to-Stanley yacht race.

Tours

Stanley Seal Cruises   WILDLIFE-WATCHING

(☑6458 1294, 0419 550 134; www.stanleyseal cruises.com.au; Fisherman's Dock; adult/child $49/19) Provides 75-minute cruises to see up to 500 Australian fur seals sunning themselves on Bull Rock. Departures are at 10am and 3pm from October to April, and at 10am in May and September, sea conditions permitting. They also do offshore fishing charters ($200 for four people, two hours), all equipment supplied.

Wilderness to West Coast Tours   NATURE

(☑6456 5200, 0427 565 200; www.wilderness towestcoasttours.com.au) This operation offers full-day 4WD wilderness tours to the Tarkine rainforests and to wild beaches near Arthur River ($249 per person), including a gourmet lunch. It also offers day fishing tours ($390) and tag-along Tarkine tours by arrangement.

Sleeping

@VDL   HOTEL $$$

TOP CHOICE (☑6458 2032; www.atvdlstanley.com. au; 16 Wharf Rd; ste $180-225; ☎) What's been done within the bluestone walls of this

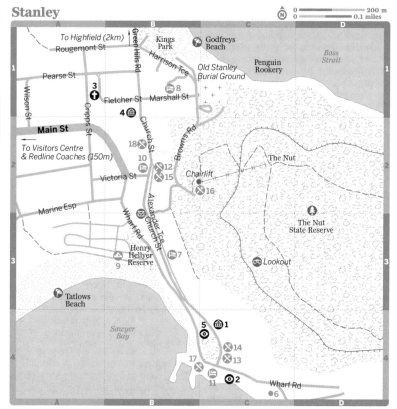

1840s warehouse is quite incredible. This ultra-hip boutique hotel has two suites and a self-contained loft apartment, which are frankly the coolest of the cool. Everything's top class, from the bedding to the artworks on the walls. If you've booked just one night you'll be disappointed. The same people run a sister property, @The Base (32 Alexander Tce, d $125-155), which is a heritage house divided into two similarly stylish suites.

Cable Station Restaurant &
Accommodation BOUTIQUE HOTEL **$$$**
(☑6458 1312; www.oldcablestation.com.au; 435 Greenhills Rd, West Beach; d $140-280, extra person $30) Having maintained a telephonic link with the mainland for over 30 years from 1935, this place now upholds a sophisticated guesthouse. Comprising private en-suite accommodation (one with a spa) and a self-contained cottage (sleeping up to four), this option offers sea views, seclusion

and peace. House guests and groups of four or more can dine at the excellent on-site restaurant.

To reach the Cable Station, depart Stanley on Browns Rd, which becomes Green Hills Rd along the waterfront. Follow Green Hills Rd (which becomes unpaved) without turning off. The Cable Station is about 400m after a sharp bend to the left.

Beachside Retreat West
Inlet CABINS **$$$**
(☑6458 1350; www.beachsideretreat.com; 253 Stanley Hwy; d $178-348; 🛜) There's luxurious and ecofriendly accommodation on a land-for-wildlife property here, just metres from a secluded beach. You'll enjoy magnificent sunsets, spot sea eagles, and thoroughly unwind in this natural haven. They also offer nature tours of the property and the Tarkine. It's located about 4km from Stanley, well signposted off the Stanley Hwy (B21).

Stanley

◎ Sights

	Ford's Store	(see 17)
1	Lyons Cottage	C4
	Plough Inn	(see 4)
2	Seaquarium	C4
3	St James Presbyterian Church	A1
4	Stanley Discovery Museum & Genealogy Centre	B1
	Stanley Hotel	(see 10)
5	Van Diemen's Land Company Store	C4

Activities, Courses & Tours

6	Stanley Seal Cruises	C4

⊜ ☼ Sleeping

7	@ The Base	B3
	@ VDL	(see 5)
8	Hanlon House	B1
9	Stanley Cabin & Tourist Park	B3
10	Stanley Hotel	B2
11	Stanley Village	C4

◉ Eating

12	Chin Wags	B2
13	Hursey Seafoods	C4
14	Kermie's Cafe	C4
15	Moby Dicks	B2
16	Nut Rock Café	C2
	Stanley Hotel	(see 10)
17	Stanley's on the Bay	B4
18	Xanders	B2

tea on arrival and also provide directions and equipment for viewing penguins that nest on the adjoining property.

Stanley Hotel PUB **$$**
(☑1800 222 397, 6458 1161; www.stanleytasmania.com.au; 19 Church St; s/d with shared bathroom $50/70, d $99-115) This historic pub has a rabbit warren of rooms. They're brightly painted and truly delightful – this has to be some of the nicest pub accommodation around. The shared bathrooms are superclean and the staff superfriendly. You can sit out on the upstairs verandah and spy down on the Stanley streetscape. They also run the six self-catering **Abbeys Cottages** (d $150-180, extra person $30).

Stanley Village MOTEL **$$**
(☑6458 1404; www.stanleyvillage.com.au; 15-17 Wharf Rd; d $130-160; ⏸) The reception here is in the old Wiltshire Junction Train Station, from where staff will lead you to a selection of motel-style rooms and self-contained apartments on the water's edge, some with good views over Sawyer Bay. Dine at the excellent on-site restaurant Stanley's on the Bay.

Stanley Seaview Inn MOTEL **$$**
(☑6458 1300; www.stanleyseaviewinn.com.au; 58 Dovecote Rd; d $116-150, extra person $20; ⏸) This welcoming option has a selection of motel rooms and self-contained accommodation with million-dollar views of the Nut and township. Its **Nut View Restaurant** (mains $19 to $35; ⊘closed Mon) serves dinner from September to May and has a great local seafood platter on its satisfying menu. To get here from Stanley's centre, leave town on Main Rd and bear left onto Dovecote Rd. The motel is situated on a sharp corner, 1.7km from the town centre.

Stanley Cabin & Tourist Park CARAVAN PARK **$**
(☑6458 1266; www.stanleycabinpark.com.au; Wharf Rd; unpowered/powered sites d $25/27, dm $26, cabins d $85-150; ⏸) With wide views of Sawyer Bay in one direction, and the Nut on the other, this park is in a spectacular spot. There are waterfront camp sites, neat cabins and a backpackers hostel comprising six twin rooms. Linen is supplied, but it's BYO towels.

Horizon Deluxe Apartments APARTMENTS **$$$**
(☑0448 251 115; www.horizonapartments.com.au; d $330; ⏸) You can hardly beat the views from these luxurious new hilltop apartments, and inside they're kitted out with spas, surround sound, luxury toiletries, fluffy robes and touch-of-a-button climate control. Chocolate truffles and personal bar are provided: you bring the romance. To get here from Stanley, take Main Rd out of town, and turn left onto Dovecote Rd. It's approximately 2km from the town centre.

Hanlon House B&B **$$**
(☑6458 1149; 6 Marshall St; d $150-200) This lovely B&B has comfortably homely en-suite rooms, one with a spa. You can enjoy sea panoramas from the breakfast table while you tuck into absolutely gourmet cooked breakfasts: think eggs Benedict, bacon fritters, pancakes or smoked-salmon scrambled eggs. Your hosts greet you with afternoon

✗ Eating

Xanders MODERN AUSTRALIAN **$$$**
(☑6458 1111; 25 Church St; mains $25-39; ⊘dinner Mon-Sat) Stanley's newest fine-dining restaurant is set in an old house on the main street with views back and front. The menu

here has an accent on fish and seafood, but Xanders also serves the area's excellent beef and specials like duck. There's a good kids menu too.

Stanley's on the Bay SEAFOOD **$$**
(☑6458 1404; 15 Wharf Rd; mains $18-35; ⊘dinner Mon-Sat Sep-Jun) Set inside the historic Ford's Store at Stanley Village, this fine-dining establishment specialises in steak and seafood. The wonderful seafood platter for two ($95) overflows with local scallops, oysters, fish, octopus and salmon.

**Cable Station
Restaurant** MODERN AUSTRALIAN **$$**
(☑6458 1312; 435 Greenhills Rd, West Beach; 2-/3-course dinners $49/59) This is a truly sophisticated dining option offering fine food in the salubrious surrounds of the Cable Station. Don't miss the wood-oven roasted Stanley crayfish or the delectable Black River lamb.

Stanley Hotel PUB FARE **$$**
(19 Church St; mains $16-38; ⊘breakfast, lunch & dinner) This pub serves better-than-bistro fare, including year-round fresh seafood – crayfish in season – and servings the size of the Nut itself. Leave room for the tempting desserts.

Chin Wags CAFE **$**
(6 Church St; mains $8-13; ⊘9am-5pm; 🖉) The folks at Chin Wags say they serve 'modern hippie gourmet', but perhaps that's just shorthand for delicious, healthy grub. Everything's homemade, and there are good vegie plus gluten-free options. They cook all day and do cakes and coffee for in between.

Kermies Cafe SEAFOOD **$$**
(2 Alexander Tce; mains $12-29; ⊘lunch & dinner) Here is the best place in Stanley for fresh crayfish, served natural or mornay ($70 to $170). Kermies also does prawns, scallops, calamari and platters to share.

Moby Dicks CAFE **$**
(5 Church St; mains $8-15; ⊘7.30-11.30am) Tuck into an enormous breakfast here before you go out and battle the wild west winds: things like cooked eggy breakfast with the lot or waffles with maple syrup...yum.

Nut Rock Café CAFE **$**
(Nut State Reserve, Brown Rd; cakes from $3; ⊘9.30am-5.30pm) To keep your energy up as you conquer the Nut, or to restore you when you come down, this cafe offers coffees, frothy hot chocolates and excellent cakes.

Hursey Seafoods FRESH FISH **$$**
(2 Alexander Tce; ⊘9am-6pm) Hurseys is awash with tanks of live sea creatures: fish, crayfish, crabs and eels – for the freshest of (uncooked) seafood takeaways.

❶ Information

There is an ATM inside **Stanley Supermarket** (cnr Wharf Rd & Marine Esplanade).

Post office (Church St) Also an agent for Commonwealth and National banks.

Visitor centre (☑6458 1330; www.stanley. com.au; 45 Main Rd; ⊘9.30am-5.30pm Mon-Fri, 10am-4pm Sat & Sun, reduced hr winter) Also offers internet access ($2 per 15 minutes).

❶ Getting There & Around

Redline Coaches (www.redlinecoaches.com.au) buses stop at the visitor centre.

Burnie ($19, 75 minutes)

Smithton ($6, 25 minutes)

Smithton & Around

POP 3361

A 22km stretch of rugged coast further west of Stanley, small-town Smithton is set on the banks of the Duck River and is a service centre for local beef farming and vegetable cropping. Forestry has always been big here, and timber milling is still one of the biggest industries in town.

For insights into Smithton's pioneer days, visit the **Circular Head Heritage Centre** (cnr Nelson & King Sts; adult/child $2/1; ⊘10.30-2.30pm Mon-Thu). The most fascinating exhibit is the skeleton of the mysterious, giant wombat–like *Zygomaturus tasmanicum*.

You'll find all the major banks (with ATMs) here, and this is good place to stock up before you head off into the rainforests and wilds to the south and west.

◉ Sights & Activities

Woolnorth FARM
Sprawling across the northwestern tip of Tasmania, 25kms from Smithton, is the 220-sq-km cattle and sheep property of Woolnorth, still a holding of the Van Diemen's Land company two centuries after it began. Today it's also home to enormous wind turbines that harness the power of the Roaring Forties. You can view them up close with **Woolnorth Tours** (☑6452 1493; www. woolnorthtours.com), which offers informative one-hour excursions (adult/child $17.50/12,

departing 10am) around the wind farm, as well as a half-day tour (adult/child $75/50) and full-day tour (adult/child $135/75). These visit Cape Grim, the Woolnorth property, and a shipwreck off Woolnorth Point, weather permitting. Take deep lungfuls of the air here: the Baseline Air Pollution Station off Cape Grim declares this to be the cleanest air in the world.

Tarkine Forest Adventures ADVENTURE CENTRE (www.adventureforests.com.au/tarkine; adult/5-16 yr $20/10; ⊙9am-5pm Nov-Mar, 10am-4pm Apr-Oct) Thirty kilometres southwest of Smithton (just off the A2) is this forest adventure centre, formerly known as Dismal Swamp. There's a 110m-long slide that provides a thrilling descent into a blackwood-forested sinkhole: sliders must be over eight and at least 90cm tall. It also has a cafe, an interpretation centre and boardwalks on the forest floor. Three mountain-bike tracks, graded from 'family' to 'expert', let you get out into it on two wheels. Bring your own bike.

South Arthur Forest Drive SCENIC DRIVING There are ancient, dripping rainforests and tannin-brown rivers in the Tarkine south of Smithton, which you can get into the heart of via the **South Arthur Forest Drive**. The drive was a circuit crossing the Arthur River in two places, at Kanunnah Bridge and Tayatea Bridge, until massive flooding washed away the latter. Until a new bridge is built, this is an out-and-back drive via the (part-gravel) C218. Highlights are the roadside **Sumac River lookout**; and the incredibly still, forest-encircled **Lake Chisholm**, a flooded dolomite sinkhole that's a 30-minute walk from the car park through man fern and myrtle forest. There's also the **Milkshake Hills Forest Reserve**, where you can take a one-hour return walk and get Serengeti-like views over **Lawson Plains**. More details on these routes can be found in the *Tarkine Activity Guide*, available in Stanley's (and most other) visitor centres.

☞ Tours

Tall Timbers Adventure Tours NATURE (☎1800 628 476, 6452 2755; www.talltimbers hotel.com.au; Scotchtown Rd) From September to May, Tall Timbers offers 4WD adventure tours to the Tarkine Wilderness ($240 with gourmet lunch, minimum two people, or $99 without lunch, minimum four people). It also offers helicopter sightseeing tours in several variations. Flight options include 30 minutes ($495), 45 minutes ($730) and 60

minutes ($960). Costs are for a minimum of two and maximum of five people. From October to March, there are also evening penguin tours ($35 including dinner).

🛏 Sleeping & Eating

Island View Spa Cottage COTTAGE $$ (☎0418 595 314; 70 Cantara Rd; d $160-180, extra adult/child $40/10) This is a real delight of a place set in peaceful waterfront bushland only 2km from town. You can hang out on the sunny deck, soak in the luxurious outdoor spa, and spot abundant wildlife as the sun goes down over the nearby Bass Strait islands. This beautiful house sleeps up to five.

Tall Timbers HOTEL $$$ (☎1800 628 476, 6452 2755; www.talltimbers hotel.com.au; Scotchtown Rd; d $145-245, extra adult/child $30/15; 🐾🖥) Some 2km south of Smithton, Tall Timbers has an impressive portico of massive timber beams and a reception area under an amazing timber cathedral ceiling. The rooms are comfortable, and a reliable bistro serves breakfast, lunch and dinner (mains $14 to $38), but perhaps the best thing about Tall Timbers is the tours it offers.

Rosebank Cottage Collection RENTAL HOUSES $$ (☎6452 2660; www.rosebankcottages.com; d $170-180) This collection comprises two delightfully rosy cottages (46 Brooks Rd, Sedgy Creek, 500m off the highway), an older-style house, and a smart modern apartment in Smithton (40 Goldie St). Breakfast – including freshly baked bread – is included.

Time Out On Emmett CAFE $ (61 Emmett St; mains $4-12; ⊙6am-5.30pm Mon-Fri, to 2.30pm Sat) This is a must for a meal or snack when you're in Smithton. It serves imaginative salads, rolls and wraps, lasagne, frittatas, sweet treats – and fabulous coffee. Try its crayfish or scallop pies baked using local recipes passed down through generations.

Bridge Hotel-Motel PUB$$ (☎6452 1389; 2 Montagu Rd; s/d without bathroom from $39/49, s/d with bathroom from $49/59, extra person $15) There are rooms in a hotel proper here and motel units round the back. Seafood, roasts and Scotch fillet steaks are served in the **restaurant** (mains $6-35; ⊙lunch & dinner).

Sheer Pleasure APARTMENT $$ (☎6452 1695; www.sheerpleasure.com.au; 121 Emmett St; d $150) This is a snazzy new self-

HEAVENLY GARDENS

As you head south on the B22 out of Smithton, just 3km north of Edith Creek you'll come upon **Allendale Gardens & Rainforest** (☑6456 4216; www.allendalegardens.com. au; Edith Creek; adult/5-16yr $10/3.50; ☺9am-5pm Oct-Apr). This place is truly a wonder of green-fingered creativity, and it's the life's work and passion of Max and Lorraine Cross, who nurture it. You can wander through an incredible variety of trees and flowering plants here: there's the glorious birch walk, a spectacular dahlia-and-rose garden, a wisteria pergola, spring blossoms, autumn colours and a panoply of trees – from Himalayan spruces to redwoods, tulip trees and the exquisite Chinese dove tree. Allen Creek ripples its way through the gardens, crossed by six bridges.

There's also a peaceful stand of rainforest where you can admire towering old-growth stringy-barks, spot a rare creeping fern and perhaps see platypuses in the creek. You should then indulge in tea, scones and cream in the teahouse, with lashings of Max's homemade raspberry and blackberry jams.

contained apartment with wonderful water views where you can hang out on the balcony and cook a feast on the barbie.

Montagu Camping Ground CAMPGROUND $ (☑0428 524 843; Old Port Rd; sites for 2 people $10, extra person $5; ☺Nov-Apr) This ground is just east of the diminutive Montagu township, which is 16km west of Smithton.

❶ Getting There & Away

Redline Coaches (☑1300 360 000, 6336 1446; www.redlinecoaches.com.au) head to Burnie ($22, 1½ hours) from Smith St opposite the police station.

Marrawah

POP 370

Untamed, unspoilt Marrawah is a domain of vast ocean beaches, mind-blowing sunsets and green, rural hills. The power of the ocean here is astounding, and the wild beaches, rocky coves and headlands have changed little since they were the homeland of Tasmania's first people. The coast here is abundant with signs of Aboriginal Tasmania – and somehow there's a feeling of lonely emptiness here, as if these original custodians have only just left this land.

It's vast ocean waves that Marrawah is best known for today. Sometimes the Southern Ocean throws up the remains of long-forgotten shipwrecks here – things tumble in on waves that sometimes reach over 10m. Experienced surfers and windsurfers come here for the challenging breaks.

🏃 Activities

Surfing

The annual West Coast Classic surfing competition is regularly decided at Marrawah in March, as is a round of the state's windsurfing championships. Surfing spots:

Green Point Is 2km from the town centre; has a break that's impressive in southerly conditions.

Nettley Bay Along the road from Green Point.

Lighthouse Beach At West Point, south of Marrawah; has good surfing in an easterly. It's reached by taking the left-hand branches of the road from the turn-off on the C214.

Bluff Hill Point Has great reef surfing in easterly conditions. The surf beach is to the right of the lighthouse off Bluff Hill Point Rd.

Walking

There's a lengthy beach walk from **Bluff Hill Point** to **West Point** (four hours one way) and a coastal walk from **Bluff Hill Point** to the mouth of the **Arthur River** (two hours one way). There's also a highly scenic walk north along the beach from **Green Point** to **Preminghana** (around three hours return).

Fishing

In winter you can catch Australian salmon at **Nettley Bay** or off the rocks at **West Point**, while in summer you can catch black-backed salmon off the beach at the mouth of the Arthur River, or estuary perch in the river itself.

Tours

King's Run Wildlife Tours   NATURE
(☑6457 1191; www.kingsrun.com.au; tours per person $100-125) Geoff King is a local character who has become famous for his unique and unforgettable devil-spotting tours. He takes visitors on evening trips to an atmospheric old fishing shack in a remote spot on his 330-hectare property to watch devils tuck voraciously into a buffet dinner of road kill. It's really a special experience and well worth travelling here for.

🍴 Sleeping & Eating

Ann Bay Cabins   CABINS $
(☑0428 548 760; 99 Green Point Rd; d from $140) These two cosy wooden cabins are just the place to hang out and get away from it all. You can sit on the deck and admire the views, or luxuriate in the deep spa bath, with bathing essentials and choccies supplied.

Arties   RENTAL HOUSE $$
(☑6457 1223; 157 Arthur River Rd; d $150, extra person $25) This is a cosy double-storey cottage set back from the road on 1.2 hectares of native bush with possible visiting wildlife. It's fully equipped for self-catering and sleeps up to six.

Marrawah Beach House   RENTAL HOUSE $$
(☑6457 1285; 19 Beach Rd, Green Point; d from $140, extra person $25) This place is secluded, view-filled and brightly decorated with starfish and seashells. The friendly owners set it up with treats like fresh flowers and maybe local honey before you arrive. Sleeps up to four.

Marrawah Tavern   PUB FARE $$
(Comeback Rd; mains $10-25; ☺lunch & dinner) You can get a good meal and a drink here. Choices include steak sandwiches, prawns, roasts, beef 'n' reef, and whole local flounders.

Camping is possible for free at beautiful Green Point, where there are toilets, water and an outdoor cold shower. You must pitch your tent by the toilets back from the beach, not on the foreshore.

🛍 Shopping

Marrawah General Store   GENERAL STORE
(800 Comeback Rd; ☺7.30am-7pm Mon-Fri, 8am-7.30pm Sat & Sun) This store sells supplies and petrol, and is an agent for Australia Post and Commonwealth Bank. Fill up on fuel here if you're planning to take the Western Explorer to Corinna as there's no other petrol outlet until Zeehan, some 200km away.

Arthur River
POP 110

There are only a few hardy souls who call Arthur River their full-time home – the rest of the population is made up of 'shackies',

---

TASMANIAN ABORIGINAL SITES

The far northwest of Tasmania has been home to the Tasmanian Aboriginal Tarkininer people for more than 35,000 years. Evidence of their habitation is clearly visible along much of the Tarkine coast, and experts call this one of the most important archaeological regions in the world.

There's a significant Aboriginal site along the road to Arthur River at West Point. Beyond the township at Sundown Point is a site containing several dozen mudstone slabs engraved with mainly circular motifs. The Arthur Pieman Conservation Area, further south, has a particularly dense concentration of middens, and, slightly further afield, there are also several important cave sites at Rocky Cape National Park.

Arguably the most significant site on the west coast is 7km north of Marrawah at Preminghana (formerly known as Mt Cameron West). At the northern end of the beach are low-lying slabs of rock with geometric carvings (or petroglyphs) dating back two millennia. Also in this area are hut depressions, stone tools, seal-hunting hides, tool quarries and middens. Natural links with Tasmanian Aboriginal culture here include boobialla, honeysuckle and tea-tree clusters – plants used to prepare food and traditional medicines.

Preminghana was returned to the Aboriginal people in 1995 – you can't visit the area independently. If you'd like to be authoritatively guided around this and other significant Aboriginal sites, contact the Tasmanian Aboriginal Land and Sea Council (TALSC; ☑6231 0288; 4 Lefroy St, North Hobart), which keeps a list of heritage officers who can accompany you.

and fishers who love the wild remoteness of the country around here. There's a **Parks & Wildlife Service ranger station** (☑6457 1225) on the northern side of the river, where you can get camping information and permits for off-road vehicles.

Gardiner Point, signposted off the main road on the southern side of Arthur River is Tasmania's official **Edge of the World**: the sea here stretches uninterrupted all the way to Argentina. There's a plaque at the point – a great place to take those leaning-into-the-wind, world's-end photos.

The town has a kiosk with limited supplies opposite the ranger station, offering fishing- rod hire (half/full day $15/25) and takeaways, and a small general store on the south side of the river where you can book river cruises.

🏃 Activities

Arthur River Canoe & Boat Hire   BOATING
(☑6457 1312; River Jetty, Arthur River) You can explore the amazing river and rainforest with watercraft hired here. This place offers information on river conditions and storage for your gear, and hires single and double Canadian canoes for $12 to $16 per hour and $50 to $70 per day. It also rents out aluminium dinghies with outboards for $25 an hour or $150 per day. Even better, they'll help you organise a downriver canoe expedition from either Kanunnah Bridge (two-day trip) or the Tayatea Bridge site (four-day trip). They'll meet you at the launching site with the boats and the river gear you'll need, and drive your car back to Arthur River (for a $100 fee).

🎫 Tours

Arthur River Cruises   CRUISE
(☑6457 1158; www.arthurrivercruises.com; cruises adult/child $92/35; ⊘10am Sep-May) The reflections on the Arthur River have to be seen to be believed, and you can get out among them on board the MV *George Robinson*, operated by Arthur River Cruises. You'll see sea eagles and kingfishers, stroll in the rainforest and enjoy a BBQ lunch.

AR Reflections River Cruises   CRUISE
(☑6457 1288; www.arthurriver.com.au; 4 Gardiner St; tours adult/child $88/48; ⊘10.15am) An alternative cruise is offered by this crew. Its attractive MV *Reflections* departs daily for a 5½-hour return trip to Warra Landing, where you also get a guided rainforest walk and gourmet lunch.

🛏 Sleeping

Arthur Riverfront & Sea Lodge   RENTAL HOUSE $$
(☑0418 595 314; www.arthurriveraccommodation.com; 22 Gardiner St; d + 1 child $115-205, extra adult/child $30/15) This smart new house can be rented as two separate apartments (one two-bedroom, one three-bedroom) or opened up into one big house, sleeping up to 12. It's absolute waterfront and also absolutely well equipped with spacious living areas, wood stoves, expansive decks, and amazing river and Southern Ocean views. One child stays for free.

Arthur River Holiday Units   APARTMENTS $$
(☑6457 1288; 2 Gardiner St; d $120, extra person $30) These comfortable, self-contained units may not have the most stylish decoration you've ever seen, but they're great for families and perfect for people less nimble on their feet, as they have level access. Accommodation and river-cruise packages are available.

Arthur River Cabin Park   CAMPGROUND $$
(☑6457 1212; www.arthurrivercabinpark.com; 1239 Arthur River Rd; unpowered/powered sites d $25/28, vans/cabins $80/95, extra adult/child $25/15) There are hot showers and a laundry for all stayers at this neat park, and the spick-and-span cabins are amazingly good value. Wildlife – including devils – visit in the evening.

Arthur River Beach House   RENTAL HOUSE $$
(☑0438 454 311; 24 Gardiner St; d $100-160) This beach house is on the banks of the Arthur River where it empties into the sea, and bills itself as a top bolt-hole for your fishing holiday. Nonfishers also welcome.

The Parks and Wildlife Service at Arthur River manages three camping areas. **Seaside Manuka Campground** is just north of Arthur River, and **Peppermint Campground** is in Arthur River itself. Both have unpowered sites ($13 for two people, $5/$2.50 per extra adult/child) with taps, cold showers and toilets. Unserviced **Prickly Wattle** has unpowered sites ($6 per adult, $3/2 per extra adult/child) and is along the road to Couta Rocks. None of these camp sites have bins: take your rubbish with you.

The Tarkine Wilderness

The Tarkine is a 4470-sq-km stretch of wild country between the Arthur River in the north and the Pieman River in the south. It's a globally significant ecosystem that encompasses the largest intact tract of temperate rainforest in the southern hemisphere, tall eucalyptus forests, endless horizons of buttongrass plains, savage ocean beaches, sand dunes and extensive coastal heathland. It's home to several endangered species and extensive, ancient archaeological sites. Because of its remoteness, ferocious weather and isolation, the Tarkine survived almost untouched by modernity well into the 20th century.

The Tarkine first entered the national psyche through the controversial construction of the 'Road To Nowhere' – now called the **Western Explorer** (p239) – in 1995, and conservation groups have been seeking full protection for it ever since. In 2005, after an election in which Tasmania's forests became a national issue, the federal government protected 730 sq km of the Tarkine's unique myrtle-rich rainforest. In 2009 the area received a National Heritage emergency listing when faced with the threat of more road building. Finally, in 2011, following the historic Statement of Principles agreement between Tasmanian forestry and conservation groups, a further 700 sq km of Tarkine forest were to be protected from logging. But as this book went to print, the Statement of Principles agreement appeared to be floundering, and the forests may not receive the protection that was proposed

Conservation groups still call for a Tarkine National Park to be added to the remote Savage River National Park (p241), as parts of the Tarkine remain vulnerable to mining, uncontrolled off-road driving and, unfortunately, arson. You can read more about the work of the **Tarkine National Coalition**, which has been instrumental in the long-running campaign to protect the area, at www.tarkine.org.

To get deep into the heart of the Tarkine, get ahold of the *Tarkine Activity Guide*, available at most tourist information centres in Tasmania. This gives further details of Tarkine driving routes, short walks, river cruises, kayak trips and guided vehicle-based tours mentioned in this guide.

Tarkine Trails (✆6223 5320; www.tarkinetrails.com.au) can take you on a number of different adventures if you want to get really remote on foot. Trips include a full-forest-immersion six-day Tarkine Rainforest walk ($1799) or a six-day Wild Tarkine Coast walk from Pieman Heads to Sandy Cape ($1799). It also offers adventures based out of its breathtakingly beautiful new Tarkine Rainforest Retreat, set deep in the forest, where you sleep in a comfortable safari tent–style standing camp and marvel at the surrounding giant tree ferns from the lodge's cantilevered verandah. A five-night/six-day trip costs $2199; the two-night/three-day trip is $1299).

Tasmanian Expeditions (✆6331 9000, 1300 666 856; www.tasmanianexpeditions.com.au; trips $1995) also offers a six-day Tarkine Experience trip, with hotel accommodation, day walks and a river cruise in the Tarkine.

In the forests behind Rocky Cape National Park, the new **Tarkine Wilderness Lodge** (✆6445 9184; www.tarkinelodge.com.au; d $270-370) offers luxury accommodation and walks into the surrounding green.

The **Tarkine Interpretation Centre** in Waratah has insider information, maps and brochures.

Western Explorer (C249) & Arthur Pieman Conservation Area

The Western Explorer is probably Tasmania's most excitingly remote road journey. It delves deep into the buttongrass wilderness of the **Arthur Pieman Conservation Area** of the western Tarkine. Dubbed the 'Road to Nowhere', it was controversially upgraded from a barely-there 4WD track into a wide gravel road in 1995, to the dismay of conservationists, who saw it as opening up this vulnerable wilderness to damage and exploitation. Predictions about its detrimental effects have unfortunately come true: more visitation has meant more frequent fires, set both unintentionally and on purpose.

Despite its troubled beginnings, the road is now a well-established means of traversing this rugged part of Tasmania, and it's an unmissable journey if you are in this region. Road conditions vary from season to season. Although it's regularly negotiated by vehicles without 4WD, it's remote, unsealed and at times rough and rocky. Some of the steepest hills now have paved sections, but there are many others where there's potential to skid on a treacherous surface: drive with great care. Don't drive the road at night or in bad weather. For an up-to-date assessment on road conditions ask at the **Arthur River ranger station** (✆6457 1225). Fill up your car at Marrawah if you're travelling

LOCAL KNOWLEDGE

PETER STEWART: PIEMAN FERRYMAN

I run the ferry across the Pieman River. On any one day, you can cross up to 80 times, usually two cars at a time. People are often amazed that this little car ferry still exists in the middle of the forest here. Some people come just for that experience. I drive the boat for the river cruises down to Pieman Heads, too, or do whatever's needed at Corinna. When you work this remote, you have to be a jack-of-all-trades. As the crow flies, it's only 120km from Burnie, but it feels a million miles from the world.

Remote? Just how remote?

There's no mobile-phone reception, no TV, no internet, no public phone. Step a few metres off the road and you're into deep forest.

The best thing about living here?

That remoteness, the beauty, the peace, the birds.

Much wildlife around?

It's everywhere: sea eagles, Tas devils, wallabies, possums, the odd wombat.

And when you're not on the river?

I do some gold prospecting in the Tarkine. I get just enough to keep the enthusiasm going. It's exciting…but also back-breaking. I'm just a hobbyist…a part-time gold prospector. If I'd found much, I wouldn't be here, would I?

south or at Zeehan, Tullah or Waratah if heading north: there's no petrol in between.

The 1000-sq-km Arthur Pieman Conservation Area takes in the remote fishing settlement of Temma, the mining ghost town of Balfour, magnificent beaches like Sandy Cape Beach, the rugged Norfolk Range, the Thornton and Interview Rivers and savage Pieman Heads. The Tarkine's wild beaches are feared for their vehicle-swallowing quicksand.

Corinna & the Pieman River

In rip-roaring gold-rush days Corinna was a humming town with two hotels, a post office, plenty of shops and a population that numbered 2500 souls. That's hard to believe now when you pull up on the forested edge of the Pieman, turn off your car's engine and absorb the unbelievable forest peace.

A wise bunch of tourism experts took over the remains of Corinna a few years ago, and have turned it, with utmost care, into a really pleasant little place to stop and stay, while retaining the deep-forest feel. There's no mobile-phone reception and no TVs: the most prevalent sound is birdsong.

While in Corinna you can't miss the Pieman River Cruise (⌧6446 1170; adult/child

$90/51; ☺10am). You'll be awe-filled by the reflections and may appreciate this more rustic alternative to the crowded Gordon River cruises out of Strahan. The tour on the MV *Arcadia II* lasts 4½ hours. Book well ahead.

Also on offer are canoe and kayak paddles on the Pieman (half day/full day $40/80); fishing (rod hire half day/full day $10/20); and boat trips (adult/child $50/25) to Lovers' Falls, where you can be dropped with a picnic hamper and sigh at the beauty of it all.

Bushwalking around here includes nearby Mt Donaldson (four hours return) and Philosopher's Falls (four hours return). The shorter Huon Pine Trail on the banks of the Pieman has some sections that are accessible by wheelchair. For details on all these activities, ask at the reception of Corinna Wilderness Experience.

🛏 Sleeping & Eating

Corinna Wilderness Experience COTTAGES $$ (⌧6446 1170; www.corinna.com.au; s $50, cottages $135-189, extra person $25) Corinna has a collection of new self-contained timber cottages, three older-style houses sleeping four ($239) and the diminutive old pub, which houses backpackers rooms' with shared facilities. One of the cottages is wheelchair accessible. Outside, there's also (unpowered) camping with toilets and showers (two/three people $20/30).

You can satisfy your hunger in the **pub-restaurant** (mains $12 to $35; ☺lunch & dinner), which serves hearty homemade meals, including gourmet pizzas, focaccia and delectable wallaby-shank pies. Picnic hampers are also available for order.

❶ Getting There & Away

The cable-driven **Fatman vehicle barge** (☑6446 1170; 2-wheelers/cars/caravans $10/20/25; ☺9am-5pm Apr-Sep, to 7pm Oct-Mar) plying the Pieman River at Corinna allows you to travel from Corinna down to Zeehan and Strahan. There's a 9m length limit on vehicles with caravans.

You can also approach Corinna from Somerset, just west of Burnie, via the Murchison Hwy through magnificent Hellyer Gorge (perfect for picnic stops).

Waratah

POP 230

Waratah has two claims to fame: the nearby tin mine at Mt Bischoff was once the world's richest, and the (presumed) last Tasmanian tiger was trapped here in 1936. This pretty lakeside town is sliced through by Happy Valley gorge and its cascading waterfall.

To get an impression of early days, visit the local **museum** (Smith St; ☺10am-3pm Mon-Sun), and for the latest on the Tarkine, visit the **Tarkine Interpretation Centre** (☑6439 7100; www.discoverthetarkine.com.au; Athenaeum Hall, Smith St; ☺10am-2pm Wed-Sun).

There's also a restored, fully working **stamper mill** (Main St; ☺7.30am-4.30pm Mon-Fri, 8am-5pm Sat) once used to break up tin ore.

Behind the post office, **Waratah Camping & Caravan Park** (☑6439 7100; Smith St; unpowered/powered sites d $16/22) has lakeside caravan and camping sites. Keys to the amenities block are available at the post office or the roadhouse–general store. **Bischoff Hotel** (☑6439 1188; Main St; s/d $44/88, mains $10-18) offers rooms and counter meals for lunch and dinner. There's also the attractive **O'Connor Hall Guesthouse** (☑6439 1472; 2 Smith St; d $110-160), with wrought-iron tracery and four-poster beds.

King Island

POP 1570

There are no traffic lights on King Island: the only traffic control is a leisurely wave of the hand from a local as you pass by. A skinny sliver of land 64km long and 27km wide, King Island (or 'KI', as locals call it) is a laid-back place where everyone knows everyone and life is mighty relaxed. The island's green pastures famously produce a rich dairy bounty, and its surrounding seas supply fabulous fresh seafood. Locals dry kelp to extract its goodies and tend lighthouses, four of which guard the rocky coastline. They also surf: KI has some of the most consistently good surf anywhere. As a visitor, your hardest decision of the day might be which secluded cove to have all to yourself, which surf beach to go to for the perfect break, or how much more of that amazing King Island cheese you could possibly consume.

◎ Sights

King Island Dairy   DAIRY
(www.kidairy.com.au; North Rd, Loorana; ☺noon-4pm Sun-Fri, reduced days winter) Low-key but top-quality, King Island Dairy's Fromagerie is 8km north of Currie (just beyond the airport). Taste its award-winning bries, cheddars and feisty blues and then stock up in its shop on cheeses that are budget priced, only here, to fuel your King Island exploring.

Cape Wickham   HISTORIC SITE
You can drive right up to the tallest lighthouse in the southern hemisphere at Cape Wickham, on KI's northern tip. This 48m tower was built in 1861 after several ships had been wrecked on the island's treacherous coastline. Most famous of all King Island shipwrecks is the *Cataraqui* (1845), Australia's worst civil and maritime disaster, with the loss of 400 lives.

SAVAGE RIVER NATIONAL PARK

Tasmania has one national park that you can't easily visit: the remote 180-sq-km **Savage River National Park**. The park protects part of the largest contiguous region of cool temperate rainforest surviving in Australia, pristine blanket bogs, undisturbed river catchments and rare wildlife. There are no roads and no facilities for visitors. Only the very hardiest of bushwalkers make it here. This is one of the few surviving tracts of true wilderness left in Tasmania – though the large Savage River open-cut iron-ore mine is not far away.

Currie Lighthouse HISTORIC SITE
(☑0439 705 610; tours adult/child $15/7.50; ☺3.30pm Wed & Sat) This lighthouse was built in 1880 in response to the *Cataraqui* calamity, and there are two more lighthouses at Stokes Point and Naracoopa.

King Island Museum MUSEUM
(Lighthouse St, Currie; adult/child $5/1; ☺2-4pm, closed Jul & Aug) There's information on lightkeeping, shipwrecks and monuments here and also in *The King Island Maritime Trail: Shipwrecks & Safe Havens* booklet, which you can pick up wherever visitor information is available.

Kelp Industries' Visitor Centre INDUSTRIAL
(89 Netherby Rd, Currie; ☺8am-5pm Mon-Fri) Come here to find out why you see tractors gathering kelp on KI's beaches. Glimpse the huge straps of bull kelp *(Durvillaea potatorum)* being air-dried here: it's exported to factories in Scotland and Norway, which extract alginates for use in products including sauces, lotions and detergents.

Calcified Forest NATURE RESERVE
From Currie, head south to the Seal Rocks Reserve (off South Rd). A 30-minute return stroll takes you to a viewing platform to survey the fossilised stumps of rainforest trees.

🏃 Activities

Ask a surfer to name the best waves in Australia and they'll likely name some KI spots. **Surfing** is brilliant in the cool, clear waters here: *Surfing Life* magazine has voted the break at Martha Lavinia as one of the top 10 waves in the world.

Surf and freshwater **fishing** almost guarantee a good catch, and you can swim at many of the island's unpopulated beaches (though beware rips and currents) and freshwater lagoons. Bring your own gear for the legendary snorkelling and diving here: there's crayfish and abalone to catch if you have a licence. Beachcombing may reveal flotsam from old wrecks – and a bounty of seashells. The prized paper nautilus shell sometimes washes up on the east coast in autumn.

There's also plenty of good, gentler **bushwalking** on KI. Pick up a map from King Island Tourism and go independently, or take a guided walk with **King Island Wilderness Walks** (☑0400 858 339; www.kingislandwildernesswalks.com).

You don't even need to get out on foot for **wildlife spotting** on KI: it's just about

everywhere you look. There are rufus and Bennett's wallabies, pademelons, snakes, echidnas and platypuses, and you may even glimpse seals. The island has 78 bird species, native and non: black swans, oyster catchers and red-capped plovers, but also turkeys, peacocks and pheasants. On summer evenings little penguins come ashore around the Grassy breakwater.

If you're keen for a spot of golf, there's an excellent nine-hole links course at **King Island Golf and Bowling Club** (☑6452 1126; 9/18 holes $15/$30, club hire $10) – it's challenging and wind-blustered and has been compared to the famous course at St Andrews.

🛏 Sleeping

TOP CHOICE **Portside Links** APARTMENTS $$
(☑6461 1134; www.portsidelinks.com.au; Grassy Harbour Rd, Grassy; apartments d $150-190, B&B $180-120) This fantastic new accommodation is the best place to stay on KI. There are two stylish and well-equipped self-catering apartments here as well as a B&B room in the owners' home. It's a short stroll to pretty Grassy Harbour and Sand Blow Beach. Penguins also nest nearby.

Naracoopa Holiday Units COTTAGES $$
(☑6461 1326; www.naracoopaholidayunits.com. au; 125 The Esplanade, Naracoopa; d $120, extra adult/child $25/15) Bright, clean and peaceful cottages on Sea Elephant Bay. The owners are mines of island information and can arrange car hire.

Devil's Gap Retreat COTTAGES $$
(☑6462 1180, 0429 621 180; Charles St, Currie; d $140) Two weathered one-bedroom cottages owned by a local artist overlooking the ocean close to Currie.

King Island Holiday Village MOTEL $$
(☑6461 1177; www.kingislandholidayvillage. com.au; 1 Bluegum Dr, Grassy; d $130-150, extra person $30) Motel rooms, self-contained villas, houses, and units of varying sizes. The owners can help with car hire and penguin viewing, and they run tours of the island.

Boomerang by the Sea MOTEL $$
(☑6462 1288; www.boomerangbythesea.com. au; Golf Club Rd, Currie; d $140, extra person $10) Recently refurbished, motel-style units with views over the golf course and sea. Breakfast is included, and you can dine in the on-site restaurant.

Bass Cabins & Campground CAMPGROUND **$**
(☏6462 1168, 6462 1474; 5 Fraser Rd, Currie; cabins d $100, camp sites per person $10) There are a few camp spots here with bathroom facilities adjacent and two two-bedroom cabins. The campground is 1.5km from the centre of Currie.

✖ Eating

KI is a foodie heaven. Must-trys include KI cheese and dairy products, but also crayfish in season (November to August), oysters, crabs, grass-fed beef, free-range pork and game. Don't forget to find some Cloud Juice: KI's pure bottled rainwater. There are two supermarkets in Currie and a store in Grassy.

Kings Cuisine at Bold Head
Brasserie MODERN AUSTRALIAN **$$**
(☏6461 1341; www.kingscuisine.com.au; 10 Main Rd, Grassy; mains $24-28; ☉lunch Fri-Sun, dinner Wed-Mon, bar open daily) Fine dining with a fine reputation.

Boomerang by the Sea MODERN AUSTRALIAN **$$**
(☏6462 1288; www.boomerangbythesea.com. au; Golf Club Rd, Currie; mains $18-40; ☉dinner Mon-Sat) Excellent menu, big on seafood; big views.

King Island Bakery BAKERY **$**
(5 Main St, Currie; snacks $5-18; ☉breakfast & lunch, dinner Fri) Best pies for miles.

Nautilus Coffee Lounge CAFE **$**
(28 Edward St, Currie; mains $6-14; ☉breakfast & lunch Mon & Wed-Sat) Healthy, delicious cafe fare; best coffee on KI.

Rocky Glen Retreat Restaurant
& Chalets MODERN AUSTRALIAN **$$**
(www.rockyglen.com.au; 1 Lovers Lane, Naracoopa; mains $14-28; ☉lunch Sat & Sun, dinner Thu-Mon) Down-to-earth, family-friendly dining.

Bert's Cafe CAFE **$**
(The Esplanade, Naracoopa; mains $6-15; ☉10am-6pm Sat & Sun) Part-time cafe serving hamburgers and more.

ℹ Information

ATMs are located at the corner of Main and Edward Sts in Currie, and at KI Foodworks Supermarket, Currie.

King Island Tourism (☏1800 645 014, 6462 1313; www.kingisland.org.au; 5 George St, Currie)

Main post office (1 Main St, Currie; ☉9am-5pm Mon-Fri)

Online Access Centre (5 George St; per hr $5; ☉10.30am-5pm Mon & Thu, to 7pm Wed, to 9pm Fri, 10am-noon Sat)

Trend (26 Edward St, Currie; ☉8.30am-6pm Mon-Fri, 9.30am-1.30pm Sat, 9.30am-12.30pm Sun) Fishing bait and tackle, petrol, and (limited) tourist information.

ℹ Getting There & Away

King Island Airlines (www.kingislandair.com.au) Melbourne Moorabbin to King Island ($160 to $173).

Regional Express (www.regionalexpress.com.au) Melbourne Tullamarine to King Island ($138 to $325).

Tasair (www.tasair.com.au) Devonport to King Island ($226); Hobart to King Island ($452).

ℹ Getting Around

King Island Car Rental (☏1800 777 282, 6462 1282; 2 Meech St, Currie; per day $63-110)

P&A Car Rental (☏6462 1603; 1 Netherby Rd, Currie; per day $66-73)

Cradle Country & the West

Includes »

Tullah 245
Rosebery 248
Zeehan. 249
Strahan 250
Queenstown 259
Franklin-Gordon
Wild Rivers
National Park 262
The Overland Track . .265
Maydena 271
Southwest
National Park 274
Melaleuca 275

Best Places to Eat

» Franklin Manor (p257)

» Linda Valley Café (p261)

» Ol' Jacks Café (p248)

» Café Serenade (p261)

Best Places to Stay

» Cradle Mountain Highlanders Cottages (p267)

» Franklin Manor (p256)

» Wheelhouse Apartments (p256)

» Penghana (p260)

Why Go?

If you imagined Tasmania as a land of soaring alpine peaks and dreamy, untouched wilderness, then you've imagined this part of Tasmania. Think endless ocean beaches, ancient mossy rainforests, whisky-tinted rivers, glacier-sculpted mountains and boundless horizons where you feel like the only soul on earth. This is Tasmania's vast outdoor playground, where your options for adventure are varied and plentiful. Come here for the toughest multi-day hikes (or gentle rainforest wanders); come to shoot rapids on untamed rivers (or cruise mirror-calm waters); kayak into some of the last untouched temperate wilderness on earth, (or fly over it all by light plane). Get out into the wilds independently, or come here with a guided group, but whatever you do, *get out there*. For more see www.tasmaniaswest-coast.com.au.

When to Go

This whole region buzzes in the warmest months. It may be busy, but the long days give you more time in the outdoors, and visitor services operate at full tilt. Tasmania's alpine heart can be gorgeously ice-encrusted in winter. Fewer souls get out for bushwalking now, and even the most-trodden tracks are hushed. If you're equipped and keen for a frosty – even snowy – highland adventure, it's a great time to visit. The southwest returns to remotest isolation in the cold months: this is when ferocious western gales arrive...and few visitors dare.

Tullah

POP 270

A quiet place offering visitors accommodation, excellent trout fishing, and some challenging mountain walks, the little town of Tullah has been long isolated in the dreamy rainforests of the West Coast Range, and is wrapped by deep, tannin-brown rivers. It was established when mineral riches were discovered here in 1887. The lead-zinc-copper-silver-ore bearing body in nearby Mt Farrell sustained the town until the mine closed in the 1970s.

The name Tullah comes from an Aboriginal word meaning 'meeting of two rivers', and indeed, Tullah is almost an island: there are bridge crossings to enter and leave town, and seven dams in the vicinity. The town shelters in the nape of majestic Mts Farrell and Murchison, and the waters of Lake Rosebery lap close.

For most of its history, Tullah was only accessible to the outside world by horse or on foot. Later came a narrow-gauge train and only in 1962, a road. In the 1970s and 1980s, Tullah was a 'hydro-town' accommodating workers building hydroelectric dams. It was a rollicking time: with 800 hardworking men in town the pub served 38 18-gallon beer kegs in one week.

Though post-hydro Tullah has been a somnolent backwater, like much of the west coast it also experiences the boom-and-bust mining cycle. When old mines reopen for a time, there's a real air of optimism about.

◉ Sights & Activities

To commemorate the days of steam when Tullah's only link to the outside world was by train, local residents have restored Wee Georgie Wood Steam Railway (☑0417 142 724; Murchison Hwy; adult/child/family $7/3/14), one of the narrow-gauge steam locomotives which operated on the town's original railway. From late September to May, on the first Sunday and the last Saturday and Sunday of the month, between 10am and 4pm, passengers can take 20-minute rides through the hills and rainforest, on part of the original track.

There are several **scenic drives** from Tullah alongside hydroelectric dams and lakes:

Reece Dam Three kilometres north of town you can follow remote (but sealed) Pieman Rd (which, after it swings south around the Reece Dam, becomes Heemskirk Rd, C249) west for about 45 minutes to the 120m high rock fill dam wall of the Reece Dam on Lake Pieman. The road continues over the dam wall another 29kms to Zeehan.

Anthony Rd Just south of Tullah, turn left into Anthony Main Rd (B28) which heads over the flanks of Mt Murchison and close to the sometimes mirror-calm waters of Lake Plimsoll. It's a scenic shortcut to Queenstown.

Mackintosh Dam Rd You can also take a side trip to Lakes Mackintosh and Murchison. Turn right onto Mackintosh Dam Rd if you're heading north to Lake Mackintosh, and then follow the road for an out-and-back-trip across the Mackintosh Dam to Lake Murchison.

The area's **best walks** include Mt Farrell (712m, three to four hours return) and the tallest mountain in the West Coast range, Mt Murchison (1275m, six hours return). The folks at Tullah Lakeside Chalet can provide walking information and may be able to guide you. There are also beautiful, short lakeside walks starting near the jetty and boat ramp. You might see local platypuses at play.

🛏 Sleeping & Eating

Tullah Lakeside Chalet   HOTEL, CABINS $$
(☑6473 4121; www.tullahchalet.com; Farrell St; dm with shared en suite $35, d $90-220, extra person $20) Set in ex-hydro workers' accommodation, this lake-edge hotel is being renovated bit by bit and has comfortable rooms – some with lake views and spas – as well as back-packers' accommodation. The chalet has kayaks you can take out on the lake (half/full day $30/50) and you can borrow fishing gear to catch Atlantic salmon and brown or rainbow trout in the lake. It also arranges guided hikes to Mt Farrell and Lake Herbert. The restaurant here (mains $18 to 28) has glorious lake views. Last dinner orders at 7.30pm.

Tullah Wilderness Gallery CAFE, APARTMENTS $$
(☑6473 4141; Murchison Hwy; d $75-100; mains $7.50-18; ⊙8am-9pm, reduced hours in winter; 🛜) The friendly cafe here serves all-day break-fasts and hearty mountain fare, such as la-sagne and schnitzel, as well as burgers and sandwiches to eat in or take away. You can browse in the attached gallery for art cre-ated from local wood. There are also two cosy self-contained apartments; book well

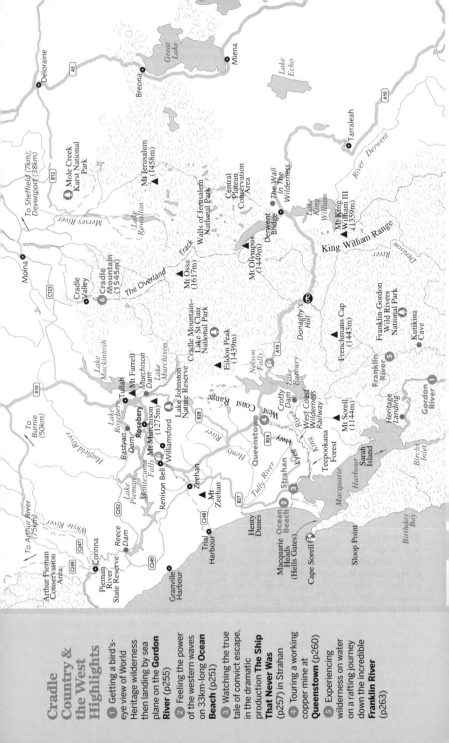

Cradle Country & the West Highlights

1 Getting a bird's-eye view of World Heritage wilderness then landing by sea plane on the **Gordon River** (p255)

2 Feeling the power of the western waves on 33km-long **Ocean Beach** (p251)

3 Watching the true tale of convict escape, in the dramatic production **The Ship That Never Was** (p257) in Strahan

4 Touring a working copper mine at **Queenstown** (p260)

5 Experiencing wilderness on water on a rafting journey down the incredible **Franklin River** (p263)

6 Cradle Mountain (1545m)

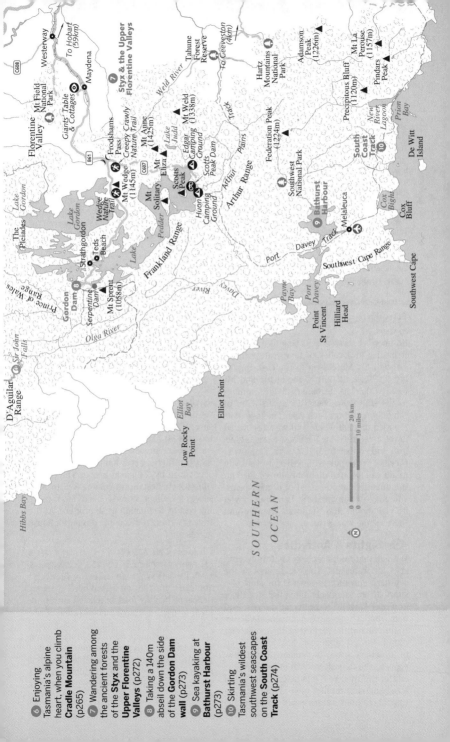

6 Enjoying Tasmania's alpine heart, when you climb **Cradle Mountain** (p265)

7 Wandering among the ancient forests of the **Styx** and the **Upper Florentine Valleys** (p272)

8 Taking a 140m abseil down the side of the **Gordon Dam wall** (p273)

9 Sea kayaking at **Bathurst Harbour** (p273)

10 Skirting Tasmania's wildest southwest seascapes on the **South Coast Track** (p274)

in advance as they're often rented out to local miners.

Tullah Village Café CAFE **$**

(Farrell St; meals $6-14; ⊙breakfast, lunch & dinner) You can get cooked breakfasts, snack take-aways, decent hamburgers, schnitzels, and fish and chips here. It also does kids' meals.

❶ Information

Tullah Wilderness Gallery (☑6473 4141; ⊙8am-9pm; reduced hours in winter; @) has a few brochures and the locals who work here are usually keen to help visitors with local information.

❶ Getting There & Away

Tassielink's (www.tassielink.com.au) Launceston–Strahan service stops at the petrol station in Tullah.

Launceston-Tullah ($51, 4 hrs)

Tullah-Strahan ($32, 3 hrs)

Rosebery

POP 1500

Rosebery's best asset is its beautiful location. It nestles in a valley of temperate rainforest with Mt Murchison to the east, imposing Mt Black (950m) to the north, and Mt Read (which has Tasmania's highest rainfall) to the south. Rosebery itself gets 3.5m of rainfall on average each year. The town was founded in 1893 when gold was discovered in the area; the mine here now extracts zinc, lead and copper from the earth, employing much of the populace. Rosebery is what you might call a rough diamond: unpolished on the outside but possessed of a good heart. You may not linger long here, but if you do you should find the locals friendly, and there's some wonderful nature nearby.

◉ Sights & Activities

With all that rain, Rosebery's naturally a top spot for waterfalls. The picnic area at the southern entrance to town is the start of a short (10-minute) walk along the Stitt River and over Park Rd to pretty Stitt Falls. And then there's incredible Montezuma Falls, 104m tall and the highest in Tasmania, that plume down a rainforest cliffside. Head out of Rosebery towards Strahan and follow signs to the falls 2km south of town. At the end of the road is Williamsford, the site of an abandoned mining town. From here an easy three-hour return walk leads to the falls. You can venture out onto the narrow swing bridge suspended over the yawning chasm to get a great view.

Tours

Hay's Adventure Tours NATURE, FISHING

(☑6473 1247; www.haytour.com.au) Hay's is the only operator allowed into Lake Johnston Nature Reserve, near Rosebery, to see an extraordinary 10,000-year-old stand of Huon pine. Its 4WD nature tours here cost $77 (2½ to three hours). Departure is usually about 11am in summer (on request – 24 hours notice needed) and in winter, whenever the fog lifts. Hay's also offers trout fishing tours on Mackintosh, Rosebery and Murchison lakes near Tullah for $165 per person for a half-day and $440 for a full day. All gear is supplied.

✪ Festivals & Events

Rosebery Festival FOLK

In late March or early April each year, the town comes alive with this folk festival. There's live music, horseback rides, a puppet theatre, food stalls, fireworks and, of course, that old Tassie favourite: wood-chopping.

🛏 Sleeping & Eating

TOP
CHOICE **Mount Black Lodge** HOTEL **$$**

(☑6473 1039; www.mountblacklodge.com; Hospital Rd; d $120-130) This rustic little lodge set in award-winning gardens is a real pleasure. It's run by friendly owners and looks towards Mt Murchison and Mt Read, so ask for a mountain-view room (extra adult/child $30/15). There's a cosy lounge where you can stay warm by the wood heater. The on-site Blue Moon Restaurant (mains $25 to $34) serves excellent home-cooked food using the best of Tasmanian fresh produce. At the time of writing it was doing dinner for house guests only.

Ol' Jacks Café & Gallery CAFE **$**

(32 Agnes St; mains $4.50-14.50; ⊙breakfast & lunch Tue-Sat) What an asset to Rosebery! You can't miss out on a stop here. It serves delicious, healthy food in relaxed surroundings: focaccias, wraps, a good range of salads, gluten free cakes and daily blackboard specials...and hands-down the best coffee on the west coast. It's big on using Tasmanian produce – organic where possible. Hang out on the sofas, peruse the art gallery, and let the small ones get into the toys in the kids corner.

Rosebery Top Pub
PUB **$**

(☑6473 1351; Agnes St; s with/without bathroom $65/40, d $80-100/60) On Rosebery's main street, this pub has clean and quiet budget rooms (extra person $20) over the bar where you can get chatting with locals. The restaurant serves counter meals (mains $20 to $30, Monday to Saturday).

Rosebery Cabin & Tourist Park
CARAVAN PARK **$**

(☑6473 1366; Park Rd; unpowered/powered sites d $20/25, cabins d $60-90) This park is surrounded by hills and has grassy campsites, a gravel caravan area and basic cabins. It's so shady it can get quite cool once it loses the sun.

ⓘ Information
ATM (Agnes St) Outside the newsagency.
Online Access Centre (⊙10am-5pm Mon-Thu, 10am-1pm Fri & Sat) In the library on Morrisby St.
Post office (Agnes St)

ⓘ Getting There & Away
Tassielink's (www.tassielink.com.au) Launceston–Strahan service stops at Mackrell's Milkbar on Agnes St.

Launceston-Rosebery ($53, 5¼ hrs)
Rosebery-Strahan ($30, 2½ hrs)

Zeehan
POP 900

For Zeehan – as for much of the west coast – the big thing in town has always been mining. In 1882, Frank Long discovered silver and lead on the banks of Pea Soup Creek, marking the first days of a boomtown that became known as Silver City with a population of 10,000 and 27 pubs, the famous Gaiety Grand theatre – seating 1000 people – and even its own stock exchange.

When boom had evolved to bust in the 1960s Zeehan revived its fortunes as dormitory town for the nearby Renison Bell Tin mine. In the 1980s, Renison Bell was Australia's largest underground tin mine and produced 46% of all the country's tin. Boom became bust again in the 1990s. In 2008 Zeehan Zinc expected to make $30 million from its open-cut zinc and lead mine in just six weeks, and the Renison Bell mine opened once again, hoping to ride high on the back of record tin prices. It's rumoured that from 2011 the Avebury nickel mine, west of Zeehan, could be in action again: townspeople look forward to a new boom...or at least a little relief from the doldrums.

Despite the recent mining activity, Zeehan now has that hushed one-horse town feel where you could be forgiven for believing you just saw some tumbleweed roll down the main street. You might stop for the excellent museum, a couple of quirky private collections, or simply to wander Main St and appreciate the period architecture: but do bear in mind much has closed here in recent years...there are more empty shops with bolted doors than ever.

◉ Sights & Activities
West Coast Pioneers Museum MUSEUM
(☑6471 6225; Main St; adult/child $15/4; ⊙9am-5pm) This excellent museum is in the 1894 School of Mines building, and is one of the best regional mining museums in the nation. It also includes displays on the west's rail and shipping heritage. The ground floor features a world-class mineral display, including samples of bright orange crocoite, which is Tasmania's official mineral emblem, only found in this area. Upstairs there's a fascinating photographic history of the west coast. To one side of the museum is an exhibit of steam locomotives and carriages from the early west coast railways, and downstairs is a display of early mining equipment.

Gaiety Grand HISTORIC BUILDING
(Main St; ⊙9am-5pm) Just down the road from West Coast Pioneers Museum and covered by the same entry fee is the Gaiety Grand complex. The Gaiety was one of the biggest, most modern theatres in the world when it opened in February 1898, and what a bonus it must have been for the miners to be able to move between the pub and the theatre through connecting doors. To mark the Gaiety's opening a troupe of 60 was brought to town from Melbourne and played to 1000 spectators every night for a week. Audiences came from as far afield as Queenstown, then a six-hour journey away. Such luminaries as Dame Nellie Melba were included on the billings.

The theatre has recently been beautifully restored to its former glory – complete with gorgeous red velvet drapes – and has occasional ballet and orchestra touring performances. There's also a very worthwhile gallery collection by Tasmanian and local

WARNING

If walking off marked tracks in the bush close to Zeehan or at Trial Harbour, beware of abandoned mine shafts hidden by vegetation.

artists of the west coast. The friendly staff are a veritable (err....) mine of information.

Spray Tunnel   INDUSTRIAL
This 100m long railway tunnel was constructed as part of silver mining operations in 1904. You can now walk through it, and spy the remains of the **Spray Silver Mine** on the other side. Head down Fowler Street from Zeehan's Main St, and park at the Golf Club, from where you'll have to walk a short distance to access the tunnel. There are plenty of other mining relics around town. Just south of town you'll see old **smelters** beside the highway.

Zeehan has two off-beat private collections that are part of local lore and popular with visitors:

Shorty's Private Collection   MUSEUM
(☑6471 6595; 22 Shaw St; admission by gold- coin donation; ☺10am-5pm) An unusual and tongue-in-cheek assemblage of minerals, mining odds and ends, and 'bushcraft oddities' – a display so all-encompassing it even includes a witches' coven!

Dr Frankenstein's Museum of
Monsters   MUSEUM
(☑6471 6580; 12 Whyte St; admission by donation) This eccentric funhouse is open afternoons: ring the doorbell to alert the monster to your arrival. Look out for the sinister two-headed Tasmanian babies. Know the joke, don't you?

✵ Festivals & Events
Zeehan Gem & Mineral Fair   GEMS, MINERALS
In November each year the town comes alive with a festival featuring gems, jewellery, minerals, crystals and fossils for sale or simply for wondering at; as well as gem-fossicking-related activities including gem-panning and crystal hunts.

⌂ Sleeping & Eating
Hotel Cecil   PUB $
(☑6471 6137; www.cecilhotel.com.au; Main St; s $55, d with/without bathroom $75/65, cottages $100-135) Characterful Hotel Cecil has pub rooms

upstairs which come with their own ghost, Maud: the owners will tell you her story. If you're wary of otherworldly happenings, you might prefer the innocuous self-contained miners' cottages just outside. You can eat at Maud's Restaurant (mains $18 to $31, open lunch and dinner Monday to Saturday) here. Its 400g Angus rib eye steak is tops.

Heemskirk Motor Hotel   MOTEL $$
(☑6471 6107; www.heemskirkmotorhotel.com.au; Main St; d $100-150) At the eastern entrance to town, this motel won't win any architectural design awards, but it does have large, clean motel rooms and the Abel Tasman Bistro (mains $15 to $30, open lunch and dinner) which serves Aussie and international fare.

Coffee Stop   CAFE $
(110 Main St; mains $5-15; ☺breakfast & lunch Mon-Sat) The light meals here include quiche, soups and sandwiches, and there are decent fish-and-chip takeaways. It also sells little ornaments made of west coast minerals.

Cribb Hutt   CAFE $$
(☑6471 6122; 79 Main St; mains $15; ☺5am-8pm) This friendly cafe-takeaway is the town's meeting place, and does pizzas, steaks, burgers and excellent homemade egg-and-bacon pies all day. In the evening it offers chicken curry, spag bol, casseroles or roasts and takeaways catering to the young miners in town.

❶ Information
There is a multicard **ATM** in the supermarket.
Visitor's information is available at the West Coast Pioneers Museum.
Online Access Centre (Zeehan Library, Main St; ☺2-4.30pm Mon, 3-7pm Wed, 2-4.30pm Thu, 11am-1pm Fri, 10am-noon Sat) In Zeehan's library.

❶ Getting There & Away
Tassielink's (www.tassielink.com.au) Launceston–Strahan service stops at Coffee Stop on the main street.
Launceston-Zeehan ($62, 5 hrs)
Zeehan-Strahan ($20, 2 hrs)

Strahan
POP 700

Strahan was once dubbed by an American travel writer 'the best little town in the world.' With its perfect location, nestled between the waters of Macquarie Harbour and the rainforest, it has faultless natural assets. Add to that the restored pioneer buildings – the cutesy shops, hotels and cottages crowding up the slope from the compact waterfront – and you've got a scene that's almost Disney-Utopian. If you're more into rugged wilderness you might find Strahan just a bit sugary-sweet, and, dare we say it – it seems Strahan has gone a bit down hill of late. With one big business owning much of the town's centre, there's not much authentic wild west coast left here. Yes, it has all the services to help get you out easily into the wilds – but when you return to town, you might find it all a bit cloyingly tacky. Still, tourists flock here because of the unbelievable beauty that surrounds it.

As the west coast's greatest drawcard, Strahan could have been very different had it not been for a turn of events in the early 1980s. When Tasmania's Hydro-Electric Commission (HEC; now Hydro Tasmania) began construction of a new mega-dam as part of the planned Gordon-below-Franklin power scheme, Strahan became the launching point for Australia's largest and most effective environmental protest. The Franklin River Blockade (see p294) lasted for months in 1982, and was eventually successful in saving from the floodwaters what's now one of the jewels of Tasmania's World Heritage Area: the mirror calm, tannin-brown waters of the lower Gordon River.

Several boats now ply these waters daily, from luxury catamarans to sailing yachts. There are also high-speed adventures to be had around Strahan in jet boats or helicopters, guided explorations by 4WD, or more slow-paced immersion in nature in the form of rainforest and beach walks. While you're here you'll hear about some of the incredible tales of mutiny and escape from the convict settlement on Sarah Island, and the swashbuckling stories of some of the early pioneers. You shouldn't miss Strahan's nightly theatrical performance that's an entertaining primer on all this history.

⊙ Sights

West Coast Reflections   MUSEUM
(Esplanade; adult/child $2/1; ⊙10am-6.30pm summer, noon-5pm winter) This is the museum section of the Strahan visitor centre. It's a creative and thought-provoking display on the history of the west coast, with a refreshingly blunt appraisal of the region's environmental disappointments and achievements, including the Franklin Blockade.

Ocean Beach   BEACH
Six kilometres from town is Ocean Beach, awesome as much for its 33km length as for the strength of the surf that pounds it. This stretch of sand and sea runs uninterrupted from Trial Harbour in the north to Macquarie Heads in the south – and is *the* place to watch the orange orb of the sun melt into the sea. The water is treacherous: don't swim. The dunes behind the beach become a **mutton bird rookery** from October, when the birds return from their 15,000km winter migration. They stay until April, providing an evening spectacle as they return to their nests at dusk.

Henty Dunes   BEACH
Fourteen kilometres along the road from Strahan to Zeehan are the spectacular Henty Dunes, a series of 30m-high sugary-fine sand dunes backing Ocean Beach. Unfortunately, the peaceful beauty is marred by the strident, peace-shattering noises of off-road vehicles, which are permitted here. You can also sandboard down the slopes of

HARBOURS & WEST COAST BACKBLOCKS

To experience the west coast in the raw, visit the tiny wave-lashed settlements of **Trial Harbour** and **Granville Harbour**. Directly west of Zeehan the gravel C248 leads to the former. This was Zeehan's port and is now a ragged collection of holiday shacks and the odd permanent home. There are coastal walks here, good fishing and great free camping in the vicinity – but no shops or facilities. The local **history room** (⊙opening times vary) gives an insight into the early days including tales of the ships that came in and colourful local identities.

Further north, tiny Granville Harbour (reached via the gravel Granville Harbour Rd off the paved C249) is one of the best spots in Tasmania for crayfish. The C249 (which becomes gravel as you head north) also leads to peaceful Corinna, which is the jumping-off point for the Pieman River Cruise (see p240) and driving the Western Explorer (see p239).

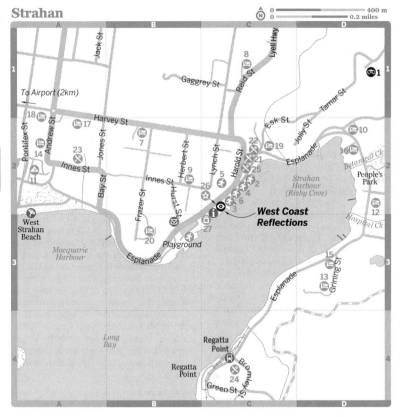

CRADLE COUNTRY & THE WEST

these sandy giants. From the picnic area take the 1½-hour return walk through the dunes and out to Ocean Beach; remember to carry drinking water. You can have fun here playing Lawrence of Arabia crossing the Sahara.

King River   RIVER
Although its condition is slowly improving, the King River has long served as a graphic example of that other west-coast feature: environmental degradation. It was used for many years as a waste sump for mining operations in Queenstown and has sterile, rust-coloured sludge along its banks. Nature is slowly healing itself here, however – it's thought that within a century, the King River could again run clean. It's surrounded by incredible rainforest and you can see much of the length of the river from the West Coast Wilderness Railway (p254) which plies its steep banks.

Hogarth Falls   WATERFALL
This is a pleasant 50-minute return walk through the rainforest beside platypus-inhabited Botanical Creek. The track starts at People's Park, off the Esplanade opposite Risby Cove.

Water Tower Hill   LANDMARK
There's a lookout over the town here, accessed by following Esk St beside the Strahan Village booking office; it's less than 1km from the Esplanade.

Cape Sorell Lighthouse   LANDMARK
The 45m-high lighthouse, at the harbour's southern head, is purportedly the second-highest in Australia. You'll need a boat to cross the heads unless you can find an accommodating fisher to take you over. A return walk of two to three hours along a vehicle track from the jetty at Macquarie Heads leads to the lighthouse.

◎ Top Sights
West Coast Reflections........................C2

◎ Sights
1 Water Tower Hill Lookout...................D1

Activities, Courses & Tours
4 Wheelers....................................(see 2)
Bonnet Island Experience...........(see 2)
2 Gordon River Cruises..........................C2
Gordon River Kayaking...............(see 2)
Shack...(see 5)
Strahan Activity Centre (Pure
Tasmania)...............................(see 2)
Strahan Marine Charters............(see 2)
3 Strahan Seaplanes &
Helicopters..............................C2
4 West Coast Yacht Charters................C2
5 Wild Rivers Jet...................................C2
6 World Heritage Cruises.......................C2

◎ Sleeping
7 Aldermère Estate................................B2
8 Aloft Boutique Accommodation.........C1
9 Crays (Innes St)..................................B2
10 Crays (on the Esplanade)..................D2
11 Discovery Holiday Parks
Strahan...A2

12 Franklin Manor.....................................D2
13 Gordon Gateway................................D3
14 Motel Strahan....................................A2
15 Piners Loft...D3
16 Risby Cove..D2
17 Strahan Backpackers.........................A2
18 Strahan Bungalows............................A1
19 Strahan Village Booking
Office...C2
West Coast Yacht Charters.........(see 4)
20 Wheelhouse Apartments...................B3

◎ Eating
21 Banjo's...C2
Franklin Manor..........................(see 12)
22 Hamer's Hotel....................................C2
23 Molly's...A2
24 Regatta Point Tavern.........................C4
Risby Cove................................(see 16)
25 Schwoch Seafoods............................C2

◎ Entertainment
26 Amphitheatre.....................................C2

◎ Shopping
Cove Gallery..............................(see 16)
27 Strahan Woodworks..........................C3

🏃 Activities

Gordon River Kayaking KAYAKING
(☑6471 4300; Strahan Activity Centre, Esplanade) If you'd like to spend a little time away from the hubbub of the cruise vessels and enjoy the silence of the river, combine a Gordon River trip with a spot of sea-kayaking on the river's mirror-calm waters. Year round, on demand, the full-day tours depart on the *Lady Jane Franklin II* at 8.30am. The kayaks are launched on arrival at Heritage Landing and you paddle upstream into the extreme peace of the river. You pull up for a rainforest lunch stop before drifting back downstream to the cruise boat – then return with the afternoon cruise boat to Strahan via Sarah Island, arriving at 8.30pm in summer, 5.30pm in winter. Tours cost $365 in summer including dinner, $310 without in winter.

Kayak hire KAYAKING
(☑6471 7396; 'The Shack', Esplanade) You can also hire kayaks to take out on your own. Arrange hire (single one hour/half day/full day $35/45/80, double one hour/half day/

full day $45/60/110) at The Shack but you'll need to get around to Risby Cove where the kayaks are kept, for launching.

Wild Rivers Jet JET BOATING
(☑6471 7396; www.wildriversjet.com.au; 'The Shack', Esplanade) This operation runs exhilaratingly speedy 50-minute jet-boat rides up the rainforested gorges of the King River, with Huon pine-spotting stops, for adult/child/family $70/42/190. Take the longer 1¾-hour combined boat/4WD trip (adult/child/family $94/50/249) and you'll also be able to visit the **Teepookana Plateau** with its ancient (and newly planted) Huon pines, and eagle's-eye forest lookout. Bookings recommended.

4 Wheelers QUAD BIKING
(☑6471 4300, 0419 508 175) With these guys, you can do 45 minutes of guided hooning over the Henty Dunes on four-wheeled motorbikes. Trips usually leave hourly in summer from the Henty Sand Dunes car park, 10 minutes' drive north of Strahan, and you can buy tickets here or from the Strahan Activity Centre. Kids can hop on a

THE WEST COAST WILDERNESS RAILWAY

Love the romance of the days of steam? The old wood-lined carriages with shiny brass trimmings, the breathy puffing of steam engines and the evocative, echoing train whistle? Then hop on board, and make the breathtaking 35km rainforest rail journey between Strahan and Queenstown.

When it was first built in 1896, this train and its route through torturously remote country was a marvel of engineering. It clings to the steep-sided gorge of the King River, passing through dense myrtle rainforest, over 40 bridges and on gradients that few other rolling stock could handle. The railway was the lifeblood of the Mt Lyell Mining & Railway Co in Queenstown, connecting it for ore and people haulage to the port of Teepookana on the King River, and later with Strahan. The original railway closed in 1963.

Today the track is magnificently restored, and steam and diesel locomotives take passengers on a four-hour journey over its entire length. Trains depart from Queenstown at 10am and 3pm and Strahan at 10.15am and 3.15pm from the end of December to the end of March. Between April and September, there's a Strahan to Queenstown trip at 10.15am on Tuesday, Wednesday, Friday and Sunday; and a Queenstown to Strahan trip on Monday, Thursday and Saturday at 11am. Costs for riding the full length one way are $111/30/228 per adult/child/family, including lunch. Alternatively, for the same cost, you can ride halfway to the rainforest station at Dubbil Barrel and then hop on the train going back to where you boarded. For one-way rides, there's a bus service back to the embarkation point costing an additional $18/10 per adult/child. There's also a Premier Carriage 1st-class service ($210 per person) which includes extra special food, drinks and service. Inquiries and ticket purchases are at **Queenstown Station** (☑6471 1700; Driffield St) or the **Strahan Activity Centre** (☑6471 4300, 1800 628 286; www.westcoastwildernessrailway.com.au; Esplanade).

buggy (adult driver/first child/second child $50/30/20) as passengers.

Shack
SAND-BOARDING

(☑6471 7396; Esplanade) The towering Henty Dunes are the spot to try your hand at a bit of sand-boarding. You climb the highest dune around, jump on your board and skid down at breakneck speed. The Shack rents boards for $20 for a half-day.

Swimming
SWIMMING

Next to the caravan park is West Strahan Beach, with a gently shelving sandy bottom that provides safe swimming.

☞ Tours

A Gordon River cruise is what most visitors come to do, and no matter how much wilderness beauty you've seen, you can't help but be inspired by the magic of this river: the perfect reflections in its treacle-darkness, the complete peace and the deeply green rainforest that surrounds it.

You can cruise the Gordon on a large, fancy catamaran in the company of a crowd of fellow river admirers (with plenty of comforts laid on) or be a bit more adventurous and visit with a small group by sailing boat. All cruises cross vast Macquarie Harbour before entering the mouth of the Gordon and proceeding to Heritage Landing for a rainforest walk. Most cruises visit Sarah Island – site of Van Diemen's Land's most infamously cruel penal colony – as well as Macquarie Heads and Hells Gates: the narrow harbour entrance. If you visit under sail, you can sneak a little further up the river than other cruise vessels are allowed to go, to beautiful Sir John Falls.

World Heritage Cruises
CRUISES

(☑6471 7174, 1800 611 796; www.worldheritagecruises.com.au; Esplanade) This business is run by the Grining family, which has been taking visitors to the Gordon since 1896, and are Strahan's true river experts. You can join the Grinings aboard their new low-wash environmentally sensitive catamaran, the *Eagle,* for a morning cruise from 9am to 2.45pm, or an afternoon cruise from 3pm to 8.30pm in the summer season (late December to March) only. Prices, depending on whether you take a window seat (premium) or one in the centre of the boat (standard), are adult/child/family at $90/48/247 (standard) and $115/63/310 (premium). All these prices include buffet lunch or dinner. There are no cruises between 15 July and 15 Aug.

Gordon River Cruises · CRUISES

(☑ 6471 4300; www.puretasmania.com.au; Strahan Activity Centre; Esplanade) Run by the conglomerate that now calls itself Pure Tasmania (which seems to own half of Strahan) is the *Lady Jane Franklin II*, departing Strahan at 8.30am and returning 2.15pm, and (in peak season only) also departing at 2.45pm and returning at 8.30pm. There are three levels of service: the Captain's Premium Upper Deck ($1210 for all tickets), a Window Recliner seat (adult/child/family $115/65/295) and Atrium seating in the centre of the vessel ($90/40/230). Lunch, tea and coffee are included in the fare.

West Coast Yacht Charters · CRUISES

(☑ 6471 7422; www.westcoastyachtcharters.com.au; Esplanade) If you'd like your Gordon River experience with a little adventure – and fewer people in the mix – then sailing on *Stormbreaker* is the way to do it. There's a wonderful crayfish lunch, kayaking and fishing cruise that departs on demand most days at noon and returns at 3pm (adult/child $80/60). There's also an overnight trip up the Gordon River, so you can be first to see the undisturbed river reflections when you wake up on the water (adult/child $320/160). The trip departs Strahan at 1pm and returns at noon the following day, with a visit to Sarah Island and meals included. The only cruise licensed to get a full 37km up the Gordon as far as magical Sir John Falls is *Stormbreaker*'s River Rafter Collection Trip (adult/child $250/125) that departs Strahan at 1pm and returns at noon the next day. You'll hear tales of rafting the west's wild rivers as you cruise back to Strahan. On all trips you can do some fishing and take a short paddle in a sea kayak. Just for fun, you could also make this yacht your floating hotel for the night when it's docked in Strahan. You can also buy crayfish at this outfit's office in Strahan.

Strahan Seaplanes & Helicopters · SCENIC FLIGHT

(☑ 6471 7718; www.adventureflights.com.au; Strahan Wharf; ☺ 8.30am-5pm Sep-May) You can't help but be excited when you hear the distinctive buzz of a seaplane: it speaks of adventure and remoteness. Strahan Seaplanes can take you on an 80-minute flight (adult/child three to 11 $199/120) over Ocean Beach and Macquarie Harbour, landing on the Gordon River at Sir John Falls. There are also 15-minute helicopter joyrides taking in Ocean Beach, Hells Gates, Cape Sorell

and Macquarie Harbour ($110/70); and 60-minute helicopter trips (with 25 minutes in the air) up to the Huon pines of the Teepookana Plateau, with hair-raising low flying over the King River ($199/120). For the same price it does another 60 minute flight with a landing on the spectacular summit of Mt Jukes (1168m). The cherry on the top is a 70 minute seaplane flight to Cradle Mountain and Lake St Clair taking in the whole of Tasmania's alpine heart before returning to Strahan (adult/child $210 to $315/$95).

Strahan Marine Charters · CRUISES

(☑ 6471 4300; Strahan Activity Centre, Esplanade) This boat will do trips on demand for $165 per hour to Sarah Island, Hells Gates, the fish farms on Macquarie Harbour or anywhere else you'd like to visit – though if you do want to go as far as the Gordon River, it could cost you an arm and a leg. It will also pick up and drop off kayakers at remote spots on the harbour or river. Fishing gear and a barbecue can be provided.

Bonnet Island Experience · CRUISES

(☑ 6471 4300; Strahan Activity Centre, Esplanade) This trip (adult/child/family $85/40/200) takes you to tiny Bonnet Island at the mouth of Macquarie Harbour where you can watch short-tailed shearwaters and penguins come ashore, and hear stories of the remote lighthouse here and its early keepers. Departure is at dusk, which varies through the year: ask at the Strahan Activity Centre.

Piners & Miners Experience · 4WD

(☑ 6471 4300, 1800 628 286) Immerse yourself in west coast history and get comfortably into the backblocks with these luxury 4WD tours offered by Pure Tasmania. You ride in a Hi-Rail (a Landrover converted to ride on the rail tracks of the West Coast Wilderness Railway before the vehicle retracts its rail-riding wheels and proceeds deep into the bush. You hike to abandoned mining sites and settlements, and learn of the unique history and nature here, before cruising back to Strahan on Macquarie Harbour. The tour costs $365 per person with gourmet food laid on.

Shopping

Strahan Woodworks · SOUVENIRS

(12 Esplanade; ☺ 8.30am-5pm) Here you can see Huon pine, sassafras and myrtle being turned, and then buy the end results, mainly kitchen knick-knacks, platters and ornamental objects.

Cove Gallery ART GALLERY

(Esplanade; ☺8am-6pm summer, 8am-5pm winter) Strahan exhibits more of its creative side here at Risby Cove, with fine woodworking, paintings and crafts to browse and buy.

🛏 Sleeping

TOP CHOICE **Franklin Manor** BOUTIQUE HOTEL $$$

(☑6471 7311; www.franklinmanor.com.au; Esplanade; d $145-250; 🐾) This beautiful historic home is the top spot to stay in Strahan. Set in well-tended gardens just back from the waterfront, it's now an elegant boutique guesthouse with fine rooms, fine dining, and equally fine service (extra person $50). There's a legendary wine cellar, and now also a Tasmanian produce room where you can taste and buy local delicacies. Its restaurant is probably the best in Strahan.

Aldermère Estate APARTMENTS $$$

(☑6471 7418; www.aldermere.com.au; 27 Harvey St; d $260-320) Impeccable Aldermère offers luxurious self-contained, one- or two-bedroom apartments, some with spas. They're absolutely immaculate: beautifully decorated, painstakingly clean, refreshingly spacious, and the friendly management offers use of the guest laundry, books, DVDs and games. A really fantastic place to stay. Extra person $40.

Wheelhouse Apartments RENTAL HOUSE $$$

(☑6471 7777; www.wheelhouseapartments.com. au; 4 Frazer St; d $220-320) Talk about a room with a view! Perched up high above the harbour, these smart and luxurious houses are designed to feel like you're on the bridge of a ship at sea and have seamless acres of glass to give you jaw-droppingly good views over Macquarie Harbour. They're the best spot in Strahan for water panoramas and peaceful seclusion, and they're also wheelchair-accessible. Extra adult $45 to $65, child $25 to $35.

West Coast Yacht Charters B&B $$

(☑6471 7422, 0419 300 994; www.westcoasty achtcharters.com.au; Esplanade; d $100, dm adult/child $50/25) If you're hankering to sleep in a floating bunk on a wharf-moored yacht, then this is a great option. Because the yacht is used for charters, it has late check-in and early check-out (be prepared to check in after 5pm and disembark before 9am). The yacht isn't moored every night, so book ahead. Prices include continental breakfast.

Risby Cove HOTEL, APARTMENTS $$

(☑6471 7572; www.risbycove.com.au; Esplanade; d $160-244) Once a waterfront sawmill complex, Risby Cove is now a smart little enclave done up in corrugated-iron cool. There's a restaurant, a gallery, and eight rooms and one- and two-bedroom spa suites, some with water views (extra adult/child $40/25). You can launch a Macquarie Harbour kayak expedition here: arrange hire at The Shack.

Aloft Boutique Accommodation

APARTMENTS $$

(☑6471 8095; www.aloftaccommodation.com; 15 Reid St; d 145-170;🐾) These are smart, contemporary apartments, with full kitchens or kitchenettes, just up the hill from Strahan's centre (extra person $30). There's free wireless internet and laundry use, and your hosts will book you Strahan activities for no extra cost. No kids please.

Strahan Bungalows APARTMENTS $$

(☑6471 7268; www.strahanbungalows.com.au; cnr Andrew & Harvey Sts; d $90-160) Decorated with a nautical theme, these award-winning bungalows are bright, light and friendly, and are equipped with everything you need for a self-contained stay. They're close to the beach and the golf course, and less than 15 minutes' walk from the centre of town. Extra person $30.

The Crays COTTAGE $$

(☑6471 7422, 0419 300 994; www.thecraysa ccommodation.com; 11 Innes St & 59 Esplanade; d $130-160) The Crays has two self-contained units on Innes St and six new bright, roomy architect-designed cottages on the Esplanade opposite Risby Cove. Extra adult/child $50/30. Guests who stay three nights are rewarded with a succulent Tasmanian crayfish on the house; and there are reduced prices for cruises on the yacht *Stormbreaker*.

Strahan Village HOTEL $$

(☑6471 4200, 1800 628 286; www.pure tasmania.com.au; d $105-330) Much of the accommodation in the centre of town, known as Strahan Village, is now run by Pure Tasmania, which has its booking office (open 7am to 7pm May to October, 24 hours November to April) under the clock tower on the Esplanade. Strahan Village has been garnering very mixed reviews of late: make sure you know exactly what you're reserving.

Strahan Backpackers
HOSTEL $

([☑]6471 7255; 43 Harvey St; unpowered sites d $15-25, dm $25-35, d $69-75, cabins $70-85; [@][🛜]) In an attractive bush setting 15 minutes' walk from the town centre, are plain bunks and doubles, and cute, A-frame cabins. There's a kitchen block, laundry and a games room.

Discovery Holiday Parks Strahan
CARAVAN PARK $$

([☑]6471 7239; cnr Andrew & Innes Sts; unpowered sites d $20-35, powered sites $25-45, cabins $95-150; [@]) Right on Strahan's West Beach, this neat and friendly park has good facilities including a camp kitchen, barbecues and a kids' playground.

Motel Strahan
MOTEL $$

([☑]6471 7555; www.motelstrahan.com.au; 3 Andrew St; d $130-175; [🛜]) The rooms in this complex are quite smart, but it seems housekeeping has got less punctilious of late. Still, it's walkable to town, there's a guests' laundry, and it's also wheelchair-friendly.

Gordon Gateway
APARTMENTS $$

([☑]6471 7165, 1300 134 425; www.gordongateway.com.au; Grining St; d $125-350, extra person $35-55) On the hillside on the way to Regatta Point, this place has motel-like studio units and larger A-frame chalets, most with water and township views. The luxury penthouse is the pick.

Piners Loft
RENTAL HOUSE $$$

([☑]6471 7036, 1300 134 425; www.pinersloft.com.au; Grining St; d $250) This handsome pole house (sleeping six) can be your own private lookout. It's built atop towering poles of three-storey, over three-storeys, so it's best for those who don't mind climbing stairs. Extra person $50.

Camping
CAMPGROUND $

(unpowered sites d $7) Camping is possible at the basic site at Macquarie Heads, 15km southwest of Strahan – follow the signs to Ocean Beach and see the caretaker. There are pit toilets and water, but no showers or kitchen facilities.

✖️ Eating

Franklin Manor
MODERN AUSTRALIAN $$

([☑]6471 7311; Esplanade; 2 courses $47.50, 3 courses $49.50; [🕐]dinner Mon-Sat) A dinner here is sure to be your dining highlight in Strahan. It serves imaginative and beautifully presented dishes in thoroughly elegant surroundings. The food is fancy, but the atmosphere and service are comfortably down to earth. In summer only (from 2pm to 5pm) you can also enjoy high tea here. Highly recommended.

Risby Cove
MODERN AUSTRALIAN $$

([☑]6471 7572; Esplanade; mains $22-36; [🕐]breakfast Dec-Mar, dinner) People come from all over to dine at the Cove. The menu features fancy dishes like red wine and juniper marinated duck breast, there's always fresh Macquarie Harbour ocean trout, and there's a good kids menu too. The views over the water are sensational.

Schwoch Seafoods
FISH & CHIPS $$

(Esplanade; mains $10-26; [🕐]11.30am-8.30pm Mon-Sat, 5-8pm Sun) This little eatery serves up the best fish and chips in town: grilled or battered and just-out-of-the-sea fresh. It serves crayfish too when it's available, and does good burgers and pizzas in the evening. Come to eat-in or for takeaways.

Regatta Point Tavern
PUB $$

(Esplanade; mains $16-35; [🕐]lunch & dinner) If you want to eat with the locals away from the glitz, make your way to this down-to-earth pub near the railway terminus 2km around the bay from Strahan's centre. There are the usual steaks and burgers as well as good fresh fish. Check out the crayfish mornay – in season – if you're after something fancy. It serves good kids meals too.

Hamer's Hotel
PUB $$

(Esplanade; lunch mains $12-22, dinner mains $18-25; [🕐]lunch & dinner) This done-up historic pub is where most tourists go to eat in Strahan and serves a solid menu of pub fare. Try the Macquarie Harbour ocean trout or the huge eye fillet steaks. It's often packed in summer, and it doesn't take bookings: get here early for meals.

Banjo's
BAKERY $

(Esplanade; light meals from $5; [🕐]6am-6pm, hr may vary in winter) This central bakery next to Hamer's Hotel serves reasonable breakfasts and all-day light meals, sandwiches, pies and pastries.

Molly's
FAST FOOD $$

(Innes St; [🕐]6.30am-9pm; [@][🛜]) Drop by for basic food supplies and takeaways.

☆ Entertainment

The Ship that Never Was
THEATRE

([☑]6471 7700; Esplanade; adult/concession/teenager or student $17.50/12.50/7.50) This unmissable production is played out nightly in the amphitheatre adjacent to the Strahan visitor centre. The play tells the story of convicts who escaped from Sarah Island in 1834 by hijacking a ship they were building. It's entertaining fun (with crowd participation) for all age groups (children under 13 years gold coin donation). Performances are held at 5.30pm year-round, and also sometimes at 8.30pm in January.

Hamer's Hotel PUB
(Esplanade) This pub *occasionally* stages live music entertainment. Ask at the Strahan Village reception.

❶ Information

ATM Outside the Strahan activity centre.

Health West (☑6471 7152; Bay St) Strahan's health clinic.

Online Access Centre (⊙12.30-4.30pm Tue, 10am-1pm Wed, 2-5pm Thu; Esplanade) In the library, housed in the Customs House.

Parks & Wildlife Service (☑6471 7122; ⊙9am-5pm Mon-Fri) Also in the Customs House building, adjacent to the library – though not open as many hours as it advertises.

Post office Also in the Customs House building; a Commonwealth Bank agent.

Strahan Activity Centre (☑6471 4300, 1800 084 620; www.puretasmania.com.au; Esplanade) Hotel conglomerate Pure Tasmania owns much of Strahan, and has its own activity/information centre and gift shop on the water in the town centre. You can book its tours as well as some others here.

Strahan visitor centre (☑6472 6800; www.westernwilderness.com.au; Esplanade; ⊙10am-6.30pm summer, noon-5pm winter) This centre incorporates an insightful display on the area's history.

Supermarket/newsagent (Reid St) Also handles ANZ accounts.

❶ Getting There & Around

Tassielink's (www.tassielink.com.au) services arrive at and depart from the visitor centre.

Launceston-Strahan ($82, 7 hrs)

Hobart-Strahan ($75, 7½ hrs)

Strahan-Queenstown ($11, 45 mins)

Strahan Taxis (☑0417 516 071) can run you to surrounding attractions like Ocean Beach (about $15 to $20 each way) and Henty Dunes ($20 each way) and do hotel pick-ups and drop-offs for the morning river cruise departures.

Bicycles are rented out by the **Strahan Activity Centre** (☑6471 4300) for $40 per day.

Cruise passengers can **park** for free at the visitor centre car park (on the concrete only) and opposite Strahan Woodworks ($2 all day).

Spaces in front of the main shopping area have 30- to 60-minute time limits: parking tickets do happen here!

Queenstown

POP 3400

The winding descent into Queenstown from the Lyell Hwy is unforgettable for its moonscape of bare, dusty hills and eroded gullies, where once there was rainforest. The area is the clearest testimony anywhere to the scarification of the west coast's environment by mining. Copper was discovered here in the 1890s and mining has continued ever since, but today pollution is closely monitored and sulphur emissions controlled. Rumour has it that when green started to creep back to these barren hills, Queenstown residents were perplexed: they felt the town's identity was so closely tied to the surrounding barrenness that hills covered in green simply wouldn't do.

Although Queenstown is now getting in on the tourism trend, unlike overcommercialised Strahan, it's still got that authentic, rough-and-ready pioneer town feel. You can spot miners in boilersuits wandering the streets and there's a rich social and industrial history that still feels alive. With the completion of the West Coast Wilderness Railway, Queenstown now has a real tourist hub that is breathing new life into the town.

◉ Sights & Activities

Iron Blow LOOKOUT
On top of Gormanston Hill on the Lyell Hwy, just before the final descent along hairpin bends into Queenstown, is a sealed side road leading to a lookout over the geological wound of Iron Blow. This decommissioned open-cut mine where Queenstown's illustrious mining career began is awesomely deep, and is now filled with emerald water. You can get an eagle's-eye view from the new 'springboard' walkway projecting out into thin air above the mine pit. The views from here are really spectacular, and well worth the short diversion off the highway.

LARQ Gallery ART GALLERY
FREE (☑6471 2805; 8 Hunter Street; ⊙2-6pm Tue-Sat mid-Jan–mid-Jun) Run by internationally renowned Tasmanian artist Raymond Arnold, Landscape Art Research Queenstown is a wonderful gallery that runs exhibitions by local and visiting artists and community workshops in printmaking and painting. Its

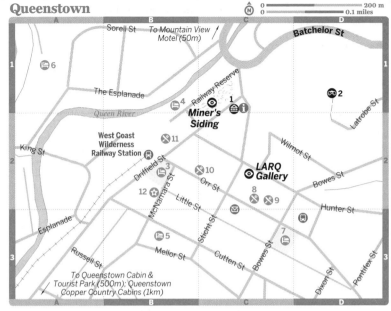

mission is to nurture a breed of art that's inspired by the powerful natural landscapes of the west coast. It's an excellent institution and definitely worth visiting.

Eric Thomas Galley Museum MUSEUM
(☑6471 1483; 1-7 Driffield St; adult/concession/family $5/2.50/12; ☺9.30am-5pm Mon-Fri, 12.30-5pm Sat & Sun, winter hours vary) This museum started life as the Imperial Hotel in 1898 and now houses an extensive photographic collection with wonderfully idiosyncratic captions showing the people and places of Tasmania's west coast, including an exposé of the Mt Lyell mining disaster which claimed 42 lives. There's also a clutter of old memorabilia, household items and clothing, right down to grandma's undies! The friendly volunteers at the counter also offer **tourist information**.

Miner's Siding MONUMENT
Opposite the museum, on the site of the original train station, is the Miner's Siding, a public monument featuring a giant mining drill, a water race and sculptures that commemorate the area's mining heritage. The locomotive that was once parked here is now restored as part of the West Coast Wilderness Railway.

Queenstown

⊙ Top Sights
LARQ Gallery C2
Miner's Siding C1

⊙ Sights
1 Eric Thomas Galley Museum C1
2 Spion Kopf Lookout..............................D1

⊜ Sleeping
3 Empire Hotel..B2
4 Greengate on Central...........................B1
5 Mt Lyell Anchorage..............................B3
6 Penghana...A1
7 Queenstown Motor Lodge..................C3

⊗ Eating
8 Cafe Serenade.......................................C2
Empire Hotel.................................(see 3)
9 Filis Pizza C2
10 Koppa Rock Cafe C2
Maloney's Restaurant ....(see 7)
11 Tracks Café..B2

⊕ Entertainment
12 Paragon Theatre..................................B2

Spion Kopf Lookout LOOKOUT
Follow Hunter St uphill, turn left onto Bowes St, then do a sharp left onto Latrobe St to a small car park, from where a short,

steep track leads to the summit of Spion Kopf (named by soldiers after a battle in the Boer War). The rhododendron-lined track features a rail adit near the car park and the top of the hill has a pithead on it. The panoramic views of town are excellent, particularly at sunset when the bare hills are flaming orange.

Mt Jukes Rd   SCENIC DRIVE
Continue south along Conlan St to Mt Jukes Rd (22km one way) which will take you to side roads leading to sections of the West Coast Wilderness Railway. Further along this scenic road (9km south of Queenstown) is **Newall Creek**, where a platform provides access to a patch of superb King Billy and Huon-pine rainforest. The bitumen section of the road ends at **Lake Burbury**, a hydroelectric dam that can be seen to magnificent effect from a lookout on the descent to its shores.

Tours

Mt Lyell Mine Tours   MINE
TOP CHOICE
(☑0407 049 612) These intensely worthwhile underground mine tours ($100 per person, two hours) take you right down into the working heart of Queenstown's copper mine with interpretation by a local who has worked here for 20 years. You'll be kitted out with gumboots, miner's cap and headlamp and you travel to 500m below sea level along 9kms of tunnels in a troop carrier. You're able to view the working machinery and get to chat with the miners themselves. Tours leave at 10am, 2pm and 7pm on demand: forward bookings essential. No kids under 14.

Mt Lyell Enviro Tours   MINE
(☑0419 104 138) During the summer season this company offers 2½-hour tours ($55 per person) departing at 10am, which interpret over 100 years of copper mining at Mt Lyell. The tours visit the mine's surface and tailings dam only, and focus on the environmental impact of, and remediation after, mining. It also arranges trips to Lakes Margaret and Burbury on request.

Sleeping

Mt Lyell Anchorage   B&B **$$**
(☑6471 1900; www.mtlyellanchorage.com; 17 Cutten St; s $80-130, d $130-160) Though you wouldn't guess from the outside, this 1890s weatherboard home has been completely transformed into a wonderful little guesthouse with quality beds, linen and luxuriously deep carpets. Two of the spacious

rooms have smart en suite bathrooms (the others have private facilities across the hall), there's a shared kitchen and comfortable lounge with wood fire. There are also two self-contained apartments ($150 for up to four people, $200 for up to six). Breakfast provisions included for all.

Penghana   GUESTHOUSE **$$**
(☑6471 2560; www.penghana.com.au; 32 The Esplanade; s $135, d from $150, ste $175; ☎) This National Trust-listed mansion was built in 1898 for the first general manager of the Mt Lyell Mining & Railway Co, and, as befits its managerial stature, is located on a hill above town amid a beautiful garden with a rare number of trees. There's comfortably old-fashioned B&B accommodation here. The house includes a billiards room and a grand dining room for enjoying hearty breakfasts and evening meals by arrangement.

Greengate on Central   APARTMENTS **$$**
(☑6471 1144; 7 Railway Reserve; apt from d $100, family of 4 $160) With shady verandahs, these meticulously tidy, quiet apartments have polished boards and are fully self-contained. They're just a hop and skip from the train station. Great value for money. Extra person $20.

Queenstown Motor Lodge   MOTEL **$$**
(☑6471 1866; www.queenstownmotorlodge.com. au; 54-58 Orr St; d from $100; ☎) While it's no architectural gem, this compact little motel has friendly owners, clean, brightly painted rooms, and is on the quiet part of Queenstown's main street. There's also a good on-site restaurant.

Empire Hotel   PUB **$**
(☑6471 1699; 2 Orr St; s $35, d with/without bathroom $75/50) The rooms here aren't as magnificent as the imposing blackwood staircase that's a National Trust-listed treasure, but they are clean and tended by friendly staff who make you feel at home. It serves excellent meals in the dining room downstairs.

Queenstown Copper Country Cabins   CABINS **$$**
(☑0417 398 343; 13 Austin St; d $95-110, extra adult $15) These self-contained timber cabins, one of which is equipped for disabled travellers, are set in flourishing gardens. Though not exactly your stylish brand of accommodation, they're incredibly neat and tidy.

LINDA VALLEY CAFÉ

In mining boom days, hundreds of people lived in Gormanston and Linda Valley, in the hills just west of Queenstown. Today there are just four residents in Linda Valley...and one unexpected gem. Next to the derelict Royal Hotel Linda Valley (about 5kms west of Queenstown on the Lyell Hwy) is the much lauded **Linda Valley Café** (☑6471 3082; mains $32-35; ☺breakfast, lunch & dinner in summer, reduced hours in winter) which locals swear serves some of the best food on the west coast. It's contemporary, delicious dining in unpretentious surrounds: things like slow roasted pork belly, lemon pepper squid, special liqueur coffees and beautiful homemade cakes. There's free camping for tents and RVs out the back.

Mountain View Motel MOTEL $
(☑6471 1163; 1 Penghana Rd or Lyell Hwy; d $80, dm $25) Parts of this age-old motel used to be single mens quarters for the mine: now converted to budget twin backpacker rooms. We recommend it just for these.

Queenstown Cabin & Tourist Park CARAVAN PARK $
(☑6471 1332; 17 Grafton St; unpowered/powered sites $20/25, on-site vans d $60, d cabins $70-90) You have to drive through run-down suburbs to get here, and though this basic, rather depressing, park is set on gravel, it does have a small grassy camping area. Extra adult $10 to $15, extra child $5, linen hire $5.

There is also **camping** at Lake Burbury.

✗ Eating

Café Serenade CAFE $
(☑40-42 Orr St; mains $10-14.50; ☺breakfast & lunch; ☑) This is hands-down the best cafe in Queenstown. The food is deliciously homemade from scratch: yummy soups, sourdough toasted sandwiches, salads and good vegetarian options; as well as hearty roasts and curries. It also does gluten-free and dairy-free sweet treats, and the coffee is excellent. What a find!

Tracks Cafe CAFE $$
(Queenstown Station, Driffield St; mains $14-20; ☺breakfast & lunch) Tracks is a good option if you're a bit of a trainspotter. It serves smooth, creamy coffee and cafe staples like gourmet pies and sandwiches, as well as cakes. You can also sit alfresco on the train platform itself.

Empire Hotel PUB $$
(☑6471 1699; 2 Orr St; mains $12-17; ☺lunch & dinner) This old miners' pub has survived the ages and includes an atmospheric heritage dining room serving a changing menu of hearty pub standards, including roasts, pastas, and fine steaks and ribs.

Maloney's Restaurant BISTRO $$
(☑6471 1866; 54-58 Orr St; mains $18-32; ☺dinner Mon-Sat) Who would expect such good food in a small-town motel? It's quite sophisticated fare here all cooked fresh to order. Try the Maloney's chicken stuffed with camembert and sundried tomatoes. It does a great sticky date pudding too.

Koppa Rock Cafe CAFE $
(☑6471 1222; 7 Orr Street; meals from $6.50; ☺7am-8pm, sometimes closed Sun) Source good hamburgers and toasted sandwiches here, and also fry-ups like country fried chicken, wedges and doughnuts. Takeaway available.

Filis Pizza PIZZA $$
(☑6471 2006; 21 Orr St; pizzas $12-26; ☺4pm-9.30pm) This friendly place offers many different takes on the humble pizza. The roast garlic and olive supreme with roasted chicken is tops.

☆ Entertainment

The Paragon Theatre CINEMA
(www.theparagon.com.au; 1 McNamara St; ☺2pm-6.30pm, reduced hrs in winter, $10 per hr) This amazingly refurbished art deco theatre shows some Hollywood films, but, more interestingly, a revolving program of short films about the west coast and Queenstown (hence the price per hour, rather than per film). You can take your coffee or a glass of vino (and popcorn of course) into the theatre with you where seating is in deep leather couches. It's been so beautifully done up, it's worth a look inside even if you aren't going to watch a film.

❶ Information

ATM (Orr St) Commonwealth Bank ATM.
Parks & Wildlife Service (☑6471 2511; Penghana Rd; ☺8.30am-9.30am) Get advice here

WORTH A TRIP

DETOUR: LAKE BURBURY

Heading south out of Queenstown along Conlan St to Mt Jukes Rd for about 15 minutes you'll come to the end of the bitumen road that leads to Lake Burbury. Built as a large hydroelectric dam, the dam's construction flooded 6km of the old Lyell Hwy. The lake is surrounded by the Princess River Conservation Area, and the scenery around it is magnificent – especially when there's snow on the nearby peaks. There are impressive vistas from the attractive shoreline **camping ground** (unpowered sites for 2 people $7) just east of Bradshaw Bridge. Here there's also a public picnic area with sheltered electric barbecues and a children's playground. Fishermen say the trout in Lake Burbury make for some of the best fishing in Tasmania.

on nearby walking tracks and buy national park passes if you haven't obtained them previously. Rafters take note: if you intend to use the Mt McCall Rd 4WD track from the southern end of Lake Burbury to the Franklin River, ask the ranger for a free permit and a gate key. Ring and book the key prior to coming to Queenstown. The office is located just out of the town centre on Penghana Rd, (which becomes the Lyell Hwy (A10) to Strahan).

Queenstown visitor centre (☎6471 1483; 1-7 Driffield St) In the Eric Thomas Galley Museum and run by volunteers. At time of writing an improved visitor centre was under construction in a new complex next door.

ⓘ Getting There & Away

Tassielink's (www.tassielink.com.au) services arrive at and depart from the milk bar at 65 Orr St.

Hobart-Queenstown ($65, 6 hrs)

Launceston-Queenstown via Strahan ($72, 5½ hrs)

Franklin-Gordon Wild Rivers National Park

The centrepieces of this environmentally awesome park are the wild, pristine rivers that twist their way through the infinitely rugged landscapes here and give the national park its name. The park is part of the Tasmanian Wilderness World Heritage Area

and encompasses the catchments of the Franklin, Olga and Gordon Rivers. It was proclaimed in 1981 after the failed campaign to stop the flooding of precious Lake Pedder under the waters of the Pedder/Gordon hydroelectric dam scheme (see p271) and p294). The park is probably best known as the site of Australia's biggest-ever environmental battle, the Franklin River Blockade, which drew national and international attention and was ultimately successful in saving the wilderness from further dams.

The battle to save the lower Gordon and Franklin Rivers was played out in Tasmania in the early 1980s. Despite national park status and then World Heritage nomination, dam-building plans here by the then-Hydro Electric Commission (HEC) continued. In the aftermath of Lake Pedder's flooding, public opinion on the matter was clear: when a 1981 referendum asked Tasmanians to decide between two different dam schemes, 46% of voters scribbled 'No Dams' across their ballot papers. Politically, the state was in turmoil, and both the premier and opposition party leader were dumped over the dams issue. A state election resulted in a change of government, but no change in plans to go ahead with a new mega-dam. When the World Heritage Committee eventually announced the area's World Heritage listing and expressed concern over the proposed dam, the new state premier attempted to have the listing withdrawn.

Antidam and proconservation lobbyists then turned their attention to the federal arena. In May 1982, at a Canberra by-election, 41% of voters wrote 'No Dams' on their ballot papers, but the federal government still refused to intervene.

Dam construction began in 1982 and protesters from all over Tasmania set off from Strahan to stage what became known as the 'Franklin River Blockade'. Press pictures from the time show flotillas of blow-up dinghies stretched across the river, blocking the HEC boats' access to the dam work site. Despite the peaceful protests, the Tasmanian government passed special laws allowing protesters to be arrested, fined and jailed. In the summer of 1982-83, 1400 people were arrested in a confrontation so intense it received international news coverage.

The Franklin River became a major issue in the 1983 federal election, which was won partly on a 'No Dams' promise by the incoming Labor party, which then fully implemented the Franklin and Gordon Rivers' World Heritage assignation, finally protecting the rivers and rainforests fully.

The national park's most significant peak is **Frenchmans Cap** (1443m), with a white-quartzite top that can be seen from the west coast and from the Lyell Hwy. The mountain was formed by glacial action and has Tasmania's tallest cliff face.

The park also contains a number of unique plant species and major Aboriginal sites. The most significant is **Kutikina Cave**, where over 50,000 artefacts have been found, dating from the cave's 5000-year-long occupation between 14,000 and 20,000 years ago. The only way to reach the cave, which is on Aboriginal land in remote forest, is by rafting down the Franklin.

Walks

Much of the park consists of deep river gorges and impenetrable rainforest, but the Lyell Hwy traverses its northern end. Along this road are a number of signposted features of note, including a few short walks that you can take to see just what this park is all about:

Collingwood River This is the usual put-in point for rafting the Franklin River, of which the Collingwood is a tributary. You can camp for free here; there are pit toilets and fireplaces.

Donaghy's Hill Located 4km east of the bridge over the Collingwood River, this 40-minute return walk leads to the top of the hill above the junction of the Collingwood and Franklin Rivers. It has spectacular views of the Franklin and Frenchmans Cap.

Franklin River Nature Trail From the picnic ground where the highway crosses the river, a 25-minute return nature trail has been marked through the forest.

Frenchmans Cap Six kilometres further east is the start of the three- to four-day return walk to Frenchmans Cap. There are two shelter huts along the way (though you'll need a tent) and much infamous mud, particularly on the plains known as the Sodden Loddons. Even if you don't intend doing the whole bush walk, you'll enjoy the initial 15-minute walk along the banks of the Franklin River. The Tassielink Hobart-Strahan service stops on request at the beginning of this walk. You can also do this walk as a guided trip (six days, $1695) with **Tasmanian Expeditions** (☑1300 666 856, 6331 9000; www.tasmanian expeditions.com.au).

Nelson River Just east of Lake Burbury, at the bottom of Victoria Pass, is an easy 20-minute return walk through rainforest to 35m-high Nelson Falls. Signs beside the track highlight common plants of the area.

Rafting the Franklin

Rafting the Franklin River is about as wild and thrilling a journey as it's possible to make in Tasmania. This is really extreme adventure. Experienced rafters can tackle it independently if they're fully equipped and prepared, but for anyone who's less than completely river-savvy (and that's about 90% of all Franklin rafters), there are tour companies offering complete rafting packages. If you go with an independent group you must contact the park rangers at the **Queenstown Parks and Wildlife Service** (☑6471 2511; Penghana Rd) for current information on permits, regulations and environmental considerations. You should also check out the Franklin rafting notes on the PWS website at www.parks.tas.gov.au.

All expeditions should register at the booth at the junction of the Lyell Hwy and the Collingwood River, 49km west of Derwent Bridge. The trip down the Franklin, starting at Collingwood River and ending at Sir John Falls, takes between eight and 14 days, depending on river conditions. Shorter trips on certain sections of the river are also possible. From the exit point at Sir John Falls, you can be picked up by a **Strahan Seaplanes & Helicopters** (☑6471 7718) seaplane or by **West Coast Yacht Charters'** (☑6471 7422) *Stormbreaker* for the trip back to Strahan. You can also just do half the river. The upper Franklin takes around eight days from Collingwood River to the Fincham Track – it passes through the bewitchingly beautiful Irenabyss Gorge and you can scale Frenchmans Cap as a side trip. The lower Franklin takes seven days from the Fincham Track to Sir John Falls and passes through Great Ravine.

These tour companies offer complete rafting packages:

Rafting Tasmania (☑6239 1080; www. raftingtasmania.com) Has five-/seven-/10-day trips costing $1750/2100/2700.

PARK ACCESS & WEATHER CONDITIONS

To keep traffic out of the park itself, most access is now by **shuttle bus**. Buses run every 10 to 20 minutes between about 8am and 8pm in summer (reduced hours in winter) from the **Cradle Mountain Transit Centre** (by the visitor centre) where you park your car. The fare is included in a valid parks pass. Buses stop at the Rangers Station interpretation centre, Snake Hill, Ronny Creek and Dove Lake. Note: it's best to visit the interpretation centre on your way out of the park as the shuttle bus will return you to the visitor centre from here and you'll have to wait for another bus into the park. There is limited parking for cars (no campervans) at Dove Lake on a first come, first served basis. You'll need a valid parks pass. The boom gate into the park closes once parking capacity is reached.

Whatever time of the year you visit, be prepared for cold, wet weather in Cradle Valley and on the Overland Track: it rains on seven out of 10 days, is cloudy on eight out of 10 days, the sun shines all day only one day in 10, and it snows in Cradle Valley on 54 days each year. You could find yourself camping in the snow at any time of year, but you also need to be aware of sunburn, not just in summer. Winds can be extreme. Be well prepared with warm and waterproof gear, and be weather savvy – check expected conditions and be prepared for these to change.

Tasmanian Expeditions (☎1300 666 856, 6331 9000; www.tasmanianexpeditions.com.au) Has nine-/11-day trips for $2595/2795.

Water By Nature (☎1800 111 142, 0408 242 941; www.franklinriver.com) This outfit provides five-/seven-/10-day trips for $1940/2240/2790 and you get to fly out of the Gordon River in a seaplane. Also offers climbs of Frenchmans Cap.

Maps
For adventures in this region, you'll need Tasmap's 1:100,000 *Olga and Franklin* and 1:25,000 *Loddon* maps, available from the Tasmanian Map Centre and Service Tasmania in Hobart (see p76).

CRADLE MOUNTAIN–LAKE ST CLAIR NATIONAL PARK

Cradle Mountain – that perfect new-moon curve of rock that photographers love to capture reflected in mirror-still waters – has become something of a symbol of Tasmania. It's perhaps the best-known feature of the island and is regarded as the crowning glory of the 1262-sq-km Cradle Mountain–Lake St Clair National Park. Its glacier-sculpted mountain peaks, profound river gorges, lakes, tarns and wild alpine moorlands extend from the Great Western Tiers in the north to Derwent Bridge in the south. The park encompasses Mt Ossa (1617m), Tasmania's

highest peak, and Lake St Clair (200m), the deepest lake in Australia, brimming with the clear, fresh waters of this pristine environment.

The legendary adventure within the park is the celebrated Overland Track – a week-long hike that's become something of a holy grail for bushwalkers. The 80km track stretching from Cradle Mountain to Cynthia Bay on Lake St Clair (Leeawuleena or 'sleeping water' to Tasmania's indigenous people), is an unforgettable journey through Tasmania's alpine heart.

Information

Cradle Mountain visitor centre (☎6492 1110; www.parks.tas.gov.au; ⏰8am-5pm, reduced hrs in winter) is just outside the park boundary. Here you can buy your parks pass, get detailed bushwalking information and maps, weather condition updates, advice on bushwalking gear, bush safety and bush etiquette. In mid-summer there's a program of free activities run by park rangers: enquire at the visitor centre. The centre has toilets, a small shop-cafe and Eftpos (cash out *may* be available). It also accepts credit card payment. There are no ATMs. There's no drinking water to fill up with here: only bottled water to buy in the shop.

Just inside the park boundary is the **Rangers Station interpretation centre** (⏰9am-5pm during Daylight Saving, 9.30am-4pm in winter). At time of writing it was building an auditorium for video presentations on the natural history of Cradle Mountain and the tracks in the area. There are also Aboriginal cultural displays here.

Cynthia Bay, on the southern boundary of the park, has the **Lake St Clair visitor centre** (☑6289 1172; ☺8am-5pm Sep-Apr, 8.30am-4.30pm May, 9am-4pm Jun-Aug, may vary). It provides park and walking information and has displays on the area's geology, flora and fauna and Aboriginal heritage. If you've forgotten your rain gear you can pick up some waterproof attire in the shop here.

At the adjacent **Lake St Clair Lodge** (☑6289 1137; www.lakestclairresort.com.au; 8am-8pm Nov-Mar, 8.30am–5pm Apr-Oct), you can book a range of accommodation in Cynthia Bay, a seat on a ferry or a lake cruise (p270).

The Overland Track

This is Tasmania's iconic alpine journey: a six- to eight- day odyssey with backpack through incredible World-Heritage mountainscapes. If you have experience of camping and multiday hikes, good fitness and are well prepared for Tasmania's erratic weather, it's a very achievable independent adventure. Inexperienced walkers should consider going with a guided group (see p266).

Most hikers walk the Overland Track during summer when alpine plants are fragrantly in flower, daylight hours are long, and one can work up enough heat to swim in one of the frigid alpine tarns. The track is also most busy at this time and is subject to a crowd-limiting booked permit system. The track is quiet and icily beautiful for experienced walkers in winter. Spring and autumn have their own charms, and fewer walkers than in summer.

Apart from in the peak time, when a north-south walking regulation is enforced, the track can be walked in either direction. The trail is well marked for its entire length. Side trips lead to features like Mt Ossa, and some fantastic waterfalls – so it's worth budgeting time for some of these. Apart from in the dead of winter, you can expect to meet many walkers each day.

There are unattended huts with bare wooden bunks and coal or gas heaters spaced at a day's walking distance along the track: but don't count on any room inside in summer, and carry a tent. Camp fires are banned and you must carry a fuel stove for cooking.

The walk itself is extremely varied, negotiating high alpine moors, rocky scree, gorges and tall forest. A detailed description of the walk and major side trips is given in Lonely Planet's *Walking in Australia*. For further notes on the tracks in the park, read *Cradle Mountain–Lake St Clair and Walls of Jerusalem National Parks* by John Chapman and John Siseman. A handy pocket-sized reference for the walk is the PWS *Overland Track: One walk, many journeys,* which has notes on ecology and history plus illustrations of flora and fauna you may see along the way. You can get all the latest on the track and walk-planning at www.overlandtrack.com.au. The reference map for the track and surrounds is the 1:100,000 *Cradle Mountain–Lake St Clair* map published by Tasmap.

Other Walks

Cradle Valley

From the interpretation centre you can take an easy but quite spectacular 10-minute circular boardwalked **Rainforest Walk**. There's another boarded path nearby leading to **Pencil Pine Falls** which may be possible for some wheelchair users. This route continues to **Knyvet Falls** (not wheelchair accessible – 25 minutes return). There's also the child-friendly **Enchanted Nature Walk** alongside Pencil Pine Creek (25 minutes return). The easy 8.5km **Cradle Valley Walk** between the interpretation centre and Dove Lake is boardwalked up to Ronny Creek only (5.5km); the rest of the track to Dove Lake can get quite muddy.

Crater Lake is a popular two-hour return walk from Ronny Creek. You can also make the spectacular climb to the summit of **Cradle Mountain**: the views are incredible in fine weather, but it's not advised in bad visibility or when it's snowy and icy in winter. Allow about eight hours from the Dove Lake carpark or Ronny Creek.

Otherwise, marvel at Cradle Mountain from below – if the weather gods oblige – from the easy two- to three-hour circuit track around **Dove Lake**. Other walks in the area involve steep climbs. The **Twisted Lakes** walk via **Hansons Peak** provides great views of Cradle Mountain.

Cynthia Bay

The **Larmairremener tabelti** is an Aboriginal cultural-interpretative walk that winds through the traditional lands of the Larmairremener, the indigenous people of the region. This easy one-hour return walk starts at the visitor centre and loops through the lakeside forest before leading along the lake's shoreline back to the centre. From Watersmeet, near the visitor centre, you can also

LICENCE TO WALK

The Overland Track is struggling under the weight of its own popularity. Recent years have seen 9000 walkers tread its paths annually. With all those feet on the ground, washing up scraps around camps, and human waste to deal with, there have been some big questions about environmental sustainability. Only careful management will prevent this route from being loved to death. To help keep walker numbers manageable and the walking experience one of wilderness, not crowd-dodging, the following rules apply:

» There's a booking system in place from 1 November to 30 April, when a maximum of 34 walkers can depart each day.

» There are fees of $160/128 per adult/child aged five to 17 and concession, to cover costs of sustainable track management (these apply from November to April only).

» The compulsory walking direction from November to April is north to south.

There's a web-based booking system for walking permits on the Overland Track website at www.overlandtrack.com.au, or call ☑6233 6047 for more information.

take the **Platypus Bay Circuit** (30 minutes return). Most other walks are fairly long: the circuit of **Shadow Lake** takes four to five hours return, while the highly worthwhile **Mt Rufus** circuit is at least seven hours return.

To take in just a little of the Overland Track magic, you can also catch the ferry to **Echo Point** (three to four hours back to Cynthia) or **Narcissus Hut** – five to seven hours' walk back to Cynthia Bay along the lakeshore.

Tours

Tasmanian Expeditions GUIDED WALKING
(☑1300 666 856, 6331 9000; www.tasmanian expeditions.com.au) Between October and May Tasmanian Expeditions does a seven-day Overland Track trek (from $2095), and a 10-day Cradle Mountain Explorer trip which includes a side trip to exquisite Pine Valley and The Labyrinth (from $2695). It also does a hut-based three-day Cradle Mountain Experience ($950) and a six-day Cradle MountainWalls of Jerusalem walk from $1695 (see 216).

Cradle Mountain Huts GUIDED WALKING
(☑6391 9339; www.cradlehuts.com.au) If camping isn't for you, then from October to May you can take a six-day guided walk in a small group (four to 10 people) along the Overland Track which includes accommodation in private huts. Trips cost $2600 October to December and April and May, $2800 January to March. The fee includes meals, national park entry fees and transfer to/from Launceston. Gear hire is also available.

Cradle Park Explorer Tour 4WD
(☑6394 3535; www.mcdermotts.com.au) A Park Explorer Tour (adult/child $15.40/10) will get you conveniently to the park's bus-accessible highlights for a spot of walking. McDermotts also do a 4WD tour for evening wildlife-spotting ($25/12.50) and one that combines watching devil feeding at Devils@ Cradle and night-time wildlife spotting in a 4WD ($40/30). Trips leave from the Cradle Mountain Transit Centre. National park entry is additional. It also does a day tour from Launceston: see its website.

Grayline BUS
(☑6234 3336; www.grayline.com) Offers a day coach tour from Launceston to Cradle Mountain (adult/child $159/79.50) including a hike around Dove Lake on Monday, Wednesday, Friday and Sunday leaving at 8.30am and returning at 5pm.

Cradle Country Adventures HORSE, QUAD BIKE
(☑1300 656 069; www.cradlecountryadventures. com.au) The country around Cradle is perfect riding territory, and travelling on the back of one of this operator's friendly horses is a perfect way to see it. Half-day, full-day and multiday riding trips are available (two hour trip $95, full-day from $220). For some muddy, wheel-spinning adventures, just outside the World Heritage areas, these guys also do quad bike tours (www.cradlemountainquadbikes. com.au; 2hr trip $110). Kids can go as passengers (two hours $66).

Cradle Mountain Helicopters FLIGHTS
(☑6492 1132; www.adventureflights.com.au) You can get a spectacular bird's-eye view over Tasmania's alpine heart by taking a helicop-

ter joy ride. The choppers leave from the airstrip next to the visitor centre, and 30-minute flights cost from $190/140 per adult/child. You can get all your postcard-perfect shots of sights like Cradle Mountain, Dove Lake and little-seen Fury Gorge. It also does longer charter flights.

🛏 Sleeping & Eating
CRADLE VALLEY
The Cradle Valley has heaps of accommodation options, but if you find yourself unable to secure a booking you could always try Gowrie Park (p217) or Tullah (p245). A lot of the accommodation here is self-catering but there's no supermarket: bring your own supplies.

TOP CHOICE **Cradle Mountain Highlanders Cottages** COTTAGES $$
(☑6492 1116; www.cradlehighlander.com.au; Cradle Mountain Rd; d $115-250) This is the best kept secret at Cradle Mountain! The genuinely hospitable hosts here have a charming collection of immaculately kept self-contained timber cottages. All have wood or gas fires, queen-sized beds, electric blankets and continental breakfast provisions (extra adult/child $30/20). Three cabins include a spa; and all are serviced daily. The surrounding bush is peaceful and filled with wildlife that will pay you a visit. A really wonderful place to stay.

Cradle Mountain Lodge HOTEL $$$
(☑6492 2103, 1300 806 192; www.cradlemountainlodge.com.au; Cradle Mountain Rd; d $310-760; extra adult $72; @) When this mountain resort of wooden cabins emerges from the swirling mist on a winter's day, you can't help but be charmed by its ambience. If you're after contemporary style, however, you might be disappointed: although some of the rooms have had a contemporary spruce-up, others are rather dated. The lodge puts on activities and guided walks and the Waldheim Alpine Spa offers relaxing massages and beauty treatments. There's hearty mountain fare in the **Tavern** (mains $16-26; ☺lunch and dinner), but the **Highland Restaurant** (2-/3-/5-course degustation menu $56/65/85, ☺dinner) is the real culinary experience here: fine dining to linger over, accompanied by Tasmanian wines. The Lodge is also the venue for the renowned winter foodie event **Tastings at the Top**, a three-day festival of gastronomic delights held in mid- to-late June.

Waldheim Chalet & Cabins CABINS $$
(☑6491 2271; 4-bed $95, 6-bed $135, 8-bed $185) Set in the forest near the original Wein-dorfers' chalet are some rustic wood-lined cabins with bunks sleeping eight, six and four. Each has kitchen facilities and there's a shared shower and toilet block. Despite its simplicity, this is a lovely place to stay in a gorgeous setting.

Cradle Mountain Wilderness Village APARTMENTS, COTTAGES $$$
(☑6492 1500; www.cradlevillage.com.au; Cradle Mountain Rd; cottages d $180, chalets & villas sleeping up to 4 $360; @) When you walk into the reception here on a clear day, you'll be treated to some exceptional views of Cradle Mountain. There are some quite luxurious chalets and cabins set peacefully in the trees, but they're painted in such perfect eucalypt greys and greens that it feels almost like army-barrack camouflage.

Cradle Mountain Chateau HOTEL $$
(☑6492 1404, 1800 420 155; www.puretasmania.com.au; Cradle Mountain Rd; standard d $131-289, spa d $144-320, ste $162-360; @🕾) This large complex is the first you come to on the way into Cradle Valley, and heralds its presence with a grand porticoed gate. Though the public areas are pleasantly timbered and log fire-warmed, the rooms are frankly rather motel-ish. Get one on the front side to ensure your morning view isn't one of the gravel car park. There's a bistro serving good nosh (open breakfast, lunch & dinner) and the Calm day spa where you can have relaxing treatments.

Wilderness Gallery
(☑6492 1404; www.wildernessgallery.com.au; Cradle Mountain Rd; admission $7, free for guests; ☺10am-5pm) The highlight of the Cradle Mountain Chateau complex is undoubtedly

DON'T MISS
DEVILS @ CRADLE
This excellent **Tasmanian devil park** (☑6492 1491; www.devilsatcradle.com; adult/child/family $15/10/40-55; ☺10am-4pm) is the place to have close encounters with these fascinating creatures and learn about the facial tumour disease that's threatening their survival. The mainly nocturnal animals are observed most spectacularly at feeding times (5.30pm, also 8.30pm during daylight saving only). Entry fees for the night feeding tours are adult/child/family $25/12.50/60-80.

If not for the forward-looking vision of one Gustav Weindorfer, Cradle Mountain might never have been incorporated into a national park. Weindorfer, an Austrian immigrant, first came to Cradle in 1910 and built a wooden cabin, Waldheim (German for 'Forest Home'), in 1912 in this rugged and isolated wonderland. Weindorfer and his Australian wife, Kate, took their honeymoon at Waldheim and fell in love with Tasmania's alpine heart. Recognising its uniqueness, they lobbied successive governments for its preservation.

Kate Weindorfer had a passion for botany and became an expert in the area's bushland and flora, encouraging Gustav's appreciation of the landscape. Their spirit was tenacious: in those days a horse and cart could only get within 15km of Cradle Mountain, and from there they walked to Waldheim while packhorses carried supplies. The Weindorfers encouraged visitors to come to this remote place and share in its marvels.

Kate died in 1916 from a long illness, and Gustav moved to Waldheim permanently, devoting his life to preserving the mountain he loved. He died in 1932, and half a century later Cradle Mountain was finally declared a national park.

The original chalet burnt down in a bushfire in 1974, but was rebuilt using traditional carpentry techniques and stands as a monument to the Weindorfers. Just inside the doorway is Gustav's original inscription: 'This is Waldheim/Where there is no time/And nothing matters.'

this impressive gallery showcasing incredible environmental photography. It also has a fascinating new **thylacine exhibition**, complete with the only thylacine-skin rug in existence.

Discovery Holiday Parks Cradle Mountain
CARAVAN PARK $$
(☑6492 1395, 1800 068 574; www.discoveryparks. com.au; Cradle Mountain Rd; unpowered/powered sites d $32/45, dm $42, cabins $160-200; @☎) This bushland complex is 2.5km from the national park. It has well-separated sites, a YHA- affiliated hostel, a camp kitchen and laundry and self-contained cabins.

Cradle Wilderness Cafe
CAFE $$
(☑6492 1024; Cradle Mountain Rd; mains $9-10; ☺8am-9pm Dec-Mar/Apr, 9am-5pm Apr-Nov) This cafe next to the visitor centre does coffee, light meals and snacks. Pick up last-minute sandwiches for your walk here. There's pasta and pizza in the evening in summer.

ROAD TO CRADLE MOUNTAIN
Lemonthyme Lodge
HOTEL $$
(☑6492 1112; www.lemonthyme.com.au; Dolcoath Rd, Moina; lodge d from $130, cabins $195-395; @) Off Cradle Mountain Rd at Moina is this secluded mountain retreat offering cabins, some with spa, and rooms in the main lodge with shared facilities – though the word is that these rooms can be noisy (extra adult/child $35/25). Hang out by the roaring fire before dinner in the restaurant (two/three

courses $47.50/60, open breakfast, lunch and dinner). There's animal-feeding nightly at 8.30pm and good walks on the property. Driving to Cradle Mountain from Devonport, turn onto the gravel Dolcoath Rd 3km south of Moina and follow it for a scenic 8km to get here.

Cradle Chalet
HOTEL $$
(☑6492 1401; www.cradlechalet.com.au; 1422 Cradle Mountain Rd, Moina; d $175-240) There are attractive timber chalets in a bushland setting here. You can soak up the peace from your own private deck or chat with the friendly hosts, who are a mine of regional advice. The rooms include continental breakfast, and evening meals are by arrangement (two/ three courses $50/63). No kids under 15.

CYNTHIA BAY
Lake St Clair Lodge
COTTAGES $-$$$
(☑6289 1137; www.lakestclairresort.com.au; unpowered/powered sites d $25/35, dm/d $35/80, cottages d $240-265) There are unpowered bush camping sites on the lakeshore here, and powered caravan spots. The backpackers lodge has two- to four-bunk rooms and kitchen facilities. There are also upmarket self-contained cottages (extra person $35). Another option is cute, old-fashioned Mimosa, bang on the waterfront, ($190 for four people) which has its own kitchen but shares amenities. In the main building opposite the Lake St Clair visitor centre there's a cafe (lunch mains $8 to $22.50, dinner

mains $18.50 to $31, open 8am to 8pm November to March, 8.30am to 5pm April to October), serving a hearty menu to fill you up before or after a bushwalk. Last orders at 6.30pm.

You can camp for free at **Fergy's Paddock**, 10 minutes' walk back along the Overland Track. You'll need your parks pass. There are pit toilets, and fires are not allowed so take a fuel stove for cooking.

DERWENT BRIDGE & BRONTE PARK

Derwent Bridge is 5km from Lake St Clair and has a few good accommodation options, otherwise the nearest place to stay is Bronte Park, 30km from Lake St Clair, in the direction of Hobart.

Derwent Bridge Wilderness Hotel HOTEL **$$** (☑6289 1144; Derwent Bridge; dm $30, linen $5, d with/without bathroom $140/120) This chalet-style pub has a high-beamed roof and a pleasingly country feel: enjoy a beer or a hot drink in front of the massive log fire. The hostel and hotel accommodation is plain but comfortable, and the restaurant (mains $20.50 to $49.50, open breakfast, lunch and dinner) serves commendable pub fare, including excellent roasts, pasta dishes, steaks and soups with inviting hot crusty bread.

Derwent Bridge Chalets & Studios COTTAGES **$$** (☑6289 1000; www.derwent-bridge.com; Lyell Hwy, Derwent Bridge; d $145-245; @) Just 5km from Lake St Clair (500m east of the turn-off), this place has one-, two- and three-bedroom self-contained cabins and studios, some with spa but all with full kitchen and laundry facilities, and bush at the back porch. Extra adult/child $40/25.

Hungry Wombat Café CAFE **$** (☑6289 1125; Lyell Hwy, Derwent Bridge; mains $6-15; ⊙8am-6pm summer, 9am-5pm winter) Part of the service station, this friendly cafe is well placed to feed the famished, serving breakfasts to keep you going all day. For lunch there are soups, sandwiches, fish and chips, pies, wraps and burgers, and there's a range of all-day snacks, coffees and cakes. Everything's homemade and jolly good. There's a small grocery section too, and it gives insiders' tourist info.

Bronte Park Holiday Village HOTEL **$$** (☑6289 1126; www.bronteparkvillage.com.au; 378 Marlborough Hwy, Bronte Park; unpowered/powered sites $15/20, d $120-130, cottage d $140) Just off the Lyell Hwy 30km east of Derwent Bridge,

this place has a variety of accommodation (extra person $30), plus a bar and restaurant. The hotel can also arrange a spot of fishing with local guides or evening wildlife-spotting tours. At time of writing the restaurant was closed for renovations, but it was serving bar meals (mains $15 to $20, open lunch and dinner).

❶ Getting There & Away

Tassielink (☑1300 300 520; www.tassielink.com.au) has services to Cradle Mountain Transit Centre from Launceston via Devonport: pick-up at the ferry terminal can be arranged.

Launceston-Cradle Mountain ($59, 3¼ hrs)

Devonport-Cradle Mountain ($41, 2 hrs)

Hobart-Lake St Clair ($51, 2½ hrs)

To get from Launceston to Lake St Clair, take the Tassielink service to Queenstown, overnight here, then take the Strahan-Hobart bus to Lake St Clair the following day ($102, eight hours).

For Overland Track walkers, there's a Launceston-Cradle Mountain and Lake St Clair-Hobart package costing $99. It also does baggage storage and transfers while you're on the track, costing $10 per bag. A bushwalkers' package from Launceston to Cradle Mountain and Lake St Clair to Launceston costs $129.

Sainty's Coaches (in association with **Maxwells**) (☑6334 6456) run a variety of bushwalker services on demand, including those shown below. Prices shown are for groups of up to four. For groups of five or more the price is per person (shown below in brackets):

> **DON'T MISS**
>
> ## WALL IN THE WILDERNESS
>
> On your journey between Derwent Bridge and Bronte Park, don't miss **The Wall** (www.thewalltasmania.com; adult/child $8.50/5; ⊙9am-5pm Sep-Apr, 9am-4pm May-Aug). This amazing creation is a work of art in progress. Wood sculptor Greg Duncan is carving a panorama in wood panels depicting the history of the Tasmanian highlands. The scale is incredible: when it's finished the scene will be 100m long, which will take an estimated 10 years to complete. Though the tableau is large-scale it's carved with breathtaking skill and detail: from the veins in the workers' hands, to the creases in their shirts, to the hair of their beards. The Wall is 2km east of Derwent Bridge, and is definitely worth making time to check out.

Launceston-Cradle Mountain $300 ($75)
Launceston/Devonport-Lake St Clair $320 ($80)
Devonport-Cradle Mountain $220 ($50)
Lake St Clair-Cradle Mountain $400 ($100)
Lake St Clair-Hobart $320 ($80)

If driving, fill up with petrol before heading out to Cradle Mountain – prices are higher there than in the towns. The road north from Bronte Park to Great Lake (35km) is mostly gravel. Though it's usually in a good condition, it's worth checking with a local before you depart.

ℹ️ Getting Around

To avoid overcrowding on the narrow road into Cradle Mountain and gridlock at the Dove Lake car park, there's now a **shuttle bus** into the park. See p264 for details.

Sainty's Coaches (in association with **Maxwells**) run an on-demand service that must be pre-booked between Cynthia Bay/Lake St Clair and Derwent Bridge ($30 per person one way). The distance is 5km.

Lake St Clair Lodge (☎ 6289 1137; www. lakestclairresort.com.au) operates bushwalkers' ferry trips to and from Narcissus Hut at the northern end of Lake St Clair (30 to 40 minutes). The one-way fare is adult/child $38/19. The boat departs Cynthia Bay three times daily (9am, 12.30pm and 3pm) October to early May (or on demand, minimum six people), stopping at Narcissus Hut about 30 minutes later. If you're using the ferry service at the end of your Overland Track hike, for which bookings are essential, you *must* radio the ferry operator when you arrive at Narcissus to reconfirm your booking. In winter there's no scheduled service, but the ferry will run on demand for a minimum of six people. If you're fewer than six, but pay the $225 minimum charge, the ferry will transport you by arrangement.

There are also 90-minute **lake cruises**, departing 9am and 3pm, weather dependent. They cost $60/30/150 per adult/child/family. You can also ride the ferry one way to Echo Point costing $32/16 per adult/child, and then walk back to Cynthia Bay (two to three hours).

THE SOUTHWEST

Tasmania's southwest corner is about as wild as it's possible to get in this plenty-wild state. It's an edge-of-the-world domain made up of primordial forests, rugged mountains and endless heathland, all fringed by untamed beaches and turbulent seas. This is among the last great wildernesses on Earth: a place for absorption in nature, adventure and isolation.

Much of the southwest is incorporated into the Southwest National Park, some 600,000 hectares of largely untouched country. Just one road enters the southwest, and this only as far as the hydroelectric station on the Gordon Dam. Otherwise, all access is by light plane to the gravel airstrip at Melaleuca, by sailing boat around the tempestuous coastline, or on foot. Despite its isolation, Tasmania's southwest has a human history. It was home to Tasmanian Aborigines for some 35,000 years, then became the territory of surveyors, miners and adventure-seekers. Apart from periodic burning here by the first inhabitants, which helped form the buttongrass plains, the southwest bore little human imprint before hydroelectric dams drowned a great swathe of it in 1972.

For the well-prepared visitor this part of Tasmania is an enticing adventure playground. There are challenging, multiday walks (as well as shorter wanders), remote sea-kayaking on the waterways of Bathurst Harbour and Port Davey, and ancient forests to explore. Those who prefer aerial pleasures can take a mind-blowing abseil down the curvaceous wall of the Gordon Dam, or swoop over the valleys and mountains on a scenic southwest joy flight.

History

When the first humans came to this part of the world, they inhabited a planet in the grip of an ice age. The southwest was then covered in frigid open grasslands – ideal for hunting game and covering large distances on foot. Between 18,000 and 12,000 years ago, as the ice retreated, the landscape changed dramatically. Rising sea levels drowned river valleys and formed landlocked waterways like Bathurst Harbour. Warmer temperatures also brought more extensive forest cover, which Aboriginal Tasmanians burnt periodically to keep it open for hunting.

European explorers were at first appalled by the landscape. Matthew Flinders, the first to circumnavigate Tasmania, described the southwest thus: 'The mountains are the most dismal that can be imagined. The eye ranges over these peaks with astonishment and horror.' Most of the early explorers were surveyors who cut tracks here and endured great hardships in the name of opening the region for development. But the acidic soils of the southwest, its remoteness and harsh weather conditions meant little farming ever got off the ground. Mineral deposits also proved less than anticipated, so although a road was cut as far as Gordon Bend in the 1880s, no permanent access to the southwest was established. Apart from the hardy few who came to Bathurst Harbour to hunt for Huon pine, and a few stalwart miners at Adamsfield and Melaleuca, early European Tasmanians left the southwest well alone. They simply regarded it as uninhabitable.

Read more about this area in *South-West Tasmania* by Ken Collins, a fascinating natural history and field guide to geology, vegetation and ecology here. There's also *King of the Wilderness: the Life of Deny King* by Christobel Mattingley, a wonderful biography of Tasmania's best-loved bushman, who made Melaleuca his home and built its small gravel airstrip which visitors still use to get to the heart of this wilderness.

Maydena

POP 250

Maydena is a quiet little town in the Tyenna Valley, surrounded by hills and eucalypt forests, just 12km west of the National Park on the way to Strathgordon and the southwest. Take Junee Rd north out of town for about 10 minutes, and you'll come to the start of the 10-minute walk to the mouth of **Junee Cave**. Here, a waterfall cascades out of the cave mouth that is part of a 30km-long series of caverns known as the **Junee River karst system**. The system includes Niggly Cave, reputedly the deepest in Australia at 375m. Cave divers make hair-raising journeys through the flooded underground passageways, but other visitors can't enter.

Back in Maydena, employment has historically been in forestry, but the town has been in the doldrums of late, and Forestry Tasmania's latest foray into tourism here is an attempt to reverse that. The new **Maydena Adventure Hub** (✆6288 2288, 1300 720 507; www.adventureforests.com.au; ⊙9am-5pm Oct-Mar, pre-booked tours only rest of year) can take you on a top-of-the-world adventure (adult/child $62/50) to the amazing Eagle's Eyrie, set in alpine vegetation at 1100m with fantastic 360-degree panoramas over the southwest mountain ranges. Travel is in a 4WD bus and you stop along the way to view heritage forest machinery.

Tours only operate for a minimum of four people – advance booking is essential. The adventure hub also rents out three-wheeler recumbent trikes, which you can use to visit Junee Caves, and mountain bikes on which you can swoop downhill from the Eagle's Eyrie ($15/25/40 per hour/two hours/full day). The most unique thing to do here, though, is to have a go on the new **rail track riders** – pedal-powered rail carts. Guided tours take these for an amble along the track to Florentine Station for a walk through the rainforest (adult/child $25/15.) There's also a cafe in the adventure hub serving lunches and snacks (mains $8 to $18).

🛏️ Sleeping & Eating

TOP CHOICE Giants' Table & Cottages
COTTAGES $$

(✆6288 2293; www.giantstable.com.au; Junee Rd; cottage d $150-170) Named for the nearby giant trees in the Styx, these were once simple workers' cottages. Now done-up, they're spacious, warmly wood-heated and come in various configurations: one sleeps up to 10 (extra adult/child $30/15). There's also a restaurant (two/three courses $40/45, open dinner Tuesday to Saturday in summer, call for winter opening times, bookings essential) serving hearty fare to fill you after a day's adventuring. Platypuses are a frequent sight in the ponds on the property.

Maydena Country Cabins
CABINS $$

(✆6288 2212; www.maydenacabins.com.au; 46 Junee Rd; d $165) There are cosy timber-lined one- and two-bedroom cabins (extra adult/child $20/15) here with glorious mountain views, and – something you don't expect in Tasmania – a small herd of friendly alpacas who are just dying to pose for a photo with you. There's also an in-house B&B option (double $165), and the friendly owners are a mine of information on the area.

Wren's Nest
RENTAL HOUSE $$

(✆6288 2280; 8 Junee Rd; d $120) A well-equipped and homey three-bedroom cottage (extra adult/child $25/15) in a peaceful garden setting. It has all self-contained necessities including laundry and wood heating, and is just 20 minutes from the Styx Valley and an hour from Strathgordon.

Lake Pedder Impoundment

At the northern edge of the southwest wilderness lies the Lake Pedder Impoundment,

THE GIANTS OF THE STYX & UPPER FLORENTINE

The Styx: even the name is evocative, speaking of the ancients and underworlds. Perhaps 'crossing the Styx' is not what you imagined doing on holiday, but if you come to the Tasmanian Styx, you'll be absorbed in a domain of ancient tall trees and forests so mysteriously beautiful you'd be forgiven for thinking you have indeed crossed to another world. Putting aside the intangible, Tasmania's **Styx River Valley**, and the nearby **Upper Florentine Valley**, have also become known for something far more of this world: the logging of old-growth forests, and the fight to save them.

In the rich and heavily watered soils of the Styx River Valley, trees grow exceptionally tall. The *Eucalyptus regnans* (swamp gum) here are the loftiest trees in the southern hemisphere, and the highest hardwood trees on Earth. Trees of up to 95m tall have been recorded in the valley, and many of the trees in what's known as the Styx **Valley of the Giants** reach over 80m above the ground.

Tasmania's forestry industry has long been cutting these giants and until recently, the Styx and the Upper Florentine have been a flashpoint of tensions between loggers and anti-forestry protesters. After years of tree sit-ins, protestors chaining themselves to logging machinery, and thousands-strong anti-logging marches, it looks like the forests in this region may be protected at last.

In 2010, conservationists and the timber industry reached an historic agreement on conserving Tasmanian forests and restructuring the industry into one that's socially, economically and environmentally sustainable. The Statement of Principles agreement would safeguard previously unprotected high conservation value old growth forest, including all of the forests under contention in the Styx and the Upper Florentine. (For more background on this, see p297.) But as this book went to press, there were new doubts about whether the on-paper Statement of Principles agreement would actually be implemented. The old growth in this area may still not be off limits for logging. Conservationists continue their campaign to fully protect both areas in a national park, which would be added to the Tasmanian World Heritage Area.

Come here and be inspired by walking among some of the world's tallest trees. Southern visitor centres stock Forestry Tasmania's *Styx* brochure and the Wilderness Society's *Styx Valley of the Giants* brochure with detailed driving directions, a walking map and interpretation, or download it from: www.wilderness.org.au/campaigns/forests/styx_walking_guide.

In the Upper Florentine, there are several walks varying from 15 minutes to two hours return. The **Tiger Valley Lookout** is one hour from the car park and has awe-inspiring views over the peaks and forests of the southwest. See www.wilderness.org.au/campaigns/forests/tasmania/upper-florentine-self-drive-guide for details of how to get here. Note: the roads here are unsealed and, though manageable by 2WD vehicles, are slippery after rain. Watch out for log trucks. Boom gates may restrict access to some of the features described in the self-drive tours.

a vast flooded valley system covering the area that once cradled the original Lake Pedder, a spectacularly beautiful natural lake that was the region's ecological jewel. The largest glacial outwash lake in the world, its shallow, whisky-coloured waters covered 3 sq km and its wide, sandy beach made an ideal light-plane airstrip. The lake was home to several endangered species, and considered so important that it was the first part of the southwest to be protected within its own national park. But even this status ultimately failed to preserve it.

In the early stages of what was known as 'hydro-industrialisation', the HEC, now Hydro Tasmania – built dams, power stations and pipelines on the Central Plateau and Derwent River. By the 1960s, when the HEC proposed flooding Lake Pedder to create a storage lake for electricity generation at the Strathgordon Hydroelectric power station, Tasmania's fledgling conservation movement had stepped up a gear. There were protests with street marches in Hobart and Melbourne. This did little to sway the HEC's agenda.

In 1972 the Tasmanian parliament collapsed under the weight of anti-dams protests, and a pro-conservation political movement called the United Tasmania Group – the world's first Green party – was formed, though it failed to win a seat in subsequent elections. Protests and political pressure were in vain: the Scotts Peak and Serpentine Dams were built and Lake Pedder was lost in the winter of 1972. Next, the HEC turned its attention to the lower Gordon and Franklin Rivers. For details of the ensuing struggle to prevent new dams here – with a remarkably different outcome to the Lake Pedder campaign – see p262 and also p294.

Together with Lake Gordon (to which Lake Pedder is connected via McPartlan Pass canal), the dams are the largest water catchment in Australia, with a surface area of 514 sq km, and a volume of 15.2 cubic kilometres – more than 20 times that of Sydney Harbour. The Gordon Power Station is the largest hydroelectric power station in Tasmania and can generate 13% of the state's electricity. Lately, however, with less rain falling in its catchment, Lake Gordon is never full and the power station operates at well below its intended capacity.

Trout fishing is popular here. The lake is stocked and fish caught range from 1kg to the occasional 20kg monster. Small boats or dinghies are discouraged because the lake is 55km long and prone to dangerously sizable waves. Boat ramps exist at Scotts Peak Dam in the south and near Strathgordon in the north.

There are two campgrounds near the lake's southern end. The **Edgar Camping Ground** (free) has pit toilets, water, fine views of the area and usually a fisherman or two – in wet weather it's less attractive as it's exposed to cold winds. There's also **Huon Campground** (d $10, extra adult/child $5/2.50) hidden in tall forest near Scotts Peak Dam.

Strathgordon

Built to house HEC employees during construction of the Gordon Dam, Strathgordon is still the base for the few souls who operate the power station today.

TOURS IN THE SOUTHWEST

There are a few tours available for those who'd like to tackle the southwest in a small group, with an experienced guide and someone else organising much of the gear and logistics.

Tasmanian Expeditions (☎1300 666 856, 6331 9000; www.tasmanianexpeditions.com.au) offers three walking tour options in the southwest. The first is a nine-day trek on the South Coast Track ($2395), flying into Melaleuca and walking out along the coastline. For hard-core trekkers there's a 16-day trek along both the Port Davey and South Coast Tracks ($3595), and the legendary Western Arthurs Traverse (13 days, $3495), one of Australia's hardest, remotest – and most spectacular – walks.

To experience this wilderness from the water, consider a sea kayaking adventure in the southwest. From November to April, **Roaring 40s Ocean Kayaking** (☎6267 5000, 1800 653 712; www.roaring40skayaking.com.au) offers kayaking and camp-based walking trips exploring **Port Davey** and **Bathurst Harbour** with access by light plane to and from Hobart. Costs vary from $2595 (seven days) to $1895 for a three-day trip, $1200 for a wilderness weekend, or $1895 for a boat-and-walking trip.

You can also swoop over the southwest from the air on a scenic small-plane flight with Hobart-based operators **Par Avion** (☎6248 5390; www.paravion.com.au). On a clear day you can see the whole of this corner of Tasmania as you buzz over wild beaches and jagged peaks before landing at Melaleuca. Prices start from $240 (child $210) for a half-day trip, and $350 (child $310) for a full-day tour including a boat cruise on Bathurst Harbour.

Tasair (☎6248 5088; www.tasair.com.au) also offers flights. Its speciality is a 2½-hour scenic flight, landing at Melaleuca for tea (adult/child $298/208). It also does a slightly longer 'gourmet' version of this flight (with two hours on the ground at Melaleuca) for $395/270 per adult/child, which gives you time to get to a scenic spot and enjoy the picnic hamper provided. There's also the 90-minute Federation scenic flight, which buzzes over this amazing southwest peak (adult/child $225/157).

About 2km past the ex-Hydro settlement is Lake Pedder Lookout, with good views over the lake. A further 10km west is the Gordon Dam itself. From the car park, walk down a flight of steps that takes you along the perfect curve of the dam wall. You can't go inside the underground power station any more, but you can plunge over the edge of the dam wall – all in the strictest safety of course – by spending a day with Hobart-based Aardvark Adventures (☑6273 7722, 0408 127 714; www.aardvarkadventures.com.au), which organises abseiling trips here ($210, suitable for beginners, minimum two people). You can do two different abseils, and then the big one: 140m right down the wall. It's the highest commercial abseil in the world.

There's a campground at Teds Beach (d $13, extra adult/child $5/2.50) beside the Lake Pedder Impoundment (toilets and electric barbecues; no fires permitted). The Hydro Tasmania visitor centre at Strathgordon (☉9am–6.30pm) has interpretation on the dams, including two huge mock-up models of the power station and maps of the mountains and the lakes in 3D.

Southwest National Park

There are few places left in the world that is as isolated as Tasmania's southwest wilderness. The state's largest national park is made up of remote, wild country – forest, mountain, grassy plains and seascapes. Here grows the Huon pine, which lives for 3000 years, and the swamp gum, the world's tallest flowering plant. About 300 species of lichen, moss and fern – some very rare – festoon the rainforests, and the alpine meadows are picture-perfect with wildflowers and flowering shrubs. Through it all run wild rivers: rapids tearing through deep gorges and waterfalls plunging over cliffs.

Each year more people venture here in search of peace, isolation and challenge. Fit, experienced bushwalkers can undertake tough multiday walks. One short walk is an easy 20-minute stroll through rainforest with child-friendly interpretive signage known as the **Creepy Crawly Nature Trail**. Its start is about 2km after the Scotts Peak turn-off from the Strathgordon Rd.

Further south, the road leaves the forest near Mt Anne, revealing wonderful views of the surrounding mountains in fine weather.

To the west lies the Frankland Range, while to the south is the jagged crest of the Western Arthur Range. The road ends at Scotts Peak Dam.

Get your national parks pass and information about the southwest at the Parks & Wildlife visitor centre (☑6288 1149) at Mt Field National Park.

◎ Sights & Activities

Day Walks

From Scotts Peak Rd you can climb to Mt Eliza, a steep, five-hour return walk, giving panoramic views over the Lake Pedder Impoundment and Mt Solitary. Another challenging eight-hour walk for experienced hikers is from Red Tape Creek (29km south of the main road, B61, along Scotts Peak Rd) to Lake Judd.

From the Huon Campground at the Lake Pedder Impoundment, the best short walk follows the start of the **Port Davey Track** through forest and buttongrass plain. Mt Wedge is a popular five-hour return walk (signposted off the main road), and has great views of the Lake Pedder Impoundment and Lake Gordon. If you're not up to that, there's the 15-minute **Wedge Nature Trail** from the car park.

Long Bushwalks

The best-known walks in the southwest are the 70km **Port Davey Track** between Scotts Peak Rd and Melaleuca (four or five days duration), and the considerably more popular, 85km **South Coast Track** between Cockle Creek and Melaleuca .

The South Coast Track takes six to eight days to complete, and hikers should be prepared for weather that could bring anything from sunburn to snow flurries. Light planes fly bushwalkers into or out of the southwest, landing at Melaleuca, and there's vehicle access to Cockle Creek on the park's southeastern edge. Detailed notes to the South Coast Track are available in Lonely Planet's *Walking in Australia,* and there's comprehensive track information on the PWS website: www.parks.tas.gov.au.

There are many other walks in the park, but you should first complete one of the better-known routes. The South Coast Track makes good preparation for the more difficult walks – these require a high degree of bushwalking skill to complete safely and enjoyably. The shortest of these is the three-day circuit of the **Mt Anne Range**, a challenging walk with some difficult scrambling.

The walk to **Federation Peak**, which has earned a reputation as the most difficult bushwalking peak in Australia, will take a highly experienced walker seven to eight days. The spectacular **Western Arthur Range** is an extremely difficult traverse, for which seven to 11 days are recommended.

ℹ️ Getting There & Away

From November through March, **Evans Coaches** (☑ 6297 1335; www.evanscoaches.com.au) operates an early morning bus to the start (and finish) of the Mt Anne Circuit, and to Scotts Peak. Evans also runs a bushwalkers' pickup/ drop off at Cockle Creek, at the end of the South Coast Track.

Melaleuca

Melaleuca is little more than a couple of houses hidden in the bush and a white quartzite gravel airstrip with a wooden shed for an airport. As you fly in, you'll see the workings of the earth from the tin mining carried out by hardy bushmen over the years. In the trees by Moth Creek is the house lived in for over 40 years by the southwest's most legendary resident, Deny King (see p270). All around are buttongrass plains, mountains, water and wilderness. Walkers can overnight in a basic hut, and there's camping nearby. You can also visit the excellent bird-hide, where you might see the rare orange-bellied parrot.

Bushwalkers' flights by Par Avion and Tasair (both $190 one way, $370 return) deposit walkers at the Melaleuca airstrip. They also pick up here by arrangement, and can leave food drops for hikers coming in to Melaleuca on the Port Davey Track. Flights run on demand, so book well ahead, especially in the summer season. Note: gas canisters and fuels like shellite and methylated spirits cannot be carried on the planes. You must purchase them at the airline offices and pick up at your destination.

Understand
Tasmania

TASMANIA TODAY 278
Fast track your understanding of the issues – big and small –
affecting Tasmania today.

HISTORY 280
Understand the often tragic history of Tasmania, closely
integrated with the story of Australia itself.

GOURMET TASMANIA 289
Discover where to source the best farm-gate produce, what
craft beers to drink, and where to eat fresh seafood.

WILDERNESS & WILDLIFE 294
Immerse yourself in Tasmania's rugged and wild scenery, and
find out where to see the island's fascinating wildlife.

ENVIRONMENTAL POLITICS IN TASMANIA 304
Anna Krien details how a man's solitary protest in 1970 has
evolved into Tasmania's compelling world of politics, industry
and environmental activism.

population per sq km

GREATER HOBART   TASMANIA   AUSTRALIA

≈ 3 people

Tasmania Today

A Renewed Respect

There's an expression from the 1980s: 'Wake up Australia, Tasmania is floating away!' These days, mainland Australia is definitely wide awake to the Apple Isle's loveliness. Sea-change migrants from the mainland are escaping to Tassie, reversing the historical legacy of Tasmanians migrating north, and savvy travellers from other Australian states and around the world are recognising the island's unique gifts. Tasmania's easygoing lifestyle, clean southern air, and astounding natural beauty are regarded as essential antidotes to the more complicated and pressured urban lifestyles to the north.

An Outdoor State of Mind

The modern Tasmanian identity is also mirrored in the island's ancient and remarkable landscape. Dark foliage and craggy peaks are whipped by notorious winds, and short winter days are infused by the stark clarity of southern light. The environment fosters a keen sense of adventure and an understated resilience. Rather than hiding indoors behind solid stone, Tasmanians embrace their wilderness beneath layers of thermals and Gore-Tex. Getting into it, over it, or on top of it, is something the Tassie work-life balance absolutely mandates.

An Evolving Urban Vibe

Hobart and Launceston's growing urban buzz is now proving irresistible to ex-Tasmanians, back home and confident they're really not missing anything that Melbourne, Sydney or London offers. Hobart has views to rival Sydney's, and continues to evolve into a cosmopolitan hub. Launceston has been busy transforming itself from colonial backwater into a boutique harbour city, and a rigorous arts scene infuses both centres.

Run by one passionate and energetic guy in Hobart, www.tasmaniantimes.com is a 'forum of discussion and dissent' and a great way to check the pulse of local politics or issues like the 'peace deal' between the pro-forestry and pro-environmental groups.

Top Books

» **In Tasmania** by Nicholas Shakespeare

» **Into the Woods: the Battle for Tasmania's Forests** by Anna Krien

» **For the Term of His Natural Life** by Marcus Clarke

Best Blogs

» **Mark's Tasmanian Bush Blog** www.tasbushblog.blogspot.com: Photos and bushwalking reports

» **Rita's Bite** www.pc-rita.blogspot.com: Incorporating Hobart Food for Thought with restaurant and cafe reviews.

Big in Hollywood

» **Errol Flynn** Born in Hobart in 1909, Flynn went on to become a big movie star. His reputation for bedding women with ease lives on in the expression 'in like Flynn'.

» **Simon Baker** Launceston-born star of TV's *The Mentalist*.

national parks & reserves
(% of land use)

national parks & reserves — 41

Other — 59

if Tasmania was 100 people ...

couples with children 41%
couples without children 40%
single-parent families 17%
other families 2%

Inspiring Australian Chefs

A highlight of any Tasmanian trip is sampling the local gourmet fare, especially fresh seafood, luscious fruits, and cool-climate wines. It's a combination that's inspiring both Australian and international chefs: local salmon is now served in the restaurants of Tokyo, and superb cheeses are providing the perfect end to a meal in Melbourne and Sydney bistros.

Inspiring & Informing Australia

Australia's wee southern isle continues to evoke increased fondness in the hearts of mainlanders, who don't mind admitting what they find precious about Tasmania. The passionate environmental debates of recent years often overflow to become federal issues. More than ever, there's conflict over what the big island thinks the little island should be protecting. Should they fight for a close-knit community, jobs for locals and a sequestered way of life? Or should it be for the wilderness, justly famous beyond these island shores? Either way, specifically Tasmanian issues continue to inspire and inform the broader Australian political debate on the melding of commercial and environmental imperatives.

Battling the Global Storm

Early in the 21st century, the exodus of young, educated Tasmanians had begun a slow reversal, with a revival of Tasmania's economy heralding a new era of optimism. But at the time of writing in early 2011, growth in tourist numbers were flat due to the global financial crisis and the strength of the Australian dollar, but the state's marketing as a tourist destination is still arguably the most distinctive and compelling in Australia.

For a quarterly list of all the latest books on Tasmanian culture, politics and issues, check out the Fullers Bookshop website: www.fullersbookshop.com.au/tasmaniana.html.

BOOKS

Top Films

» **Van Diemen's Land (2009)** About the escape of Alexander Pearce and seven other convicts from the Macquarie Harbour penal settlement. He was the last survivor after the group murdered and cannibalised each other.

Local Lingo

» **Chigger** Hobart's version of a hoon or a bogan.

» **'I'm going out scrub'** On the Australian mainland, they'd say 'I'm going out bush'.

» **Abs** Not a group of muscles, but the colloquial Tasmanian contraction for abalone.

Newspapers

» **The Mockery** What Hobartians call the city's daily newspaper, the *Mercury*

» **The Exaggerator** Launceston nickname for the daily *Examiner*.

» **The Aggravate** Also known as the *Advocate*, local newspaper around Devonport and Burnie

History

Tasmania's short written history is bleak and powerful. But like the rest of Australia, it has a much longer story, that of its *palawa,* or 'first man': the term some Tasmanian Aborigines use to describe themselves. Depicted as a people all but wiped out in an attempted genocide, their culture survives today, despite the fact that their home became Britain's prison island in the first years of the 19th century.

In 1804 74 convicts were shipped out to Van Diemen's Land (as Tasmania was then known), with 71 soldiers, plus their 21 wives and 14 children. Early Tasmania was dominated by the mentality, 'If it grows, chop it down; if it runs, shoot it'. Penal settlements were built in the island's most inhospitable places. Macquarie Harbour, on the harsh west coast, became Tasmania's first penal site in 1822, and by 1833 roughly 2000 convicts a year were sent to this end of the earth as punishment for often trivial crimes.

The community quickly developed a very particular character: lawlessness and debauchery were rife. Yet it was also defined by great pioneering innovation and courage. Tasmanian culture has undergone a transition from shame, and an increasing number of Tasmanians of European descent now identify with their convict past. There has also been an increase in pride in being Tasmanian, and driven by compelling tourism marketing and a burgeoning food and wine scene, the state's positive and cosmopolitan profile is far removed from the negative preconceptions of just a few decades ago.

Since the early 1970s, the key influence on Tasmanian history has been the ongoing battle between pro-logging companies and environmental groups. Tasmania is a state that's poorer and has less employment opportunities than its northern partners in Australia's federal alliance, but it's also an island with world-beating wilderness and scenic beauty. With these two contemporary markers of Tasmanian history, the ideological fault lines often evident in Tasmanian society are not difficult to understand.

Trying to find a convict in your family tree? To help with genealogy searches, check the website of the Tasmanian Family History Society (www.tasfhs.org).

TIMELINE	60,000–35,000 BC	12,000–8000 BC	1642
	Aborigines settled in Australia sometime during this period. It is thought that the original indigenous settlers of the Australian continent crossed by a land bridge.	Tasmania's Aborigines are separated from the mainland when sea levels rise dramatically during the end of the of the last ice age.	Abel Tasman discovers Tasmania and names it Van Diemen's Land after a Dutch governor. During the later arrival of convict ships, the name becomes shorthand for 'Hell on Earth'.

Tasmanian Aborigines

The Land Bridge & the Ice Age

Tasmania was part of the supercontinent Gondwana until it broke away and drifted south 160 million years ago. Aboriginal people probably migrated across a land bridge that joined Tasmania to the rest of Australia at least 35,000 years ago. The sea level was much lower then and the Tasmanian climate much drier and colder. Aborigines settled the extensive grasslands on the western side of Tasmania, where they hunted wallabies. When the last ice age ended between 18,000 and 12,000 years ago, the glaciers retreated, sea levels rose and tall forests became established in the western half of the island, while in the east, rainfall increased and new grasslands developed. Tasmania 'floated away' from mainland Australia, and a distinctive existence began for the people, animals and plants of the island.

Life on the Smaller Island

The culture of the Tasmanian Aborigines diverged from the way people were living on the mainland, as they developed a sustainable, seasonal culture of hunting, fishing and gathering. They produced more sophisticated boats and used them to hunt seals and mutton birds on and around the offshore islands.

Those who remained in the west lived mainly on the coast. Aboriginal women collected shellfish (mussels, abalone and oysters), the remains of which make up the enormous middens around Tasmania's coastline. Both men and women wore necklaces of shell. They sheltered in bark lean-tos and protected themselves from the island's cold weather by rubbing a mixture of ochre, charcoal and fat on their skin.

Sails, Guns & Fences

European Discovery

The first European to spy Tasmania was Dutch navigator Abel Tasman, who bumped into it in 1642. He named this new place Van Diemen's Land after the Dutch East Indies' governor. It's estimated there were between 5000 and 10,000 Aborigines in Tasmania when Europeans arrived, living in 'bands' of around 50 people, each claiming rights over a specific area of land and being part of one of the nine main language groups.

European sealers began to work Bass Strait in 1798 and they raided tribes along the coast, kidnapping Aboriginal women for forced labour and sex slaves. The sealers were uninterested in Aboriginal land and eventually formed commercial relationships with the Aborigines, trading dogs and other items so they could take Aboriginal women back to their islands.

Along the west coast there are sites with stone engravings, thought to be important symbols of Tasmanian Aboriginal beliefs; the Aborigines also had knowledge of astronomy.

ENGRAVINGS

HISTORY TASMANIAN ABORIGINES

1700s	1788	1798	1803
Captain Bligh cleverly plants the isle's first apple tree. Three centuries later the orchardists of the Huon Valley still toast their good fortune with zingy cider.	The First Fleet arrives at Sydney with its cargo of convicts. Around 200 years later, these earliest colonial settlers will be a badge of honour for contemporary Australians.	'Straitsmen', a rough bunch of sealers, make their home and their living in Bass Strait. It's a tough life, characterised by long periods working an unforgiving stretch of water.	The *Lady Nelson* arrives in Risdon Cove, and Australia's second British penal settlement is established. The site north of Hobart on the Derwent River is farmed until 1948.

The Black Wars

Risdon Cove, on the Derwent River, became the site of Australia's second British colony in 1803. One year later, the settlement moved to the present site of Hobart.

During this period, despite initial friendly exchanges and trade, an unknown number of peaceable Aboriginal people were killed as European fences and farming encroached on their hunting grounds and significant places. In return, Aboriginal people began to carry out their own raids. In 1816 Governor Thomas Davey produced his 'Proclamation to the Aborigines', which represented settlers and Aborigines living together amicably – in direct contrast to the realities of a brutal conflict.

By the 1820s these territorial disputes had developed into the so-called Black Wars, as Aboriginal people increasingly refused to surrender their lands, women and children without a fight. In 1828 martial law was declared by Lieutenant-Governor Arthur. Aboriginal groups were systematically murdered, arrested or forced at gunpoint from districts settled by whites; arsenic on bread and steel traps designed to catch humans were used. Many succumbed to European diseases they had no immunity against.

Meanwhile, a disapproving Tasmanian establishment contemptuously termed the descendants of sealers and Aboriginal women 'half-castes', and even though Cape Barren was designated an Aboriginal reserve in the 1880s, there was continual pressure on the islanders to adopt European farming ways and assimilate with mainlanders.

Historic Bridges

» Richmond Bridge

» Ross Bridge

» Campbell Town's Red Bridge

The Black Line

By now, the British were concerned by how it might look to the world if their actions led to the extinction of an entire people. In 1830, in an attempt to contain all Aborigines on the Tasman Peninsula for their security and to preserve their culture, a human chain of about 2200 men known as the 'Black Line' was formed by settlers and soldiers, moving through the settled areas of the state from Moulting Lagoon, through Campbell Town, to Quamby's Bluff. Three weeks later, the farcical manoeuvre had succeeded in capturing only an old man and a boy, and confirmed settlers' fears that they couldn't defeat the Aborigines by force of arms. The *Hobart Courier* mocked the exercise: it had cost half the annual budget. In turn, it must have given the Aboriginal people an awful sense that their time was running out.

A Parallel Prison

As a result, Lieutenant-Governor Arthur consented to George Augustus Robinson's plan to 'conciliate' the Aboriginal people. In effect Robinson enticed and cajoled virtually all of the Aborigines in mainland Tasma-

1804	1807	1811	1822–53
Tasmania's first permanent colonial settlements are established at Sullivans Cove (Hobart) and George Town (Tamar Valley).	First settlers arrive from Norfolk Island on the *Lady Nelson* and found New Norfolk. A replica of the *Lady Nelson* now offers tall-ship sailing on the Derwent River.	Governor Lachlan Macquarie arrives from Sydney and draws up initial plans for Hobart streets. Public buildings erected at this time include the Mt Nelson Signal Station.	Convicts are imprisoned at various penal settlements around the state, including at Sarah Island and Port Arthur. For some it (eventually) presents the opportunity of a new start.

nia to lay down their arms, leave their traditional lands and accompany him to new settlements. In doing so, he became the first European to walk across much of the state, adding the title of 'explorer' to that of missionary. There is strong historical evidence that the people of Oyster Bay, including their prominent chief Tongerlongetter, whom Robinson regarded as 'a man of great tact and judgement', followed him to a succession of settlements in the Furneaux Islands based on the promise of sanctuary and land. Instead, they were subjected to attempts to 'civilise' and Christianise them, and made to work for the government.

After enduring a number of moves, including to Sarah Island on the west coast, they were finally settled at Wybalenna (Black Man's Houses) on Flinders Island. One by one, the people began to die from a potent mixture of despair, homesickness, poor food and respiratory disease. In 1847 those who had managed to survive petitioned Queen Victoria, complaining of their treatment and referring to the 'agreement' they thought Robinson had made with Lieutenant-Governor Arthur on their behalf. Wybalenna was eventually abandoned and the survivors transferred to mainland Tasmania. Of the 135 who had been sent to Flinders Island, only 47 lived to make the journey to Oyster Cove, south of Hobart. The new accommodation here proved to be substandard, and the Aborigines once again experienced the criminal neglect of the authorities, and growing demoralisation. Within a decade, half of them were dead.

Historic Pubs

» Knopwood's Retreat, Hobart
» Bush Inn, New Norfolk
» Man O'Ross, Ross
» Stanley Hotel
» Deloraine Hotel
» Royal Oak, Launceston

Mapping Van Diemen's Land

Nearly 130 years after Abel Tasman's able efforts, Tasmania was sighted and visited by a series of other European sailors, including captains Tobias Furneaux, James Cook and William Bligh. Between 1770 and 1790 they all visited Adventure Bay on Bruny Island and believed it to be part of the Australian mainland, rather than an island off an island (off an island). In 1792 Admiral Bruni D'Entrecasteaux explored the southeastern coastline more thoroughly, mapping and naming many of its features. Most major Tasmanian landmarks still bear the French names he gave them.

In 1798 Lieutenant Matthew Flinders circumnavigated Van Diemen's Land and proved that it was an island.

Australia's Second Settlement

In the late 1790s Governor King of NSW decided to establish a second settlement in Australia, south of Sydney Cove. Port Phillip Bay in Victoria was initially considered, but the site was rejected due to a lack of water on the Mornington Peninsula and, in 1803, Tasmania's Risdon Cove was chosen. A year later, the settlement was moved 10km away to the present site of Hobart. The threat of French interest in the island suggested the

» Abel Tasman statue, Hobart

CHRIS MELLOR/LONELY PLANET IMAGES ©

1824	1830	1853
The Cascade Brewery opens in Hobart under the shadow of Mt Wellington, making it Australia's oldest continuously operating brewery. Cheers to that!	The Black Line, a human chain of 2200 men, fails to flush out Tasmania's Aborigines. The intention was to 'corral' all Aborigines to the Tasman Peninsula south of Eaglehawk Neck.	The Anti-Transportation League lobbyists suceed in ending convict transportation. In the 50 years from 1803, an estimated 75,000 convicts made the forced journey south to Tasmania.

need for a settlement up north, on a site proclaimed 'George Town' on the Tamar River.

The reference to 'Truganini in chains' in the Midnight Oil song *Truganini* is not factually correct: it's more likely to be a metaphor for the appalling treatment of Tasmania's Aboriginal people.

Exploring Coast to Coast

The establishment of George Town in 1804 attracted new settlers, resulting in a demand for more land. Settlers initially spread along the southern coast towards Port Arthur, along the east coast and around the Launceston area. By 1807 an overland route from Hobart to Launceston had been forged. Stone was readily available for construction work and many early stone buildings have survived; some of the best examples of these buildings can be found in Richmond and along the Midland (Heritage) Highway.

To the settlers, Tasmania's big unknown was its rugged hinterland, where difficult, mountainous country barred the way. The first Europeans to cross the island were escapees from Macquarie Harbour; many escaped, but only a few survived the journey across to Hobart Town.

TRUGANINI'S LEGACY

Reckoned to be the last surviving full-blooded Tasmanian Aborigine, Truganini's life was lived out during the white invasion and her death became a symbol for the attempted genocide of her people. By all accounts an intelligent and lovely-looking woman, she was born on Bruny Island in either 1803 or 1812, the daughter of Mangana, the chief of the Nuenonne people. Along with her husband, Woureddy, she left her island home to travel with George Robinson; accounts also suggest she lived with sealers as a young woman, an experience which left her unable to bear children. When she was older, Truganini lived with fellow Tasmanian Aborigines in the derelict environment of Wybalenna on Flinders Island and afterwards at the disastrous Oyster Cove settlement.

It is remarkable given the times that Truganini lived into her 70s. When she died in Hobart in 1876, the Tasmanian Government declared that she was the last of the island's Aborigines and that her race was extinct (in fact, she was outlived by Suke and Fanny Cochrane, two women of tribal parentage). The announcement of her death, and the resulting funeral procession through Hobart, aimed to 'end the native problem'; this demise was taken as fact – and still is in some encyclopedias and school history lessons.

Against her wishes to be buried in the mountains behind Oyster Cove or dropped deep into the D'Entrecasteaux Channel, Truganini's 4ft-tall skeleton was instead displayed for many years as a public curio in the Tasmanian Museum. Much to the chagrin of the Royal Society in Tasmania, other parts of her contested remains were shipped to Britain by the Royal College of Surgeons in London and were only repatriated in 2002. It took more than a lifetime for Truganini's wishes to be granted and her ashes finally scattered in the channel beside her beloved Bruny Island. You can visit a memorial to Truganini at The Neck on Bruny Island, and there is a memorial on Mt Nelson, at the top of the Truganini Track.

1856	1870s	1916	1932
The state changes its name from Van Diemen's Land to Tasmania to remove stigma. A popular word play of the time was that the island was 'Van Demonian'.	Gold and tin are discovered in the state's north, signalling the beginning of mining interests in Tasmania. Organised opposition to the industry only begins to take hold a century later.	Tasmania's first national parks are established at Freycinet and Mt Field, laying a strong foundation for the state's future reputation for pristine wilderness areas for outdoor activities.	Born in Stanley in 1879, Joseph Lyons becomes Australia's first (and only) Tasmanian prime minister. The suburb of Lyons in Canberra is named after him in 1965.

In 1828, George Frankland was appointed Tasmania's surveyor-general. Determined to map the entire state, he sent many surveyors on long, arduous journeys during the 1830s, often accompanying them. By 1845, when Frankland died, most of the state was roughly mapped and catalogued.

Building roads across the mountainous west was difficult and many were surveyed across all sorts of landscapes before being abandoned. But in 1932 the Lyell Hwy from Hobart to Queenstown was finally opened for business, linking the west coast to Hobart.

Convict Life

Sarah, Maria & Arthur: the Worst of the Worst

The actual site of the first penal settlement in Tasmania was on small Sarah Island, in Macquarie Harbour on the west coast. The prisoners sent there were those who had committed further crimes after arriving in Australia. Their severe punishment was the manual labour of cutting down Huon pine in the rainforest. It's believed conditions were so dreadful here that some prisoners committed murder in order to be sent for trial and execution in Hobart.

The number of prisoners sent to Van Diemen's Land increased in 1825; in the same year the island was recognised as a colony independent of NSW, and another penal settlement was established, this one on the east coast of Maria Island, where prisoners were treated more humanely.

In 1830 a third penal settlement was established at Port Arthur on the Tasman Peninsula. Shortly after its construction, the other two penal settlements closed – Maria Island in 1832 and Sarah Island in 1833.

Punishments meted out to convicts at Port Arthur included weeks of solitary confinement. The worst prisoners were sent to work in the coal mines of the nearby Saltwater River where they were housed in miserably damp underground cells. A visit to Port Arthur evokes the terrible conditions suffered by prisoners during this era.

A Name Change & A New Image

In 1840 convict transportation to NSW ceased, resulting in an increase in the number of convicts being sent to Van Diemen's Land; there was a peak of 5329 new arrivals in 1842. In 1844 control of the Norfolk Island penal settlement (in the Pacific Ocean, 1610km northeast of Sydney) was transferred from NSW to Van Diemen's Land and by 1848 'VDL' was the only place in the British Empire to which convicts were still being transported.

Vociferous opposition to the continued transportation of convicts came from free settlers, who in 1850 formed the Anti-Transportation

Experience Convict Life

» Port Arthur Historic Site

» Coal Mines Historic Site

» The Female Factory sites in Hobart and Ross

» Maria Island Penitentiary

1934	1935	1945	1967
Construction of the 7km Pinnacle Rd up Mt Wellington begins, creating employment for thousands of men during the Depression. Now mountain biking down the spectacular road is a Hobart attraction.	Tasmanian Errol Flynn stars in *Captain Blood*, in which his character is sold as a slave to Olivia de Havilland, escapes, and becomes a pirate. (Art mirrors life?)	Arguably the world's toughest open-ocean yacht race, the Sydney-to-Hobart Yacht Race is run for the first time. *Wild Oats'* 2005 winning time of just under 43 hours is the race record.	Tasmania's deadliest bushfires kill 62, injure over 900, and leave more than 7000 homeless. The 'Black Tuesday' fires impacted on 2640 sq km from the Midlands to the D'Entrecasteaux Channel.

League to successfully lobby for change. The last convicts transported to the colony arrived in 1853.

Van Diemen's Land had been the most feared destination for British prisoners for more than three decades. During those years a total of 74,000 convicts had been transported to the island. The majority of these people had served out their sentences and settled in the colony, yet so terrible was its reputation that in 1856 – the year it achieved responsible self-government – it changed its name to Tasmania in an attempt to free its image once and for all from the shackles of its past.

Gold, But No Great Rush

In the 1870s gold was discovered near the Tamar River, as was tin in the northeast. These discoveries prompted a deluge of international prospectors. In the northeast a number of Chinese miners arrived, bringing their culture with them. Tourism authorities are constructing a themed 'Trail of the Tin Dragon' through the northeast to highlight this aspect of the state's history.

Mining was a tough way of life, and most people didn't make their fortunes. Individual prospectors grabbed the rich, easily found surface deposits, but once these were gone the miners had to form larger groups and companies to mine deeper deposits, until eventually these either ran out or became unprofitable to work. Remains of the mine workings at Derby and the mine at Beaconsfield can be visited today.

Once it was realised that there was mineral wealth to be found, prospectors randomly explored most of the state. On the west coast, discoveries of large deposits of silver and lead resulted in a boom in the 1880s and an associated rush at Zeehan. In fact, so rich in minerals was the area that it ultimately supported mines significant enough to create the towns of Rosebery, Tullah and Queenstown. Geological exploitation went unchecked, however, and by the 1920s, copper mining at Queenstown had gashed holes in the surrounding hills, while logging, pollution, fires

Historic Museums
» QVMAG, Launceston
» TMAG, Hobart
» Narryna Heritage Museum, Hobart
» Anglesea Barracks, Hobart
» Low Head Pilot station

TRUST IN THE NATIONAL TRUST

As you explore Tasmania you'll often come across gracious old heritage homes and properties managed by the **National Trust** (☑6344 6233; www.nationaltrusttas.org.au; 413 Hobart Rd, Launceston). Many are staffed by volunteers and have rather specific opening hours, but if you do fancy a spot of time travel, be sure to talk with the attendants as they are often passionately knowledgeable about stories in the area. Step onto the well-worn flagstones of the Georgian Regency mansion, Clarendon near Evandale, the convict-built Franklin House in Launceston, and the colony's first lawyer's digs, Runnymede in Hobart. All are well worth a visit.

1972	1975	1982	1982–83
Lake Pedder is flooded as part of hydroelectric industrialisation. The Lake Pedder Restoration Committee (www.lakepedder.org) is now committed to restoring the lake to a natural wilderness state.	Hobart's Tasman Bridge collapses, killing 12, when the ore carrier *Lake Illawarra* crashes into it. Seven of the dead were crew members.	Taking in the South-West, Franklin-Lower Gordon Wild Rivers and Cradle Mountain-Lake St Clair National Parks, the expansive Tasman Wilderness World Heritage Area is established.	The Franklin River Blockade is staged to oppose construction of a dam in the area, and is ultimately successful. The action is a substantial boost to Tasmania's pro-conservation lobby.

and heavy rain stripped the terrain of its vegetation and topsoil. The environment has only begun repairing itself over the past few decades.

The rich belt of land from Queenstown to the northern coast is still being mined in several places, but this is now being done with a little more environmental consideration and fewer visible effects than in the past.

Tasmania in the 20th Century

Although it was ignored in the initial Federal ministry, Tasmania officially became a state when Australia's Federation took place in 1901. For Tasmanians, as for mainlanders in the new Commonwealth of Australia, the first half of the 20th century was dominated by war, beginning with the dispatch of a contingent of 80 Tasmanian soldiers to South Africa and the Boer War, through the Great War and WWII, with the Depression of the late 1920s thrown in for bad measure.

The state's post-WWII economy was reassuringly buoyant, with industrial success embodied by Bell Bay's aluminium refinery and the ongoing developments of the powerful Hydro-Electric Commission. However, by the 1980s it had suffered a worrisome decline. Subsequent years saw economic unease reflected in climbing 'emigration' levels to the mainland (especially among the under-30s) and falling birth rates.

Saving the Wilderness

In 1910 an Austrian, Gustav Weindorfer, reached the summit of Cradle Mountain. Throwing his arms out, he declared that the magnificence of the place, 'where there is no time and nothing matters', was something the people of the world should share – it later became a national park. In the 20th century, the extinction of the thylacine (see p301) and the flooding of Lake Pedder in the late 1960s and early '70s led to the birth of the green movement in 1972, when concerned groups got together to form the United Tasmania Group. Ten years later, thousands of people acted to stop the damming of the Franklin River in 1984–85. Leaders in these movements became a force in Australian federal politics, the Greens Party, under the leadership of Bob Brown, who has been a senator since 1996.

The long-running debate between pro-logging groups, pro-pulp mill corporations and conservationists keen to protect Tasmania's old growth forests and wild heritage continues. In 2010, a breakthrough was achieved with the signing of the 'Statement of Principles' agreement – a 'peace deal' between pro-forestry and pro-environmental groups. By March 2011, the deal was still in limbo as several key Tasmanian environmental groups had withdrawn their support following a delay in the signing of a government moratorium on logging in

» Hobart Historic Walks

» Female Factory, Hobart

» Runnymede, Hobart

» Launceston Historic Walks

1986	1996	1997
Snow falls at sea level around Hobart and is so deep that one intrepid local is able to ski on the Tasman Bridge across the Derwent River.	The massacre of 35 people at the Port Arthur Historic Site stuns the nation and the world and eventually results in stricter gun-control laws in Australia.	Homosexuality is finally decriminalised in Tasmania. In 2010, Tasmania becomes the first state to recognise same-sex marriages performed in other jurisdictions as registered partnerships.

» Memorial cross, Port Arthur

high-conservation-value forests. See p297 to understand the likely impact of this agreement on the forests and wilderness of Tasmania.

In 1997 the Tasmanian parliament became the first in Australia to formally apologise to the Aboriginal community for past actions connected with the 'Stolen Generation'.

Tasmania in the 21st Century

Backed by strong tourism campaigns, vocal supporters in mainstream media, a respected arts scene and the emergence of several excellent local brands that wind up in shopping trolleys across the country, Tasmania's image change is well under way as it fosters its reputation as a 'pure' holiday isle and lifestyle haven.

Indigenous Rights

While tourism expands, Tasmanian Aborigines continue to claim rights to land and compensation for past injustices. Acknowledgement of the treatment meted out to Aborigines by Europeans has resulted in the recognition of native titles to land. In 1995 the state government returned 12 sites to the Tasmanian Aboriginal community, including Oyster Cove, Kutikina Cave and Steep Island. Wybalenna was added to this list in 1999, and areas of Cape Barren and Clarke Islands in 2005.

1998	2004	2008	2010
The Sydney-to-Hobart yacht race is marred by tragedy when hurricane force conditions causes five boats to sink with the loss of six lives.	Launceston-born Ricky Ponting becomes captain of Australia's test cricket team. By the summer of 2010–2011 he'll have skippered the 'Baggy Greens' to two consecutive Ashes losses to England.	Prime Minister Kevin Rudd apologises to Australia's Aboriginal 'Stolen Generation'. Tasmanian Aboriginal activist Michael Mansell questions whether financial compensation will follow. By early 2011, none had.	Signed in December 2010, the 'Statement of Principles' agreement is promoted as a 'peace deal' between the pro-forestry and pro-environmental groups in Tasmania.

Gourmet Tasmania

The Providore Island

Tasmania was dubbed the 'Providore Island' in the excellent 2008 book of the same name. It's a wonderfully accurate description of Tasmania's blossoming food and wine culture, showcasing superb seafood, juicy berries and stone fruits, award-winning dairy products and cheeses, an emerging craft-beer scene, and excellent cool-climate wines.

Farms, orchards, vineyards and small enterprises are busy supplying fresh local produce, and buyers (restaurants, markets, providores and individuals) are snapping it up. Dishes on menus throughout Australia feature Tasmanian oysters, scallops and salmon, and King Island cream appears on dessert menus from Sydney to Perth. Hobart and Launceston eateries offer even more in the way of locally sourced and seasonal goodies.

Visitors may find themselves sometimes underwhelmed menu-wise in some country towns, especially if the local pub is the only eatery. However, this is rapidly changing, and excellent providores are popping up around the island. A Tasmanian picnic or a DIY dinner party is never far away if the local pub fails to impress.

Local Produce

Seafood

Tasmania's best food comes from the sea, garnered from some of the purest waters on the planet. Genuine specialities include oysters on Bruny Island, at Coles Bay, and at Barilla Bay near Hobart, or ocean trout from the waters of Macquarie Harbour.

Fish like trevalla (blue eye) and striped trumpeter are delicious, as is the local Atlantic salmon, largely farmed in the Huon estuary. Rock lobster (usually called crayfish), abalone, scallops, mussels and oysters are also available.

From a humble curried scallop pie or fish and chips at Hobart's Constitution Dock, to an innovative meal at Hobart's Marque IV restaurant, Tasmania is a true seafood star.

Travellers who want to eat their way around the Apple Isle should go to www.discovertasmania.com.au, click on 'Activities & Attractions', then 'Food & Wine', and start salivating.

BILLS & TIPPING

The total at the bottom of a restaurant bill is all you really need to pay. It should include GST (as should menu prices) and there is no 'optional' service charge added. Waiters are paid a reasonable salary, so they don't rely on tips to survive. Often, though, especially in urban Australia, people tip a few coins in a cafe, while the tip for excellent service can go as high as 15% in whiz-bang establishments.

ESSENTIAL FOODIE EXPERIENCES

Here are some of our island-wide favourites. Also check out the smorgasbord of gourmet delights in the 'Tasting Tasmania' itinerary (p126).

» Pick your own fresh berries at the **Sorell Fruit Farm**

» Slurp oysters fresh from the **Freycinet Marine Farm** or at **Get Shucked** on Bruny Island

» Attend a Tasmanian food and wine festival – get salivating for **The Taste** or **Savour Tasmania** in Hobart, or **Festivale** in Launceston

» Pan-fry the trout you just caught yourself in a highland lake

» Scoff down fresh fish and chips from the floating fish punts at Hobart's **Constitution Dock**

» Develop your culinary skills with cookery classes at the **Agrarian Kitchen** near New Norfolk or the **Red Feather Inn** in Hadspen

» Explore Tassie's foodie credentials on a guided tour with Hobart's **Herbaceous Tours** (www.herbaceoustours.com.au). Options include Bruny Island, the Huon Valley, Hobart and Richmond

Meat

Tasmania is known for its high-quality beef, based on a natural, grass-fed (as opposed to grain-fed) production system and free from growth hormones, antibiotics and chemical contaminants. Beef from King Island and Flinders Island is sublime, and if you see it on a menu and the wallet allows, tuck into premium Wagyu beef from Robbins Island in Bass Strait. Flinders Island also farms prime lamb. These meats are available Tasmania-wide and in upmarket restaurants throughout Australia, and command a ransom in overseas markets like Tokyo.

Game meats feature on menus, with quail, wallaby and farmed venison often available. Wallaby meat is tender, lean and has a mild flavour. The Bruny Island Smoke House specialises in smoked meat, poultry and seafood.

Download the *Tasmanian Fruits Farm Gate Guide* from the Fruit Growers of Tasmania website (www.fruitgrowerstas.com.au). The annual publication lists the best place to secure a drive-in, pick-your-own summertime bounty of stone fruit, cherries, and berries.

Fruit

Tasmania's cold climate means its berries and stone fruit are sublime, and picking your own (in season) is a great way to enjoy them. Sorell Fruit Farm near Hobart is a favourite – it gives visitors the opportunity to pick all sorts, including raspberries, cherries, apples and pears. Roadside stalls in the Huon and Tamar Valleys offer the chance to buy freshly picked fruits. Other places worth a visit include Christmas Hills Raspberry Farm Café near Deloraine, Kate's Berry Farm outside Swansea, and Eureka Farm in Scamander.

Jams, sauces, fruit wines, ciders and juices made from Tasmanian fruits are also excellent. Many varieties are available at gourmet food stores and providores and from stalls at Hobart's Salamanca Market. Fleurtys in Woodbridge also has lots of tasty fruity by-products.

Cheese

Tasmania has a brilliant cheese industry, somewhat hampered by the fact that all the milk must be pasteurised, unlike in Italy and France. Despite that, the results can still be great: just slap some local leatherwood honey over a slice of blue cheese for tasty confirmation.

Visit Pyengana Cheese Factory, not far from St Helens, for sensational cheddar. Grandvewe Cheeses, just south of Woodbridge, produces organic cheese from sheep and cow's milk. Ashgrove Farm Cheese near Deloraine conjures up traditional cheeses like Rubicon red, smoked cheddar and creamy Lancashire, and the Bruny Island Cheese Company produces Italian and French styles. In providores and restaurants, also keep an eye out for King Island Dairy's superb brie.

New Directions

Locals are getting creative and showing off their agricultural skill, growing or harvesting some wonderfully diverse products, including buckwheat, wasabi, wakame (a type of seaweed) and saffron. Black truffles are even being harvested in the north of Tasmania, with an idea to capture the European market during the French off-season.

Tasmania also produces fantastic honey, chocolate and fudge, mushrooms, asparagus, olive oil, walnuts, and mustards and relishes. Check out the Salamanca Market in Hobart or the providores listed in this chapter.

Where to Eat

Fine Dining

Tasmania's best fine-dining restaurants rival anything on the Australian mainland, and local chefs are renowned for making the most of the excellent local produce. Menu items can be expensive (mains exceeding $35), but diners are guaranteed innovative and thoughtful interpretations of local seafood, beef and lamb, partnered with the best of Tasmanian wines.

In Hobart consider Marque IV, Restaurant 373, and Garagistes, while Stillwater and Novaro's deliver Launceston's most interesting high-end tastes. Elsewhere on the island, Cygnet's Red Velvet Lounge, Ripple in St Helens, and the Piermont Restaurant in Swansea are all excellent.

Cafes

Like the rest of Australia, Tasmania has fallen head over heels with coffee, and the humble bean is taken very seriously indeed at cafes like Retro, The Cupping Room and Pigeon Hole in Hobart, and at tant pour tant and the Blue Café Bar in Launceston.

Listing wineries, breweries, distilleries and other purveyors of gastronomic bounty, the *Tasmania Wine & Gastronomy Map* is essential for the comprehensive foodie visitor. See www.australianwinemaps.com or Hobart's main bookshops.

GOURMET TASMANIA WHERE TO EAT

TOP FARM GATES & ARTISAN FOOD PRODUCERS

Chat with the farmer, baker or orchard owner at these top spots to pick up the freshest of local Tasmanian produce.

» **Kate's Berry Farm**, Swansea
» **Freycinet Marine Farm**, Coles Bay
» **The Cherry Shed**, Latrobe
» **Ashgrove Farm Cheese**, Deloraine
» **41 Degrees South Salmon**, Deloraine
» **House of Anvers Chocolate**, Devonport
» **Honey Farm**, Chudleigh
» **Bruny Island Cheese Company**, Bruny Island
» **Bruny Island Berry Farm**, Bruny Island
» **Bruny Island Smokehouse**, Bruny Island
» **Get Shucked Oyster Farm**, Bruny Island
» **Grandvewe Cheeses**, Woodbridge
» **Companion Bakery**, Oatlands
» **Thorpe Farm Dairy**, Bothwell
» **Sorell Fruit Farm**, Sorell

Cafes are travellers' best options for breakfast and brunch. Expect to pay around $12 to $18 for main-course menu items. Outside of Hobart and Launceston, options for breakfast are more limited, but most hosted accommodation provides a hearty start to the day.

Pubs

The quality of Tasmanian pub food varies enormously. Upmarket city pubs provide ethnic flavours and innovation, while standard country pubs proffer schnitzels, roasts and basic seafood. Bistro meals ($18 to $28) come with the added ambience of a dining room, while bar-counter meals ($10 to $18) are more no-frills meals.

In Hobart, the Shipwright's Arms and the New Sydney Hotel offer the city's best pub food, while Launceston's finest meal with a cold beer can be found at the Sportsman's Hall Hotel. The Man O'Ross Hotel in Ross is also very good.

Vegetarian Dining

Vegetarian eateries and vegetarian menu selections are becoming common in large towns and areas visited by tourists. Cafes usually have vegetarian options, but vegans will find the going much tougher. For the best vegetarian and vegan eating in Tasmania, head to Sirens and Nourish in Hobart, or Fresh in Launceston.

See p314 for more information of restaurant prices and opening hours.

BLOG

Before your journey to Tasmania, check out Rita's Bite (www.pc-rita.blogspot.com), an authoritative online labour of love that's bursting with information about new restaurant openings in Hobart.

Tasmanian Wine

Since the mid-1950s Tasmania has gained international recognition for producing quality wines, characterised by their full, fruity flavour, along with the high acidity expected of cool, temperate wine regions. Today vineyards across the state are producing award-winning Pinot Noirs, Rieslings and Chardonnays, and Tassie wineries are growing grapes for many of the top Australian sparkling-wine brands.

Tasmania can be split into two main wine growing regions: the north and east around Launceston and Bicheno, and the south around Hobart. Throughout these areas are a growing number of larger operators with sophisticated cellar doors. There are also many smaller, family-owned vineyards – some open to the public by appointment only, others with restricted opening hours.

Start with wine tastings right at the cellar door. Some wineries' tastings are free, but most charge a small fee that is refundable if you purchase any wine.

The North & East

The Tamar Valley and Pipers River area is home to a number of well-established wineries, including Rosevears Estate, Tamar Ridge Wines and Pipers Brook. Wineries are also dotted down the east coast from Bicheno to Dunalley, including the well-respected Freycinet Vineyard.

TOP FIVE VINEYARD RESTAURANTS

A few places worth heading to for a long, leisurely lunch with some beaut Tassie wines (definitely book ahead):

» **Meadowbank Estate**, in Cambridge in the Coal River Valley
» **Home Hill Winery Restaurant**, near Huonville in the southeast
» **Moorilla Estate**, near Hobart
» **Strathlynn**, Rosevears in the Tamar Valley near Launceston
» **Pipers Brook**, Pipers River near Launceston

BREWING UP A TASSIE STORM

Beer lovers may want to time their Tasmanian sojourn around November's Tasmanian Beerfest. In October 2010, the inaugural Tasmanian Micro Brew Fest was also held in Hobart.

Here's a handy summary to kick off Beer Tourism Tasmania-style. See the breweries' main entries in destination chapters for details on tastings and brewery tours.

Moo Brew's (p53) standout beers include a zingy hefeweizen and a hoppy pilsner. Try the beer on tap at Hobart's Lark Distillery or the IXL Long Bar at the Henry Jones Art Hotel in Hobart.

Seven Sheds (p220) specialises in a malty Kentish ale, and also produces regular seasonal brews and honey-infused mead. Hobart's New Sydney Hotel usually has Seven Sheds on tap.

On the east coast, the **Ironhouse Brewery** (p161) makes beers that include a nicely hoppy pale ale and a Czech-style pilsner. In Hobart it's usually available at the Lark Distillery.

Two Metre Tall (p84) makes real ale and ciders, with ingredients sourced locally from its farm in the Derwent Valley. Try its Forester Real ale at Lark Distillery or at its Friday night 'Farm Bar' sessions from September to April.

Van Dieman Brewing (www.vandiemanbrewing.com.au) is based near Evandale, and produces six beers, including the Jacob's Ladder English-style Amber Ale. Try it at Knopwood's Retreat in Salamanca Place in Hobart, or see the Van Dieman website for stockists. And yes, the brewery does prefer to spell Dieman with the letter 'a'.

Around Hobart & The South

A major producer in the Derwent River Valley is Moorilla Estate, established in 1958, making it the oldest vineyard in southern Tasmania. Check out its tasty Moo Brew beers as well. The Coal River Valley, easily accessed from Hobart, is home to an increasing number of wineries, among them Meadowbank Estate and Puddleduck Vineyard.

Further south, in the Huon Valley area you'll find Hartzview Vineyard, Panorama Vineyard, and Home Hill. Cross on the ferry to Bruny Island Premium Wines – Australia's southernmost vineyard – or continue south to Dover and St Imre's Hungarian-style wines.

To learn more about the state's wine industry – and sample lots of local wines – visit Hobart's Tasmanian Wine Centre (p75), which can arrange worldwide shipping of wine purchases.

Tasmanian Beer

The definitive example of Tasmanian parochialism is the traditional local loyalty to regionally brewed beer. In the south it's Cascade from Hobart, and in the north, Launceston's James Boag's flies the flag. A few years ago, you could draw a line from Strahan through Ross to Bicheno, north of which no sane publican would serve Cascade. South of this hoppy division any mention of Boag's would provoke confusion and ridicule. These days things are much less definitive, and you'll find Cascade and Boag's both freely available in 'enemy territory'.

Cascade produces the very drinkable Cascade Premium Lager and Pale Ale. Visitors tend to ask for 'Cascade' expecting to get the bottle with the distinctive label bearing a Tasmanian Tiger, but you're unlikely to get Premium unless you ask specifically for it – you'll probably get Cascade Draught. Boag's produces similar-style beers to the Cascade brews, such as James Boag's Premium Lager and Boag's Draught. See p52 for details of tours of the Cascade Brewery, and p179 for information on touring the Boag's Brewery.

When We Eat: A Seasonal Celebration of Fine Tasmanian Food and Drink, by Liz McLeod, Bernard Lloyd and Paul County, is the companion guide to *Before We Eat*. This title covers the availability of seasonal foods in the state, accompanied by great recipes and photographs.

Wilderness & Wildlife

Tasmania's relatively small surface area is no barrier to packing in an incredible diversity of flora and fauna. The island's wilderness areas are recognised as comprising some of the planet's most important natural heritage areas, and a roll call of quirky wildlife species also reinforces Tasmania's unique appeal to travellers keenly interested in the surrounding natural environment.

The Tasmanian Wilderness

Australia's Only Island State

Adrift some 240km south of Victoria across tumultuous Bass Strait, Tasmania is Australia's only island state. To the east is the Tasman Sea, separating Australia and New Zealand; to the west the Southern Ocean roils nonstop to Antarctica. Including its lesser islands, Tasmania's surface area is 68,332 sq km, slightly smaller than Ireland and slightly larger than Sri Lanka.

The website of the Parks & Wildlife Service (www.parks.tas. gov.au) is an absolute gold mine of information. Download fact sheets on all parks, walks, plants and wildlife, campgrounds within parks and loads more.

Rugged But Beautiful

Although Tasmania's highest mountain, Mt Ossa, stands at only 1617m, much of the island's interior is extremely rugged. One indication of the lack of flat land is the proximity of central Hobart and Launceston to extremely steep hills.

Tasmania's coastline is studded with coves and beaches, shallow bays and broad estuaries, the result of river valleys being flooded by rising sea levels after the last ice age. By contrast the Central Plateau was covered by a single ice sheet during that ice age. Now it harbours a harsh environment, dotted with lakes and completely unsuitable for farming.

Showing the scars of recent glaciation, most of Tasmania's west is a twisted nest of mountainous ranges and ridges. The climate here is inhospitable, with annual rainfall greater than 3m, and the region is often pummelled by uncompromising seas. The west's cliffs, lakes, rainforests and wild rivers are among Tasmania's greatest attractions, and essential temptations for walkers, adventurers and photographers. Conversely, the rain-shadowed east coast is usually dry, sunny and beachy-keen. Welcome to Australia's most compact, yet versatile, state.

National Parks & Reserves

Australia's Most Wild State

A greater percentage of land is allocated to national parks or reserves in Tasmania than in any other Australian state. The Tasmania Parks & Wildlife Service (PWS) manages 423 reserves (including 19 national parks) covering 25,083 sq km. More than 2000km of superb walking tracks, unique flora and abundant fauna combine to create a mecca for naturalists, bushwalkers, wildlife-watchers, campers and photographers. Roughing it in the wild is an option, but guided walks, scenic flights and river cruises open this world up to the soft-option seeker. Rugged outdoorsy types can trek through inspiring natural beauty in the challenging southwest, or escape civilisation on the free-flowing Franklin River.

National Parks

Tasmania's outstanding feature is the state's 19 national parks. Walk on their trails and trek to their peaks, or just take in the environmental diversity encompassing highland lakes and surging rivers, ocean-swept beaches and craggy coves, wildlife-rich islands, jagged mountain ranges and lush temperate rainforest. Most of the parks are easily accessed by vehicle, but two (Savage River, in the heart of the Tarkine Wilderness, and the Kent Group, (a group of Bass Strait islets) are virtually inaccessible. Walls of Jerusalem National Park has no road access directly into the park itself, but there is a car park a steep walk of 30 minutes from the park boundary.

Public access to the national parks is encouraged as long as the safety and conservation regulations are observed; don't damage or alter the natural environment, and don't feed the wild animals.

When to Visit

Most people visit during summer (December to February) to enjoy long days and warm weather (although Tasmania has received snow in December!) Visiting outside these months sees smaller crowds and seasonal diversity. Autumn showcases the changing colours of foliage, winter sees snow on the peaks, and spring brings out a surge of wildflowers.

Park Fees

Visitors fees apply to all national parks, even when there's no ranger's office. Funds from the park entry fees remain with the Parks & Wildlife Service and go towards maintaining and making improvements to walking tracks, campgrounds, toilets, lookouts and picnic facilities, as well as funding a program to train new rangers and the popular summer 'Discovery Ranger' activities for younger visitors.

There are two types of passes: per vehicle and per person. A vehicle pass includes up to eight passengers, and costs $24/60 for 24 hours/eight weeks. An individual pass costs $12/30 for 24 hours/eight weeks. Annual passes are also available if you're a frequent return visitor.

For most visitors, the eight-week holiday pass is the best bet. Passes are available at most park entrances, at many visitor centres, aboard the *Spirit of Tasmania* ferries, at Service Tasmania (p76) and online at www.parks.tas.gov.au.

Access & Facilities

Information centres with walking information and history and ecology displays are at both ends of the Cradle Mountain–Lake St Clair National Park, as well as at Freycinet, Mt Field, and Narawntapu National Parks.

The 16 most accessible parks (ie not the Savage River, Kent Group and Walls of Jerusalem national parks) all have short walking tracks, toilets, shelters and picnic areas for day-visitors to enjoy; many also have barbecues. The entire World Heritage area and most national park areas have been declared 'fuel-stove-only' to protect the area's natural environment – this means no campfires. Dogs are definitely not allowed in any of the national parks.

WILDERNESS & WILDLIFE NATIONAL PARKS & RESERVES

If you plan on camping in Freycinet National Park from mid-December to Easter (early April), you'll need to fill out a ballot online at www. parks.tas.gov.au.

CAMPING

Camp sites are available in all accessible parks except for the Hartz Mountains, Mole Creek Karst and Rocky Cape national parks. Some sites are free, while others have a small charge per person ($3 to $7) in addition to park entry fees. Ben Lomond, Cradle Mountain–Lake St Clair, Freycinet, Maria Island and Mt Field national parks also have accommodation options inside their boundaries, ranging from basic huts to five-star resorts. See the regional chapters for more information and search for 'Camping' on www.parks.tas.gov.au for detailed information for each park.

Short walks suitable for wheelchair users and some prams are at the Cradle Mountain–Lake St Clair, Freycinet, Mt Field, Tasman and Franklin -Gordon Wild Rivers national parks (though wheelchair users may require assistance on these walks).

World Heritage Area

The internationally significant Tasmanian Wilderness World Heritage Area contains the state's four largest national parks – Southwest, Franklin -Gordon Wild Rivers, Cradle Mountain–Lake St Clair and Walls of Jerusalem – plus the Hartz Mountains National Park, the Central Plateau Conservation Area, the Adamsfield Conservation Area, a section of Mole Creek Karst National Park, the Devils Gullet State Reserve and part of the Liffey Falls State Reserve.

The region achieved World Heritage status in 1982, acknowledging that these parks make up one of the planet's last great, temperate wilderness areas. An area nominated for World Heritage status must satisfy at least one of 10 criteria, and the Tasmanian Wilderness World Heritage Area fulfilled a record seven categories. In 1989 the World Heritage area was enlarged to 13,800 sq km, around 20% of all of Tasmania.

In December 1997 the Macquarie Island World Heritage Area was proclaimed for its outstanding geological and faunal significance. See p320 for details of cruises to this remote sub-Antarctic island 1500km southeast of Tasmania.

Several of Tasmania's national parks comprise the Tasmanian Wilderness World Heritage Area. There are only 166 such natural World Heritage areas in the world; to find out what gives these places 'outstanding universal value', see http://whc.unesco.org/en/list.

Access & Tours

Most of the area is managed by the Parks & Wildlife Service as a publicly accessible wilderness. Being so large however, most of it is accessible only to bushwalkers with at least one week's food. For considerably less demanding ways to visit, see information on guided walks, kayaking tours and scenic flights (including landings and walking time), on p273. There are also scenic flights over the area out of Hobart, Strahan, and Cradle Valley near Cradle Mountain.

Other Protected Areas

Apart from the national parks, the Parks & Wildlife Service also manages a further 423 reserves of land. These reserves are usually established around one significant, protected feature – often wildlife – but have fewer regulations than national parks and allow some mining, farming, forestry or tourism development. Many are very small and include caves, waterfalls, historic sites and some coastal regions. Usually there are no entry fees to these areas, except where the government has actively restored or developed the area.

Categories of Reserves

Categories of reserves managed by the PWS include **state reserves** such as the Hastings Caves in the southeast and the Nut in Stanley; **conservation areas** including the Arthur Pieman Conservation Area in the state's northwest and the Bay of Fires in the northeast; **nature reserves**, cover

ing marine reserves; and **historic sites** including high-profile spots like
Port Arthur and the Richmond Gaol.

Forest Reserves

On small protected areas inside larger state forests, these reserves include waterfalls and picnic areas. During weekdays some forestry roads
are closed to private vehicles. If the roads are open, drive slowly and give
way to logging trucks.

Marine Reserves

Fishing or collecting living or dead material within Tasmanian marine
reserves is illegal. Reserves include Tinderbox near Hobart, around the
northern part of Maria Island, around Governor Island off the coast at
Bicheno, at Port Davey and Bathurst Harbour in the southwest on Macquarie Island. See www.parks.gov.tas.au for other marine reserves, including Sanctuary Zones and Habitat Protection Zones, in which fishing
is either banned outright or limited.

Tasmanian Wildlife

Like Australia, But Also Very Different

The distinctive mammals of mainland Australia – the marsupials and
monotremes isolated for at least 45 million years – are also found in
Tasmania. Marsupials, including wallabies and pademelons, give birth to
partially developed young that they then protect and suckle in a pouch.
Monotremes (platypuses and echidnas) lay eggs but also suckle their
young. Most are nocturnal and the best time to see them in the wild is
around dusk. The smaller mammals can be difficult to find in the bush,
but there are plenty of wildlife parks around the state where they can
be seen.

Tasmania's fauna is not as varied as that of the rest of Australia and
it has relatively few large mammals. Its best-known marsupial the Tasmanian tiger resembled a large dog or wolf and had dark stripes and a
stiff tail. It was officially declared extinct in 1986, but hadn't been sighted
with any certainty since 1936.

Birdwatching

Tasmania has a wide variety of seabirds, parrots, cockatoos, honeyeaters
and wrens, and birds of prey (hawks, owls, falcons and eagles) are also on
the prowl. See this book's index for the best places for birdwatching on
the island, and if you're a mad-keen twitcher, sign up for a comprehensive week-long tour of Tasmania with Bruny Island's Inala Tours (www.
inalabruny.com.au). Inala is also a driving force behind October's annual
Bruny Island Bird Festival (www.bien.org.au). Birding highlights of a Tasmanian visit include the following:

Black Currawongs

The black currawong *(Stepera fuliginosa)*, found only in Tasmania, lives
primarily on plant matter and insects, but will sometimes kill small
mammals or infant birds. You'll often see this large, black, fearless bird
goose-stepping around picnic areas.

Mutton Birds

The mutton bird is more correctly called the short-tailed shearwater
(Puffinus tenuirostris). It lives in burrows in sand dunes and migrates
annually to the northern hemisphere. These small birds fly in spectacular flocks on their way back to their burrows (the same ones every year)

*The Mammals of
Australia,* edited
by Ron Strahan,
is a complete sur-
vey of Australia's
somewhat offbeat
mammals. Every
species is illus-
trated and almost
everything known
about them
is covered in
individual species
accounts, written
by the nation's
experts.

TASMANIA'S NATIONAL PARKS

PARK	FEATURES	ACTIVITIES	BEST TIME TO VISIT
Ben Lomond National Park	alpine flora, the state's main ski field	walking, skiing, rock climbing	year-round
*Cradle Mountain-Lake St Clair National Park	moorlands & mountain peaks, the famed Overland Track, Australia's deepest freshwater lake	walking, scenic flights, wildlife-spotting	year-round
Douglas-Apsley National Park	dry eucalypt forest, river gorges, waterfalls, wildlife, waterhole-swimming	walking, swimming	summer
*Franklin-Gordon Wild Rivers National Park	two grand wilderness watercourses, deep river gorges, rainforest, Frenchmans Cap, Aboriginal sites	rafting, cruises (from Strahan)	summer
Freycinet National Park	picturesque coastal scenery, Wineglass Bay, granite peaks, great beaches, walks	walking, abseiling, sea-kayaking, scenic flights, fishing	summer
*Hartz Mountains National Park	alpine heath, rainforest, glacial lakes, views of the southwest wilderness	walking	spring, summer
Kent Group National Park	Bass Strait islets (mostly inaccessible), fur seals, sea birds, historical significance	wildlife-watching	year-round
Maria Island National Park	traffic-free offshore island with convict history, peaceful bays, fossil-filled cliffs	walking, cycling, swimming	summer
Mole Creek Karst National Park	more than 200 limestone caves & sinkholes, some open to the public	walking, caving	year-round
Mt Field National Park	abundant flora & fauna, alpine scenery, high-country walks, Russell Falls, Mt Mawson ski field	walking, skiing, wildlife-watching	year-round
Mt William National Park	long sandy beaches, protected grey Forester kangaroos	walking, fishing, swimming	spring-summer
Narawntapu National Park	north-coast lagoons, wetlands, tea-tree mazes, native wildlife	swimming, walking, wildlife-spotting	summer
Rocky Cape National Park	bushland, rocky headlands, caves used by Aborigines, exceptional marine environment	swimming, fishing, walking	summer
Savage River National Park	cool temperate rainforest inside the Tarkine wilderness; utterly secluded, no road access	walking	summer
South Bruny National Park	wild southern cliffs, surf & swimming beaches, heathlands, wildlife	walking, swimming, surfing, wildlife-spotting, ecocruises	spring-summer
*Southwest National Park	vast multi-peaked wilderness; one of the world's most pristine natural wonders	walking, swimming, scenic flights, mountaineering, kayaking	summer
Strzelecki National Park	mountainous slice of islandscape, rare flora & fauna	walking, rock-climbing, wildlife-watching, swimming	summer
Tasman National Park	spectacular sea cliffs and rock formations, offshore islands, forests, bays & beaches	walking, diving, surfing, ecocruises, fishing, sea-kayaking	spring-summer
*Walls of Jerusalem National Park	spectacular, remote alpine & mountain wilderness, no road access	walking	summer

* Part of the Tasmanian Wilderness World Heritage Area

at dusk. They are still hunted by some Tasmanians, notably around Flinders Island, and there are certain places where you will occasionally see cooked mutton bird advertised for sale.

Penguins

The fairy penguin *(Eudyptula minor)* is the smallest penguin in the world, and lives in burrows in Tasmania's sand dunes. Penguin-spotting is a popular activity for tourists and is particularly fun for the young (and young at heart!). Visitors can see Tassie's penguins waddle from the ocean to their nests just after sunset at Bruny Island, Burnie, and Penguin (naturally). Take a picnic, settle in to watch the sun go down and enjoy the show.

Pouches & Bouncers
Kangaroos & Wallabies

Both the kangaroo and wallaby species found in Tasmania are related to those found on the mainland, but are usually smaller. The largest marsupial is the forester kangaroo *(Macropus giganteus)*. Following increasing pressure from the growth of farming in the area, the Narawntapu National Park and Mt William National Park have been set aside to preserve this impressive animal.

The Bennetts wallaby *(Macropus rufogriseus)* thrives in colder climates (Tasmania certainly fits the bill), and is often seen angling for food at Cradle Mountain–Lake St Clair National Park or Freycinet National Park. They may seem cute and straight out of central casting from *Skippy* but please don't feed them because the animals are wild and should be feeding themselves. Giving them processed foods such as bread crusts or biscuits not only teaches them to rely on the occasional visitor as their main food source, it actually causes a fatal disease called 'lumpy jaw'. Bennetts wallabies stand just over 1m in height and can seem very friendly, but along with other native animals can sometimes be aggressive. It is best to approach with caution.

Possums

There are several varieties of possum in Tasmania. The sugar glider *(Petaurus breviceps)* has developed impressive webs between its legs, enabling it to glide effortlessly from tree to tree. The most common and boldest of the species is the brushtail possum *(Trichosurus vulpecula)*, which lives and sleeps in trees but descends to the ground in search of food. Possums show little fear of humans, and regularly conduct late-night food heists at campgrounds. You've been warned! Don't forget to zip up your tent and carefully store any leftover food. You may also be alarmed to hear something very similar to a Darth Vader impersonation as they hiss and growl at one another, particularly during mating season. A shyer relation is the smaller ringtail possum *(Pseudocheirus peregrinus)*.

Uniquely Tasmanian

The Tasmanian pademelon *(Thylogale billardierii,* also known as a rufous wallaby), is a smaller, rounder species sometimes seen hiding in forests. It's a notoriously shy creature, which you'll be lucky to see in the wild – tread quietly if you do spot it. Other endemic Tasmanian marsupials include the Tasmanian bettong *(Bettongia gaimardi)*, found exclusively in the east of the state and growing only to a compact 2kg, and the eastern quoll *(Dasyurus viverrinus)*, approximately the size of a domestic cat. The eastern quoll was reported extinct on the Australian mainland in 1964 – the last known sighting was believed to be in Sydney's exclusive Vaucluse neighbourhood – but is common and fully protected in Tasmania.

Wombats

Wombats *(Vombatus ursinus)* are very solid, powerfully built marsupials with broad heads and short, stumpy legs weighing up to 35kg. They live in underground burrows that they excavate, and are usually very casual, slow-moving animals, partly because they don't have any natural predators to worry about.

(Slightly) Scarier Species

In 2010, the Tasmanian state government presented a plan to the Australian Federal Government for 100,000 brushtail possums a year to be killed and processed for overseas sale.

There are only three types of snake found in Tasmania, but they're all poisonous. The largest and most dangerous is the tiger snake *(Notechis scutatus)*, which will sometimes attack, particularly in late summer. The other snakes are the copperhead *(Austrelaps superbus)* and the smaller white-lipped whip snake *(Drysdalia coronoides)*. Bites are very rare, as most snakes are generally shy and try to avoid humans. If you do get bitten, don't try to catch the snake, as there's a common antivenene for all three – instead, get to hospital for treatment.

The eight-legged critter with the longest reach (up to 18cm) on the island is the Tasmanian cave spider *(Hickmania troglodytes)*, which spins horizontal mesh-webs on the ceiling of a cave to catch insects such as cave crickets. Other local species include the Tasmanian funnel-web, huntsman and white-tailed spiders.

Tasmania's Threatened Icon

The Tasmanian devil *(Sarcophilus harrisii)* mostly eats insects, small birds and mammals, and carrion, and can often be seen at night feasting on roadkill (a habit that unfortunately often leads to it becoming roadkill itself). It's about 75cm long and has a short, stocky body covered in black fur with a white stripe across its chest.

Devil Facial Tumour Disease (DFTD, a fatal, communicable cancer) infects up to 75% of the wild population. Quarantined populations have been established, but efforts to find a cure are ongoing. Check out www.tassiedevil.com.au for more DFTD info. To make a tax-free donation to the devils' cause, log on to www.devilsindanger.com.au.

The Weird & Wonderful

The platypus *(Ornithorhynchus anatinus)* and echidna *(Tachyglossus aculeatus)* are the only living monotremes – mammals which lay eggs.

Monotremes are often regarded as living fossils, and although they display some intriguing features of their reptile ancestors (egg-laying, and that their reproductive, defecatory and urinary systems utilise a single outlet), they suckle their young on milk secreted from mammary glands.

Platypus

The platypus lives in water and has a ducklike bill, webbed feet and a beaverlike body. You're most likely to see one in a stream or lake, searching out food in the form of crustaceans, worms and tadpoles with its electro-sensitive bill.

Echidnas

Echidnas are totally different and look similar to porcupines, covered in impressively sharp spikes. They primarily eat ants, and have powerful claws for unearthing their food and digging into the dirt to protect themselves when threatened. They're common in Tasmania but if you approach one, all you're likely to see up close is a brown, spiky ball. However, if you keep quiet and don't move, you might be lucky. They have poor eyesight and will sometimes walk right past your feet.

Visitors from Antarctica

Southern right whales *(Eubalaena australis)* migrate annually from Antarctica to southern Australia to give birth to their calves in shallow waters. So named because they were the 'right' whales to kill, they were hunted to the point of extinction while sustaining a lucrative industry around Tasmania. They are still seen off the Tasmanian coast (sometimes in Hobart's Derwent River estuary) and occasionally beach themselves.

Long-finned pilot whales *(Globicephala melas)* are more commonly involved in beach strandings in Tasmania. In 2009 up to 140 pilot whales died in a mass stranding on King Island, while in 2011 around 15 died on the southern beaches of Bruny Island.

The original cartoon run of the Taz, the Looney Tunes Tasmanian devil character was only five short episodes in 1964. He was then brought back for three seasons of his show in 1991.

A Unique & Diverse Flora

Tasmania's myriad flora ranges from the dry forests of the east, through the alpine moorlands of the centre, to the rainforests of the west. Many of the state's plants are unlike those found in the rest of Australia and have ties with species that grew millions of years ago, when the southern continents were joined at the hip as Gondwanaland. Similar plants are found in South America and fossilised in Antarctica.

See the Parks & Wildlife Service (www.parks.tas.gov.au) for comprehensive information on Tasmania's diverse array of flora.

Ancient & Unique Pines

Many of Tasmania's trees are unique to the state – the island's native pines are particularly distinctive. The best known is the Huon pine which can live for thousands of years, but there are other slow-growing island pines, including the king billy pine, celery-top pine and pencil pine, all of which exist commonly at higher altitudes and live for around 500 years. Some pencil pines on the Central Plateau have managed to hang in there for 1000 years, but they're especially vulnerable to fire.

TIGER, TIGER, BURNING BRIGHT

The story of the Tasmanian tiger (*Thylacinus cynocephalus*, or thylacine), a striped, nocturnal, doglike predator once widespread in Tasmania, has two different endings. Version one says thylacines were hunted to extinction in the 19th and early 20th centuries, the last captive tiger dying in Hobart Zoo in 1936. No specimen, living or dead, has been conclusively discovered since then, despite hundreds of alleged sightings.

Version two maintains that thylacines continue a furtive existence deep in the Tasmanian wilderness. Scientists ridicule such suggestions, but the tantalising possibility of remnant tigers makes them prime corporate fodder. Tasmanian companies plaster tiger imagery on everything from beer bottles to licence plates and record labels.

In recent years, scientists at Sydney's Australia Museum began scripting another possible ending to the tiger saga. Kicking off version three, biologists managed to extract DNA from a thylacine pup preserved in alcohol since 1866. Their aim was to successfully replicate the DNA, with the long-term goal of cloning the species. Needless to say, there were many obstacles, and the project drew criticism from those who would rather have seen the money spent on helping current endangered species. In early 2005 the project was shelved due to the quality of the extracted DNA being too poor to work with, but new work done by the University of Melbourne in 2008 has again raised the possibility of success in the future.

You can see incredible black-and-white footage of a tiger in captivity at the Tasmanian Museum & Art Gallery in Hobart (p50) and on YouTube (search for 'thylacine').

WOMBATS

Beech & Eucalyptus

The dominant tree of the wetter forests is myrtle beech, similar to European beeches. Tasmania's many flowering trees include the leatherwood, which is nondescript most of the year but erupts into bright flowers during summer. It's white and pale-pink flowers yield a uniquely fragrant honey.

Many of Tasmania's eucalyptus trees also grow on the mainland, but down on the island they often grow ludicrously tall. The swamp gum (*Eucalyptus regnans,* known as mountain ash on the mainland) can grow to 100m in height and is the tallest flowering plant in the world. Look for it in the forests of the southeast, where you'll also find the state's floral emblem, the Tasmanian blue gum (*Eucalyptus globulus*).

In autumn you might catch an eye-full of the deciduous beech, the only truly deciduous native plant in Australia. It usually grows as a fairly straggly bush with bright green leaves. In autumn, however, the leaves become golden and sometimes red, adding a splash of colour to the forests. The easiest places to see the display are the Cradle Mountain and Mt Field National Parks.

Challenges For Bushwalkers

If threatened, a wombat dives headfirst into a tunnel, blocking the entrance with its extremely tough rear end with extra-thick skin.

A notable component of the understorey in Tasmanian forests is the infamous horizontal scrub, a plant that can make life hell for bushwalkers attempting to avoid established tracks. More familiar, and considerably more benign, is buttongrass. Growing in thick clumps up to 2m high, this uniquely Tasmanian grass prefers broad, swampy areas like the many flat-bottomed valleys pressed out by ice ages. Buttongrass plains are usually so muddy and unpleasant to walk over, that in many places the Parks & Wildlife Service has incorporated sections of elevated boardwalk into tracks crossing such areas.

Another interesting specimen is the cushion plant, which is found in alpine areas and at first sight resembles a green rock. In fact, it's an extremely tough, short plant that grows into thick mats ideally suited to helping it cope with its severe living conditions. It's not so tough, however, that it can tolerate footprints – stepping on one can destroy thousands of tiny leaves, which take decades to regenerate.

THE IMPACT OF HUMANS

Since Europeans arrived, Tasmania has lost more than 30 species of plants and animals – most famously, the thylacine, or Tasmanian tiger. Currently, over 600 types of flora and fauna are listed under the state's Threatened Species Protection Act.

Among Tasmania's threatened birds are the forty-spotted pardalote, orange-bellied parrot and wedge-tailed eagle. Tasmania is also home to the largest invertebrate in the world, the giant freshwater crayfish, whose numbers have been so depleted by recreational fishing and habitat destruction that it's now illegal to take any specimens from their natural habitat.

Introduced species are also having an impact, and in 2001 it was reported a fox had been spotted near Longford in the state's north. Fox predation puts nearly 80 of the island's indigenous land species at enormous risk because of their vulnerability to attack from an animal against which they have no defence. Subsequent reports of the European red fox in other parts of the state confirmed foxes had been deliberately introduced to Tasmania, probably for the purposes of hunting. A full-time fox taskforce has been set up by the state government. If you see a fox, phone the **Fox Hotline** (☎1300 369 688).

Only in Tasmania

Horizontal Scrub

The skinny horizontal scrub *(Anodopetalum biglandulosum)* is a feature of the undergrowth in many parts of Tasmania's southwest. It grows by sending up thin, vigorous stems whenever an opening appears in the forest canopy. The old branches soon become heavy and fall, then put up shoots of their own. This continuous process of growth and collapse creates dense, tangled thickets – bushwalkers have been rumoured to completely disappear into it when venturing off the beaten track. You can see twisted examples of horizontal scrub in the southwest's forests and in the Hartz Mountains.

Huon Pine

Prized by shipbuilders and furniture makers for its rich golden hue, rot-resistant oils, and fine grain, Tasmania's Huon pine *(Lagarostrobos franklinii)* is one of the slowest-growing and longest-living trees on the planet. Individual trees can take 2000 years to reach 30m in height and live to 3000 years, a situation overlooked by 19th-century loggers and ship builders who plundered the southwest forests in search of this 'yellow gold'. Fortunately it's now a protected species. Most of the Huon pine furniture and timberwork you'll see around the state is recycled, or comes from dead trees salvaged from riverbeds and hydroelectric dams. Some older trees remain, and one 2500-year-old beauty can be viewed during cruises on the Gordon River.

King's Lomatia

This endemic Tasmanian plant, a member of the *Proteaceae family,* has flowers similar to those of the grevillea, and grows in the wild in only one small part of the Tasmanian Wilderness World Heritage Area. Studies of the plant's chromosomes have revealed that it's incapable of reproducing sexually, which is why it must rely on sending up shoots to create new plants. Further research has shown that there's absolutely no genetic diversity within the population, which means that every king's lomatia in existence is a clone. It's the oldest known clone in the world, thought to have been around for at least 43,600 years.

David Owen's little hardback *Thylacine* investigates the great fascination with the Tasmanian tiger, hunted to extinction and now a treasured symbol of Tasmania and of the conservation movement worldwide.

WILDERNESS & WILDLIFE A UNIQUE & DIVERSE FLORA

Environmental Politics in Tasmania

Anna Krien
Anna Krien's debut book, *Into the Woods: The Battle for Tasmania's Forests,* was published by Black Inc in 2010 and is shortlisted for the Douglas Stewart Prize.

It was the loss of Lake Pedder that first divided Tasmanians. In spite of its national park status, the glacial lake with a pink quartz beach was flooded in 1972 to create the Gordon Dam. Tasmania was, and still is, consistently passed over for manufacturing investments, and the state government was intent on luring industry to the island with the offer of cheap electricity. But the 1960s was also a heady time of naturalist and hiking groups as a newfound appreciation of the Australian landscape was emerging and protesters seemed to converge at the lake. Ignoring a nationwide petition to save Lake Pedder (with over 250,000 signatures, it was the largest conservation petition at the time in Australia's history), both state political parties declared the lake a 'non issue'. This led to the formation of the United Tasmania Group (later to become the Greens), which became the first political Green party in the world and has haunted the island's entrenched two-party political system ever since.

See the website of Forestry Tasmania (www.for estrytas.com.au) for its views on how both sides of the Tasmanian logging debate – economic and environmental – can be managed.

Saving the Franklin River

In 1976, when the Franklin River fell in the sights of the Hydro Electric Commission, the activists were ready. Lessons learnt from the failure of saving Lake Pedder came to the fore as they ignited a nationwide campaign that would become the most famous environmental fight in Australia's history. At its peak, hundreds of people swarmed to the wild river's edge in the west to protest as workers and bulldozers cut a path to the banks. A core political team, led by Greens leader Bob Brown, pushed for a national referendum on the river's fate. In 1981, the pressured federal Liberal party offered a compromise – voters could choose between a 'big' dam and a 'little' dam. Almost half of Australian voters scrawled 'NO DAM' across the scrap of paper and dropped them into the ballot boxes with disdain. A third of Tasmania's voters did the same. Sniffing the wind, leader of the federal Labor opposition Bob Hawke told a crowd gathered at a 'Save the Franklin' rally, that he would protect the Franklin if he were elected. His wife, standing beside him, wore yellow dangly earrings with 'No Dam' placarded on them. Finally in 1983, after 1272 protesters had been arrested, 1324 charges laid and 447 jailed in the island's maximum-security prison including Bob Brown, who went from prison to taking a seat in state parliament in a four-week turnaround, the federal election swung to the Labor party. Tasmania's state government tried to repeal federal orders to reverse construction on the river in the High Court, but lost by one vote. It was the local conservation movement's first victory, and the Wilderness Society was formed – now a nation-wide advocacy group and major player in the island's conservation. But the victory was not without a large degree of trauma and bitter division. Hours after the river's safety was ensured and hundreds of jobs therefore dismissed, a 2000-year-old protected tree was axed, drilled and filled with diesel and set alight.

Logging & Woodchipping Industries

To this day, the division continues. But the conservation movement's enemy is no longer hydro-electricity. It is the logging industry, in particular – woodchippers. In 2007, according to the *Wood Resource Quarterly,* Australia exported a record quantity of woodchips, over 6 million tonnes, almost 70% of which came from native forests.

In 1972, four companies had locked in contracts for 30 million tonnes of Tasmania's native forest woodchips to the value of $460 million. Initially promoting their work as an act of frugality, woodchip companies claimed they were simply using the 'waste on the forest floor' left behind by loggers. But while loggers today present a united front against attacks from the conservation movement, this was not always the case.

In the late '60s and '70s, loggers who had been selectively felling mature trees for sawlogs for generations accused the newcomers of taking

SIMPLE STEPS FOR SAVING THE FORESTS *SENATOR BOB BROWN*

Tasmania's wild and scenic beauty, along with a human history dating back 30,000 years, is a priceless heritage available to all of us. The waterfalls, wild rivers, lovely beaches, snowcapped mountains, turquoise seas, and wildlife are abundant and accessible for locals and visitors alike.

Because we are all creations of nature – the curl of our ears is fashioned to pick up the faintest sounds of the forest floor – we are all bonded to the wilds. Yet around the world, wilderness is a fast-disappearing resource and Tasmania is no exception.

This year 150,000 truckloads of the island's native forests, including giant eucalypt species producing the tallest flowering plants on earth, will arrive at the woodchip mills, en route to Japan. After logging, the forests are firebombed and every wisp of fur, feather and flower is destroyed. These great forests, built of carbon, are one of the world's best hedges against global warming. They are carbon banks. Yet they are being looted, taken from our fellow creatures and all who come after us. The log trucks on Tasmania's highways are enriching banks of a different kind.

Over two decades ago, people power saved Tasmania's wild Franklin and Lower Gordon Rivers (p262), which nowadays attract hundreds of thousands of visitors to the west coast. Those visitors, in turn, bring jobs, investment and local prosperity. Saving the environment has been a boon for the economy and employment.

The rescue of Tasmania's forests relies on each of us, and there are plenty of ways we can help. We can help with letters or phone calls to newspapers, radio stations or politicians; with every cent donated to the forest campaigners; and in every well-directed vote. The tourist dollar speaks loudly in Tasmania, so even overseas travellers, who cannot vote, should take the opportunity to write letters to our newspapers and politicians. With each step we take, we move toward ending this destruction of Tasmania's wild and scenic heritage.

Senator Bob Brown was elected to the Tasmanian parliament in 1983 and first elected to the Senate in 1996. His books include The Valley of the Giants (The Wilderness Society, with Vica Bayley, 2005). Read more about Bob Brown at www.bobbrown.org.au.

away their future yield. Woodchippers had introduced 'clearfelling' – wherein they literally mowed a logging coupe flat by carting away useful trees and burning the rest. It became clear that the 'waste' the loggers left behind, was the actual forest. Fights broke out between the two crews but the chippers took priority. Woodchips were an accountant's dream – cheap public forest, a resource extraction method that requires little delicacy or skill, quick turnaround, and a seemingly insatiable market in Japan, who turned the high volume, low-value product into pulp and paper. Soon loggers were instructed to cut all sawlog trees in one swoop, whether the resource was mature or not, and let the chippers take the rest.

Today this practice continues. Excepting a few mills on the mainland licensed to chip the butts and heads of trees felled for sawlog purposes (as well as use of the residue from sawmills) this ideology of waste efficiency is mostly spin.

Read the perspective of the loggers on the Gunns website (gunns.com.au). 'Making Sustainability is Our Business' is its motto. Make it yours to understand both sides of this important debate. Up until recently Gunns Limited ran 85% of the island's timber industry.

Semantics & Stickers

Many Australians refer to Tasmania's forests conflict as the 'forest wars' and in this vein, like all wars, visitors to the island will need to wade through a significant amount of propaganda and spin.

It can be a semantic nightmare. Conservation groups produce aerial shots of scarred charcoal swathes of land, using words such as 'Hiroshima' and 'rape', while pro-timber organisations respond with photographs revealing a 'tapestry' of new growth. Even more confusing are the statistics. From state forestry and the timber industry, you'll hear that 45% of the island's forests are protected, 95% of 'high quality' wilderness is in reserves and 79% of all old growth forest is safe from logging. From green groups however, 30% of Tasmania's original forest is protected from logging and 70% has either been destroyed or is still available for logging.

It's often said that each glut of car stickers in Tasmania signals a new chapter in the feud. Visitors to the island may want to keep an eye out for these as well as for the wildlife. The Franklin River campaign produced pro-dam stickers that read 'Save a job, shoot a Green', 'Fertilise the Forest: Doze in a Greenie' and 'Keep Warm This Winter: Burn a Greenie'. In response, 'No Dam' was plastered defiantly across the country. Today's stickers include 'Save the Styx', 'Tasmania: The Corrupt State' and 'I love Tassie's forests, so SUE me', alluding to the Gunns 20 case in 2004 which saw the local woodchipping giant, Gunns Limited, bring a $6.3 million lawsuit against 20 protesters.

Gunns & the Pulp Mill

Tasmania's Gunns Limited is one of the world's largest native hardwood woodchippers. The most recent addition to bumpers and rear windscreens is a 'No Pulp Mill' sticker, in regards to a $2.9 billion pulp mill proposed by Gunns. And while a pulp mill doesn't have quite the same romantic appeal as the Franklin River or Lake Pedder, it has, however, broadened the depth of the island's green movement into a coalition of convenience. In particular, residents of the Tamar Valley, the proposed location for the mill, have proven more difficult than Gunns expected, as many disbelieve the company's claims that their health, their economies and the environment has been taken into consideration and will be unaffected by the mill.

Its monopoly compromised local timber workers' bargaining power when it came to their rights, wages, and compensation. The company also leased vast swathes of state land, enjoyed first buyer's rights over much of the state's unprotected native forest and was the biggest private landowner on the island. Its directors also appeared to have had a direct line to the state's political powerbrokers.

Recently, prior to Gunns' announcing its pulp mill proposal in 2005, the state government rolled out a 'Pulp Mill Taskforce'. The $1.4 million tax-paid initiative, which included a touring promotional minibus, sought to convince locals that the island needed a pulp mill. Controversially, Labor premier Paul Lennon appeared on pro-pulp-mill TV advertisements and it was reported in the *Tasmanian Times* that he also had a Gunns' building subsidiary do his home renovations during an independent assessment of the company's mill proposal. During this time, the independent panel was blighted with numerous resignations, as three key members – Christopher Wright, a retired Supreme Court judge, Dr Warwick Raverty, known as the country's 'go to' pulp mill expert, and Julian Green, a senior bureaucrat – accused the state government and Gunns of intimidation and bullying.

Today, the site for the Gunns' pulp mill is empty. The company has shrunk in size, its influence diminished, and its controversial board members – former premier Robin Gray and director John Gay – have been forced to resign by its own investors. In state parliament, the Greens party currently holds the balance of power. Gunns vows that the pulp mill will be built – but its finances continue to say otherwise and its much-needed investors are demanding the company receives globally recognised ethical certification before any deal can be struck.

The Statement of Principles

In 2010, the Statement of Principles agreement regarding the state's forest wars, was negotiated. This pact – largely driven by broad opposition to the pulp mill – is widely believed to be different to the past 30 years of forestry inquiries, impact statements, court cases, legislation and subsequent amendments, and agreements, all of which also claimed to be the last of their kind but seemed only to further entrench the conflict. This recent roundtable discussion between the forest industry, timber workers *and* conservation groups, has produced a carefully worded statement proposing to phase out logging the island's native forests for commodities such as woodchips and has called for a moratorium on the logging of high-conservation-value forests. This pact, however, is waiting on federal funding, and with considerable reason, the federal government is not handing it over without careful thought. After all in 2005, in a deal struck between then-prime minister, John Howard, and premier Paul Lennon, $250 million was given to the island's timber industry to restructure and shift into a sustainable future. A subsequent investigation by the Australian National Audit Office suggested that the distribution of these funds was rushed, not transparent and failed commonly accepted standards for grants. The proposed deadline for this most recent moratorium has since come and gone, with high-conservation-value forests still being logged.

But more than money, a change of attitude on the island is required. Tasmania is a beautiful, but poor state. Many of those that want to protect the wilderness say the island can survive on tourism, whilst those who are 'pro-development at all cost' rely on short-term job creation via government capitalisation projects and natural resource extraction. In truth, neither of these economies can keep the island afloat alone, and nor are they the only options. As many locals will tell you, there is a lot more to Tasmania than trees.

The Tasmanian Conservation Trust (www.tct.org.au) is the state's primary nongovernmental conservation organisation. In addition to managing its own campaigns, the TCT hosts the Tasmanian offices of two other Australian environmental organisations: the National Threatened Species Network, and the Marine and Coastal Community Network.

Survival
Guide

DIRECTORY A–Z....310

Accommodation..........310

Activities 312

Business Hours 312

Climate..................312

Dangers & Annoyances...312

Discount Cards..........314

Electrical 314

Food 314

Gay & Lesbian
Travellers 314

Health...................314

Holidays.................315

Insurance................315

Internet Access..........315

Legal Matters 315

Maps....................315

Money...................316

Post.....................316

Solo Travellers...........316

Telephone 316

Time 317

Tourist Information 317

Tours....................317

Travellers with
Disabilities..............318

Visas....................318

Women Travellers........319

Work 319

TRANSPORT...... 320

GETTING THERE & AWAY 320

Entering Tasmania...... 320

Domestic Air Travel 320

Sea 320

GETTING AROUND.......321

Air.......................321

Bicycle 322

Boat 322

Bus 322

Car & Motorcycle....... 323

Hitching 325

Local Transport......... 325

Train 325

Directory A–Z

Accommodation

Accommodation in Tasmania includes campgrounds, hostels, B&Bs, guesthouses, ecoresorts, heritage hotels and motels. Main tourist centres are often fully booked in summer, at Easter and on public holidays, so booking ahead is recommended. High-season prices are quoted in this book unless otherwise indicated. Weekend visits are popular with mainland Australians, so look for cheaper midweek and off-peak packages for good discounts.

In most areas you'll find seasonal price variations. Over summer (December to February) and at school and public holidays, prices are the highest. The cooler winter off-peak season (June to August) offers lower rates.

This book's Sleeping reviews are ordered in preference:

$	under $100 per double
$$	$100 to $200 per double
$$$	greater than $200 per double

Most accommodation in Tasmania offers nonsmoking rooms or is 100% nonsmoking. Ask about car parking when booking accommodation for central Hobart and Launceston.

Key websites:

Discover Tasmania (www.discovertasmania.com) Tasmania's official tourism website offers online booking of accommodation.

Ecohotel (www.ecohotel.com.au) Concise listings of environmentally aware accommodation.

Luxury Oz Stays (www.luxuryozstays.com.au) Top-end boutique hotels, lodges and rental properties.

RACT (www.ract.com.au) The Royal Automobile Club of Tasmania.

Take a Break (www.takeabreak.com.au) Everything from campgrounds to hotels and motels.

Tasmanian Accommodation (www.tasmanianaccommodation.info) Specialised B&B listings.

Tasmania Luxury Accommodation (www.tasmanialuxuryaccommodation.com.au) Resorts, boutique hotels and luxury B&B accommodation.

Wotif (www.wotif.com) Last-minute deals.

Camping & Caravan Parks

Camping in most national parks requires you to purchase a park pass (see p295) and then pay a small (unpowered) site fee ($15/10/5 per family/couple/child, additional adult $5). A few parks with minimal facilities don't have site fees, and Forestry Tasmania also offer a few simple camp sites.

Tasmania has many camping and caravan parks. Nightly costs for two campers are between $18 and $26, slightly more for a powered site. Most caravan parks are well maintained and equipped with hot showers, kitchens and laundry facilities. Some parks offer cheap dorm-style accommodation and more expensive on-site cabins. Cabin sizes and facilities vary, but expect to pay $90 to $150 for two people in a cabin with kitchenette.

Key websites:

Camping Tasmania (www.campingtasmania.com) Discovering Tasmania by camping.

Caravan Tasmania (www.caravantasmania.com.au) Specialist caravanning website including discussion forums.

Forestry Tasmania (www.forestrytas.com.au) Look under 'Visiting Our Forests'.

Parks & Wildlife Service (www.parks.tas.gov.au) Click on 'Outdoor Recreation', then 'Camping and Caravanning'.

Guesthouses & B&Bs

Tasmania's B&Bs fill everything from restored convict-built cottages to upmarket country manors and beachside bungalows. Some places advertised as B&Bs are actually self-contained cottages with breakfast provisions supplied. Only in the cheaper B&Bs will bathroom facilities be shared. Some B&B hosts may cook dinner for guests (usually 24 hours' notice is required). Rates range from $120 to $300 per double.

Key websites:

Beautiful Accommodation (www.beautifulaccommodation. com) Luxury B&Bs and self-contained rental properties.

Oz B&B Directory (www. ozbnbdir.com) Nationwide website with good Tasmanian listings.

Tasmanian Bed & Breakfast (www.tasmanianbedan dbreakfast.com) B&Bs, homestays and farmstays.

Hostels

The YHA network in Tasmania comprises six hostels, but backpacker accommodation is found in most major towns. Often you'll need to supply your own bed linen, or sheets can be rented for around $5.

INDEPENDENT HOSTELS

Tasmania has plenty of independent hostels and the standard can vary enormously. Look for ones that are purpose-built, as these often have the best facilities. Other good places tend to be smaller, more intimate hos-

tels where the owner is also the manager. Some places are run-down hotels or pubs trying to fill empty rooms, while others are converted motels with units containing four to six beds.

Independent backpacker establishments typically charge $23 to $30 for a dorm bed and $60 to $80 for a twin or double room (usually with shared bathroom).

Key websites:

Backpacker Tasmania (www.backpackertasmania. com) Information on accommodation and also on securing part-time work.

Hostel Bookers (www. hostelbookers.com)

Hostelworld (www.hostel world.com)

Workstay (www.workstay. com.au) Hostels offering accommodation in exchange for work.

YHA HOSTELS

At the time of research, Tasmania had six hostels as part of the **Youth Hostels Association** (www.yha.com. au). YHA hostels offer dorms, twin and double rooms, and cooking and laundry facilities. Many also have notice-

boards offering shared rides and advertising seasonal and part-time work.

Nightly charges start at $26 for members; most hostels also take non-YHA members for an extra $3. Australian residents can become full YHA members for $42 for one year. Join online or at any YHA hostel. Families can also join, and kids under 18 receive free membership.

The YHA is part of the **International Youth Hostel Federation** (www.hihostels. com), also known as Hostelling International (HI), so if you're already a member of that organisation in your own country, your membership entitles you to YHA rates in Tasmanian hostels.

Hotels & Motels

Hotels in Tasmania's cities are generally comfortable and anonymous, in a multi-storey block. Aimed at business travellers and tourists, they tend to have a restaurant/cafe, room service, gym and various other facilities. A few more luxurious options are also emerging.

For comfortable midrange accommodation, motels have similar facilities (tea- and coffee-making, fridge, TV, bathroom). Prices vary and there's rarely a cheaper rate for singles, so they're a better option if you are travelling as a couple or a group of three. The price will indicate the standard, but you'll mostly pay between $120 and $160 for a room.

Key websites:

Innkeepers Collection (📞1300 130 269; www.inn keeper.com.au) Hotels, motels, lodges and apartments.

Pure Tasmania (📞1800 420 155; www.federalresorts.com. au) Upmarket hotels and resorts in Hobart, Launceston, Strahan, Cradle Mountain and Freycinet National Park.

PRACTICALITIES

» For newspapers, the *Mercury* (www.themercury. com.au), covers Hobart and the south, and the *Examiner* (www.examiner.com.au) covers Launceston and the north.

» *Tasmania 40° South* (www.fortysouth.com.au) is a glossy quarterly magazine ($12.50) with food, travel and wildlife stories.

» On TV, watch the ad-free ABC, the multicultural SBS, or one of two commercial stations, WIN (the equivalent of Channel Nine) or Southern Cross (the equivalent of Channels Seven and Ten) plus additional digital channels.

» Plugs have three flat pins; the electricity supply is 220-240V AC, 50Hz.

» The metric system is used.

» The Australian dollar is made up of 100 cents. There are 5c, 10c, 20c, 50c, $1 and $2 coins, and $5, $10, $20, $50 and $100 notes.

Pubs

Pub rooms are invariably cheap, upstairs, small, and with shared bathrooms. A few pubs like the Cygnet Art Hotel have also undergone recent makeovers making the heritage rooms more comfortable.

Standard pubs have singles/doubles with shared facilities starting at around $60/90. Few pubs have a separate reception area; just ask in the bar if rooms are available. If you're a light sleeper, never book a room above the bar, especially on Friday and Saturday nights when live music is often on offer. A key website:

Tassie B&B (www.tassiepubs.com.au) Properties around Tasmania.

Self-Contained Apartments & Cottages

Holiday units are largely self-contained, with many rented on either a daily or weekly basis. They often have two or more bedrooms, making them cost-effective for families and groups. The prices given in this guide are for single-night stays and are mostly in the range of $140 to $170 a double. Historic cottages can be anything up to about $220 a double. Unlike prices for holiday units, prices for historic cottages usually include breakfast (with cook-your-own provisions supplied).

Key websites:

Cottages of the Colony (www.cottagesofthecolony.com.au) Self-contained historic cottages.

Stayz (www.stayz.com.au) Self-contained rental properties and private homes.

Tas Villas (www.tasvillas.com) Self-catering accommodation.

Other Accommodation

In country areas, farmers may be willing to rent out a room in exchange for some labour or just to supplement their income (see p319).

If you want to stay a bit longer in Tasmania, noticeboards in universities, hostels, bookshops and cafes are good to check out. Another place to look for a shared flat or a room is in the classified advertisements section of the daily newspapers: Wednesday and Saturday are usually the best days.

Activities

See Walking in Tasmania, p22, and Outdoor Adventures, p28.

Business Hours

Banks	8.30am-4pm Mon-Thu, 9.30am-5pm Fri
Post offices	9am-5pm Mon-Fri
Pubs & bars	11am to midnight daily
Restaurants	breakfast 8-10.30am, lunch noon-3pm, dinner 6-9pm
Shops	9am-5pm Mon-Fri, 9am to noon or 5pm Sat, open for late-night shopping to 9pm Thu or Fri

Sunday trading for retailers is becoming more common, but is limited mainly to Hobart and Launceston.

Restaurants in the main restaurant strips of Hobart and Launceston keep longer hours than usual, but in regional Tasmania most eateries adhere to limited hours. Outside of the peak tourist season, it's sometimes necessary to book for dinner to make sure that a particular establishment opens.

Climate

Because Tasmania is small and also an island, it enjoys a maritime climate, which means that it's rarely extremely hot or extremely cold. However, many Australians find it much colder than the mainland, and storms can deposit wintry conditions in any month.

Tasmania experiences four distinct seasons. Summer (December to February), with its generally warm days and mild nights, is the most pleasant time of year. In general, the east coast of Tassie is nearly always warmer and milder than other parts of the state, and Hobart is actually Australia's second-driest capital (after Adelaide).

Tasmania is in the path of the 'Roaring Forties', a notorious current of wind that produces very changeable weather. The west and southwest can be blasted by strong winds and drenched by heavy rain.

Dangers & Annoyances

Animal Hazards

You're unlikely to see many of Australia's more notorious creatures in the wilds of Tasmania, much less be attacked by one.

INSECTS

In the warmer months of the year, expect mosquitoes, especially around sunset. Insect repellents will deter them, and calamine lotion can soothe the bites, but it's best to cover up. Ticks, parasites that feed on human or animal blood, are found in moist bushy areas and can be avoided by covering up in light clothing. Most people experience little or no symptoms of bites, but occasionally paralysis or allergic reaction to their toxins can occur. If you find a tick lodged somewhere on your body, gently remove it with a pair of fine-pointed tweezers by grasping as close to the skin as possible.

LEECHES

Leeches may be present in damp rainforest conditions. Trekkers often get them on their legs or in their boots. Salt or a lighted cigarette end will make them fall off. Do not pull them off, as the bite is then more likely to become infected. Clean and apply pressure if the point of attachment is bleeding. An insect repellent may keep them away and gaiters are a good idea when you're trekking.

SHARKS

Attacks are rare, with only four deaths in the last 50 years in Tasmanian waters.

SNAKES

Tasmania's bushland is home to three species: tiger, white-lipped and lowland copperhead snakes (see www.parks.tas.gov.au/wildlife/reptile/snakes.html). Although all snakes in Tasmania are venomous, they are not aggressive and, unless you have the bad fortune to stand on one, it's unlikely you'll be bitten. February is the month when snakes are at their most active.

To minimise your chances of being bitten, always wear boots, socks and long trousers (ideally gaiters) when walking

CRADLE VALLEY

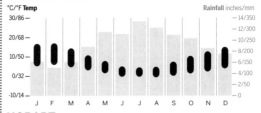

HOBART

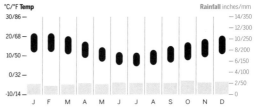

LAUNCESTON

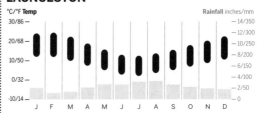

through undergrowth where snakes may be present. Don't put your hands into holes and crevices, and be careful when collecting firewood.

SPIDERS & ANTS

There are only a couple of spiders to watch out for in Tasmania. The large, grey brown huntsman spider is quite common in the bush and often enters homes. It can bite, resulting only in transient swelling and pain, but is generally shy and harmless. The white-tailed spider is a long, thin, black spider with a white tip on its tail. It has a fierce bite that can lead to local inflammation. It is a ground scavenger rather than a web dweller, and can sometimes crawl into piles of stuff left on the floor. A spider found only in Tasmania is the Tasmanian cave spider.

Jack jumper ants have a brown body and orange pincers; they are quite aggressive and can sometimes 'jump' from the vegetation. They sting rather than bite, causing a severe allergic reaction. Signs of an ant nest can include small pebbles at the entrance to the hole.

Crime

Tasmania is a relatively safe place to visit, but you should still take reasonable precautions. Don't leave hotel rooms or cars unlocked, and don't leave your valuables unattended or visible through a car window. Avoid walking around in cities by yourself after dark.

Swimming

Surf beaches can be dangerous places if you aren't used to the conditions. Undertows (or 'rips') are the main problem. If you find yourself being carried out by a rip, the important thing to do is just keep afloat; don't panic or try to swim against the rip, which will exhaust you. In most cases the current stops within a couple of hundred metres from the shore and you can then swim parallel to the shore for a short way to get out of the rip and make your way back to land.

Discount Cards

The **International Student Travel Confederation** (ISTC; www.istc.org) issues the International Student Identity Card (ISIC) to full-time students aged 12 years and over, providing discounts on accommodation, transport and admission to various attractions.

Senior travellers and travellers with disabilities who reside in Australia are eligible for concession cards; most states and territories issue their own version and these can be used Australia-wide (for more, see p318).

See Tasmania Card

The **See Tasmania Smartvisit Card** (☑1300 661 711; www.seetasmaniacard.com; per adult/child for 3 days $179/125, for 7 days $259/180 & for 10 days $349/245) allows free or discounted entry to over 50 attractions and activities around the state (including national parks, National Trust properties and big-ticket drawcards such as the Port Arthur Historic Site and the Tahune AirWalk). Children's rates apply to those aged four to 15.

The card is not cheap, however, and it's worth noting that the card can only be used on consecutive days, so before purchasing, do some research to determine if it's a worthwhile investment. You'll need to be pretty busy (and organised) to get your money's worth. Cards can be purchased online.

Electricity

240v/50 hz

Food

Eating is generally good in modern cafes, pubs and more expensive restaurants showcasing the state's fabulous local produce. In this book, eating options are listed in order of preference and categorised by the following indicators for the average cost of a main dish.

$	less than $15
$$	from $15-30
$$$	greater than $30

General opening hours:

Breakfast	8am-10.30am
Lunch	noon-3pm
Dinner	from 6pm

Note that outside of Hobart and Launceston, dinner service in restaurants and pubs may end around 8pm. See the Gourmet Tasmania chapter (p289) for more information on the Tasmanian food scene.

Gay & Lesbian Travellers

Tasmania is now considered by gay- and lesbian-rights groups to have greater equality in criminal law for homosexual and heterosexual people than most of the other Australian states.

Key websites:

Gay & Lesbian Community Centre (www.taspride.com) Based in Hobart, but a Tasmania-wide support group; a good source of information on upcoming events, including November's annual TasPride Festival. Get recorded info from its **Gay Information Line** (☑6234 8179).

Gay Tasmania (www.gaytasmania.com.au) Accommodation and travel information.

Tasmanian Gay & Lesbian Rights Group (www.tglrg.org) Led the successful campaign for antidiscrimination legislation and same-sex relationship laws from 1988 to 1997.

Health

Availability & Cost of Health Care

Tasmania's excellent healthcare system combines privately run medical clinics and hospitals alongside a government-funded system of public hospitals. The Medicare system covers Australian residents for some health-care costs. Visitors from countries with which Australia has a reciprocal health-care agreement are eligible for benefits specified under the Medicare program. Search for 'Reciprocal' on www.medicareaustralia.gov.au to see if your home country is covered.

Self-Care

In Tasmania's remote locations, there could be a significant delay in emergency services reaching you in the event of serious accident or illness. An increased level of self-reliance and preparation is essential.

Consider taking a wilderness first-aid course, such as those offered at the **Wilderness Medicine Institute** (www.wmi.net.au). Take a comprehensive first-aid kit that is appropriate for the activities planned; and ensure that you have adequate means of communication. Tasmania's often limited mobile-phone coverage can mean that additional radio communication is important for remote areas.

Holidays
Public Holidays
The holidays listed are statewide unless otherwise indicated:

New Year's Day 1 January
Australia Day 26 January
Hobart Regatta Day 2nd Monday in February (southern Tasmania)
Launceston Cup Last Wednesday in February (Launceston only)
Eight Hour Day 2nd Monday in March
Easter March/April (Good Friday to Easter Tuesday inclusive)
Anzac Day 25 April
Queen's Birthday 2nd Monday in June
Burnie Show 1st Friday in October (Burnie only)
Launceston Show 2nd Thursday in October (Launceston only)
Hobart Show 3rd Thursday in October (southern Tasmania)
Recreation Day 1st Monday in November (northern Tasmania)
Devonport Show Last Friday in November (Devonport only)
Christmas Day 25 December
Boxing Day 26 December

School Holidays
The Christmas holiday season, from mid-December to late January, is part of the summer school vacation and is the time when accommodation often books out. There are three shorter school holiday periods during the year, but they vary by a week or two from year to year, falling from early to mid-April, late June to mid-July, and late September to early October. Book early for accommodation and transport, especially the *Spirit of Tasmania* ferry services.

For a list of school holidays in all Australian states, see www.australia.gov.au. Enter 'School Term Dates' into the website's search box.

Insurance
If you're from overseas, and plan on doing any outdoor activities in Tasmania, make sure the policy you choose fully covers you for scuba diving, motorcycling, skiing and even bushwalking (some policies specifically exclude designated 'dangerous activities'). Check also that the policy covers ambulances and emergency medical evacuations by air.

Worldwide travel insurance is available at www. lonelyplanet.com/bookings.

Internet Access
You'll find internet access in libraries, cafes, hotels and hostels, and government-funded Online Access Centres operate in 66 of the state's towns. For a complete listing of these centres, pick up the *Tasmanian Communities Online* brochure at many visitor centres, or visit the scheme's website at www.tco.asn.au.

Wi-fi access is fast becoming a given in most Tasmanian accommodation, but access is still limited in more isolated areas like Bruny Island and the southeast. If you're a Telstra customer, you should be able to secure wi-fi access in most parts of the island.

Legal Matters
There is a significant police presence on the state's roads, with the power to stop your car and ask to see your licence, check your vehicle for roadworthiness, and also to insist that you take a breath test for alcohol (the legal limit in Australia is 0.05%).

If you are arrested, it's your right to telephone a friend, relative or lawyer before any formal questioning begins. Legal aid is available only in serious cases and only to the truly needy (for links to Legal Aid offices see www.legalaid.tas.gov.au).

Maps
One of the best road maps of the state (1:500,000) is produced by the **Royal Automobile Club of Tasmania** (☑13 27 22; www.ract. com.au) and is on sale in the organisation's offices around the island. This sheet map includes detail of main city centres.

For more detail, including contours, the maps (1:250,000) published by **Tasmap** (www.tasmap.tas. gov.au) are recommended. Tasmap also produces more detailed 1:25,000 topographic sheets appropriate for bushwalking, ski touring and other activities requiring large-scale maps.

Many of the more popular sheets, including day walks and bushwalks in national parks, are usually available over the counter at shops specialising in bushwalking gear and outdoor equipment, and also at urban and national park visitor centres, Service Tasmania (p76) and the Tasmanian Map Centre p76).

The best atlas is the *Tasmania Country Road Atlas* ($31), published by UBD. It contains clear, detailed maps of over 45 significant towns in the state.

Money

ATMs

In smaller Tasmanian towns, banks are often open only two or three days a week. Local post offices act as agents for the Commonwealth Bank, although they are open only restricted weekday hours. In towns where there are no banks, you'll usually find a multicard ATM in the local grocery store or petrol station.

For international travellers, debit cards connected to the international banking networks – Cirrus, Maestro, Plus and Eurocard – will work fine in Tasmanian ATMs.

Credit Cards

Credit cards such as Mastercard and Visa are widely accepted for most accommodation and services, and a credit card is essential (in lieu of a large deposit) to hire a car. They can also be used to get cash advances over the counter at banks and from many ATMs, depending on the card, but be aware that these incur immediate interest. Charge cards such as Diners Club and American Express are not as widely accepted.

Taxes & Refunds

The Goods and Services Tax (GST) is a flat 10% tax on all goods and services – accommodation, eating out, transport, books, furniture, clothing (but basic foods such as milk, bread, fruits and vegetables are exempt). By law, the tax is included in the quoted or shelf prices, so all prices in this book are GST-inclusive. International air and sea travel to/from Australia is GST-free, as is domestic air travel when purchased outside Australia by nonresidents.

If you purchase goods with a total minimum value of $300 from one store no more than 30 days before you leave Australia, you are entitled under the Tourist Refund Scheme (TRS) to a refund of any GST paid. The scheme only applies to goods you take with you as hand luggage or wear onto the plane or ship. For more details, contact the **Australian Customs Service** (☑1300 363 263; www.customs.gov.au).

Post

Australia Post (www.auspost.com.au) offices are usually open from 9am to 5pm Monday to Friday. There are also post office agencies lurking within general stores and newsagencies.

There are four international parcel zones and rates vary by distance and class of service. Airmail offers reliable delivery to over 200 countries in three to 10 working days. If it's not urgent, the cheapest way to send larger items back home is by sea mail (everywhere except New Zealand and Asia).

Express Post delivers a parcel or envelope interstate within Australia by the next business day; otherwise allow two days for urban deliveries, longer for country areas.

Solo Travellers

Women travelling on their own should exercise caution when in less populated areas, and may find that guys get annoyingly attentive in some drinking establishments; see also Women Travellers (p318).

Telephone

Information & Toll-Free Calls

Numbers starting with ☑190 are usually recorded information services, charged at anything from 35c to $5 or more per minute (more from mobiles and payphones).

Toll-free numbers beginning with ☑1800 can be called free of charge from anywhere in the country, though they may not be accessible from certain areas or from mobile phones. Calls to numbers beginning with ☑13 or ☑1300 are charged at the rate of a local call – the numbers can usually be dialled Australia-wide, but may be applicable only to a specific state or STD (Subscriber Trunk Dialling) district. Telephone numbers beginning with either ☑1800, ☑13 or ☑1300 cannot be dialled from outside Australia.

International Calls

The **Country Direct service** (☑1800 801 800) connects callers in Australia with operators in nearly 60 countries to make reverse-charge (collect) or credit-card calls.

When calling overseas, you need to dial the international access code from Australia (☑0011 or ☑0018), the country code and the area code (without the initial 0).

If calling Australia from overseas, the country code is ☑61 and you need to drop the 0 in the state/territory area codes.

Local Calls

Calls from private phones cost 15c to 25c, while local calls from public phones cost 50c. Calls to mobile phones attract higher rates and are timed.

Long-Distance Calls & Area Codes

For long-distance calls, Australia uses four STD area codes. STD calls can be made from virtually any public phone and are cheaper during off-peak hours, generally between 7pm and 7am. Long-distance calls (to more than about 50km away) within these areas are charged at long-distance rates, even though they have the same area code.

STATE/ TERRITORY	AREA CODE
ACT	☑02
NSW	☑02
NT	☑08
Qld	☑07
SA	☑08
Tas	☑03
Vic	☑03
WA	☑08

When calling from one area of Tasmania to another, there's no need to dial 03 before the local number (and you don't need to add the 03 when calling Victoria either). Local numbers start with the digits 62 in Hobart and southern Tasmania, 63 in Launceston and the northeast, and 64 in the west and northwest.

Mobile (Cell) Phones

Local numbers with the prefix ☑04 belong to mobile phones. If you're not on the **Telstra** (www.telstra.com.au) mobile network, coverage can be patchy, and other network coverage is limited outside of Hobart, Launceston, Burnie, Devonport, and the Midland Hwy. It may be worth purchasing a Telstra prepaid SIM card – you'll still struggle in more remote parts of the state, but overall coverage will be markedly better than **Optus** (www. optus.com.au) or **Vodafone** (www.vodafone.com.au). Coverage is being upgraded (slowly), so see the websites of all three companies for up-to-date coverage maps.

Australia's digital network is compatible with GSM 900 and 1800 (used in Europe), but generally not with the systems used in the USA or Japan. For overseas visitors, GSM 900 and 1800 mobiles can be used in Australia if set up at home first – contact your service provider before you travel.

It's easy enough to get connected short-term, though, as the main service providers (Telstra, Optus and Vodafone) all have prepaid mobile systems. Just buy a starter kit, which may include a phone or, if you have your own phone, a SIM card and a prepaid charge card. Shop around between the three carriers for the best offer.

Phonecards

A wide range of phonecards is available. These can be bought at newsagents and post offices for a fixed dollar value (usually $10, $20 or $50) and can be used with any public or private phone by dialling a toll-free access number and then the PIN on the card. Shop around, as call rates vary from company to company. Some public phones also accept credit cards.

Time

Australia is divided into three time zones: Western Standard Time (GMT/UTC plus eight hours) applies in Western Australia; Central Standard Time (GMT/UTC plus 9½ hours) covers the Northern Territory and South Australia; and Eastern Standard Time (GMT/UTC plus 10 hours) covers Tasmania, Victoria, NSW and Queensland. During the Tasmanian summer things get slightly screwed up when Daylight Saving time comes into play.

Tourist Information

Tourism Tasmania (☑6230 8235, 1300 827 743; www.discovertasmania.com) Tassie's official tourism promoters.

Tasmanian Travel & Information Centre (☑6238 4222, 1800 990 440; www.hobarttravelcentre.com.au) Hobart's information centre is also great for pretrip planning statewide.

Tasmanian Travelways (☑6336 7275; www.travelways.com.au) The online version of the Tasmanian Travelways tourist information newspaper.

Local Tourist Offices

Tasmania's visitor information centres supply brochures, maps and other information, and can often book transport, tours and accommodation. They are generally open from around 8.30am or 9am to 5pm or 5.30pm weekdays and slightly shorter hours on weekends. Some centres are staffed by volunteers, resulting in irregular opening hours.

Tours

Many travel agents arrange package deals from the mainland that include transport to Tasmania (either by air or sea), car rental and accommodation. Contact Tourism Tasmania (p317) or **TasVacations** (☑1800 030 160; www.tasvacations.com).

In Tasmania, many operators guide you on or off the

DAYLIGHT SAVING

Daylight Saving in Tasmania begins on the first Sunday in October and ends on the last Sunday in March. This start date is three weeks earlier than the Victoria, NSW, SA, WA and ACT commencement date, and this end date is a week earlier. Daylight Saving does not operate in Queensland or the NT.

beaten track, often with a wilderness or activity-based spin. See p25 for companies specialising in bushwalking.

Adventure Tours (☎1800 068 886, 08-8132 8230; www.adventuretours.com.au) An Australia-wide company offering three- to seven-day tours in Tasmania. For hostel accommodation travellers can choose between twin/ double rooms or dorms; prices for a three-day tour start at $445.

Herbaceous Tours (☎0416 970 699; www.herbaceous tours.com.au; per person from $130) Specialist food and wine tours across Tasmania, including Hobart, the Coal River Valley wine region, Bruny Island and the Huon Valley.

Island Cycle Tours (☎6234 9558; www.islandcycletours. com) Offers guided cycling trips from seven to 13 days.

TASafari (☎1300 882 415; www.tasafari.com.au) Offers four-, five- and 10-day, ecocertified 4WD tours that visit both the well-known and more remote parts of the state. There's bushwalking, bush camping and off-road driving. A four-day tour of the state's east is $720; five days in the west is $920.

Tasmanian Expeditions (☎1300 666 856, 6331 9000; www.tas-ex.com) Offers an excellent range of activity-based tours – bushwalking, cabin-based walks, rafting, rock climbing, cycling and sea-kayaking.

Tasmanian Wilderness Experiences (☎1300 882 293; www.twe.travel) Lots of one-day and multiday walks across the island. Bushwalking gear is also for sale and for hire.

Tours Tasmania (☎1800 777 103; www.tourstas.com. au; one-day tours $120-140) Small-group, backpacker-oriented full-day trips from Hobart: Cradle Mountain, Wineglass Bay or Mt Field National Park. Also offers

longer two- to five-day itineraries.

Under Down Under (☎1800 064 726, 6362 2237; www.underdownunder.com. au) Offers pro-green, nature-based, backpacker-friendly trips. There are tours from three to nine days.

Travellers With Disabilities

Many accommodation providers and key attractions provide access for those with limited mobility, and tour operators often have the appropriate facilities: call ahead to confirm. Also check out the *Hobart CBD Mobility Map* from Hobart's visitor information centre.

Several agencies also provide information:

National Information Communication and Awareness Network (☎1800 806 769; www.nican. com.au) Australia-wide database providing information on access issues, accommodation, sporting and recreational activities, transport and specialist tour operators.

ParaQuad Association of Tasmania (☎6272 8816; www.paraquadtas.org.au) Information for disabled travellers. Download *The Wheelie Good Guide*.

Parks & Wildlife Service (☎1300 135 513; www.parks. tas.gov.au) *Parks for all People* (PDF download) outlines access for mobility-impaired visitors to Tasmania's national parks and reserves. Search for 'Disabled Access' on the website.

Visas

All visitors to Australia need a visa (New Zealand nationals are exempt but receive a 'special category' visa on arrival). Visa application forms are available from Australian diplomatic

missions overseas, travel agents or the website of the Department of Immigration and Citizenship (☎13 18 81; www.immi.gov.au). On average, applications are processed within seven to 10 days, though some can be processed in two days. Visa types are as follows:

Electronic Travel Authority

(ETA; subclass 976) For people outside Australia who want to visit for tourism or business for up to three months. It's free but a service charge applies ($20); available to passport-holders in eight countries, including the USA, Canada, Japan, South Korea and Singapore. Apply online at www.eta.immi.gov. au. British and European passport holders should apply for an **eVisitor** visa, providing the same entry privileges. See www.immi. gov.au/e_visa/evisitor.

Tourist Visas

For people who want to visit Australia for tourism, to see family and/or friends or short-term study. Tourist visas (subclass 676; $105) are available for three months. If you're from a country not covered by the ETA or eVisitor programs, you'll need to apply for this visa.

Working Holiday Maker (WHM) Visas

Travellers who are single, aged between 18 and 30, and from Belgium, Canada, Cyprus, Denmark, Estonia, Finland, France, Germany, Hong Kong, Ireland, Italy, Japan, Korea, Malta, the Netherlands, Norway, Sweden, Taiwan or the UK can apply to work for up to 12 months in Australia with this visa (subclass 417).

Apply online ($235) at www.immi.gov.au/visitors/ working-holiday/417.

Visa Extensions

Visitors are allowed a maximum stay of six months, including extensions. Visa extensions are made through the Department of Immigration and Citizenship, and it's best to apply at least two or three weeks before your visa expires. The application fee is $215. It's nonrefundable, even if your application is rejected.

Women Travellers

Tasmania is generally a safe place for women travellers, although the usual sensible precautions apply. It's best to avoid walking alone late at night in major towns. When the pubs close and there are drunks roaming around, it's probably not a great time to be out on your own.

Lone female hitchers are tempting fate. Hitching with a male companion is safer, and increasingly travellers are not hitching at all.

Work

Casual work can usually be found during summer in the major tourist centres, mainly working in tourism, hospitality, labouring, gardening or farming. Seasonal fruit-picking is hard work and pay is proportional to the quantity and quality of fruits picked. Harvest is from December to April in the Huon and Tamar Valleys. Grape-picking jobs are sometimes available in late autumn and early winter, as some wineries still hand-pick their crops. Visit **Australian Job Search** (www.jobsearch.gov.au). See also the information about the WHM visa.

Volunteer Work

Volunteering is an excellent way to meet people and visit some interesting areas of the country, with a number of worthy projects active in Tasmania.

Key contacts:

Conservation Volunteers Australia (☎1800 032 501, 03-5330 2600; www. conservationvolunteers.com. au) Organises volunteers (including overseas visitors) to get their hands dirty with tree-planting, walking-track construction and flora and fauna surveys.

Greening Australia (www. greeningaustralia.org.au) Encourages volunteers to get involved with environmental projects.

Willing Workers on Organic Farms (www.wwoof. com.au) Exchange a few hours' work each day on a farm or cottage business in return for bed and board, often in a family home.

Transport

GETTING THERE & AWAY

Tasmania is the land beneath 'the land down under'. It's a long way from just about everywhere except Antarctica, and getting here usually means a long-haul flight.

At the time of writing, there were no international flights to Tasmania, and overseas visitors to the island state will need to fly to one of Australia's mainland cities and connect to a Tassie-bound domestic flight to Hobart, Launceston or Devonport. Melbourne and Sydney airports have the most frequent direct air links to these cities. Also popular is the *Spirit of Tasmania* passenger and car ferry linking mainland Victoria to Devonport in Tasmania's north.

Flights, tours and rail tickets can be booked online at lonelyplanet.com/travelservices.

Entering Tasmania

With increased security in mainland Australian airports, both in domestic and international terminals, Tasmania's arrivals procedures are generally less time-consuming.

Domestic Air Travel

There are major airports located at Hobart and Launceston, as well as smaller operations at Burnie/Wynyard and Devonport. (Burnie/Wynyard airport is officially known as Burnie airport but is actually located 20km west of Burnie near the town of Wynyard. Due to the fact that some Tasmanians call the airport 'Burnie' and others call it 'Wynyard', we refer to it as 'Burnie/Wynyard' throughout this book).

Flights are getting ever cheaper and it's straightforward to find a one-way flight to Hobart or Launceston for around $100 to $150 from most Australian gateway cities.

Airports

Hobart (☑6216 1600; www.hobartairpt.com.au)

Launceston (☑6391 6222; www.launcestonairport.com.au)

Airline

Jetstar (☑13 15 38; www.jetstar.com.au) Qantas' low-cost airline. Direct flights from Melbourne and Sydney to Hobart and Launceston.

Qantas (☑13 13 13; www.qantas.com.au) Direct flights from Sydney, Brisbane and Melbourne to Hobart and Launceston. QantasLink (the regional subsidiary) offers flights from Melbourne to Launceston and Devonport.

Regional Express (☑13 17 13; www.regionalexpress.com.au) Flies from Melbourne to Burnie/Wynyard and King Island.

Sharp Airlines (☑1300 556 694; www.sharpairlines.com.au) Flights four days a week from Melbourne Essendon to Flinders Island.

Tiger Airways (☑9335 3033; www.tigerairways.com.au) Flies from Melbourne to Hobart.

Virgin Blue (☑13 67 89; www.virginblue.com.au) Direct flights from Melbourne, Sydney, Brisbane, Canberra and Adelaide to Hobart, and from Melbourne, Brisbane and Sydney to Launceston.

Sea

Cruise Ship

Just about the only way to see the spectacular diversity of wildlife on remote, sub-Antarctic Macquarie Island, proclaimed Tasmania's second World Heritage area in 1997, up close is to take one of the sub-Antarctic islands cruises scheduled by New Zealand-based Heritage Expeditions (www.heritageexpeditions.com).

Ferry

There are two high-speed *Spirit of Tasmania* ferries operated by TT-Line (☑1800 634 906; www.spiritoftasmania.com.au) that ply Bass Strait nightly in each direction between Melbourne and Devonport on northern Tasmania's coast. The regular crossing takes around 11 hours, departing either mainland Australia or Tasmania at 7.30pm and arriving at 6.30am. During peak periods including Christmas, Easter and key holiday weekends, the schedule is amended to two sailings per day, departing at 9am and 9pm. Check the website for exact timings.

DEPARTURE POINTS
The Devonport terminal is on The Esplanade in East Devonport; the Melbourne terminal is at Station Pier in Port Melbourne. Each ferry can accommodate 1400 passengers and around 650 vehicles and has restaurants, bars and games facilities. The public areas of the ships have been designed to cater for wheelchair access, as have a handful of cabins.

CABIN & SEATING OPTIONS
There is a range of seating and cabin options. 'Ocean view recliner' seats are the cheapest and resemble airline seats. Cabins are available in twin or four-berth configurations, with or without porthole windows, or you can opt for a 'deluxe' cabin (with a queen-size bed and complimentary bottle of sparkling wine). All cabins have a private bathroom. Child, student, pensioner and senior discounts apply to all accommodation except for deluxe cabins. Prices do not include meals, which can be purchased on board from an à la carte restaurant or cafeteria.

FARE OPTIONS
Fares depend on whether you're travelling in the peak period (mid-December to late January and Easter), or in the off-peak period (all other times). For the peak season and holiday weekends, booking ahead as early as possible is recommended.

One-way prices (per adult) are as follows. Booking online saves a further $5 each way. Fares listed here (except for deluxe cabins) are the less flexible, non-refundable 'ship saver' fares (conditions are similar to discount airlines). Look online for regular specials.

FARE	PEAK	OFF-PEAK
Ocean-view recliner seat	$97	$90
Inside 4-berth cabin	$102	$90
Inside twin cabin	$205	$105
Deluxe cabin	$338	$105
Daytime sailings (seats only)	$97	$90
Standard vehicles	$79	$79
Campervans up to 5m length	$135	$135
Motorcycles	$54	$54
Bicycles	$6	$6

GETTING AROUND
Driving is the easiest, most flexible way to see Tasmania. Don't make the mistake of drawing up exhaustive itineraries with carefully calculated driving times between each destination. Though this is sometimes necessary to catch a particular tour on a particular day, or to check in at a prebooked B&B, it runs contrary to the best way of exploring Tasmania:

stopping for a spontaneous photo, or diverting down a side-road to discover the unfamiliar.

Many people also make the mistake of thinking they can see all of Tasmania's top attractions in one week, madly dashing from the west coast to the east (via Cradle Mountain, Hobart and Port Arthur). Slow down, otherwise you may need a holiday when you get home.

Public transport is adequate between larger towns and popular tourist destinations, but visiting remote sights can be frustrating due to irregular or nonexistent services. Consider renting a car to make the most of your time; competition keeps rental prices reasonable.

Air
As distances within Tasmania are far from huge, air travel within the state is not very common. Of more use to travellers are the air services for bushwalkers in the southwest, and links between major towns and King and Flinders Islands.

There are a few small regional airlines within the state:

Airlines of Tasmania (☑6248 5490; www.airtasmania.com.au) Links Cape Barren Island and Launceston on Tuesdays and Thursdays ($248 return).

INTERSTATE QUARANTINE

There are stringent rules in place to protect the 'disease-free' status of the agriculture of this island state, and fresh fruit, vegetables and plants cannot be brought into Tasmania. Tourists must discard all such items prior to their arrival (even if they're only travelling from mainland Australia). There are sniffer dogs at Tasmanian airports, and quarantine inspection posts at the Devonport ferry terminal; while quarantine control here often relies on honesty, officers are entitled to search your car for undeclared items.

Par Avion (☑6248 5390; www.paravion.com.au) Flies from Hobart to Melaleuca in the southwest wilderness (adult one-way $190). Good for scenic flights and bushwalker pick-ups/drop-offs; also offers a southwest off-season special ($220, May to October).

Sharp Airlines (☑1300 556 694; www.sharpairlines.com. au) Flies to Flinders Island daily from Launceston (adult one-way $157) and Melbourne's Essendon airport on Monday, Wednesday and Friday (one-way $212).

Tasair (☑1800 062 900, 6248 5088; www.tasair.com. au) Flies daily to King Island from Devonport (adult one-way $226, student discounts apply). Flies four times a week between Devonport and Hobart (one-way $226). Also offers charters and scenic flights, plus a bushwalkers' service to Melaleuca (one-way $190).

Bicycle

Cycling Tasmania is one of the best ways to get close to nature (and, it has to be said, to log trucks, rain and roadkill). If you're prepared for steep climbs and strong headwinds in certain sections, you should enjoy the experience immensely.

It's worth bringing your own bike, especially if you're coming via ferry as transport on one of the *Spirit of Tasmania* ferries costs $6 each way any time of year.

Another option is buying a bike in Hobart or Launceston and reselling it at the end of your trip.

Bike rental is available in the larger towns, and there are also a number of operators offering multiday cycling tours or experiences such as mountain-biking down Mt Wellington in Hobart. See p31 for more information.

Note that bicycle helmets are compulsory in Tasmania, as are white front lights and red rear lights if you are riding in the dark.

See www.biketas.org.au for more information.

Boat

A car ferry runs at least eight times a day from Kettering to Bruny Island in Tasmania's southeast ($32 one way). To effectively explore Bruny, you'll need your own car or bicycle.

At the time of writing there was a twice-daily service from Triabunna on the east coast to Maria Island, which is a national park, carrying only passengers and bicycles as vehicles aren't allowed on the island. The services may be limited during winter.

There is also a small weekly passenger and car ferry from Bridport in Tasmania's northeast to Flinders Island (the ferry continues on to Port Welshpool in Victoria on demand).

Bus

Tasmania has a reasonable bus network connecting major towns and centres, but weekend services are infrequent, which can be inconvenient for travellers with limited time. There are more buses in summer than in winter, but smaller towns are still not serviced terribly frequently.

The main operators are the following:

Redline Coaches (☑1300 360 000; www.redlinecoaches. com.au) Services the Midland Hwy between Hobart and Launceston, the north coast between Launceston and Smithton, north from Launceston to George Town, and to the east coast.

Tassielink (☑1300 300 520; www.tassielink.com.au) Runs from both Hobart and Launceston to the state's west (Cradle Mountain, Strahan, Queenstown, Lake St Clair) and to the east coast (St Helens, Bicheno, Swansea), from Hobart to Port Arthur, and south from Hobart down the Huon Valley. It also runs the 'Main Rd Express', an express service connecting Bass Strait ferry arrivals/departures in Devonport to Launceston, Hobart and Burnie. Over summer, Tassielink buses also run to popular bushwalking destinations offering drop-offs and pick-ups from key trailheads. Buses take the link road from Devonport past Cradle

---

CLIMATE CHANGE & TRAVEL

Every form of transport that relies on carbon-based fuel generates CO_2, the main cause of human-induced climate change. Modern travel is dependent on aeroplanes, which might use less fuel per kilometre per person than most cars but travel much greater distances. The altitude at which aircraft emit gases (including CO_2) and particles also contributes to their climate change impact. Many websites offer 'carbon calculators' that allow people to estimate the carbon emissions generated by their journey and, for those who wish to do so, to offset the impact of the greenhouse gases emitted with contributions to portfolios of climate-friendly initiatives throughout the world. Lonely Planet offsets the carbon footprint of all staff and author travel.

Mountain to the Lyell Hwy; and services also run from Hobart past Mt Field and Maydena to Scotts Peak; and from Hobart past Dover to Cockle Creek in the south. See the website (click on 'Walking Track Links') and these destinations in the relevant chapters for more information.

Hobart Coaches (☎13 22 01) Runs regular services south from the capital as far as Woodbridge and Cygnet, and north to Richmond and New Norfolk.

Smaller transport operators offer useful bus services on important tourist routes (eg between Bicheno and Coles Bay, or within the Cradle Mountain–Lake St Clair region).

Bus Passes

Tassielink (☎1300 300 520; www.tassielink.com.au) offers an Explorer Pass valid on all scheduled services for unlimited kilometres. The pass can be bought from Tasmanian travel centres, YHA and STA Travel offices, most other travel agents or directly from Tassielink. If you intend to buy an Explorer Pass, ask for Tassielink's timetables in advance or check the company's website and plan your itinerary carefully before making your purchase – this is the best way to ensure you'll be able to get where you want to go within the life of the pass.

EXPLORER PASS	VALID FOR	COST
7-day pass	travel in 10 days	$208
10-day pass	travel in 15 days	$248
14-day pass	travel in 20 days	$286
21-day pass	travel in 30 days	$329

Car & Motorcycle

Travelling by car gives you the freedom to explore according to your own timetable. You can bring cars from the mainland to Tasmania on the ferry so renting may only be cheaper for shorter trips. Tasmania has many international, national and local car-rental agencies. See p321 for information on the cost of bringing your own car on the ferry compared with the cost of flights and a rental car.

Motorcycles are another popular way of getting around, and the climate is OK for bikes most of the year.

Automobile Associations

Royal Automobile Club of Tasmania (☎13 27 22; www.ract.com.au) provides an emergency breakdown service to members and has reciprocal arrangements with services in other Australian states and some from overseas. It also provides tourist literature, excellent maps and detailed guides to accommodation and camping grounds.

Key contacts are the following:

Roadside Assistance Number (☎13 11 11)
RACT Hobart Address (cnr Patrick & Murray Sts)
RACT Launceston Address (cnr York & George Sts)
Australian Automobile Association (☎02-6247-7311; www.aaa.asn.au)

Driving Licence

You can generally use your own home-country's driving licence in Australia, as long as it's in English (if it's not, a certified translation must be carried) and has an identifying photograph. Alternatively, it's a simple matter to arrange an International Driving Permit (IDP), which should be supported by your home licence. Just go to your home country's automobile association and it can issue

one on the spot. The permits are valid for 12 months.

Fuel

In small towns there's often just a pump outside the general store, while the larger towns and cities have conventional service stations and garages. Most are open from 8am to 6pm weekdays, but fewer are open on weekends, and fewer still are open late at night or 24 hours, something to keep in mind if you intend travelling long distances at night.

In small rural towns, unleaded petrol prices can rise about 10c a litre compared to larger cities and towns. Fill up before leaving a bigger centre.

Insurance

In Australia, third-party personal injury insurance is always included in the vehicle registration cost. This ensures that every registered vehicle carries at least minimum insurance. It's wise to extend that minimum to at least third-party property insurance as well.

When hiring a car, find out exactly what your liability is in the event of an accident. Rather than risk paying out thousands of dollars if you do have an accident, you can take out your own comprehensive insurance on the car, or (the usual option) pay an additional daily amount to the rental company for an 'insurance excess reduction' policy. This brings the amount of excess you must pay in the event of an accident down from between $2000 and $5000 to a few hundred dollars.

Be aware that if you're travelling on dirt roads you will not be covered by insurance unless you have a 4WD – in other words, if you have an accident you'll be liable for all the costs involved. Also, most companies' insurance won't cover the cost of damage to glass (including

the windscreen) or tyres.
Always read the fine print.

Purchase

If you're touring for several
months, buying a second-
hand car may be much
cheaper than renting.

You'll probably get any car
cheaper by buying privately
online rather than through a
car dealer. Buying through a
dealer does have the advantage of some sort of guarantee, but this is not much use
if you're buying a car in Sydney for a trip to Tasmania.

When you come to buy or
sell a car, there are usually
some local regulations to
be complied with: see www.
justice.tas.gov.au/fair_trad
ing/motor_vehicles.

Online, check out the following buying and selling
sites:

Auto Market (www.automar
ket.com.au)

Carpoint (www.carpoint.
com.au)

Car Sales (www.carsales.
com.au)

Drive (www.drive.com.au)

Rental

Ask about any kilometre limi-
tations and find out exactly
what the insurance covers.
Ensure there are no hidden
seasonal adjustments and
also note that some com-
panies do not cover acci-
dents on unsealed roads, and
hike up the excess in the case
of damage or an accident on
such a road; a considerable
disadvantage as many of
the best Tasmanian destinations can only be reached via
unsealed roads. Some com-
panies also do not allow their
vehicles to be taken across to
Bruny Island.

International company
standard rates start at about
$60 for a high-season,
multiday hire of a small car.
Booking in advance usually
produces the best price, but
check the websites for deals.

AutoRent-Hertz (☎1800
030 222; www.autorent.com.
au)

Avis (☎13 63 33; www.avis.
com.au)

Budget (☎1300 362 848;
www.budget.com.au)

Europcar (☎1300 131 390;
www.europcar.com.au)

Thrifty (☎1800 030 730;
www.tasvacations.com.au)

Small local firms rent cars
for as little as $35 a day,
depending on the season and
how long you hire the vehicle
for. The smaller companies
don't normally have desks at
arrival points, but can usually
arrange for your car to be
picked up at airports and the
ferry terminal in Devonport.

Lo-Cost Auto Rent
(www.locostautorent.com);
Hobart (☎6231 0550);
Launceston (☎6334 3437);
Devonport (☎6427 0796)

Selective Car Rentals
(☎www.selectivecarrentals.
com.au) Hobart (☎6234
3311); Launceston (☎6391
8652); Devonport (☎1800
300 102)

CAMPERVANS

Hiring four-berth camper-
vans costs around $700
per week from May to mid-
September, rising in stages
to a hefty $1110 in the peak
period from Christmas to
January.

Autorent-Hertz (☎1800
030 222; www.autorent.com.
au)

Britz (☎1800 331 454; www.
britz.com)

Cruisin' Tasmania (☎1300
664 485; www.cruisin-tas
mania.com.au).

Maui (☎1800 200 80 801;
www.maui-rentals.com)

**Tasmanian Campervan
Hire** (☎1800 807 119; www.
tascamper.com) Specialises in
two-berth vans.

Wicked Campers (☎1800
24 68 69; www.wickedcampers.
com.au) Backpacker friendly.

MOTORCYCLES

**Tasmanian Motorcycle
Hire** (☎6391 9139; www.
tasmotorcyclehire.com.au; 17
Coachmans Rd, Evandale) has a

range of touring motorbikes
for rent from $110 per day
(cheaper rates for longer
rentals and half-day rentals
also available); full pricing
details are listed on the
website. Evandale is south of
Launceston, not far from the
airport.

Road Conditions &
Hazards

WILDLIFE

Watch out for wildlife while
you're driving around the
island – the huge number of
carcasses lining main roads
is sad testimony to the fact
that many drivers don't use
enough caution. Many local
animals are nocturnal and
often cross roads around
dusk, so try to avoid driving
in rural areas when darkness
falls and if it's unavoidable,
remember to slow down.

DISTANCES

Distances may appear short
when looking at a map of
Tasmania (especially in
relation to distances on the
mainland), but roads are
often narrow and winding,
with many sharp bends
and, occasionally, one-lane
bridges that aren't clearly
signposted. This can make
trip durations considerably
longer than anticipated.
There are also many un-
sealed roads leading to sites
of interest throughout the
state.

CYCLISTS

Cycling is popular on some
roads (particularly on the
east coast) and when en-
countering bicycles you
should wait until you can
pass safely. Log-trucks piled
high and coming around
sharp corners also demand
caution. Finally, in cold
weather be wary of 'black ice',
an invisible layer of ice over
the bitumen, especially on
the shaded side of mountain
passes.

4WD DRIVING

Anyone considering travelling on 4WD tracks should

ROAD DISTANCES (KM)

	Burnie	Deloraine	Devonport	Geeveston	Hobart	Launceston	New Norfolk	Oatlands	Port Arthur	Queenstown	St Helens	Scottsdale	Smithton	Sorell	Strahan	Swansea
Deloraine	100															
Devonport	50	50														
Geeveston	381	281	331													
Hobart	328	228	278	53												
Launceston	137	51	87	254	201											
New Norfolk	290	190	240	91	38	197										
Oatlands	246	146	196	136	83	118	79									
Port Arthur	386	286	336	148	95	258	133	140								
Queenstown	148	204	198	312	259	251	221	261	354							
St Helens	293	207	243	304	251	156	247	168	299	407						
Scottsdale	197	111	147	314	261	60	257	178	318	311	96					
Smithton	88	188	138	469	416	225	378	334	474	236	381	285				
Sorell	316	216	266	78	25	188	63	70	70	284	229	248	404			
Strahan	183	222	209	353	289	271	253	370	388	41	405	330	224	325		
Swansea	264	164	214	189	136	136	174	114	181	395	118	214	352	111	352	
Triabunna	314	214	264	139	86	186	124	131	131	345	168	264	402	61	249	50

These are the shortest distances by road; other routes may be considerably longer.
For distances by coach, check the companies' leaflets.

read the free publication *Cruisin' Without Bruisin'*, available at visitor centres around the state or online from the website of the **Parks & Wildlife Service** (www.parks.tas.gov.au). It details 20 tracks (graded easy to hard) and explains how to minimise your impact on the regions you drive through. Type '4WD' into the website's search box

Road Rules

Driving in Tasmania holds few surprises, other than the odd animal caught in your headlights. Cars are driven on the left-hand side of the road (as they are in the rest of Australia). An important road rule is 'give way to the right' – if an intersection is unmarked (which is unusual), you must give way to vehicles entering the intersection from your right. Also watch for carefully concealed speed cameras.

Hitching

Travelling by thumb in Tassie is generally good, but wrap up in winter and keep a raincoat handy. Many of the state's minor roads are unsurfaced and traffic on them can be very light, so although some of these roads lead to interesting places, it could be a frustrating exercise in going nowhere fast. That being said, hitching is never entirely safe in any country and we don't recommend it. Travellers who decide to hitch should understand that they're taking a small but potentially serious risk. People who do choose to hitch will be safer if they travel in pairs and let someone know where they are planning to go.

People looking for travelling companions for car journeys around the state often leave notices on boards in hostels and backpacker accommodation. The website

www.needaride.com.au is a good resource.

Local Transport

Metro (☑13 22 01; www.metrotas.com.au; ⊙information line 5am-11.30pm Mon-Thu, 5am-1.30am Fri, 5.30am-1am Sat, 8am-10.30pm Sun) operates bus networks in Hobart, Launceston and Burnie, offering visitors inexpensive services enabling them to reach some out-of-the-way attractions. See online for schedules and price lists of its Hobart services.

Train

For economic reasons there are no longer any passenger rail services in Tasmania, except for the West Coast Wilderness Railway between Queenstown and Strahan (a scenic 34km).

behind the scenes

SEND US YOUR FEEDBACK

We love to hear from travellers – your comments keep us on our toes and help make our books better. Our well-travelled team reads every word on what you loved or loathed about this book. Although we cannot reply individually to postal submissions, we always guarantee that your feedback goes straight to the appropriate authors, in time for the next edition. Each person who sends us information is thanked in the next edition – and the most useful submissions are rewarded with a free book.

Visit **lonelyplanet.com/contact** to submit your updates and suggestions or to ask for help. Our award-winning website also features inspirational travel stories, news and discussions.

Note: We may edit, reproduce and incorporate your comments in Lonely Planet products such as guidebooks, websites and digital products, so let us know if you don't want your comments reproduced or your name acknowledged. For a copy of our privacy policy visit lonelyplanet.com/privacy.

OUR READERS

Many thanks to the travellers who used the last edition and wrote to us with helpful hints, useful advice and interesting anecdotes:

Jack Bayliss, Bart Benschop, Graeme Brock, Helga Campbell-Waite, Tannith Cattermole, Claire Davis, Sinead Falvey, Frans Flippo, Jayne Gardiner, Sophie Houghton, Donald Hunt, Paul Key, Brandon Lane, Anita Lasocki, Yann Le Beguec, Paul Marchment, Boris Marrone, Anthony Morel, Russell and Mitty O'Shea, Valerie Petersen, Evie Pottage, Jack Russell, Dick Sandvik, Alison Schultz, Adam Stanford, Annette Suter, Ellen Ten Dam, Brett Tollis, Peter Turnham, Ivan Valencic.

AUTHOR THANKS

Brett Atkinson

Huge thanks to all the staff at the visitors centre in Hobart who answered all my questions – before, during and after research – with authority and patience. Thanks also to Maryanne Netto at Lonely Planet, and to Gabi Mocatta, my superb author partner on this book. Your combined energy and input made my coordinating role very easy, and it's been great working together. Final thanks to Carol for the ongoing love and support.

Gabi Mocatta

Thank you to the wonderful folks at Lonely Planet, Maryanne Netto, Liz Heynes and David Connolly. Huge thanks to Brett Atkinson, brilliant co-ordinating author. So many Tasmanian locals have helped unearth hidden gems – this book is so much the richer for those chance conversations, directions and tips. Thank you to friends and loved ones for tolerating my absence. To Phil – you are so amazing. Your patience and late-night cups of tea and your irreverence kept me going.

ACKNOWLEDGMENTS

Climate map data adapted from Peel MC, Finlayson BL & McMahon TA (2007) 'Updated World Map of the Köppen-Geiger Climate Classification', *Hydrology and Earth System Sciences*, 11, 163344.

Cover photograph: Snow gums, Navarre Plains, south of Lake St Clair, Rob Blakers/ Lonely Planet Images. Many of the images in this guide are available for licensing from Lonely Planet Images: www.lonelyplanetimages.com.

THIS BOOK

This is the 6th edition of Tasmania. The 1st edition was researched and written by John and Monica Chapman; Lyn McGaurr updated the 2nd edition, and Paul Smitz researched and wrote the 3rd edition. Research on the 4th edition was led by Carolyn Bain, and the 5th edition by Charles Rawlings-Way and Meg Worby. Brett Atkinson was the coordinating author on this edition, joined by coauthor Gabi Mocatta; see Our Writers (p336) to find out which destinations each of them researched. Anna Krien wrote the Environmental Politics in Tasmania chapter.

Senator Bob Brown wrote the boxed text 'Simple Steps for Saving the Forests' on p305.

This guidebook was commissioned in Lonely Planet's Melbourne office, and produced by the following:

Commissioning Editor Maryanne Netto

Coordinating Editors Karyn Noble, Katie O'Connell

Coordinating Cartographers Joelene Kowalski, Tom Webster

Coordinating Layout Designer John Taufa

Managing Editor Liz Heynes

Managing Cartographer David Connolly

Managing Layout Designer Jane Hart

Assisting Editors Sarah Bailey, Amy Karafin, Andi Lien, Alan Murphy, Martine Power, Elizabeth Swan

Assisting Cartographer Andras Bogdanovits

Cover Research Naomi Parker

Internal Image Research Aude Vauconsant

Thanks to Chris Girdler, Lisa Knights, Julie Sheridan, Peter Shields

index

A

Aboriginal culture
  history 280-8
  museums 111-12, 205
Aboriginal sites 237, 288
  Freycinet Peninsula 150
  Great Western Tiers 214
  Kooparoona Niara 214
  Larmairremener tabelti 265
  Marakoopa Cave 215-16
  Maria Island (Toarra Marra Monah)
    145
  North Cave 230
  Pyengana 168
  South Cave 230
  Southwest 270
abseiling 31, see also rock climbing
accommodation 18, 310-12, see also
    individual locations
activities 28-32, see also individual
    activities
Agrarian Kitchen 69, 81
air travel 320, 321-2
  to/from Tasmania 320
  within Tasmania 321-2
animals 17, 297-301, see also
    individual animals
Antarctica 62
  Australian Antarctic Division 89
antiques 75
ants 313
area codes 316-17
art galleries, see museums &
    galleries
Arthur Pieman Conservation Area
    239-40
Arthur River 237-8
ATMs 316
Australian Three Peaks Race 184
Australian Wooden Boat Festival 19,
    61, 125

B

Barnbougle Dunes 172
Bathurst Harbour 13, 13
Batman Bridge 193
Battery Point 51
Bay of Fires 12, 166-7, 12
Bay of Fires Walk 122, 167, 123
beaches 18, 30, see also swimming
  Bakers Beach 195
  Bay of Fires 12, 166-7, 12
  Beaumaris 163
  Binalong Bay 167
  Blackmans Bay 89
  Boat Harbour Beach 229
  Boronia Beach 88
  Cockle Creek 120
  Freycinet National Park 11,
    150-1, 11
  Friendly Beaches 151
  Henty Dunes 251-2
  Kingston Beach 88
  Mt William National Park 169
  Ocean Beach 251
  Orford 143
  Randalls Bay 111
  Redbill Point 159
  Rice Beach 158-9
  Scamander 163
  Seven Mile Beach 87-8
  Sisters Beach 230
  Tinderbox 88
  Verona Sands 111
  Waubs Beach 158-9
  White Beach 100
  Wineglass Bay 154, 11
Beaconsfield 193-4
Beaumaris 163
Beauty Point 194
beer 16, see also breweries
  Boag's Centre for Beer Lovers 179
  Tasmanian Beerfest 21, 62
  Weldborough Hotel 168
Ben Lomond National Park 203
Bicheno 157-61, **158**
bicycle travel, see cycling
Binalong Bay 167-8
birdwatching 297-8
  Bridport Wildflower Reserve 172
  Bruny Island Bird Festival 108
  Lime Bay 100
  Loon.tite.ter.mair.re.le.hoin.er
    Walk 147
  Maria Island 146
  Moulting Lagoon 151
  Ocean Beach 251
  Springlawn Nature Trail 195
black currawong 297

Blessing of the Harvest Festival 201
blogs 278
Boag's Centre for Beer Lovers 179
Boat Harbour Beach 229
boat travel 320-1, 322, see also
    ferries
boat trips
  Arthur River 238
  Bicheno 159
  Gordon River 254-5
  Launceston 181
  Maria Island 146
  Orford 143
  Wineglass Bay 152
books 278-9
Bothwell 136-7
breweries 293, see also beer
  Boag's Centre for Beer Lovers 179
  Cascade Brewery 52, **128**
  Iron House Brewery 161
  Moorilla Estate 53
  Seven Sheds 220
  Two Metre Tall 84
Bridport 172-3
Brown, Bob 287, 304, 305
Bruny Island 8, 105-10, **106**, 8
  Bruny Island Bird Festival 21, 108
  food 107
  tours 107-8
budget 14
Burnie 223-7, **224**
  Savour Tasmania 20
bus travel 322-3
bushfires 25, 285
bushwalking 9, 16, 22-7, 122, 161
  Bay of Fires Walk 122, 167, 123
  Ben Lomond National Park 203
  Bicheno 158
  Blue Tier 168-9, **121**
  books & brochures 23
  Cataract Gorge 178-9, 12
  Cockle Creek 120
  Deloraine 214
  Douglas-Apsley National Park 161
  Exeter 193
  Franklin-Gordon Wild Rivers
    National Park 263
  Freycinet Peninsula Circuit 151
  Great Walks 23
  Hartz Mountains National Park 117
  Holwell Gorge 194
  Lake Leake 135
  Loon.tite.ter.mair.re.le.hoin.er
    Walk 147
  Maria Island National Park 145, 146
  Marrawah 236
  Mt Amos 151
  Mt Field National Park 13, 85-6

Narawntapu National Park 195
Noel Jago Walk 228
Overland Track 122, 265-6, **122**
Penguin Cradle Trail 222
Rocky Cape 230
South Bruny National Park 105
South Coast Track 122, 274, **9**
Southwest National Park 274-5
St Helens 164
St Marys 162
Tahune Forest Reserve 116-7
Tarkine Wilderness 122, 239
Tarn Shelf Track 86
Tasman Coastal Trail 94
Tasmanian Trail 32
Waterfall Bluff 94
Weldborough Pass Rainforest
   Walk 168
Wineglass Bay Walk 151
business hours 312

C
Cadbury Chocolate Factory 54
Callington Mill 131
Campbell Town 134-6
camping 26, 41, 310,
   Ben Lomond National Park 203
   Fingal Valley 163
   Flinders Island 174
   Freycinet National Park 157
   Mt William National Park 169
   Richardsons Beach 153-4
   St Helens 165
canoeing 28, 238, 240
car travel 323-5
   road distance chart 325
Carrick 198-9
Cascade Brewery 52, **128**
Cataract Gorge 178, **12**
caves 30
   Hastings Caves State Reserve 119
   Kutikina Cave 263
   Mole Creek area 215-16
   Remarkable Cave 100
cell phones 15, 317
cheese 290-1
cheese-makers
   Ashgrove Farm Cheese 213
   Bruny Island Cheese Company 107
   Cheese Tasting Centre 224
   Grandvewe Cheeses 110
   King Island Dairy 241
   Pyengana Dairy Company 168
   Thorpe Farm 136
children, travel with 18, 36-8
   Hobart 58
   Launceston 181, 185
Chinese history 169, 286

chocolate factories 54, 95, 212
Chudleigh 215
churches
   Scots Uniting Church 92
   St Andrews Anglican 202
   St Andrews Uniting Church 202
   St George's Anglican 51, 92
   St James Presbyterian Church 231
   St John's Church 78
   St Luke's Church of England 78, 134
   St Matthew's Church 82
climate 14, 25, 312, see also
   individual regions
climate change 322
Cockle Creek 120
Coles Bay 150-7, **152**
cooking schools 69, 81, 198
Corinna 240-1
Cradle Mountain 41, 264-70, **10**
Cradle Mountain–Lake St Clair
   National Park 264-70
credit cards 316
cricket 55
cruise ships 320
culture 278-9
currency 14, 311
cycling 31-2, 55, 322
   Hobart 55
   Launceston 180-1
   Maria Island National Park 145
   tours 165
Cygnet 111-13

D
dangers, see safe travel
Deloraine 213-15
Denison Canal 93
D'Entrecasteaux, Bruni 283
Derby 169-70
Derby River Derby 170
Derwent Valley 138-40
Devonport 41, 204-12, **208**
disabilities, travellers with 318
discount cards 314
diving, see scuba diving & snorkelling
Dockside Festival 231
Doo Town 95
Douglas-Apsley National Park 161
Dover 117-18
drinks 292-3, see also beer,
   breweries, whisky, wine, wineries
driving, see car travel
Dunalley 93

E
Eaglehawk Neck 93-5
East Coast 40, 141-75, **142**
   highlights 142

echidnas 300-1
electricity 311, 314
emergencies 15
environmental issues 287-8, 304-8
   Franklin River 262
   Lake Pedder 272-3
   pulp mill 197
   Recherche Bay 119
   Tarkine Wilderness 239
Evandale 201-3
events, see festivals & events
exchange rates 15
Exeter 193

F
Falls Festival 21, 62
ferries 15, 320-1
Festival of Voices 20
Festivale 19, 184
festivals & events 19-21, 214, 231
   Australian Three Peaks Race 184
   Australian Wooden Boat Festival
      19, 61, **125**
   Blessing of the Harvest Festival 201
   Bruny Island Bird Festival 21, 108
   Campbell Town Show 134
   Cygnet Folk Festival 19, 112
   Derby River Derby 170
   Dockside Festival 231
   Evandale Village Fair & National
      Penny Farthing Championships
      19, 202
   Falls Festival 21, 62
   Festival of Voices 20
   Festivale 19, 184
   Fingal Valley Festival 163
   Glover Art Prize 202
   Henley-on-the-Mersey Carnival 212
   Hobart Summer Festival 21, 61
   Latrobe Chocolate Winterfest
      20, 212
   Latrobe Wheel Race 212
   Launceston Cup 184
   Longford Garden Festival 201
   Longford Revival Festival 201
   Lumina 20, 62
   MONA FOMA 19, 61
   Mural Fest 219
   Rosebery Festival 248
   Royal Hobart Regatta 19, 61
   Royal Hobart Show 21, 62
   Royal Launceston Show 21, 184
   Savour Tasmania 20
   Sydney to Hobart Yacht Race 21,
      52, 61
   Table Cape Tulip Festival 21
   Tasmanian Beerfest 21, 62
   Tasmanian Craft Fair 21, 214

festivals & events *continued*
   Taste, The 21, 61, **124**
   Taste of the Huon 20
   Ten Days on the Island 20, 62
   Tulip Festival 228
   Zeehan Gem & Mineral Fair 250
films 279
Fingal Valley 163
fishing 29, 30-1
   Bicheno 159
   Currawong Lakes 135
   Dover 117
   internet resources 137
   Lake Leake 135
   Lakes, The 137
   Marrawah 236
   Orford 143
   St Helens 164
   tours 108, 138, 164
Flinders, Matthew 283
Flinders Island 173-5
food 16, 112, 115, 189, 289-93, 314,
   8, **126**, **127**
   books 293
   cheese & cheese-makers 107, 110,
      136, 168, 213, 224, 241, 290-1,
   chocolate factories 54, 95, 212
   cooking schools 69, 81, 198
   festivals & events 20, 21, 61,
      184, 212
   oyster farms 87-8, 107, 151
   providores 93, 107, 110, 135, 189
   tours 58, 88, 152, 183
Fortescue Bay 96
foxes 302
Franklin River 304, **10**
   damming of 262
   rafting 28-9, 263-4
Franklin-Gordon Wild Rivers National
   Park 262-5
Freycinet National Park 11, 150-7,
   155, **11**

G
galleries, *see* museums & galleries
gardens, *see* parks & gardens
gay travellers 314
Geeveston 115-16
geography 294
George Town 195-6
Glover Art Prize 202
golf 136, 172
Gowrie Park 217
Greens Party 287, 304

H
Hadspen 198-9
Hamilton 138-9
Hartz Mountains National Park 117
Hastings Caves & Thermal Springs 119
health 314-15
Henley-on-the-Mersey Carnival 212
hiking, *see* bushwalking
historic buildings & sites 47
   Allport Library & Museum of Fine
      Arts 47
   Battery Point 51
   Bothwell 136
   Brickendon 200
   Campbell Town 134-5
   Cape Wickham 241
   Cascade Brewery 52, **128**
   Coal Mines Historic Site 100
   Darlington 145
   Derby History Room 170
   Eaglehawk Neck Historic Site 94
   Evandale 201-3
   female factories 52, 133
   Ford's Store 231
   Franklin House 179
   Gaiety Grand 249-50
   George Town Heritage Trail 195
   Hamilton Heritage Centre 139
   Highfield 231
   Hobart Waterfront 50
   Hobart's Real Tennis Club 47
   Launceston 184
   Oatlands 131
   Officers Quarters 94
   Old Colony Inn 82
   Old Umbrella Shop 179
   Penitentiary Chapel Historic
      Site 46
   Plough Inn 231
   Port Arthur Historic Site 97-8, **7**
   Red Bridge 134
   Richmond 78
   Ross Bridge 132
   Runnymede 54
   Salamanca Place 47-51
   Theatre Royal 46, 75
   Van Diemen's Land Company
      Store 231
   Willow Court Historic Site 82
   Woolmers 200
   Wybalenna Historic Site 173
history 17, 280-8
   Chinese immigration 169, 286
   early settlement 282-7
   recent past 287-8
hitching 325
Hobart 39, 44, 56, **45**, **48**, **50**, **56**,
   59, **7**

   accommodation 44, 62-8
   activities 55-8
   attractions 46-55
   climate 44
   drinking 73-4
   entertainment 74-5
   festivals & events 19, 20, 21,
      61-2
   food 44, 68-73
   highlights 45
   history 46
   internet resources 76
   planning 44, 47
   shopping 75
   tourist information 76
   tours 58-61
   travel seasons 44
   travel to/from 76
   travel within 77
   walking tours 58, 60, **59**
Hobart Aquatic Centre 58
Hobart Summer Festival 21, 61
holidays 315
horizontal scrub 303
horse riding
   Huon Valley 114
   Koonya 100
   Narawntapu National Park
      195
   St Marys 162
   Tasmanian Trail 32
hot springs 119
Huon pine 301, 303
Huonville 113-15
hypothermia 27

I
insurance 315
internet access 315
internet resources 15, 76, 278
itineraries 33-5

J
jet-boat rides 82
   Hobart 61
   Huon River 114
   King River 253
   New Norfolk 82

K
kangaroos 298-9
kayaking 17, *see also* sea-kayaking
   Gordon River 253
   tours 273
Kempton 132
Kettering 104-5
King Island 241-3

king's lomatia 303
Kingston 88-9
Koonya 100-1

L

Lady Franklin Gallery 54-5
Lake Barrington 217-18
Lake Country 136-8
Lake Leake 135
Lake Pedder Impoundment 271-3
Lakes, The 137-8
language 14, 279
Lark Distillery 50
Latrobe 212-13
Latrobe Chocolate Winterfest 20, 212
Launceston 12, 41, 176-91, **177**, **180**, **182**
  accommodation 176, 185-7
  activities 180-1
  attractions 178-80
  climate 176
  drinking & entertainment 188-9
  festivals & events 19, 20, 21, 184
  food 176, 187-8
  highlights 177
  history 178
  planning 176
  shopping 189-92
  tourist information 190
  tours 181-4
  travel seasons 176
  travel to/from 190
  travel within 190-1
  walking tours 181, 183-4
Launceston Cup 184
legal matters 315
Legana 192-3
Legges Tor 203
leeches 313
lesbian travellers 314
Liffey Valley 200-3
lighthouses
  Cape Bruny Lighthouse 107
  Cape Sorell Lighthouse 252
  Cape Tourville Lighthouse 151
  Currie Lighthouse 242
  Eddystone Point Lighthouse 167, 169
  Low Head 196
  Table Cape Lighthouse Tour 228
Lilydale 197-8
Lime Bay 100
Longford 200-1
Longford Garden Festival 201
Longford Revival Festival 201
Low Head 196-7
Lumina 20, 62
Lune River 119-20

M

magazines 311
maps 315
Margate 104
Margate Train 104
Maria Island National Park 13, 144-6, **144**, **13**
marine reserves 297
  East Coast 145
  Tinderbox Nature Marine Reserve 88
Maritime Museum of Tasmania 46
markets
  antiques 75
  Dunalley fish market 93
  Esk market 190
  Evandale market 202
  farmers' market, Hobart 73
  Penguin market 222
  Salamanca Market 7, 53, **50**
Marrawah 236-7
Mary, Princess of Denmark 87
Maydena 271
measures 311
Melaleuca 275
Midland (Heritage) Hwy 131-6
mobile phones 15, 317
Mole Creek Karst National Park 215-16
MONA 6, 53, **6**
MONA FOMA 19, 61
money 14, 316
  discount cards 314
Moonah Arts Centre 54
Moorilla Estate 53
motorcycle travel 323-5
mountain biking 31-2
  Blue Tier 168-9
Mt Arthur 197
Mt Field National Park 13, 85-7, **13**
Mt George 195
Mt Nelson 53
Mt Roland 217
Mt Strzelecki 174
Mt Tanner 174
Mt Wellington 52-3
Mt William National Park 169
Mural Fest 219
museums & galleries
  Allport Library & Museum of Fine Arts 47
  Australasian Golf Museum 136
  Australian Antarctic Division 89
  Bark Mill Museum Swansea 147
  Bass & Flinders Centre 195
  Beaconsfield Mine & Heritage Centre 193-4
  Bicheno Motorcycle Museum 158
  Bligh Museum of Pacific Exploration 107
  Bruny Island History Room 107
  Burnie Regional Art Gallery 223-4
  Cygnet Living History Museum 111
  Design Centre of Tasmania 179
  Devonport Maritime Museum 205
  Devonport Regional Gallery 205
  Don River Railway 205
  Dr Frankenstein's Museum of Monsters 250
  Eric Thomas Galley Museum 259
  Forest & Heritage Centre 116
  Furneaux Museum 173
  Heritage Centre 147
  Heritage Highway Museum 134
  History Room 131
  Huon Apple & Heritage Museum 114
  John Temple Gallery 199
  Kentish Museum 218
  King Island Museum 242
  Lady Franklin Gallery 54
  LARQ Gallery 259
  Living History Museum of Aboriginal Cultural Heritage 111-12
  Makers' Workshop 223
  Maritime Museum of Tasmania 46-7
  Military Museum of Tasmania 51
  MONA 6, 53, **6**
  Moonah Arts Centre 54
  Mural House 218
  Narryna Heritage Museum 52
  National Automobile Museum of Tasmania 179
  Pilot Station Maritime Museum 196
  Pioneer Village Museum 224
  Port Arthur Museum 97
  Queen Victoria Museum & Art Gallery 178-9
  Southern Design Centre 116
  Stanley Discovery Museum & Genealogy Centre 231
  Tasmanian Copper & Metal Art Gallery 198
  Tasmanian Cricket Museum 55
  Tasmanian Museum & Art Gallery 50
  Tasmanian Transport Museum 54
  Tasmanian Wool Centre 133
  Tiagarra 205
  Tin Centre 170
  Vintage Tractor Shed Museum 199
  West Coast Pioneers Museum 249
  West Coast Reflections 251
  Wooden Boat Centre 114
mutton birds 297

N

Narawntapu National Park 195
national parks & reserves 294-7, 298-9
  Ben Lomond National Park 203
  Bridport Wildflower Reserve 172
  Bruny Island Neck Game Reserve 105, 107
  Cradle Mountain–Lake St Clair National Park 264-70, **10**
  Douglas-Apsley National Park 161
  Evercreech Forest Reserve 163
  Fern Glade 225
  Franklin-Gordon Wild Rivers National Park 262-5
  Freycinet National Park 11, 150-7, **11**
  Hartz Mountains National Park 117
  Lime Bay State Reserve 100
  Lost Falls 135
  Maria Island National Park 13, 144-6, **144**, **13**
  Meetus Falls 135
  Mole Creek Karst National Park 215-16
  Mt Field National Park 13, 85-7
  Mt William National Park 169
  Narawntapu National Park 195
  Rocky Cape National Park 229-30
  Savage River National Park 241
  South Bruny National Park 105
  Southwest National Park 274-5
  Tahune Forest Reserve 116-17
  Tamar Island Wetlands 179-80
  Tasman National Park 96
  Walls of Jerusalem National Park 216-17
New Norfolk 81-4, **82**
newspapers 279, 311
Nubeena 100-1

O

Oatlands 131-2
opening hours 312
Orford 143
Overland Track 122, 265-7, **122**

P

pademelons 299
parks & gardens
  Allendale Gardens & Rainforest 236
  Burnie Park 224-5
  Cataract Gorge 178, **12**
  City Park 179
  Emu Valley Rhododendron Garden 225
  Mt Nelson 53
  Mt Wellington 52-3
  Princes Sq 179
  Queen's Domain 53-4
  Royal Tasmanian Botanical Gardens 53-4
  Salmon Ponds Heritage Hatchery & Garden 84
  Trevallyn State Recreation Area 180
Parliament House 46
Penguin Observation Centre 225
penguins 159, 205, 221-3, 298
  tours 159, 196, 225
Penitentiary Chapel Historic Site 46
phonecards 317
Pieman River 240-1
planning
  budgeting 14
  bushwalking 22-7
  calendar of events 19-21
  children 36-8
  internet resources 15
  itineraries 33-5
  Tasmania's regions 39-41
  travel seasons 14
plants 301-3
platypuses 300
  Geeveston Circuit Platypus Walk 116
  Platypus House 194
politics 287, 307
population 279
Port Arthur 39, 90-2, 96-101, **91**, **98**
Port Arthur Historic Site 7, 97, **7**
possums 299
postal services 316
Princess Mary 87
providores
  Alps & Amici 189
  Fleurtys 110
  Hiba 107
  Mill Providore & Gallery 189
  Red Bridge Café & Providore 135
  Sorell Providore 93
public holidays 315
pulp mill 306-7

Q

quad biking 172, 253-4
quarantine regulations 321
Queen's Domain 53-4
Queenstown 258-62, **259**

R

rafting 10, 17, 28-9, **10**
Remarkable Cave 100
Richmond 77-81, **78**
Richmond Bridge 78
rock climbing 31, 174, 181, 203
Rocky Cape National Park 229-30
Rosebery 248-9
Rosevears 192-3
Ross 132-4
Ross Bridge 132-3
Royal Hobart Regatta 19, 61
Royal Hobart Show 21, 62
Royal Launceston Show 21, 184
Royal Tasmanian Botanical Gardens 53-4
Runnymede 54

S

safe travel 312-14
  bushwalking 25-7, 156
sailing 29, 58
  Australian Three Peaks Race 184
  Hobart 58
  Royal Hobart Regatta 19, 61
  Sydney to Hobart Yacht Race 21, 52, 61
Salamanca Market 7, 53
Salamanca Place 47-51, **50**
Saltwater River 100
Savage River National Park 241
Savour Tasmania 20
scenic flights
  Coles Bay & Freycinet National Park 153
  Flinders Island 174
  George Town 196
Scottsdale 171
scuba diving & snorkelling 29-30
  Bicheno 158
  Binalong Bay 167
  Eaglehawk 94
  Fossil Bay 145
  St Helens 164
sea-kayaking 29, 55, *see also* kayaking
  Coles Bay 152
  Hobart 55-7
  Kettering 104
  Tasman Peninsula 92
seals 107
  tours 195-6, 231
senior travellers 314
sharks 313
Sheffield 218-20
skiing 20, 31
  Ben Lomond National Park 203
  Mt Mawson 86

000 Map pages
000 Photo pages

Smithton 234-6
snakes 300, 313
snorkelling, *see* scuba-diving & snorkelling
solo travellers 316
Sorell 92-3
Sorell Fruit Farm 92
South Bruny National Park 105
South Coast Track 122, 274, 9
Southport 118-19
Southwest National Park 274-5
spiders 300, 313
sport, *see individual sports*
St Helens 163-6, **164**
St Marys 162
Stanley 230-4, **232**
Strahan 250-8, **252**
Strathgordon 273-4
Styx River Valley 272
surfing 30
  Binalong 167
  King Island 242
  Marrawah 236
  Sorrel 94
Swansea 146-50, **148**
swimming 18, 30, 58, 178, 313-14
  see also beaches
Sydney to Hobart Yacht Race 21, 52, 61

T
Table Cape Tulip Festival 21
Tahune Eagle Glide 116-17
Tahune Forest AirWalk 116
Tahune Forest Reserve 116-17
Tamar Valley 191-200, **191**
Taranna 95-6
Tarkine Wilderness 122, 238-9
Taroona 88
Tarraleah 139-40
Tasman, Abel 281
Tasman National Park 96
Tasman Peninsula 9, 39, 90-101, **91**
Tasmanian Beerfest 21, 62
Tasmanian Craft Fair 21, 214
Tasmanian Cricket Museum 55
Tasmanian devil 122, 179, 267, 300, 122
  tours 237
Tasmanian tiger 297, 301
Tasmanian Trail 32
Tasmanian Transport Museum 54
Tasmanian Wilderness World Heritage Area 296
Taste, The 21, 61, 124
Taste of the Huon 20
taxes 316

telephone services 316-17
Ten Days on the Island 20, 62
Theatre Royal 46, 75
thylacines, *see* Tasmanian tiger
time 317
tourist information 317
tours 58, 317-18 *see also* walking tours
  Bruny Island 107-8
  Callington Mill 131
  Cradle Mountain–Lake St Clair National Park 266-7
  cricket 55
  Curringa Farm 139
  cycling 165
  distilleries 50, 136, 224
  diving 158
  Eaglehawk Neck 94-5
  fishing 108, 138, 159, 164
  Flinders Island 174
  food 58, 88, 152, 183
  Gordon River 254-5
  Hastings Caves State Reserve 119
  Hobart 58, 60-1
  kayaking 273
  Launceston 181-4
  penguins 159, 196, 225
  Port Arthur 91-2, 97-8
  quad bike 152, 172
  seals 195-6, 231
  southwest 273
  St Helens 165
  Tasman Peninsula 90-1
  whisky 50, 136, 224
  wine 152
train travel 325
travel to/from Tasmania 320-1
travel within Tasmania 321-5
Triabunna 143-4
Truganini 105, 284
Tulip Festival 228
Tullah 245-8
TV 311

U
Ulverstone 220-1
Upper Florentine Valley 272

V
vacations 315
vineyards, *see* wineries
visas 318-19
volcanoes 231

W
walking, *see* bushwalking
walking tours 25

Bay of Fires Walk 167, 123
  Freycinet Experience 151
  Hobart 58-61, **59**
  Launceston 181, 183-4
  Maria Island Walk 146
  Narawntapu National Park 195
wallabies 298-9
Walls of Jerusalem National Park 216-17
Waratah 241
waterfalls
  Guide Falls 225
  Hogarth Falls 252
  Holwell Gorge 194
  Horseshoe Falls 85
  Lady Barron Falls 85
  Liffey Falls 200
  Lilydale Falls 197
  Mathinna Falls 163
  Montezuma Falls 248
  Preston Falls 222
  Ralphs Falls 168
  Russell Falls 85, 13
  St Columba Falls 168
  Stitt Falls 248
  Waterfall Bluff 94
weather 14, 25, 312
Weindorfer, Gustav 268, 287
Weldborough 168-9
Westbury 199-200
Western Explorer 239-40
whales 61, 301
whisky 16, 136
  Hellyers Road Whisky Distillery 224
  Lark Distillery 50
  tours 50, 136
Wilderness Society 305
wildlife, *see* animals
wildlife parks & sanctuaries
  Bonorong Wildlife Centre 79
  East Coast Natureworld 158
  Guide Falls Alpaca and Animal Park 225
  Something Wild 85
  Tasmania Zoo 179
  Trowunna Wildlife Park 215
  Wings Wildlife Park 222
  ZooDoo Wildlife Fun Park 78
wine 16, 292-3
  Artisan Gallery & Wine Centre 193
  Pinot Shop 189
  Tamar Valley Wine Route 191
  Tasmanian Wine Centre 75
Wineglass Bay 154, 11
wineries 292
  Bay of Fires Wines 197
  Brookfield Vineyard 104

wineries *continued*
Bruny Island Premium Wines 107
Coombend Estate 147
Craigie Knowe Vineyard 147
Craigow Vineyard 80
Dalrymple 197
Darlington Vineyard 143
Delamere 197
Freycinet Vineyard 147, **128**
Goaty Hill Wines 193
Hartzview Vineyard 111
Herons Rise Vineyard 104-5
Home Hill 114
Jansz Wine Room 197
Kinvarra Estate Wines 85
Leaning Church Vineyard 198

Leven Valley Vineyard & Gallery 222
Meadowbank Estate 80
Milton Winery 147
Moorilla Estate 53
Ninth Island Vineyard 192
Panorama Vineyard 113
Pipers Brook 197
Providence Vineyards 197-8
Puddleduck Vineyard 80
Rosevears Vineyard 192
Spring Vale Vineyards 147
St Imre 118
Tamar Ridge Wines 193
Tamar Valley Wine Route 191
Unavale Vineyard 174
Valleybrook Wine Tours 183

Velo Wines 192
wombats 300
women travellers 319
Woodbridge 110-11
work 319
World Heritage sites
Brickenden 200
Maria Island 144, **13**
Tasmanian Wilderness 296
Woolmers 200
Wynyard 227-9

Z
Zeehan 249-50

000 Map pages
000 Photo pages

how to use this book

These symbols will help you find the listings you want:

⊙ Sights
🕴 Activities
🍃 Courses
👉 Tours

📸 Festivals & Events
🛏 Sleeping
🍴 Eating
🍺 Drinking

☆ Entertainment
🛍 Shopping
ℹ Information/
Transport

Look out for these icons:

TOP Our author's
CHOICE recommendation

FREE No payment
required

🌱 A green or
sustainable option

Our authors have nominated these places as demonstrating a strong commitment to sustainability – for example by supporting local communities and producers, operating in an environmentally friendly way, or supporting conservation projects.

These symbols give you the vital information for each listing:

📋 Telephone Numbers
⊙ Opening Hours
🅿 Parking
⊜ Nonsmoking
❄ Air-Conditioning
@ Internet Access

📶 Wi-Fi Access
🏊 Swimming Pool
🥗 Vegetarian Selection
📖 English-Language Menu
👪 Family-Friendly
🐾 Pet-Friendly

🚍 Bus
⛴ Ferry
Ⓜ Metro
Ⓢ Subway
⊖ London Tube
🚊 Tram
🚆 Train

Reviews are organised by author preference.

Map Legend

Sights
⊙ Beach
🔺 Buddhist
🔲 Castle
✝ Christian
🕉 Hindu
☪ Islamic
✡ Jewish
❶ Monument
🏛 Museum/Gallery
⊗ Ruin
🍷 Winery/Vineyard
🐾 Zoo
⊙ Other Sight

Activities, Courses & Tours
⊙ Diving/Snorkelling
⊙ Canoeing/Kayaking
⊙ Skiing
⊙ Surfing
⊙ Swimming/Pool
⊙ Walking
⊙ Windsurfing
⊙ Other Activity/
Course/Tour

Sleeping
⊙ Sleeping
⊙ Camping

Eating
⊗ Eating

Drinking
⊙ Drinking
⊙ Cafe

Entertainment
⊙ Entertainment

Shopping
⊙ Shopping

Information
⊙ Post Office
ℹ Tourist Information

Transport
✈ Airport
⊗ Border Crossing
🚍 Bus
Cable Car/
Funicular
Cycling
Ferry
Ⓜ Metro
Monorail
🅿 Parking
Ⓢ S-Bahn
Taxi
Train/Railway
Tram
⊙ Tube Station
Ⓤ U-Bahn
• Other Transport

Routes
Tollway
Freeway
Primary
Secondary
Tertiary
Lane
Unsealed Road
Plaza/Mall
Steps
Tunnel
Pedestrian
Overpass
Walking Tour
Walking Tour
Detour
Path

Boundaries
International
State/Province
Disputed
Regional/Suburb
Marine Park
Cliff
Wall

Population
⊙ Capital (National)
◉ Capital
(State/Province)
⊙ City/Large Town
• Town/Village

Geographic
⊙ Hut/Shelter
⊙ Lighthouse
⊙ Lookout
▲ Mountain/Volcano
⊙ Oasis
⊙ Park
)(Pass
⊙ Picnic Area
⊙ Waterfall

Hydrography
River/Creek
Intermittent River
Swamp/Mangrove
Reef
Canal
Water
Dry/Salt/
Intermittent Lake
Glacier

Areas
Beach/Desert
+ + + Cemetery
(Christian)
× × × Cemetery (Other)
Park/Forest
Sportsground
Sight (Building)
Top Sight
(Building)

OUR STORY

A beat-up old car, a few dollars in the pocket and a sense of adventure. In 1972 that's all Tony and Maureen Wheeler needed for the trip of a lifetime – across Europe and Asia overland to Australia. It took several months, and at the end – broke but inspired – they sat at their kitchen table writing and stapling together their first travel guide, *Across Asia on the Cheap*. Within a week they'd sold 1500 copies. Lonely Planet was born.

Today, Lonely Planet has offices in Melbourne, London and Oakland, with more than 600 staff and writers. We share Tony's belief that 'a great guidebook should do three things: inform, educate and amuse'.

OUR WRITERS

Brett Atkinson

Coordinating Author, Hobart & Around, Tasman Peninsula & Port Arthur, The Southeast, Midlands & Lake Country Brett has been 'crossing the ditch' to Australia from his hometown of Auckland for more than 30 years now, and jumped at the chance to return to Tasmania, definitely his favourite Aussie state. He loves Tassie's wild and spectacular scenery, the laid-back and upfront nature of the locals, and the island's brilliant food and wine scene. Brett has previously written about Tasmania's wine and wildlife for New Zealand magazines, but for his first extended Lonely Planet research trip to the state, he ventured south to Bruny Island and the Tasman Peninsula, and conducted diligent investigation of the local beer scene in Hobart's great pubs. When he's not adding to his total of more than 20 Lonely Planet guidebooks, Brett is exploring the world as a freelance travel writer. See www.brett-atkinson.net for his latest articles and travel plans.

Gabi Mocatta

East Coast, Launceston & Around, Devonport & the Northwest, Cradle Country & the West It was 10 years ago that Gabi first walked across the Hobart airport tarmac and breathed champagne-fresh Tasmanian air. She didn't know then, but that arrival was the start of many from far-flung travels, and the air is always as good as it was the first time: an exhilarating welcome home. Gabi now calls Hobart her base: with its forest and sea surrounds, it's the perfect city for someone who loves the outdoors. For this edition, Gabi beachcombed the east and west Coasts, savoured delicious Launceston; was wind-lashed in the wild northwest; and was breathtaken in the even wilder southwest – a sea kayaker's delight and one of the last temperate wildernesses on earth.

Contributing Author

Environmental Politics in Tasmania

Anna Krien's debut book, *Into the Woods: The Battle for Tasmania's Forests*, was published by Black Inc in 2010 and is shortlisted for the Douglas Stewart Prize. Her writing has appeared in the *Big Issue*, *Frankie*, the *Monthly*, the *Age* newspaper, *COLORS*, *Griffith Review* and has been selected for *Best Australian Essays* and *Best Australian Stories*.

Published by Lonely Planet Publications Pty Ltd
ABN 36 005 607 983
6th edition – Aug 2011
ISBN 978 1 74179 461 8
© Lonely Planet 2011   Photographs © as indicated 2011
10 9 8 7 6 5 4 3 2 1
Printed in China

Although the authors and Lonely Planet have taken all reasonable care in preparing this book, we make no warranty about the accuracy or completeness of its content and, to the maximum extent permitted, disclaim all liability arising from its use.